THE
GREAT
CRUSADE

H. P. WILLMOTT

THE
GREAT
CRUSADE

A NEW COMPLETE HISTORY OF
THE SECOND WORLD WAR

THE FREE PRESS
A Division of Macmillan, Inc.
NEW YORK

Maxwell Macmillan International
New York   Oxford   Singapore   Sydney

The Free Press
A Division of Macmillan, Inc.
866 Third Avenue, New York, N.Y. 10022

Collier Macmillan Canada, Inc.
1200 Eglinton Avenue East
Suite 200
Don Mills, Ontario M3C 3N1

First American Edition 1990

Printed in the United States of America

printing number

1 2 3 4 5 6 7 8 9 10

Library of Congress Cataloging-in-Publication Data

Willmott, H. P.
   The great crusade : a new complete history of the Second World War
/ H. P. Willmott.—1st American ed.
       p.   cm.
   Originally published: London: M. Joseph, © 1989.
   Includes bibliographical references.
   ISBN 0-02-934715-7
   1. World War, 1939–1945.   I. Title.
D743.W524   1990
940.53—dc20
                                                            90-35738
                                                            CIP

CONTENTS

LIST OF ILLUSTRATIONS

LIST OF MAPS

PREFACE AND ACKNOWLEDGEMENTS

A singularly destructive commentary that appeared in the September 1985 edition of *Reviews in American History* included the reviewer's observation, "It has long been my view that it is impossible for a single volume history to do justice to the war against Japan." By the same logic, a single volume history cannot deal properly with the much greater subject of the Second World War. But when, in March 1987, I was asked to write such a history of this greater subject I accepted, in the sure knowledge that my earlier comment would be used against a work that, limited to 200,000 words in length, permitted only sustained analysis.

The decision to accept the challenge of writing such a book was made for several reasons. Nearly two decades of study and teaching had coincided with a massive outpouring of publications about the Second World War, not a little of it of dubious value and even less taste. I was thus aware that any newcomer to this subject, indeed even the historian with a reasonable working knowledge of events, was confronted by an intimidating volume of material, massive diversity and even grave uncertainty on such mundane matters as places, dates and events. Moreover, I was aware, from my teaching experience, of a lessening familiarity with the subject matter on the part of second- and third-generation students and their untutored, selective and ethnocentric views of this war that seem, more often than not, the product of exposure to third-rate television than first-rate scholarship. Indeed, given the fact that the Second World War was the first radio-cinema war, it may be that the power of image and of the spoken word has so impressed itself upon the collective subconsciousness of successive generations that the written word of the historian no longer commands the power of redress.

This may be the last book-reading generation, but the Second World War nevertheless demands the reconsideration that historians alone can provide. We are now into the sixth decade since the outbreak of war in Europe, yet our main themes of historical interpretation remain today much as they were when set down in the first glut of post-war memoirs and the writings of the first generation of historians after 1945. This is somewhat surprising. The process of re-evaluation and re-interpretation of events is the essence of History, but the

Second World War has not been subjected to the critical re-examination to which the reputations of Frederick the Great and Napoleon were subjected within twenty years of the deaths of these men or, indeed, to a cycle of appraisal and re-appraisal which has been the fate of such conflicts as the Franco-Prussian and even the First World War. It may be that, in the case of the Second World War, ethnocentric and ideological considerations have affected historiography more than History itself, yet it is legitimate to question both the place that the Second World War holds in History and the conventionally-held wisdoms of this conflict which society entertains.

We are still too close to events to understand the historical context of the Second World War but future generations may well come to see the war merely as the most important and destructive single part of a series of conflicts, waged between 1931 and 1975, that resulted in the destruction of one world order and the erosion of its replacement to the extent that, for the first time in man's history, no important part of the land surface of this planet was not part of indigenous, sovereign territory and the various regional issues brought to the fore between 1931 and 1945 were resolved, for the moment, with little or no reference to the Great Powers. The diffusion of power and the right of societies to arrange their affairs with little let or hindrance on the part of major powers arose from the process of which the Second World War was the greatest and most important single part.

This possible re-appraisal of the context of the Second World War has been raised in order to dismiss it from further consideration: for the moment there remain more obvious and pressing needs, and these provide the terms of reference for this work. There is a need for an account of this war that may serve as a basic reference and guide and at the same time provide a balance between the two partially concurrent conflicts that together made up the Second World War. Equally there is the need in this process to present a subordinate balance between the component parts of each of these conflicts. Moreover, these needs must be met by a chronological narrative that not merely avoids the "and then" approach but explains not so much what happened as why events unfolded in the manner in which they did, and does so by time rather than theatre in order that these events may be set in their proper sequence.

Such, then, were the initial terms of reference for the work on which I embarked, but to these I added others. The balance I sought within the work could only be achieved by reference to the relationship between power and military force, defined within the context of struggle rather than war, and limitations of length precluded comprehensive treatment of military events. An attempt had to be made to provide an analysis of the war economies of the powers, but in the hand of a military historian such esoteric subject matter threatened a general readership with death by statistics, while any attempt to examine the detail of major campaigns threatened to be exhausting long before it was exhaustive. This account, therefore, sought to provide a general overview of military events and to relate them to political and economic factors, and it sought to do so while deliberately refusing to accept the "great men" approach to the presentation of history. Anglo-American historiography has never escaped Carlyle's legacy, but just as this history had repudiated an ethnocentric interpretation of events so it has refused to portray these events in the gladiatorial terms of national champions that so beset western histories. War in the modern age is between systems and societies, and in this history individuals, with one exception, receive little consideration. In this account, and despite the element of inevitability thus imparted to proceedings, events are related in terms of organization and the underlying currents of History.

If any single aspect of the Second World War can be said to form the thread of this history then I must admit to a contempt for that popularly accepted but pernicious myth of German military excellence which, in THE GREAT CRUSADE, is presented for what it is, both pernicious and a myth. The easy facility with which an uncritical view of German performance in the Second World War has gained widespread acceptance in western society since 1945 has been a source of alternating amusement and irritation to me for obvious reasons. If the German military was as good as conventional wisdom would have us believe, then why did it lose, and in defeat is there not confirmation of a suitably amended Wilde witticism: "To lose one world war may be regarded as a misfortune: to lose both looks like carelessness"? Expounded at various parts of this text is the view that the German military genius was in fighting, not in war, that indeed Germany's failure stemmed from her inability to understand the nature of war. In terms of organizing for war Germany was totally outclassed by her enemies, and those who cite the extent of German conquest as evidence of military proficiency fail to note the obvious, that the destruction of the German state after such conquest is evidence of a fundamental German misappreciation of the nature of war itself.

THE GREAT CRUSADE attempts to provide the perspective of fifty years in a manner that presents a balanced account of events and relates their causes to matters that fall beyond the normal terms of reference of military history. In setting down such an account I wish to acknowledge the debt I owe to many individuals who, either over the years or in the specific preparation of this book, have shaped my ideas and perspectives, enhanced my factual knowledge and, not least, corrected my errors of understanding, fact and expression. Too often acknowledgements seem to be used as the means of casting a cloak of respectability around an otherwise dubious product by the naming of names, and I trust that this is not the case in acknowledging my debts to Charles Dick, Christopher Donnelly and Michael Orr of the Soviet Studies Research Centre; various members, past and present, of the War Studies Department at RMA Sandhurst, and specifically to Nigel de Lee, Christopher Duffy and John Keegan; to other members of the Sandhurst faculty, and specifically Anthony Clayton and John Sweetman; the members of the Naval Historical Branch and Library, especially

PREFACE AND ACKNOWLEDGEMENTS

David Brown and Arnold Haig; and various people from various countries, such as Lawson Clare, Willem Duijnhouver, Anthony Gorst, Riley Sunderland and Jack Sweetman. Together these and others over the years have convinced me of the wisdom of the observation that truth is never pure and rarely simple. As always in these matters, without their patient advice errors of fact and interpretation would have abounded in these pages: those that remain are my responsibility alone. For their unfailing co-operation and patience I would acknowledge the help that I have received from the staff of various institutions, most obviously the Institute of Historical Research, the Public Record Office, the School of Oriental and African Studies, and the Sandhurst, Staff College and MOD Whitehall libraries.

Finally I would add two acknowledgements, to my family, which endured much that could have been avoided in the course of the preparation of this book, and to Everton, Sherry and Kondor, for the joy and happiness they brought in their short lives.

H. P. Willmott

1

A NEW WORLD AND A NEW WAR

The verdict of history on the Treaty of Versailles has not been favourable. Preceded as it was by bitter inter-Allied wranglings and repudiated by the greatest of the victorious powers, the Treaty of Versailles has been widely derided as nothing more than a hollow truce. But the most cursory comparison of the territorial arrangements of Europe of 1929 and 1989 reveals that for all its shortcomings, the settlement that ended the First World War provided boundaries that have changed little in 60 years: moreover, the changes that have occurred reflect a realignment of power within Europe that was the product of the second, not the first, of the great European conflicts of the twentieth century.

Nevertheless, the settlement that ended the First World War was undoubtedly flawed, and on two counts. Germany after 1919 remained both potentially the strongest power within Europe and unreconciled to her defeat. The grievance that Germany nurtured against Versailles and proclaimed throughout the inter-war period stemmed not so much from the terms of the Treaty, which in any event had been largely set aside by 1939, but from the reality of defeat in 1918. It was this reality that Germany constantly denied between the wars, and in fact the Treaty of Versailles, even allowing for some of its more questionable provisions, was very moderate, especially when contrasted with the terms of treaties that a victorious Germany had dictated to Romania and Russia in 1918. Moreover, the main aspects of the settlement that ended the First World War – its redrawing of the frontiers of Europe; its reconfirmation of European primacy outside Europe; and its attempt to return to pre-1914 economic practices – were based upon a premise, an Anglo-French ability to maintain the peace, that could not be sustained in face of

1

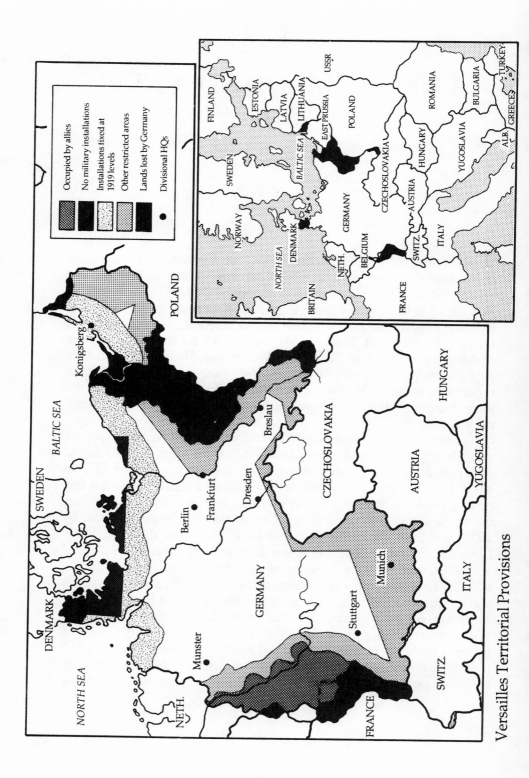

Versailles Territorial Provisions

differences between Britain and France and in light of the changes that had taken place during and in the period immediately after the First World War.

The period between July 1866 and May 1944 was the era of German pre-eminence within Europe, notwithstanding the outcome of the First World War. It was an era, however, when two of the traditional features of the international order had broken down, namely the balance of power within Europe and European domination of the outside world. Europe could no longer decide the outcome of events beyond her shores, and Germany was too strong to be checked by the powers of Europe. Much of the history of the troubled inter-war period stems from this fact, and from one related matter: that two powers, crucial to the Allied victory of 1918, were largely excluded from the inter-war diplomatic process. By her own choice, the United States, and by the choice of others the Soviet Union, as successor state to Imperial Russia, stood apart from the process whereby Britain and France shouldered responsibility for the re-ordering of Europe after 1919. Britain and France, however, were divided on the crucial question of how this was to be achieved, whether the post-war treaties were to be enforced or modified. Without any Anglo-American guarantee of her security, France saw the re-ordering of Europe in terms of ensuring herself against defeat: she thus sought to maintain a post-war settlement that provided for her continuing military superiority over Germany and to underpin this with alliances that were concluded with Belgium, Poland, Czechoslovakia, Romania and Yugoslavia between 1920 and 1927. Britain, primarily concerned with imperial and naval matters, saw her security in terms of ensuring herself against war, and in the context of Europe this involved revision of Versailles and the restoration of Germany as a great power within the community of nations.

Thus except for the period of Franco-German *rapprochement* between 1925 and 1930, Britain and France were seldom in step in dealing with European problems for most of the inter-war era, but even this period of Franco-German accommodation, which followed a futile Franco-Belgian attempt to enforce the Treaty of Versailles by the occupation of the Ruhr between January 1923 and August 1925, was riddled by inconsistencies and ambiguities. The series of treaties, known collectively as the Locarno pact, that inaugurated this period had four main provisions: a treaty of guarantee of their common borders by Belgium, France and Germany, which further pledged themselves to use specified arbitration procedures to resolve disputes; separate German arbitration treaties with

3

Czechoslovakia and with Poland with respect to common borders; France's provision of guarantees of their borders to Czechoslovakia and Poland; and an Anglo-Italian guarantee of the first but of no other set of arrangements.

At the time Locarno seemed to meet the requirements of the various signatories of its treaties. For Germany the various negotiations marked the first step in her rehabilitation within the international community, and her admission to the League of Nations followed in September 1926. Czechoslovakia and Poland had their borders and security guaranteed anew by France which, with Belgium, secured a voluntary German renunciation of territorial ambitions in Western Europe. Britain and France were able to present themselves as impartial guarantors of both France and Germany and thus the powers that ensured the peace of Europe. But the various treaties nevertheless failed to address fundamental issues. Germany's position of inferiority relative to France remained unchanged, and Germany served notice that she regarded the question of her borders with Czechoslovakia and Poland as unresolved: German concessions to France raised obvious question marks against the credibility of France's guarantees to her allies; the Anglo-Italian guarantees were practically worthless since they applied just as long as there was no danger of war between France and Germany. But these matters were, or seemed at the time, of relatively small account when set against the spirit of reconciliation and future hope that prevailed at Locarno, and therein lay the real significance of the pact. Locarno in 1925 seemed to open the way for a peaceful solution of European problems.

Events were to show that not all of Europe's problems could be resolved by negotiation: diplomacy ensured that Versailles was a dead letter by 1939 but still proved unable to prevent the outbreak of war. But the first proof of the limitations of diplomacy and of a continuing recourse to armed force in order to resolve disputes was provided in the 1920s outside Europe. It is inevitable that the story of the inter-war period and the Second World War should be recounted primarily in terms of Europe: the figure of Adolf Hitler dominates the era, and serves as a reminder of the primacy of Europe in international affairs. But the fact remains that just as the Second World War was in reality two partially concurrent conflicts, a European war and a war fought in both Asia and the Pacific, so the inter-war period saw the emergence of challenges to Versailles and the principle of negotiated change both in the Far East and within Europe. It was the challenge in the Far East that was the first to present itself, and it emerged as a result of developments inside the one

4

country that alone amongst the Allied nations refused to sign the Treaty of Versailles in 1919: China.

Developments within China during the 1920s assumed international significance because of the challenge that emergent Chinese nationalism presented to the position of privilege that foreign powers had created for themselves over the previous 80 years. The exercise of the rights that had been extracted from China in that time was dependent, however, upon a delicate set of balances, both between the various powers and within China between weakness and strength on the part of central authority. Chinese governments had to be too weak to challenge the position of the powers but strong enough to maintain order sufficient to allow their exploitation of their rights: the powers for their part were obliged to exercise a certain restraint in their dealings with China relative to one another.

These balances did not survive the revolution of 1911, which led to the inauguration of the republic in 1912, and the First World War. The revolution marked a rearrangement of political, economic and social forces within China that by its very nature was certain to clash with entrenched foreign interests in the country, and the First World War, by weakening the Western powers throughout the Far East because of their enforced preoccupation with European events, strengthened the position of Japan throughout eastern Asia. Indeed, as early as 1915 the extent of Japanese ambitions on the mainland had been revealed in the infamous 'Twenty-one Demands', which aimed at the reduction of China to little more than a Japanese dependency or protectorate. In the event Japan, aware of the international suspicion that her claims had provoked, withdrew the more exacting of her demands and settled for a Chinese acceptance of most of her terms while reserving her position on other matters. At the same time, having taken over various German concessions in China, she secured both Chinese and American endorsement of her claims on these concessions, which by law should have reverted to China. It was the Allied acceptance of Japanese claims to these concessions at Versailles that provoked China's decision not to be a party to the Treaty and which led to violently xenophobic, specifically anti-Japanese, demonstrations throughout the country. China, however, proved not merely volatile but very unstable, and this instability was crucial in shaping Japanese policy towards China in the inter-war period.

By 1919 Japan had acquired extensive interests in China and hers was the dominant, almost exclusive, influence in Manchuria where her control of the southern railroads gave her a stranglehold over the economy of China's richest provinces. Her various investments in and trade with China was crucially important to Japan in financing her import trade, but by 1919 her overseas development had assumed a character very different from that of other powers. It was exclusively regional and was directed at the expense of societies with which Japan shared a common political, cultural and ethnic heritage and which were economically similar to herself. It was also different in that it was led by considerations of national security, yet these considerations were open-ended and, in the last analysis, recognised no limitations other than that imposed by superior force. Thus a not unnatural preoccupation with Korea and southern Manchuria had led after 1905, when Japan secured control of these two areas, to a deepening involvement in the affairs of Inner Mongolia and northern China in order to ensure their security. At various times specifically political or economic considerations proved important in shaping Japanese attitudes towards China, but the *leitmotif* running through the evolution of Japanese policy on the Asian mainland was an obsession with physical occupation of space and a restless encroachment upon China in order to consolidate and further develop national interests.

But there proved to be an Asian equivalent of Locarno: the seven accords known as the Washington Treaty. Of these seven, four – the four-power treaty of 13 December 1921, the nine-power and Sino-Jananese treaties of 4 February 1922, and the naval limitation treaty of 6 February 1922 – were of particular significance. The naval limitation treaty fixed capital ship strengths at ratios of 5:5:3:1.67:1.67 for Britain, the United States, Japan, France and Italy respectively; imposed maximum displacement and armament for battleships and aircraft carriers; and prohibited the construction of naval bases by Britain beyond Singapore, by the United States beyond Hawaii and the Aleutians, and by Japan outside her home islands. The four-power treaty bound these three countries and France to respect one another's rights and possessions in the Pacific and to consult in the event of future disputes. The nine-power and Sino-Japanese treaties both reaffirmed the principle of China's sovereignty and territorial integrity. The first also reaffirmed the principle of equal access to China's markets and gave various undertakings to China regarding her future recovery of customs and revenue rights and other concessions. The Sino-Japanese treaty saw Japan agree to the evacuation of her forces from Shantung and to recognise certain Chinese claims in return for guarantees of her substantial economic interests in the province.

The naval treaty enabled Japan to avoid a prohibitively expensive arms race with the United States, curbed American construction and ambition, and provided Japan with an undisputed superiority in the western Pacific. It thus ensured for Japan a measure of security that she could never have provided for herself in an unrestricted building race with the United States, but while this was recognised by those with the power of decision in Japan in 1922 the ending of the Anglo-Japanese alliance, the suspicion of Anglo-American collusion and racism, and the belief that national interests had been sacrificed at Western insistence subsequently gained widespread currency in Japan. The Shantung issue provoked similar if muted resentment: Japan's involvement in the Russian civil war had proved costly and unrewarding, and by 1922 she was somewhat wary of entanglements on the mainland. But the various accords dealing with China that had been concluded at Washington were based on the premise that China was stable and would meet the political and administrative obligations involved in any restoration of her rights: in reality, China was slipping ever more deeply into chaos, and it was into this chaos that Japan was increasingly and not too unwillingly drawn.

Between 1916 and 1926, the worst years of 'the warlord era', ordered government in China all but ceased to exist as a bewildering number of factions fought and manoeuvred for power. This period presented Japan with a difficulty of options: whether to support or to undermine any current government in Peking; which regional or local faction to support and to what end; whether to consolidate existing rights or to use China's weakness to secure fresh concessions. In its dilemma the Japanese leadership had no clear definition of national interest in China, and it was subjected to pressure from a number of vested interests at a time when control over its agencies in China was somewhat precarious. Moreover, Tokyo was not blind to a Chinese nationalism that threatened Japanese interests and made impossible any attempt to mobilise Chinese opinion in support of Japan's interests. Like the warlords, Japan had no programme that could attract popular support and she hesitated to tap grass-root feelings for fear that emotion, once roused, might ultimately be turned against herself.

After 1926, however, Japan's position in China became increasingly difficult. She had become closely associated with the Manchurian warlord, Chang Tso-lin. Her support for Chang had not been without ambiguity, but she was generally prepared to support him and to accept his machinations south of the Great Wall as long as he maintained order throughout Manchuria. After 1926, however, Chang's rule was increasingly erratic, incompetent and corrupt; moreover, he proved unwilling or unable to check anti-Japanese agitation inside Manchuria. The situation

7

in Manchuria thus increasingly invited some form of direct action on the part of the Japanese after 1926. By this time also, 10 years of civil war had thrown up a faction that seemed capable of ending the chaos within China. This was the Kuomintang, a loose coalition of political parties and associated interest groups with its power base at Canton. In October 1926 its armies, commanded by Chiang Kai-shek, established themselves on the middle Yangtse: by April 1927 they had secured Nanking and Shanghai, and were preparing for a campaign into northern China.

The emergence of an organisation capable of reuniting China and which claimed to be both radical and nationalist posed an obvious threat to Japanese interests, but two years were to elapse between the KMT armies' arrival on the Yangtse and the inauguration of a KMT government in Nanking with at least nominal authority over the whole country excluding Tibet, Sinkiang and Manchuria. In reality, KMT authority was limited to a handful of provinces on the lower Yangtse and theoretical national unity was achieved by deals struck between Chiang and local warlords who were confirmed in positions of power after suitable declarations of loyalty. Chiang, in fact, was no more than a warlord who owed his national position to control of some of China's richest provinces, to possession of a good army and administration, and to his shrewd awareness of the realities of power. The latter included a recognition of Japan's power and her desire to sever all links between China and Manchuria, and in January 1928 Chiang tacitly acknowledged Manchuria's exclusion from the process of national reunification. In order to dispel doubt on the matter Japanese formations were landed in Shantung in April 1928 to save Chang's forces from defeat by KMT armies; and in June, in order to preserve Manchuria from further involvement in China's wars, a Japanese military detachment, on orders from Tokyo, murdered Chang outside Mukden.

This action brought about the result it was designed to forestall: Chang's successor and eldest son, Chang Hsueh-liang, aligned himself with Nanking in December. This declaration of loyalty had no practical effect upon the situation inside Manchuria where Japanese pre-eminence was assured, and at this time the Japanese were prepared to wait upon events. They watched Chang Hsueh-liang provoke a war with the Soviet Union in November 1928 and the Soviets overrun north-west Manchuria with contemptuous ease, and they noted the lack of any Western response to support China in this crisis. They recognised the underlying weakness behind the façade of Chinese unity, and in 1930 and 1931, as both northern and southern China were gripped in rebellion and a resumption of civil war, the Japanese military in Manchuria set in

8

hand preparations for a campaign to bring Manchuria under its undisputed control. In the process of this campaign, the Japanese military inflicted blows upon the post-war settlement and upon representative, responsible government in Japan from which neither recovered.

Of the various factors that led to the Japanese conquest of Manchuria two were of crucial importance, if only in deciding the timing of events. The first was the Great Depression, which hit Japan quickly and hard. Faced by recession, Japan's markets in China and Manchuria assumed ever greater importance, and very quickly the idea of the conquest of Manchuria as the answer to Japan's economic problems gained widespread support in Japanese society. The second was the fact that constant involvement in Chinese domestic politics had left the Japanese army with a liking for unauthorised action and immunity from cabinet control, and after 1930 sections of the army wanted action in Manchuria in order to bring down the Hamaguchi government because of its success in curbing the military. This administration imposed cuts upon the armed forces, negotiated the 1930 London naval limitation treaty despite the objections of the naval general staff, and sought to re-establish the primacy of parliamentary and cabinet government. Sections of the military saw unauthorised action in Manchuria as the means of reversing these successes, but in fact the Depression was more effective in undermining representative government in Japan than the military: Hamaguchi had been removed from the scene before the Manchurian campaign began. Party government, closely associated with major business interests, was inevitably blamed for the country's economic problems, and Hamaguchi was shot and seriously wounded by a right-wing fanatic in November 1930. Though he partially recovered, Hamaguchi was forced to resign in April 1931 and died in August: his successor, Wakatsuki Reijiro, proved incapable of controlling the military once the campaign in Manchuria began. Thus the combination of a search for assured markets and economic self-sufficiency and of military restiveness with democratic government provided the impetus for the Japanese conquest of Manchuria after September 1931.

The conquest of Manchuria was both rapid and easy, but the Japanese were to find that the dictum that it is easy to conquer but hard to occupy had not lost its validity. For all its great size, Manchuria had relatively few cities, most of which were concentrated in Liaoning (Fengtien) province and linked by railroads under Japanese control at the start of hostilities. The rail network dictated the course of the campaign as the Japanese, attacking at a time of their own choosing, cleared Chang Hsueh-liang's forces from the South Manchuria Railroad, between Port Arthur and

9

Changchun, during September and secured Kirin and the Mukden–Kirin line in October. Only on the Siping–Tsitsihar line did the Japanese experience any serious resistance, but Tsitsihar was nevertheless occupied in November. Thereafter, with some forces detailed to mopping-up operations around Mukden and Kirin, the Japanese turned to the southwest to drive Chang Hsueh-liang's remaining forces south of the Great Wall. The Manchurians completed the evacuation of their homeland in the first week of January 1932, and the main campaign effectively ended with the Japanese occupation of Harbin on 5 February.

Though the Japanese committed only the equivalent of a corps to Manchuria, the campaign had significance beyond its scale and length. It fatally compromised the Wakatsuki government, which was obliged to send reinforcements to Manchuria while claiming it sought an end to hostilities. From this the military drew the obvious conclusion, that any action on its part could not be repudiated by the authorities in Tokyo. Wakatsuki was forced from office in December 1931 and replaced by Inukai Tsuyoshi, who was assassinated on 15 May 1932. His offence was a desire to end operations in Manchuria, and his death marked the end of party government in Japan. Under the terms of the Japanese constitution the armed forces had to provide cabinets with their respective service ministers, and after 1932 the army used what amounted to the power of veto to destroy civilian authority. By resignation or refusal to nominate a minister the army could bring down or prevent the formation of a cabinet, and by these means the army was able to ensure the formation of cabinets and policy along lines that met with its approval.

For Chiang Kai-shek the loss of Manchuria, which had not properly been a part of China since 1916, was not immediately serious. Aware that China could not consider armed resistance to Japan at this stage, Chiang sought to unite China under his own single leadership before turning to face the Japanese: his policy was to deal with domestic enemies, specifically the communists, before tackling the foreign invader. This policy was arguably correct, but in practical terms it ran three very obvious risks, all of which were realised in the coming decade. Given the Kuomintang's lack of a genuine programme of radical social reform, it risked compromising Chiang's strongest claim to rule China, namely the Kuomintang's exclusive title to represent Chinese nationalism. It offered nothing to those regimes in the northern provinces now forced to live alongside the reality of Japanese power in Manchuria, and it presupposed that there would be no further Japanese moves before the process of Chinese reunification was complete. Japanese operations at Shanghai,

Tsingtao and Foochow during the Manchurian campaign clearly showed that Japanese ambitions were not limited to Manchuria.

As early as 24 September 1931, just six days after the start of operations in Manchuria, the Japanese installed a puppet administration in Mukden: on 18 February 1932 a Japanese-sponsored assembly proclaimed the independence of Manchoukuo. Significantly, this declaration defined the new state as incorporating the four north-west provinces of Liaoning, Kirin, Heilungkiang and Jehol, the last of which was thus far outside Japanese control. 1932 saw the start of Japanese incursions into Jehol which culminated, in January and February 1933, with the invasion and conquest of the province. It was subsequently incorporated into Manchoutikuo when Manchoukuo was reconstituted as an empire on 1 March 1934. But acquisition of Jehol led the Japanese into an increasingly active role in the northern provinces. With scarcely any reference to Tokyo, the Japanese armies in Manchoutikuo and northern China were able to use a number of incidents as the means of forcing increasingly extensive concessions from the Chinese, the latter being obliged to withdraw their garrisons from Hopei in June 1935 and from Charar the following month. With a pattern of piecemeal Chinese surrender in the north well established, the Mongolian princes of Charar and Suiyan became increasingly receptive to Japanese overtures after this time.

The Manchurian campaign thus had profound effects for both China and Japan, but it also had far-reaching significance for the international community. The Japanese action in Manchuria was a deliberate breach of various undertakings given by Japan since 1919 and was a defiance of the powers, both individually and as represented by the League of Nations. It was a challenge to the principle of collective security and the idea of the renunciation of the use of force to resolve disputes which had taken root over the previous decade. None of the powers responded positively to Japanese aggression with the result that the League failed its first major test as guardian of peace. The Japanese began the Manchurian campaign at a time when the other powers were confronted by other, seemingly more important, matters. The summer of 1931 saw the failure of major German and Austrian banks, and Britain embarking on a bitterly divisive election campaign. The United States was in the grip of the political, social and economic crisis that stemmed from the 1929 crash, and, like the Soviet Union, was not a member of the League and would not associate herself with the other powers on the Manchurian issue. The United States confined herself to the January 1932 declaration that she would not recognise the results of aggression, a statement of principle that, by combining inactivity with moral posturing, could only offend and draw contempt from Japan. The Soviet Union was more practical: she set about selling her assets in Manchuria.

American and Soviet absence from the League of Nations was a reflection of the fact that the League, for all its claims to encompass the full international order, was European-orientated and did not possess any power of decision with regard to the Far East. Without a lead provided by any of the great powers, the League could do no more than pass resolutions calling for an end to hostilities in Manchuria and the withdrawal of Japanese forces to their original positions, and when Japan ignored these summons it contented itself with the despatch of a commission of enquiry to the Far East. The Lytton Commission reported in September 1932, by which time it was far too late for any form of effective action, but its report, for all its judicious phrasing, branded Japan an aggressor. The League adopted the report on 24 February 1933 whereupon Japan withdrew from the organisation. There was no countermove on the part of the League or any single nation, perhaps a tacit recognition by all concerned that the principle of collective security had been mortally wounded by the episode. In Manchuria the Japanese demonstrated that aggression could go unchecked, that the League, and primarily Britain and France, lacked the means and will to maintain the post-1919 system. The lesson did not go unheeded by Germany's new rulers.

Just as the Manchurian affair is partially explicable in terms of the onset of the Depression, so the latter provides partial explanation of the rise of Hitler to the position of supreme authority in a state of which he was not a citizen until 1931 and in which he never held a directly elected office. At the election of May 1928 his Nazi Party took just 13 seats in the *Reichstag* and was the eighth largest party in Germany with less than 3 per cent of the popular vote. At the September 1930 election the Nazis emerged as second only to the Social Democrats, and in the July 1932 poll, when unemployment in Germany was climbing through the 5,000,000 barrier, the Nazis emerged as the largest single party in Germany. The Depression provided Hitler with the opportunity to seize power by compromising a parliamentary system saddled with responsibility for the defeat of 1918 and the economic disasters of the post-war era, but Hitler and Nazism were more than a mere reaction to unemployment and national humiliation. Hitler's strength lay in the fact that far from being some nightmarish aberration he was the embodiment of certain values and beliefs deeply entrenched in German tradition, culture and political consciousness. Hitler tapped that romantic strand of German values that repudiated liberal democracy, that stressed leadership at the expense of consensus, will as opposed to reason, race and society at the expense of the individual, force rather than restraint. In 1933 few, even amongst those responsible for bringing him to power, took Hitler at his word. He was regarded as an extremist but one who would be tamed by the obligations of office, and very few took seriously the ideas and policies Hitler had set down in his autobiography-cum-political-testament, published in 1925, to which he adhered and which he put into effect with remarkable consistency. To a world that had yet to experience mass deportation and extermination, the ill-organised and undisciplined utterances of a semi-educated Austrian were incomprehensible in what they foreshadowed.

In essence, however, Hitler's philosophy was simplicity itself. The right to life was secured through racial struggle. This struggle was territorial, of earth and blood, and the German race would earn its right to survive in a struggle of annihilation with the inferior Slavonic peoples of eastern Europe. Not for Hitler was Germany to be confined even to the limits set down in the national anthem – *Von der Maas bis an die Memel, Von der Etsch bis an den Belt* – but was to be very literally *über alles* as she reached from the North Sea to the Urals. Thus established, Germany would secure herself 'living space' (*Lebensraum*) and the resources necessary for the survival of 'the thousand-year *Reich*'. Only war could provide Germany with her needs, and war was the social cathartic, the supreme test for which a people was organised, and which was the acid test of racial resolve. For Hitler the military aspects of war were but a reflection of the will to survive and conquer. Hitler's ideology was the embodiment of amoral violence that was unaccountable and that justified itself by victory or through self-immolation in the event of defeat. Armed with such nihilistic beliefs and at the head of potentially the most powerful state in Europe, Hitler was to dominate European affairs from the time that he became German chancellor on 30 January 1933 to the moment, 11 years later, when the reality of American and Soviet power served notice on the limitations of military force in the conduct of international affairs and of German national power in the world at large. Between 1934 and 1941, however, nothing in Europe, not even the sophisticated duplicity of the Quai d'Orsay in combination with the consent and evasive cynicism of the British Foreign Office, could withstand Hitler's singleness of purpose. In these years Hitler, as he both promised and threatened, imposed his will upon Europe, and in so doing precipitated a conflict that Germany showed no sign of losing.

13

Though these years were marked by a growing Germany stridency and assertiveness within Europe, they opened quietly with Hitler intent on consolidating his authority within Germany and forestalling preventive action on the part of neighbours. On the first score Hitler encountered little difficulty. On 23 March 1933 the *Reichstag* invested him with the power to rule and enact any law and constitutional change without reference to itself for four years. At a single stroke the *Reichstag* thus bypassed presidential authority and made Hitler dictator of Germany, and when President von Hindenburg died on 2 August 1934 Hitler merged the offices and powers of president and chancellor in his own person. Whilst the full apparatus of the police state was imposed upon Germany in this 20-month period, Hitler's actions were for the most part circumspect. The brutality of his regime was no less real for its being selective and implicit rather than open and immediate, but the same threatening characteristics were to apply to Hitler's conduct of foreign policy, at least until March 1936.

Between January 1933 and March 1936 Hitler largely waited upon events and used them to destroy the cohesion and determination of potential enemies. By use of legitimate German demands for the restoration of sovereign rights Hitler was able to confuse the issues that arose as the European powers dealt with problems of disarmament and security. Thus, in response to proposals in February 1933 to set limits on the armed forces of all League members Hitler proposed total disarmament, an aim set down in the Treaty of Versailles, or acknowledgement of Germany's right to determine for herself the size of her military establishment. These twin-track proposals, that tapped the desire of Germany's neighbours for peace yet presented them with an unenviable choice, were complicated in the spring of 1933 by the suggestion of Benito Mussolini, dictator of Italy since 1924, that Britain, France, Germany and Italy should assume responsibility for the re-organisation of Europe and the preservation of its peace. In the event France diluted this suggestion, the four-power pact of June 1933 going no further than recognition that the Versailles settlement might need amendment but that revision should be by agreed procedures and conducted under the aegis of the League. Yet when Hitler on 14 October denounced the inconclusive disarmament negotiations and announced Germany's withdrawal from the League, there was no countermove by France and her allies. Indeed, the links between France and her associates had been strained even by the June pact because any revision of the Versailles settlement and return to a concert of Europe could only be at the expense of France's allies in eastern Europe, and after France declined to accept

14

a Polish suggestion that the two powers mount a pre-emptive attack to destroy Nazism Poland concluded a 10-year non-aggression treaty with Germany on 26 January 1934.

This pact did much to draw the sting of the Franco-Polish alliance, as the French came to appreciate in the course of 1934, but in March 1935 France made no move when Hitler used the occasion of the return of the Saarland to Germany to make public the existence of a German air force, proscribed by the Treaty of Versailles. Immediately afterwards, Hitler announced the reintroduction of conscription, a parallel assurance that Germany had no claims on France and justification of this measure in terms of token British and French rearmament programmes serving to confuse issues. Britain, France and Italy met at Stresa to determine a common response, but beyond referring the matter to the League – a supine, pointless gesture – the three powers did no more than protest. That these three countries had no common ground in dealing with Germany became patently obvious very quickly. With indecent haste Britain concluded a naval limitation treaty with Germany, the first occasion when a German violation of Versailles was condoned by an Allied power. Even more importantly, as 1935 unfolded so did the crisis in which Hitler took no direct part but which nevertheless effectively destroyed the League of Nations: the Abyssinian crisis of October 1935– May 1936.

The main outline of this crisis can be simply told. Italy had long harboured ambitions in East Africa, but had been restricted to possession of Eritrea and part of Somaliland and had concluded a treaty of friendship and arbitration with Abyssinia in 1928. In December 1934 a clash over a remote and ill-defined part of Abyssinia's border with Italian Somaliland resulted in Italy's refusal to accept arbitration under the terms of the 1928 treaty, and the issue was referred by Abyssinia to the League on 17 March 1935 – an action that thus coincided with the announcement of German rearmament. The League subsequently passed the issue to Britain, France and Italy to resolve, but despite an Anglo-French proposal that would in effect have reduced Abyssinia to an Italian protectorate Italy opened hostilities on 3 October. After an initial mishandling of the campaign that drew international derision and scorn, the Italians completed the conquest of Abyssinia in seven months and installed King Victor Emmanuel as emperor on 9 May 1936.

The Italian refusal to consider anything other than a military solution to the Abyssinian question after January 1935 stemmed in part from a genuine, if mistaken, belief that in talks with the French that month the latter had dealt the Italians a free hand in Abyssinia. In the course of

15

1935, however, it became clear that France's ambiguity, for all her friendliness towards Italy, had to be balanced against a hostile British attitude. For France there was no point in alienating Italy over Abyssinia at a time when German restiveness was assuming an ominous form. It had been Italy, not France, that in July 1934 had moved military forces to ensure the independence of Austria after an abortive Nazi coup, and again in the crisis of March 1935 Italy had associated herself with Britain and France. To the French a deal over Abyssinia would ensure Italy's continued cooperation in Europe, but they were both dismayed and irritated by the sudden British conversion to the merits of the League and the principle of collective security over Abyssinia. Britain's moralistic stance failed either to impress or to deter Mussolini and was discredited, in December 1935, by her being party to the notorious Hoare-Laval pact which proposed the partition of Abyssinia and the ceding of two-thirds of that country to Italy. This obvious abandonment of morality for expediency was accompanied by a refusal to deny Italy rights of passage through the Suez Canal and to impose punitive sanctions after Italy was condemned as an aggressor by the League in October. Britain, in effect, shrank from any action that threatened a direct confrontation with Mussolini but by her actions alienated Italy and compromised France's attempt to retain Italian cooperation in dealing with European problems. In such a situation the only winner from the episode was Hitler, who used the opportunity presented by the others' distraction to reoccupy the demilitarised Rhineland on 7 March 1936.

French policy towards Italy over the Abyssinian crisis was amoral but had the virtue of consistency. It sought to ensure Italian friendship and cooperation but this was only one part of a two-fold French response to Germany's withdrawal from the League and pact with Poland: the other was the redefinition in the spring of 1935 of the non-aggression treaty that France had concluded with the Soviet Union in 1932. That treaty bound the signatories not to join an alliance directed against the other, but under the terms of the treaty signed on 2 May 1935 the two powers pledged themselves to consult in the event of either being threatened and to render immediate military assistance if the other was subjected to unprovoked attack in Europe. The meaning of these provisions was obvious but partially dissipated by the provision whereby the implementation of these arrangements in the event of German aggression would be dependent upon definition of that aggression by Britain and Italy as guarantors of the Locarno Pact.

The Franco-Soviet alliance (and the Soviet-Czech treaty of 16 May 1935 that gave Czechoslovakia a Soviet guarantee conditional on French action) was significant in several ways. It represented a return by France to the alliance that had been the cornerstone of her security and independence between 1892 and 1916; it combined in a military convention the only two powers in Europe that together might be able to check Germany; it completed the rehabilitation of the Soviet Union after years of being the outcast from the councils of Europe. But the treaty also provided Hitler with the opportunity to claim the advance of communism in France, a point directed as much to an increasingly divided French society as to the wider international audience. Hitler's violent anti-communism attracted right-wing admiration in many countries, and his claims to be the guardian of Western civilisation against the Bolshevik menace impressed and confused those who feared a resurgent Germany but nevertheless hesitated to make common cause with the Soviet Union against her.

The twin-track policy that Hitler had employed during disarmament negotiations in 1934 was used again at the time of the German move into the Rhineland when Hitler repudiated the Locarno pact, on the grounds that the Franco-Soviet treaty had nullified the agreement, but at the same time he offered Belgium and France a 25-year non-aggression pact and treaties with Germany's neighbours on the lines of the German-Polish treaty. These offers served to confuse the issue presented by the German reoccupation of the Rhineland: France either had to respond to the move or adbicate the position of supremacy within Europe that had been hers since 1919. If France's concern for her security and her guarantees to her allies meant anything German aggression had to be countered. Her failure to respond to the German action ensured a profound change in the balance of power in Europe: with one action Hitler neutralised the French army and destroyed French credibility with her allies. Belgium sought and obtained formal release from her 1920 alliance, and for three years after the Rhineland episode the Franco-Polish alliance was a dead letter as Poland sought to ensure good relations with Germany. For France, however, there was no respite because hardly had German troops taken up positions along her frontier than another crisis, immediately exploited by Hitler, served to weaken and distract her still further.

Sheltered behind the Pyrenees Spain and Portugal had long ceased to be involved in the mainstream of European events, but in February 1936 a general election in Spain resulted in a decisive victory for the Left though the campaign itself and the balance of votes cast showed Spain to be bitterly and evenly divided. In the aftermath of the election Spain quickly became ungovernable as the Right took its fight into the streets, the Left replying in kind. Amid mounting chaos the army in Spanish

17

Morocco rose in revolt on 16 July and on the following day garrisons throughout Spain joined the rebellion. In a matter of weeks the army was able to conquer half of Spain, but with the bulk of the population rallying to the Republic neither side was able to secure the upper hand and Spain was condemned to the horrors of a civil war that was to last until March 1939 when Nationalist forces finally secured Madrid and Valencia.

At the start of this war Britain and France sought to limit the conflict to Spain itself and to ensure that the war did not assume international dimensions. They took the lead in proposing and then following the principle of non-intervention in Spanish affairs, but this policy quickly assumed the mantle of craven weakness in light of Italian and then German involvement in the war. Italy supported the army revolt from the outset, and may well have been involved in preparations for the uprising: German involvement followed that of Italy and never matched the latter's scale but was nevertheless a substantial factor in the Nationalist victory. Between them Germany and Italy flouted the principle of non-intervention, as did the Soviet Union on behalf of the Republic, but in terms of the events that were to lead to the outbreak of a general war in Europe in 1939 the Spanish civil war was of obvious significance: the Nationalist cause in Spain provided Germany and Italy for the first time with common cause. There was an equally obvious difference between Germany and Italy over Spain in that Italy sought a Nationalist victory *per se* whereas Germany's priority was to ensure Italy's estrangement from Britain and France, plus the latter's distraction, but as a result of those interests that they shared Germany and Italy came together to thwart the policy of non-intervention. In so doing, German and Italian attraction was mutual, at least at the exalted level of *Führer* and *Duce*, while their earlier and separate successes over the democracies provided the momentum for a deepening friendship and cooperation. As a result, on 24 October 1936 Germany and Italy agreed to recognise the Nationalist regime at Burgos and to divide Europe into German and Italian spheres of influence, and on 1 November Mussolini, in a speech at Milan, referred appropriately to 'the Rome–Berlin axis'. He used the phrase, rightly, to predict that the future of Europe would revolve around decisions made by Germany and Italy but the phrase implied, wrongly, a basic equality between the two countries.

Nevertheless the re-orientation of Italian policy was of obvious significance. Italy had associated herself with Britain and France in their ineffectual protests in March over the Rhineland affair and Italy had no good cause to support a resurgent Germany against her traditional allies. As Mussolini shrewdly appreciated, Italy's ability to mould events to her advantage lay in exploiting the balance of power between France and Germany, not by acquiescing in French supremacy and still less its German alternative. Moreover, as the events of July 1934 had shown, German and Italian interests clashed over Austria, and for that matter over Hungary, which Mussolini liked to think lay within an Italian sphere of influence in central Europe, but after October 1936 Italy was irrevocably committed to Germany and a reorganisation of Europe just as much as she and Germany were committed to the Spanish Nationalists. On 18 November the two powers recognised the Burgos junta and thereafter adopted an increasingly open role in Spain. On 27 April 1937 German aircraft destroyed the Basque town of Guernica and, even more brazenly, German warships shelled the port of Almeria on 31 May. By then, however, the international community was less than six weeks from what was in effect, if not in law, the outbreak of the Second World War.

In the two years between the agreements whereby they secured the withdrawal of Chinese forces from Hopei and Charar and the outbreak of general hostilities in China in July 1937 the Japanese, by a combination of political, economic and timely military action, came to assert a largely unchallenged control of China north of the Great Wall. In these same years, however, there developed within Japan, and particularly within the Imperial Army, a belief that the nature of Japan's relationship with China had to be settled, and settled by armed force.

As in 1931, the Japanese action in 1937 was the product of an interplay of developments within Japan, within China and within the wider international community, though those developments within China served as a catalyst rather than a cause of Japanese actions. The major factors that shaped Japan's decision to settle accounts with Chiang Kai-shek's regime at Nanking were Japanese in origin and mostly stemmed from the upsurge of violent nationalist sentiment within Japan triggered by her successful occupation of Manchuria and international condemnation of her action. But however much this disapprobation contributed to a laager mentality, intense patriotism was neither a Japanese monopoly nor unknown in Japan before 1932. After the Manchurian episode, however, nationalism in Japan acquired an added dimension that reflected both an accumulated grievance against the international order and a self-confidence in Japan's right to direct the affairs of eastern Asia. This change ran in parallel, inevitably, with an increasing regimentation of Japanese society and the growing domination of the army of the Japanese polity.

During the 1930s the Depression and the quest for autarchy were the most potent single factors in rising nationalist sentiment in Japan, but economic nationalism ran alongside an ethic that stressed Japan's uniquely divine character and her right and duty to present herself as leader of an eastern Asia purged of Western influence and presence. The imposition of Shinto orthodoxy became increasingly evident in the 1930s, and this period saw the rise within the army of a faction, the *tosei-ha* or control group, intent on conquest in China. By their very nature these developments proved self-fulfilling. To a society hit hard by the Depression and forced to make considerable sacrifices in order to provide for the armed services, the use of force as the means of solving economic problems and discharging a national, if self-imposed, duty was natural and justified, and Japan's decision, announced on 29 December 1934, that she would not accept limitation on her future naval construction programmes reflected and reinforced these developments. The end of limitation represented an assertion of national rights relative to powers that had denied Japan the principle of racial equality and was the cause of intense patriotic satisfaction: the dangerous implication of freeing the United States from any limitation relative to Japan and the fact that Japan, as a result of her various actions, was isolated in a way without precedence in 40 years counted for little in comparison.

An increasingly strident nationalism that recognised no restriction other than the limit of available military force thus proved the main impetus for Japanese aggression in China after July 1937, but this campaign also marked the completion of the process whereby the army secured for itself a position of dominance in the Japanese decision-making process. The Inukai government was followed by four administrations in five years, and there would have been more had all the coups and assassinations planned by members of the armed forces been successful. This brief period between 1931 and 1937, often known as a period of 'government by assassination' but noted also for the growing power of the army and for *Gekokujo* or manipulation of senior officers by their juniors and the breakdown of discipline within the army, came to an end after the last assertion of its independence by the Diet. After the government of General Hayashi Senjuro was defeated at the April 1937 election, the two main political parties, the *Minseito* and *Seiyukai*, which in the past had done much to discredit the democratic process, combined to force Hayashi from office. This move was countered by an army that ensured that the cabinet that came to power on 5 June was heavily weighted in its favour and headed by a premier, Prince Konoye

Fumimaro, known to be, for all his moderate reputation, sympathetic to the army's aims and interests.

Two international developments marked the lurch of Japan into war in China in 1937. First, on 24 November 1936 Japan joined Germany in the Anti-Comintern Pact. The pact's aim was to neutralise the Soviet Union both in Europe and the Far East by dividing her attention between both, but its real significance for Japan lay in the fact that it was negotiated by the army, not the foreign ministry, and marked the victory of the *tosei-ha* within the army. The *tosei-ha* had no wish to become embroiled in a war with the Soviet Union and sought if not friendly then correct relations with Moscow or a check on Soviet power because it saw China as Japan's natural area of interest and expansion. The Anti-Comintern Pact, therefore, was an acknowledgement of the army's power within the state and the *tosei-ha*'s power within the army, but it was also the means whereby the army sought to secure its flank and rear in the event of a general war in China.

Second, in early 1937 the Japanese authorities could not avoid becoming aware that China appeared to be on the point of halting her interminable civil wars in order to prevent further Japanese incursions into northern China: such a development served as a temptation to act before Chinese preparations were completed. This change in the domestic Chinese situation was forced upon Chiang Kai-shek who, though under no illusions about Japanese intentions, between 1931 and November 1936 more than doubled the area under his direct control and brought the communists to the very brink of defeat. In the course of five major offensives Chiang was able to eliminate communist strongholds south of the Yangtse. Between October 1934 and October 1935 his fifth offensive forced the communists in Kiangsi and Fukien into a withdrawal to north-west China that is known to history as the Long March. Though the communist armies avoided total annihilation in the course of their withdrawal to Shensi, they were weakened severely during this campaign and found on their arrival in the north-west that their programmes of social and political reform had very limited appeal. In November 1936 Chiang was on the point of launching a sixth offensive against the communists in every expectation that it would be his last.

The cutting edge for this offensive was to have been provided by the Manchurian troops of Chang Hsueh-liang, but on 12 December the Manchurians arrested Chiang at Sian and presented him with the choice between his offensive and his life. Not surprisingly, Chiang chose the latter, the price of his release being his agreement to a united front to oppose the Japanese. Chiang was released on 25 December, and

Japan's 'Special Undeclared War': China, 1937 - 38

negotiations between his government and the communists proceeded throughout the early months of 1937 to the very obvious alarm of the Japanese. Indeed, as early as 28 December, when it was far from clear what had been agreed at Sian, the Japanese army unequivocally stated that in the event of Chiang allying himself with the communists and assuming an anti-Japanese policy it would 'devise whatever measures it deems necessary for . . . the preservation of peace throughout east Asia'. By July 1937 the army had devised at least some of the measures it deemed necessary, though whether these were necessarily those that would ensure peace throughout east Asia was quite another matter.

'The China Incident' arose from a minor clash between Chinese and Japanese forces on 7 July 1937 at Wanping, just outside Peking. This clash, which became known as the Lukouchiao or Marco Polo Bridge Incident, was just one of many such skirmishes that had taken place since 1932 and which had been used by the Japanese to browbeat local Chinese authorities into concessions. At the time this familiar pattern seemed certain to repeat itself. Though Japanese responsibility for the clash was obvious, the Chinese indicated a willingness to meet Japanese demands and in Tokyo, both within the government and the army general staff, there was a willingness to settle the matter locally. Even the Japanese forces in northern China, aware of the small number of formations immediately available for operations, were reluctant to escalate the affair, but in the event three developments – the determination of the Japanese army in Manchoutikuo to force the Inner Mongolia issue; the massacre of several hundred Japanese soldiers and civilians at Tungchow in late July; and the outbreak of fighting in Shanghai on 13 August – combined to ensure that the Lukouchiao Incident could not be limited either by area or scale. The reality was that there were only too many Japanese willing to use any pretext to begin their country's 'special undeclared war' with China, but in the five weeks after the Wanping clash the Japanese, notwithstanding their occupation of Tientsin on 30 July and Peking on 8 August, made no attempt to mobilise or move beyond the Suiyuan–Peking–Linghai line. Mobilisation was not ordered until 17 August as the fighting at Shanghai proved the decisive factor that drew Japan into full-scale war in China. Once the commitment to Shanghai was undertaken the China Incident began in earnest, a total of 15 divisions being sent from Japan to northern and central China by the end of September.

From such inauspicious beginnings developed a war that lasted eight years. It was to pass through several phases in that time but the bulk of

Japanese conquest was registered between August 1937 and October 1938. This opening phase of the war, however, divided into two distinct parts separated, or linked, by the fall of Suchow in north-west Kiangsu in May 1938. Between July 1937 and May 1938 the Japanese fought what were in effect two quite separate campaigns in China, one in the northern provinces of Shansi, Hopei and Shantung and the other on the lower Yangtse. It was only in spring 1938, after Japanese forces converged on Suchow, that the Japanese were able to link their conquests and secure direct overland communications between Peking and Shanghai. Thereafter the Japanese carried the war up the Yangtse and through the Tapiehshan mountains, securing Hangchow in October and Yoyang and Tungshan in November. Though the Japanese tide of conquest continued to inch forward in certain areas after October 1938 with various operations that included the occupation of Hainan in January 1939 and various coastal towns in Kwangsi and Kwantung in 1941, the main Japanese effort in China was at an end with the taking of the Wuhan cities in autumn 1938.

At the outset of the war the Japanese forces in the northern provinces amounted to no more than a corps equivalent, but in the absence of Chinese regular formations in the area the Japanese had no difficulty in securing the Peking–Tientsin line and their entry into Peking was unopposed. At this time the Japanese High Command had no plans to move against Chahar, still less against Suiyuan, and by its own terms of reference – if not those of others – its designation of the Paoting–Tuliuchen line as the limit of its interests was a token of its restraint.

Even before the outbreak of fighting at Shanghai changed the character of the Lukouchiao Incident, however, the Manchoutikuo-based *Kwantung Army*, by convention the most important and independently minded of Japanese commands, made clear its designs on Chahar and Suiyuan, and its initial moves in Chahar were contrary to explicit instructions from Tokyo. But as in 1931, the *Kwantung Army* proceeded on the premise that its actions could not be repudiated and would be approved retrospectively, as was the case. It moved forces from Chengte to Tolun and Changpei in western Chahar before being ordered to secure the Nankow Pass and to begin operations within the Outer Great Wall. This it did with its occupation of Kalgan on 27 August and of Tatung, gateway to Shansi province, on 13 September. The presence of Manchoutikuo and Mongolian forces with the Japanese in these operations indicated that the *Kwantung Army*'s interest lay not in Shansi but in Suiyuan, and with the scope of the war rapidly widening its assorted formations advanced along the Peking–Suiyuan railroad securing Pingti-chuan on 23 September, Kueisui on 14 October and Paotow on the seventeenth. The *Kwantung Army*'s ambitions in Inner Mongolia were revealed as early as 23 October when it sponsored, 'in year 732 of the era of Genghis Khan', the proclamation of Suiyuan's independence by a collection of Kueisui's citizens of somewhat uncertain status. With the creation of the Mongolian Federated Autonomous Government at Kueisui in December the Japanese idea of Man-Mo, the linking of Japan with Manchuria and Mongolia that dated back at least to 1912, had been realised if only with respect to eastern Inner Mongolia.

In northern China the various commands were reinforced and reorganised in the course of August, the *North China Area Army* of General Terauchi Misaichi being activated on 31 August with the *1st* and *2nd Armies* under command. *The 1st Army*, supported on its right flank by a formation from the *Kwantung Army*, was ordered to develop an attack along the Peking–Paoting axis while the *2nd Army* secured Tuliuchen, but from the outset both armies, undeterred by the move of some 400,000 Chinese troops into positions around Chohsien in order to block any advance by the *1st Army*, sought to extend the scope of operations by striking at objectives far beyond those approved by the high command. The *1st Army* set Shihchiachuang as its objective while the *2nd Army* assigned the Chengtin–Tehchow line for itself. With the *gekokujo* principle asserting itself in the form of Terauchi's subsequent demand that Japanese efforts could only be justified if the whole of China north of the Yellow River was reorganised within an enlarged Japanese sphere of influence, the end of September found the Japanese army committed to a major campaign in China.

The army, however, was also committed to a short war: it believed that China could not offer sustained or effective resistance and that Chiang Kai-shek would come to terms quickly in accordance with the past practice of his subordinates. At least the first part of Japanese calculations was correct: Chinese forces around Chohsien simply melted away in the face of the *1st Army*'s advance, Paoting being taken on 24 September and Shihchiachuang on 10 October. In taking the latter the Japanese rendered the defence of Shansi impossible, and converging attacks from the north via the Inner Great Wall by the *5th Infantry Division* and from the east by the *20th Infantry Division* resulted in the capture of the provincial capital, Taiyuan, on 9 November, after which the Japanese forces in Shansi went over to the defensive. In Hopei, however, the *1st Army* continued its southwards advance after taking Shihchiachuang and occupied Anyang on 31 October. To the east the *2nd Army* found its operations restricted as a result of decisions taken in Tokyo. While some of its formations moved up the Tseya to link up with the *1st Army* around Chaohsien, its *10th Infantry Division* was halted after it secured Tehchow, immediately inside Shantung, on 5 October. In fact it was able to creep forward in order to secure first Pingyuan and then Yucheng, the latter on 31 October, but the *2nd Army* was specifically ordered not to move against the provincial capital, Chinan.

The restriction on operations in Shantung appears to have been the result of the decision to reinforce the *Shanghai Expeditionary Army* which faced a very large Chinese force in an area which, with its heavy concentration of population and maze of waterways, was not well suited to mobile operations. Moreover, the *SEA* had been fed piecemeal into the battle around Shanghai – two divisions were committed to battle in August and another three in early September – with the result that the *SEA* had been forced to respond to events dictated by a numerically stronger army. It was thus decided that operations in Shantung should be halted while the situation at Shanghai was resolved, the Japanese intention being to turn the Chinese positions around the city by two amphibious attacks, one against Paimaochiang and the other against Chuankungting.

The decision to commit four divisions to these two landings was made on the basis that operations on the lower Yangtse were to be limited to the clearing of Shanghai, and the decision was vindicated by the fact that the city was secured as a result of these operations. The landings in Hangchow Bay were carried out by the *10th Army* on 5 November, and with Japanese units threatening a close investment of Shanghai with the capture of Paihokang on the eleventh the Chinese began the evacuation of Shanghai two days before the *16th Infantry Division* (detached from the *2nd Army*) came ashore at Paimaochiang. But unknown to most senior officers of the Japanese High Command, the commander of the *SEA*, General Matsui Iwane, and certain members of the army general staff, had secretly agreed that after Shanghai was secured Japanese forces would strike deep into Chinese territory. Indeed, the renaming of the *Shanghai Expeditionary Army* as the *Central China Expeditionary Army* was an indication of widening Japanese ambitions in the Yangtse valley and of the continuing effectiveness of *gekokujo*. Senior officers duly provided the necessary authorisation for a forward strategy on the lower Yangtse when presented with the demands of their subordinates. They did so in the belief that the loss of Nanking would force Chiang Kai-shek to come to terms, but by the time that Shanghai fell in mid-September there were signs that the China Incident was not going to be ended by a final battle or the capture of a single city.

The defence of Shanghai cost the Chinese armies an estimated 270,000 killed and wounded, including the equivalent of four years' supply of junior lieutenants, but while this defeat exposed Nanking to attack Chiang made no response to Japanese overtures for negotiations and refused to consider a German offer of mediation. Nanking fell on 13 December amid scenes of mass murder, torture, rape and pillage that were to become the hallmarks of the Japanese army over the next five years. An estimated 200,000 Chinese were butchered by the Japanese in the seven weeks after the fall of the city, but on 26 December Chiang publicly and in very great detail rejected any possibility of a negotiated settlement with Japan. By that time the Japanese had sponsored the first of several puppet regimes that they were to establish in northern China with the installation of a provisional government at Peking on 14 December. Chiang's hardline refusal to consider negotiations nevertheless came as a surprise to Tokyo. On 16 January 1938 the Japanese announced that in future it would have no dealings with Chiang and would eliminate 'once and for all the cause of disturbance' in China. Perhaps the only real surprise at this stage was that Tokyo should ever have considered that its terms for a settlement – Chiang's recognition of the puppet regimes in northern China and Inner Mongolia; Japan's sole right to garrison northern and central China; the economic integration of Japan, Manchoutikuo and China; and a Chinese reparation for the cost of the war – could ever have been accepted by Chiang, but the fact of the matter was that for all of its bravado Chiang's refusal left Tokyo with a series of dilemmas not dissimilar from those that Japan had faced in the warlord era a decade earlier. The Japanese political and military leadership really had no clear idea of its objectives in China: it did not know whether to seek the destruction of Chiang's regime or its preservation as the only authority with which it could negotiate a settlement: it did not know whether to sponsor rival regimes in an attempt to put pressure upon the Kuomintang in order that it might come to a settlement or to present genuine alternatives to Chiang's regime.

These dilemmas were compounded by the illusion that one last effort would ensure the decisive victory that would end resistance, but by the end of 1937 Japan was in a position unlike any other that she had faced in China over previous years. She could still find individuals, even of national standing, with whom to deal, but Chinese mobilisation for continuing resistance meant that ultimately Japan had to deal directly with Chiang Kai-shek, and by his refusal to negotiate Chiang denied the

Japanese the means to end the China Incident by political means. This refusal left the Japanese with no alternative other than to seek their decisive victory, but this presented three complications. First, impressive though Japanese conquests in 1937 undoubtedly were, the Japanese occupation of northern China was one of cities and lines of communication and by the beginning of 1938 insurgency had begun to take hold in areas nominally under Japanese control. Second, the campaign in northern China in 1937 had involved a reduction of Japanese garrisons in Manchoutikuo, and the consequence was a revival of banditry and insurgency throughout Japan's client state. Third, at the back of every Japanese military problem in China was the question of relations with foreign powers, and specifically with the Soviet Union, and indeed Chiang's refusal to come to terms with Japan was largely shaped by this same issue. Chiang genuinely believed that a protracted war would end with the defeat of Japan if only because in the course of such a war Japan would involve herself with enemies that would crush her. In December 1937 it indeed seemed likely that Japan would involve herself in a war with other powers as a result of attacks by Japanese army and naval air units on four American and five British warships above Nanking. In naval circles in both London and Washington there were advocates of intervention, but neither the Americans nor the British were prepared in December 1937 to act without the other and by the time that joint staff talks opened in London the Japanese had defused the issue by apologies and offers of compensation.

These incidents were thus smoothed over and Chiang was forced back on 'the sustained strategy of attrition' that had been proclaimed on 7 August. But the Soviet Union presented a more persistent and substantial problem for the Japanese. Border clashes along the ill-defined frontier between Manchoutikuo and the Soviet Union were frequent, and as early as August 1937 the Soviet Union made clear her intention not to be intimidated by the Anti-Comintern Pact. In that month she concluded a non-aggression treaty with China and subsequently occupied Sinkiang and used the old Silk Route through the province to supply the increasingly beleaguered Kuomintang regime at Chungking with military equipment, stores and advisers. Her occupation of Sinkiang and Mongolia left the Soviet Union well placed to counter any Japanese move into western Suiyuan, and while 1938 was not to pass without a serious clash between Japanese and Soviet forces the year presented in more acute form the problem that the Japanese had faced since July 1937: whether operations in China were to be restricted in order to ensure the security of Manchoutikuo or developed without reference to the prospect of a clash with the Soviet Union.

The immediate reality of Japan's situation, however, dictated that operations in China proceeded, and the first quarter of 1938 saw the Japanese complete the conquest of Shansi, overrun virtually the whole of northern and central Shantung, and in Anhwei secure Hwaiyuan and Pengpu in readiness for operations against Suchow. In Shansi, where the Japanese had already occupied Taiyuan and Anyang, the *109th Infantry Division* struck westwards from Taiyuan to secure Lishih on 24 February while the *20th Infantry Division* advanced southwards to take Pingyaohsien on the thirteenth and Linfen on the twenty-sixth, where it was joined by units from the *106th Infantry Division*. This had advanced from Hantanhsien, having taken Changchih on 20 February. At the same time the *14th Infantry Division* had advanced southwards along the line of the railroad to secure Sinsiang on the seventeenth before turning westwards along the northern bank of the Yellow River, taking Tsinyang on the twenty-first, Yuanku on the twenty-seventh and Pinglu on 9 March. Around Pinglu its advance converged with that of the *20th Infantry Division* which, having taken Linfen, secured Anyi and, on 6 March, Yungtsi. With Hotsin also taken on the fourth, the various Japanese advances resulted in their securing the line of the Yellow River and the clearing of Shansi.

The clearing of Shantung, however, proved more difficult. Having taken Chinan on 26 December the *2nd Army* continued to advance to the south, securing Tsining on 5 January while naval units, supported by the ubiquitous *5th Infantry Division*, secured Tsingtao on the tenth. But the defence of Shantung to date by its warlord, Han Fu-chu, had been so irresolute as to raise suspicion of collusion with the Japanese, and after Han was arrested and executed on orders of Chiang Kai-shek the *2nd Army* encountered stiffening resistance. Having taken Tangtoucheng on 5 March the Japanese moved against Suchow on the twenty-fourth only to have the *5th Infantry Division* repulsed with heavy losses around Tierhchuang in the first week of April. On the main axis of advance the *2nd Army* was not able to secure Tsowhsien until early May. By then, however, three divisions of the *Central China Expeditionary Army* had begun an offensive against Suchow from the south, and on 18 May the *13th Infantry Division* secured Yungcheng and joined up with the *2nd Army* on the following day. With the loss of Suchow Chinese resistance slackened with the attempt to avoid encirclement and annihilation, but in fact the Japanese were too thin on the ground to trap the bulk of Chinese forces which escaped to the west or went to ground in the coastal areas:

the Japanese completed a general, if temporary, pacification of Shantung by September.

The moves against Suchow coincided with operations by the *1st Army* against Lanfeng, but only after formations from the *2nd Army* were released for an advance to the west after the fall of Suchow did the advance along the railroad to Kaifeng and Chengchow prosper. Kaifeng fell on 7 June and Chengchow on the tenth, and with the capture of the latter the Japanese had the choice of developing their offensive either to the west, against Loyang, Tungkwan and Sian, or to the south, against the Wuhan cities. The Chinese, their forces scattered and unable to oppose the Japanese on either front, opened the dykes of 'China's Sorrow', diverting the Yellow River hundreds of miles to the south until it met the Hwai above Pengpu. By this action the Chinese devastated the countryside and killed countless fellow countrymen, but halted Japanese operations in the direction of the Chengchow–Hangchow railroad until 1944.

This Chinese action led to the regrouping of the *2nd Army* and its move to Hefei in central Anhwei, which had been secured by *CCEA* on 14 May. From there the *2nd Army* prepared to advance around and through the Tapiehshan mountains in order to get astride the Chengchow–Hangchow railroad in the area of the Honan–Hupeh border. It opened its offensive with the capture of Liuan on 28 August and then, using two axes of advance, secured Shangcheng on 16 September and Hwangchwan on the seventeenth. Thereafter this outflanking attack was continued with the railroad being reached on 10 October at Sinyang. Avoiding the Washengkwan Pass, the Japanese moved off the railroad and secured Yingshan and Yingchen on 26 and 30 October. The attempt to force the Schwangmen Pass predictably made only slow progress: Sungfow was not secured until 26 October, the day on which two of the Wuhan cities, Wuchang and Hanyang, fell to Japanese formations that had advanced up the Yangtse. Hangkow, abandoned as a temporary capital in June, had fallen the previous day.

The main drive on the Wuhan cities had begun in early June, the Japanese making their main effort on the right bank of the Yangtse while the *6th Infantry Division* operated independently north of the river and secured Tsienshan on 13 June and Hwangmei on 2 August. On the line of the river the Japanese secured Anking on 12 June and then, after the Chinese made no attempt to hold the heavily fortified Matang position on 2 July, Hukow on the fourth and Kiukang on the twenty-sixth. In August the Japanese reorganised their forces around Kiukang in readiness for the final stage of the advance on the Wuhan cities. With the *6th Infantry*

Division remaining north of the river, the *11th Army* deployed two of its four infantry divisions to guard the open flank to the south while it advanced on a double front, securing Wuchang and Hanyang on 26 October and Sienning on 31 October. The fact that the *6th Infantry Division* occupied Hangchow on the twenty-fifth was evidence of the most obvious aspect of these operations: the Japanese took the Wuhan cities by marching, not fighting: indeed, the Chinese had abandoned the middle Yangtse as a result of the landings by the *21st Army* in Bias Bay on 12 October. The value of the Wuhan cities to the Kuomintang depended on their links with Canton and foreign trade, and the patent inability of forces in Kwangtung to prevent the loss of Canton – which fell on 21 October – prompted the Chiang regime to abandon the Wuhan cities in favour of a withdrawal into the mountains of Szechwan. As a result of this decision and the continued refusal of Chiang to come to the negotiating table, the Japanese remained unable to end the China Incident by either military or political means. In fact, Chiang's withdrawal to Chungking clearly pointed to the lengthening of the war into the indefinite future, and this at a time when perhaps no more than 10 per cent of the area that Japanese armies had overrun since July 1937 was under effective Japanese control. By October 1938, however, events in central China were overshadowed by developments in Europe, and for two years after the fall of the Wuhan cities events in eastern Asia were of secondary importance as Europe took centre stage.

The final stages of the Japanese advance on the Wuhan cities coincided with the greatest of Europe's inter-war crises, the very name of which remains synonymous with the reassertion of German primacy within Europe and an abject Anglo-French compliance in the process. The Munich crisis of September 1938 saw a return to the concept of the concert of Europe on the lines that had been proposed by Mussolini in 1933, but as such it proved the swansong of Europe: it was the last occasion when European problems were handled by Europeans without the involvement of the United States and the Soviet Union. But it was a crisis that was handled and settled in a manner that ensured it remains, even after 50 years, a subject of controversy and emotion, not because it involved a failure to ensure the peace of Europe but because by their deeds Britain and France forfeited any claim on morality as the basis of their actions and decisions.

The Munich crisis was unlike any other episode in the process that led to war in 1939 in that it did not burst suddenly upon the European scene. The crisis of September 1938 was predictable, and indeed much of the

31

moral slime that has attached itself to Anglo-French appeasement at Munich stems from the fact that after March 1938 Britain and France took the lead in forcing Czechoslovakia into concessions in anticipation of unspecified German demands. In principle the Anglo-French policy of appeasement was not unreasonable, but in practice it was flawed by the fact that the concessions made by Britain and France were at the expense of a third nation in order to preserve a peace that was doomed. The rationalisations used by Britain when the failure of this policy became clear – that Munich provided Britain and France with a year in which to rearm themselves and that in September 1938 it was not clear that nothing could preserve the peace of Europe in the long term – are at best irrelevant and at worst deliberately disingenuous. The strategic position of Britain and France relative to Germany deteriorated rather than improved between Munich and September 1939, and if Britain was unaware in September 1938 of the nature and long-term ambitions of Nazism then she was virtually alone in her illusions.

For a year that was to see not one but two major European crises, 1938 opened quietly, but by the time it did so Hitler had already taken the decision to hasten the pace of German aggrandisement and was thinking of war not in or after but before 1943. Though he had no immediate intention of provoking a general conflict in Europe, Hitler thought in terms of advancing his ambitions with respect to Austria and Czechoslovakia and was presented with the opportunity to absorb Austria by events in that country. His success in Germany had considerable appeal within Austria and throughout 1937 acts of terrorism in Austria increased as local Nazis sought to provoke the government of chancellor Kurt von Schuschnigg into measures that could be used as a pretext for German intervention. By January 1938 the situation inside Austria was such that Schuschnigg sought Hitler's personal commitment to restrain the Austrian Nazis, but he was to find that Hitler sought nothing less than the destruction of Austria as an independent state. In the course of their meeting of 12 February Hitler threatened to turn Austria into 'a second Spain' unless the Austrian Nazis were allowed to operate legally and their leader, Arthur Seyss-Inquart, was made Minister of the Interior. Unwilling either to risk civil war in Austria or war with Germany Schuschnigg agreed to these demands, but with Nazi strength in Austria growing as a result of his concessions Schuschnigg, on 9 March, announced a plebiscite on the thirteenth on the question of whether Austrians wished their country to remain independent. On 11 March, with the Austro-German border closed and German troops massed in

Bavaria, Nazi ministers in his cabinet presented Schuschnigg with Hitler's demand that the referendum be cancelled, and when this was conceded the demand for the chancellor's resignation followed immediately. With Seyss-Inquart installed as chancellor the invitation to Germany to intervene in Austria was automatic, and German forces crossed the border on 12 March when the chancellor of one day proclaimed the *Anschluss* and the end of a distinct Austrian identity and independence that dated from the thirteenth century.

In the course of the meeting on 12 February Hitler had warned Schuschnigg that Britain and France would not oppose a German occupation of Austria. As was so often the case at this time, events proved Hitler correct: Britain and France did not even bother to convene the League of Nations for the ritual condemnation of this latest German breach of an international treaty. At the time of the *Anschluss* France was between governments and Britain took the view that it was simply a domestic German affair and in accordance with the principle of national self-determination established at Versailles. But not even the British government could ignore the fact that the *Anschluss* had altered profoundly the strategic geography of central Europe, yet on 14 and 28 March the British prime minister, Neville Chamberlain, specifically refused either to guarantee Czechoslovakia or to guarantee France in the event of her supporting Czechoslovakia in accordance with her treaty obligations. Moreover, on 28 March Chamberlain refused a Soviet request for consultations on the subject of joint action in the event of German aggression. Chamberlain thus indicated that Britain was not prepared to go to war for Czechoslovakia and would not be a party to any collective security arrangement intended to ensure peace through deterrence. Given French subservience to Britain in dealing with Germany, Chamberlain effectively stated that the alliance system on which Czechoslovakia depended for her security was dead and that German demands upon her would not be opposed by Britain and France.

On 28 March Hitler instructed the leader of the Sudeten Nazis, Konrad Henlein, 'always to demand so much that we can never be satisfied', and after this date the three great powers began to act upon the logic explicit in the events of this day. As Hitler set about confusing the issue he intended to raise – the independence and integrity of Czechoslovakia – by presenting it as a dispute between an oppressed German minority and an authoritarian Czech state that demanded German intervention rather than unprovoked aggression by Germany against a neighbour, German planning for an invasion of Czechoslovakia began on 21 April, and on 24 May Hitler indicated to his senior commanders his determination to destroy Czechoslovakia 'by military action in the near future'. But in April British and French leaders met to decide a joint approach to a Czechoslovakian problem that they recognised as certain to emerge by the time of the annual Nazi Party rally in September and both separately assured Germany of their intention to resolve the Czech question, Britain going so far as to ask Germany to restrain Henlein while she pressed the Czechs to agree to Nazi demands.

Hitler spent the summer of 1938 allowing events to gather momentum as Britain set about dismantling Czechoslovakia on his behalf. His concern was lest his potential enemies find common ground and the will to oppose him, specifically that France, the Soviet Union and Czechoslovakia would stand by their various alliances with one another. Given his hostility towards the Soviet Union there was no bilateral means by which he could neutralise her, but in trusting that the differences that divided his neighbours would prevent their combining effectively against Germany he was rewarded. Without direct access to Czechoslovakia the Soviet Union could only support that country if she was granted rights of transit through Poland and Romania, an eventuality that they regarded as only marginally different from direct invasion. In any case, Poland and Hungary had claims on Czechoslovakian territory that they were quietly encouraged by Germany to press. The cordon of small states that for two decades had shielded Europe from the Soviet Union thus served to isolate Czechoslovakia from possible Soviet help in 1938, but even without this Hitler was assured that the Western democracies would not associate themselves with the Soviet Union over Czechoslovakia. France attempted to do so during June, but was blocked by Britain. Motivated by an extreme distrust of the Soviet Union, Chamberlain refused to consider any approach to the latter until 23 September, and France felt obliged to go along with British wishes. For her part Britain, despite her identification of her own security with the maintenance of France as a great power, was not prepared to endorse either the alliances that were the basis of French security or an understanding with the Soviet Union, and given these views Britain had no alternative but to force the Czechs into concessions if war was to be avoided.

As a result of Anglo-French pressure Czechoslovakia conceded on 4 September the substance of Nazi demands only to find that, like the famous definition of another problem, every time she provided the answer Germany changed the question. On the twelfth Hitler repudiated Czech concessions with the clear implication of a willingness to use force against Czechoslovakia, and on the thirteenth, when the Czech army put down a Sudeten rising without difficulty, Chamberlain offered to fly to Germany to meet Hitler in an effort to resolve the developing crisis. This he did on the fifteenth and again on 22 September, on each occasion being greeted by increased German demands. Though in the second meeting Chamberlain made clear his view that the borders of Czechoslovakia shorn of the Sudetenland need not be considered final, he was not empowered to agree to the German demand for the immediate occupation of the Sudetenland. On his return to London, however, Chamberlain found that British public opinion had hardened in the face of this latest German demand and on 26 September he felt obliged to announce that in the event of France honouring her commitments to Czechoslovakia Britain would be obliged to support France. At the same time the British government sought Mussolini's help in avoiding a general war over Czechoslovakia, and on 28 September the Italian dictator advised Chamberlain that Hitler had agreed to a four-power conference to settle the Sudetenland issue. Accordingly, on 29 September the leaders of Britain, France, Germany and Italy met at Munich, and in the early hours of the thirtieth concluded a treaty that provided Hitler with all he wanted other than the destruction of Czechoslovakia by force. The task of informing the Czechs of their fate fell to the British and French, and within two months Czechoslovakia had all but fallen to pieces. In October the Poles demanded and occupied Teschen and in November German-Italian arbitration gave Hungary lands in southern Czechoslovakia to which she laid claim. That same month Prague conceded Slovak and Ruthenian claims for autonomy.

At the time the Munich agreement was not regarded in Britain and France as a capitulation: the prevailing mood in both countries was one of relief that war had been avoided and that there would be, as Chamberlain proclaimed, 'peace in our time'. Yet within six months the illusion was to be destroyed by two German actions. First, beginning on 14 March 1939 German forces occupied Czechoslovakia with the result that Bohemia-Moravia was declared a German protectorate on the fifteenth and a nominally independent Slovakia concluded a treaty of alliance with Germany on the twenty-third. Second, on 20 March Germany demanded from Lithuania the return of Memel, which had been ceded to the Baltic state in February 1923. On 26 March the city was restored to Germany.

The initial reaction of the British government to the German occupation of Prague was very restrained: Chamberlain expressed the opinion that the demise of Czechoslovakia may well have been inevitable and, by implication, was not to be regretted or taken very seriously. But this somewhat casual attitude changed with the realisation of public outrage at the course of events. British opinion was shaped by two matters. The Munich agreement had included an Anglo-French guarantee of Czechoslovakia's revised borders, and to demonstrate the Anglo-German friendship and understanding that was part of the agreement Hitler had asserted that he had no further demands on Czechoslovakia and had no wish to incorporate the Czechs within Germany. Technically, Hitler did not break either provision, but in reality he quite deliberately destroyed Czechoslovakia in March 1939. This was not lost upon a British public which realised that it had deceived itself over Munich and that 'whetting the appetite of the insatiable is mere suicidal folly'. With the German occupation of Prague there was belated British recognition that there could be no peace in Europe as long as Hitler ruled in Germany, and on the last day of March Chamberlain personally wrote a guarantee of Polish independence, sovereignty and territorial integrity. For good measure he included France in this guarantee, not that the Daladier government had been consulted on the matter.

The guarantee was given almost nonchalantly, and most certainly with no awareness of what it might entail: Chamberlain most assuredly did not foresee war as the direct and inevitable consequence of his action. The issuing of the guarantee was no more than a reaction to the occupation of Prague and Mezel, and it was the product of the hope that a display of resolution on the part of the democracies would cause Hitler to show a moderation that had been notably absent over Czechoslovakia. It was also an attempt to reassure the Poles whose dealings with Germany had clearly reached a critical point at this time. As early as 24 October, just after the Poles had pocketed Teschen, the Germans had raised with Poland the issue of the future status of the League of Nations' free state of Danzig and German rights of transit through Posen and Silesia between the two parts of Germany. Long accustomed to regard Danzig as the indicator of German intentions towards themselves, the Poles refused to consider the return of the city state to Germany despite the seemingly attractive *quid pro quo* of an alliance against the Soviet Union and Polish compensation in the east. On the immediate issues, the sympathies of the British government lay with German claims which, with respect to Danzig, were the most reasonable of German inter-war grievances, but by providing Poland with an unconditional guarantee on 31 March the British government denied itself the means of influencing the Poles on these two issues, not that the Poles would have yielded on either of them. Poland regarded herself as the Christ-nation of Europe because she was fated to be crucified between two thieves and had no wish to choose between neighbours which, in historical terms, had never wished to preserve and maintain her. Both Germany and Russia had sought to extinguish Polish national consciousness and to absorb Polish territory within themselves, and however attractive the German offer of an anti-Soviet alliance the Poles knew that acceptance would involve ultimate subjugation to Germany.

The weakness of the British guarantee to Poland was that while it sought to deter Germany it could not be made effective if it failed to check Hitler unless the Soviet Union was in some way associated with it. But the guarantee was as much a pledge of Poland's eastern border with the Soviet Union as it was a promise to preserve Poland's western borders with Germany, and Poland had no wish to rely upon the Soviet Union for support in dealings with Germany. In early spring this was not a serious concern to Chamberlain: the British government's calculation was that Soviet support in dealing with Germany would be forthcoming 'if desired'. The British concern was to ensure that the Soviet Union fought at Anglo-French behest, but Britain was not prepared to force the Poles to accept Soviet assistance and she most certainly was not prepared to support the Soviet Union if the latter was involved in war with Germany on her own behalf. For her part, the Soviet Union was well aware of the one-sided arrangement that Britain sought after negotiations between the two countries opened in April, and she was equally aware of the fact that in some Western circles there was a real hope that Germany and the Soviet Union would clash in a mutually exhausting war. The Soviet Union, therefore, was wary of any arrangement other than a reciprocal and binding alliance, and thus the search for an agreement between Britain, France and the Soviet Union in 1939 was doomed on two counts. From the start Britain and the Soviet Union sought mutually unacceptable arrangements, and in the final analysis Britain would not consider any device whereby the power of decision regarding the implementation of an alliance rested with the Soviet Union.

Two developments provided the essential element of urgency in Anglo-Soviet negotiations. First, on 28 April Hitler abrogated the German-Polish non-aggression and Anglo-German naval treaties. Though he made no specific demands on Poland, and indeed there were no diplomatic contacts between Germany and Poland from 28 March to 31 August, the pattern of German behaviour before Munich began to repeat itself with respect to Poland. Second, in an attempt to restore a position in the Balkans that had been weakened at Munich, Italy unexpectedly occupied Albania on 7 April. But Mussolini's attempt to restore the balance between the two Axis powers was countered on 13

April by British offers of guarantees to Greece and Romania and, on 12 May, by the conclusion of an Anglo-Turkish mutual assistance pact. This attempt to stabilise the Mediterranean situation nevertheless had the effect of completing the Italian alignment with Germany. Despite Mussolini's suspicions of Germany and the course on which she was embarked, on 22 May Italy joined her in a treaty by which the two powers promised one another 'full military support' if either was involved in war. Given the fact that Mussolini knew that Italy dared not consider war before 1943 but that in October 1938 Germany had raised the possibility of war in autumn 1939, the Pact of Steel was an act of folly on Italy's part: the day after the alliance was concluded Hitler committed himself to war, the plans for an attack on Poland on 1 September having been under preparation since his provisional directive of 3 April.

But if these developments provided urgency to the search for an alliance between the Democracies and the Soviet Union only the latter appreciated the fact. Throughout the summer Britain sought to delay proceedings while the Soviet Union forced the pace of negotiations, and confronted by British half-heartedness the Soviet Union moved to the conclusion that the premise on which Britain negotiated with her was flawed. Just as Britain had the choice between appeasing or opposing Germany so did the Soviet Union, which had the choice of joining Britain and France in 1939 or standing aside in the hope of avoiding or postponing war with Germany. As early as 17 April the Soviet Union indicated to Germany that past hostility and present ideological differences need not prevent the future improvement of relations between the two countries, and in May and June, as Germany and the Soviet Union grappled with the problems presented by Britain's obduracy in that country's very different dealings with them, Hitler and Stalin very slowly moved towards an otherwise unthinkable conclusion: a non-aggression treaty on the part of the two arch-enemies in Europe at the expense of their neighbours.

Both sides approached the idea of a pact with the other with reluctance: habits born of years of mutal vilification were difficult to discard. Despite her initial overtures, the Soviet Union made little attempt to explore the possibilities of an arrangement with Germany and only turned to this option after 14 August, on which date it became clear that Britain would never enter a reciprocal alliance with her. Hitler likewise only committed himself to seeking an arrangement with Stalin on that same 14 August after weeks of procrastination in which he alternated between aversion to, and the lure of, a Nazi–Soviet understanding. In the end it was the prospect of a diplomatic coup that would deter Britain and France from supporting Poland – thus leaving Germany with a local war – that led Hitler to seek a treaty with Moscow and to accede, on 18 August, to the Soviets' demand for a prior definition of respective spheres of influence as the price of their signature on a treaty with Germany. On the twentieth Hitler asked Stalin to receive his foreign minister in Moscow on the twenty-third, and with Stalin's agreement to this request on the twenty-first the Soviet Union committed herself to a pact with Germany. On 24 August the two countries concluded a treaty that for 10 years bound them not to involve themselves in any form of action against the other and to resolve differences by arbitration. Secret protocols allocated Finland, Estonia and Latvia to the Soviet sphere of influence and Lithuania to that of Germany; recognised the primacy of Soviet interest in the northern Romanian province of Bessarabia; and provided for a partition of Poland along the line of the Narew, Vistula and San rivers.

With the conclusion of this pact Hitler hoped that Anglo-French determination to support Poland would collapse, but on the afternoon of 24 August Chamberlain declared Britain's intention to honour her guarantee to Poland. In one sense the Nazi–Soviet Pact made no difference to Britain and actually eased her position: it ended the complications that had arisen from a search for an alliance that Poland did not want and which Chamberlain had pursued unenthusiastically, and Britain took the view that she would honour her guarantee for no very good reason other than the fact that Poland was certain to be attacked: if war was inevitable then it might as well come over Poland and at once. But the failure to secure an alliance with the Soviet Union in 1939 – characterised by one historian as the most calamitous failure of British foreign policy since the loss of the American colonies – was a disaster for Britain and France, arguably for Poland and perhaps even for the Soviet Union. The failure to conclude an alliance was the direct consequence of the British government's distaste not just for the Soviet Union, which was perhaps understandable, but for the principle of collective security, which under the circumstances was not, and it was the product of a view of Europe that failed to realise that the real alternative to an alliance with the Soviet Union in 1939 was defeat in detail and the German occupation of the Low Countries and northern France in 1940.

The last week before the outbreak of hostilities witnessed the failure of various appeals to the leaders of the great powers to prevent war and the failure of Hitler to detach Britain and France from their Polish connection. In this week Britain rejected a German offer of a guarantee of herself and her empire in return for a free hand over Poland, but this

Europe, June 1939

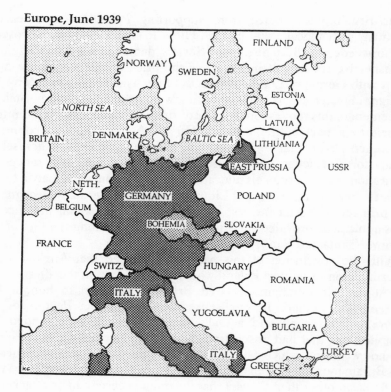

did not prevent Britain from pressing the Poles to open negotiations with the Germans. On 28 August the Poles agreed to do so though they had no intention of making any concessions to German demands. This the Germans knew because of their ability to read the signals that passed between Warsaw and the Polish embassy in Berlin, but the very fact that Poland committed herself to negotiations caused the Germans considerable embarrassment because it forced them, for the first time, to define their terms for a settlement. No such terms existed: Hitler wanted a war, not an agreement. By 31 August, when the Polish envoy sought and was granted a meaningless interview at the German foreign ministry and Mussolini, having reneged on the May treaty, proposed a great power conference to settle the Polish question, the issue of war and peace had been resolved. At dawn on 1 September German forces began the invasion of Poland without any previous declaration of war and on the third, after a series of unseemly delays, Britain and France declared war on Germany.

In a speech to country and empire on this day King George VI spoke in terms of a war for civilisation, justice and humanity that would involve sacrifice and defeats before final victory was won. Chamberlain's address to the nation was very different in content and tone from that of the King and was remarkable for its revelation of a lack of understanding of the forces that were at work in plunging Europe into war. After announcing that a state of war between Britain and Germany existed, Chamberlain went on:

> You cannot imagine what a bitter blow it is to me that all my long struggle to win peace has failed. Yet I cannot believe that there is anything more . . . that I could have done.

Having thus informed his listeners of the personal disappointment and irritation that the outbreak of war had caused him, Chamberlain continued:

> The government has made plans under which it will be possible to carry on the work of the nations . . . But these plans need your help. You may be . . . in the fighting services or . . . in one of the branches of civil defence. If so you will report . . . in accordance with the instructions you have received. You may be engaged in work essential to the prosecution of the war, for the maintenance of the life of the people – in factories, in transport, in public utility concerns or in the supply of other necessities of life. If so, it is of vital importance that you should carry on with your jobs . . . I know that you will all play your part with calmness and courage . . .

Early in the war the British government withdrew a propaganda poster that simply read: 'Your efforts will bring us victory.' Its subconscious 'us and them' theme was the product of a class system that obviously took its lead from the top. The distinction that Chamberlain drew between government and the governed – as if the British people were domestic servants whose only right was to know what was expected of them – was one that could not have been made by Hitler. Moreover, the implication that the prosecution of the war was distinct from the work of the nation showed that Chamberlain did not grasp that Britain had involved herself in a war in which forces of unprecedented power and virulence were to add new dimensions of violence and destruction to the conduct of war. The British declaration of war and Chamberlain's speeches of that day contained no recognition of this fact: indeed the British

41

declaration of war of 3 September was no such thing because it announced the outbreak of hostilities but did not pledge Britain to wage war. The real British declaration of war on Germany came on 8 May 1940 at the end of a momentous House of Commons debate, in the course of which Chamberlain was destroyed politically and physically. But on 1 September 1939 a new war and a new world began, and six years and one day were to pass before both came to an end after the bloodiest and most destructive conflict in history ended in a way that was unimaginable to all but a very select few who heard Chamberlain's broadcast of 3 September 1939, and even these could not have glimpsed the unbelievable horror and depravity that were to be unleashed in the intervening years.

2

CONQUEST BY INSTALMENTS

If, as von Clausewitz laid down,

> the first, the most decisive act of judgement which the statesman
> exercises is rightly to understand [the nature of] the war in which he
> engages [and] not to take it for something, to wish to make of it
> something, which . . . it is impossible for it to be

it is possible to argue that Hitler in the first two years of the European
conflict displayed statesmanship of the first and grandest order. The war
that began on 3 September 1939 was not the war that Hitler wanted, but
within a month its scope and nature were trimmed to proportions that
accorded with his perspective and wishes. Thereafter, until the autumn
of 1941, his was the dominant influence in determining its course, and
hence the paradox: for all his success between 1939 and 1941 Hitler
never understood the nature of the war he had unleashed and was intent
on making it something which it was not and could never be.

Although Hitler saw himself in terms of a warlord he was not. Because
of the weaknesses he deliberately built into the state system in order to
ensure his personal authority, Hitler could not wage war, a fact that
became increasingly obvious with the passing of time. Hitler's great and
undoubted talents lay in his ability to conduct individual campaigns and
to provide the political conditions whereby these campaigns were isolated
in time and area from one another: the conflict in Europe between
September 1939 and September 1941 was not so much a war as a series of
separate campaigns linked by the constancy of Anglo-German hostility.
Yet because of Hitler's view of war the seeds of final defeat were present
even in this period of easy, overwhelming German victories. To Hitler the
state existed for the purpose of making war – an insane transposition of
Clausewitzian criteria – but the racial struggle that was the basis of
Nazism involved an open-ended commitment to war denying Germany

43

the means to consolidate her victories because Nazism could offer the conquered peoples of Europe nothing but death and enslavement. The racism that provided the cutting edge of German military power in the first two years of the European conflict was arguably the most important single factor in Nazism's final defeat.

Scarcely less formidable than his ability to conquer by instalments was Hitler's ability to forge an instrument of conquest that was able to exploit effectively the advantageous political conditions he conjured into existence. In terms of the organisation and tactical doctrine of armed forces Hitler was not an innovator, but his knowledge of what he wanted to achieve provided him with the insight necessary to identify and support individuals and ideas that offered the prospect of quick victories.

The tactical doctrine that emerged under Hitler's sponsorship and upon which he relied to defeat Poland in weeks rather than months – *Blitzkrieg* – was one that sought to restore a mobility conspicuously lacking on Belgian and French battlefields during the First World War by concentrating mobile, overwhelming firepower against a single part of an enemy front. *Blitzkrieg* involved the use of mobile firepower, achieved by the close cooperation of all arms – assault engineers, infantry, artillery and close air support – to make a breach in an enemy front through which armour and motorised supporting arms could pass in order to carry the battle into enemy rear areas. Infantry and anti-armour units were to eliminate remaining pockets of resistance in and around the breach and to hold the flanks from the breach against counter-attack. Bombers operating against lines of communication (interdiction) were to destroy the enemy's command facilities and means of reinforcement, thereby leading to the paralysis and defeat in detail of enemy field forces.

The key technical development in the evolution of *Blitzkrieg* involved neither the tank nor the aircraft – both of which acquired in the 1930s the reliability, range and speed needed for deep penetration operations – but the miniaturisation of the radio. Carried on vehicles that could operate at the head of an advancing column, the radio made possible accurate and timely reporting from the point of contact and effective command and control from the rear. The key organisational development was the creation of armoured divisions, though it must be noted that in September 1939 one-third of all operational German tanks were outside such divisions and that for most of the war this non-organic element never fell below one-fifth of the German armoured establishment.

But unlike other armies that developed light tanks for reconnaissance and dispersed battle tanks in support of the infantry, the German army raised armoured divisions, each with about 240 tanks and supported by a balanced force of motorised infantry, artillery and assault engineers, in order to maximise the advantages of mass and shock action. The key personnel development lay in the intensive training of armoured forces in a deliberate attempt to offset German quantitative and qualitative inferiority to potential enemies by superior leadership, technique and initiative.

It was the combination of these elements with this new, revolutionary form of warfare that Hitler was prepared to unleash upon Poland in order to achieve two aims: to destroy the Polish army before mid-October when the onset of autumn rains would render the majority of Poland's primitive roads impassable to military traffic, and to present Britain and France with a *fait accompli* at the outset of hostilities. Hitler, for all his selective use of history, knew that for Germany the lesson of the First World War was that she had to avoid a protracted, two-front war, and he believed and hoped that the rapid defeat of Poland would destroy Anglo-French determination to continue the fight. Just as German propaganda before September tried to convince the Democracies that Danzig was not worth a war, so Hitler hoped that a quick victory over Poland would convince Britain and France that continuing the war was pointless.

For their first campaign German air and ground forces possessed potentially decisive organisational and tactical advantages over an enemy that based its strength on conventional infantry divisions and cavalry brigades, and which was dependent upon the mobilisation of reserves for mass. For most of the inter-war period Polish defence planning had been geared to a war against the Soviet Union in the wetlands of eastern Poland, hence the large cavalry element within the Polish army. As a nation Poland lacked the industrial base and time to provide armoured and mechanised forces for defence against a German army that did not emerge as a threat until 1937. These German advantages, moreover, were supplemented by numerical superiority. In the course of the September campaign the German army deployed the equivalent of 70 divisions against the Pole's nominal 40, but in reality the disparity of numbers was much greater than a simple comparison of orders of battle would suggest.

At the outbreak of war the German army had under command 66 field divisions and another 23 either in the process of forming or of second-grade status. The 59 divisions in the east included seven armoured, four light, four motorised, two mountain and 37 infantry formations, the balance being five infantry divisions in the process of being formed. The

Polish army numbered two mountain and 38 infantry divisions plus 11 cavalry, two mechanised and three mountain brigades. But the failure of Poland to mobilise before 30 August led to probably no more than 40 per cent of the Polish army being mobilised at the start of hostilities, and the speed of German advances into Poland once war began meant that eight divisions could not be constituted in the course of the campaign. Moreover, in terms of combat effectiveness – firepower, logistical support, mobility and communications – a Polish infantry division was probably no more than half the value of its German counterpart, despite a rough equality of numbers of men and rifles between the two formations. The German armed forces thus held an overwhelming numerical advantage over their opponent, and to this was added the advantage conferred by position: the German army was able to concentrate on selected axes of advance while the Poles, surrounded on three sides and committed to the defensive, were obliged to deploy their forces along virtually the entire length of their 930-mile border with Germany.

The bulk of the Polish army, commanded by Marshal Edward Smigly-Rydz, was organised into seven armies, geographically located and named. On the southern border of East Prussia, and around one of the very few parts of the frontier that was fortified, was Army Modlin, with two infantry divisions and two cavalry brigades. To the west, in the Polish Corridor, were the five infantry divisions and one cavalry brigade of Army Pomorze, while to its south was Army Poznan, with four infantry divisions and two cavalry brigades under command. Along the borders with Silesia and Slovakia the Polish High Command deployed three armies. Opposite Lower Silesia and covering its name city was Army Lodz, which counted one mountain and five infantry divisions, plus three mountain brigades, in its order of battle. Facing Upper Silesia and western Slovakia were the one mountain and six infantry divisions and single cavalry, mechanised and mountain brigades of Army Krakow. Army Karpaty had two infantry divisions and one mechanised and two mountain brigades with which to cover the border with eastern Slovakia. The remaining formation, Army Prusy, was nominally constituted with eight infantry divisions and one cavalry brigade as the strategic reserve, and was deployed around Ptrkow in front of Warsaw, on the main road between the capital and Czestochova. The balance of Polish divisions was held in various detached forces. Overall, the Polish army had 475 tanks, 774 anti-tank and 2,065 field guns with which to meet the German attack, and it was supported by 315 combat and 130 auxiliary aircraft, most of which were obsolescent. Apart from the east being all but denuded of army formations, the two most obvious features of the Polish order of battle and deployment were the Polish army's over-centralisation of command, brought about by the lack of an intermediate level of command between supreme headquarters and the field armies, and the fact that German forces in East Prussia were appreciably closer to Warsaw than all of the Polish armies with the exception of Army Modlin.

German forces facing Poland were under the operational control of the commander-in-chief of the army, Colonel-General von Brauchitsch, head of *Oberkommando des Heeres* (*OKH* or Army High Command), and were divided between *Army Group North* (Colonel-General von Bock) and *Army Group South* (Colonel-General von Rundstedt). Bock's command consisted of the *3rd* and *4th Armies* and a reserve of one armoured and three infantry divisions. The *3rd Army*, in East Prussia, consisted of one armoured and seven infantry divisions; the *4th Army*, in Pomerania, of one armoured, one motorised and six infantry divisions. *Army Group North*, therefore, had a total of four mobile and sixteen infantry divisions under command. *Army Group South* had three armies and a reserve of eleven infantry divisions in its order of battle. The *8th Army*, in Lower Silesia, was the weakest of Rundstedt's armies with just four infantry divisions. The *10th Army*, opposite Czestochova, had two armoured, three light, two motorised and six infantry divisions under command, while to the south and in Slovakia the *14th Army* had a mixture of two armoured, one light, one motorised, two mountain and five infantry divisions under command. Overall, the German formations facing Poland comprised 2,511 tanks, 4,019 anti-tank and 5,805 field guns, and were supported by 1,393 combat aircraft. The air force, commanded by Field Marshal Hermann Göring, head of *Oberkommando der Luftwaffe* (*OKL* or Air Force High Command), deployed 219 Stuka dive-bombers, 648 light and medium bombers, 426 fighters and a total of 762 auxiliary aircraft. The two most obvious features of the German order of battle were the heavy concentration of mobile formations with *Army Group South* and the fact that while the majority of the armour was concentrated in armoured divisions, the latter were dispersed between no fewer than four of the five armies and one of the two reserves committed to the invasion of Poland.

Of the seven armoured divisions involved in this campaign only two, the *1st* and *4th Panzer Divisions*, served in the same formation, and then only in the company of two ordinary infantry divisions. The 15 armoured, light and motorised divisions used were dispersed between one reserve and seven corps, and only two of the latter deployed solely mobile formations. Such a deployment was evidence that the Polish campaign was not a *Blitzkrieg* campaign in the sense that the term came to be understood by 1942. For the first test of mobile forces the German High Command refused to authorise deep penetration of enemy rear areas by armoured forces operating independently of the remainder of the army, being content to attempt the encirclement of Polish forces within the line of the Vistula and using armour as the means of raising the fighting power of the army (i.e. the infantry) as a whole. With *Blitzkrieg* in its infancy, the smallness of the operational area west of the Vistula plus the German advantages of numbers, position and mobility enabled a cautious and orthodox *OKH* to insist upon a distribution of forces and plan of campaign that were very conventional. German forces were to eliminate the Polish corridor; to strike against Warsaw from East Prussia and Silesia; to secure Krakow and to advance to the Deblin–Lublin–Chelm line. The German High Command was to seek the encirclement of Polish forces within the line of the Bug as a result of the issue having been decided in the first week of the campaign, though such were the German advantages over the Poles that in reality the campaign was effectively decided before its first shots were fired.

The mythology of the Second World War holds that the Polish campaign opened with the bombardment of the Polish base of Westerplatte in Danzig by the battleship *Schleswig-Holstein*, but in fact operations began a few minutes before when Stukas prematurely attacked the Tczew bridge over the lower Vistula. Be that as it may, operations along the length of Poland's borders with Germany and Slovakia began at 0445 on 1 September, the most immediately obvious German effort being made in the attempt to win air supremacy over Poland.

On the first day of the campaign German air operations were not particularly successful: early morning mists shrouded most Polish airfields, and only at Krakow and Puck were Polish formations caught on the ground. Nevertheless, from the start of hostilities the logic of the air battle was remorseless. Though in the first week of the war the Polish fighter element accounted for 105 German aircraft in air combat while losing 63 of its number, the imbalance of relative losses and the overrunning of Polish airfields by advancing German ground forces effectively destroyed the Polish army air force within seven days. On the sixth most of what remained was withdrawn to the Lublin area where its impact on the subsequent campaign was negligible. From the first day of the war, therefore, the *Luftwaffe* enjoyed an overwhelming superiority in the air and its bombers were able to range over the battlefield virtually at will, although its losses in this short campaign against modest opposition were nevertheless very heavy. With 285 aircraft shot down and another 279 heavily damaged or written off, the *Luftwaffe* lost more than a quarter of its strength in the course of this campaign, but its effectiveness in terms of providing close air support to ground formations was impressive. It was the air force, rather than the armoured columns, that led the way into Poland, and incessant air attack was the most important single factor in destroying the cohesion of Polish ground forces.

The first day of the war in the north brought mixed results for Bock's two armies. The *3rd Army* found itself held on the fortified Mlawa position, but to the west the *4th Army*, advancing through heavily wooded areas with armour, forced the weakly held Brda line and savaged the 9th Infantry Division in the process. Here in the north a pattern of operations that was to repeat itself throughout the campaign on every front manifested itself from the outset. However successful a local Polish defence, superior numbers and mobility enabled the Germans to wear down or bypass opposition with the result that slow-moving Polish formations were either isolated and destroyed or forced to withdraw to shorter defence lines that were outflanked. By the second the *3rd Army* both broke and sidestepped the Mlawa position forcing Army Modlin to pull back from the border with the aim of re-establishing itself on a main line of resistance immediately in front of Warsaw: by the fifth the *3rd Army*, by widening its frontage, had secured Rozan and was moving on Pultusk, thereby isolating Polish forces in the north-east and providing *OKH* with the chance to attempt a deep encirclement of Polish forces by an armoured thrust against Brest. To the west the *4th Army* continued to harry the hapless Polish forces in the corridor and by the fifth had secured Bydgoszcz, thus bringing the campaign in the corridor to an end and securing overland communications between East Prussia and Pomerania. Thereafter the *10th Panzer Division*, from Bock's reserve, and *XIX Motorised Corps*, part of the *4th Army*, moved into East Prussia and to the left flank of the *3rd Army* in readiness for the move on Brest.

To the south Rundstedt's armies recorded a series of advances on the first day of the campaign, but only in two sectors were significant results achieved. Along most of the frontier the Poles made no attempt to defend the immediate border area and were content to stand on tactically strong defensive positions anything up to 15 miles behind the frontier, but at Nowy Targ they found themselves outflanked by the *2nd Panzer Division*, which covered 50 miles in one night along undefended forest tracks. Moreover, at the naturally strong defensive position around Mokra, just to the north of Czestochova, Army Krakow was outfought by the two armoured divisions of *XVI Panzer Corps*. Attacking just to the south of the

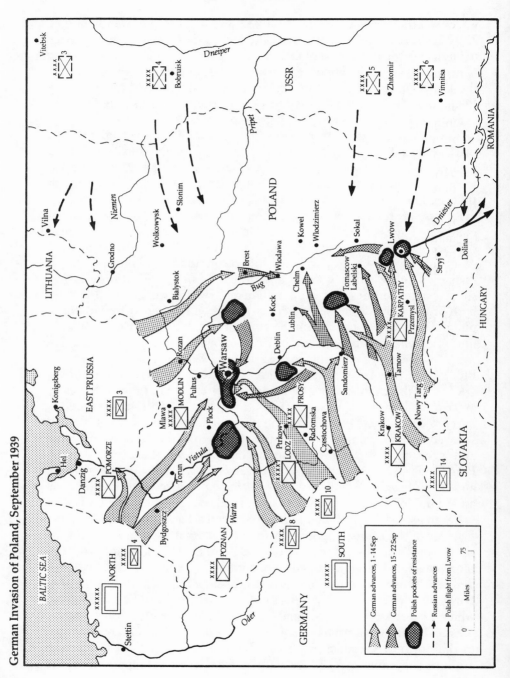

German Invasion of Poland, September 1939

line of weakness presented by the boundary between Army Krakow and Army Lodz, the *10th Army* in the first two days of the campaign broke through the Mokra position, mauled the 7th Infantry Division on the left flank, and then split the two Polish armies asunder by an overwhelming attack that brought the *XVI Panzer Corps* control of the road to Ptrkow. On the second Army Krakow was forced to pull back its right flank – thus widening the gap between itself and Army Lodz – but despite the attentions of the *14th Army* it was able to withdraw in relatively good order towards Krakow and at the same time maintain contact with Army Karpaty. Nevertheless, within two days of the start of the campaign the position of Polish forces in the south had become very ominous: such was the speed of the German advance that mobilisation of reserves could not keep pace with the worsening tactical situation. Further, superior German mobility ensured that Polish forces once bypassed were in effect lost to the defence. By the fifth the Polish position had deteriorated to the extent that the Polish High Command had to stabilise the situation on the Czestochova–Ptrkow road, but its attempted counter-attack with armour was frustrated by German exploitation of earlier success. Instead of being able to counter-attack Polish forces were obliged to respond to German moves, and to do so with armour that was too weak and dispersed to impose more than a brief halt on German progress. With the collapse of this attempted counter-attack on the fifth the Polish High Command ordered a general withdrawal to the east bank of the Vistula.

By the time this order was given it was too late to be effected. With their forces established around Ptrkow and driving on Warsaw from the north, the Germans were already on the point of encircling three complete Polish armies and parts of two more. Moreover, by securing Krakow on the sixth and Tarnow on the seventh the *14th Army* established itself not merely behind Army Krakow and between it and Army Karpaty but behind the upper Vistula itself. To confound matters, on the seventh the Polish High Command took the decision to move to Brest in order to maintain communications with the field armies. With *XVI Panzer Corps* then approaching the outskirts of Warsaw, this decision was justified, but with no division of the field armies into army groups and a duplication and confusion of commands during the move itself, the move cost the Polish armies the communications that it intended to preserve. As a result, after the seventh there was a progressive collapse of Polish command facilities as each Polish army was forced increasingly to fight its own battle for survival without reference to the High Command and its neighbours.

51

In the first week of the campaign only one Polish army, Army Poznan, was not heavily engaged. Like Army Pomorze to the north, Army Poznan had been deployed in an untenable sector of the corridor, while the main German efforts had been made to the north and south. For the most part the battle had flowed around Army Poznan. By the end of that week, of course, both its flanks had been turned with the collapse of Army Pomorze and the forced retreat of Army Lodz, and Army Poznan had no option but to conform to the movements of its neighbours. Thus, when it began to withdraw to the south-east along the Lodz–Radom axis in order to get behind the Vistula, Army Poznan was largely intact and in good order, though its rear was under increasing pressure from the *4th Army* as it closed from the north after taking Torun.

As Army Poznan approached the Bzura the situation to its front, across its line of withdrawal, was that the *14th Army* had advanced to the Radom–Sandomierz–Rzeszow–Sanok line while the *10th Army* had established itself at various points along the Vistula between Warsaw and Deblin. In fact, as Army Poznan reached the Bzura, the *4th Panzer Division*'s armoured regiments made a rash attempt to rush the Polish capital without waiting for artillery and infantry support. These attacks were beaten back with heavy loss by the city's garrison, then being strengthened as various formations pulled back into Warsaw, on the eighth and ninth. But the resultant deployment of German formations in the northern sector of *Army Group South*'s area of responsibility – the armour halted on the Vistula with the infantry divisions of the *10th Army* and trailing *8th Army* strung out on the line of march – presented Army Poznan with an opportunity that was unique in the campaign. While it stood in obvious danger of encirclement as it came to the Bzura, it had the chance to achieve overwhelming superiority against part of the thinly spread German forces, and on the ninth its formations fell on the *24th* and *30th Infantry Divisions* of the *8th Army*. In two days it had mauled these divisions and driven them south of the river. At this stage it was Army Poznan's intention to strike towards Lodz in an attempt to extricate itself and hope that Army Pomorze could escape into Warsaw, but superior German technique and mobility very quickly trapped both armies as *Army Group South* switched its formations on the line of march, not to support the threatened divisions but to work around the open left flank of Army Poznan.

By the twelfth the Polish advance south of the Bzura had been halted, and with the *4th Army* pressing on the rear of the mass of Polish divisions caught within the Plock–Sochaczew–Leczyca triangle, Army Poznan abandoned its attempt to escape southwards and chose instead to strike eastwards, through Sochaczew, to Warsaw. When it made its effort on the fourteenth, however, it ran into the *4th Panzer Division*, which found the plains more to its liking than Warsaw's suburbs. With the first of the reserve divisions committed against Army Poznan's western flank and rear, the German encirclement of nine Polish divisions – drawn from four armies – was completed on the sixteenth. Under incessant attack from all sides and from the air, Polish resistance within the Bzura pocket collapsed on the eighteenth. German mopping-up operations continued until the twenty-first.

The Bzura counter-attack, the only major Polish operation of its kind during the campaign, thus ended with the destruction of a quarter of the Polish army; even as it came to an end the collapse of the Polish armies in the south also became reality. There the *14th Army*, having smashed three Polish divisions around Radom on the twelfth and having then secured Rzeszow and Sanok, struck towards Zamosc with *XVIII Corps* and towards Lwow with the *1st Mountain Division* in attempts to encircle Army Krakow and the remnants of Army Karpathy. By the fifteenth Army Krakow was surrounded on three sides. On the eighteenth it made a last despairing attempt to break out of the trap that was forming around it by attacking, with its armour, in the direction of Tomaszow Lubelski, but this effort to reach Lwow was halted by the *2nd Panzer Division*. This attempted breakout resulted on the twentieth in the biggest armoured clash of the campaign, but by the end of the day Army Krakow was forced to capitulate. To the south Army Karpathy was heavily engaged around Przemysl, and in the running battle that developed between the sixteenth and twentieth as it tried to fight its way into Lwow this army, along with various formations that had come from the east to give support, was destroyed.

After the destruction of the southern armies various remnants and detached formations remained in the field and continued to resist, but for the most part their main concern was to avoid contact and to escape to the safety of neutral Romania. Organised resistance by the Polish army within the country did not end until 6 October when some 16,000 men from Group Polesie, one of the formations raised in eastern Poland after the start of hostilities, surrendered to the *XIV Motorised Corps* around Kock, just to the north of Lublin. But after the collapse of major resistance in the south, the remainder of the campaign was fought on the Hela peninsula until 2 October, and in and around Warsaw. The greatest battles of the campaign were fought for Warsaw and ended, predictably, with the destruction of the Polish army and state before the end of September.

The counter-attack and battle of encirclement on the Bzura spared Warsaw the ordeal of a direct assault for two weeks by drawing off the *10th Army* formations approaching the capital on 9 September. In the end no fewer than 19 German divisions were committed on the Bzura, and their diversion from Warsaw ensured that the final assault on the capital, which began on the twenty-third, was conducted by forces from both German army groups.

The *3rd Army*, having secured Mlawa and the lower Narew, made only slow progress towards Warsaw. Army Modlin, with the support of formations moving into Warsaw from the west, was able to slow the German advance on the most direct and obvious approach to the capital, but German numerical superiority and command of the air prevented Army Modlin holding the German advance on any line while its failure to regain the lower Narew left it vulnerable to the wide outflanking attack against Brest that began on 9 September. With *10th Panzer Division* leading the *XIX Motorised Corps*, the Germans crossed the upper Narew, masked Bialystok on the eleventh – the city falling on the sixteenth to second-echelon forces – and secured the town, but not the fortress, of Brest on the fifteenth. Thereafter a detachment moved south along the Bug to link up with *14th Army* formations at Wlodawa, thus completing the deep encirclement of Polish forces. On the fifteenth, however, the *3rd Army* closed upon Warsaw from the east and over the next two days was involved in a battle for control of Praga. The German attacks were held, but nevertheless succeeded in seriously eroding the strength of a garrison that at this same time lost contact with its forces at Modlin and Palmiry.

Moreover, during this period, and indeed from the start of the campaign, Warsaw was subjected to indiscriminate terror bombing. On the thirteenth the Germans announced their intention to bomb cities irrespective of open status, and at this same time Hitler ordered that an exodus of refugees from Warsaw be prevented. Both decisions were the result of the calculation that Poland's surrender would be hastened by deliberate terror bombing. Two days after the main bombardment of Warsaw began, the *Luftwaffe* flew some 1,150 sorties against the city. With the garrison overwhelmed by the scale and ferocity of these attacks, the city surrendered on 27 September with nearly 150,000 troops being taken prisoner. On the twenty-ninth the 25,000-strong garrison at Modlin capitulated, the surrender here, as at Warsaw, being prompted by humanitarian considerations. From the first day of the campaign, however, the presence of one *Einsatzgrüppe der Sicherheitspolizei* per army served notice of future German intentions towards Poland and the normal conventions of war, but with the piecemeal destruction of the

Polish army the casual murder of civilians and prisoners gave way to the systematic policy of mass executions and deportations in those parts of Poland under German control. Eastern Poland, as a result of Soviet military operations after 17 September and the Nazi–Soviet treaty of the twenty-eighth, was occupied by the Soviet Union and then incorporated into that country on 1/2 November.

Despite the Nazi–Soviet pact of 23 August and a Soviet mobilisation after 11 September, Soviet intervention came as a shock to the Polish High Command. The Warsaw authorities had not anticipated such a move, and various formations in eastern Poland initially believed that Soviet forces entering the country were coming to their support. In reality, the Soviet intervention was the direct result of the August pact, even though its terms did not oblige the Soviet Union to move against Poland: she had to secure for herself, and not be beholden to Germany for, the 75,000 square miles and 12 million inhabitants of eastern Poland that she was to acquire under this latest partition of the country.

In military terms, the Soviet intervention was irrelevant to the outcome of the campaign: the Polish army had been effectively defeated by the seventeenth and those Polish forces in the east were few in number and without military significance. The only strategic consequence of the Soviet move into eastern Poland was that it ended any last, unrealistic Polish hope of forming 'the Romanian bridgehead' in the Lwow area where the army could remain in the field while waiting for relieving attacks to be mounted by the French. Such attacks were scheduled for the third week of war, after French mobilisation was complete. Pre-war Polish planning, which had recognised that Poland's only hope of survival lay in the French offensive into the Rhineland that drew upon itself the bulk of German military power, had foreseen a withdrawal into the south-east in order to preserve the army and keep it in the field. The order for this general withdrawal was not issued until the eleventh: the Soviet move into eastern Poland ended any lingering possibility of continuing resistance by the Polish army on its own soil.

Formations from seven armies, divided between the Byelorussian and Ukrainian Fronts, were involved in operations in eastern Poland in September 1939, but overall strengths and orders of battle are not readily available in Soviet military histories that pass over this campaign in obvious embarrassment. A minimum of 25 infantry and 16 cavalry divisions saw service in Poland, and it appears that these were divided between two armies and three mobile groups with the Byelorussian Front and two armies and at least two mobile groups or independent forces with the Ukrainian Front. North of the Pripet Marshes the Byelorussian Front had two front-line armies, the 3rd Army, at Vitebsk, and the 4th Army, at Bobruisk. The 3rd Army was given the task of securing Vilna, and was apparently supported by groups that operated along the Sventsyany–Mikhalishki and Ushmyany–Grodno axes. The 4th Army was given the twin objectives of Bialystok and Brest, while one group advanced along the Slonim–Wolkowysk axis. South of the Pripet Marshes the Ukrainian Front tasked the 5th Army, based at Zhitomir, with securing Lublin, and the 6th Army, based at Vinnitsa, with the occupation of Lwow. One mobile group, seemingly drawn from the 12th Army, operated as the Front's vanguard force, and other groups apparently operated in the wide gap between the main axes of advance of the 5th and 6th Armies. One or more force was tasked with the closing of the Polish–Romanian border and the clearing of the area of the Dnestr and northern Carpathians.

The Soviet advance into eastern Poland was extremely rapid. Brest was reached on 18 September; Vilna was occupied on the nineteenth and Grodno on the twentieth. On the twenty-first Soviet forces occupied Bialystok after German forces had withdrawn from the area, while the Soviet occupation of north-east Poland was completed on the twenty-third with the securing of Turmont, on the border with Latvia. South of the Pripet Marshes the 6th Army reached Lwow on the nineteenth while the Kowel–Wlodzimierz–Sokal line was secured by the twenty-first, but Soviet forces did not cross the Bug. To the south of Lwow the occupation of the border areas was necessarily slow and not fully effective in preventing isolated groups of Polish soldiers crossing into Romania, but with the occupation of Stryj and Dolina by the twenty-third the major phase of Soviet operations in eastern Poland came to an end. Though isolated clashes with scattered Polish forces continued until the end of the month, Soviet operations were largely unopposed and resulted in 200,000 Polish troops being taken prisoner.

At various places clashes between German and Soviet forces were only narrowly averted, and in order to prevent incidents representatives of the two High Commands agreed that the line of the Narew, Vistula and San should serve as the operational boundary between the two armies. Seven days later, on 28 September, however, the formal partition of Poland between Germany and the Soviet Union moved the political boundary eastwards to the Pissa–Narew–Bug–Vistula–San line, leaving the Soviet Union with slightly less rather than slightly more than half of Poland but still in possession of Galicia and the Polish Ukraine. The Soviet Union thus emerged, if only for the moment, as the real winner of the Polish campaign, and she immediately consolidated her position by forcing mutual assistance pacts upon Estonia that same day, on Latvia on 5 October and Lithuania on the tenth. With Soviet forces occupying bases in the Baltic states after mid-October, the Nazi–Soviet spheres of influence agreement of August assumed reality: the Soviet surrender of Vilna to Lithuania as part of this process was no more than giving up the shadow whilst retaining the substance.

For Germany, the transfer of Lithuania to the Soviet sphere of influence and the Soviet acquisition of eastern Poland were the price of the August pact but were more than balanced by a concurrent trade agreement that ensured Germany access to Soviet raw materials, thereby offsetting the effects of the Allied naval blockade. With a war to be fought in the west, Germany would not press her claims in the east and would not resist the Soviet Union on the question of the reconstitution of a rump Polish state. In August this issue had been left open, but with the defeat of Poland it presented itself for a decision. Hitler was not averse to the creation of a Polish client state, the very existence of which could only confuse and divide his enemies, but the Soviet Union was hostile to any idea of a reconstructed Polish state. Thus once his peace offer of 6 October to Britain and France was rejected, Hitler decreed on the eighth that 35,000 square miles of Poland – including the Augustow triangle, the Corridor and Teschen – were to be incorporated into Germany, and on the twelfth, that the remainder of Poland (less suitable crumbs that were provided for Slovakia) was to be administered by a civilian authority known as the Government-General. This authority came into existence on 26 October, and was to be the main agency of Nazi terror and barbarism in Poland. As a state, therefore, Poland was destroyed as effectively as her army, which lost 200,000 killed and wounded and 600,000 prisoners of war in the course of the September campaign. But Polish nationalism, nurtured over centuries by foreign occupation and oppression, was not destroyed quite so easily: even before the end of September resistance groups were being formed in German-occupied territory. Moreover, the Polish government had crossed into Romania on 18 September. Some 80,000 Polish military personnel managed to reach that country before the border was closed, and they were able to make their way to France and Britain in order to continue a struggle that had only just begun.

Other than the British and French declarations of war on Germany, the Soviet intervention of 17 September was the most important single development to emerge from the Polish campaign, yet this intervention, which marked the beginning of the end of one campaign, coincided with an act of war that served notice that another campaign was on the point of acquiring its own pace and significance. This was the conflict at sea, which proved to be the longest single campaign of the European war. The act of war involved the first loss of a British fleet unit to enemy action in the course of the Second World War, the unit being the fleet carrier *Courageous*, which was torpedoed and sunk by the submarine *U-29* in the south-west approaches. Thus the Soviet intervention in Poland and the loss of the *Courageous*, both on the same day, provide a neat juxtaposition between campaigns: one that was fading into history and the other still in its skirmishing phase preparatory to battle being joined in earnest after June 1940.

At the outbreak of hostilities Britain and France possessed potentially decisive advantages over Germany with respect to the prosecution of the war at sea. The two Allied powers stood astride German trade routes beyond Europe, and their possession of world-wide empires enhanced a positional advantage that was as important as force itself in driving German commerce from the high seas. In terms of warships in service moreover, the German navy, with four battleships, three armoured, one heavy and three light cruisers, 34 destroyers and torpedo boats, and 57 submarines, was more than matched by a good, high-quality French navy even before the Royal Navy's 12 capital ships, six aircraft carriers, 58 cruisers, 201 destroyers and escorts, and 69 submarines were added to the scales. But notwithstanding the handicaps under which it was forced to operate, the German navy was determined to wage an active war and was confident that, as a result of its overhaul of strategic and tactical doctrine since 1919 and the quality of its units, it had the means of securing victory in the struggle at sea.

The outcome of the war at sea was decided by a combination of many factors. Like a rope that is the product of the weaving together of many strands, so the ultimate German failure at sea was the result of many elements coming together over a long period of time. Yet if certain of these are to be identified as particularly significant, then four – all related to doctrinal, structural and technical weaknesses of the German navy itself – naturally recommend themselves for serious consideration as the key to any understanding of why the *Kriegsmarine*, despite its confidence, found itself condemned after 1939 to a futile stern chase. The fact of the matter was that the German navy entered the war with a balanced fleet, but one that was too small to achieve major strategic success, still less defeat the greatest naval and maritime power in the world. By the time that it grew into the strength necessary to give it a chance of victory, however, its balance had been destroyed, and its effort was shouldered by one arm of the service that could not achieve victory nor even sustain itself in the face of Allied sea power. Very literally, the *Kriegsmarine* operated throughout the war two years behind a schedule that would have provided it with victory, and its failure was primarily the result of the combination of mistiming and flawed doctrine.

The doctrine with which the *Kriegsmarine* entered the war had emerged as a result of a deliberate attempt to rethink the strategic policy that had failed the Imperial Navy in the First World War. In reality, it was no more than a carbon copy of the makeshift ideas that not merely failed in 1917 but which ensured Germany's defeat in 1918. By a very odd process, German naval thought in the inter-war period came round full circle despite the navy's attempt to provide itself with a doctrine that would enable it to escape its fate in the First World War when, for all its strength, it was no more than a coastal defence force without strategic purpose and capacity. In large measure the confusion that surrounded the navy's inter-war deliberations arose because while it rid itself of its old obsession with battle, the *Kriegsmarine* could not provide itself with a policy that would enable it to secure command of the sea and thereby ensure German seaborne lines of communication while severing those of its enemies. In a sense such confusion was unavoidable: the German navy's problems were insoluble as long as it operated under conditions of geographical and numerical inferiority. In the inter-war period, however, the ideas of seizing Denmark and Norway, in order to push back a British blockade, and of securing northern French ports, from which to counter-blockade Britain, took hold.

The esoteric nature of naval doctrine ensured that such practical solutions to Germany's strategic problems contained the flaw that by stressing one aspect of warfare (namely geographical position) to offset strategic inferiority, the idea of command of the sea being divisible and capable of being localised gained acceptance. Moreover, because this line of argument was joined by the parallel idea that naval warfare was economic in nature, the debate within the inter-war navy moved inexorably to the conclusions that command of the sea was solely identifiable in terms of lines of communication; that battle was to be avoided because it distracted forces from the all-important task of waging war on commerce; that it would be possible to win a war at sea by waging 'tonnage warfare' despite Germany's positional and numerical inferiority to her enemies; and, crucially, that the denial of command of the sea to an enemy in terms of either time or area was as effective as Germany exercising command of the sea. These varied conclusions, which were very confused because of the tendency throughout this debate to regard the struggle for and exercise of command of the sea as identical, were directly contrary to historical experience: in no war had a navy committed to a *guerre de course* defeated a navy committed to winning command of the sea. Moreover, though the basis of 'tonnage warfare' – the belief that Britain could be defeated if 750,000 tons of her shipping could be destroyed every month over a one-year period – may well have been valid, the idea of cumulative damage proving fatal to an enemy with time to counter the threat it faced was dubious, as had been proved in 1917.

A fundamental doctrinal weakness thus lay at the heart of the German naval effort in the Second World War, and to this was tied the fact that many of the *Kriegsmarine*'s problems stemmed from war coming at least five years too soon for the navy. But these factors were related to three other sources of weakness, of which the first and most important was the junior status of the navy in the German military hierarchy. It was also a service that its commander-in-chief, Grand Admiral Erich Raeder, deliberately kept outside Nazi politics. It was thus ill-placed in the struggle for resources, and with perverse logic it was denied priority for its construction programmes at times when it had realistic chances of winning its war but secured priority treatment when its chances of success had gone. Second, the navy lacked its own organic air arm, and its relations with the *Luftwaffe* were always difficult in part because of Göring's prejudice against the navy and Raeder, in part because the *Luftwaffe* was ignorant of naval requirements and was both structurally and technically ill-suited to conduct maritime operations. With its carrier programe in effect abandoned in April 1940, the *Kriegsmarine* fought its war without carrier aviation and with only limited shore-based air support, especially after June 1941. Third, while the submarine, the main instrument of commerce warfare, proved formidably effective in the first three years of the war, it also proved incapable of in-service development at a pace that equalled the advances made in anti-submarine warfare in those years.* Though the massive Allied losses of 1942 served to obscure this reality, the changing balance between escort and submarine began to make itself felt in the last quarter of 1941 and was recognised by the German naval staff in March 1942. The submarine nevertheless achieved results that at various times seemed likely to vindicate 'tonnage warfare' because of the diversity of British naval commitments, the

*See Appendix A

slenderness of British defensive resources, and certain tactical advantages that the submarine held over escort forces in the first three years of war.

On the day that Britain declared war on Germany the submarine *U-30* torpedoed and sank the liner *Athenia*: Germany, by comparison, lost three-quarters of her 400-odd merchantmen in foreign ports or on the high seas. Over the next few months 76 merchantmen of 463,122 tons, using the long hours of winter darkness of northern latitudes, eluded British patrols and returned to Germany, 22 of their compatriots being caught in the attempt. The greater part of Germany's oceanic merchant marine, however, sought safety in neutral ports in the expectation that the war would be short, but because this proved unfounded Allied sea power drove German commerce from the oceans from the outset of war. In the following weeks, moreover, the Allied powers, using precedents set in the First World War, sought to prevent Germany trading via neutral countries by denying the latter the right to carry German cargoes and by a rationing system that limited them to pre-war import levels. Germany, too, found herself following First World War precedents. At the start of hostilities she declared her intention to abide by the 1936 prize regulations, even though these severely restricted U-boat operations, but such restraint was abandoned with the realisation that Britain and France would not make peace. Though the formal elimination of the distinction between Allied and all neutral shipping in the eastern Atlantic had to await August 1940, the German navy in effect waged an unrestricted submarine campaign against commerce after November 1939.

In this opening phase the Germans carried the war to Allied commerce in three ways: by raiders, mines and submarines. The first of these threats, and the one that most alarmed the Allies, proved short-lived and exaggerated. Before hostilities began two German armoured cruisers, the *Deutschland* and *Admiral Graf Spee*, sailed to the North and South Atlantic respectively, in order to prey upon Allied commerce. Before reaching home on 15 November the former accounted for just two merchantmen of 7,000 tons. The *Admiral Graf Spee* took nine merchantmen of 50,000 tons before seeking the safety of Montevideo after incurring damage on 13 December in the course of an action with three cruisers off the River Plate. Denied sanctuary in Uruguay, she scuttled on the seventeenth rather than fight the force that awaited her in the estuary. Ten months were to elapse before another warship sailed on a similar raiding mission. In the meantime, six auxiliary raiders took up the fight, the first sailing on 31 March 1940, but it was not until July that raiders accounted for more than 10 merchantmen in a single month. Herein lay one of the more obvious failures of the attempt to wage 'tonnage war'. At a time when Allied commerce was all but defenceless against raiders, the German navy could not mount the appropriate effort. Though raiders sank a total of 891,980 tons of shipping in 1940 and 1941, their efforts were belated and increasingly marginal as independently sailing merchantmen became fewer and Allied counter-measures more effective.

The mining campaign against shipping was similar to the raider effort in that it provided diminishing returns, but unlike the former it both peaked very quickly and continued to take a toll of shipping until April 1945. During the war mines accounted for 79 warships and 534 merchantmen of 1,406,087 tons, but only in the period between September 1939 and April 1940, when mines accounted for 128 merchantmen of 429,899 tons, did this campaign pose a serious threat to the Allied cause. Thereafter its real effectiveness lay not in sinking ships but in disrupting traffic and tying down a disproportionate number of warships and auxiliaries – a total of 717 in May 1945 – on defensive duties: after December 1941 mines accounted for less tonnage than in the first seven months of the war.

German success in this opening phase, when the port of London was all but closed and massive disruption was caused to British trade along the east coast, was the result of surprise and British unpreparedness. The element of surprise was both tactical and technical, achieved by the use of influence mines to which there was no immediately available counter. In November 1939, when the mine threat was at its greatest, 27 ships of 120,958 tons were sunk and many more were damaged, but the recovery of an intact magnetic mine on 23 November provided the key to the neutralisation of this threat. Thereafter, Allied losses were reduced to irritant proportions though the Germans achieved notable local successes as a result of their use of acoustic mines in autumn 1940 and their sowing distant Indian and Australasian waters, but such success declined as the initial advantage of surprise was dissipated.

The submarine campaign, on the other hand, was protracted and bitterly contested, yet it began at a time when the British were confident that it would be countered effectively. Indeed, in 1937 the Admiralty had predicted that the submarine would never again pose the threat that it had in 1917 when Britain was brought within six weeks of defeat. The basis of this confidence was the faith vested in Asdic – a means of underwater detection – and the depth charge. Both had been developed during the

First World War and, with the introduction of convoy, had contained the German submarine offensive of 1917 and 1918.

In 1939 and 1940, however, the submarine threat was contained more because of the lack of German numbers than by any other factor. War showed that the effectiveness of Asdic had been exaggerated, while new depth charges and firing patterns had to be developed in order to deal with the new generation of boats in German service. Moreover, escorted convoy barely existed in the opening phase of the war. In September 1939 there were some 4,000 oceanic and coastal ships in British service; the British navy had but 43 escorts of which only 26 were in the Western Approaches. Though the first convoy from Britain sailed on 2 September and the first inward convoy, from Freetown, arrived on the fourteenth, the scale of defence afforded these and other convoys was necessarily slender, particularly in light of the priority given to escorting troopships to France and to raising anti-submarine patrols. Thus in the opening months of the war, when 500,000 troops were moved to France without loss and patrols accounted for just two submarines, British merchant shipping in the Atlantic was all but undefended, and even the minimum protection provided to outward-bound convoys ended some 600 miles west of Ireland at the limit of endurance of escort forces.

It was from the ranks of independently sailing merchantmen that the U-boats claimed 102 of their 114 victims in 1939. In return they lost nine of their number, three on the mine barrage that after mid-October closed the Straits of Dover. By the end of March 1940, at the cost of another eight boats, the submarines had accounted for a further 108 merchantmen, but by this time a cyclical pattern of operations had been established that revealed an obvious weakness in the submarine campaign. Allied losses to submarine attack declined in November and December 1939 from their September/October levels, rose in January and February 1940, and fell back again in March, mainly because a maximum deployment of operational submarines in September 1939 had an inevitable knock-on effect in subsequent months. Seventeen of Germany's 27 ocean-going boats were deployed on station on 1 September 1939 and this number could not be sustained because of the operational cycle, refitting programmes and the withdrawal of units for training and the expansion of the arm. Given the various demands and overheads, it was not until the second quarter of 1941 that German operational strength passed the 49 with which the *Kriegsmarine* began the war, and this lack of submarine numbers with which to prosecute the campaign at sea was a vital factor in ensuring British survival in the opening 18 months of the war when shipping losses exceded 500,000 tons in a month on only one occasion.

While the opening exchanges taught both sides certain tactical lessons, four realities crucial to the outcome of the campaign against shipping were barely touched. The British capacity to absorb losses was considerable even though her construction capacity, cut by naval building and refitting programmes, was no more than 2,000,000 tons a year. Although she could not match a 'tonnage warfare' rate of loss, in 1939 she had 21,000,000 tons of shipping with which to meet import demands that totalled some 60,000,000 tons of food, raw materials and finished goods in 1938. Careful planning and stringent rationing ensured by 1944 that Britain could survive and make war on 27,000,000 tons of imports. This halving of shipping requirements meant, in general terms, that of every two British merchantmen sunk by enemy action only one represented real loss. In addition, such was the German concern to sink ships in order to wage 'tonnage warfare' that the *Kriegsmarine* made no distinction between inward- and outward-bound shipping, yet by definition the former was the more important. In reality, the immensity of the ocean and the difficulty of finding targets denied the submarine the luxury of choice in such matters, but had German submarines been able to concentrate against heavily laiden merchantmen proceeding to Britain their results would have been infinitely more damaging than those recorded by the less discriminating practices that were followed. Further, the 'tonnage warfare' concept that stressed the need to avoid battle extended to submarines declining to tackle escorts. In the first seven months of the war no escorts and only two destroyers were sunk by submarines, and during the entire war submarines sank only 37 escorts and 34 destroyers. Had German submarines deliberately embarked upon a policy of tackling escort forces in order to strip merchantmen of their cover – as did American submarines in the Pacific – then the long-term destruction of Allied commerce might well have been assured. Moreover, despite the policy of declining battle in order to concentrate against commerce, German submarines could not avoid specifically military commitments. The most obvious such commitment in the opening phase of the war was the carefully planned operation that resulted in the sinking of the battleship *Royal Oak* in Scapa Flow by *U-47* on 14 October, but in March 1940 the decline of U-boat numbers in the North Atlantic was not solely the result of the inroads made into their strength by the demands of the operational cycle: it was partly the result of the diversion of submarines from the war against commerce to the support of military operations, in this case the occupation of Denmark and Norway.

The operations for which German submarines were withdrawn from the North Atlantic constituted the second of two campaigns fought in Scandinavia in the first nine months of the European war, the first being the Winter War between Finland and the Soviet Union. The second campaign was the product of the first despite their being separated in time and having no party common to both. Between them these campaigns resulted in the humiliation of three great powers, the fall of three governments, the exile of one of Scandinavia's three kings and the imprisonment of another in his own capital. They also provided in Quisling a name that became synonymous with the word 'traitor' in many languages, and in military terms resulted in a reorientation of power that initially favoured Germany but which, in the long term, probably drained rather than strengthened her. These various results thus represented no mean achievement for a part of Europe that Hitler in 1939 wanted to preserve as a neutral backwater, and the fact that he failed in this aim is significant in terms of the limits of his power of decision. At a time when he sought to settle accounts with Britain and France, the lateness of the year prevented his doing so while the decisions and actions of others brought war to countries that only wished to be left alone.

The first of these campaigns was the Finnish–Soviet, or Winter, War that lasted 105 days between 30 November 1939 and 13 March 1940. It came about for no very good reason other than the determination of one great power to impose its will on a small neighbour, and was the outcome of the Nazi–Soviet agreements of 23 August and 28 September that temporarily ended the historical German role as counter-balance to Russia in the Baltic area. The German victory over imperial Russia in the First World War had provided the basis of the post-war independence of the Baltic states and Finland, and German acceptance in 1939 that these ex-Russian possessions lay within the Soviet sphere of influence unwittingly led to the Winter War as a result of the Soviet Union's overplaying her hand in trying to force Finland into concessions that recognised this fact.

The Soviets opened negotiations with the Finns on 12 October with the aim of securing a mutual assistance treaty, concessions in the Gulf of Finland that would ensure the security of the sea approaches to Leningrad, and a restoration of the 1721 border on the Karelian Isthmus. In return the Soviets offered to cede eastern Karelia, in territorial terms twice as much as they demanded. In *realpolitik* terms, Soviet demands were not unreasonable, but with Soviet behaviour over Poland and the Baltic states to serve as their guide, the Finns suspected correctly that Soviet security and territorial demands were underpinned by ideological and Russian nationalist calculations that aimed at the Sovietisation of Finland and her total subjugation. While she was prepared to make certain concessions, Finland was not prepared to accept the Soviet demand for a treaty and bases at Hanko and on the Aland Islands.

Finland's refusal to compromise her neutrality ensured that negotiations with the Soviet Union ended on 13 November with no result other than Soviet exasperation with what the Kremlin saw as unwarranted Finnish obduracy, and from this stemmed two Soviet errors that were to be critical in ensuring that the Winter War's second phase of operations was disastrous for the Soviet army. The Soviet Union, probably because of the ease with which eastern Poland had been occupied – at a cost of 2,600 killed and wounded – and with which concessions had been obtained from the Baltic states, underestimated Finnish national resolve and military capacity. Moreover, because the Soviets had made public their intentions towards Finland on 31 October, the failure to achieve results by diplomatic means left them with little option but to use force against Finland, and to do so quickly and at the very time of the year least suited to the conduct of operations in Karelia. November and December are months of heavy cloud over this area, and the wet, broken ground and rivers, lakes and sea are not sufficiently frozen to bear the weight of armoured and mechanised forces. As the Russians had shown in the last war in this area in 1809, February was the best month for operations in Karelia, but the unfolding of events in 1939 ensured that the Soviet Union could not wait for three months before dealing with Finland. She was thus obliged to begin operations when much of the terrain was impassable, and to this basic error was added misfortune: once her offensive stalled her armies were to be engulfed by the harshest winter since 1828, the severity of which contributed massively to the débâcle that overwhelmed Soviet forces in the second phase of the war.

For her attack on Finland the Soviet Union deployed an estimated 600,000 men formed into four armies. The 7th Army, on the crucially important Karelian Isthmus, deployed 12 infantry divisions, a mechanised corps, and three tank brigades, but three of its divisions were still forming on 30 November. The 8th Army, north of Lake Ladoga, had six infantry divisions and two tank brigades under command, while on its right, opposite the waist of Finland, were the five infantry divisions of the 9th Army. In the Arctic, opposite Petsamo, were the three infantry divisions of the 14th Army. The Soviet plan of campaign envisaged the main effort being made on the Isthmus with the aim of securing Viipuri, Finland's second city and gateway to Helsinki. The 8th Army, operating from the Petrozavodsk area, was to come round the northern shore of Lake Ladoga in order to fall upon the rear of the Finnish defenders in front of Viipuri, while to the north the 9th Army was to advance on three widely separated axes to the Gulf of Bothnia, thereby isolating Finland from Sweden and splitting her into two. In the far north the 14th Army was to secure Petsamo and its seaward approaches and then move south to join the 9th. With perhaps 1,000 tanks and twice that number of aircraft committed to this attack, the Soviet plan was imaginative, flexible and totally unrealistic.

In the north the tenuous line of communication provided by the distant Murmansk railroad was wholly inadequate to maintain the 9th Army, while this formation and the 14th Army were to be plagued by an inability to deploy off the forest tracks. To the south broken ground similarly limited the various axes of advance, while on the Isthmus the unfrozen Vuoksi effectively channelled the 7th Army's attack into a very restricted frontage. The obvious weakness of the plan, however, was the false assumption that the Finns were incapable of sustained and effective resistance. The other faults would have counted for little but for a confidence that anticipated victory inside 10 days and the gift-wrapping of Finland as 'Stalin's birthday present' on 21 December. Less obviously, a major weakness of Soviet arrangements was the fact that overall command of operations was vested in Lieutenant-General Kirill Meretskov, who was commander of both the Leningrad military district and the 7th Army, a diversity of command appointments that is explicable only in terms of an overwhelming Soviet confidence that the war would be short and uncomplicated.

In the first 10 days of the campaign the Soviets recorded advances that suggested that their confidence was not misplaced. In the north Petsamo was secured, and Soviet forces began to move south down the track with the grandiose title of the Arctic Highway. The 9th Army pushed forward to secure Kemijarvi with the 132nd Rifle Division, Soumussalmi with the 163rd and 44th Rifle Divisions, and Kuhmo with the 54th. On the northern shore of Lake Ladoga, however, the 8th Army found its progress blocked while successive attempts to outflank Finnish positions were checked at Kollaa, Tolvajarvi and Ilomantsi. But if these attacks failed to bring the 8th Army into the rear of Finnish positions on the Isthmus they served to prevent the movement of forces from this area and also forced the Finns to commit reserves to the support of *IV Corps*'s two divisions. On the Isthmus itself the initial Soviet advance was not opposed, but it was not until 5 December that the 7th Army arrived on the main Finnish defences of the Mannerheim Line. Held on the right flank by the three divisions of *II Corps* and on the left by the two divisions of *III Corps*, these positions had been strengthened in the weeks following the breakdown of negotiations but remained no more than a series of field works rather than fortifications. The Soviets nevertheless took 10 days to reconnoitre and prepare for a setpiece attack, and by the time this attack was delivered the 9th Army had been routed. The attack itself foundered disastrously, but it was not until 26 December, by which time the weather had broken, that it was discontinued as part of a reorganisation of the armies in the north-west.

Of the Finns' 10 divisions at the outbreak of war seven were with their three corps, one was in reserve on the Isthmus, and the others, at Viipuri and Oulu, were held as strategic reserve. Only small detachments had covered the north, but by the simple expedient of blocking the forest tracks the various Soviet advances were brought to a halt. With Soviet forces immobilised and deployed along miles of track, the reserves were committed against flanks and rear positions with the aim of breaking down Soviet formations into packets – *mottis* – that could be destroyed. Thus both the 163rd and 44th Rifle Divisions were annihilated between 27 December and 6 January around Suomussalmi, while to the south the 139th was destroyed at Talvajarvi as early as 15 December. The 18th Rifle Division, around Pilkaranta on the northern shore of Lake Ladoga, was similarly destroyed, but not until 29 February and only after a desperate effort to save itself.

These disasters, plus the failure of the main offensive on the Mannerheim Line, were the basis of the abiding impression of Soviet military incompetence created by the Winter War, yet in the final analysis it was the fact that such formations as the 168th Rifle Division at Ketila, the 54th at Kuhmo and the 75th at Aittojoki similarly held their ground that was strategically significant. Where Soviet formations could provide themselves with space and be supplied by air they could hold out, and it was only around Suomussalmi that the Finns won a clear-cut victory that enabled them to return formations to the reserve: elsewhere they found themselves besieging forces that they could not destroy for want of armour and heavy artillery. Moreover, because of their lack of numbers the Finns could not follow up their defensive victory on the Isthmus with the result that Soviet forces there were given time to reorganise, re-equip and retain in readiness for a resumption of the offensive. In the five weeks between the two main Soviet offensives a fresh army, the 13th, moved into the eastern sector while medium tanks replaced the light tanks used in first-phase operations. In addition, considerable attention was paid to the close coordination of armour, infantry and artillery, a feature and major cause of the initial attack having been the ease with which Soviet armour had both penetrated Finnish defences and lost the infantry in the process, the consequence being that both were destroyed in detail. The various changes put into effect after 26 December had results that were immediately apparent when the Soviets made their second major effort on 11 February, the Finnish army holding the view that the formations that attacked were unrecognisable from those that had attacked in December. Herein lay one of the three realities of the campaign that were missed or ignored amidst the overall impression of Soviet mismanagement, the second being that whether in attack or defence Soviet formations displayed an aggressiveness and determination that indicated that Soviet morale had not been affected by the Stalinist purges to anything like the extent assumed at that time.

The third reality was that however costly her defeats the Soviet Union had both the means to make good her losses and the will to continue the war: indeed first-phase defeats ensured that for reasons of national prestige the Soviet Union had to continue the war until these defeats were reversed. Finland, for her part, could not fight a protracted war. However impressive her initial victories Finland's ultimate defeat was assured, and this fact slowly impressed itself upon the Finnish government with the result that it sought to use its army's victories to moderate what would otherwise be total defeat and a draconian peace. It therefore opened secret negotiations with the Soviets on 29 January and immediately reaped the benefits of the army's success: the Soviet Union made clear that as part of a settlement it would abandon the puppet regime it had installed at Terijoki on 1 December and with which it had concluded a formal treaty of alliance on the second. Finnish independence was thus assured, but the logic of the war decreed that the Soviets had to be seen to be victorious and the Finns had to realise that they had been brought to the brink of defeat before hostilities could be ended.

The initial round of negotiations lasted until 9 February, by which time the battle on the Isthmus had been resumed. Beginning on 1 February the 7th and 13th Armies, with 21 infantry divisions and 10 tank brigades between them, mounted three setpiece attacks aimed at wearing down the Finns in a battle of attrition. The first attack was made between the first and third, the second between the fifth and eighth: the third attack, begun on the eleventh, immediately yielded Summa, the strongest sector of the Finnish defences in the centre of the Line, and by the thirteenth a clean breach had been made through the Finnish position. The 7th Army nevertheless adhered to very slow, deliberate advances with the result that the Finns were able to withdraw to their second line of resistance by the seventeenth, where the process repeated itself. On the twenty-fifth the Finns were forced to abandon their positions in favour of their last line of defence before Viipuri. By this stage, however, they had been reduced from an original November strength of 150,000 troops to 80,000 exhausted men, lacking effective artillery support and manning positions that could be outflanked by attacks across the frozen sea. The result of the final attack, which began on 2 March, was a foregone conclusion: by the thirteenth, when the war was ended by the Treaty of Moscow and the Finnish army was perhaps only hours away from total collapse, the 13th Army had forced the Vuoksi and the 7th Army had fought its way into central Viipuri, though most of the city remained in Finnish hands.

The territorial concessions exacted from Finland under the terms of the Treaty of Moscow were greater than those demanded by the Soviet Union during the negotiations of October–November 1939. In addition to the restoration of the 1721 border on the Isthmus, the Finns surrendered their islands in the Gulf of Finland, the area around Salla and, in the far north, the Rybachiy peninsula. In addition, the Soviet Union secured a military lease on Hanko and various economic concessions. As spring gave way to summer, however, it became clear to Finland that far from having abandoned her ambitions, the Soviet Union regarded the March treaty as no more than a halfway house and that she sought to secure by threats and pressure what had been denied her in war. Her display of relative moderation in March was the result of the calculation that the price of the conquest and occupation of Finland was too great relative to the Soviet Union's other commitments, but her various actions in 1940 ensured that she secured the worst of every eventuality. The territorial gains she made were marginal and obtained at the twin cost of an estimated 600,000 casualties and making an enemy of a neighbour that before 1939 had no aggressive intention towards her. After March 1940 the Soviet Union was obliged to maintain a minimum of 15 infantry divisions along an 800-mile border where previously no threat had existed. It was not until the spring of 1941 that the Soviet Union belatedly realised the consequences of her actions. By then, Finland, seeking to reverse the verdict of the Winter War if a suitable opportunity presented itself, had associated herself with a Germany free from major commitments in western Europe, and which was in possession of Denmark and Norway.

The Soviet Union's willingness to accept a negotiated solution to the Finnish problem in March 1940 was in part the result of an awareness that Britain and France harboured intentions towards Finland in general and Scandinavia in particular that threatened to destabilise the area. A similar awareness on the part of Germany, however, provided the imperative for her moves against Denmark and Norway on 9 April.

This Allied interest in Scandinavia was the product of various, inter-related considerations that emerged as a result of the Winter War, but the goad to Allied action in this area was provided by a political imperative that was itself the result of the Allied commitment to a strategically defensive policy in north-west Europe. In September 1939 it was Britain's intention to raise 32 metropolitan and 23 imperial divisions, of which 39 would be in France in September 1940. Though the total of 55 was trimmed to 36 in February 1940, Allied policy in the opening phase of the war was not to provoke large-scale operations but to build up strength, and remain on the defensive until 1941. The obvious weakness of this intention was that it left the initiative in German hands. Britain and France were uneasily aware that until 1941 they would be the weaker side awaiting attack by an enemy with superior numbers, mobility and air power. A passive policy and the certainty that they would be attacked at a time of Germany's choosing were positive incentives to the Allies to act decisively somewhere, and that somewhere in the winter of 1940 was Scandinavia.

Allied attention focused upon Scandinavia because of the belief that her neutrality worked to Germany's advantage. German oceanic shipping used Norwegian territorial waters to evade British patrols in the Norwegian Sea, but with the onset of winter, when Swedish iron ore, which by volume in 1938 accounted for 19.6 per cent of all German imports and 37.9 per cent of all her seaborne imports, moved to Germany via ice-free Narvik, British irritation gave way to a determination to cut this trade. Narvik and the Lapland Railroad to Boden and Oulu, however, provided a route into Finland, and the various Scandinavian pieces of the Anglo-French jigsaw puzzle began to fall into place after 14 December when the Soviet Union was expelled from the League of Nations. With an enthusiasm that was shameful in light of past behaviour, Britain and France rediscovered the cause of collective security over Finland, particularly Article XVI of the covenant of the League that obliged member countries to grant rights of transit to states going to the aid of a victim of aggression.

The cause of Finland, rationalised in terms of weakening Germany by striking at the interests of her Soviet accomplice, was seen therefore as a cloak for an attempt to secure a major strategic interest, namely the

71

Scandinavia

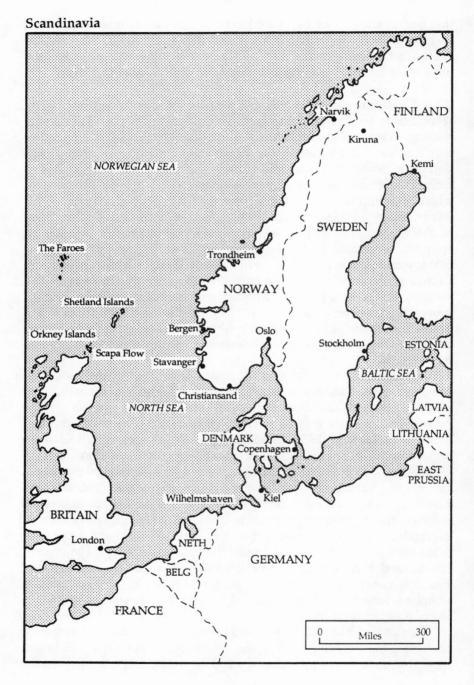

Narvik

FINLAND

Kiruna

Kemi

NORWEGIAN SEA

SWEDEN

The Faroes

Trondheim

Shetland Islands

NORWAY

Bergen

Oslo

Orkney Islands

Stockholm

ESTONIA

Scapa Flow

Stavanger

BALTIC SEA

Christiansand

LATVIA

NORTH SEA

LITHUANIA

DENMARK

Copenhagen

EAST
PRUSSIA

Wilhelmshaven

Kiel

BRITAIN

London

NETH

GERMANY

BELG

FRANCE

| 0 | Miles | 300 |

occupation of Narvik, the fields of Kiruna and Gallivare, and the railroad. Given the Allies' defensive policy a Scandinavian operation, with its promise of small investment and large return, was an irresistible temptation to two powers that sought to seize the initiative. France, in particular, saw in such a venture a means of distracting German attention away from herself with an operation that would involve the British navy while she provided reconstituted Polish forces and the Foreign Legion.

In their Scandinavian deliberations the Allies were faced by a number of unknown factors, the most important of which was Norwegian and Swedish reaction to any Allied move on the peninsula. Between 1935 and 1938 Norway and Sweden had repudiated the various articles of the covenant that placed a price on their membership of the League of Nations, and in the winter of 1940 the Allies had no means of knowing whether Norway and Sweden would oppose or acquiesce in any move supposedly intended to aid Finland. For their part the Finns, as the British and French discussed in national newspapers the merits and problems of moving to their country's support, slowly but rightly concluded that either Allied promises were fraudulent or Allied aid would prove inadequate. At a time when the Allies tried to stiffen Finnish resolve with promises of unspecified but substantial help, their plans envisaged taking Narvik with two regiments, securing Namsos, Trondheim and Bergen with two more, and passing a single regiment into Finland while two divisions were held to move into central Norway to frustrate any German counter-move. In their final form, however, Allied plans sought to secure only Narvik, the central Norwegian ports being occupied only when German intervention provided a suitable pretext. With the Finns undeceived by Allied inducements, it appears that only the British and French were beguiled by their own promises.

The Allied failure to support Finland brought down the ineffectual Daladier government, which invested much of what little credibility it retained by 1940 in this lost cause. But the close of the Winter War, while it denied the Allies a pretext for intervention and ended any thought of a move into Sweden, found them too deeply committed to an operation in Scandinavia to turn back and, paradoxically, it increased rather than eased the pressure on them to undertake some form of aggressive action against German interests in this area. On 28 March the Allies resolved upon a scaled-down version of their earlier plans, to mine Norwegian waters and, should this act provoke a German response, to occupy Narvik with a regiment and Trondheim, Bergen and Stavanger with five battalions. The mining of the Narvik approaches and the Stadlandet headland was carried out on the night of 7/8 April, but the sighting on the morning of the seventh of a German naval task group in the North Sea led to the ground forces being stood down while the Home Fleet sailed to prevent the German ships breaking into the North Atlantic. In fact the German ships were bound for Narvik and Trondheim, and belonged to two of twelve task groups that were to be employed in the occupation of Denmark and Norway.

German intentions towards Norway ran almost parallel to those of Britain, even down to details of timing, but the final German decision to move in Scandinavia, taken on 26 March, was the direct result of knowledge of Allied intentions. From the start of the war the *Kriegsmarine*, true to its inter-war ideas, had sought Hitler's approval for the occupation of Denmark and Norway. Though not unsympathetic to the navy's arguments, Hitler after the Polish campaign had to decide between seeking a decision to fight on land against France or making a naval war against Britain his priority. Not unnaturally, Hitler chose to play to strength rather than weakness, and it was not until 14 December that he ordered his personal planning staff, *Oberkommando der Wehrmacht* (*OKW* or Armed Forces High Command), to consider the problem of how to secure Norway. Urgency and realism were given to this study by Allied approaches to Norway and Sweden in January 1940 and, critically, by the interception of a German auxiliary in Norwegian waters by British destroyers on 17 February. On the nineteenth Hitler took the decision to proceed with the occupation of Norway, and on the twenty-ninth took the crucial step of separating the administrative arrangements and force allocations for such an operation from those in hand for the attack on France. With the latter scheduled for May, Hitler thus provided himself with the means to move north before the attack in the west, and on 26 March, after hesitations caused by the hope that the end of the Winter War would kill Allied interest in Scandinavia, Hitler formally authorised *Operation Weserübung*, its date of 9 April being set on the second.

For this operation the German armed forces committed the whole of the surface fleet less three cruisers, 28 submarines, some 500 combat aircraft and a similar number of transports, and as many infantry divisions (eight) as the British planned to use battalions for their operations in northern and central Norway. The German plan of campaign against Denmark – *Weserübung Sud* – involved the *170th Infantry Division*, supported on its left flank by naval landings at Esbjerg and Thyboron and on its right by a motorised brigade, securing the Jutland peninsula while the *198th Infantry Division* occupied the islands with landings at Middelfart, Nyborg and Korsor, Gedser and Vordingborg, and Copenhagen. The plan of campaign against Norway – *Weserübung Nord* –

involved initial landings of some 8,800 troops from three divisions. The *3rd Mountain Division* was to divide its two regiments between Narvik and Trondheim, and was tasked to occupy the Tromso-Harstad area; the *69th Infantry Division* was to land at Bergen and secure Stavanger and Egersund; and the *163rd Infantry Division* was to occupy Oslo, Arendal and Kristiansand. The three second-echelon divisions were to be moved into Norway after the 11, 15 and 17 April and were to complete the occupation of central and southern Norway and thus relieve the three divisions committed to the initial landings. With some 2,000 troops committed to the initial landings at Oslo, the Germans planned to move 24,700 troops to the Norwegian capital by sea and air in the first week of operations and some 40,000 troops thereafter.

Operation Weserübung was notable on several counts, not least for its representing a number of significant 'firsts'. It was the first tri-service operation in German history, and it was the first operation planned by *OKW* outside the established military planning staffs. *OKH* and *OKL* were not consulted about the operation before 1 March, and the chief of the general staff and Göring were not informed of Hitler's intentions until 2 and 5 March respectively: the Foreign Ministry was not informed until 3 April. *Operation Weserübung* thus marked the first intrusion of the *Führer Prinzip* into those areas of professional expertise that were the proper preserve of the armed forces, a precedent with very serious implications for the long-term conduct of the German war effort. *Operation Weserübung* was also the occasion of the first use of parachute and airlanded forces in war, Soviet use of small sabotage teams in the Winter War notwithstanding. Aalborg and Vordingborg in Denmark, and Oslo and Stavanger in Norway, were all assaulted by airborne units drawn from the *Luftwaffe's 22nd Infantry Division* and airlanded elements from the other divisions, all of which made their operational début in this campaign.

The most notable feature of *Operation Weserübung* was its complexity and range, involving as it did simultaneous landings against widely separated objectives, the most distant of which was 1,200 miles from German naval bases. An exact synchronisation of landings was sought on two counts: to secure Trondheim, Bergen, Kristiansand and Oslo at the same time in order to paralyse a Norwegian army that was obliged to mobilise five of its six divisions in these cities; to secure northern and central Norway before an alerted British fleet could intervene. While *Weserübung Sud* presented no problems because of the short distances involved in the occupation of Denmark, *Weserübung Nord* necessarily involved a high element of risk because it involved a two-way movement of warships and transports through waters dominated by British naval power. Surprise and the cover of dark worked initially to German advantage, but the lengthening hours of daylight hampered British submarine operations in the North Sea and Skagerrak and German forces north of Bergen alike. The balance of danger, however, was not exact, and in the event was to be set aside by air power.

The Norwegian campaign began with air power an unknown factor in the conduct of naval warfare, yet it ended in part as the result of the British navy's inability to sustain itself in northern waters in the face of German command of the air. The British lost only one cruiser and two destroyers to air attack in the course of the campaign, but it was the threat of German air power and its ability to neutralise British naval superiority that proved decisive. At the outset the Germans secured advantages of time and position that enabled them to concentrate sufficient air power in central and southern Norway to insure themselves against defeat, and the campaign lasted as long as it took the Allies to recognise and act upon that fact.

German ultimata to Denmark and Norway were presented at 0520 on 9 April, a matter of minutes after German forces entered both countries. Threatened with the bombing of Copenhagen unless it complied with German demands, the Danish government accepted German terms under protest within two hours. The Norwegians rejected German demands out of hand, and in so doing denied Hitler his primary aim – the unopposed occupation of Norway – and condemned the Germans to a serious campaign. Norwegian defiance, however, could not prevent the Germans from securing their immediate military objectives on the ninth. At Narvik mountain troops were put ashore after their escorts sank two coastal defence ships that had opposed them, and Trondheim was occupied without difficulty despite the *Admiral Hipper*'s having been damaged in an action with a British destroyer on the eighth. At Bergen two German warships were damaged by shore batteries but the town was secured, and Stavanger and Sola airfield were taken without problems. Fog prevented the taking of Kristiansand until mid-afternoon, and the German grip on Oslo by nightfall on the ninth was no more than tentative as a result of the only major German loss during this phase of operations: the cruiser *Blücher* was sunk with heavy loss of life by gunfire and torpedoes in the approaches to the Norwegian capital.

Other than the *Hipper* action there was only one contact between British and German warships in this initial phase of operations, but with the commitment of the British fleet and the ending of restrictions on British submarine activity in the North Sea and Skagerrak, encounters and German losses began to mount. Two warships were sunk by submarine attack as they tried to return to Germany, and an armoured cruiser was crippled though she was ultimately towed to safety. At Bergen on the tenth the light cruiser *Königsberg* gained the unsought distinction of being the first major warship to be sunk by air attack when she was despatched by shore-based aircraft, and at Narvik the entire force of 10 destroyers committed to the capture of the port was destroyed in the course of actions on the tenth and thirteenth by British surface forces, which lost two destroyers in the process. British operations also accounted for nine transports and merchantmen committed to the initial landings. The Narvik force was particularly badly hit by the loss of ships carrying its ammunition and transport, while amongst the second-echelon shipping bringing supplies and reinforcements across the Skagerrak submarines sank eight merchantmen prior to the fourteenth. During the remaining two months of the campaign, however, submarines were able to sink only another 13 merchantmen as German counter-measures became increasingly effective and shipping to Norway hugged Swedish territorial waters. A total of 249 successful sailings carried 108,000 troops and 109,000 tons of supplies to Norway in the course of the campaign.

Though the Germans failed to achieve an unopposed occupation of Norway they realised their secondary aim on the ninth, the paralysis of the Norwegian army, sufficient to insure themselves against effective counter-attack. But it was their successful occupation of the airfields at Sola and Oslo that proved decisive for the outcome of the campaign. As early as the tenth the British took the decision not to commit the fleet south of Bergen, a tacit recognition of the loss of southern Norway, while the occupation of Oslo provided the Germans with the means to rush reinforcements by air into the Norwegian heartland. While the British sought to secure northern and central Norway by landings at Namsos on the fourteenth and at Andalsnes on the eighteenth – the aim being to mount converging attacks on Trondheim – and near Narvik on the twenty-fourth, the Germans, with some 15,000 troops in the Oslo area by the fourteenth, set about securing south-east Norway in readiness for an advance to Bergen and a twin drive towards Trondheim. These moves, conducted with improvised forces – led by light tanks – in countryside still covered by thick snow, began in mid-April and included the use of parachute forces at Dombaas on the fourteenth. Though this unit was forced to surrender on the nineteenth the other German efforts were uniformly successful. Elements of the *163rd Infantry Division* from Oslo and the *69th* from Bergen linked up around Haugastal on 2 May while in the Gudbrandsdal and Osterdal valleys German forces secured both Lillehammer and Rena on the twenty-first, the former after their first clash with British forces around Lundehogda on the twentieth. The speed of these advances prevented the two British regiments landed at Andalsnes moving against Trondheim while the force landed at Namsos never advanced beyond the Steinkjer area, and this failure to secure Trondheim, combined with German possession of the initiative and total command of the air, convinced the Allies that the Germans could not be denied control of central Norway. British forces thus began the evacuation of a heavily bombed Andalsnes on 30 April, the same day that German forces from Trondheim and the Osterdal valley linked up at Berkaak, the withdrawal being completed on 2 May when the Germans occupied the town. By 3 May the Allied evacuation of Namsos was similarly completed, the Germans capturing the port the following day. With the last remaining Norwegian forces in southern and central Norway surrendering at Lommen on 1 May and at Hegra on the fifth, and the *2nd Mountain Division* being airlifted into Trondheim at the end of April in order to develop an overland offensive towards Narvik, by the first week of May German control of the key strategic areas of central and southern Norway was undisputed.

In the north, however, the German position was precarious after the naval actions of 10 and 13 April, and had the British committed forces to an assault landing at Narvik when they arrived on the fourteenth they might well have taken the port from a demoralised and disorganised German force under orders to seek internment in Sweden as the alternative to defeat. Not until the twenty-fourth, however, was a major landing attempted, and then the effort was made not at Narvik or even in Ofotfiord but at Salangen, Lavangen and Elvenes, and it was not until 13 May, when French and Polish forces were present in strength, that Allied forces came ashore at Bjerkvik. But by that time German forces at Narvik had been reinforced and resupplied, partly by air and partly by courtesy of Swedish railroads, while the *2nd Mountain Division* had pushed forward to the Mosjoen–Elsforden area, sweeping aside the first of five independent units that the Allies had landed between Mosjoen and Bodo in an attempt to slow or halt the German advance.

With scarcely any night in which to hide from German aircraft, the Allied position at Narvik was little better in real terms than that of the German defenders, but it was the increasingly serious situation in Belgium and France, where the German offensive had opened on 10 May, that on 24 May prompted the Allies to abandon the Norway venture. They resolved, however, to secure and then destroy Narvik before they did so, and on the twenty-eighth the port was taken after a major assault throughout the beachhead area. Thereafter the Allies set about the liquidation of the whole Narvik expedition, Narvik itself being wrecked to the extent that it was out of service for seven months. The port was evacuated between the 7 and 9 June and Harstad on the eighth, the same day the King of Norway and his government were evacuated by a British cruiser from Tromso. Norwegian forces remaining in the north concluded an armistice with their conquerors on the ninth.

Thus ended a campaign that the Allies had initiated but which they lost decisively, though in many ways the worst single disaster of the campaign came in its last hours when a fleet carrier and its two escorting destroyers were sunk by battleships. The loss of so valuable a unit was disastrous for Britain, but in an odd sense, with so much shipping involved in withdrawing forces from Norway, the notable feature was not perhaps the loss of the *Glorious* on 8 June but the fact that Allied losses were not greater. As it was, in the whole of the campaign the Allies lost one carrier, two cruisers, nine destroyers and six submarines, about 110 aircraft, and 5,300 killed. The Norwegian campaign also cost Chamberlain his post as British prime minister, though ironically his replacement, Winston Churchill, bore a greater responsibility for the disasters incurred in this campaign than any other single minister. The only factor that served to disguise the extent of the Allied defeat in Norway was the fact that an even greater defeat had overwhelmed the Allies in France at the same time.

The Germans lost about 5,700 dead and 200 aircraft destroyed as the price of conquering Norway, but the immediate and real cost of the campaign was borne by the *Kriegsmarine*, which was reduced to an operational strength of three cruisers and four destroyers by the end of the struggle. It lost a total of three cruisers, 10 destroyers and six submarines, and had two battleships and three cruisers out of service for periods of up to 12 months. In return for these losses, however, the *Kriegsmarine* secured Trondheim as a base for its submarines, but other than this acquisition Norway proved something of a strategic cul-de-sac. The securing of the ore route from northern Sweden was an obvious gain, but the conquest of France and the gain of Lorraine's ore lessened German dependence upon Sweden. The acquisition of bases for fleet operations counted for little after the cancellation of the carrier and battleship building programmes in April 1940. Norway itself came to require a garrison of 12 first-grade divisions, which with the passing of time Germany could ill-afford. But while these matters were or became self-evident, the three aspects of Germany's real failure in the Norwegian campaign were not so readily apparent and in any event were hard to quantify. While German military prestige rose, Hitler's political capital amongst the neutrals, particularly the United States, was eroded as a result of aggression against two inoffensive neighbours, the initial British infringement of Norwegian neutrality being superseded by Norway's allegiance to the Allied cause. Moreover, the German seizure of Denmark left Britain free to take over Danish possessions, and British forces occupied Reykjavik on 17 May and Torshavn in the Faeroes on the twenty-third. Perhaps the major failing of *Operation Weserübung* was that it made no provision for airlanding a battalion at Reykjavik, which certainly could have been taken but perhaps not held by such a force. In Allied hands, however, Iceland and Greenland furnished air bases that were crucial to the defeat of the German submarine offensive in 1943, and in political terms the severing of links between German-occupied Denmark and Allied-occupied Iceland was arguably the most important single event in the process that led to Icelandic secession from Denmark and self-proclaimed independence in June 1944.

But the most significant aspect of German failure in the Norwegian campaign was the fact that by its own terms of reference the *Kriegsmarine* lost a nominal 16 months in its prosecution of 'tonnage warfare'. In 1939 Norway possessed the fourth largest merchant navy in the world with 1,987 ships of 4,863,813 tons registered under her flag. From the start of the war part of this navy was chartered, according to accepted maritime practices, by Britain, and prior to 31 March 1940 49 Norwegian merchantmen of 106,868 tons were sunk by German action. Over the next three months the Germans sank or seized another 43 ships of 149,106 tons, but the balance of Norwegian shipping placed itself at British disposal. The German attack on Norway thus resulted in 4,607,839 tons of shipping being added to Allied resources, and the aggregate of Allied losses from all causes did not reach this total until December 1940 while sinkings by German submarines did not exceed this figure until December 1941. In terms of time, therefore, the Norwegian campaign proved as disastrous for the *Kriegsmarine* as its immediate battle losses.

No major European war in modern times has been decided in Scandinavia, and for all its importance to the Allies at the time the campaign in Norway was never more than a sideshow that assumed its proper proportions when operations began in the main theatre of war on 10 May with the German invasion of the Low Countries. Within seven weeks the

Netherlands, Belgium and Luxembourg had been occupied, the French army had been destroyed and France itself partitioned, and Britain had been reduced to impotent irrelevance. Few campaigns in history have been so swift and conclusive as the German spring offensive of 1940, and in the course of the Second World War only the Japanese campaign in south-east Asia between December 1941 and April 1942 stands comparison in terms of speed of execution, comprehensiveness and a finality that went with the ultimate defeat of the victor. In one other matter, moreover, these two campaigns are similar in that both were characterised by a precision and symmetry that render them amongst the most inspired examples of the military art, though the aesthetic qualities of the campaign that humbled the Western powers in the first months of the Pacific war have received less critical acclaim than those of the *Sichelschnitt* of 1940.

The professional finesse of *Fall Gelb* (Plan Yellow) was ironic in view of the fact that had Hitler had his way after the Polish campaign Germany would have attacked in the west in 1939 with a plan of campaign vastly inferior to the one executed with devastating effect in the spring of 1940. With the end of the Polish campaign and the brusque Allied refusal to consider his peace offer of 6 October, Hitler wanted to turn immediately upon France and on the ninth ordered the preparation of a plan of campaign for an offensive in the west. The plan submitted by *OKH* on the nineteenth was not to Hitler's liking, being conservative and orthodox to the point of predictability. It was in reality an updated but significantly modified version of the plan with which Germany had gone to war in 1914. On that occasion Germany, while standing on the defensive in the east, had invaded Belgium and Luxembourg in order to provide space in which to deploy four armies that then advanced into France west, and in the rear, of the French defensive system that extended between Verdun and Belfort.

The 1939 plan provided for the invasion of the Netherlands as well as Belgium and Luxembourg by two army groups. With the main effort to be made through southern Holland and central Belgium while a secondary thrust was staged through the broken Ardennes country of eastern Belgium and Luxembourg, the plan envisaged a frontal attack on the Anglo-French field armies on the Franco-Belgian border. But whereas both plans provided for an anti-clockwise advance to contact, the 1914 edition had been geared to fighting a battle of encirclement and annihilation in eastern France six weeks after the outbreak of war: the 1939 version was directed westwards, towards the Channel ports, and the conventional wisdom amongst senior German commanders, who at this stage of proceedings retained a healthy respect for the French army, was that the bases that the *Kriegsmarine* sought in order to prosecute its war against Britain might not be secured for two years. At very best, the plan of 19 October reflected the reluctance of the German military to force a decision in the west and it held out no more than the prospect of partial success in a protracted campaign.

The plan did not recommend itself to Hitler, though its failure to provide the means of conducting 'the last decisive battle' that would end in 'the final military annihilation' of France stemmed in part from the vagueness and relative moderation of Hitler's own directive of the ninth. But the plan, or at least the plan as modified on 29 October, was one that Hitler was obliged to accept if he persisted in his intention to settle accounts with France in 1939. It was this plan of campaign that Hitler ordered to be put into effect on no fewer than 29 occasions before, on 16 January 1940, it was abandoned. At every stage over the preceding three months Hitler was opposed by senior commanders who stressed that the army needed time to reorganise, re-equip and retrain in order to profit from the lessons of the Polish campaign while the *Luftwaffe* similarly used the opportunity to make good its losses. The army, moreover, needed time to increase its overall strength, a campaign in the west representing a considerably greater commitment than the Polish campaign. But it was the adverse weather of late autumn and early winter, not the objections of his generals, that forced Hitler to cancel *Fall Gelb* on every occasion but the last. The decision of 16 January was the result of the compromising of the plan of campaign when two *Luftwaffe* officers, with one set of plans, were obliged to make a forced landing at Mechelen in Belgium on the ninth. The outcome of this decision was the recasting of Plan Yellow in February 1940 along lines that accorded with ideas that Hitler had propounded in November, the end product being a plan of campaign that offered every prospect of a final, cataclysmic encounter battle in the spring.

In its final form Plan Yellow rested upon three assumptions: that the Allies would move to support Belgium in the event of a German invasion; that the French army, despite its size and reputation, lacked fighting spirit; and that the shattering of the French front at one point would be irreparable and decisive. The key to success lay in its first assumption, which was correct in that the Allies indeed planned to advance their field armies into Belgium and the Netherlands to meet a German onslaught, but the element of finesse was provided by the fact that the point of the German attack – the *Schwerpunkt* – was directed against the pivot of the

Allied deployment, on the middle Meuse between Dinant and Sedan. The very strength of this strategem lay in the reasons that made Hitler's original suggestion of 25 November that the main axis of advance should be along the Sedan–Amiens line so unacceptable at that time to conventional military opinion, namely the difficulty of moving armoured forces through the Ardennes, the problem of making an opposed crossing of the Meuse, and the dangers inherent in leaving an open left flank in the course of an advance to the Somme. The very detailed staff calculations of force levels and road availability that led to these objections being overcome during February 1940 were crucial in providing the element of strategic surprise essential to the plan's success, the German intention being to cross the Meuse over a 45-mile front in a strength that would deny the French the means and time to mount an effective response.

The German plan of campaign for the offensive against the west in May 1940 envisaged the use of all but 21 of the *Wehrmacht*'s 154 divisions. These 133 formations were divided between three army groups and a strategic reserve of 41 infantry divisions shared between the *2nd* and *9th Armies*. In the north, with its southern boundary set on the Namur–Liège–Eupen–Cologne line, was *Army Group B* (Bock) with the *18th* and *6th Armies*, plus a reserve of two motorised and five infantry divisions, under command. The role of this army group was to draw the Allied field armies into southern Holland and central Belgium, but with nine divisions in the *18th Army* and 16 in the *6th*, Bock's command was expected to grip the various enemies that opposed it and prevent their turning southwards against the breach that was to be opened above Namur. In the south, with its northern boundary fixed on the Trier–Koblenz line, was *Army Group C* (Colonel-General von Leeb). This formation deployed the four divisions of the *7th Army* in fixed defences on the east bank of the Rhine while the 11 infantry divisions of the *1st Army* faced the Maginot Line defences in Lorraine. The role of *Army Group C* was to mount holding attacks that would prevent the French from moving formations on this front to other sectors.

Between Bock and Leeb was Rundstedt's *Army Group A*, which had three armies, three armoured and one motorised corps, and a reserve of three infantry divisions under command. The *4th Army* deployed nine infantry divisions and the two armoured divisions of *XV Panzer Corps*, and was assigned the task of providing flank guard for the main effort to the south. The *XV Panzer Corps* was tasked to secure Dinant. The *12th* and *16th Armies*, with 10 and 12 infantry divisions respectively, were to provide the supporting role for Colonel-General von Kleist's *Panzer Group*, which was the *Schwerpunkt* of the whole German effort. The *Kleist*

Panzer Group detailed the two armoured divisions of *XLI Panzer Corps* to secure Monthermé while *XIX Panzer Corps*, with three armoured divisions and a reinforced motorised regiment, secured Sedan. The *XIV Motorised Corps*, with three motorised divisions, was to operate as the second-echelon formation behind *XIX Panzer Corps*, thereby bringing the total of German armoured and motorised divisions in this single sector to 10.

Beyond the Meuse the Germans had no detailed plans, and indeed such was the scepticism within the ranks of senior commanders that some of their number doubted if the Meuse could be crossed and dismissed the idea that the armoured formations could force the river without conventional infantry support. The unwillingness of the German High Command to make provision for the campaign beyond the Meuse was one of the obvious weaknesses of the plan, though the omission also reflected one of its strengths. With the options of making for the Channel ports, driving on Paris or wheeling eastwards to take the Maginot Line from the rear, the crossing the Meuse would present the German High Command with an enviable choice of how best to exploit success, and by the same token would present the French army with a series of dilemmas as it tried to respond to the enemy's initiative in trying to cover various axes of advance without being able to anticipate German intentions and without having at its disposal the means of countering German firepower and mobility.

The 133 German divisions committed to *Fall Gelb* were matched exactly by those available to the Belgium, Dutch and Allied armies in France in May 1940, and one of the best known facts about this campaign is that in overall numbers of men, tanks and artillery the four democracies actually held a margin of superiority over the *Wehrmacht*. In terms of formations on the ground, the Dutch army in May 1940 had 10 infantry divisions; the Belgium army two cavalry, two light motorised and 18 infantry divisions; and the French army the equivalent of 14 divisions in the Maginot Line and 77 infantry, five cavalry, three light armoured and three armoured divisions in the north-east. The French also had various formations on their other borders. The British Expeditionary Force had nine infantry divisions plus one more in the Maginot Line, and had three more infantry divisions, which were without organic artillery, detailed to labour duties. The British also had one armoured division in the process of being raised in France in May 1940, and one Canadian infantry division of similar status in Britain.

But the Democracies' ability to equal Germany on a divisional basis was not matched in terms of combat effectiveness. The lack of standardisation of equipment and doctrine, the absence of a common command structure, and, of critical importance, the failure of the four democracies to align themselves together and coordinate their policies before the start of the campaign lowered their military effectiveness relative to a *Wehrmacht* that enjoyed the advantages of single-nation identity. With Belgium and the Netherlands clinging to their neutrality until they were attacked, there was no close coordination of planning between these two countries and the Allies of the kind necessary to provide any chance of countering German aggression. Given the Belgian refusal to sanction any Allied move into Belgium in anticipation of a German invasion, the British and French had to be content with an informal arrangement with Belgium whereby in the event of a German attack on the Low Countries their forces would move into southern Holland and to the Dyle line. This undertaking was given on the understanding that the Belgians would hold the line of the Albert Canal, west of which there was no natural line of defence, for some eight days, which was the time the Anglo-French armies of Army Group 1 (General Billotte) needed to advance the 60 miles to the Dyle and then prepare and stock defensive positions on this unassuming little river. Though the French commander-in-chief, General Gamelin, and his immediate subordinates, including Billotte, were not unduly concerned by this arrangement, various commanders whose forces would be involved in this movement into central Belgium recognised the weakness of this plan. If the Belgians failed either to buy sufficient time for their move or to prepare defensive positions on the Dyle in readiness for their forces, the Allied armies would face the unwelcome prospect of an encounter battle in central Belgium against an enemy with superior mobility and after an advance that was certain to be made in the face of concerted air attack.

This weakness of the Allied plan of campaign has attracted relatively little comment alongside the more obvious failure to provide an adequate covering force on the right flank, which was where the Germans made their main effort. This was indeed the greater weakness, and in the event proved decisive to the outcome of the campaign, but recognition of the danger implicit in an encounter battle in central Belgium was an unconscious acknowledgement of superior German operational doctrine and recognition of German command of the air. Whereas the Germans had some 2,400 tanks with their armoured divisions, plus a number of older PzKw Is in an infantry-support role with formations in *Army Group B*, the British and French between them deployed some 3,100 tanks but none in divisions that were more than four months old in May 1940. The first two French armoured formations were raised in January 1940, the third and last only as late as March, and in the time that was left to them before the German onslaught these could not learn lessons and techniques that German armoured formations had absorbed since 1937. Moreover, though with the Char-B and Matilda the Allies had tanks that in terms of firepower and armour were amongst the best in the world in 1940, their tanks were generally inferior to those of the Germans with regard to gunsights, radios and turret arrangements. Allied armoured divisions were thus inferior in numbers and technique to their German counterparts and had no qualitative margin to offset these disadvantages, while overall Allied numerical preponderance was dissipated by the employment of the majority of British and French tanks in the infantry-support role. Most Allied tanks were deployed where no serious German effort was mounted and in those sectors selected by the Germans as their main axes of advance Allied tanks were not present in sufficient numbers to have any chance of achieving strategically significant results.

Only in the air, where the Democracies had some 2,000 aircraft to oppose the 4,200 of the *Luftwaffe*, did the Germans possess a clear numerical superiority over their enemies. Ranged against some 200 Belgian, 1,300 French and 416 British aircraft, of which less than 1,000 were fighters, the *Luftwaffe*, in addition to some 650 liaison-reconnaissance aircraft and 1,000 transports, had some 1,100 fighters, 400 dive-bombers and 1,200 medium bombers. In qualitative terms German aircraft were generally superior to those of the Allies, only the latest British fighters being the equal of their opposite numbers, and in terms of technique and operational doctrine the *Luftwaffe* held overwhelming advantages over the British and French air forces. The Allied air forces had no combat experience to set against that acquired by the *Luftwaffe* in Poland, but whereas Allied doctrine stressed the importance of fighter cover for ground forces German philosophy emphasised the concentration of combat aircraft in the offensive.

On both sides there was an element of self-fulfilment of doctrine in that the role of the fighter was justified in terms of the state of the air defences of ground forces. The Allied ground forces, and particularly the French, were poorly provided with anti-aircraft guns, the French army having no more than 1,500 flak pieces in the whole of the north-east. German flak defence, which was provided by *Luftwaffe* ground forces and not the army, mustered a total of 9,300 guns, and such a lavish establishment not only presented obvious problems for Allied attack aircraft, which for the most part were unescorted on missions, but freed German fighters to operate in the escort and air supremacy role. In the event the *Luftwaffe* was unable to destroy the British and French air forces that opposed it during this campaign but was nevertheless able to secure a general command of the air, operate effectively against Allied positions and lines of communication and, critically, deny the Allies a significant reconnaissance capability over the Rhineland and Ardennes in the first days of operations.

Such was the balance, or imbalance, of *matériel* and doctrine of the two sides, but the question that has attracted the attention of historians and commentators since the time the campaign was fought is why the German victory was so rapid and one-sided, or, in its alternative form, why it was that the French army, for three centuries the warrior host of Europe and for the previous two decades the most prestigious army in the world, collapsed in the way it did in May 1940. Inevitably, invidious comparisons have been drawn between the French failure of 1940 and French tenacity in the First World War, particularly in front of Verdun in 1916, and it is generally acknowledged that the French defeat of 1940 was due in part to the effort that France had made in the previous conflict. As a result of France's losses in that war – 27 per cent of all Frenchmen between 18 and 26 years of age were killed – there was undoubtedly a growing belief in France in the inter-war period that 'this western front business couldn't be done again, not for a long time', and this abhorrence of war had its unavoidably baleful effect when France was forced to go to war in 1939.

But this lack of commitment, which so impressed itself upon British commanders in the period of the 'Phoney War' between September 1939 and April 1940, was the product of more than just a reaction to the fearful blood-letting of the previous war. The bitter social divisions within France in the 1930s, the open preference of the French right for Hitler rather than for French socialists, the debilitating effect of both the Depression (which lasted longer in France than elsewhere) and the political instability of the dying Third Republic, all had their part to play in weakening French resolve before the clash of arms. Yet perhaps the most immediately important factor in the crumbling of French spirit was that by May 1940 France had become accustomed to defeat and the habit had acquired its own aura of apathetic fatalism. As late as 1937 British military observers of the French army remained convinced of its moral stamina, but by the spring of 1940 there was a belief in France in the inevitability of defeat to follow those that had been incurred, unbroken, since the German reoccupation of the Rhineland. The *Anschluss*, Munich, the Spanish imbroglio, the Nazi–Soviet pact, Poland, the Winter War and finally the débâcle that was unfolding in Norway bred defeatism. The French army's inactivity during the winter of 1939–40 in the aftermath of Gamelin's wretchedly inadequate move against the Saarland in September 1939 completed the process of self-demoralisation.

A lack of resolve, and not just on the part of the French, would seem to account, at least in part, for one of the more surprising facts about this campaign: while the Allied armies in the west in 1940 were much better equipped and placed in terms of strategic geography than had been the hapless Poles in 1939, the toll of German dead exacted in these two campaigns was not significantly different. In Poland the *Wehrmacht* lost 16,000 dead; in the west in 1940 it lost 27,000 killed. In terms of relative scale and duration the totals are roughly balanced, and that this is so in light of the greater Allied material strength relative to the *Wehrmacht* in 1940 than that of the Poles in 1939 points to an obvious conclusion that needs no elaboration.

Inevitably, certain codicils have to be entered in the presentation of this argument. Many more Germans (about 110,000) were wounded in the west than the 32,000 wounded in Poland. The *Wehrmacht* in 1940 was more formidable than it had been in 1939 in Poland, and between campaigns it had unwittingly stumbled across a doctrine, economical in terms of German lives, that is best summarised in terms of 'the more you use the less you lose'. But the fact that Germany conquered France and the Low Countries at a cost of 150,000 casualties, and conversely the BEF lost no more than 4,500 dead in the whole campaign in Flanders and France, suggests that more than matters of superior technique and economy of effort were involved in accounting for the relative lightness of battle casualties. France, in military terms, was beaten in the first four days of this campaign, but her defeat was as much political and psychological as it was military. Like Poland before her, but for very different reasons, France was beaten before the fighting began, and she was beaten because as a nation she was not prepared to make the sacrifices necessary to wage war, because she had an army that had not kept abreast of technical change, and because in 1940 she lacked allies that compared to those that had sustained her in 1917 and 1918.

The German invasion of the west opened in the early hours of 10 May with air raids upon airfields, major ports and communications centres, and main rail lines throughout north-east France and the Low Countries, and with parachute and glider landings on certain key tactical objectives in Belgium, Luxembourg and the Netherlands. The initial German moves into Luxembourg, which were made soon after midnight and included the seizure of Esch on the French border, served to alert the Allies, but in fact Belgium intelligence had been warned on the ninth of the impending attack by anti-Nazi elements within the German High Command and the Belgians had passed this information to the British and French. For their part, the French had been warned as early as 30 April that the German main effort would be made at Sedan, but such alarms had been frequent during the winter 'war of nerves' and no great reliance was placed upon these last-minute warnings. The Belgians, however, began the recall of libertymen on the ninth and manned certain key defensive positions, but it was not until the Germans showed their hand in Luxembourg that the French High Command readied its forces to move, and it was not until mid-morning, more than seven hours after the first reports of German activity had been received and two hours after German ground forces had begun to move into the Low Countries, that British and French forces began to move into Belgium.

The Allied move into the Low Countries involved the advance of the 7th Army into southern Holland, specifically into the Breda area; the BEF and the 1st Army secured the Dyle Line; the 9th Army occupied the Meuse above Namur; and the 2nd Army secured the latter's right flank around Sedan.

From the start, however, Allied intentions miscarried. The 7th Army, though it was able to secure Walcheren and Breda, was badly shaken by repeated bombing attacks in the course of its advance, and its formations were unable to eliminate the Moerdijk and Dordrecht positions secured by German airborne forces on the southern approaches to Rotterdam. The move to the Dyle was complicated by the late assembly of various units, lack of sufficient transport to move all the earmarked formations into central Belgium, and increasingly congested roads. On the Meuse the 9th Army could not cover all possible crossing points: only the flanks, immediately around Namur and Charleville-Mézières, were occupied in any strength. Allied reconnaissance forces were able to take up positions east of the Dyle and the Meuse on the afternoon of the tenth in accordance with Allied intentions, though in the south the French were to be surprised by immediate contact with German forces that had passed through Luxembourg. On the tenth German forces actually reached French soil, but the crucial development on this the first day of the campaign was German success in neutralising Fort Eban Emael, the key to the defences along the Albert Canal, and in seizing intact three bridges over this waterway. Although the Dutch blew the Maastricht bridges on the tenth and the Belgians recaptured and destroyed the Briegden bridge on the eleventh, the loss of the Vroenhoven and Veldwezelt bridges provided the *6th Army* with immediate access into central Belgium with the result that Belgian possession of the Albert Line became untenable

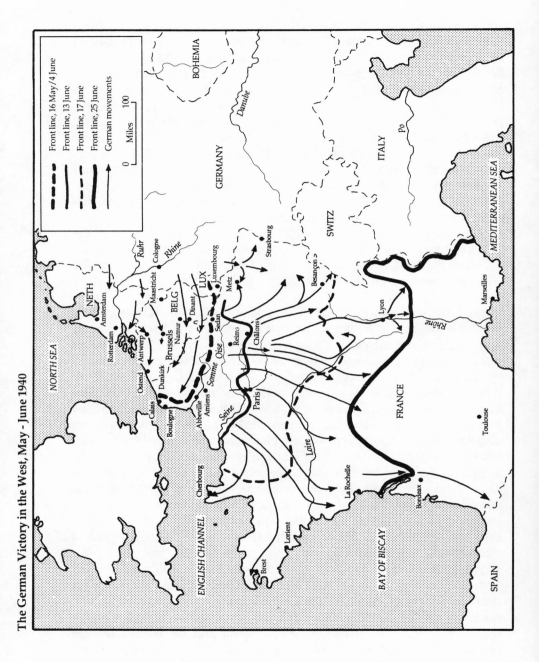

The German Victory in the West, May – June 1940

and *XVI Panzer Corps* reached Tongres on the eleventh. With the *9th Panzer Division* spearheading the *18th Army*'s advance into the Netherlands with its drive on Tilburg, Breda and Moerdijk, German success in breaking through the Albert Canal defences within two days of the start of operations destroyed the premise of the Gamelin plan as ruthlessly as German armour destroyed Allied cavalry and reconnaissance units east of the Dyle and Meuse on the twelfth and thirteenth.

By 13 May the 7th Army had begun to withdraw from the Breda area, and by the fourteenth, when the reconcentration within the Dyle position of the 18 Belgian divisions north of the Sambre was completed but offset by the surrender of the Dutch on this same day, German forces were moving up to the Allied main line of resistance, which remained unoccupied along parts of its length. It was not until the morning of the fifteenth that the last French units detailed to man the Dyle Line took up their positions, and then only after exhausting forced marches along roads crammed with refugees. By the time that these latecomers arrived on the Dyle, however, Army Group 1 had decided that a withdrawal to the Dendre and then to the Escaut was unavoidable, though it delayed issuing the appropriate orders until the sixteenth. This decision was prompted in part by a realisation of the inadequacies of the Dyle Line and the strength of German forces moving into central Belgium, but in reality neither the Dendre nor the Escaut were better prepared for defence than the Dyle. In part, however, the decision to withdraw from central Belgium was the result of the awareness that virtually the whole of the front along the Meuse between Yvoir and Wadelincourt had been destroyed and that German armour was operating virtually unopposed west of the river.

The success of *Army Group B* in the first three days of the campaign in fighting its way into the Dutch heartland and through the Albert Canal defences was substantial, but it counted for little in comparison with its real success in attracting and holding Allied attention at the very time that the main threat to the Allies developed through the Ardennes. On 10 and 11 May *XV Panzer Corps*, operating at times in echelon because of the paucity of roads in the northern Ardennes, advanced beyond the Ourthe and reached the Meuse to the north of Dinant on the afternoon of the twelfth. Franco-Belgian demolition and denial programmes in this sector had not been particularly effective, and infantry from the *5th Panzer Division* was able to cross the river at Houx on the night of the 12/13 May. Elements of the *7th Panzer Division* were similarly able to cross the Meuse on the morning of the thirteenth at Leffé. Although French formations counter-attacked both bridgeheads, German command of the air and the French inability to muster substantial and balanced forces against the German positions inevitably resulted in the French failure to push *XV Panzer Corps* back into the Meuse on the thirteenth, German armour being left free to move across the river during the night. On the following morning, when no fewer than three German infantry divisions arrived around Dinant in order to consolidate the bridgeheads, *XV Panzer Corps* set about the twin tasks of levering the French from their downstream positions and consolidating their gains by advances to the west. By nightfall on the fourteenth the two French formations facing the Dinant position, II and XI Infantry Corps, had been reduced to a state of collapse. To the south the attack of *XLI Panzer Corps* developed later than those of its neighbours, this formation having been forced to concede priority to *XIX Panzer Corps* on the roads through Luxembourg and eastern Belgium. It did not reach the Meuse until the afternoon of the thirteenth, though its intentions had been signalled to the French by a pulverising air attack on positions around Monthermé during the morning. It crossed the river on the thirteenth and withstood an immediate French counter-attack, a second and more substantial counter-attack on the following morning being shattered by the *Luftwaffe*. Thereafter *XLI Panzer Corps* limited itself to relatively light patrolling while it brought its full strength across the river and prepared for the next phase of operations. During the day its position was consolidated by the arrival of *III Infantry Corps* at Nouzonville, though in reality it no longer faced serious opposition: by dusk on the fourteenth *XLI Panzer Corps* had effectively destroyed the third and last of 9th Army's corps.

German success around Dinant and Monthermé was substantial but not critical to the outcome of the campaign, but the efforts of *XV* and *XLI Panzer Corps* had never been intended to be more than complementary to the main attack made by *XIX Panzer* and *XIV Motorised Corps* at Sedan, and even as early as the morning of the twelfth, just two days into the offensive, *XIX Panzer Corps* had secured a potentially overwhelming advantage of position, timing and concentration in being able to drive French screening forces behind the Samois and back to Sedan itself. Indeed, on 12 May the 2nd Army, recognising the threat that was developing on its front, destroyed the bridges in the Sedan sector and secured the release of four first-grade divisions, including the 3rd Armoured and 3rd Motorised Divisions, from the reserve in order to underwrite X Infantry Corps around Sedan. By the time the release of reserves was authorised, however, it was too late for the French to restore the situation. X Infantry Corps was a low-grade formation, many of its troops being B-category reservists, and most of its defences on the

Meuse were incomplete. The reinforcements, moreover, needed time to reach the front and immunity from air attack as they made their way forward, but in the event they had neither. While the 2nd Army realised that a German assault crossing was inevitable, it appreciated neither the scale of the impending attack nor the speed with which *XIX Panzer Corps* would mount its effort.

On the morning of the thirteenth the *Luftwaffe* launched a series of heavy attacks behind Sedan before conducting a sustained assault on the French positions on the Meuse in mid-afternoon. Under the cover of this attack infantry from the *1st Panzer Division* crossed the river at Gaulier, just below Sedan, and captured most of the defenders as they sheltered from air attack and before they had a chance to reoccupy their positions. With the infantry working its way downstream in order to take French positions from the rear, German armour crossed the river and moved to the south, passing in front of the Bois de Marfée position covering the Bar valley to the south and causing the French to abandon prematurely their heavy artillery around Bulson. On the morning of the fourteenth, as the *10th Panzer Division* crossed the Meuse at Wadelincourt scattering the 71st Infantry Division as it did so, a French counter-attack on the *1st Panzer Division* was repulsed and *2nd Panzer Division* crossed the river below Donchery. By late afternoon *XIX Panzer Corps* had crossed the Ardennes Canal and Bar and was moving westwards, *10th Panzer Division* having been detached to secure the left flank while *XIV Motorised Corps* secured the rear. The leading German infantry divisions bound for Sedan were at this stage some 36 hours from the Meuse.

If the defeat at Sedan was not to become a disaster the Allies had to respond immediately to the situation, but apart from the counter-attack on the *1st Panzer Division* no major French response was mounted on the fourteenth. British and French bombers tried to eliminate the German bridgeheads, and in the course of its second such attack on the fourteenth the Royal Air Force incurred the greatest rate of loss it ever sustained in any single operation when 40 of its 71 Battle light bombers were lost. With the *Luftwaffe* committing some 850 aircraft over Sedan on this day and the German spans over the Meuse heavily ringed by flak defences, the only result of these raids was the crippling of Allied air power: on the fifteenth the French air force was able to fly a bare 200 sorties compared to the 370 flown on the fourteenth, and the British effort showed a similar decline.

But the real Allied failure on 14 May was on the ground. During the day X Infantry Corps disintegrated while French plans to counter-attack the Dinant and Sedan bridgeheads came to nothing. The French

93

intention was to use the 1st Armoured Division, then at Charleroi, against Dinant; the 2nd, after it reached Charleroi from the reserve, against Monthermé; and the 3rd against Sedan. By definition, however, the formations detailed for these attacks were inadequate and the attacks themselves would be too late to be effective. In the event none of the attacks took place. The 1st Armoured Division moved to attack the Dinant bridgehead on the fourteenth, but in doing so its units became separated and on the following day the heavy units had the misfortune to be refuelling when German armour was encountered. Despite their immobility these units avoided heavy losses but were simply bypassed. Lacking adequate supply and without infantry and artillery support, the various units of 1st Armoured Division slowly broke down into smaller packets lacking overall control and direction. By the sixteenth the 1st Armoured Division had ceased to exist.

On the Sedan front, however, the failure of the 3rd Armoured Division to move against the bridgehead on the fourteenth was compounded by two disastrous decisions by the 2nd Army that effectively sealed the fate of Army Group 1. Despite its orders to attack during the morning, the 3rd Armoured Division was unable to reach its start lines until late afternoon, and even by that time it was all but unsupported. It was then ordered not to attack and to disperse its tanks amongst neighbouring infantry. Thus the only division that was available for the counter-attack was destroyed without battle. Moreover, with the collapse of X Infantry Corps the 2nd Army took the decision to pull back its left flank and centre in order to block any German attempt to work around the open flank and threaten 2nd Army, and by extension eastern France, from the rear. However orthodox the decision, its effect was to abandon those positions that the 2nd Army still retained in the immediate vicinity of Sedan at the very time when German armour moved to expand its bridgehead not to the east but to the west, through the remnants of the 9th Army. For all their success, the Germans had broken through the French defences at Sedan across a front of only five miles. By pulling back from Sedan, the 2nd Army helped to widen the breach to a distance of 15 miles, and it withdrew its remaining formations to positions from which the German bridgeheads could not be taken under effective artillery fire.

These two decisions cost the French what slender chances of avoiding defeat remained to the Allies by the fourteenth, but their immediate effect was to present the Allied armies on the Dyle with a series of dilemmas. With no reserve in northern France capable of holding German armour as it broke clear of the Meuse, and since by dusk on 17 May *Army Group A* had all but cleared the area bound by the Sambre,

Sambre–Oise canal and Aisne, the only chance of restoring a continuous front rested upon 1st Army attacking southwards from its positions on the Dyle, contacting fresh forces brought against the German left flank, and cutting off the *Schwerpunkt* before German infantry had the chance to line the sides of the breach. But the 1st Army could only be freed for an offensive role if the British and Belgians to the north extended their fronts and provided flank protection as French columns moved across the Gembloux gap, and if the 1st Army was successful the British and Belgians would have to conform to French movements and come south. Leaving aside the fact that any French reconcentration against the lengthening German left flank was problematical at best, the immediate military implications of this situation were obvious. With the 7th Army in southern Holland in disorderly retreat and the Allied left flank crumbling as a consequence, any thinning of the British and Belgian positions on the Dyle ran a fearful risk in light of *Army Group B*'s being poised to attack the Line. Moreover, the decision of Army Group 1 to abandon central Belgium merely increased Allied difficulties because any withdrawal from the Dyle Line served only to widen the gap between the 1st and 2nd Armies and correspondingly reduce the chances of restoring the front.

Underlying the military dilemmas, however, were political issues that reflected conflicting national interests and tensions within the anti-German alliance and which came to the surface with the strains imposed by defeat. To the French it was inconceivable that the British and Belgians could even consider refusing to extend their fronts, dangerously overstretched though their divisions were, when the fate of all depended – or at least appeared to depend – upon the French stemming the breach in the centre. Any move to the south, however, would involve the Belgian army abandoning Brussels and the heartland of Belgium without a fight in order to provide France with the opportunity to save herself. For its part, the BEF, in the words of its chief of staff, 'didn't give a bugger what happens to the Belgians', as long as they held the British left flank. The British army in Belgium, however, looked not to the south but either to the south-west, and the possibility of a reconstituted defence on the line of the Somme, or, more relevantly, to the west and the Channel ports. One aspect of this divergence of national interest manifested itself in the immediate aftermath of the French collapse at Sedan. Having despatched 12 fighter squadrons to France between 10 and 15 May, on the fifteenth the British war cabinet took the unpalatable decision that no more Hurricanes would be sent across the Channel. Moreover, on the seventeenth the Chief of the Imperial General Staff, General Sir Edmund Ironside, informally asked the navy to put in hand arrangements for the evacuation of the BEF from the continent. This development, however, had no immediate effect upon the situation in Belgium and France, but the issue it raised became ever more urgent after 20 May when, after a 60-mile advance in a single day, the *1st Panzer Division* secured Amiens and the *2nd Panzer Division* took Abbéville and then both Eu and Noyelles.

The speed of the German advance to the Channel was both remarkable in its own right and decisive in keeping the Allies wrong-footed and unable to mount any effective countermove. It was particularly impressive in that the armoured columns were effectively halted for much of the seventeenth while the German High Command decided its future course of action. Hitler, anxious about the lengthening left flank, wanted to halt the armour while the infantry came forward. *OKH*, conscious that the French were beyond salvation, wished to press on with the armour and even to wheel to the south-west, towards and beyond Paris, in the hope and expectation that France could be finished with a single blow rather than in the two phases that had been anticipated. In effect these arguments resolved themselves: the armour was to proceed with its advance to the coast without waiting for the infantry, the only results being a further souring of relations between Hitler and *OKH* and one day's rest, reorganisation and refitting for the armour that stood it in good stead in the coming week. Compensation for the armour's halt was provided by the occupation of Louvain and Brussels by *Army Group B*, the counter-attack by the newly raised 4th Armoured Division at Montcornet on this same day being scarcely noted at the time and not reported to Kleist until the eighteenth. A second counter-attack by the same formation on the Serre near Laon on the nineteenth, after German armour had resumed its advance and was approaching the Canal du Nord, similarly had no effect other than to provide the mythological basis of the combat reputation of the divisional commander, a certain Colonel de Gaulle.

With *XVI Panzer Corps* removed from the *6th Army* and *Army Group B* at this time in order to reinforce success in the centre, the French needed more than two separate regimental-sized counter-attacks to stem the tide of defeat, and this they recognised. Despite the chaos that was beginning to engulf the upper reaches of the French High Command at this time but with the withdrawal from the Dyle to the Escaut completed between 16 and 19 May, the Allies planned to counter-attack on the twenty-first with two British and eight French divisions at Arras and Cambrai respectively. Instead of a coordinated assault by 10 divisions, however, only two British infantry battalions and 74 tanks counter-attacked on the twenty-first, the French being unable to make their effort – in regimental strength – until the twenty-second. Although the British effort caused the Germans some initial alarm, the only practical result of these attacks was the denial of Arras until 23 May, by which time German armour was approaching Calais from the south and the Aa canal from the south-west.

At this time the British planned to resume their attack, but the enforced withdrawal from Arras effectively ended this intention, exposed the French on the lower Scarpe to attack and led to bitter French accusations of having been betrayed even though the French themselves had abandoned the intention to resume their offensive. On the afternoon of the twenty-fifth, however, General Gort, commander of the BEF, moved the two divisions concentrated for the resumption of the offensive to cover a gap that had opened in the Allied line between Ypres and Menin. In effect, this decision placed the preservation of a British line of withdrawal to Dunkirk above the requirements of an attack to re-establish contact with the French on the Somme. Given the isolation of the northern armies after the twentieth, the only surprising feature of this decision was that it was not made until the twenty-fifth.

By the time Gort decided his priorities, however, German spearheads were closer to Dunkirk than most British formations and total disaster threatened the BEF as a result of the partial collapse of Belgian resistance on the left flank. History, or at least Anglo-American and French versions of it, has not been generous in its treatment of Belgian efforts in May 1940, but the fact was that as in the First World War the Belgian army's defence of its homeland was dogged and determined. It was always outnumbered and subjected to consistently heavier attack than the BEF, and after the twentieth its front had been extended as the British turned to the south. After two weeks' constant fighting and marching, its divisions were overcommitted and exhausted. On the twenty-fourth it was subjected to overwhelming attack on the Lys by *Army Group B*, and by the following morning the Germans had broken through Belgian positions across a 14-mile front.

Other than by its own efforts, the BEF was to be saved by a combination of the Belgian army's ability to keep fighting until the national capitulation on 28 May, the sacrifice of French forces that fought to the end, and the German decision to halt the armoured forces on the twenty-fourth. For long the subject of controversy, this decision had been foreshadowed by the *OKH* order of 19 May that made provision for the reorganisation of forces in readiness for second-phase operations, but in reality it was the unwillingness of commanders at ivisional, corps and group levels to commit armour in heavily built-up coastal areas that led to the halting of the armour when the total annihilation of all the Allied armies in the north was within its grasp. When the decision was confirmed by Hitler it was rationalised in terms of fighting the last battle on French as opposed to Belgian soil, of denying the army total victory by allowing the *Luftwaffe* to administer the *coup de grâce*, and of leaving *Army Group B* to administer the last rites over the Allied corpse. By 27 May when the armour of *Army Group A* was ordered to resume a short-lived offensive – the product of the twin realisation that a major evacuation had begun and that Bock's armies could not come immediately against the beachhead – the Allies had been given time to improvise a defence where none had existed on the twenty-fourth.

By the twenty-sixth, when the concentration of all three British corps within the beachhead perimeter was completed and *Operation Dynamo* officially began, what started with the modest objective of rescuing perhaps 45,000 men had already resulted in the evacuation of some 27,936 British troops from various ports and beaches north of the Somme. In the event, the loss of 177 British fighters over Dunkirk and the sinking of 10 fleet units, including eight Allied destroyers, proved the price of the rescue of a further 338,226 Allied troops by 4 June, of which some 53,000 were Frenchmen evacuated after the last British troops departed on the night of 2/3 June. To the total of 366,162 men evacuated from the north between 20 May and 4 June were to be added another 191,870 Allied troops evacuated from France during and after the second phase of operations. Of the overall total of 558,032 Allied military personnel evacuated from the continent between 20 May and 14 August, when British evacuations on the French Mediterranean coast finally came to an end, 368,491 were British.

By 4 June, when fighting around Dunkirk finally ended, both the French and the Germans had reorganised and redeployed their armies in readiness for the next phase of operations, the start of which was less than 24 hours away. The result of this phase of the campaign was a foregone conclusion: having failed with its full strength to prevent the German advance to the coast, a much weakened French army, with no natural line of defence between the Channel and the Meuse on which to stand, could not hope to hold an enemy of superior strength and with all the advantages bestowed by possession of the initiative and command of the air.

Having failed to eliminate the crucially important German bridgeheads over the Somme at Abbéville, Amiens and Péronne after 20 May and having lost the equivalent of three full-strength armies and a total of

22 infantry, four armoured, three light and two cavalry divisions in first-phase operations, the five French armies covering the 172 miles of front between the Channel and the Meuse on 4 June numbered some 37 infantry, three cavalry and four reconstituted armoured divisions. With just one British division remaining from the total of 37 Belgian, British and Dutch divisions that had been in the line on 10 May, the total of 45 field divisions available for the defence of France was less than that available to *Army Group B*, which was to lead the advance south of the Somme–Aisne line with three of the five available armoured corps. Bock's command mustered 48 divisions, with another 12 held in its area of responsibility, and was tasked with the destruction of the French left flank, after which *Army Group A*, itself only marginally inferior to the French armies across the whole of the front, was to attack on the upper Aisne. Content to mask and pass either side of Paris, the German intention was to reduce the remaining French armies to debris at the very start of proceedings and then to secure the Channel and Atlantic coasts with *Army Group B* and to encircle the Maginot Line and occupy eastern and central France with *Army Group A*.

Though events did not work out according to plan, results exceeded expectation in that while the forces of Bock and Rundstedt achieved the success that was expected of them, *Army Group C*, hitherto quiescent apart from its destruction of the La Ferté position on 18/19 May, succeeded in breaching the Maginot Line between Faulquemont and Wittring on 14/15 June. Moreover, while the *1st Army* pressed forward almost to the Marne–Rhine canal before turning eastwards into the Vosges where its formations accepted the surrender of XLIII Infantry Corps at the Donon on the twenty-third, the *7th Army* crossed the Rhine on the fifteenth and secured Colmar two days later. The German success in breaking through the very symbol of inter-war French greatness was overshadowed, however, by other events. On the day that Colmar fell the *29th Motorised Division*, part of the *XXXIX Panzer Corps*, reached Pontarlier on the Franco-Swiss border, thus completing the encirclement of eastern France and the Maginot Line, while on the previous day, the sixteenth, the pugnacious Paul Reynaud was replaced as prime minister by the octogenarian Marshal Henri Pétain. With the French government then at Bordeaux, having abandoned Paris on the eleventh, Pétain's first actions on assuming office included the appointment of ministers known to oppose the continuation of the war and a request via Spain for German terms. Moreover, in the course of a radio broadcast to the French people in which he stated that the fighting had to be ended, Pétain destroyed what little resolve was left to the French army. While nothing could stem the German onslaught, Pétain's initial actions after taking over from Reynaud, combined with his known antipathy towards Britain, ensured that France would not attempt to continue the war from North Africa.

Of second-phase operations little need be noted other than that they conformed to a simple pattern. Neither *Army Group B*, which opened proceedings on 5 June on the Somme front, nor *Army Group A*, which attacked on the upper Aisne four days later, recorded much success on the respective first day of operations in the face of very determined French resistance. But lacking the means of conducting a mobile defence, the French armies deployed in the path of Bock and Rundstedt were capable of making no more than a single defensive effort. With the very tenacity of that effort massively and immediately eroding French capacity, the French front between the Channel and the Meuse was very quickly broken and, once broken at any single point along its length, a general collapse ensued with the result that German armoured formations advanced almost unopposed into rear areas and occupied one historic French city after another with bewildering rapidity. Thus on the Somme, where the *Kleist Panzer Group*'s *XIV Panzer Corps* at Amiens and *XVI Panzer Corps* at Péronne made very little impression on French defences on the fifth, the success of *XV Panzer* and *XXXVIII Infantry Corps* either side of Hangest proved immediately decisive. With the infantry formation securing Poix on the eighth, *XV Panzer Corps* was freed to advance and secure Rouen and Elbeuf on the following morning but not before the bridges over the lower Seine were destroyed. With *XV Panzer Corps* thereafter turning north in order to prevent the withdrawal of IX Infantry Corps to Le Havre, the destruction of the 10th Army's centre and the progressive reduction of French positions masking the Amiens and Péronne bridgeheads on the sixth left the 7th Army with little option but to retreat. Its front had been withdrawn behind the Oise and lower Aisne by the time that *Army Group A* opened its offensive.

On 9 June the attacks of *Army Group A* fared no better than those of *Army Group B* on the fifth, but the shallow bridgeheads that were secured around Rethel were just sufficient to allow the newly raised *Guderian Panzer Group* to move formations from *XXXIX Panzer Corps* across the river during the night and, with *XLI Panzer Corps*, in the second echelon, to develop advances to the east of Rheims on the tenth. On the following day the *Kleist Panzer Group*, having been withdrawn from the Somme front and *Army Group B*, came into the line in order to develop offensives to the west of Rheims, which fell that same day. It was the speed of these various offensives, by both *XV Panzer Corps* and the two armoured groups of *Army Group A*, that ended any possibility of a French withdrawal into either a Cotentin or Breton redoubt, and also confounded the British intention to send a second expeditionary force to France, the leading elements of which arrived at Cherbourg on 5 June.

It was the speed of these offensives, moreover, that provide the lasting impression of this campaign, namely of German armoured units passing long columns of dishevelled, dispirited *poilus*, but, most important of all, it was the speed of the armoured advances into France that after the ninth rendered the French military situation utterly impossible and which made the French request for an armistice only a matter of time. Châlons-sur-Marne on 12 June, Paris on the fourteenth, Verdun on the fifteenth, Besançon and Dijon on the sixteenth, Belfort, Rennes and Tours on the eighteenth, Brest and Cherbourg on the nineteenth and Lyon and Nantes on the twentieth were to fall to German forces before the German terms of an armistice were made known to the French at Réthondes on the twenty-first. The terms were harsh and humiliating, designed as they were 'to provide Germany with the guarantees required for the enforced pursuit of the war against Britain' and 'to create the conditions necessary for the establishment of a fresh peace, the main object of which will be the reparation of the wrongs inflicted by force on the German Reich'. Thus the obstinacy of Britain in refusing to come to terms was to be made the immediate cause of France's misfortune in being partitioned and partially occupied, but the terms deliberately avoided the one demand – the surrender of the French fleet – that might have prevented the Pétain government, intent on surrender at almost any price, from accepting the German *diktat*. The French plenipotentiaries at Réthondes signed the armistice terms on the twenty-second, the ceasefire coming into effect shortly after midnight on 25 June. As one German diarist noted at the time: 'The battle for France is over. It lasted 26 years.'

At first sight there seems to be no difficulty in distinguishing the victor of the 1940 campaign from the vanquished: the German triumph was evident and overwhelming while the defeats of Belgium, France and the Netherlands and the partial defeat of Britain were beyond dispute. But wars, as von Clausewitz has taught us, have the habit of acquiring their own logic and of producing results very different from those anticipated by participants. The 1940 campaign had aspects and ramifications that blurred the images of defeat and victory, none more obviously than the fact that the US defence establishment, and particularly the US Navy, emerged as the real winners of the 1940 campaign in Europe. As France went down to defeat in May and June the United States, conscious that

101

the prevention of the domination of Europe by any single power represented a supreme American security interest, authorised the massive expansion of her army and navy and their respective air forces. The army was to be transformed from its status of eighteenth in the list of military rankings, behind Portugal, by fixing its establishment at 2,000,000 men and the raising of 10 motorised and 45 infantry divisions. The navy was to be expanded by 1947 from its existing strength of 15 battleships, six carriers, 37 cruisers, 237 destroyers and 102 submarines to an establishment of 35 battleships, 20 carriers, 88 cruisers, 378 destroyers and 180 submarines. The air forces were to receive 19,000 aircraft above the currently authorised expansion limits. In a rare display of national unity, therefore, the Americans, as a direct result of German control of Europe from the North Cape to the Pyrenees and from the Vistula to Finisterre, looked to their own defences, and in the process placed themselves on a collision course with the chief beneficiary of the German victory in western Europe: Japan.

If the Maginot Line had been the first line of defence of the United States until May 1940, it had been even more significant in underwriting the British, Dutch and French empires in the Far East. These were rendered defenceless by the collapse of Allied power in Europe in the spring of 1940. France's defeat left Indo-China in pawn to the Japanese, and on 8 August the British High Command concluded that Britain could not oppose any Japanese move against either Indo-China or Siam and that British possessions in the Far East, Malaya and Singapore included, were indefensible. The eclipse of Allied power thus provided Japan with maximum temptation and minimum risk – other than that explicit in the measure providing for a doubling of the US Navy which received presidential assent on 20 July and was called 'the two-ocean naval expansion act'. The American definition of global intention after the fall of France thus carried implications for the Pacific and south-east Asia that impressed themselves upon Japan over the next 14 months, and were a major factor in the process of transforming concurrent Asian and European wars into a global conflict in December 1941.

The fall of France marked the end of European domination in world affairs. That domination, the product of European industrial, technological and naval superiority over non-European societies, had been acquired in a previous age. By 1939 that domination was no more than a convicted man on parole, and 1940 saw an end that had been foreseen. Yet, oddly, the change in the balance of power between Europe and the non-European world and within Europe as a result of the 1940 campaign obliquely confirmed the correctness of Allied strategic policy before

1940: defeat did not invalidate its soundness. The essence of Allied policy had been that a major industrialised power such as Germany could only be defeated in a protracted war, and that the issue between Germany and her enemies would not be tested until 1942 or 1943. This, of course, was exactly what was to happen, but not in the way that Anglo-French planners had envisaged. By these years Germany had established a dominance within Europe that was too great to be challenged by any single European state or combination of European states. Indeed, by 1942 only one wholly European state remained both at war with and unoccupied by Germany. But German hegemony within Europe was tested in 1942 and 1943, and it was tested – and found wanting – by an alliance headed by two states, one wholly non-European and the other extra-European, that between them reduced Britain by 1943 to a position of *minor inter pares* within Allied councils. The German domination of Europe thus coincided with the contraction of European power, and the destruction of German pre-eminence within Europe was to be achieved by a process that resulted in the future of Europe being decided, for the first time, by outsiders.

The question of Britain's role in the Second World War after France's defeat brings into focus the major flaw of the German plan of campaign of 1940. Reference has already been made to the fact that *Fall Gelb* contained two weaknesses, the first being its lack of detailed provision for operations after the Meuse was crossed. This lack of definitive policy was a contributory factor in the halting of forces and the various arguments within the German High Command after 14 May. But while the advantages of flexibility and the handicaps of uncertainty probably cancelled each other out in the conduct of operations, *Fall Gelb* was only a plan of campaign and not a coherent strategy for the conduct of the war in which Germany was engaged. With so much of Germany's emotional capital invested in reversing 1918 and France's inter-war ascendancy, it was perhaps inevitable that in 1940 German military attention was myopic in its concentration upon France. But the failure of German planning to provide any means of dealing with Britain, or perhaps more accurately the failure of German planning to provide any means of dealing with Britain at the same time as accounts with France were settled, was nevertheless a weakness. In retrospect it can be seen that between 20 May and 4 June Germany had as favourable an opportunity to destroy British power – certainly with respect to the BEF and perhaps even in terms of establishing an air- or beachhead in south-east England – as any that presented itself during the war. The failure to deal decisively with Britain at the time of her greatest vulnerability meant that with the end of the campaign in France and Flanders the

103

Wehrmacht could not complete its victory, and in the event Hitler did not await the outcome of his attempt to carry the war to Britain by means of an air offensive before deciding his next move.

On 29 July the German operational planning staffs received orders to prepare for an attack on the Soviet Union in the spring, an eventuality that had been foreshadowed since 18 October 1939, when Hitler instructed *OKH* to consider occupied Poland 'as an assembly area for future operations'. The spring 1941 schedule nevertheless represented an unwelcome concession on Hitler's part: his inclination, as the prospect of victory over France hardened into certainty but before the campaign was over, was to move against the Soviet Union in the autumn of 1940, and it was only with considerable difficulty that he was deflected from such a timetable.

Hitler's desire to move against the Soviet Union was in part an inevitable reaction to the fact that Stalin took the opportunity presented by German commitments in the west to occupy the Baltic states on 14/15 June and to relieve Romania of Bessarabia and northern Bukovina on the twenty-eighth. But for all these short-term gains, the Soviet Union was one of the main losers of the 1940 campaign because her security in part rested upon France. France's defeat owed itself to some extent to the fact that in 1940, unlike 1914, she had no eastern ally to help divide German strength and attention between two fronts: her defeat placed the Soviet Union in exactly the same relative position after June 1940. Stalin had been under no illusion that Hitler, if provided with the opportunity, would turn upon the Soviet Union, and indeed in formulating his ideas in November 1939 for an attack on France Hitler had set down the defeat of France as the *sine qua non* for an attack on the Soviet Union. The fall of France thus provided Hitler with his opportunity. By denying France a second front in 1940 and failing to allow for an outright German victory in the west Stalin condemned the Soviet Union to face the full power of the *Wehrmacht* without the support of an effective military ally.

The implications of France's defeat for Nazi–Soviet relations were obvious: scarcely less obvious, and more immediate because of Soviet action against Romania in June, were the implications of Germany's victory for central and south-east Europe, and in this area, as with the case of the United States, the German victory over France set off a sequence of events over which Hitler had only partial control. The obvious implication of Germany's victory over France lay in the fact that the independence and sovereignty of the Balkan states – even their right to continue their incessant feuding with one another and, in the case of Yugoslavia, within her own borders – had rested upon a balance of power within Europe. France's defeat left the Balkan states very much dependent on German largesse. But this, plus the Soviet demands on Romania, ruptured the fragile *status quo* within the Balkans, and in July both Bulgaria and Hungary laid claims on Romanian territory.

While having no sympathy for a Romania which, until 1 July, was still guaranteed by Britain, Hitler could not be indifferent to these developments. Germany was dependent upon Romania for oil, and could not afford to see an outbreak of war in the Balkans that might provoke Soviet intervention. As a result Hitler forced Bulgaria and Romania into an agreement that on 21 August gave Bulgaria the southern Dobrudja and restored the 1878 border between the two countries. Nine days later the Hungarian–Romanian dispute was settled by German–Italian mediation in the form of the Vienna Award, the greater part of Hungarian claims being met with the transfer of more than half of Transylvania from Romania. In return Romania was guaranteed and promised military assistance by Germany, and during October German forces proceeded to occupy the country.

Balkan issues, however, involved more than Franco-German and Nazi–Soviet dimensions and domestic, intra-Balkan concerns. The Soviet interest in the Balkans was an inheritance of a traditional Russian involvement in south-east Europe. Scarcely less well-established was a British involvement in the eastern Mediterranean that dated back to the end of the eighteenth century. Moreover, there was an Italian interest in the Balkans that had been actively pursued in the inter-war period and which Hitler had acknowledged in 1939. In the event it was this Italian interest that was to be decisive in inadvertently plunging the Balkans into war in the spring of 1941. Herein lies the most important aspect of Italian participation in the Second World War. Though the least of the eight major powers that engaged in this conflict, Italy undertook four major military commitments in the course of hostilities and of those, three – in the Balkans, in the Libyan–Egyptian theatre, and in East Africa – provide the link between discontinuous mainstream events to the north of the Alps. Like Britain, with whom she fought after June 1940, Italy was peripheral to the unfolding and outcome of the European war, but in their war with one another Italy and Britain provided the vital element of continuity between otherwise disparate, disjointed campaigns in other theatres where the issue of defeat and victory was decided.

Although Italian action accounted for one British cruiser and three submarines within 10 days of Italy's entering the war, the Italian declaration of war on Britain and France on 10 June 1940 was not accompanied by major offensive action on any front. Italian strategic policy in June 1940 was essentially defensive, Mussolini's calculation being that the outcome of the war had been decided and that Italy was destined to make considerable gains at British and French expense without undue effort on her part. Mussolini was not alone in making such calculations: in June 1940 the dictator of Spain, General Francisco Franco, came to exactly the same conclusion and in response to German overtures indicated a willingness to enter the war on the side of the Axis powers at some future date. A promise in principle by Franco, however, concealed a refusal to do anything in practice, at least not until the lion was certified dead. Having declared war, Mussolini, in contrast, was to be frustrated in his expectation of gain in part by the Italian army's failure to record more than the most derisory of gains along the border of France; in part by Hitler's refusal to share Germany's victory over France with Italy and his unwillingness to force France into colonial concessions at Italian behest; in part because of Britain's refusal to surrender as expected. Thus Italy's defensive policy gave way to offensive action only slowly, though local factors, not considerations of national policy, dictated the timing of the first Italian offensive moves in East Africa.

The approach of the rainy season prompted the move into eastern Sudan to secure the border towns of Kassala and Gallabat on 4 July and Kurmuk on the seventh, while in the south Italian formations advanced into Kenya and occupied Moyale on the fifteenth. It was not until 3 August, by which time the neutrality of French Somaliland was assured, that Italian forces crossed the border into British Somaliland on three axes of advance, securing Zeila and Hargeisa on the fifth and Odweina on the sixth. Having forced the Tug Argan defile, the Italians occupied Berbera on the nineteenth after the last British units in the colony had been evacuated to Aden. On the Libyan–Egyptian border, however, minor patrol activity did not give way to major operations until 13 September when the *10th Army*, with five divisions under command, began a ponderous offensive that within five days carried it 60 miles to Sidi Barrani, where it halted. It had been the Italian intention to begin an offensive into Egypt on the same day as German forces landed in southern England, but the inability of the *Wehrmacht* to undertake *Operation Seelöwe* left Mussolini with little alternative but to proceed with the invasion of Egypt. The fact that the invasions of Egypt and Britain had been timed to coincide was nevertheless a tacit admission that the Axis campaigns in North Africa were marginal to the outcome of the war.

With the fall of France Hitler reasoned, quite correctly, that Britain's strategic position had been rendered hopeless, but his parallel belief, that

106

with the defeat of France there was no good reason why Anglo-German hostilities should continue because there was no longer any clash of British and German interests, was altogether mistaken: Britain had declared war in order to resist German aggression, not acquiesce in German success and assume a position of dependence upon Germany. Britain's refusal to come to terms in the aftermath of France's defeat thus came as a surprise to Hitler and left him with an option of difficulties in trying to bring about her surrender.

Reliance upon an intensification of the campaign against shipping was not really an option open to Hitler: political considerations – the product of past German success, present British defiance and world expectation – meant that Hitler had to break British resistance by direct attack, and in effect this narrowed German choices to alternatives: either to invade Britain or to destroy her will and capacity to wage war by sustained air attack. The *Luftwaffe*, however, had not been conceived, developed, equipped or trained to amount a strategic air offensive, and in any case neither Hitler nor the air staff believed that Britain could be forced to make peace as a result of an unsupported bombing campaign. But if the *Luftwaffe* was not capable of making a strategic effort, the absence of a powerful surface fleet that could guarantee the security of an invasion force in the Channel meant that Hitler's decision of 16 July to proceed with the invasion of southern England necessarily involved the *Luftwaffe*'s being committed to another almost impossible task. In order to neutralise British naval supremacy in the narrow seas, the *Luftwaffe* had to win air supremacy over southern England, and to do so in weeks rather than months by destroying an air force that was the equal of itself in numbers of operational, single-engined fighters.

Without heavy bombers and long-range single-engined fighters the *Luftwaffe* was ill-prepared to make such an effort, and as bombing campaigns later in the war indicated, the *Luftwaffe* in 1940 simply lacked the massive numbers of aircraft and aircrew needed to sustain a campaign that, by definition, could not be won in a single, overwhelming effort. In addition, in even making such an attempt the *Luftwaffe* faced difficulties and handicaps that were not immediately apparent at the time.

The Royal Air Force was technically the equal of the *Luftwaffe*; its first-line fighters were as good as those of the German air force; and with Fighter Command the RAF had developed the instrument of defence that was intended to defeat the very form of attack that the *Luftwaffe* now intended to carry out. Moreover, the seven weeks that elapsed between the surrender of France and the first attacks on British airfields and installations provided the RAF with just enough time to reorganise and refill its depleted ranks – a total of 931 British aircraft were lost in the course of the campaign in France and Flanders – and face the *Luftwaffe* on the basis of a rough equality of front-line fighters. With British aircraft factories outproducing those of Germany by 2.1:1 between June and October and two inbuilt positional factors – the British ability to draw upon reserves that were beyond the range of German attack and to recover shot-down pilots and damaged aircraft – working to Britain's advantage throughout the campaign, the scales were tipped slightly but decisively against the *Luftwaffe* even before it opened proceedings with the *Kanalkampf* on 7 July.

These underlying British advantages that ultimately decided the outcome of the Battle of Britain were nevertheless countered by the fact that throughout the campaign the *Luftwaffe* possessed advantages inherent in its holding the initiative and operating offensively. It had choice in the matter of target selection and when and in what strengths to mount its attacks. Moreover, in the initial phase of operations Fighter Command laboured under the handicap of not necessarily being able to deploy its aircraft before German attacks materialised, though this was in part offset by the fact that the *Kanalkampf* involved much more than attacks on British coastal shipping. In this phase the *Luftwaffe* carried out extensive mining operations, mounted fighter sweeps over south-east England, attacked key port installations, and bombed various non-military targets, and it was in the course of these other operations that the pattern of the Battle of Britain was set. Faced with the choice of making the maximum possible or minimum necessary effort to counter German raids, Fighter Command committed its squadrons sparingly and directed its fighters against German bombers. With the standard German single-engined fighter of 1940, the Bf 109, limited to 30 minutes' endurance over southern England and coordination between German bombers and fighters leaving much to be desired, the RAF accounted for 297 German aircraft between 7 July and 11 August for the loss of 175 of its own.

In the course of these operations, however, the German High Command came to appreciate for the first time not just that the campaign was not going to be the four-day walk-over that had been anticipated but that the radar stations established throughout southern England were the key to the unexpected effectiveness of the RAF. In fact these stations and Fighter Command and subordinate headquarters in southern England were in effect the prototype Combat Information Centers that came to fruition with the US carrier task force in the latter stages of the Pacific war. It was against these stations and RAF airfields that the *Luftwaffe* turned its attention after 12 August in a deliberate attempt to destroy the

RAF's capacity to maintain combat air patrols. The *Luftwaffe* came very close to success in its attempt. Between 12 and 23 August the RAF continued to inflict disproportionate losses upon the *Luftwaffe*, accounting for 299 German aircraft for the loss of 177, but thereafter losses came roughly into balance with 294 German and 269 British aircraft destroyed between 24 August and 5 September, the difference being that the vast majority of British losses were sustained by Fighter Command whereas those incurred by the *Luftwaffe* were shared between its bombers and fighters. In fact, by 5 September Fighter Command, despite the care with which it was committed to battle, had been brought to the edge of destruction.

Both its original front-line and its reserve squadrons were savaged in the course of the August fighting, but more serious than its aircraft losses were the problems posed by pilot exhaustion and replacement. By September Fighter Command was reduced to committing to battle pilots with as little as 10 hours' flying time in fighters, but it was to be saved from defeat by a combination of three factors: the *Luftwaffe*'s inability to mount sustained attacks on the scale needed to achieve success because of its losses; intervals of bad weather that broke the thread of continuity essential to German efforts; and the inability of Göring, in personal command of the *Luftwaffe*'s effort, to concentrate upon single targets for the time needed to achieve decisive results. By constantly switching targets Göring secured a measure of tactical surprise at every stage and ensured the continued attrition of Fighter Command's strength, but he also confused and demoralised his own formations in the process and prevented any single British target being attacked to destruction: no British radar station or airfield was put out of service for a protracted period.

In part this failure of command was the result of exaggerated claims made by *Luftwaffe* aircrew, in part the result of Göring's limitations as an operational commander, but in reality the confusion of targets and policy stemmed from the fact that the *Luftwaffe* was committed to three divergent objectives. It was attempting to win air supremacy over southern England, to pave the way for an invasion, and to destroy the British means of counter-attacking an invasion force. The obvious elements of overlap of these objectives were more than counter-balanced by the corresponding elements of contradiction, yet all were to be further confused after 7 September as a result of the *Luftwaffe*'s attempt to pursue a fourth objective: the breaking of Britain's will to resist by the destruction of her cities.

This change of policy, to an objective that the *Luftwaffe* had already stated to be beyond its capabilities, was the result of an accident. On the night of 24/25 August London was bombed over a wide area by formations that erred in their navigation. Believing that the attacks had been deliberate, the RAF retaliated by bombing Berlin for the first time the next night, and thereafter the *Luftwaffe* found itself committed to response in kind. On 7 September it began a series of systematic attacks on London, abandoning the strikes against radar stations and airfields that had brought it unknowingly to within measurable distance of victory. This change of policy provided Fighter Command with a week-long respite when it was on the point of defeat, and it was this respite that enabled it to gather its strength and inflict upon the *Luftwaffe* the decisive defeat of 15 September.

It was on this date, selected on 31 July by Hitler as the date when German forces would land in southern England, that the *Luftwaffe* lost 56 aircraft in the course of two major attacks on London. This was not the greatest daily loss incurred by the *Luftwaffe* in the course of the campaign – it lost 71 aircraft on 15 August and 60 three days later – but the losses sustained on 15 September were endured by a *Luftwaffe* that on this day made a supreme effort as it came to the end of its strength. After two months of heavy fighting and unacceptable losses – between 7 July and 15 September it lost 1,116 aircraft to the 779 lost by the RAF – the *Luftwaffe* found itself opposed on 15 September by unprecedented numbers of British fighters. On both the morning and afternoon of the fifteenth Fighter Command put more than 300 aircraft into the air over southern England, and it was this apparently inexhaustible supply of British fighters that finally convinced the *Luftwaffe* that the battle could not be won. It continued to attack British cities throughout the autumn and winter, concentrating on night operations after October in order to minimise losses, but with a further 527 German and 323 British aircraft destroyed between 16 September and 31 October the scale and effectiveness of German operations gradually declined with passing weeks. Though individual German attacks proved extremely destructive in this further phase of operations – the attacks on Coventry (14/15 November) and Liverpool (20/21 December) were particularly severe – both sides recognised that the issue was decided on 15 September. On the sixteenth Hitler ordered the postponement of *Operation Seelöwe*, and on the following day British intelligence deciphered a German signal ordering the dispersal of shipping that had been assembled for the invasion of Britain. Though *Operation Seelöwe* was not formally cancelled until January 1942 it was dead from the time that Hitler and the *Luftwaffe* concluded, as a result of the exchanges of 15 September, that German losses could not justify a continuation of the battle.

The outcome of the Battle of Britain neither surprised nor greatly concerned Hitler. The campaign was the first German offensive of the war in which Hitler did not involve himself, and distance from the conduct of its operations enabled him to see clearly results that have been distorted with the passing of time and the campaign's elevation into the ranks of British national mythology. In military terms, the Battle of Britain was both small-scale and of limited significance. In the course of the campaign the RAF lost 520 pilots; within three years both Bomber Command and the 8th US Army Air Force would lose such numbers in single missions over Germany. *Luftwaffe* losses, though heavier, were to be quickly eclipsed by those incurred in the Battle of Moscow during the autumn of 1941. The only practical result of the campaign was that after September the RAF possessed a greater measure of superiority over southern England in daylight hours than it had in August: in every other respect Britain's position was unchanged. At no point could she challenge Germany's control of western Europe. Never in British history, not even at the height of British naval supremacy, had British sea power alone been able to challenge, still less defeat, a great continental power, and by 1940 the superiority of overland communications over seaborne lines of communication meant that German military forces could be moved in greater numbers and more quickly than any British force that attempted to establish itself on the European mainland. In addition, the reality of the situation was that British naval power in 1940 was barely able to ensure Britain against defeat by the strangulation of her trade. The acquisition of air and submarine bases in France and Norway by the *Wehrmacht* reversed the previous positional advantage held by Britain in the war and enabled the *Kriegsmarine*, as it had predicted in the inter-war period, to reach into the Atlantic with its submarines far beyond the range of British escorts, and by October 1940 it was ready to recommit warships to oceanic operations.

The failure of the *Luftwaffe* in the Battle of Britain had no immediate effect upon the existing military situation within Europe, and likewise it had no effect upon Hitler's decision to attack the Soviet Union in 1941, though it forced Hitler to attempt to consolidate the German position in western Europe and to continue to take the war to Britain by indirect means before preparing for the 1941 campaign in the east. Hitler's persistence in seeking to destroy the Soviet Union before completing the defeat of Britain has been portrayed generally as one of the major errors of the war. This was not the case. The decision to attempt the destruction of the Soviet state in a single campaign was not unreasonable, though it might have been better for the *Wehrmacht* to have made the attempt in two campaigns rather than one, and there is no good reason to suppose that had those forces committed to the prosecution of the war against Britain in 1941 been available for the attack on the Soviet Union then the course and outcome of this campaign would have been altered in any significant way. Only 23 of the 55 German divisions not committed to *Operation Barbarossa* were considered by the German High Command as suitable for service in the east and the fact of the matter was that the forces committed to *Barbarossa* represented the maximum, indeed even more than the maximum, that could be handled and maintained effectively on the Eastern Front at that time; extra formations would not have added to German capacity and effectiveness. Moreover, whilst the decision to proceed with an attack on the Soviet Union while the war against Britain continued is seen generally as Hitler's voluntary acceptance of the problems inherent in waging a two-front war, there is no overlooking the fact that the forces held in the west in 1941 represented a force of occupation, the means of ensuring that the countries of western Europe were milked of their resources and output to German benefit. This commitment was never going to disappear, but it was not until 1943, by which time France was contributing some 25 per cent of German war production, that German forces in the west assumed the dual roles of occupation and defence. By then the error not of attacking the Soviet Union before Britain was defeated but of failing to despatch the Soviet Union as intended was obvious.

By itself, Hitler's decision to attack the USSR without waiting for the defeat of Britain was sound, particularly when it was underscored by the calculation that the defeat of the Soviet Union would further weaken Britain by eliminating the only power in Europe capable of disputing German domination. But Hitler's decision was flawed in that he failed in his various attempts to tie up the situation in western Europe after the Battle of Britain and he failed to ensure that the timing and context of operations against the Soviet Union were in accordance with German requirements. These failures stemmed from the political consequences of the *Luftwaffe*'s failure in the Battle of Britain which presented Hitler with problems that he could not resolve to Germany's advantage, and most certainly not within the timetable to which he was working.

In political terms the events of the summer and autumn of 1940 were seen as a German failure, most obviously by Britain which saw in her own immediate survival the first Allied victory of the war and confirmation of her undiminished, indeed enhanced, status. The disappointment caused to the German High Command, not just to Hitler, by Britain's refusal to come to terms was confirmation of the accuracy of Britain's views about herself, though this in no way lessened the German belief that ultimately Britain would go the way of her allies. But Britain's ability to survive in 1940 was crucially important in buying time for the United States to embark upon industrial and military mobilisation, and it was decisive in convicing a sympathetic American High Command that Britain would not surrender. Even in June 1940, as France went down to defeat and there was no certainty that Britain would not follow her, the Roosevelt administration directed the transfer of large stocks of First World War material – all that was available to the US Army after two decades of financial parsimony and political insularity – to Britain, but until the Battle of Britain was won the United States, despite her material support, was only too conscious that any aid could be lost in a matter of weeks at the cost of material that was necessary to ensure America's own defences. Once the Battle of Britain had been won, and Roosevelt returned to the White House for an unprecedented third term, the administration set out to achieve what Britain could not: Britain's survival. Even after drawing upon the resources of her empire, Britain could not sustain herself in a war with Germany. By April 1941 Britain's gold reserves had been reduced to a level insufficient to cover one day's trading, but by then the Roosevelt administration had devised Lend-Lease (11 March) and was embarked upon a forward policy in the North Atlantic that by the end of the year was to see the United States' involvement in the war as Britain's ally.

The most immediate consequence of the German failures of the summer of 1940, however, was the fact that Hitler's attempts to consolidate the German position in western Europe and to continue the war against Britain by indirect means in the wake of these setbacks were confounded by these very failures. In an attempt to close the western Mediterranean to the British and to ensure the security of west and north-west Africa against British or even American attack, Hitler sought an alliance with Spain and to bring Pétain's regime to his side. These two efforts were mutually incompatible: Spain could only gain at French expense, but Hitler was unprepared to force France into concessions if she could be persuaded to support Germany. Moreover, as long as the French empire in the Maghreb was not under Axis control the western Mediterranean could not be closed to the British, and Britain's continued resistance served to make Spain and Pétain's regime doubly cautious.

Hitler's personal attempt to persuade Franco to join the war at their meeting at Hendaye on 23 October was met by evasion until, on 10 January 1941, the German request for rights of transit for an attack on Gibraltar was met with an unequivocal refusal. Hitler's overtures to Pétain on 24 October were not pressed, and despite the challenge to its authority presented by de Gaulle's Free French and the British attempts to neutralise French naval power by the attacks on the French fleet at Mers el-Kabir on 3 and 6 July, the Vichy authorities did not pursue the matter. But the obvious implication that if necessary Hitler would support the French empire against Italian claims irritated Mussolini, though this development in fact merely completed the process whereby the Italian dictator attempted a *coup de théâtre* designed to demonstrate his independence of Germany. In the event, however, Mussolini reduced Italy to the status of German satellite and thwarted German hopes of stabilising the situation in the Balkans.

In September and at their meeting at the Brenner Pass on 4 October Hitler impressed upon Mussolini the need for Italian restraint in the Balkans at that time, the *quid pro quo* being German support for Italian ambitions at Greek and Yugoslav expense. Hitler's deception in not warning Mussolini of his intentions towards Romania, which was occupied on the seventh, thus provoked Mussolini to invade Greece on the twenty-eighth as the means of restoring Italian standing. With both Bulgaria and Yugoslavia having claims on Greek territory, the Italian action threatened to upset the Balkans at the very time when Hitler was on the point of ensuring its stability, and the Italian act had obvious implications in that the British were certain to involve themselves in Greece if only to secure airfields from which to bomb Romania. Hitler nevertheless offered Italy full support in her war with Greece, but when this was declined he took the precaution of earmarking German air and ground formations for moves to southern Italy, Albania and North Africa in order to stiffen Italian forces. In these matters Hitler pursued the same aim as in his dealings with Franco and Pétain: limited German commitment in support of other national forces that were expected to realise German aims at Hitler's demand. Both Franco and Pétain saw through Hitler's intention, and in the final analysis he could not force either to declare war on Britain. Mussolini, already half ensnared by being in the war, was to be stripped of all freedom of action when within six weeks of moving against Greece disaster overwhelmed Italian arms in the Balkans, in North Africa and at sea.

While many factors contributed to the disastrous Italian failure in Greece, one, a fatal underestimation of Greek determination to resist attack, was all-important. Throughout the summer the Italians had subjected the Greeks to constant provocation, which included the deliberate sinking of a cruiser off Tinos on 15 August; the lack of response was interpreted as weakness by the fascist hierarchy. Mussolini's decision to attack Greece was based on the calculation that the dictatorship of General Ioannis Metaxas was crypto-fascist and pro-Axis in sentiment and that the Greek public would welcome Italian occupation. In reality the Greeks wished to avoid war but were neither intimidated by nor prepared to acquiesce meekly in Italian aggression.

The misreading of Greek temper, leading as it did to the instigation of a campaign without sufficient forces to complete the defeat of the Greek army in the field, was the fundamental error from which all other Italian mistakes and misfortunes flowed. Italy boasted two armies – the *9th* and *11th* – in Albania in October 1940 but only eight of the 20 divisions that the Italian general staff calculated were needed to conquer Greece if half the Greek army's one cavalry and 15 infantry divisions were tied down on the Bulgarian border. The Italian armies in Albania were thus wholly inadequate for the task of conquering Greece and, indeed, given the air force's failure to prevent or delay Greek mobilisation they were outnumbered 2:5 within two weeks of the start of hostilities. Moreover, while bad weather prevented naval operations that might have tied down Greek formations in defensive positions away from the border area, the Italian armies were over-equipped for fighting in this wild and inhospitable theatre. The extent of Italian mechanisation confined formations to the valleys and left the *9th* and *11th Armies* vulnerable to infiltration and encirclement through the mountains in the opening phase of operations: conversely, it also secured these armies against total defeat because Italian mechanisation ensured control of the main lines of communication in December.

Mussolini's determination to attack Greece in October 1940 compounded Italian military problems in two other fields. First, two weeks' notice of operations condemned the Italian armies to an offensive before adequate supplies had been accumulated in Albania, and by December, by which time another eight Italian divisions had arrived in that country, the Italian supply system had collapsed. Second, and more immediately important, Mussolini's timetable committed the Italian armies to attack at the very worst time of the year. Torrential, freezing rain accompanied the Italian invasion of Greece, and by December the thermometer stood at

20 below zero. Raging rivers, bottomless mud and bitter cold completed the destruction of an Italian offensive that was politically inept and militarily underprepared.

The Italian advance into Greece was made on the Koritsa–Florina, the Franshnei–Metsovon and coastal axes of advance, the main Italian effort with four divisions being made in Epirus. Only in this area did the Italians make much progress. The *9th Army* quickly secured Filiates and Paramithia, but with the Italian offensive in the centre halted in the first couple of days and the Florina sector quiet, the Greeks went on to the offensive as early as 31 October. With mobilisation rapidly adding the 13 reserve divisions to the Greek army's order of battle and Thrace barred despite Bulgarian ill-will, the Metaxas regime chose to carry the war into Albania because it knew that a defensive policy would condemn Greece to long-term defeat. By securing the mountain ridges above Italian formations, the Greeks were quickly able to counter-attack in the east and centre, defeating an alpine division around Vovoússa as early as 3 November before going over to a general offensive along the length of the frontier on the fourteenth. This attack opened three days after a notable British victory – the sinking of three Italian battleships at their moorings at Taranto by carrier aircraft during the night of 11/12 November – and began to draw to its close three days before the start of the first British land offensive of the Second World War.

Both Allied offensives were successful, but separately, and neither proved irreversible. Though British forces occupied Crete on 2 November and thereafter neutralised the Dodecanese, as long as he lived – until 29 January 1941 – Metaxas refused to allow the British on the mainland on the grounds that any British troops in the Balkans were too big to be ignored by the Germans and too small to avoid defeat. In the short term this was of little consequence as the Greek army overran a quarter of Albania and reduced the Italian army to building defence lines *north* of Valona by December, but in the long term the Metaxas attitude, and the position of Greece, was untenable. The success of V Infantry Corps in securing Koritsa on 22 November and Pogradec on the twenty-ninth, destroying three Italian divisions in the process, plus the parallel successes of II Infantry Corps in taking Përmet on 3 December and of I Infantry Corps in occupying Argyrokastron on the eighth ensured German intervention: Hitler could not afford to see his only ally defeated.

On the tenth, three days after a formal Italian request for assistance, Hitler committed one bomber formation to southern Italy and on the thirteenth took the decision to occupy Bulgaria and to invade Greece in March. With these decisions Hitler, under the pressure of events, reversed his previous policy of relying on Italy to secure the eastern Mediterranean before turning on Greece, but still maintained limited aims: Greece and Crete represented the limits of German ambitions and were not stepping stones to points east.

By the end of December, however, the second part of Hitler's original policy had similarly collapsed. Whilst the Greeks continued to inch their way forward in Albania, securing Himara on the twenty-fourth, Kelcyre on 10 January and subsequently Tepelini, the Italian *10th Army* in North Africa collapsed in dramatic and humiliating fashion. Beginning on 9 December after an approach march through Italian positions which allowed British forces to attack the Italian encampments around Sidi Barrani from the west, the Western Desert Force was in two months to advance some 560 miles to El Agheila, securing Bardia on 3 January, Tobruk on the twenty-second, Derna on the thirtieth and Benghazi on 7 February in the process. By advancing on either side of the Jebel Akhdar, British forces were able to reach Beda Fomm via Mekili and Msu ahead of Italian formations that had withdrawn along the coast road. As a result, a British force that never numbered more than two divisions completed a battle of encirclement and annihilation of Italian forces in Cyrenaica on 5 February. In 60 days the British forces destroyed four Italian corps and nine divisions and captured 130,000 prisoners, some 400 tanks and 1,290 guns at a cost of less than 2,000 casualties. To add to Italian humiliation, defeat in Cyrenaica coincided with the start of British operations in East Africa which, within two months, were to result in the capture of Addis Ababa and the restoration of Haile Selassie as Emperor of Abyssinia after an exile of five years.

British operations began in mid-January with the recapture of lost border towns in Kenya and the Sudan but were not to end until 27 November 1941 when Italian resistance came to an end at Gondor in north-west Abyssinia. The paradox between the very rapid conquest of Italian Somaliland – the border was crossed on 10 February, the Juba on the nineteenth and Mogadishu was captured on the twenty-fifth – and of the Abyssinian heartland and the difficulty that British, imperial, Belgian and Free French forces encountered both in Eritrea and in bringing the campaign to an end was evidence of an unevenness of Italian military performance that extended beyond East Africa in the course of the Second World War. After the crushing victories in Cyrenaica and in Somaliland British propaganda went to considerable lengths to denigrate Italian military effectiveness, to the fury of British forces whose own achievements were correspondingly belittled and whose experience often suggested otherwise. The Italian defence of Keren in Eritrea, where the

4th and 5th Indian Divisions were committed, was protracted and determined, and the final withdrawal on 26 March, after a defence of 52 days, was skilfully executed. The fact that the campaign in East Africa lasted for seven months after the fall of Addis Ababa reflected to Italian credit, and indeed, even in the course of the Cyrenaica débâcle certain units and arms fought bravely if ineffectively.

The fact remains, however, that Italian military performance in the Second World War was totally inconsistent. The Italian army ultimately raised some 84 divisions, of which some were very impressive and were used by the Germans in North Africa as parts of the *Afrika Korps*. On the Eastern Front, which claimed more Italian dead than North Africa, the Germans regarded the Italians as the best and most reliable of their allies, though admittedly the competition for this accolade was not particularly fierce. Yet the greater part of the Italian army was distinctly unimpressive. The performance of the air force in various theatres was similarly undistinguished, though in its dealings with the British navy its aircraft bombed consistently with accuracy but no luck. At sea the Italian *forte* was obviously individualistic and small scale. The sinking of two British battleships at Alexandria on 19 December 1941 was the Italian navy's greatest achievement, but the Italian fleet consistently failed in circumstances when it held advantages – the second battle of Sirte on 22 March 1942 being an obvious example of failure to press home an attack despite enormous superiority of strength – yet it fought gallantly in the last desperate months of the North African campaign in the face of overwhelming Allied air and naval superiority. Its overall performance was nevertheless mediocre.

Obviously local factors played their part in the Italian defeats in Cyrenaica and East Africa. The latter's isolation, apart from a few aircraft flown to Abyssinia from southern Libya, was a major factor in the Italian defeat, as was Italian concern for the safety of white communities in Abyssinia as war came to the region. The Italian cause was not helped by the fact that 70 per cent of the army in East Africa, at peak strength in August 1940 some 370,000 men, were drawn from native peoples of dubious reliability and value, though it should be noted that Eritrean troops and some Abyssinians – too deeply implicated with Italian rule to entertain doubts about their fate under a restored Haile Selassie – proved trustworthy and fought well. In Cyrenaica the Italian *10th Army* was surprised and never allowed to recover its balance by an aggressive, professional, well-commanded enemy, and if the scale of the subsequent débâcle was inordinate then the *10th Army* was in good company in North Africa in being consistently outfought by numerically inferior forces. But

Italian defeats in the Second World War were too consistent for there to be anything other than fundamental weaknesses that struck at Italian military efficiency, and certain major flaws within the Italian military establishment can be readily identified.

The most obvious of these was the person of Mussolini and the nature of his regime, both of which despite outward appearances were shallow and incompetent. Like his stronger ally in Berlin, Mussolini was incapable of working through a system that could correlate political, economic and military policies and he similarly surrounded himself with individuals noted for personal loyalty rather than professional competence: in Mussolini's case the weakness of Italy as an industralised and military power immediately manifested itself in battlefield failures whereas the weaknesses inherent in the German system were disguised for many years by greater national power and early victories.

The weaknesses within the High Command were complemented at the field officer level. German liaison officers with the Italian armies were forcefully struck by the low standards of training and lack of initiative of junior officers. German officers were similarly conscious of the disparity between divisions raised in southern Italy and those from the north which were much superior. It may be that Italy's relative backwardness, at least in terms of lacking a large, educated, professional middle class on which to draw for officer material may have been the cause of these weaknesses, but the lack of a strong industrial base was most certainly the cause of the wretchedly inadequate equipment with which Italian forces were expected to fight after 1940. Italy had been the first major power to rearm in the early and mid-1930s, but such were the qualitative improvements in weaponry in the late 1930s that the Italian forces in 1940 were using equipment that was comprehensively outclassed by that of other nations, the corollary being that Italy lacked the financial strength and development capacity to re-equip herself with a new generation of weapons.

The various structural and material weaknesses of Italy were compounded by a weakness of morale that was three-fold in origin, though in effect these amounted to much the same thing: a general lack of interest in war in 1940. Despite the initial patriotic outbursts that greeted Mussolini's declaration of war, the Italian population had no enthusiasm for war in 1940 and most certainly had no enthusiasm for a war alongside Italy's traditional enemy – Germany via Austria – against traditional friends. Indeed, many Italians were positively embarrassed by the war and by Mussolini's timing of his entry into it; in any event migration from southern Italy across the Atlantic ensured that few Italians welcomed the adding of the United States to their country's list of enemies in December 1941. Moreover, though Mussolini had been in power for nearly two decades by 1940, fascism had no solid foundations in Italian society, in large measure because, unlike Nazism, it had no real philosophic basis and appeal and was merely a cloak for Mussolini's shrewdness and opportunism. The *Duce* and fascism were not causes for which rank-and-file Italians were prepared to fight and die, and most certainly there was a genuine war-weariness in Italy even before she entered the war; Italy had been involved in wars and foreign adventures since 1935 and the sacrifices demanded of her people since that time had been considerable. Like every other nation, Italy could not fight a six-year war, and in Cyrenaica and East Africa Italian soldiers seem to have taken Mussolini at his pre-war word. Mussolini's frequent complaint before 1939 was that in the scramble for Africa Italy had been left with the deserts, and his assertion of the intrinsic worthlessness of Italy's imperial possessions could hardly have been an encouragement to the armed forces to fight to the finish in their defence. For the ordinary Italian soldier there was no good reason to die in defence of Abyssinia, and under the circumstances the fact that the British occupation of Addis Ababa on 6 April 1941 was unopposed was not altogether surprising, though overshadowed by the start of the German offensive in the Balkans on that same day.

The period during which British forces cleared Cyrenaica and prompted a voluntary Italian withdrawal to positions around Sirte in Tripolitania coincided with a series of British and German decisions and an unfolding of events throughout the Levant that collectively resulted in a reversal of Allied successes in Albania and Cyrenaica and in the eclipse of Allied power in the eastern Mediterranean. In some small part this snatching of defeat from the jaws of victory was self-inflicted in that the British, having cleared Cyrenaica, closed down operations in this theatre in order to send forces to Greece. Just as the 4th Indian Division had been withdrawn from North Africa for service in Eritrea after it had helped make the initial breakthrough at Sidi Barrani, so Australian and New Zealand formations were to be sent to Greece after the capture of Benghazi and El Agheila in order to support an ally whose defeat was assured – and at the very moment when German ground formations arrived in North Africa for the first time. On balance, however, the British decisions were marginal to the outcome of events because the real power of decision lay with Hitler, and in the first quarter of 1941 he was able to dictate events by virtue of geography: in this time Germany established an ascendancy in the Balkans that made the defeat of Greece a formality while the shortness of Axis lines of communication to North Africa, combined with British exhaustion after the advance into western Cyrenaica, handed the initiative in this theatre to the Axis powers. Thus, while in this period the British won a notable victory – the sinking of three Italian heavy cruisers and two destroyers off Cape Matapan on the night of 28/29 March – and moved to occupy Iraq after a pro-Axis coup on 1 April, the tide of war in the main theatres of operations flowed relentlessly against the Allies.

In fact, notice of the changes explicit in a German commitment south of the Alps was served as early as 10 January 1941 when the first *Luftwaffe* operations from bases in Sicily resulted in the crippling of a British fleet carrier: the period of easy British naval superiority in the Mediterranean was over. Likewise, with the arrival of German armoured formations at Tripoli on 14 February the immediate crisis for the Italian High Command in North Africa came to an end, as did the crisis in Albania following the failure of the Greek offensive to take Valona on 5 February. In March the Italians resumed the offensive in the Balkans, but despite having some 28 divisions in Albania by this time the Italians failed to secure Tepelene. They were successful, however, in further weakening an enemy exhausted by its efforts of the winter, and which was obliged, in March, to move forces into Thrace in order to meet the threat presented by the German occupation of Bulgaria at this time. This latter development was seen by Hitler as the penultimate move in the process whereby Mussolini's ill-judged Greek venture could be brought to an end. While not losing sight of his main aim – the attack on the Soviet Union in the spring – between November 1940 and March 1941 Hitler was able to bring the various Balkan states into the Axis fold by a skilful mixture of inducements, bribery and intimidation. Using as the basis of his efforts the formal alliance concluded by Germany, Italy and Japan on 27 September 1940, Hitler secured the adherence of Hungary to the Tripartite Pact on 20 November, of Romania and Slovakia on the twenty-third, and of Bulgaria on 1 March 1941, after German forces moved to occupy her in the last week of February. Thereafter the only task facing Hitler was to reduce Yugoslavia to a similar position of dependence, and it was in this attempt that German plans miscarried.

Hitler's attempts to bring Yugoslavia into the Axis camp during the winter months was both patient and skilful, and it was a tribute to his perception and self-control that in dealing with a state whose very name must have been anathema to him that Hitler's formal demands on Belgrade were very moderate. He sought from Yugoslavia her adherence to the Tripartite Pact, not rights of transit, but his skill in attempting to ensnare Yugoslavia in an entangling alliance was matched by the skill shown by Belgrade in playing for time and in avoiding such a commitment. By March 1941, however, Yugoslavian procrastination had to end: spring and the German occupation of Bulgaria in readiness for an attack on Greece forced Yugoslavia to come to a decision. The reality of German strength and Allied weakness, combined with Hitler's offer of Greek Macedonia in return for her signature, determined Yugoslavia's decision, and on 25 March she aligned herself with Germany. Two days later, however, the Yugoslavian government was overthrown by a military coup that received widespread popular support, and without waiting for a formal repudiation of the Tripartite Pact by the new authorities in Belgrade Hitler saw the coup for what it was and acted accordingly.

The coup was an assertion of Yugoslavia's independence and a deliberate defiance of Hitler personally, and Hitler resolved to deal with Yugoslavia 'with merciless harshness'. Within a day of the coup the necessary directives and preliminary orders for the simultaneous invasion of Greece (*Operation Marita*) and Yugoslavia (*Operation '25'*) had been issued, and Hitler had begun the process of ensuring that Bulgaria, Hungary and Italy played the roles allotted them in the destruction of Yugoslavia. The Hungarian prime minister, Pál Teleki, killed himself rather than be a party to 'cowardice that places us in alliance with scoundrels', but those with the power of decision in Budapest, Rome and Sofia had no such scruples: within 10 days of the Belgrade coup the *Wehrmacht* was ready to begin operations against Greece and Romania and Germany's allies were preparing for operations that would entitle them to a share of the spoils.

For the conquest of Greece and Yugoslavia the German High Command planned to use 32 divisions, of which 10 were to be armoured and four motorised, but in the event it used only 24, such was the haste in which these offensives were mounted and the speed with which they were concluded. German strength was divided between the *2nd* and *12th Armies*, the *2nd Army* having three corps in southern Germany and one in Hungary and the *12th Army* five in Bulgaria and one in Romania. In support were 15 divisions of the *2nd Italian Army* in the Venezia Giulia, one division at Zara, and in Albania the *9th* and *11th Armies*, which were expected to pin down the Greek and Yugoslav divisions that opposed them. The *3rd Hungarian Army*, which committed the equivalent of four divisions against Yugoslavia, and one Bulgarian division which was attached to the *12th Army* for cosmetic purposes completed the Axis order of battle. On paper Axis forces were opposed by three cavalry and 28 infantry divisions of the Yugoslavian army and 14 Greek divisions, but the latter were at half-strength after the winter fighting and the Yugoslavian army needed three weeks to mobilise. Organised into seven armies, each the equivalent of a corps, the Yugoslavian army had no more than 11 divisions fully mobilised and deployed on 6 April.

A lack of armour in the Greek and Yugoslav armies was just one aspect of a general material weakness that was compounded by three handicaps other than those imposed by German possession of the initiative and command of the air. For political reasons, the Yugoslavian army was obliged to attempt the defence of the kingdom at its frontiers rather than concentrating in the interior. Yugoslavia's border with her seven neighbours was some 1,020 miles long, and was indefensible over much of its length. The dangers inherent in deploying infantry in forward positions against an enemy with superior mobility were obvious; suffice to note that after the deployment of the army Yugoslavia's defences consisted of a series of gaps held apart by the occasional formation. Further, the political considerations that dictated a policy of forward defence reflected the major flaw within the Yugoslavian state and army, namely their division along racial, religious and cultural lines between bitterly opposed nationalities with little in common but their hatred for one another. Such, indeed, were the divisions in Yugoslavian society that after 1929 the country had been ruled by royal dictatorship as the only practical alternative to civil war. The outbreak of the European war in 1939 had seen leaders of the two major nationalities within Yugoslavia, the Croats and Serbs, try to resolve their differences in the knowledge that failure could only invite foreign intervention, but with Mussolini sheltering and supporting fascist Croat exiles, and Bulgaria, Hungary and Italy having historical irredentist claims on Yugoslavian territory, Yugoslavia was threatened by both foreign and domestic enemies and was ready to fragment on racial lines in the event of attack.

The third and most immediate handicap under which the Allied powers laboured was the fact that Greek and Yugoslavian forces were not able to support one another and, critically, Macedonia was in effect covered by neither. The Yugoslavian 3rd and 5th Armies, almost at full strength on 6 April, covered the borders with Albania and with Bulgaria and south-west Romania respectively, but while the Greek 1st Army occupied southern Albania the deployment of the 2nd Army on the Metaxas Line in eastern Macedonia within the line of the Nestbos left a gap of about 150 miles between the Greek armies which British forces could not cover. After 5 March two Anzac infantry divisions and one British armoured regiment arrived in Greece, but the subsequent British employment on the Aliaknon Line, between the Varos Mountains and the Gulf of Salonika on the direct route of an invasion from Bulgaria, rendered them vulnerable to an advance via the Monastir gap but unable to cover the rear of the Metaxas Line against an advance down the Vardar valley. Thus, in addition to the various material and numerical weaknesses that plagued the Allies, their forces were effectively divided and liable to defeat in detail. The German High Command needed no second invitation to settle its plan of campaign under these circumstances, and the initial German attacks, accompanied by massively destructive air raids on Belgrade and Piraeus, were directed from western Bulgaria against these lines of obvious weakness.

The initial German effort was made by the *12th Army*; the *2nd Army*, having been activated only after the coup of 27 March, was unready between the 6 and 9 April for anything more than minor bridgehead operations. The *12th Army* struck on three separate fronts: against an undefended Thrace with *XXX Infantry Corps*; against the Metaxas Line with *XVIII Mountain Corps*; and against eastern Macedonia with *XL Motorised Corps*. Other than on the Metaxas Line the initial German attacks met with immediate success, the critical breakthrough being registered by *XL Motorised Corps* which crushed the Morava and Bregalnica Divisions on the frontier and secured Skopje and Veles on the seventh. With the *2nd Panzer Division*, part of *XVIII Mountain Corps*, advancing via the Strymon plain into Yugoslavia and thence down the Vardar valley to secure Salonika on the eighth, *XL Motorised Corps* advanced to the south-west to secure Monastir on the ninth and to link up with the *9th Italian Army* at the mouth of Lake Okhrida on the eleventh. With the Metaxas Line turned and both the 1st Greek Army and the Aliaknon Line in danger of being outflanked by a single thrust through the centre, the Germans had secured an overwhelming positional advantage within three days of the start of the campaign, but another three days were to elapse before *XL Motorised Corps* was able to break clear of the Monastir gap and secure Ptolemais. On the twelfth, moreover, the *Kleist Panzer Group*, having crossed into Yugoslavia on the eighth and taken Nis on the ninth, Cuprija on the tenth and Kragujeval on the eleventh, secured Belgrade, a matter of hours ahead of *XLI Motorised Corps*, which had crossed the Romanian border on the previous day. On the thirteenth these formations were joined by elements from *XLVI Motorised Corps*, which had been committed to battle on the tenth. Breaking from its bridgehead at Barcs in the face of virtually no opposition from the 4th Army, this formation occupied Osijek, Srem Karlovca and Srem Mitrovica on the eleventh before driving south on a double axis of advance to take Zvornik and Valijevo on the fourteenth.

These efforts were part of a deep encircling movement that was to result in the *16th Motorised Division* securing Sarajevo on the fifteenth and the *8th Panzer Division* the Kotor area on the nineteenth.

By the time that the *8th Panzer Division* reached the coastal area, however, the *Wehrmacht* was poised between surrender acceptances, the formal capitulation of the Yugoslav army having been signed on 17 April. The punishing advance of the *8th Panzer Division* through Bosnia and Montenegro thus proved unnecessary, but in reality the whole of the German intention to encircle the northern armies was superfluous because whole formations from the 7th, 4th, 2nd and 1st Armies simply disbanded themselves, actively sought to surrender and even welcomed and immediately collaborated with the invaders as two decades of Italian and Hungarian sedition reaped its reward as Yugoslavia's internal divisions opened under the impact of defeat. The main German effort in the north began on the tenth, and with the capture of Zagreb and the German proclamation of an independent Croatia on the same day Yugoslavian resistance collapsed, the advance by the *14th Panzer Division* to Sarajevo via Kadovac and Banja Luka being little more than a test of mechanical reliability.

This phase of operations saw the entry of Hungarian and Italian forces into the fray, the Hungarians securing the Vojvodina between 11 and 13 April. The *2nd Italian Army*, having crossed the border on the eleventh, occupied Ljubljana on the twelfth, linked up with the *Zara Detachment* at Knin on the thirteenth, secured Split two days later and then advanced to Dubrovnik, which was occupied by the *9th Infantry Corps* advancing from Albania on the seventeenth. This phase of operations passed easily enough for the Italians, their only difficulty having been in the first days of the campaign when the 3rd Army had attacked into northern Albania, but the discomfiture suffered by the Italians during this opening phase was little compared to that suffered on the twelfth when Mussolini received from Hitler the lines of demarcation of the various Axis armies in occupied Yugoslavia. Superficially, Italian ambitions appeared to have been realised with the direct annexation of southern Slovenia and parts of Dalmatia, a considerable enlargement of Albania, Italian suzerainty over Montenegro and the decision to install an Italian prince as King of Croatia. But with Bulgaria and Hungary correspondingly compensated for their efforts and Germany annexing northern Slovenia, occupying the Banat, sponsoring a puppet Serb state and retaining certain key rights in Croatia, Hitler's unilateral arrangements for the disposal of Yugoslavia ensured German primacy in that country and confirmed Italy's status as a satellite state on a par with Bulgaria, Hungary and Romania. In

The Axis Conquest and Division of Greece and Yugoslavia 1941

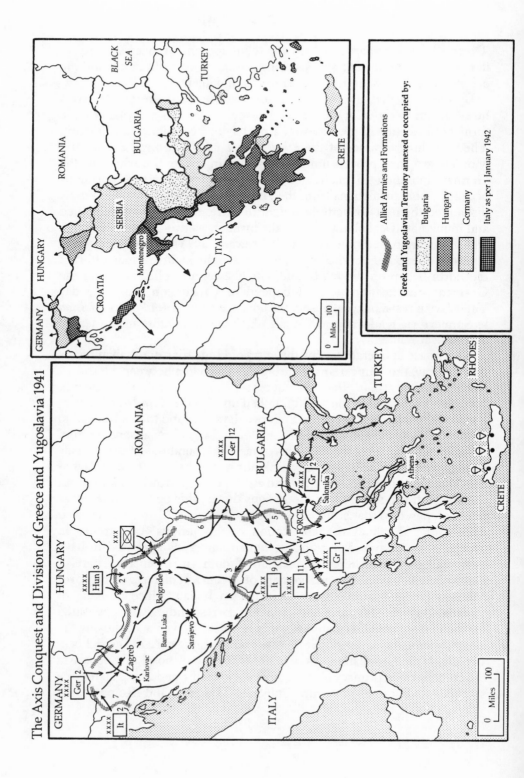

GERMANY

xxxx
It 2

xxxx
Ger 2

7

Zagreb
Karlovac
Banta Luka
Belgrade
Sarajevo

xxxx
Hun 3

2

4

HUNGARY

xxx

ROMANIA

1

6

xxxx
It 9

xxxx
It 11

3

5

W FORCE

xxxx
Gr 1

BULGARIA

xxxx
Ger 12

Salonika

xxxx
Gr 2

Athens

TURKEY

ITALY

0 ___ Miles ___ 100

CRETE

RHODES

Inset map

GERMANY
HUNGARY
CROATIA
SERBIA
Montenegro
ROMANIA
BULGARIA
BLACK SEA
TURKEY
ITALY
CRETE

0 ___ 100
Miles

Legend

Allied Armies and Formations

Greek and Yugoslavian Territory annexed or occupied by:

- Bulgaria
- Hungary
- Germany
- Italy as per 1 January 1942

Yugoslavia as elsewhere, Germany's allies were expected to occupy on her bidding while she exploited all and reserved the power of decision for herself.

The capitulation of the Yugoslavian army on 17 April coincided with Allied recognition of defeat in Greece, Churchill on this day approving, subject to formal Greek agreement, the suggestion made by the Greek army commander on the sixteenth that the British should begin the evacuation of their forces from the mainland. The immediate military cause of a defeat that the Allies realised by the seventeenth was inevitable lay in the fact that the surrender of the 2nd Greek Army on the Metaxas Line on the ninth had allowed the *12th Army* to develop two offensives, one along the coast with *XVIII Mountain Corps* and the other through the mountains with *XL Motorised Corps*, the under-strength Allied formations on the Aliaknon Line being unable to concentrate against either without overreaching themselves. Though the 1st Greek Army abandoned offensive operations in southern Albania on the ninth, its failure to begin to withdraw in response to the German advance to Monastir rendered it unable to release formations in any number to cover the critically important Monastir–Ptolemais–Grevená axis, but in reality much more than depleted formations from the 1st Greek Army was needed to stabilise the situation in northern Greece. As early as the tenth, with *XL Motorised Corps* trying to force the Veve–Ptolemais position, the decision was taken to abandon the Aliaknon Line in favour of defences astride Mount Olympus, but while these began to be occupied on the fourteenth the German success in taking Kozani on that day and the fight for Servia on the fifteenth pointed to the fact that the new line was no more defensible than the old. On the fifteenth, therefore, the Allies took the decision to withdraw across the exposed Plain of Thessaly to stand at Thermopylae, but by the time this withdrawal began on the eighteenth the realisation of impending defeat went alongside an appreciation of the need to hold Thermopylae for sufficient time to allow the evacuation of British forces to begin. The decision to abandon Thessaly nevertheless ensured the encirclement of the 1st Greek Army, and after the Germans occupied Yanina on the twentieth this formation surrendered on the twenty-first despite explicit orders not to do so. With Greek resistance in Epirus brought to an end, *XL Motorised Corps* resumed its southward advance, reaching the Gulf of Corinth and securing Missolonghi on the twenty-sixth.

Though *XVIII Mountain Corps* secured Larissa on the nineteenth and *XL Motorised Corps* occupied Trikkala on the twentieth it was not until the twenty-second, four days after Allied troops first took up their new defensive positions, that the *12th Army* was able to move against Thermopylae, and two more days were to elapse before its formations were able to move into Ellas. The time that was bought by the defence of Thermopylae thus allowed the British and Greek governments to agree on 21 April to an evacuation of forces from the mainland, the caveat being that Crete was to be held in strength. The Greek king and government moved to the island on the twenty-third, and the evacuation of British, Greek and occasional Yugoslavian forces began from minor ports around Athens on the twenty-fourth. The loss of Thebes on the twenty-sixth and of Athens on the twenty-seventh, however, forced the Allies to withdraw into the Peloponnesus; the German attempt to secure the bridges over the Corinth Canal on the twenty-sixth by parachute forces was frustrated by their demolition. The evacuation of forces from ports in southern Greece continued until the night of 28/29 April, after which time effective Allied resistance in the Peloponnesus came to an end although British destroyers managed to rescue another thousand men from Kalamatha and Milos during the next two nights. A total of 52,000 Allied troops were evacuated from Greece, some 18,000 to Crete, but the cost was substantial with no fewer than 45 transports and merchantmen – all but four of them Greek – and two destroyers being sunk between 23 and 30 April in Greek and neighbouring waters.

The conquest of Greece and Yugoslavia cost the *Wehrmacht* some 5,100 casualties, but its real cost was in terms of time and preparations with respect to the attack on the Soviet Union. The *Luftwaffe* lost some 220 aircraft in the course of operations, and their commitment in Greece meant that the *2nd* and *9th Panzer Divisions* missed the start of operations against the Soviet Union. On 30 April Hitler set 22 June as the date for *Operation Barbarossa*, but he also ordered, without consulting the army and navy, that airborne forces close Greek proceedings with the occupation of Crete. For all the island's obvious importance as a base for air operations over the Balkans and eastern Mediterranean, this decision presented the *Luftwaffe* with a major commitment at a time when it was to complete its arrangements for *Operation Barbarossa*, while the operation itself contained a high element of risk. Airborne forces had never before been used independently to secure a strategic objective, and would have to rely in part on the movement of reinforcements and heavy equipment by sea across waters disputed by the *Luftwaffe* and Royal Navy.

In reality *Operation Merkur* incorporated two further risks: an ability to read German operational signals provided the British with a full account of German plans, timings and order of battle, and Allied forces were present on Crete in numbers that exceeded German expectation. With the Germans prepared to commit the reinforced *7th Infantry* and *5th Mountain Division*s to this operation, the 42,000 Allied troops on the island outnumbered the attackers by 2:1. What perhaps should have been decisive advantages for the defence, however, were balanced by overwhelming German air superiority, the enforced dispersal of the defence amongst various key positions in order to guard against both airborne and seaborne invasions, a lack of transport and roads that made the concentration of a mobile reserve all but impossible, and the fact that the British had but 20 guns and 24 tanks on Crete. Moreover, after Greece Allied morale was low and was further eroded by the absence of air cover after the *Luftwaffe* began softening-up operations on 14 May.

Operation Merkur began with landings near Maleme and Khania on the morning of 20 May and near Rethymnon and Herakleion during the afternoon. At each place the issue was fiercely contested, but what decided the battle was the British failure to eliminate the German forces that overran and occupied part of the Maleme airfield on the twentieth and twenty-first and the German decision to land forces at Maleme under fire. Despite the fact that the British navy savaged one reinforcement convoy to the north of Crete on the night of 20/21 May and forced another to turn back on the twenty-second, German success at Maleme proved decisive, though it was not until the twenty-seventh that the British admitted defeat and began to evacuate their forces. Over the next four days some 18,600 men of the British garrison of 32,000 men on Crete were withdrawn to Egypt, but the cost to the British navy was considerable: during the whole Crete operation three British cruisers and six destroyers were sunk; one fleet carrier, two battleships and four cruisers and destroyers were damaged beyond local repair; and nine cruisers and destroyers were less severely damaged. Such losses were almost crippling, as were those incurred by the *7th Infantry Division*. The scale of German losses, about 6,000 casualties, convinced Hitler that any repetition of *Operation Merkur* was out of the question, a fact of immense significance in 1942 when Malta might well have been taken by airborne assault, possibly with critical results for the conduct of the war in the Mediterranean.

For the Allies, defeat in the Balkans coincided with defeat in Cyrenaica, and one of the major factors in the British decision to abandon Greece was the need to reconcentrate forces in North Africa in order to deal with the invasion of Egypt on 11 April. The dramatic reversal of fortunes in Cyrenaica within two months was the result of the changed balance of power in North Africa brought about by the arrival in Tropolitania of three first-grade Axis divisions at the very time when the two divisions responsible for the destruction of the *10th Army* were withdrawn from the theatre; the over-extension of raw replacement British divisions in Cyrenaica; and Axis initiative in developing a full-scale offensive when a reconnaissance-in-force revealed the extent of British weakness.

With one German and two Italian divisions under the command of a German general, Lieutenant-General Rommel, the Axis formations secured El Agheila on 24 March and then divided, with the *21st Panzer Division* advancing via Mekili while Italian forces secured Benghazi on 3 April and Derna on the sixth. Bypassing Tobruk, Axis forces reached Bardia and Sollum on the eleventh, but thereafter the drag of Axis logistics and stiffening British resistance halted the advance, the battle being continued through May and June in the Halfaya–Capuzzo area astride the border. Tobruk, however, was to resist assault and withstand siege until relieved on 28 November.

While the Allies slithered to simultaneous defeats in the Balkans and North Africa the decision to abandon Crete on 27 May coincided with a British naval victory that was to have profound strategic consequences, but before dealing with the Battle of the Atlantic an account of the Balkan campaigns must be concluded with a statement of the obvious: in April 1941 the Axis powers conquered Greece and Yugoslavia and thereafter the real struggle for the control of these countries began. Since this part of the world produced the saying (as a result of the activities of Basil the Bulgar-slayer) that in the country of the blind the one-eyed man is king, the character of these struggles leave little to the imagination. Hungarian operations in the Vojvodina in April shocked even the country's dictator, Admiral Miklós Horthy, while the Bulgarian occupation of Macedonia and Thrace was marked by widespread massacres. The Italian army proselytised and handed out death in the manner of sixteenth-century *conquistadores*, but the worst atrocities were perpetrated by the fascist Croat militia, the *Ustače*, which, it is estimated, slit 250,000 Serbian throats in the three months following Yugoslavia's conquest. With the Moslems of Bosnia killing Christians of any persuasion and the Serbs taking steps to ensure their own self-preservation, Yugoslavia was engulfed in a series of civil wars within a war of national liberation that collectively claimed the lives of one in ten of the population by 1945. In Greece, too, the war against occupying powers was to contain a civil war, but in contrast to Yugoslavia the Greek civil war did not assume significant proportions until 1944 and was not decided until 1949.

The British naval victory that coincided with the decision to abandon Crete was the sinking by units of the Home Fleet of one of two German warships that had sailed six days earlier from Bergen for operations in the North Atlantic against Allied shipping. The operation was the fifth of its kind since 23 October, the previous four having resulted in the sinking of 47 merchantmen of 254,759 tons and the massive disruption of convoy sailings in the North Atlantic. The toll of Allied shipping would have been greater but for the neutralisation of the Italian fleet at Taranto, the two British battleships at Gibraltar that were freed for duties in the North Atlantic saving two convoys from certain destruction by raiders. But on 27 May the German aim of concentrating a fleet at Brest for raiding operations ended with the sinking of the battleship *Bismarck*, and from the loss of this ship the German naval staff concluded that the extension of British maritime reconnaissance over and growth of carrier power in the North Atlantic rendered raiding operations too hazardous. Despite the huge element of luck involved in the destruction of the *Bismarck* this conclusion was correct, and after May 1941 no German warship sailed against shipping in the North Atlantic.

May 1941 also saw a second British naval victory in the North Atlantic, but one that was won by default. Between January and May 1941 Allied shipping losses averaged 490,456 tons per month, and in that period the *Luftwaffe* accounted for 269 merchantmen of 750,972 tons. Though the *Luftwaffe*'s successes were swelled by those registered in April in the Mediterranean, in this period it accounted for 30.6 per cent of Allied tonnage losses and was an increasingly important factor in the war at sea. Its successes were remarkable given the fact that when it began operations under the direct control of the U-boat arm in February 1941 it allocated only forty Fw 220 Condor bombers for maritime duties, but after *Operation Barbarossa* began *Luftwaffe* numbers and effectiveness declined dramatically. Between June and December 1941 monthly Allied shipping losses fell to an average of 268,039 tons, a decrease of 45.4 per cent from the average of the five previous months, while the *Luftwaffe*'s share of sinkings declined by 53.4 per cent to 14.3 per cent. In 1941 as a whole the *Luftwaffe* accounted for 23.5 per cent of Allied shipping losses by tonnage; in 1942 for 8.98 per cent. Though this share rose in 1943, primarily as a result of declining U-boat returns, the fact of the matter was that the *Luftwaffe*'s contribution to the German effort at sea was in irreversible decline after May 1941.

The strategic implications of these two developments are hard to underestimate, involving as they did the loss of two major means whereby the *Wehrmacht* could prosecute the war against shipping. With German mining reduced to irritant status and auxiliary raiders even by the end of June 1941 experiencing difficulty in finding potential victims as the Allied convoy system was extended, the burden of waging tonnage warfare fell increasingly upon the U-boat service. In its turn, however, the U-boat service found itself operating under increasingly less favourable conditions, in large part because the extension of the convoy system for the first time denied the U-boats a rich harvest amongst unescorted merchantmen. Though U-boats continued to exact a steady toll of stragglers and ships sailing independently, and were to register their most spectacular successes in the very special circumstances of the first six months of 1942 and again on either side of the turn of that year, the inauguration of continuous two-way escort across the Atlantic in July 1941 served notice that the period of easy German success was coming to an end. Between September 1939 and June 1941 U-boats sank 848 merchantmen of 4,058,909 tons for the loss of 43 of their number, but in the next six months 23 German submarines were destroyed in accounting for 169 merchantmen of 621,510 tons.

Four major factors were at work in eroding the advantages of the U-boat service in the prosecution of the Battle of the Atlantic in the course of 1941, arguably the most important being the increasingly un-neutral activities of the United States. In April she proclaimed waters west of 26° West to be part of her defence zone, and after 19 July American warships escorted merchantmen of any nationality to and from Iceland, which the Americans occupied that same month. After 16 September American warships escorted British convoys in the western Atlantic. To date German submarines had extended their operations westwards, beyond the reach of escorts from Britain, but Hitler had no wish to risk a clash with the United States and with each American action the activities of the U-boats were curtailed in order to avoid incidents. As a result German submarines were directed either to the Mediterranean or to more distant waters and to the eastern Atlantic, where British escort forces were operating in slowly increasing numbers and to ever growing effect.

The extension of the convoy system was the result of the increasing number of escorts, particularly corvettes, entering the battle. In July 1941, after 20 months of war in which eight escorts and 55 destroyers had been lost, the Royal Navy had no fewer than 395 oceanic escorts in service or refitting and another 306 under construction. Moreover, radar went to sea with escorts for the first time in January 1941 while depth charges with new and more powerful explosive and changed firing patterns further enhanced the effectiveness of escorts. The most significant material development, however, was the deployment of long-range patrol aircraft in Iceland after April 1941. These remained few in numbers and lacked an effective means of attacking submarines, but their very presence over convoys was a deterrent in itself.

In terms of the conduct of the battle, 1941 saw a series of British intelligence successes with the capture of documents and equipment from various German warships, supply ships and submarines that allowed the Admiralty to read German signals. German cryptanalysis had broken British naval codes even before the war, and German captures had enabled them to stay ahead of the British in intelligence matters in the first 20 months of the war, but in the course of 1941 there was an equalising of the intelligence accounts and the German naval staff became increasingly aware of the growing British success in routing convoys away from known U-boat concentrations.

In contrast German operational strength throughout 1941 remained wholly inadequate to prosecute tonnage warfare with realistic hopes of success, just 21 U-boats being operational in February 1941. The quarterly commissioning of new units did not exceed single figures until October 1940 and operational strength did not reach the September 1939 level until April 1941. The total and operational strengths of the U-boat service did show dramatic increases in the course of 1941, but in the second half of the year there was a stand-off in the Battle of the Atlantic. The U-boats sank very few ships in convoy whilst their sinkings of unescorted ships declined but the escorts in their turn sank very few submarines. Indeed, between 22 November 1940 and 6 March 1941 no German submarine was lost, and in the first six months of 1941 only 12 were destroyed and only eight more were sunk in the following four months. After June 1941 neither side was able to impose its will on the battle, and with both unable to make inroads on the other's strength both added to their forces in readiness for the trial of strength that was in the offing. Thus by June 1941 the relative position of the two sides was little changed since the start of the war. For all its increase in numbers the Royal Navy was seldom able to provide a convoy with more than five escorts, usually of very mixed abilities, while the *Kriegsmarine*, despite the sinking of 7,631,188 tons of Allied shipping since the start of hostilities and its acquisition of bases in France and Norway, could not mount a balanced assault on shipping in the North Atlantic and remained too weak to cut British lines of communications with North America.

Hitler's decision to attack the Soviet Union and his setting of 22 June 1941 as the date for the start of *Operation Barbarossa* have been noted in our consideration of the course of the campaigns in the west in 1940 and in the Balkans in 1941. Both the reasons for Hitler's decision and the details of his plan of campaign, plus the explanation of why the *Wehrmacht* failed to win the victory that was expected of it, share a common characteristic: all three aspects of *Operation Barbarossa* – cause, detail and failure – are simplistic but not simple. Complicated, inter-related factors were involved in every aspect of *Operation Barbarossa* – conception, planning, execution and failure.

Reference has been made to the fact that in deciding to move against the Soviet Union in 1941 Hitler thought in terms of completing Britain's isolation by the destruction of the only power in Europe capable of disputing his domination of the continent. With respect to the British, this calculation was a rationalisation for a decision taken on other grounds: the part of the calculation that dealt with the Soviet Union was genuine. The Soviet Union in 1941 was the last threat to German security within Europe, and for that reason alone Hitler would have turned against her at some stage. In reality, however, Hitler's decision was not the product of the situation that arose in the course of 1940: it originated from those incoherent, half-light concepts that he had peddled for two decades. To Hitler, Germany had to pursue her historic destiny in the east. Her right to survive was to be decided in a struggle of annihilation with Slavonic Europe. The *Untermenschen* of the east had to be subjugated in order to create the new order in Europe whereby the *Herrenvolk* secured for itself the mineral resources, foodstuffs and slave labour that were synonymous with the idea of *Lebensraum*, and which would ensure Germany's survival against the worst that Britain and an increasingly unfriendly United States could do. Herein was the cause of Hitler's decision to attack the Soviet Union, unchanged from the time that it had been set down in his autobiography almost two decades earlier: the situation that arose during 1940 provided opportunity, not reasons.

The German High Command had more time to prepare *Operation Barbarossa* than any other offensive of the war, and it was given twice as long to perfect its plan of campaign than it allowed for the campaign itself. A little over 10 months elapsed between *OKW*'s being ordered to begin staff studies and the start of the campaign, and only five months were allowed for the *Wehrmacht* to secure the Archangelsk–Kotlas–Gorkiy–Volga–Astrakhan line. Within this simple definition of final-phase objectives lay a confusion of aims and intentions that reflected the complicated problems presented by geography, distance and time to any attempt to invade and conquer the Soviet Union. Inevitably, the German plan of campaign was an uneasy compromise between divergent, irreconcilable objectives set in response to these problems, not that the full extent of these difficulties were appreciated properly by German planning staffs.

The most obvious compromise in the German plan of campaign was between geographical and military objectives. In its three major campaigns to date the *Wehrmacht* had aimed at the defeat of enemy armies in the field, and in each campaign geographical constraints denied Germany's foes space in which to manoeuvre in order to avoid defeat. On the Eastern Front, however, the space available to the defence dictated that Soviet forces in the border areas had to be encircled and annihilated before the Dvina–Dnepr line. But while the penetration of the Soviet front could only be achieved by armour, encirclement and annihilation could only be undertaken by infantry – which needed armour support and which had been stripped of transport and support in order to provide for new armoured formations. Any restriction of the armoured advance into the interior, however, provided the Soviets with time in which to deploy fresh forces across the line of advance, but any attempt to forestall Soviet mobilisation by deep armoured thrusts ran obvious risks of counter-attack against undefended flanks and exhaustion of armour at the tip of a dead *Schwerpunkt*.

In that period when, Hitler safely dead, it was popular to lay responsibility for every German defeat at his door, it was usually argued that had armour been freed from supporting the infantry the outcome of this campaign would have been very different. This may have been so, but the fact remains that the need to fight a battle of encirclement and annihilation before Soviet forces could withdraw into the interior posed an operational dilemma to which there was no simple solution. A fully mechanised army might have been able to penetrate and encircle at one and the same time, but of the 173 Axis divisions between the Baltic and Black Seas in June 1941 only 13 were motorised and 19 were armoured. The latter had been obtained only by halving the tank establishment of an armoured division from its 1940 level. Mobile formations, which were not properly mechanised, formed less than 17 per cent of the establishment of German ground forces, and lacked sufficient fighting strength to remain effective in the course of the campaign that was about to unfold.

The operational dilemma confronting German planning was compounded by an equally intractable strategic predicament. Geography ordained that the German effort had to be divided, the Pripyat Marshes in the very centre of the front forming a natural obstacle to movement eastwards. To the south lay the Ukraine and the Donets valley with the foodstuffs and mineral wealth Germany needed to sustain herself and here, too, were powerful Soviet forces that menaced the Balkans. Thus the southern sector could not be assigned secondary status, and in the event the Axis concentration between Lublin and the Black Sea, with Rundstedt's *Army Group South*, was the largest single Axis command involved in *Operation Barbarossa*. But the historic heartland of the Russian state and potentially the decisive theatre of operations lay to the north and east of the Pripyat Marshes, and in the final analysis German strategic policy and priorities were reduced to the question of whether or not to make Moscow the main objective.

Moscow presented itself as the obvious target of German attentions on three counts. It was the hub of the Soviet railroad system west of the Urals; it was a great industrial centre and home of vitally important armaments factories; and it was the capital of a highly centralised state. With so much of the Soviet state's power and mystique vested in this single city, a German capture of Moscow in autumn 1941 might well have decided the campaign. Yet any proposal for a direct advance on Moscow along the highway via Minsk and Smolensk raised at a strategic level the same problems that had presented themselves at the operational level: an unsupported advance in the centre invited counter-attack against extended, unsecured flanks, but any attempt to secure the flanks before moving against Moscow necessarily involved rendering the main effort dependent upon the success of supporting operations. With Moscow made the main objective of the campaign, the answer to this problem was provided in the inherently unsound arrangement whereby the drive on Moscow in the centre would begin once the left flank had been secured.

In its final form the German plan for the invasion of the Soviet Union involved the use of 190 Axis divisions of which 158 were provided by the *Wehrmacht*. Of these 153 were deployed between the Baltic and Black Seas and divided between three army groups, each of which was allocated three security divisions for duties in rear areas, and a reserve, the *2nd Army*, that numbered no fewer than two armoured, two motorised and 20 infantry divisions. Sandwiched between the Baltic and the Poznan–Lötzen line were the three armoured, two motorised and 24 infantry divisions of Leeb's *Army Group North*. Having the *18th*, *4th Panzer* and *16th Armies* under command,* *Army Group North* was to secure the Baltic states and advance on Leningrad with the aim of linking with Finnish forces in the Volkov–Lodeynoye Pole area. With the Finnish army scheduled to begin operations once German forces crossed the Dvina,

---

*Originally the armour was organised into panzer groups, but in the course of the 1941 campaign these groups were redesignated armies. For the purposes of simplicity, their final designation has been adopted.

Army Group North was to use the *16th Army* to secure the middle Dvina between Daugav'pils and Polotsk and to secure the flank of *Army Group Centre*. Bock's command consisted of one cavalry, nine armoured, six motorised and 33 infantry divisions divided between the *3rd Panzer*, *9th*, *4th* and *2nd Panzer Armies*. The concentration of two armoured armies and almost half of Germany's mobile formations with this army group was evidence that the main German effort was to be made in this sector. The expectation that the Soviets would do the same dictated the deployment of armour on the flanks of *Army Group Centre* for deep encirclement operations behind Baranovichi, Minsk and Smolensk. After taking Smolensk, however, *Army Group Centre* was to cede formations to *Army Group North* in order to ensure its own flank protection before the advance on Moscow began. To the south of the Pripyat Marshes *Army Group South* was tasked to secure Kiev and the middle and lower Dnepr but was also to develop its offensive within the bend of the Don. Rundstedt had under command five armoured, three motorised and 34 infantry divisions allocated between the *6th*, *1st Panzer*, *17th* and *11th Armies*, plus the equivalent of 14 divisions, 12 of which were infantry, of the *3rd* and *4th Romanian Armies*. Romania alone of Germany's allies and associates was asked before the start of *Operation Barbarossa* to provide forces for the attack on the Soviet Union and did so, the *quid pro quo* for her participation being the promise of the acquisition of Soviet territory as far as the Bug.

Such was the original Axis order of battle for the attack on the USSR other than the two divisions of *Mountain Group Norway* that were tasked to secure Petsamo and Murmansk, but which did not begin operations until 29 June. By then, however, *Army Group South* had been supplemented by corps equivalents provided, without enthusiasm, by both Hungary and Slovakia. In August one partially motorised Italian corps joined Rundstedt's command. The arrival in September of one Spanish infantry division on the Leningrad front completed the initial contribution of Germany's lesser partners.

To the north, Finland, as a result of negotiations with Germany between 25 May and 14 June, was prepared to play host to German formations, to involve herself on her own account in the attack on the Soviet Union, but not to conclude a formal treaty of alliance with Germany. The plans that were developed by Finnish and German staffs either side of 22 June involved the use of a corps in the Soumussalmi–Kuusamo sector to support the operations of the two German divisions of *XXXVI Infantry Corps* on the Salla–Kandalaksha axis while the bulk of the Finnish army was committed to offensive operations on either side of

137

Lake Ladoga. With one German division earmarked to move to Finland to serve as a reserve, these arrangements benefited Finland and Germany equally. Finland sought to recover territory lost in 1940 but had to avoid a costly commitment in Karelia and the Isthmus; Germany sought Finnish action to tie down Soviet forces in these areas and to prevent their redeployment to other fronts. The lateness of Finnish–German negotiations prevented a Finnish move on 22 June. The date of 10 July for Finnish intervention with no fewer than 18 infantry divisions was settled on the fourth. A state of war between Finland and the Soviet Union nevertheless existed after 25 June as a result of Soviet air raids on cities in southern Finland, *XXXVI Infantry* and *III Finnish Corps* opening proceedings on the central sector on 1 July.

In recent years the myth of German military excellence in the Second World War has become widely disseminated throughout Western histories. This development rests upon two undeniable facts: the extent of German conquests (plus the effort that was needed to bring about Germany's defeat) and a technique, initiative and flair at both tactical and operational levels that enabled German ground formations to outfight consistently superior enemy forces – at least until 1944. *Operation Barbarossa*, in both its planning and failure, is critically important in providing a corrective to this view of German military performance in the Second World War, but because of the undoubted fighting qualities of the *Wehrmacht* this operation poses formidable problems of interpretation. From today's perspective it seems incredible that Germany could have conquered so much of the Soviet Union in 1941 and 1942 and that on two separate occasions should have brought her to within measurable distance of defeat. Hindsight provides the element of inevitability that suggests that Germany's defeat in this campaign was assured because, for the first time, Hitler raised the scale of conflict to levels that Germany could not sustain. But this view presupposes the German failure to defeat the Soviet Union in a single campaign, and herein lies a paradox: before the campaign began there would seem to be no means whereby Germany could prevail, yet once the campaign started it would seem to have been impossible for her to lose. Given this contradiction and the various considerations of the German military performance in the Second World War, an examination of *Operation Barbarossa*, its planning and failure, must draw together the aspects of Nazism and Hitler's leadership that beset the planning and conduct of this campaign. Together these account in large measure for the German failure to conquer the Soviet Union in 1941.

The fact that the *Wehrmacht* failed in its attempt to overrun the Soviet Union in 1941 despite holding the strategic initiative for most of the campaign suggests that *Operation Barbarossa* was flawed in terms of objectives and direction. By any standard, however inexacting and far below those that should have been imposed by normal staff procedures, the selection of three objectives on divergent axes of advance at distances between 500 and 900 miles from start lines, followed then as the campaign unfolded by a chronic inability to decide between them, constitutes a cardinal weakness of *Operation Barbarossa*. The German plan of campaign was riddled by a confusion of priorities that was the direct result of the general chaos explicit in *Führer Prinzip*, which worsened the longer the war lasted. Hitler's lack of mental discipline, his distrust of the judgement and competence of subordinates, and his total inability to work through a cabinet system and logical chain of command were reflected in a failure to pursue a settled strategic policy. As the campaign unfolded this lack of consistency served to deny the *Wehrmacht* time, and time worked against Germany in this campaign partly because of the lateness of the start of *Barbarossa*, partly because once the offensive began logistical problems imposed delays that could not be afforded. Indecision exacerbated this problem, but Hitler's insistence upon the simultaneous pursuit of widely separated objectives with forces that were marginal to tactical requirements but greater than could be maintained in the field placed his armies in a well-nigh impossible position from the start of the campaign.

The other aspect of Nazism that contributed directly to the failure of *Operation Barbarossa* was its very nature and philosophy. Ideas of racial struggle and annihilation, the *leitmotif* of Nazism, formed the basis of Hitler's decision to attack the Soviet Union. Since the end of the Second World War it has been generally acknowledged that German brutality on the Eastern Front in 1941 was counter-productive and, in the long term, may well have been the most important single factor in ensuring German failure in the east. This general point cannot be disputed. Within the Soviet Union in 1941 were national and social groups that welcomed the Germans as liberators from the tyranny of Russian communism, only to be thrown back into Soviet arms by the appalling cruelty of the invaders. German behaviour in 1941 closed the gaps that opened in Soviet society under the impact of defeat by denying Soviet society the right to collapse.

With so much attention paid to German atrocities in the east, it is too easy to miss the fact that specific, military problems explicit in any attempt to conquer the Soviet Union in a single campaign were over-ridden by the blind faith that the campaign would be won. A complete campaigning season had been allowed originally for the defeat of the Soviet Union – which was to be destroyed by 15 October 1941 – but staff planning from the start showed that Germany lacked the means to conduct a campaign lasting five months in a theatre 900 miles in depth and 800 miles across its front. As plans were elaborated it became clear that the supply available to the *Wehrmacht* would be sufficient to take the armour and motorised divisions to the Dvina–Dnepr line only if no attempt was made to resupply the infantry divisions. Irrespective of the situation on the ground, a halt would have to be called at Smolensk, if not before, and given the margins on which the *Wehrmacht* would be obliged to operate any advance beyond the Dvina and Dnepr was problematical. Yet by the time that *Operation Barbarossa* opened it was widely assumed within the German High Command that six weeks would suffice to complete the destruction of the Soviet Union. The amazing inconsistency inherent in this view – what could not be achieved, even in five months, would therefore be done in six weeks – is explicable in certain bureaucratic terms: the process of filtering out and filtering up, the hypnotic effect generated in the preparation of major campaigns. Yet the real explanation lies in the self-deceiving and self-defeating aspects of Nazi ideology that filtered down and imposed themselves on staff planning. The belief in will as the decisive factor in the conduct of war and the inability to contemplate effective resistance and anything other than easy, total victory are the basis of this massive failure to recognise the limits of national and military power, to reconcile national policy with strategic realities and tactical objectives. In the case of *Operation Barbarossa* this inability to correlate aims and resources at the highest level of strategic direction primarily stemmed from the influence of Nazi ideas, yet it must be noted that the situation that arose in 1941 was a repeat of what had happened between 1915 and 1918 when the Army General Staff had ruled Germany in effect if not in name. For all its much vaunted efficiency, the *Wehrmacht* in preparing *Operation Barbarossa* demonstrated that it understood fighting but not the waging of war.

Post-war examination of the Soviet dimension of *Operation Barbarossa* has tended to concentrate upon the two matters most immediately relevant to the unfolding of the campaign on the Eastern Front after 22 June 1941. First, the state of the Soviet army in 1941 has been the subject of exhaustive analysis and comment. Second, the fact that the *Wehrmacht* registered complete strategic surprise on 22 June despite Stalin's having been warned over the previous four months by a number of independent sources of German intentions has exercised a fascinated bewilderment on two generations of historians. Any examination of this campaign must begin by addressing these two matters which, along with the campaign itself, have served to obscure a third aspect of the Soviet side of *Operation Barbarossa*, namely that on 21 June 1941 no fewer than 11 of the 12 armies stationed in western Soviet Union were west of the Riga–Minsk–Zhitomir–Odessa line and hence in positions to be encircled within a matter of days of the start of the German offensive. Even allowing for the need to garrison territories only recently acquired by the Soviet Union, the scale of Soviet deployment in the border areas cannot be justified in terms of the needs of military occupation, while the forward deployment of virtually all available front-line formations cannot be deemed part of a coherent defensive policy. In any examination of *Operation Barbarossa*, problems of interpretation are not confined to German calculations and conduct of operations.

The state Lenin founded in 1917 and led through civil war and foreign intervention was one that measured power and security in numbers of divisions. It looked to superior military strength, plus vigilance, to provide for its security, and in June 1941 its order of battle numbered some 240 field divisions, of which 213 were in the western theatre of operations. In terms of numbers of tanks and aircraft, perhaps 21,000 and 14,500 respectively, the Soviet Union held advantages of 3:1 or 4:1 over the *Wehrmacht*, while on a simple formation count the Soviet Union in June 1941 could meet the combined forces of Finland and Germany on the basis of equality without calling on its reserves.

In terms of quality and organisation, however, the Soviet armed forces were considerably inferior to the *Wehrmacht*, while the advantage of superior numbers was largely illusory because of the obsolescence of much Soviet equipment, the slow rate of delivery of new aircraft and tanks to field forces, and the low rates of serviceability in front-line units. With an estimated 74 per cent of all front-line armour undergoing repair or major overhaul at any time in spring 1941 and the new, very powerful KV heavy and T-34 medium tanks entering service slowly and in very small numbers,* the Soviet armies in the border areas, for all their nominal strength, probably held no advantage of overall numbers and were massively inferior to German forces on selected axes of advance. Moreover, very few defensive positions and fortifications had been completed in the border area by June 1941 and Soviet divisions on the frontier lacked adequate signals equipment, were poorly trained at all

---

*The front-line tank strength of the Soviet army was between 8,800 and 9,300 tanks in the Baltic, Western and Kiev districts, of which 1,475 were either T-34s or KVs. The air force deployed 1,540 modern combat aircraft.

levels and, by definition, were inferior to their opposite numbers in terms of combat experience. But the two most serious weaknesses of the Soviet army on the eve of *Operation Barbarossa* were, first, fact that it was caught in June 1941 in the process of reorganising its armour into tank divisions on the German 1940 pattern. As a consequence it was saddled with all the weaknesses and none of the strengths of two very different doctrines and organisations, with much of its armour deployed in the infantry support role. The overall result was a very uneven quality in Soviet formations, some armies having fully equipped armoured and mechanised divisions while many infantry divisions were at little more than half-strength and lacked proper field and anti-tank artillery.

The other major weakness of the Soviet army in June 1941 was one of leadership and command, and was in large measure the result of the purges that Stalin unleased upon Soviet society after 1937. It has been estimated that between 1937 and 1953 there were never fewer than eight million people in Soviet prisons at any one time and that in the war years the gulags accounted for a million lives annually. The great purges between 1937 and 1940 claimed an estimated million lives. No fewer than 402 generals died in the process, and thousands of officers were imprisoned and those that were not were reduced to an obedience that bordered on witlessness. Initiative and innovation, hallmarks of the army before 1937, disappeared with the purges, to be replaced by an unthinking compliance with orders enforced by the political commissars and the NKVD.*

Though the purges cut a massive swathe through the officer corps, on the eve of *Operation Barbarossa* there was no indication that they had permanently impaired the morale and discipline of the army. The rank and file of all armies are notoriously indifferent to the fate of generals, and in 1938 and 1939 in clashes with the Japanese and in the Winter War the Soviet army displayed a bravery, tenacity and lack of squeamishness about casualties that suggested that the traditional qualities of Russian soldiery had not been undermined by Stalin's tyranny. Paradoxically, the very brutality of the Stalinist state, established as it was on a stoicism and fatalism themselves the products of a harsh, unrelenting way of life, was to stand the Soviet army in good stead in the ordeal that was to come: the nature of discipline and punishment was such that, in the words of Stalin, it took a brave man to be a coward in the Soviet army. In the course of the Great Patriotic War a total of 238 generals and admirals were shot or died

---

Narodny Kommissariat Vnutrennykh Deyl, the People's Commissariat for Internal Affairs or the Soviet secret police. Gallows humour decreed that NKVD stood for *Nikogda-ne Vernyesh Domoy*: 'You will never return home.'

in penal battalions as a result of failure in battle, and for men under stay of execution – as were all Soviet commanders – the lives of subordinates could not have been of very great account. The toughness of the Soviet system and soldier, and indifference to losses, ensured that the Soviet army fought from the start, if not skilfully then desperately and with increasing effect as it acquired technique the hard way.

Even in the first days of the campaign the *Wehrmacht* was subjected to counter-attacks on a scale and of a ferocity unknown in its previous operations, and if these seldom achieved their aim then they inflicted losses, disrupted German plans and delayed advances. At Smolensk, for example, surrounded Soviet forces did not meekly surrender but fought, and in so doing blocked the main supply routes to German armour beyond Smolensk for three weeks when time was vital to both sides. Though the Soviet army wavered in mid-campaign and suffered as a result of separatist sentiment amongst its non-Russian formations, it fought from the outset, and if Hitler was correct in his belief that will was the determinant of war then *Operation Barbarossa* was doomed from the start. Despite the cruelty and excesses of the Stalinist regime, the *Wehrmacht* had only military technique to sustain itself and rape, pillage and mass murder to offer Soviet society whereas the Soviet state, once the non-Russian territories of the west had gone, was sustained by a primeval nationalism deeply embedded within Russian consciousness: for all its success the *Wehrmacht* barely penetrated beyond the Russian marches.

Soviet resilience, however, would have counted for nothing had the *Wehrmacht* at the start of the campaign been able to inflict a defeat upon the Soviet armed forces of such proportions that there could be no recovery. Such a victory was almost placed within German grasp by those aspects of Stalin's policy to which reference has been made: his discounting the warnings of German intentions and the incomprehensible deployment of the mass of the army against the frontier. Both defy rational explanation. Stalin was warned by the Americans in March and by the British in April of what was afoot, but if a not unnatural distrust of these sources allowed Stalin to discount these warnings he had no reason to doubt reports from Soviet agents. From Richard Sorge in the German embassy in Tokyo came reports on 19 May and 1 and 15 June, while from eastern Europe came reports of a deliberate slowing of exports to the Soviet Union during the spring. Moreover, while it is inconceivable that the German build-up along the border was unknown to Soviet intelligence, the Red Trio network run by Rudolf Rössler in Switzerland provided Moscow in the spring with the complete German order of battle down to the names of all commanders at corps level, German objectives, and even the date of the German onslaught before it was finally settled by Hitler. Few nations have been better warned of impending invasion than the Soviet Union in June 1941, yet despite this, and despite the fact that the Soviet Union had spent more than two decades trying to insure herself against surprise attack, the Soviet army was totally surprised by the German invasion on 22 June 1941. Only in the last hours of peace did the Soviet High Command try to alert its forces, but it needed 20 days to complete its initial mobilisation, and the German attack found bridges unguarded, aircraft not dispersed and defensive positions unmanned.

In the 40 years that have elapsed since the end of the Second World War the conventional wisdom amongst historians has held the reason for this state of affairs to have been a delusion on Stalin's part. This explanation asserts that Stalin's three calculations – that Hitler would not attack the USSR in 1941 because of Germany's unfinished war with Britain and the increasingly hostile attitude of the United States; that Hitler could be appeased; that the Soviet Union had to avoid war in 1941 because of the unreadiness of her army – translated themselves into the belief that war would not come in 1941, and that having come to this conclusion Stalin was not prepared to consider anything that suggested otherwise. Supporting evidence for this explanation is deemed to lie in Stalin's own observation to the effect that he realised war with Hitler was inevitable but that he hoped to postpone it for 'six months or so'. Given that not even Hitler would have begun the invasion of the USSR in December it must be assumed that the 'or so' qualification is somewhat more important than the 'six months' assessment.

Stalin's comment, however, begs the main question, as does an alternative version of events that suggests that far from trying to avoid war in 1941 Stalin intended to launch a pre-emptive attack on Germany that summer. This thesis, which was published in 1985 and seized upon by certain West German and neo-Nazi circles as justification for Hitler's attack on the Soviet Union, rests upon five main supports: the undeniable fact that Soviet military doctrine in 1941 was offensive, not defensive; the movement of 114 divisions from the second strategic echelon to the immediate border areas after 13 June; the secret mobilisation of reserves after April and the movement of forces from outlying military districts that by 10 July would have resulted in eight armies (with 69 divisions) being concentrated in the second strategic echelon in the western Soviet Union; the lack of sheltered accommodation for 170 divisions in the border area which meant that they could not stay in position beyond the summer; and a cost to the economy that could only be justified by an overwhelming national requirement, such as the preparation for an offensive war. This thesis presumes, however, that all those German actions in the winter of 1940–41,* interpreted by two generations of historians as matters that convinced Stalin of the need to appease Hitler, have been miscasted, and that Stalin's apparent appeasement of Hitler in the first half of 1941 was no more than an elaborate cover. Even allowing for the twin facts that in his many years in power Stalin was often badly out of touch with events and that in spring 1941 he most obviously did misread German intentions, it seems unlikely that Stalin could seriously have considered starting a preventive war in 1941 and that so many eminent historians and commentators could have been so badly misled on this matter for so long. This new interpretation of Soviet policy in 1941 cannot be dismissed lightly, but at present (1988) it remains non-proven. The obvious unreadiness of the Soviet army in June 1941 for offensive operations, and the fact that nearly 60 per cent of Soviet front-line armour was held in the Kiev military district and hence was not in a position to undertake immediate offensive operations against the *Wehrmacht*, logically suggests that the Soviet deployment in mid-1941 was defensive and precautionary, and incoherent and self-defeating.

For whatever cause, Soviet deployment on 21 June 1941 resulted in 15 armies being stationed in the five frontier districts of the western Soviet Union. The Leningrad military district, with responsibilities unchanged since the Winter War, had under command the 14th Army around Murmansk, the 7th Army in the central sector, and the 23rd Army on the Isthmus approaches. The Baltic Special Military District, covering the Baltic states and extending as far south as the Grodno–Ushmyany line, deployed two first-echelon and one second-echelon formations. The 8th Army was stationed on the right on the coast with the 11th Army on the left around Vilna, the 27th Army being held in the Pytalovo area. Each of these armies had one mechanised corps under command, as did three of the four armies of the Western SMD. With its southern boundary settled along the Vlodava–Sarny line, the Western SMD deployed the 3rd and 10th Armies in the Bialystok salient and the 4th Army at Brest. The 13th Army was around Minsk itself. To the south, as far as the upper Bug, were the armies of the Kiev SMD. Around Kovel', with a mechanised corps under command, was the 5th Army, but to the south, in the most dangerously exposed part of the line where Stalin personally prohibited

---

*The overtures to Finland; the occupation of Romania and Bulgaria; the abrasive exchanges between Hitler and Molotov in November 1940 when the Russian visited Berlin; and Germany's subsequent refusal to be drawn on the question of a new treaty that she had raised on that occasion.

the preparation of defensive positions, were three armies – the 6th, 26th and 12th – and four mechanised corps. Three more mechanised corps were held in the Zhitomir area, but with the 16th Army from the Trans-Baikal MD not having reached Berdichev before the start of hostilities the Kiev SMD had no second-echelon army. Completing the Soviet order of battle were the 9th Army and two mechanised corps of the Odessa MD and the Baltic and Black Sea fleets.

German intelligence in spring 1941 credited the Soviet army with about 150 divisions, but the Soviet Union deployed about this number with its front-line armies between the Baltic and Black Sea alone. She had about 4,500,000 men under arms in June 1941, but within six weeks of the start of the Great Patriotic War no fewer than 10 more armies entered the battle. While the 18th Army moved from Kharkov to relieve the 9th on the middle and upper Prut, before the end of June the 22nd (North Caucasus MD), 16th, 20th (Orlov MD) and 21st (Volga MD) Armies had arrived at Vitebsk, Smolensk, Orsha and Chernigov respectively. In July five more reserve armies arrived in the Staraya Russa–Smolensk–Moscow area where the German threat was at its greatest, and other armies were to be raised or arrive from the east before the end of the year.

In terms of scale the Nazi–Soviet conflict was unprecedented, and it was infinitely more important in deciding the outcome of the Second World War than any other theatre, perhaps even more important than all others combined. Some 8,000,000 troops were involved in the first clash of arms, and perhaps 15,000,000 men were committed to the Eastern Front at its peak. It was a conflict fought with a barbarism unknown in Europe since the Thirty Years' War, perhaps appropriately since this clash, like that previous conflict, was a war of religion. It was a conflict that claimed 15,000 Soviet lives for every day that it lasted, and if the total dead from all causes during this conflict could have been laid along the road from Moscow to Berlin each corpse would have been afforded 1.6-inches, less than the thickness of a headstone. It was, in Hitler's own words, 'the greatest of all struggles'; the phrase, used on 22 June 1941, is curious because of its implication of protracted conflict. Nothing was further from Hitler's thoughts, and at least in the opening month of the campaign events seemed to justify his confidence as the *Wehrmacht* won victories that promised to bring this conflict to as rapid and successful a conclusion as each of its previous campaigns.

Between 22 June and 5 December 1941 *Operation Barbarossa* divided both by geography and time into two separate but related parts. To the north of the Pripyat Marshes German success was immediate and overwhelming, Sabsk, on the Luga, and Yartsevo, east of Smolensk, being secured on 14 and 15 July respectively. Thereafter, however, the German offensives halted and never regained their former momentum, the twin objectives of Leningrad and Moscow, the fall of which seemed certain in July, ultimately proving beyond German reach. To the south of the Pripyat Marshes the offensive of *Army Group South* was slower to develop than those to the north, but as that either stalled or lurched fitfully forward, so Axis forces in the south secured a victory around Kiev that equalled any won by *Army Group Centre*, subsequently developing their advance to and beyond the middle and lower Don.

To the north of the Pripyat Marshes advances to depths of 60 miles were recorded by German armour on the first day of the campaign. By 26 June, when *XLI Panzer Corps* completed the destruction of the 2nd Armoured Division around Raseynyay, clearing the way for its advance to Yekabpils and Livani, *LVI Panzer Corps* had secured bridgeheads at Daugav'pils over the Dvina. It was not until 2 July, however, that the *4th Panzer Army* crossed the Dvina, and after securing Ostrov on the fourth and crushing an armoured counter-attack by the 27th Army east of the town on the fifth and sixth, its formations reached the lower Luga, just 80 miles from an undefended Leningrad, on the fourteenth. In the centre the *3rd Panzer Army* secured Alitus on 23 June and Vilna on the twenty-fourth, and with *2nd Panzer Army* taking Slonim on the same day and both Rogachev and Borisov, after forcing the Berezina, on 1 July, the two armoured formations of *Army Group Centre* completed the deep encirclement of three enemy forces, at Bialystok, Volkovysk and Novogrudok, when they joined hands west of Minsk on 29 June. With the offensive resumed on 3 July, the *3rd Panzer Army* reached the Dvina, cleared the west bank and secured Vitebsk on the ninth before taking Yartsevo on the fifteenth and Smolensk itself on the sixteenth. With the *2nd Panzer Army* forcing the Dnepr at Shklov and Stary Sykhoy on the tenth, a deep encirclement of Soviet forces west of Smolensk was achieved with the capture of Yelnya on 27 July.

For all this success, the failure of *Army Group Centre* to close the trap around Smolensk for 12 days after the capture of Yartsevo produced the first major German crisis of the campaign, involving as it did specific problems of command and policy and general tactical and technical difficulties thrown up in the course of the first month's fighting. In large measure the slowness with which the noose around Smolensk was drawn was the result of the deliberate refusal of the *2nd Panzer Army* to close the pocket from the south, which in turn was the result of its desire to secure

147

'Barbarossa'; The German Offensive, June to December 1941

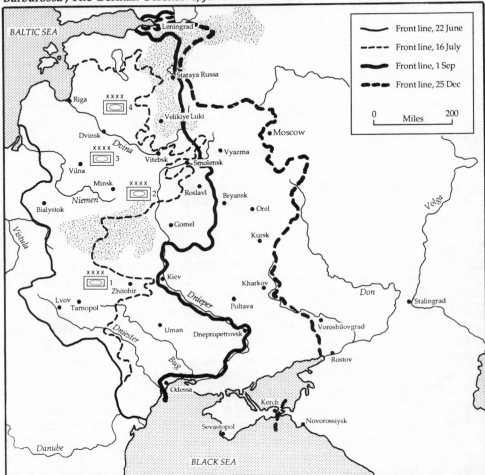

positions from which it could continue its advance on Moscow in the next phase of operations. This attitude on the part of the *2nd Panzer Army* indicated a willingness on the part of Bock and his armour to disregard unpalatable orders that was unacceptable to Hitler and *OKH*.

The advance of *Army Group North*'s armour beyond the Dvina had been possible only by curtailing the operations of the *16th Army*, though by mid-July part of this formation, plus part of Leeb's reserve, had to be switched to *Army Group Centre* to help in the defensive battles that were developing around Nevel as a result of counter-attacks by the 22nd Army. By the time the Luga was reached it was clear to *Army Group North* that an offensive over the river was possible only if supply to both the *18th* and *16th Armies* was ended, yet at the same time infantry from some source had to be made available to support an attack on Leningrad on two counts: armour could neither hold ground nor take a city, while swamp and the thickening forests channelled German advances and provided Soviet forces with positions that could only be reduced by infantry in set-piece attacks. As early as 5 July unfavourable terrain had forced *Army Group North* to abandon its intention of developing a two-pronged drive on Leningrad by denying *LVI Panzer Corps* the Opochka–Novorzhev–Staraya Russa axis, but by mid-July the infantry of *18th* and *16th Armies* were fully committed in clearing operations and far behind *4th Panzer Army*.

In the centre German problems, though different, were no less acute. Although six Soviet divisions were annihilated in each of the Bialystok and Volkovysk pockets and a further 15 were to be destroyed on the upper Dvina, the inability of the *9th* and *4th Armies* to complete the close encirclement of pockets quickly meant that *Army Group Centre* found itself committed to a series of untidy actions, particularly around Volkovysk where Soviet forces made a number of partial breakouts. In every encirclement the Germans found that Soviet forces resisted furiously, and Brest withstood attack until 24 July. Though the three pockets in front of Minsk were eliminated before 30 June, Soviet resistance inflicted unprecedented losses on German infantry, strained inadequate lines of supply – the *2nd Panzer Army* had to be resupplied by air as early as the second day of the campaign – and caused the German High Command much anxiety for good tactical reasons.

The conflict of operational doctrines that had been latent within the *Barbarossa* plan thus emerged within a matter of days of the start of the campaign precisely because of the speed and extent of German success, while by the time that Smolensk and Yelnya were secured additional problems of infantry exhaustion and Soviet resistance in the northern Ukraine imposed themselves on the German High Command. Four weeks of marching and fighting in the extreme heat and dust of a Russian summer reduced German infantry to the point of exhaustion, and by mid-July just two infantry corps from the two army groups north of the Pripyat Marshes and the *2nd Army* remained uncommitted.

By this time, too, about 50 per cent of all German armour had been lost or rendered unserviceable, and because of the army's refusal to move its workshops eastwards from Poland and Hitler's decision to reserve engine production for new tanks rather than provide replacements for armour in service, attrition that could have been absorbed within the 1940 establishment imposed obvious problems in 1941. With regard to soft-skinned vehicles casualty rates of 40 per cent in the first month of operations imposed crippling problems on an already inadequate logistics tail, and German difficulties were exacerbated by the appalling state of Soviet roads, petrol consumption 30 per cent above anticipated needs, and an inability to restore the railroad system quickly. With Soviet railroads limited to 17-ton axle loadings compared with the 24-ton limits general in western Europe and conversion to standard gauge automatically ending the German ability to use captured Soviet locomotives, the Germans found themselves confronted with a series of increasingly complicated logistical problems, largely unanticipated before the start of the campaign, and at a time when success at Smolensk posed the question of how *Barbarossa* was to be developed in coming weeks.

This problem was brought to a head by events south of the Pripyat Marshes. In the first two days of the campaign, when between them the three *Luftwaffe* air fleets on the Eastern Front accounted for an estimated 2,000 Soviet aircraft, the armour of *Army Group South* split the Soviet front before Lvov, the *6th Army* developing a 30-mile breach between the 5th and 6th Armies and the *17th Army* a 20-mile breach between the 6th and 26th. The Soviet response, however, was immediate and in some measure successful in that armour concentrated against the German breaches and attacks over the next five days brought the German advances to a halt and allowed the Soviet front to be withdrawn to a shorter line in front of Zhitomir. By the first week of July the Soviet High Command had extricated its forward armies and had re-established the front along the Korosten–Novograd–Volynsky axis, but the armour that had been used to contain the German breakthroughs had been largely eliminated in the process. A combination of *Luftwaffe* action, poor terrain for counter-attack purposes and the uncoordinated attacks by Soviet armour exacted a massive toll in what was the biggest armoured battle in the first two weeks of the campaign. The gain of space and time for Soviet infantry did not compensate for the armour losses and the fact that the *1st Panzer Army*, despite being roughly handled in some exchanges, remained intact and was ready to resume its offensive when the battles on the frontier came to an end. Thereafter, with the *11th Army* striking across the Prut on 1 July against the juncture of the 18th and 9th Armies, *Army Group South* attacked eastwards between the Bug and Dnepr, securing Berdichev on 7 July and Zhitomir on the tenth only to find that Kiev was too strongly held to be secured by a *coup de main* when armour reached Irpen, ten miles away, on the eleventh. It also found that it was then being drawn into a second running battle around Novograd, Volynsky and Zhitomir as the 5th and 6th Armies counter-attacked. Though an advance to the south-east held out the prospect of working around the right flank and rear of the Soviet armies gathering around Uman, the fact that the 5th Army remained unreduced on the left flank and that a 200-mile gap threatened to develop between *Army Group South* and *Army Group Centre* as both emerged east of the Pripyat Marshes aroused obvious and well-justified misgivings within the German High Command.

Given that in the first three weeks of the campaign the *Wehrmacht* had destroyed more than half the original Soviet order of battle in the four western military districts and that *Army Group South* had dealt with the best that the 5th Army could do, it may be that the Germans could have developed an offensive against Uman without regard to the left flank and rear. But as early as 1 July formations from *Army Group Centre* had to be detached to reduce Soviet forces around Pinsk and Hitler's anxiety about unreduced Soviet forces in rear areas, plus a natural staff caution, dictated that the threat posed by the 5th Army around Korosten had to be eliminated before *Army Group South* could develop its offensive. On 9 July, therefore, *OKH* suggested to Hitler that the *2nd Panzer Army* be diverted southwards to eliminate the Soviet formations around Kiev and the southern Pripyat Marshes. While this idea was shelved as the advances of both *Army Group Centre* and *Army Group South* accelerated in the second week of July, once conceived the idea never went away, particularly because it accorded with Hitler's strategic prejudices that placed no great value on the capture of Moscow.

On 19 July, therefore, with *Army Group North* on the Luga, *Army Group Centre* having secured the upper Dvina and Smolensk, and *Army Group South* in possession of Kazatin, Hitler ordered *2nd Panzer* and *2nd Armies* to deal with Soviet forces around Gomel and then continue southwards in order to link up with *Army Group South* thereby completing the encirclement of Soviet forces in the northern Ukraine. At the same time Rundstedt's forces were to encircle and annihilate Soviet forces around Uman and then head for the middle Don and a meeting with the *2nd Panzer Army*. With the *3rd Panzer Army* simultaneously ordered to assist *Army Group North* in its attack on Leningrad, the advance on Moscow was to be continued by *Army Group Centre*'s infantry armies. It was this directive, with its effective abandonment of the advance on Moscow, that

Army Group Centre, and particularly the *2nd Panzer Army*, tried to evade, and it took Hitler until 21 August to enforce his decision upon the generals of *OKW*, *OKH* and *Army Group Centre* who wanted to keep the Moscow option alive. By the time that Hitler was able to force his commanders into line, however, the immediate need for the diversion of forces from *Army Group Centre* had passed.

On the Leningrad front the offensive over the lower Luga on 8 August, and the advance that secured Novgorod on the sixteenth and Chudovo on the twentieth took place without the involvement of *XXXIX Panzer Corps*, and the final drive to the Gulf of Finland and the close investment of Leningrad from the south were again carried out without the use of forces detached from Bock's command. In the south the battles around Zhitomir and Berdichev were emphatically resolved in German favour even as Hitler issued his directive on 19 July, and on 3 August *1st Panzer* and *17th Armies* met at Pervomaisk, thereby encircling 20 divisions drawn from three armies around Uman. With this particular pocket reduced by 5 August, Hitler nevertheless chose to persist with the diversion of forces from *Army Group Centre* to the south and even to widen the scope of operations by moving against Kharkov. Somewhat incredibly, the commander of the *2nd Panzer Army*, having spent weeks trying to prevent the diversion of part of his army southwards, suggested on 23 August to Hitler that the whole of his command be committed to operations in the Ukraine. The suggestion was accepted immediately. This development, which infuriated a bypassed *OKH*, was an indication that for all his authority, powers of command and settled priorities, Hitler did not direct a campaign that was being increasingly improvised as a result of conflicting personal influences and of events on the battlefield.

Although the response of Soviet armies on the border to the German attack was necessarily fragmented and varied, Soviet strategic policy in the first three months of the campaing was coherent and simple. Though *Army Group North*'s offensive carried all before it and forced Soviet armies in front of Leningrad to operate defensively, elsewhere Soviet intention, once the battle of the frontiers was lost, was to counter-attack and stabilise the front as far to the west as possible. The obvious political considerations that dictated this policy were underwritten by the economic and military need to keep the invader from the main centres of production and population. It formed no part of Soviet policy at this stage to trade space for time and the preservation of field armies. From a very early stage of the campaign the Stavka appreciated the weakness of the *Barbarossa* concept, the vulnerability of the flanks of three advances that were not mutually supporting, and resolved to act accordingly. The desire to stabilise the front and attack German flanks thus ensured that the Soviet response to the partial encirclement of its forces at Smolensk in mid-July was a series of counter-attacks intended not to extricate those forces but to reinforce them and restore the front. Only in the very last days before resistance in the Smolensk pocket ended on 5 August was an attempt made to withdraw formations from this cauldron, and by that stage the *2nd Panzer Army* was in the process of completing two more encirclements, around Roslavl between the third and eighth and at Krichev on the fourteenth.

Soviet policy survived defeat around Smolensk and the temporary exhaustion of reserves. It was the Stavka's intention to reinforce the Leningrad front, to counter-attack around Gomel and Yelnya while concentrating forces at Bryansk, and to hold existing positions around Kiev. What remained of Yelnya was retaken on 6 September, but this achievement counted for little when set against the consequences of trying to hold positions around Kiev for too long. By 31 August both the *17th* and *11th Armies* had established themselves on the Dnepr below Kiev, the *17th* having crossed the river at Kremenchug, while the 21st Army's advance towards Gomel was shattered by the *2nd Army*. The *2nd Panzer Army*'s southward advance, though fiercely contested in the last week of August, quickly assumed an ominous form in September, and with the loss of Gomel and Starodub on the twelfth the Stavka ordered and then counter-ordered a withdrawal of forces around Kiev. The final authorisation for a withdrawal was given on the nineteenth, the day resistance around Kiev came to an end though the city fell on the twenty-sixth, the Germans taking a total of 210,000 prisoners. In the northern Ukraine as a whole the Germans captured some 600,000 prisoners in what was one of the greatest encirclement battles of the 1941 campaign.

If the Stavka was slow to recognise and act upon events east of the Pripyat Marshes and on the Dnepr in the first 10 days of September, the German High Command was not. The anticipation of a Soviet collapse around Kiev, plus the favourable development of the battle around Leningrad where on 1 September the city was first taken under direct artillery fire, enabled Hitler to turn his attention back to *Army Group Centre* and the possibility of a resumption of the drive on Moscow. On the eighth, the day that the Finns reached the Svir and *Army Group North* cut Leningrad's last overland link with the outside world, Hitler issued a directive that ordered *Army Group Centre* to resume its offensive against Moscow, but this order was accompanied by instructions to *Army Group North* to reduce Leningrad by siege and to *Army Group South* to break into the Crimea and to continue its advance into the eastern Ukraine. This directive represented a dangerous widening of objectives and commitments without any corresponding increase of resources, but the full extent of this development was obscured by the fact that the German victory around Kiev had two immediate repercussions. The collapse of Soviet resistance around Kiev bared Kharkov and left the eastern Ukraine and the Donets open to a German advance. Second, and more importantly, defeat around Kiev cost the Soviet army the one clear advantage that it had held over the *Wehrmacht* since the start of the campaign, its superiority in numbers of men under arms. Defeat on the Dnepr coincided with a temporary exhaustion of Soviet reserve capacity, and left the Soviet army, already forced to conform to the enemy's initiative, to face the *Wehrmacht* on the basis of bare equality of manpower and considerable inferiority of technique and numbers of aircraft and tanks.

Hitler's decision of 8 September to reduce Leningrad by starvation rather than assault released armour from the north for the offensive against Moscow. By the time that *Operation Teifun* began between 30 September and 2 October *Army Group Centre* had secured a potentially decisive superiority of numbers over the four Soviet fronts between it and the capital. These four fronts had between them 15 armies and 80 divisions, but by October 1941 Soviet armies and divisions were mostly shadows of their July selves, and the 800,000 Soviet troops guarding the approaches to the capital represented probably no more than 25 effective divisions. With three panzer and two infantry armies under command, *Army Group Centre* had 14 armoured, nine motorised and 44 infantry divisions available for *Operation Teifun*. Even allowing for its formations to be at no more than 70 per cent establishment Bock's command had clear numerical superiority both overall and on selected axes of advance. The same situation prevailed in the south where, on the same day as the *2nd Panzer Army* opened *Operation Teifun* with an advance between Bryansk and Orel, the *1st Panzer Army* broke from the Dnepropetrovsk-Novomoskovk bridgehead and the *11th Army* crossed the lower Dnepr. By 8 October the 9th and 18th Armies, and part of the 12th, had been destroyed around Orekhov, and in the aftermath of this collapse the *6th Army* secured Kharkov on the twenty-fourth while the *17th Army* occupied Slavyansk. Without the means to contest the advances of the *6th* and *17th Armies*, the Stavka had no option but to trade space for time, but in front of Rostov-on-Don Soviet resistance was more substantial, and it was not until 21 November that *1st Panzer Army* secured this gateway to the Caucasus.

But if the Stavka could trade space for time in the south, a lack of depth in front of Moscow allowed it no such luxury there, the formal decision to defend the capital being taken on 10 October though all decisions made since July had tacitly been based on the assumption that Moscow would be held to the last. For its defence of the capital the Soviet army had certain advantages to set against German numerical superiority and possession of the initiative. By the time *Operation Teifun* opened summer was over, and the shortening hours of daylight heralded the approach of winter and less time for the conduct of operations. The seemingly endless forest in front of Moscow restricted German deployment in certain areas, and on the Smolensk–Moscow highway, as in front of Leningrad, Soviet forces were to fight a series of very costly but ultimately effective delaying actions against German infantry. Moreover, as the front moved closer to Moscow so factors of time and distance worked increasingly to Soviet advantage, the relative ease of Soviet resupply – and after mid-November reinforcement – contrasting sharply with the growing chaos behind *Army Group Centre* after mid-October. While the Germans were to blame many factors, and particularly the *rasputitsa*, for the failure of *Operation Teifun*, the fact was that logistically the German attack on Moscow was in difficulty even before it began. German rail and road facilities were not sufficient to sustain the offensive beyond Smolensk, and two months had not been long enough to accumulate at Smolensk stores sufficient to maintain 70 divisions in an advance of 240 miles in the autumn.

The last factor affecting the conduct of *Operation Teifun* was that with autumn came rains that turned the unmetalled roads between Smolensk and Moscow into a sea of mud – the *rasputitsa*, or season of slush. Throughout the summer German advances had been halted periodically by sudden, torrential downpours, only to resume after the sun had dried the ground. In October and November the hardening of the ground was dependent upon frost, and the first severe frost of the autumn had to await the night of 5/6 November. The onset of the *rasputitsa* on 8 October did not prevent *Army Group Centre* from securing the Kalinin–Naro–Fominsk–Aleksin–Tula line by the twenty-fifth, when *Operation Teifun* was temporarily halted in order to deal with the mounting administrative disorder behind the German front, but despite its allegedly baleful effect upon the German conduct of operations the *rasputitsa* did not prevent *Army Group Centre* winning what was perhaps the greatest single victory of the 1941 campaign.

The *2nd Panzer Army* completed the encirclement and destruction of three Soviet armies around Bryansk between 3 and 7 October, and on the seventh the *3rd* and *4th Panzer Armies* trapped six Soviet armies west of Vyazma when they combined to capture that town. Another week was to pass, however, before the Vyazma pocket was eliminated and the Germans subsequently claimed to have taken some 675,000 prisoners in these actions. Though this figure has been disputed in Soviet accounts, the twin facts that the German army sustained 134,999 battle casualties between 3 October and 17 November and that by mid-November the Soviet forces outside Moscow appear to have been reduced to just 90,000 men suggests that German claims had some substance, and that the battles around Vyazma and Bryansk were, for the Soviet army, the most costly of the 1941 campaign. Certainly the panic and unauthorised flight of people from Moscow in mid-October, which prompted the imposition of martial law on the capital on the nineteenth, indicates the Vyazma defeat was massive. By the end of October, certainly, when its left flank held Kalinin and the upper Volga and its right flank was just short of Tula, *Army Group Centre* seemed assured of taking Moscow with its next effort.

Just six armies remained to the defence of Moscow when *Operation Teifun* was resumed between 15 and 19 November, but from the start of this last attempt to secure Moscow before the onset of winter the Tula position, held by the 50th Army, resisted repeated attacks by the *2nd Panzer Army*. Tasked to link up with the *4th Panzer Army* at Noginsk, the *2nd Panzer Army* had to secure Tula in order to free its lines of communication, but despite all but encircling Tula the *2nd Panzer Army* could not oust the 50th Army from the town while its attempt to secure Kashira on the twenty-seventh resulted in an unusual and very sharp defeat at the hands of the armour of 2nd Cavalry Corps. With the implications of the *2nd Panzer Army*'s double failure at Tula and Kashira immediately obvious and no fuel sent forward to this army after the twenty-seventh, German hopes rested upon the *4th Panzer Army*, which secured and crossed the Volga canal at Yahroma on 25 November and then occupied Krasnaya Polyana and pushed patrols into Khimki, less than 15 miles from the Kremlin. On 1 December the *4th Army* made one final effort to break the Soviet front in the centre, around Novo Fominsk, but in the course of a four-day battle the 33rd Army prevented a breakthrough. On the fifth and only after protracted argument with *OKH*, Hitler recognised the inevitable, halted the offensive and ordered *Army Group Centre* to prepare to withdraw to safer defensive positions for the duration of the winter. By then, however, the 37th Army had retaken Rostov (29 November) and Soviet counter-offensives at both Leningrad and Moscow were less than 24 hours away.

On the Leningrad front Soviet efforts resulted in the partial lifting of the siege when Tikhvin was taken on 9 December after one month in German hands. After the loss of Tikhvin in November the resupply of Leningrad had been attempted by an improvised road from Zaborie to Novaya Ladoga and thence across Lake Ladoga itself, but it was not until 26 November that the first lorries had been able to cross the frozen lake and enter Leningrad. By retaking Tikhvin the Soviet army freed the railroad as far as the Volkhov and thus allowed lorry convoys to cross Lake Ladoga near its mouth. This success came too late, however, to prevent 250,000 citizens of Leningrad starving to death between December 1941 and February 1942, but for the moment the city was saved.

The Moscow counter-offensive similarly achieved only partial success, but the impact of even limited victory in December 1941 outside Moscow had profound repercussions. The Soviet counter-attack, delivered by the Kalinin, West and South-west Fronts along the length of the front from Kalinin to Yelets between the sixth and ninth, was initially directed against the salient made by the *3rd* and *4th Panzer Armies* north of Moscow. With no overall superiority of numbers, the 17 Soviet armies ultimately committed to operations in front of Moscow aimed to make a series of limited advances against the flanks of German armour and then to complete the latter's encirclement and destruction, but neither in the north nor around Tula were the Soviet armies able to realise their aim. In temperatures that reached −36°C and with snow to a depth of three feet German armour evaded encirclement with a clear demonstration of its superior technique over an infantry-heavy opponent. Neither Klin nor Ruza, two objectives immediately behind the front line on 6 December which had to be taken quickly if Soviet plans were to succeed, could be secured before 15 December, while to the south the *2nd Panzer Army*, though forced to abandon its positions around Tula when Yelets fell on the ninth, was able to fight its way slowly back to the Oka line.

By the end of December the whole of the northern salient east of the Starytsa−Ruza line had been cleared while in the south Kaluga and Belev had been recovered, but the limited nature of Soviet success in these operations can be judged from the fact that in the last three weeks of 1941, when *Army Group Centre* was on the very edge of defeat, German battle casualties totalled only 55,825 and the number missing showed no appreciable increase on previous returns. Even in defeat the German withdrawal was orderly, and over the next four months the *9th* and the *4th Panzer Armies* were able to retain Rzhev and Vyazma. Nevertheless, if a crushing defeat of *Army Group Centre* proved beyond the Soviet army in

December 1941 its victory was sufficient to ensure the immediate security of Moscow and hence the survival of the Soviet Union herself.

The Soviet victory outside Moscow in December 1941 condemned Germany to enter 1942 with unfinished wars both in the west and on the Eastern Front, indicating that the terms of reference of this war were not solely Hitler's to decide. On 6th November Stalin committed the Soviet Union to a war of annihilation: the counter-attack of 6 December was proof of intention. No less significant than notice that the Soviet Union was not going down to defeat in December 1941 was the fact that within two days of the start of the Moscow counter-offensive the Second World War acquired truly global dimensions with the start of the Pacific war.

3

GLOBAL CONFLICT

During 1942, when for a brief period it seemed possible that she might be called upon to shoulder the burden of both the European and Pacific wars, the United States planned to raise a 1,000-regiment army. In the event, however, the survival of the Soviet Union ensured that the main effort on land against Germany did not have to be undertaken by the United States, but while this correspondingly reduced the American military mobilisation to more modest proportions, the unchallengeable industrial superiority of the United States provides the Pacific conflict with an incomprehensible aspect. Wars are invariably fought long after their outcome has been decided: the outcome of the Pacific conflict was determined before its outbreak. Such was the disparity of resources available to Japan and the United States that the latter never doubted that she had the beating of Japan. Britain shared that certainty, and part of the Japanese High Command suspected that a war with the United States and Britain would prove a *kamikaze* effort on a national scale. By the rationalist, materialist criteria applied in Western societies the Japanese decision to go to war with the United States is inexplicable and, indeed, tantamount to criminal folly in that the decision to challenge the greatest industrial power in the world stemmed directly from her inability to bring her war in China to a successful conclusion.

Such a portrayal of events is neither mendacious nor an historical *reductio ad absurdum.* Japan's difficulties in 1941 that led her to attack Britain and the United States flowed largely from the fact that for all her success in 1937 and 1938 her 'special undeclared war' in China obstinately refused to be won, but by 1941 this had been overlaid by various other considerations, some of which were historical and of long standing while others related to events in Europe and the United States that provided Japan with a 'window of opportunity' yet at the same time threatened to close it upon her.

159

Historically, the situation that arose in 1941 was the result of Japan's desire to secure for herself the markets and resources of eastern and south-east Asia that she regarded as essential to her long-term security and status as a great power. Such acquisitiveness was accompanied by the belief that it was both her right and duty to reorganise eastern Asia under her own leadership after her expulsion of the Western imperial powers from the region, and for much of the inter-war period Japanese aspirations were directed inevitably against British interests, which were the most extensive of all the occidental powers. In political and military terms, however, Japanese ambitions clashed primarily with the interests of the United States in two respects that were critical to the unfolding of events in 1941. First, American–Japanese relations throughout the inter-war period were soured by intense, mutually reciprocated racial antagonism. Second, while the idea of a war with Britain gained widespread acceptance in Japan before 1941 the idea that war with the United States was inevitable provided the crucial rationale for the decision to go to war in September 1941. For more than three decades Japanese naval planning had been based upon comparison with the United States, and from 1916 the Imperial Navy had been planned, built, equipped and trained for a defensive war in the western Pacific against 'the hypothetical enemy'. In the second half of 1941, when events conspired to present Japan with the stark choice between acceding to American demands or going to war with the United States neither the nation nor the navy could admit that the massive sacrifices demanded of the Japanese people over the previous two decades had been for nought: the element of inevitability proved self-fulfilling in the summer of 1941 in the sense that Japan chose to fight rather than tamely submit to American dictation.

Japan's problems in China originated from the miscalculation, made in 1937, that military success would quickly enable her to impose a settlement that would ensure her effective control of her greater and more populous neighbour. Chiang Kai-shek's withdrawal into the interior after the loss of the Wuhan cities in late 1938 left the Japanese armies in control of China's major centres of production, ports and sources of revenue yet denied them the means of enforcing a military solution to their self-imposed China problem, but a refusal to share power with possible rivals to Chiang Kai-shek predictably prevented Japan from sponsoring alternative Chinese regimes that could attract widespread popular endorsement. It was not that Japan did not try to establish rival bodies to the Chiang regime; perhaps inevitably, given the rivalry between Japanese military commands in China, after December

160

1937 there were never less than two client Chinese governments in addition to the puppet government in Manchoutikuo and the princes of Inner Mongolia. Indeed, the manner in which the Japanese dealt with the potential alternatives to Chiang Kai-shek's government provides the reason for their ultimate failure not just in China but throughout the so-called 'Greater East Asia Co-Prosperity Sphere' after 1942.

The provisional government of the Chinese Republic was installed in Peking on 14 December 1937 by the *North China Area Army* while on 28 March 1938 the *Central China Expeditionary Army* contributed the new Reformed Government of the Republic of China. Both were filled with nonentities who posed no threat to the Japanese exercise of real power, yet when Wang Ching-wei, for a long time second only to Chiang Kai-shek in the Kuomintang hierarchy, defected in 1939 and made himself available to the Japanese, their response was to deny his central government that they inaugurated at Nanking on 1 April 1940 control of Hopei, Shantung, Shansi and Kaifeng: these were left under the control of a Peking-based advisory authority that was, predictably, neither an authority nor capable of an advisory role.

The divide-and-rule policy, the determination to retain power by a refusal to share it, ultimately had its inevitable result: power itself diminished. In part the Japanese problem in dealing with any client regime in China was insoluble. Chinese officials lacked the skills needed to administer effectively and Japanese personnel were infinitely more honest and capable than their opposite numbers, but Japanese rapacious-ness in exploiting Chinese resources and labour and the sheer savagery with which the Japanese army dealt with the civilian population provided the lie to Japanese claims that they sought to create 'an Asia for the Asiatics'. Just as Nazism was to find in occupied Europe, the assumption of racial superiority and the right to rule other peoples denied the conqueror the ability to offer potential friends genuine cooperation and friendship. In the critical period between 1937 and 1941 Japanese attitudes prevented them from developing, in the area under their command, a credible alternative to the Chungking regime.

The fact that victory in China proved elusive left Japan with a double problem on the Asian mainland after November 1938. Failure by definition imposed on Japan the dual commitment to continue operations against Chiang's field armies but also to maintain her present occupation of conquered provinces. By 1941 this commitment was to cost Japan a ruinous $5,000,000 a day, but with 500,000 troops in China and Manchoutikuo her hold on her conquests was never more than tenuous. The efforts made in 1937 and 1938 had involved a thinning of forces in

Manchoutikuo, which in turn resulted in a revival of banditry and insurgency, and in northern and central China a numbers-to-space ratio of one soldier per hectare of conquered China left Japan with an insoluable security problem. Conventional operations continued nevertheless, indecisively around Changsha in 1939, but even in this year the illogical pattern that was to impose itself so fatefully upon events in 1941 asserted itself: unable to secure victory in the north and along the Yangtse, the Japanese sought to extend the war to the south. In February 1939 naval forces occupied Hainan and subsequently sought to establish themselves around Nanning, but it was not until the spring of 1941 that the Japanese army undertook a series of amphibious operations that brought it control of the more important coastal areas of southern China.

Stalemate in China further compounded Japanese difficulties in dealing with the Soviet Union, and, indeed, Japanese problems on this score worsened and became acute in the course of 1939. From 1933 onwards border incidents between Japanese-Manchurian and Soviet forces occurred with increasing frequency, but while Soviet aid to Chiang Kai-shek after August 1937 added a certain edge to proceedings it was not until July 1938, around Changkufeng on the Korean– Soviet border, that fighting assumed really serious proportions. On this occasion, firm action by Tokyo and the fact that the fighting quickly went against the *19th Infantry Division* resulted in a very speedy liquidation of the incident, but in 1939 the Japanese army's Mongolian ambitions provoked a much more serious clash, one that had important implications for the course of the Second World War.

In May 1939 detachments from the *Kwantung Army* occupied positions around Nomonhan, near the Khalkhin Gol, to a depth of some 10 miles inside eastern Mongolia. Despite and perhaps because of events in Europe, the Soviet Union did not hesitate to accept this challenge to her primacy in Mongolia. While the Japanese ultimately deployed the equivalent of an infantry corps from the *6th Army* around Nomonhan, by August the Soviet army had concentrated, some 400 miles from the nearest railhead, one motorised, two infantry and two cavalry divisions, plus armoured and mechanised battalions, against the Japanese positions in front of Nomonhan. Beginning on 20 August, the 1st Army, in a series of deliberate, systematic attacks, destroyed the *Komatsubara Force*, and Mongolia was cleared of Japanese forces with the total destruction of the *6th Infantry Regiment* on the Hulasmen between 28 and 31 August.

The consequences of this defeat for the Japanese were three-fold and immediate. At the tactical level, the Soviet victory was the result of overwhelming material superiority, and recognising this fact the Japanese

162

army set about developing armoured forces of its own. More importantly, defeat ended ideas of fighting the Soviet Union even while the war in China remained unfinished, and it confirmed the conventional wisdom in Tokyo that the Soviet Union was not to be underestimated. This was a lesson that remained with the Japanese even in 1941 when the Soviet Union seemed to stagger to inevitable defeat. But more importantly, the day – 23 August – when Japanese flank positions around Nomonhan collapsed under the weight of Soviet armoured attacks was the same day that Ribbentrop arrived in Moscow to conclude the Nazi–Soviet pact, and Japanese outrage at German behaviour at this time of humiliation was very real. The German action cut the ground from under the feet of those within the Japanese High Command who wanted to conclude a binding alliance with Germany, and it persuaded the government of General Abe Nobuyuki, when the European war broke out, that Japan's best interests were served by waiting upon events.

Japan was not blind, however, to the fact that her interests would not be served by an Allied victory, but apart from squeezing the British and French from certain of their holdings in China she made no sustained attempt to profit from Anglo-French distraction until June 1940. But with the collapse of France in the spring the Japanese wasted no time in seeking to complete the isolation of Chiang Kai-shek's regime. Even before the French signed the armistice at Réthondes they had been forced to agree to the closure of the Hanoi–Nanning railroad, and in July the British were similarly obliged to close the Burma Road between Lashio and Chungking. In September the Vichy authorities gave way to the Japanese demand for occupation rights in northern Indo-China, but it was as a result of her association with Germany in the Tripartite Pact that same month that Japan was to come into possession of intelligence material that lured her further southwards and in so doing set in train the events that led to the outbreak of the Pacific war one year later.

This material, taken by a German raider from the British ship *Automedon* in the Indian Ocean, was the record of the British war cabinet meeting of 12 August 1940 that endorsed a chiefs of staff report which concluded that Britain had to avoid war with Japan, could not oppose any Japanese move against Indo-China or Siam, and could not send a fleet to the Far East in the event of war with Japan. In addition, the record revealed that the British High Command believed that while an inability to send a fleet to the Far East placed an additional premium upon the defence of Malaya as opposed to Singapore, Malaya itself was indefensible on the basis of available resources. These documents were passed to the Japanese presumably because at this time Hitler wanted Japan to attack British possessions in the Far East as the means of increasing indirect pressure on his last enemy in Europe. If indeed this was Hitler's hope he was not to be disappointed. The exact fate and influence of the *Automedon* documents once they began to circulate within the Japanese High Command are somewhat obscure, but their arrival in the relevant ministries would appear not unrelated to three developments: the start of jungle training on Formosa by the army in spring 1941; the intensification of pressure for a move in south-east Asia by the navy after February 1941; and the first serious consideration by the fleet command of a suggestion made in October 1940 by the naval general staff for a pre-emptive attack on the US Pacific Fleet at Pearl Harbor.

The last two developments were of the utmost significance. Since the end of the Second World War Western histories have for the most part carried as an unquestioned fact the relative moderation of the Imperial Navy, its being dragged unwillingly into war by a boorish army, and its misgivings about the outcome of a war with the United States. This portrayal of the Imperial Navy has rested in large measure upon the known views of its Combined Fleet commander, Admiral Yamamoto Isoroku, but the process whereby the opinions of Yamamoto have become the alibi of the Imperial Navy is distinctly misleading: the navy was by no means as cautious and moderate as its reputation suggests; it had spent 20 years preparing for a war with the US Navy and was not convinced that it was doomed to lose such a war; and in 1941 it was the navy, not the army, that forced the pace of Japanese policy towards south-east Asia and led Japan to the impasse of the summer. Certainly, the naval high command had hesitated before 1939 and again in 1940 on the question of the German alliance, and until late 1940 it was strongly opposed to any action that might result in war with both Britain and the United States, but its assumed moderation on account of its attempts to restrain the army in China stemmed primarily from its view that the war in China was not the war Japan had to fight. From the early 1930s, when it converted from coal to oil, the Imperial Navy's concern was with south-east Asia. The *Automedon* documents appear to have provided the Imperial Navy with its first glimpse of the opportunity that now presented itself, and the insight into the extent of British weakness removed a crucial restraint on its ambitions. After February 1941 Yamamoto, hitherto very cautious in his calculations about south-east Asia, pressed this option upon the Japanese naval ministry with increasing firmness, and the latter, in its dealings with the army, similarly pressed for a more assertive policy in the south, doing so in the sure knowledge that Britain could not oppose it.

This increasingly aggressive stance towards south-east Asia was to produce the crisis of July 1941 which in turn led ultimately to war because it ran in parallel with the slow unfolding of a crisis that arose from two matters: the US naval construction programme of July 1940 and the progressive imposition by the United States of restrictions on her trade with Japan after September 1940. In terms of the deterioration of American–Japanese relations in the course of 1941 the two American actions were of roughly equal importance, but in terms of the timing of their separate impact the naval programme was the more significant because, by the summer of 1941, it brought the Imperial Navy to the realisation that it faced a 'go now or never' dilemma. In 1941, as Japan neared completion of her 1937 programme and a 13-month mobilisation of the fleet, the Imperial Navy realised that by the end of the year it would stand at 7:10 relative to the US Navy, but that in order to maintain itself at that level it would have to double its projected 1942 programme. It calculated, however, that even the existing provisions of that programme were beyond Japan's resources, and that as American programmes were completed so its strength relative to the US Navy would fall to 50 per cent in 1943 and to a disastrous 30 per cent in 1944. The 1:2 ratio was critical in Japanese calculations because the Imperial Navy believed that this represented the minimum on which it could fight a successful campaign in the western Pacific. On the basis of these various estimations a pre-emptive attack on Pearl Harbor became not simply attractive but essential – not only as the means of demoralising the Americans at the start of a war and of eliminating the only force capable of disputing Japanese control of the western Pacific but also of putting back American preparations by perhaps 10 years.

The idea of attacking Pearl Harbor at the start of a war for control of south-east Asia did not command unquestioning acceptance within the Japanese High Command. In the heated arguments that took place before Japanese strategic policy was settled, Yamamoto's demands for this operation were resisted by those who believed that no American government could take the United States into a war in defence of British and Dutch colonies in south-east Asia. There can be little doubt that these individuals were correct: isolationist sentiment and congressional hostility would have prevented the Roosevelt administration from going to war for Batavia and Singapore. But what decided the Japanese High Command to move against the United States was the belief that war between the two countries was inevitable and had to be induced rather than delayed, plus the situation created by the total trade embargo imposed upon Japan on 25 July by the Roosevelt administration as a result of the announcement on the twenty-third of the creation of a joint Franco-Japanese protectorate over Indo-China and the Japanese occupation of bases around Saigon.

The Japanese decision to force the French into these concessions was part of a more assertive policy pursued by Japan in south-east Asia after January 1941. In that month Japan brought to a halt a four-week war between Siam, which was bound to her by a non-aggression treaty concluded on 12 June 1940, and the French, and then imposed a treaty that provided Siam with most of her demands. In April, as the prerequisite for any move in the south, Japan concluded a non-aggression treaty with the Soviet Union, and in early June further pressure on the French yielded Indo-China's surplus rice harvest. On 25 June, three days after the start of *Operation Barbarossa*, the two Japanese services agreed to press the south-east Asia option before turning to deal with whatever situation was created by the Nazi–Soviet conflict. With this agreement the navy was ceded the power of decision, and on 21 July it formally decided to accept the risk of war with the United States over southern Indo-China.

The Japanese occupation of northern Indo-China in September 1940 had resulted in the United States imposing restrictions on certain items of her trade with Japan, and the navy suspected an American reaction to its proposed acquisition of bases around Saigon. It did not know, however, that not merely was the Roosevelt administration aware of Japan's intentions through its ability to read Japanese diplomatic signals but that in effect the Americans had made southern Indo-China its *ne plus ultra* line. The American response to the Japanese move was to freeze Japanese assets and to end all trade with Japan. With the British and Dutch falling into line with American moves, the Imperial Navy was presented with its acid test. As diplomacy revealed that the American price for a resumption of normal trading arrangements was Japan's withdrawal from her mainland conquests, so the impossibility of avoiding war with the United States impressed itself on the Japanese High Command.

Until 25 July a number of options were open to Japan. She could try to use her alliance with Germany to defy the United States or she could abandon her alliance as the price of an accommodation with the Americans. She could try to deal with just the British and Dutch, by threat or by war, without involving the United States, or she could act against all three. Such choices effectively ended on 25 July. For the previous decade Japanese industry had depended upon captive markets on the mainland, and by 1941 Manchoutikuo's vastly favourable trade balance in effect financed Japan's deficit trading with the outside world. For economic reasons alone, Japan could never accept American terms, yet these terms inadvertently provided Japan with her operational timetable. Between September 1940 and June 1941 the United States prohibited trade with Japan in a growing number of commodities, but the July ban automatically included oil, and Japan depended upon the United States for 80 per cent of her oil imports. In June 1941 a joint services' study had concluded that on the basis of projected consumption and production Japan would exhaust her oil stocks in June 1944 if all imports were stopped immediately.* Thus after July 1941 every month that passed without her securing an alternative source of oil was one month that lessened Japan's capacity to resist an American military superiority that could only grow. From this simple fact stemmed the ultimate absurdity implicit within Japanese policy: unable to win a war in China, Japan sought to extend conflict to south-east Asia, and in order to secure south-east Asia Japan deliberately chose to try to fight the greatest industrial power in the world to a standstill in a war of attrition in the central and western Pacific.

In the course of 1941 the hardening American attitude towards Japan ran in tandem with a deepening commitment to Germany's enemies, and this increasingly obvious hostility to the Axis powers on the part of the Roosevelt administration was the product of a single calculation: at a time when the United States' population of 140,000,000 compared to the 95,000,000 of Japan and 85,000,000 of Germany, American security interests could only be compromised by a German victory in Europe and Japanese supremacy in the Far East. The United States rightly feared a realignment of resources and power to her disadvantage if the Axis powers won their respective wars, but in moving to oppose Japanese ambitions American calculations were flawed. The policy of the Roosevelt administration was one of deterrence based upon the future certainty of overwhelming American military power: it lacked the present means of effectively resisting Japanese aggression in the event of deterrence failing. Further, the Roosevelt administration failed to read Japanese intentions and capabilities correctly. It was very slow to realise that its

---

*This was the first time that the Japanese armed forces had considered the oil problem, and in a very close parallel to aspects of German planning for *Operation Barbarossa* the findings of this study were set aside, a new study by the navy was ordered, and its conclusions were accepted when it glibly reported that while oil stocks would be severely depleted in the period between September 1943 and September 1944 rising production from the Indies would see Japan through this danger period. In reality, even the June study proved wildly optimistic, and Japan in effect exhausted her oil reserves in October 1943.

trade embargo denied the Japanese any choice but to fight, and in common with the British High Command it did not set any great store on Japanese military capacity. In the long term this dismissive Anglo-American attitude was vindicated: Japan could not sustain a protracted war effort. But in the short term the Japanese armed forces were far more formidable than the British and Americans suspected, and as events were to show, in 1941 Japan had better assessed relative strengths and weaknesses than her potential enemies.

Facing the Japanese in south-east Asia in autumn 1941 were the equivalent of single divisions in Burma and Hong Kong, two divisions in the Dutch East Indies, three divisions in Malaya, and four divisions in the Philippines. After meeting their various commitments in Korea, Manchoutikuo, China and Indo-China, the Japanese had the equivalent of eleven divisions for operations throughout south-east Asia by Terauchi's *Southern Army*. With a single regimental group, supplemented by marine units, earmarked for operations against various islands in the central and south-west Pacific, Terauchi's command consisted of four armies only two of which were at full establishment in the initial phase of operations. Simultaneous with the attack on Pearl Harbor the *25th Army* was to land in northern Malaya and southern Siam while units from the second-echelon *15th Army* were to secure the Kra Isthmus. The *14th Army* was to occupy the islands between Formosa and Luzon and to land in northern and southern Luzon and in southern Mindanao. The *25th* and *14th Armies* were then to secure Malaya and the Philippines and subsequently to flesh out the *15th* and *16th Armies* for their respective operations in Burma and the Dutch East Indies, the *16th Army* also being scheduled to receive the *38th Infantry Division* (from the *23rd Army*) after it secured Hong Kong.

Even with various attached units, *Southern Army* possessed no margin of numerical superiority over its various enemies, but while in every theatre Japan's enemies possessed an absolute superiority of numbers the Japanese held a potentially decisive numerical advantage in every campaign for three reasons. Whereas Japan as the aggressor held advantages bestowed by the choice of time and place of attack, her enemies were obliged to deploy defensively and thus disperse their forces with no guarantee of timely and effective concentration once the Japanese showed their hand. Also, the primacy of seaborne communications throughout south-east Asia and the vulnerability of defensive positions to outflanking movements from the sea rendered local Allied superiority of numbers of little account in the face of Japanese superiority of numbers in the air and at sea. Finally, the Japanese held the advantage of strategic surprise in that while their various enemies anticipated a Japanese attack they could not envisage either the extent of first-phase Japanese operations or the speed with which the Japanese were able to develop their various offensives. This fundamental underestimation of Japanese capabilities by the Allies was crucial to the unfolding of the south-east Asia campaign after 8 December because from its outset underrated Japanese forces seized the initiative, denied their enemies the time and means to reinforce their garrisons on any significant scale, and secured their objectives more quickly than they themselves had anticipated.

The extent of these Japanese advantages, plus the formidable level of attainment of the Japanese armed forces in 1941, can be gauged by the Pearl Harbor attack, failure though it was. Thus far in the European war no naval operation had involved the use of two fleet carriers or more than a dozen obsolescent biplanes in a single offensive mission. For the attack of 7 December 1941 the Imperial Navy committed its six front-line fleet carriers and no fewer than 355 modern, high-performance monoplanes, of which 272 were bombers, in a two-wave attack. Operating some 3,900 miles from their main base and 6,500 miles from northern Malaya, the Japanese achieved complete strategic and tactical surprise, the American ability to read part of Japanese signals traffic not being sufficient to allow the sighting of Japanese forces in the Gulf of Siam to be interpreted as warning of an impending attack on Pearl Harbor. This attack sank or damaged 18 warships and auxiliaries and accounted for 347 of the 394 aircraft on Oahu at the time of the strike. To a world accustomed to measure naval power by battleship numbers the loss of five represented a shattering defeat for the United States, but in reality American losses were relatively light and of no particular strategic and tactical significance. The lost battleships, and only two proved total losses, were old, slow and no match for the new generation of fast battleships then coming into service, and, crucially, no carrier, heavy cruiser or submarine was so much as damaged in the Japanese attack. Concentration on the prestige targets in Battleship Row meant that the greater part of the Pacific Fleet emerged from the attack unscathed and, more importantly, the Japanese made no attempt to follow their attacks on the warships with strikes against Pearl Harbor's base facilities, the destruction of which would have forced the Pacific Fleet's withdrawal to California. For all its apparent success, the Japanese attack on Pearl Harbor failed either to neutralise the Pacific Fleet or to destroy American capacity to wage war, while for the United States the loss of 18 units and the equivalent, by 1943, of two days' aircraft production was a small price to pay for the sense of national unity and purpose generated by this attack.

Westwards across the Pacific, and into 8 December, Pearl Harbor ran in tandem with landings by the *15th* and *25th Armies* between Prachuab and Kota Bharu. Only at the latter did they encounter difficulty as a result of opposition and bad surf conditions. With one formation moving on Bangkok by sea and rail, the Japanese overawed Siam, secured the railroad south from the capital, and provided themselves with a crucial advantage of timing over British forces in northern Malaya. As early as 1937 the British had realised that because the fortress guns made a direct attack on Singapore impossible, any Japanese move against the base had to be directed through Terengganu, Kelantan and southern Siam. The denial of Singora and Patani in southern Siam was therefore essential to Singapore's defence, but in December 1941 the occupation of these two ports in southern Siam could not be attempted by a Britain intent on avoiding war and denying Japan a pretext for hostilities. The landings of the *5th Infantry Division* in southern Siam soon after midnight on 8 December were therefore unopposed by the British, and the Japanese formation, with light armour support, was able to develop a twin offensive from Singora towards Jitra and from Patani towards Betong. In front of both places on the eleventh it encountered British formations that had been held on the border for advances into Siam and which, as a result, had not been able to prepare defences in depth in either sector.

With the failure to secure southern Siam ahead of the Japanese the British High Command in Malaya had either to reinforce the 11th Indian Division and hold the *25th Army* in the border area or withdraw quickly from the north to a shorter defence line served by a shorter line of communication. Political considerations, the desire to retain the rice-surplus provinces of the north, and the need to deny the Japanese the northern airfields precluded a withdrawal, but the slow British response to events and the speed with which the Japanese advanced into Malaya produced a disaster on the borders from which the British never recovered.

On the eleventh the *5th Infantry Division* encountered British defenders on both its axes of advance, and on this day and the twelfth it sliced through the British positions in front of Betong. Defeat forced the defenders westwards to cover Baling, and with this success Japanese forces turned south along the track to Grik, thereby threatening to secure Kuala Kangsor and thereby turn the whole British position north of the Perak. In front of Jitra at the same time, however, the 11th Indian Division sustained a defeat that compromised the British ability to hold northern Malaya even without the defeat around Betong. Both at Jitra and at Gurun (14/15 December) the 11th Indian Division lost single brigades – plus its cohesion and much of its confidence – even before the Japanese were able to develop the full weight of their attacks. On the seventeenth British formations in the north were given permission to withdraw to the Perak if necessary; four days later, as the threat from Grik materialised, they were granted permission to withdraw behind the river.

At this stage it was the British intention to fight a series of delaying actions at Ipoh, Kampar, Tapah and Bidor on the main road south to Kuala Lumpur while defensive preparations were put in hand in central and southern Malaya. But the pattern of operations established by the Japanese advance via Grik could not be confined to the north because British forces, once behind the Perak, could not cover all the roads and tracks available to the Japanese advance. Moreover, after the fall of Penang the whole of Malaya's west coast was vulnerable to infiltration, the Japanese having brought assault boats across the Kra from Singora for this very purpose. Thus British attempts to stand on certain selected positions were in constant danger of being outflanked, initially by the Japanese advance down the lower Perak to Telok Anson by 2 January. With no attempt until then to withdraw the 9th Indian Division from eastern Malaya to support its sister division on the main road it was only a matter of time before the strains imposed by constant withdrawals and rearguard actions on the 11th Indian Division ended in disaster. This duly occurred on 7 January when two brigades were annihilated at the Slim river in central Malaya.

By this time the British situation in Malaya was beyond recall, but so, too, was the American position in the Philippines, and indeed such was the ineffectiveness of American resistance on Luzon in the first month of the Pacific war that the Japanese High Command recast its plans in order to develop its offensive into the Indies without awaiting the end of the Philippines campaign rather than adhering to its original phased time-table. Though not intended, the effect of this decision was to leave the American forces in the Philippines 'to wither on the vine', but this bypass strategy miscarried in that the final collapse of American resistance in the Philippines proved much delayed. Continued American resistance on Luzon until April was important in terms of American domestic morale and was used as the basis of the fatuous claim that this resistance had saved Australia from invasion, but the military logic of this campaign suggests that American defence of the Philippines was no more effective than that of the British in Malaya.

The initial Japanese moves in the Philippines took the form of an unopposed landing on Batan, a strike by carrier-borne aircraft against the

Davao seaplane base, and a massed attack by naval bombers from Formosa on the Clark and Nichols airfields in central Luzon. In one of the more obscure episodes of the Pacific war, this attack caught the greater part of the American air force in the Philippines on the ground and undispersed eight hours after the Pearl Harbor attack. 103 American aircraft were destroyed and American strength in the Philippines was reduced to some 50 aircraft by the end of the eighth day. With air superiority thus ensured, the *14th Army* thereafter undertook a series of small landings in northern Luzon on the tenth, at Legaspi on the twelfth, and at Davao on the nineteenth that provided the Japanese with an overwhelming positional advantage and stranglehold on the Philippines even before the *48th Infantry Division* came ashore at Lingayen Gulf on the twenty-second and the *16th Infantry Division* landed in Lamon Bay on the twenty-fourth.

The Japanese expectation was that the Americans would stand in defence of Manila, and their plans had been devised to ensure the dispersal of American forces and the rapid encirclement of the capital, but on 23 December the US commander in the Philippines, Lieutenant-General Douglas MacArthur, ordered Manila to be abandoned and his forces to begin a withdrawal into the Bataan peninsula. Through a combination of the singular ineffectiveness of the Japanese air force in reporting and disrupting American movements after the twenty-third, an effective covering operation by the forces facing the *48th Infantry Division* as it came south from Lingayen Gulf, and the failure of the *14th Army*, in its obsession with taking Manila, to realise what was happening to its front, the Americans were successful in withdrawing some 80,000 troops into Bataan by 2 January, although virtually no effort had been made to stock the peninsula in advance of their arrival.

The completion of the American withdrawal into Bataan coincided with the fall of Manila and the Japanese decision to strip the *14th Army* of its air support and the *48th Infantry Division* for operations in the Indies. At this stage the Japanese did not anticipate any problems in wrapping up the campaign on Luzon, but the change of plan left the *14th Army* outnumbered 3:1 on Bataan and unable to complete the speedy destruction of the garrison. It was nevertheless able to breach the American main line of resistance astride Mount Natib between 10 and 22 January, the Americans completing their withdrawal to the Bagac–Orion reserve line by the twenty-sixth. But despite major assaults either side of Mount Samat and three separate attempts to land on the southern tip of the Bataan peninsula the depleted *14th Army* lacked the strength to force the surrender of the American I and II Corps. Obliged to assume the defensive after 10 February while fresh formations were moved to Luzon, the *14th Army* relied upon a two-month siege to weaken the defenders before resuming the offensive on 3 April. The rapid collapse of American resistance on the Bagac–Orion line led to the general surrender of the Luzon force on the eighth.

While events were unfolding in central Luzon the Japanese completed the conquest of Hong Kong between 8 and 25 December; they used a detached force to secure Miri on the fifteenth and Kuching on the twenty-fifth and also occupied Jolo on Christmas Day. Heralding the approach of the Indies campaign, Jolo was secured in order to serve as a staging post for an offensive through the Makassar Strait just as Davao was to provide support for an advance through the four seas that wash eastern and southern Celebes. It was the Japanese intention to develop a synchronised offensive either side of Celebes in order to divide Allied attention and resources, each effort being made by ground and naval forces that would be re-employed in successive operations. This offensive opened on 10/11 January with attacks on Tarakan and Menado, just four days before a joint Allied command in south-east Asia – the ABDA (American–British–Dutch–Australian) Command – was activated in Java.

With no reserve, minimal air power and a scratch assortment of naval units at its disposal, this new command could do no more than preside over an unfolding disaster in the 41 days of its brief existence, although the second Japanese operation in the Makassar Strait, at Balikpapen on the twenty-fourth, was opposed by Allied air and naval units. Six Japanese transports and auxiliaries were destroyed or damaged in engagements that included the first American surface action since 1898, but the Japanese landing at Balikpapen was accompanied by an assault on Kendari and, off eastern New Guinea, by the occupation of Rabaul and Kavieng. Poossession of Rabaul provided the Japanese with a base from which to move against the Solomons and eastern New Guinea, but with attention centred on the Indies the Japanese, supported by carrier forces, moved to secure Amboina and its airfield on the last day of the month.

By the 31 December, while the Americans fought to maintain themselves on the Bagac–Orion line, the British rout in Malaya was completed with the last of the formations on the peninsula withdrawn to Singapore Island on this day. Even before the Slim river débâcle the British had taken the decision to abandon central Malaya, but despite the equivalent of two divisions arriving at Singapore after 3 January the losses incurred at the Slim, plus the amphibious threats developing along the Malaccan coast, rendered northern Johore indefensible. The 8th Austra-

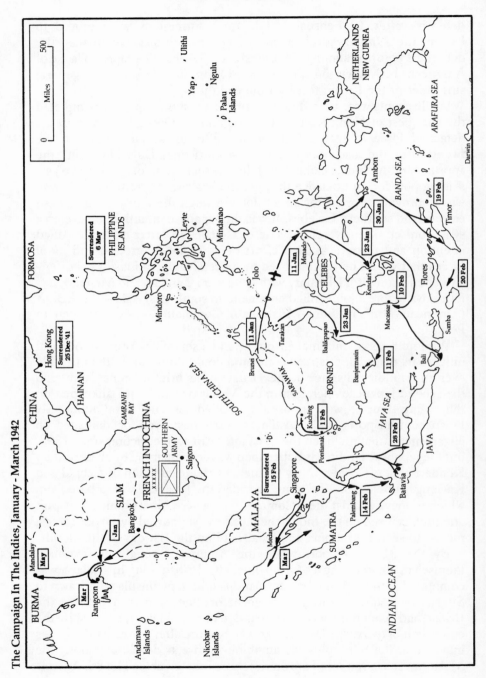

The Campaign In The Indies, January - March 1942

lian Division inflicted a sharp defeat at Gemas on the *5th Infantry Division* when it moved into Johore on 14 January, but with the *Imperial Guards Division* simultaneously breaking through British positions on the lower Muar and landing a battalion behind Batu Pahat on the sixteenth, the Australians found themselves further from the crucial crossroads at Kluang and Ayer Hitam than the Japanese and were forced to withdraw. Though the Japanese thrust on Ayer Hitam was delayed – at very heavy cost to the defenders – around Parit and Pelandok between 20 and 23 January long enough for the 8th Australian Division to avoid encirclement from the west, the occupation of Endau by the *18th Infantry Division* after an advance from Kuantan had the effect of turning the eastern flank, thereby ending any hope of standing in defence of southern Johore. The British inability to keep the Japanese at arm's length from Singapore and acceptance of defeat on the mainland carried the obvious corollary: Singapore could not be denied the Japanese. The defeat of the British forces gathered on Singapore Island was explicit in the withdrawal from the mainland and the destruction of the causeway between Johore Bahru and the island, which carried the water supply of Singapore itself.

The reduction of Singapore was considered by the Japanese to be the prerequisite for operations against Sumatra, Java and the islands of the lesser Sundras. On 8 February, the day when the *25th Army* opened its attack across the Straits of Johore, Japanese marines from Kendari secured Makassar. With the occupation of Banjarmasin on 10 February by a force that advanced overland having first secured Laut Island, the Japanese were able to dominate the approaches to Java, and on the fourteenth, with the fall of Singapore less than one day away, Japanese airborne and amphibious forces landed at Palembang in southern Sumatra. The occupation of the town and its refineries, and the Allied evacuation of southern Sumatra, were completed on the seventeenth. For the naval side of the Palembang operation the Japanese provided substantial escort forces, including a light fleet carrier, but the main Japanese naval effort was made to the east when, within a matter of 24 hours, aircraft from six carriers and from Amboina and Kendari flattened much of Darwin and Japanese forces came ashore on Bali and in Dutch and Portuguese Timor. With Japanese forces also working their way around the west coast of Borneo, the defeat of the Allies on Java was assured well before the *2nd Infantry Division* came ashore between Bantam Bay and Eretan Wetan and the *48th Infantry Division* landed at Kragan on the night of 28 February/1 March.

Various Japanese landings in the Indies had been disputed by Allied naval forces but in no instance successfully. By the time that Japanese

175

forces gathered around Java and ABDA Command dissolved itself Allied warships had to seek a decisive action, but their attempt to get amongst the transport carrying the *48th Infantry Division* to Kragan only resulted in the loss of two cruisers and three destroyers, one-third of the force remaining to them by the end of February. After this action in the Java Sea surviving Allied warships north of Java were quickly hunted down by Japanese naval forces while to the south Japanese carrier forces accounted for 175,000 tons of Allied shipping and various warships trying to escape from the island, bombing Broome on 5 March for good measure. Only at Bantam Bay did Allied cruisers manage to engage Japanese transports, and paid the inevitable price for their fleeting success; the *2nd Infantry Division* was able to establish itself ashore in western Java across a wide front and to take Batavia on the fifth. With the Dutch surrendering throughout the Indies on the ninth and the other Allied forces doing the same on the twelfth, the Japanese were able to proceed with the unopposed occupation of northern Sumatra by the *Imperial Guards Division* on the twelfth and of northern New Guinea between Boela and Hollandia between 31 March and 19 April.

Simultaneous with their operations in Malaya, the Philippines and the Indies but only when success in Malaya was assured, the *15th Army* opened its own campaign in Burma and effectively won it with the capture of Rangoon on 8 March. With detached units securing Point Victoria on 16 December, Tavoy on 19 January and Mergui on the twenty-fourth, the *15th Army* opened proceedings along the trail to Moulmein at the end of January against a defence divided between this front and the Shan States and obliged to hold and cover Rangoon. Probably the best military course open to the defence would have been to stand west of the Sittang, in open country where the armour that was arriving at Rangoon in February 1942 could have been used to greatest effect, but unless forces could be gathered to block a Japanese advance into central Burma via the Sittang valley a policy of defending Burma west of the river ran the risk of losing the country *en passant*. In any event, political considerations dictated that Burma be defended east of the Salween, but the decision to fight for Moulmein, the Salween and the Bilin left an overcommitted and understrength 17th Indian Division to face two Japanese divisions able to develop an attack on separate axes, thereby repeating the situation that had arisen in Malaya. These advantages of position and initiative more than compensated the *33rd* and *55th Infantry Divisions* for the fact that in the two months after they crossed into Burma both were seriously understrength and between them had the numbers of a single division.

176

Initial Japanese advantages of surprise and concentration resulted in the rapid capture of Moulmein (31 January), but the British attempt to hold Martaban, on the direct route to Sittang, was quickly frustrated by the *33rd Infantry Division*'s crossing the Salween at Pa-an. With this formation seeking to envelop the open flank, a series of actions was fought as British forces withdrew to Bilin. There, in accordance with orders not to retreat, British forces came close to ruin in the course of a three-day battle (16–20 February) before resuming their retreat to Sittang. This withdrawal was complicated because as a result of outflanking movements that provoked the British decision to break off the Bilin action the Japanese were closer to Sittang than the British at the start of this withdrawal and were in constant contact with British columns during the retreat. The 17th Indian Division was nevertheless able to break clear of the Bilin but in an episode that was Burma's equivalent of the Slim river disaster, the one bridge over the Sittang was blown on the night of 23/24 February with most of the division trapped on the wrong side of the river and under attack by an enemy with little propensity to take prisoners.

The destruction of the 17th Indian Division effectively ended British hopes of retaining Rangoon, which was the key to control of Burma. Because of the total absence of road and rail links between India and Burma British forces in Burma could be reinforced and maintained only through the capital, and while four brigades were moved to Burma before 7 March the weakness of British forces between Rangoon and the Sittang after the loss of the 17th Indian Division rendered the city indefensible against an enemy that intended to secure Rangoon, to advance up the Irrawaddy valley with the *33rd Infantry Division* and up the Sittang with the *55th*, and to reinforce these formations with forces released from other theatres. After crossing the Sittang on 2 March the Japanese secured Pegu and then, fortunately for the British, carried out a wide encirclement of Rangoon before taking the city on the eighth after an approach from the north-west. In executing this extravagant manoeuvre the Japanese left the road north from Rangoon unguarded with the result that the equivalent of two British divisions were able to escape from Rangoon behind the rear of the *33rd Infantry Division* as it advanced across the Rangoon–Tharrawaddy road.

With the capture of Rangoon the Japanese all but tripled their forces in Burma in the next two months, their original formations being brought to full strength and reinforced by the arrival of the *18th* and *56th Infantry Divisions* and two tank regiments. With such strength the Japanese were able to develop their offensives into central Burma despite the presence, in the Sittang valley, of Chinese forces that were sent into Burma after January to bolster the defence. The Chinese were to move three armies, each the equivalent of a division, into eastern Burma, but their divisions in the Sittang valley were committed piecemeal and while the 200th Chinese Division fought desperately for Toungoo for 12 days it could not prevent the town and its bridge falling to the *55th Infantry Division* on 31 March. With British formations in the Irrawaddy valley unable to contain the Japanese division that opposed them, the capture of the Toungoo bridge allowed the *15th Army* to destroy the whole of the Allied left flank with an offensive on three fronts, a fourth being added in late April when Siam committed three divisions of its *Northwest Army* to clearing operations around Kengtung in the eastern Shan States.* With the *56th Infantry Division* conducting a lightning campaign through the mountains and annihilating Chinese formations in its path, Lashio was secured on 28 April before the *18th* and *55th Infantry Divisions* were able to occupy Mandalay. By this time Allied forces were withdrawing from Burma on all fronts, just ahead of the pursuing Japanese and the start of the monsoon. By very narrow margins the Allies managed to keep ahead of both, but hundreds of thousands of civilian refugees perished in their attempt to reach the safety of India.

By 4 May Japanese forces had reached the lower Chindwin and the last British formations in Burma were in the process of withdrawing to Imphal, but by this time a new phase of the Pacific war was about to begin with history's first carrier battle. This clash had been foreshadowed since the start of 1942 when, with Japanese arms successful throughout south-east Asia, the attention of the Japanese High Command had turned to the question of how the war was to be continued once the initial phase of conquest was complete. Before the war Japanese plans envisaged the creation of a defensive perimeter around Japanese possessions and conquests in south-east Asia and the central and south-west Pacific, the Japanese expectation being that American counter-attacks would be ensnared amidst the web of bases that would be established until such a time as the Americans, tiring of their losses, would come to accept a compromise peace that would confirm Japan in her gains. In early 1942 the flaws in this concept – the lack of resources to create and maintain

---

*This little-known episode had one very important sequel. The Chinese 6th Army did not withdraw completely from the Shan States when the *Northwest Army* entered Burma, and the two armies settled down to what amounted to a joint and very lucrative occupation of the area. When the Siamese withdrew from the Shan States at the end of the war the Chinese, who were in effect beyond the reach of Chungking, remained, and the various arrangements made during and after the war still exist in the form of the Golden Triangle.

bases along the length of a 6,000-mile perimeter; no guarantee that the fleet would always be available for counter-attack; and the inferiority of any single base to any force committed against it – were not apparent to the Japanese High Command, but two facts had become clear. First, on New Year's Day 26 states declared adherence to the Declaration of the United Nations that they would wage total war until victory was won over the Axis powers. Thus, while operations then in hand throughout southeast Asia would go forward to an end both sides could foresee, the United States served notice on Japan that the war would be fought to a finish, not to a stalemate. Second, the first weeks of the war revealed the extent to which the outcome of the conflict would be determined by carrier formations. The Japanese were able to secure Guam on 10 December, various islands in the Gilberts, and, after a false start, Wake on the twenty-third without interference by American carrier forces, but American operations against the Marshalls, Rabaul, Wake and Marcus between 1 February and 4 March, while inflicting minimal damage, served to underline the threat presented by these formations and the extent of the failure of the Pearl Harbor attack.

These two developments had the effect of convincing the Japanese naval command of the need for offensive action in order to bring American carrier forces to battle, where they would be destroyed, and to compel the United States to come to terms despite her declared intentions. In March, Yamamoto settled for an attack in June on Midway Islands in order to force the Pacific Fleet to give battle. In the course of that month his staff devised an extremely complicated plan for an attack on the Aleutians to serve as bait, a carrier strike to neutralise Midway's defences, and the occupation of Kure and Midway by Japanese air and ground units. With submarines covering the approaches from Pearl Harbor, Japanese forces gathered off Midway would then fight and win the ensuing battle with their opposite numbers, after which the carrier forces would proceed to Truk. In July Japanese forces would secure New Caledonia, Fiji and Samoa, and in August Johnson, the main Hawaiian islands being the obvious target of future operations.

By any standard this plan of campaign was a poor one, involving as it did a dispersal of effort in June over a quarter of the Pacific; the division of the *Combined Fleet* into a plethora of tactical formations that were not mutually supporting; the commitment of a carrier strike force at the point of contact with virtually no reconnaissance capability; and a fatal ambiguity of aim in that the carrier force was to neutralise Midway and destroy American carrier formations with no guarantee that the battle would develop in a way that gave it time to deal with its enemies in turn.

But for all its faults the plan was forced upon the naval staff, and events only served to add an extra dimension to Japanese preparations: the Doolittle raid on Tokyo, Kube, Yokohama and Nagoya by medium bombers from an American carrier on 14 April simultaneously halted opposition to the Midway plan and convinced the naval high command of the need to eliminate the obvious and immediate challenge to Japanese primacy in the western Pacific. Yet in the immediate aftermath of this raid a decision was taken in response to events in the south-west Pacific that undermined the whole Midway plan. While the first American carrier operations amounted to no more than pinpricks, on 10 March two carriers combined to inflict significant losses on Japanese assault shipping supporting operations in Huon Gulf. Indeed, such were the losses inflicted upon the admittedly small resources available to the *4th Fleet* during this attack that it was obliged to abandon its intention to proceed with the occupation of Tulagi in the Solomons and Port Moresby in New Guinea. The fact that the Midway operation would not begin until late May prompted the decision to detach two carriers to support this two-pronged operation, which was rescheduled for early May. Given the intelligence appreciation that two American carrier operations continued to operate in the south-west Pacific, the Japanese decision to proceed with the seizure of Tulagi and Port Moresby and to use just two carriers for the operation was neither here nor there: the operation had to be properly invested or postponed. Moreover, as the plan for the assault of Tulagi and Port Moresby took shape it incorporated many of the bad features of the Midway plan and some of its own, namely tasking an inadequate air group at Rabaul to ensure the neutralisation of Port Moresby and assault landings against targets within range of enemy land-based bombers by forces that were to advance to contact in front of their carrier support – and with the whereabouts of American carrier forces unknown.

Flawed though both the Moresby and Midway plans were, their greatest single weakness was that both were known to the Americans. During the first months of the war US naval cryptanalysts slowly worked their way into Japanese signals until in April they could confidently predict the general Moresby plan and in May had recovered virtually every aspect of the order of battle and timing of the Midway plan. As a result, the Americans were able to deploy in the Coral Sea in May and off Midway in June formations that were to fight and win history's first carrier battles. In the course of the May action the two carriers committed to the defence of Port Moresby first harried the shipping used to secure Tulagi (4 May) and then sank a light carrier (7 May) before clashing with

180

their opposite numbers on the eighth. In the course of this action the Americans mauled both Japanese air groups and severely damaged one Japanese carrier. The loss of one American carrier equalised the tactical account, but while the Japanese were forced to abandon the enterprise their real loss lay in that their self-imposed timetable for Midway prevented their undamaged carrier being readied with a new air group in time for this operation. In an odd, perverse way, the Americans could better afford in May 1942 the loss of a carrier than the Japanese could afford to have a carrier out of action for a month; the failure to have a fifth carrier with the strike force bound for Midway was crucial because this ship and its aircraft represented the margin of superiority that the Japanese should but did not have off Midway on 4 June. In fact the absence of the carriers committed to the Coral Sea from the Midway order of battle need not have mattered. For the complete Aleutians–Midway operation the *Combined Fleet* had eight fleet and light fleet carriers with a total of 319 aircraft and overall numerical superiority but not where it mattered: at the point of contact its four carriers and 229 aircraft met three American carriers with 234 aircraft at a marked tactical advantage as a result of US intelligence success.

This disadvantage and the flaws within the Midway plan came together on the morning of 4 June when the Japanese carrier force despatched almost half its aircraft against Midway before conducting reconnaissance and failed to find either of the two American carrier formations off Midway before these had flown off the strike missions that were to destroy three of the Japanese carriers. While the Japanese carriers beat off attacks by Midway-based aircraft and the first carrier strikes, the very last attack by carrier aircraft found and wrecked the Japanese strike force just when it was about to fly off its own strike against A American carrier force. The one Japanese carrier that escaped destruction continued the battle and its aircraft severely damaged one American carrier on two separate occasions during the afternoon. It was the Japanese misfortune, however, that these partial successes were misinterpreted as two carriers savaged, this error being compounded by the failure to realise that three and not two American carriers were in action. By the time these errors were appreciated and the surviving Japanese carrier had tried to put distance between herself and the Americans, it was too late to seek safety in flight. American aircraft caught this carrier just before sunset and left her sinking like her three colleagues: all four Japanese carriers sank or were scuttled during the night.

Though Japanese surface forces tried to fight a night action after the loss of their carriers and then lure the Americans westwards for two more days in the hope of exacting some compensation for their defeat, the only result was the destruction of a Japanese cruiser and damage to three other units. A Japanese submarine accounted for the American carrier that had been damaged on the fourth, but this belated success* did not affect the outcome of the battle: Midway was the first irreversible Axis defeat of the war even though it did not provide the Americans with the initiative. Midway resulted in a rough equalisation of forces in the Pacific and left the two sides evenly matched in the struggle to seize the initiative in the next phase of operations.

In this next phase, however, Japan would have none of the advantages with which she had begun the war and which in large part accounted for her success in its first six months. Her peacetime intelligence sources had been lost and those available after December 1941 were wholly inadequate. In future she would not be opposed by understrength, poorly trained and ill-equipped divisions, as had been the case throughout south-east Asia after December 1941. The element of surprise had been largely dissipated by mid-1942. After June 1942 she never had the time that had been available before December 1941 to develop her plans effectively. But more importantly, Japan, for all her success, lacked the financial and industrial resources to expand her war production to levels needed to sustain the conflict she had initiated. Moreover, before the war her fleet and plans evolved in a way that precluded their being restructured to take account of the situation that presented itself after Midway. Various weaknesses of procurement, particularly of aircraft and auxiliaries, could not be made good; the inadequacies of the submarine arm could not be rectified; the smallness of pre-war naval aviation precluded rapid and effective expansion after 1942. In terms of strategic policy after Midway the navy was in the ironic position of having pioneered a naval *Blitzkrieg* yet being forced to rely upon a Maginot Line strategy for the defence of Japan's conquests. In terms of national resources, organisation and plans, Japan was poorly placed to regain the initiative after June 1942 though this was not readily apparent until November.

The underlying cause of the Allied disaster throughout south-east Asia in early 1942 was that the outbreak of war resulted in an immediate expansion of Allied responsibilities without providing the Allied powers

*The *I-168* torpedoed the *Yorktown* on the sixth but the carrier did not sink until the seventh. It was a measure of the *Combined Fleet*'s tactical failure at Midway that the *Yorktown* was the only American warship attacked in the whole of the battle, although one destroyer was sunk by a torpedo aimed at the carrier.

with the time and resources necessary to meet them. The most obvious and far-reaching of these was the American acceptance of responsibilities in the south and south-west Pacific that ended, on 14 February, with the United States assuming responsibility for the defence of Australia. Yet this expansion of American commitments into what had been a traditional British preserve was not limited to the Pacific and Australia: it extended to the North Atlantic as a result of the declaration of war on the United States by Germany and Italy on 11 December 1941.

These declarations of war by Germany and Italy did no more than formalise the situation that had existed in the North Atlantic since September 1941. American escort of British convoys and the extension of the American security zone into the eastern Atlantic in the course of 1941 indicated a widening American commitment to Britain that Hitler, after showing considerable restraint, regularised in December 1941 even though Germany had no formal obligation to join Japan in her war with the United States. In so doing, Hitler resolved the greatest single difficulty facing the American High Command after Pearl Harbor. For a year American war plans had set down the principle that in the event of war in two oceans the main American effort would be directed against Germany. This definition of priorities was based upon the calculation that whereas any number of Japanese victories could be reversed and the defeat of Japan would not ensure that of Germany, a German victory could prove irreversible but her defeat would doom Japan. The Pearl Harbor attack left the United States at war with Japan but the Roosevelt administration was in no position to secure a declaration of war on Germany and Italy from Congress. Hitler resolved an insoluble problem for the administration by his declaration of war on 11 December, but by his action he ended those very conditions that had been the basis of his earlier victories. To date German success stemmed from Hitler's ability to isolate successive conflicts, thereby ensuring German superiority and victory on every battlefield: his declaration of war on the United States was to escalate the scale and potential intensity of warfare to levels that Germany could not sustain. With his armies being savaged around Moscow, December 1941 was hardly the time for Hitler to add the world's greatest industrial power to the ranks of his enemies, but there was a logic to this decision that was a mirror image of Japanese calculations. In the course of conferences in 1941 Hitler, under no illusions about American enmity, frequently expounded on the theme that American mobilisation would be complete after 1943 and that therefore Germany had two years in which to subjugate Europe before

American power could make an impact on the battlefield: in December 1941 Hitler made the same decision as had the Japanese three months before, to go to war with the United States before she grew into her full strength.

The German–Italian declarations of war on the United States had the effect of increasing American responsibilities in the North Atlantic by ending the immunity of shipping in the western Atlantic from attack: the United States was forced to fight for those rights that she claimed and enjoyed before the outbreak of hostilities. But the extension of the war brought to an end the advantage that the British had secured for themselves in the eastern Atlantic in the second half of 1941, partly because of American activity in the western and central Atlantic. This activity had forced German submarines either to work in the eastern Atlantic, where British escorts were at their most numerous and effective, or to extend their operations into more distant waters where contact with American ships, and British escorts, could be avoided. In the event the Germans followed both courses, and under their own terms of reference, because 'tonnage warfare' drew no distinction between sinkings in different theatres, diversion into secondary waters represented no loss if the previous rates of sinkings could be maintained.

In real terms, however, the second half of 1941 represented a major German reverse because not only did sinkings in the North Atlantic fall in this period – from 345 ships of 1,800,190 tons in the first half of the year to 151 ships of 621,510 tons – but because compensatory results could not be secured outside this critically important theatre. In fact, merchant losses in British waters, the Mediterranean, South Atlantic and Indian Oceans showed a 66.3 per cent fall between half-years, from 1,082,830 tons to 364,897 tons. Moreover, the decline of Allied losses after June 1941 was accompanied by a rise in U-boat losses with the result that two of the most accurate indicators of the course of the battle – the exchange rate between merchantmen and submarines and the return secured in terms of operational U-boat numbers – both showed the battle in the Atlantic moving in favour of the British in the course of 1941. In the first half of 1941 submarines claimed 21.9 victims for each loss they sustained, but by the second half of the year this figure had fallen to 7.3 and in November and December it touched 2.6 in each month. In January 1941 0.95 merchantmen were sunk for every operational U-boat, but by December this figure had shrunk to 0.29. Though German losses remained small – just 35 in the whole of 1941 and 66 between 3 September 1939 and 31 December 1941 – the loss of 15 in the last two months of 1941 confirmed an ominous long-term trend for the *Kriegsmarine*. Its submarines could not maintain their previous rates of sinkings as the number of independent sailings declined nor could they secure returns outside the North Atlantic to make good their decline in that theatre, yet any resumption or intensification of effort in the North Atlantic was certain to result in major losses. The German naval staff was not slow to recognise the long-term implication of these developments, and in March 1942 it predicted the ultimate failure of its offensive against shipping.

The German declaration of war upon the United States completely altered this situation because lack of convoy off the American coasts presented German submarines with the chance to claim victims at little risk to themselves. The *Kriegsmarine*, however, was ill-placed to take advantage of this opportunity. At the end of 1941 it had 91 operational U-boats, but of these 26 were in, or bound for, the Mediterranean, six were off Gibraltar, four were deployed defensively off Norway and only 22 were in the Atlantic. In January 1942 it had but five boats with which to begin operations off the American coast, but between 12 and 31 January these sank 46 merchantmen, and as more boats were committed to the western Atlantic losses rose until they reached 121 merchantmen in June. In May and June, the Gulf of Mexico and the Caribbean were worked by no fewer than 20 U-boats, virtually the entire German strength in the Atlantic, and in these two months they accounted for 148 ships of 752,109 tons. In the event, June 1942 proved to be the high point of the German effort at sea in the Second World War: 173 merchantmen of 834,196 tons were sunk by all forms of Axis action with German U-boats accounting for 144 merchantmen of 700,235 tons for the loss of three of their number.

June 1942 was the most disastrous single month in a singularly disastrous period for the Allies. Between September 1939 and November 1941 monthly shipping losses exceeded 400,000 tons on eight occasions, but every month between December 1941 and June 1942 saw this figure surpassed and, indeed, in five successive months Axis activity accounted for more than 650,000 tons of Allied shipping. Yet however heavy the losses of this period, there was some comfort for the British in the fact that except off the American coast shipping enjoyed a remarkable degree of immunity from attack and destruction. Though this was in large measure the result of German concentration against shipping sailing independently in the western Atlantic, only two merchantmen were lost in the North Atlantic other than in American waters in January 1942; in June only three. In July, however, the Americans introduced the

185

interlocking convoy system between the St Lawrence and the Caribbean, an action that is usually presented as having led to an immediate reduction of Allied losses. Allied shipping losses did show a decline from the peak June 1942 figures in the next five months yet even in this period the average monthly losses remained above 658,200 tons – only some 33,000 tons below the monthly average for the first half of the year and a figure exceeded only in one month before February 1942.

The introduction of convoy along the western seaboard had the effect of reducing losses in those waters and of diverting the main battle to the central Atlantic. Faced with convoys throughout the North Atlantic, the U-boats had no real incentive to waste time on passage to American waters and therefore gathered for a resumption of battle in mid-ocean, beyond the range of Allied shore-based aircraft. In fact, the German submarine service might have been well advised to continue its effort in the western Atlantic because throughout 1942 American and Canadian escort forces were poorly organised, equipped and trained, lacked experience and were wedded to a flawed doctrine that placed the destruction of submarines above the safe and timely arrival of shipping. As it was, the resumption of battle in mid-Atlantic saw the U-boats all but maintain their previous rate of sinkings but at the cost of their own losses returning to December 1941 levels. In the first six months of 1942 the *Kriegsmarine* lost 21 submarines, while in the second half of the year 66 U-boats were sunk, 14 inside the Mediterranean. These losses, the first consistently heavy U-boat losses of the war, did not prevent a massive expansion of the U-boat arm, from 91 boats in commission in January 1942 to 212 in January 1943. This tripling of the arm in 1942 in large measure explains why the U-boats were able to maintain their high rate of sinkings after June: German operational numbers in the North Atlantic doubled between June and December 1942.

This expansion of the German submarine service during 1942 was countered on the Allied side, although the number of British escorts in the North Atlantic actually declined in the second half of 1942 because of the needs of the *Torch* landings in North Africa in November. But this decline, from 384 operational units in a total of 465 on 1 January to 332 operational ships in a total of 425 on 31 December, was only temporary, though it largely accounts for the submarines' richest monthly harvest of the war, some 729,160 tons of shipping in November 1942. More significant was the fact that overall British numbers were rising through-out 1942 and that a new type of escort with a corvette's handling capabilities and endurance and the speed to match a surfaced submarine had gone to sea in the spring, though it was to be a full year before it appeared in any numbers in the North Atlantic. Moreover, by 1942 escorts were becoming efficient in the use of radar and radio direction-finding equipment that had entered service in 1941 while in the course of 1942 their effectiveness was enhanced by the introduction of fast-sinking, more powerful depth charges.

While patrol aircraft similarly benefited by the introduction of radar, lights and shallow-pattern depth charges, the most significant technical development of 1942 was the entry into service in October of the Type 144 asdic set. This was a major improvement over earlier asdic sets in that it operated through two planes and could provide very accurate readings of the bearing and depth of a submerged submarine, and, crucially, could hold a contact as range closed. With no corresponding technological developments available to the U-boat, British escort forces came to enjoy a growing technical superiority over German submarines in the course of 1942.

To this was added an equally pronounced superiority of technique and training. By mid-1942 the British had established their various training schools and programmes and had begun to acquire a formidable body of combat experience. The lightness of escort losses – just 11 destroyers and six corvettes in the North Atlantic and British home waters in the whole of 1942 – ensured a continuity of experience that was denied German submarines, the losses of which were total. Indeed, in terms of training and experience the position of the U-boat service by late 1942 was little short of disastrous because the massive expansion of the U-boat service during the year was possible only by dilution: it was not uncommon for German submarines at this time to embark upon their operational careers under the command of captains with only two operational cruises to their credit. Thus by the end of 1942, with American shipyards poised for the first time to build ships more quickly than German submarines could sink them, the situation in the Battle of the Atlantic heavily favoured the Allies despite the loss of 1,664 ships of 7,790,697 tons in the course of the year.

At the time, however, this was not readily apparent to the Allies. The various imperfections of British organisation, the fact that the scale of protection afforded a convoy seldom exceeded five escorts, and the rising number of U-boats that could be directed against single convoys meant that losses amongst escorted shipping rose in the second half of 1942 despite the great improvement of equipment, training and organisation amongst British forces in the course of the year. Indeed, such were the losses sustained by convoys in late 1942 as a result of German retention of numerical advantage and the tactical initiative in individual convoy battles that in early 1943 the British were presented with their supreme crisis of the war – the seemingly inevitable collapse of the convoy system in the North Atlantic. By that time, however, they and the Americans stood on the verge of an overwhelming victory in the Mediterranean theatre of operations.

The Mediterranean theatre was last considered in connection with the German occupation of the Balkans and the Axis advance to the Libyan–Egyptian border in spring 1941. For the next three years German primacy in the Balkans remained undisputed other than by indigenous guerrilla forces, but in North Africa and at sea mastery was disputed with neither side able to secure the upper hand until the last quarter of 1942. Thereafter the Allies secured the initiative and within six months cleared North Africa and stood poised to carry the war into southern Italy.

The story of the Mediterranean campaign has been beset since the end of the Second World War with two historical problems. Because this was the only theatre in which British forces were involved in major operations against the European Axis powers in 1941 and 1942, the Mediterranean theatre of operations has come to assume a strategic significance that it did not possess in those years and a status that rivals that of the Eastern Front – the old idea of Alamein and Stalingrad being the turning point of the European conflict. Second, Anglo-American histories have always been concerned with the 'great commanders' interpretation of events and with the portrayal of war as a gladiatorial contest between national champions. The most obvious example of this is MacArthur, but in the Middle East theatre this approach to the presentation and interpretation of history has resulted in the depiction of events as a personal competition between Montgomery and Rommel. While not denying the importance and often crucial influence of individual commanders in the conduct of operations, total warfare in the twentieth century has been waged by states, societies and systems, not individuals whose reputations have rested in large measure upon media presentation to societies needing heroes. Moreover, the British portrayal of this campaign in personal terms has had a deleterious effect in concealing certain unpalatable facts about the British conduct of operations in North Africa in 1941 and 1942. Presentation of Rommel as a tactical genius has served to divert attention from fundamental weaknesses in the British army's organisation and doctrine that led to its being consistently outfought by enemies that were outnumbered in men and equipment. It has also served to gloss over the failure that allowed Italian intelligence to pass to Rommel, often on a daily basis, reports of British deployment, strength and intentions from a compromised American source. While this obviously poses the question of just what is left of Rommel's reputation if he was so informed in the period of his greatest success – the end of which coincided with the loss of this insight into British orders of battle – the removal of the personality element from the story of the campaign allows the course and outcome of events to be placed in their proper perspective in terms of relative importance and of alliance and national policies.

Between June 1940 and October 1942, and indeed until May 1944 under Anglo-American terms of reference, the Mediterranean theatre was significant because only there were Allied and Axis ground forces in contact with one another. In this initial period Britain, expelled from the continental mainland and unable to carry the war to Germany, was obliged to fight where she could rather than where she would. As a consequence most of her military effort against the European Axis powers and their associates was invested in North Africa against the lesser of the Axis, Italy, which was supported by her senior partner to the extent of a single corps in the combat zone. The limited extent of German involvement in this theatre is evidence that the Mediterranean campaign was a sideshow, of very limited strategic relevance. Compared to the 34 armies that did battle on the Eastern Front in June and July 1941, North Africa absorbed the attention of perhaps 10 divisions at this time, and if this massive imbalance between these two theatres narrowed after October 1942 then it did so only to a limited extent that left the relative importance of the two campaigns unaltered. No number of British victories in North Africa before November 1942 could have affected the situation in Europe because, however important North Africa was in terms of its being strategically part of Europe, the superiority of German lines of communication across the continent over British maritime lines of communication around Europe and Africa provided Germany with the means of ensuring the timely movement of forces sufficient to prevent defeat in the Mediterranean theatre: it was not until November 1942, by which time the *Wehrmacht* was over-committed on the Eastern Front, that the deadlock in the Mediterranean theatre was broken by an operation that effectively doubled the size of Allied forces in North Africa and extended the combat zone along the length of the North African coast.

The Mediterranean theatre nevertheless possessed a complexity that belied its importance because operations involved an inter-dependence of military, naval and air efforts unmatched in any other theatre, the south-west Pacific included. This complexity stemmed from both sides' total dependence upon supply by sea for the means to wage war in a desert, and herein a neat contrast was provided by a major British undertaking some 12,000 miles from source and a substantial Italian effort, made on the basis of inferior national resources and power, at a distance of 600 miles from Italy's southern ports. What should have proved a decisive Axis advantage of position was counter-balanced, however, by the British ability to operate air, surface and submarine forces from Malta against Italian shipping. The Italian superiority of position and warship numbers was offset by inadequate air support for most operations, by the Italian navy's poor anti-submarine capabilities, and by its lack of equipment and training for night fighting. British advantages bestowed by retention of Malta were similarly diluted by the limited offensive power that could be concentrated on Malta, by the fact that many of the submarines based in the Mediterranean in 1940 and 1941 were large oceanic boats ill-suited for operations in restricted waters, and by the scale and effectiveness of Axis air attacks on Malta. Conversely, of course, retention of Malta imposed responsibility for supplying the islands when the approaches were dominated by Axis aircraft based in Sardinia, Sicily, southern Italy and Crete. The very extent of these holdings, however, prevented the Axis from exacting full benefit from this positional advantage because the Italian air force and the one German air corps in the theatre after 1941 lacked the strength simultaneously to neutralise Malta, cover shipping, support the armies in Libya and attack strategic and tactical targets in Egypt.

On land, similar checks upon relative advantages existed. British numerical and German tactical superiorities cancelled one another, and both sides could not escape the limitations imposed by the 'diminishing force of the offensive' in their respective exploitation of alternating success. The drag of logistics during an advance and the strengthening of the enemy during a withdrawal imposed a natural balance in the course of the various advances to and from El Agheila after December 1940, yet the possession of Cyrenaica was crucial to both sides alike for the outcome of the struggle in North Africa. Possession of Benghazi and Tobruk allowed the Axis to concentrate their resupply forward: possession of the airfields of the Jebel Achdar area enabled the British to provide any attempt to resupply Malta from the east with air cover for the duration of most of the voyage. With corresponding disabilities stemming from the enemy occupation of Cyrenaica, both the Axis and the British main efforts on land were directed to the holding of this vital area.

While history has correctly paid considerable attention to the struggle for control of Cyrenaica in terms of its effect upon the outcome of the

Mediterranean campaign it has seldom, if ever, acknowledged that no less important in deciding this campaign in favour of the Allies was French retention of the Maghreb between June 1940 and November 1942. Had the Axis occupied French North Africa in the summer of 1940 or had the French adopted a hostile attitude to the British after the attack on Mers el-Kebir in July 1940 it is hard to see how the British could have held Malta. As it was, the British ability to operate in the western Mediterranean and to dominate Cyrenaica at various times allowed the supply of Malta to continue for three years after the Italian entry into the war, and herein lies a double irony. First, Malta proved the key to the whole campaign in the Mediterranean and British retention of the islands was decisive, yet before the war the British had planned to abandon Malta on the grounds that it could not be sustained in the face of Italian air power. Second, while the battle forces of the British and Italians ultimately proved marginal to the outcome of the campaign, the Italian desire to retain 'a fleet-in-being' and caution in committing the fleet to the struggle for the central Mediterranean ultimately ensured its defeat without battle.

The campaign in the Mediterranean theatre between December 1940 and October 1942 divided into five phases of alternating success. The initial phase, between December 1940 and June 1941, witnessed the rout of the *Xth Italian Army* in Egypt and Cyrenaica, the British advance to El Agheila, and the Axis counter-offensive that drove the British back to the Egyptian frontier and resulted in the isolation and siege of Tobruk. At sea this period saw the *Luftwaffe* dominate the central and eastern Mediterranean, its greatest success being registered in April off Greece and in May off Crete. In this phase Axis air power neutralised Malta, Matapan being an isolated British victory in what was otherwise a period of constant Axis success.

The second phase, between June 1941 and February 1942, saw fortune change sides, though the initial exchanges on the Libyan–Egyptian frontier – the *Brevity* counter-attack of 15/17 May and the *Battleaxe* offensive of 15/17 June – gave no indication of future trends as Axis forces easily contained both British efforts. In the second half of 1941, however, the weakening *Luftwaffe* commitment in the Mediterranean in the wake of *Operation Barbarossa* led to Malta's revival and the return of light forces to the base in October. As a result, Axis shipping losses, which had totalled 21 per cent in October, rose to 63 per cent in November, such losses causing Axis forces in North Africa to postpone an assault on Tobruk first from September and then from October, until

191

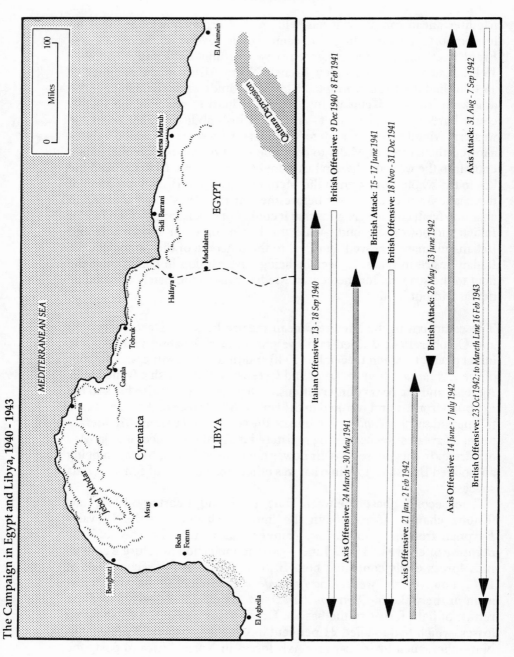

The Campaign in Egypt and Libya, 1940 - 1943

by November the 8th British Army was ready to begin a major offensive to effect the relief of Tobruk.

This effort, *Operation Crusader*, began on 18 November with attacks by two British corps on separate axes of advance, the British intention being to pin German armour in the south, bypass Sollum and Bardia and raise the siege of Tobruk. In the initial exchanges Axis forces outfought five poorly coordinated British armoured columns and brought the 8th Army to the verge of defeat, but the *Crusader* offensive was saved from disaster first by German forces having to reimpose the siege of Tobruk after it was partially raised on 21 and 27 November and then by the German mistake in trying to encircle British formations without having the means to accomplish so ambitious a task. German distraction and error provided the British with time to recover from their initial reverses, and thereafter British numerical superiority imposed its own logic on the battlefield. On 4 December, after failing to relieve the Italian garrisons at Bardia and Sollum, *Panzerarmee Afrika* abandoned its positions in front of Tobruk and withdrew to a line west of the port. On the seventh it began to withdraw to Gazala, the siege of Tobruk being raised after 242 days on the eighth. Threatened in their new positions by an outflanking attack, Axis forces voluntarily abandoned the Gazala line on the fifteenth and by New Year's Eve were back at El Agheila, from where Rommel and his German formations had set out nine months earlier.

Operation Crusader represented a partial British victory but one that coincided with Hitler's decision on 2 December to check any further deterioration of the Mediterranean situation by redeploying *Fliegerkorps II* from the Eastern Front to Sicily and with the eclipse of British naval power in the theatre. In September, partly to stiffen Italian resistance and partly to order to avoid confrontations with the Americans in the North Atlantic, U-boats had been ordered to the Mediterranean for the first time since November 1939, and in November the newcomers sank a fleet carrier off Gibraltar and a battleship off Tobruk. In December, at a time when disaster overwhelmed British arms in and off Malaya, Italian frogmen sank two battleships in Alexandria harbour while Force K, the surface formation operating from Malta, was for practical purposes removed from the British order of battle after blundering into a minefield off Tripoli. Though British sinkings of Italian shipping in December 1941 were heavier than in any of the three previous months, these British losses, plus the return of the *Luftwaffe* to Sicily, clearly pointed to a revival of Axis fortune in the new year, and indeed as early as 21 January, after replenishment on a short line of communication from Tripoli and just four days after Bardia and Sollum fell, Axis forces resumed the offensive.

193

Like *Operation Crusader* before it, this offensive lacked the means to register decisive results, and having cleared Benghazi on January 29 it was halted around Gazala in the first week of February.

The third operational phase, between February and May 1942, witnessed a stalemate on land as both sides prepared for a resumption of the offensive, but in the central Mediterranean the battle swung decisively against the British. The return of the *Luftwaffe* to Sicily resulted in a quickening offensive against Malta, the heaviest German attacks being timed to coincide with sailings to Libya. This belated coordination of the Axis effort produced immediate results: British air power on Malta was neutralised and in April the submarine flotilla began to withdraw to Alexandria. April 1942 proved the most successful month of the war for Italian sailings to North Africa, while in the previous month Axis forces enjoyed one of their most successful operations against a Malta convoy. In March 1942, with supplies on Malta running low six months after the arrival of the *Halberd* convoy, the British attempted to bring a four-ship convoy to Malta from the east. Italian warships so delayed the progress of this convoy in an action in the Gulf of Sirte that aircraft accounted for all four merchantmen, although some 5,000 tons of supplies were recovered from two ships sunk on arrival in harbour. In the event, however, these few thousand tons of stores were just enough to see Malta through the next three months until the tide turned, finally and decisively, in favour of the Allies.

Impressive though Axis success in this period was and despite the fact that the worst British defeats in North Africa still lay in the future, by May 1942 the basis of a conclusive Allied victory in this theatre had been established as a result of various errors on both sides, inside and outside the Mediterranean. Perhaps the most important of these was the least obvious – the Japanese raid on Ceylon in April 1942. For all its apparent success, this raid achieved nothing of strategic value at a time when British India and the western Indian Ocean, with its routes to the southern USSR and Egypt, were defenceless. Any interruption of British military sailings to Egypt at this time would have rendered impossible the British recovery in the eastern Mediterranean in the second half of the year, yet this unique opportunity to destroy the British position throughout the Middle East, and perhaps even drive Britain from the war, passed by default. More immediately relevant, however, was the Axis failure in the first half of 1942 to settle aims and priorities in the Mediterranean theatre. Hitler's decision in December 1941 to send an air corps to Sicily was a stop-gap, an opportunist's response to an irritant in a secondary theatre of operations. One air corps was a substitute for a policy because as Rommel's command prepared to renew its offensive its terms of reference allowed for an advance to the Egyptian frontier in June, a pause for consolidation while Malta was secured by airborne assault in July and, circumstances permitting, the subsequent resumption of the offensive into Egypt. As the Italian High Command appreciated, this programme had no clear priority, while any offensive that offered the British any respite in Egypt threatened to lead only to a repeat of the events of December 1940 and November 1941. But the power of decision did not rest with the Italian High Command, and by the spring of 1942 Italy had weakened to an extent that was largely unsuspected by all parties to the conflict. Between January 1941 and May 1942 the Italian merchant marine lost 43.6 per cent of its tonnage available in the Mediterranean – 254 merchantmen of 961,689 tons – and such losses, concentrated amongst its better ships, could not be covered by new construction and captures. Limited repair and maintenance facilities, plus fuel shortages, made further inroads into the strength of a service that even without enemy activity could not maintain its April 1942 performance into the summer.

On the Allied side this third phase of operations saw the British remedy their most glaring deficiency in the Mediterranean theatre and win, on 10 May, one of their most significant victories of the Mediterranean campaign. German dominance of the central basin after January 1942 was the result of the *Luftwaffe*'s numerical and qualitative superiority in the battle over Malta. This was at a time when the RAF had some 120 Spitfire squadrons in southern England achieving very little because of the Spitfire's limited endurance and the lack of an enemy in British skies. Until February 1942 Malta had to make do with 'second eleven' aircraft, the Hurricane by this time being totally outclassed by the Me 109, the mainstay of *Fliegerkorps II*. In March three operations resulted in 31 Spitfires being flown to Malta from carriers in the western Mediterranean, and on 20 April 46 Spitfires were flown to Malta from an American carrier operating with the British Home Fleet. Considerable though these totals were in 1942 British naval terms, they were wholly inadequate when set alongside the average seven raids and 170 aircraft directed against Malta on every day in the second half of April. Within three days of the April consignment arriving in Malta all but six had been destroyed by an enemy that deliberately set out to eliminate this threat to its command of the air. As a result, two Allied carriers flew 60 more Spitfires to Malta on 9 May, and while some of these were in action within an hour of arriving on the island on the tenth, the RAF was able for the first time to meet incoming German attacks on the basis of numerical and qualitative equality, and therefore losses reflected this new balance. Without adequate reinforcement and, more importantly, without a high command, unlike the Italians, that realised the need for intensive operations to keep Malta ineffective, the air battle on 10 May pointed to an Axis loss of air supremacy in the central Mediterranean at the very time when *Panzerarmee Afrika* stood on the brink of its greatest victories in North Africa in the fourth phase of operations between May and July 1942.

This fourth phase of operations in mid-1942 saw the low point of British fortunes in the Second World War. After two years' fighting in this theatre and coming hard on the heels of a series of disasters throughout the Far East, the 8th Army was defeated in humiliating circumstances at Gazala by an enemy that proceeded to take Tobruk and then advance deep into Egypt, thereby presenting such a threat to the British position in the eastern Mediterranean that at the end of June the British fleet began to abandon its base at Alexandria. In military terms, the defeat incurred at Gazala between 26 May and 18 June was amongst the worst sustained by the British army in the course of the war because, on ground of its own choosing and despite having brought German armour and the élite *XX Italian Corps* to the brink of defeat by the end of May, the 8th Army was routed by a numerically inferior enemy without bringing one of its two corps into serious action. The defeat at Gazala led directly to the surrender of Tobruk on 21 June and to the decision, taken by the German High Command, that saved the British from defeat.

The capture of Tobruk yielded 6,400 tons of military stores and 2,000 serviceable vehicles, and this sudden ending of German logistical problems, plus the obvious disorder of British forces, prompted Rommel to ask, and Hitler to give, permission, for Axis forces to continue their offensive into Egypt. Tactical success at Gazala and Tobruk blinded the German, but not the Italian High Command, with the possibility of a decisive victory in Egypt at the expense of the proposed attack on Malta. With the main strength of *Fliegerkorps II* still in Italy, however, the Axis forces in North Africa lacked adequate air support for this effort. At first this did not seem too serious as *Panzerarmee Afrika* swept through Mersa Matruh on 27 June in the face of feeble opposition but around El Alamein, some 60 miles from Alexandria and reached by Axis forces on the thirtieth, the 8th Army was able to improvise a defensive position that could not be turned on either flank. Between 1 and 27 July the Axis and British armies together mounted six major offensives around El Alamein, but while the month ended with both armies in a state of collapse the implications of this drawn battle were obvious and immediately appre-

196

ciated by *Panzerarmee Afrika*: the failure to secure Malta, the assault on which was abandoned on 21 June; mounting Axis supply problems; the effectiveness of British air power which throughout July hammered away at Axis supply lines and formations on the Alamein front; and growing British strength in Egypt left the initiative firmly in British hands.

The extent of Axis strategic failure even in this period of overall success was even greater than indicated on the Alamein battlefield in July because at this time of crisis for the 8th Army two factors worked to British advantage. First, British success in previously having ensured the security of their rear area by the occupation of Iraq in May 1941, of Syria in June/July 1941 and of southern Iran in August* allowed the British to draw upon formations throughout the Middle East as the struggle for control of the Mediterranean theatre narrowed down to a battle across a 38-mile front between the sea and the Qattara Depression. Second, the Americans undertook two actions to help their allies at this time of defeat. The fall of Tobruk resulted in the despatch of 400 tanks and self-propelled guns, earmarked for American forces, to the 8th Army, and in June American air formations entered the Mediterranean theatre for the first time. On 12 June American heavy bombers, originally *en route* for China, bombed the oil fields at Ploesti, and on the fifteenth American and British bombers combined in an attack on Italian surface units off Malta. On the nineteenth the US army activated its Middle East headquarters in Cairo, and two days later American bombers attacked Benghazi for the first time. While the scale of American air operations was necessarily very small at this stage, the very fact of American involvement in this theatre had obvious implications: more significantly, the fall of Tobruk coincided with the Anglo-American decision to proceed in the autumn with the invasion of French North Africa.

The *Torch* commitment represented the second most important American decision of the war, involving as it did confirmation of the Germany-first principle when it was threatened by Britain's refusal to consider any form of landing on the European mainland in 1942. To an American High Command convinced that the United States had the measure of any foe, Britain's refusal to commit herself to an invasion of north-west Europe and insistence that in 1942 the German-first principle meant concentration against Italy passed beyond mere incomprehension, but what was at issue between the two allies was a fundamental difference of military philosophy. To the United States,

*The Soviet Union simultaneously occupied northern Iran, a neutral zone separating the two Allied areas of occupation.

wedded to a concept of war that stressed mass, firepower and shock action, the invasion of Europe was essential in order to meet and defeat the German army in the field: to Britain, a tradition shaped by maritime power and limited military resources decreed that invasion should not be attempted until the enemy's defeat was assured. In June 1942, however, issues were more immediate and practical, and lack of command of the sea and the skies, plus the lack of shipping for an invasion, rightly convinced Roosevelt that an assault on the continental mainland could not be attempted that year. The invasion of French North Africa emerged as the only offensive option open to the United States in the European war in 1942 other than in the air, but the decision to proceed with *Operation Torch*, while it had obvious implications for the Mediterranean theatre, had no impact upon events in the fifth and last phase of operations in this theatre between 28 July and 22 October. It nevertheless had one consequence for Britain in that the certainty of an Allied victory in the Mediterranean in the autumn made essential a prior British, as distinct from Allied, victory in Egypt in order to restore a national prestige much damaged by the events of a disastrous year.

The final phase of operations in the Mediterranean theatre before 23 October thus provides a link between two quite separate parts of a campaign, and it witnessed two quite separate efforts. First, in August the British were successful in fighting the *Pedestal* convoy into Malta, and this success enabled surface and submarine forces to return to the island later that month. Second, on 30 August *Panzerarmee Afrika* made one last attempt to break through the Alamein position before the 8th Army acquired the strength to make the result of a British offensive a foregone conclusion. In making this effort, however, *Panzerarmee Afrika* made the 8th Army fight the one type of battle it could win, perhaps the only type of battle it could win at this time, by forcing it to fight defensively for the Alam Halfa ridge in an action in which concentrated artillery and anti-tank firepower and close air support were at a premium and German superiority in mobile operations was at a discount. With virtually no air cover and lacking sufficient fuel for protracted operations, *Panzerarmee Afrika* abandoned its offensive on 2 September, the British making no serious attempt to follow up their success. With the action ending on the sixth, the failure of the Axis offensive went some way to restoring the 8th Army's confidence after its recent defeats, left the initiative firmly in British hands, and found British plans for an offensive that would drive Axis forces from Egypt well advanced.

The significance of the *Pedestal* convoy and the Alam Halfa action was obvious, but the common feature of both and the theme running through this fifth and final phase of operations was the massive expansion of the scale of the battle for control of the Mediterranean theatre in these three brief months. The August convoy, coming soon after an ambitious and dubiously successful attempt to fight convoys to Malta simultaneously from the west and east, was the largest British carrier operation before January 1945, four fleet carriers being involved in the passage of this 14-ship convoy. British losses were correspondingly heavy with two carriers, four cruisers, one destroyer and nine merchantmen sunk or damaged, but while the *Pedestal* effort was not one that the British could repeat very easily it nevertheless represented an escalation of the naval war in the Mediterranean to a level at which the Axis could not respond effectively. The subsequent success of naval and air forces against Axis shipping bound for North Africa ensured that *Panzerarmee Afrika* similarly could not counter the massive build-up of British forces in Egypt after July. At the battle of Gazala Rommel's command numbered 113,000 men, the 8th Army about 125,000, but between first and second Alamein the latter almost doubled in size while *Panzerarmee Afrika* declined in strength.

With 10 divisions in the line at El Alamein on 23 October, the 8th Army numbered 220,000 men and 1,300 tanks compared to the 108,000 men and 200 German and 300 Italian tanks of *Panzerarmee Afrika*'s four German and eight Italian divisions. Equally important, by the start of this second battle of Alamein the 8th Army had been reorganised under new leadership with the aim of eliminating two of the worst features of recent British performances. In large measure the Gazala defeat was the result of the British army's failure to develop a coherent tactical doctrine based upon the all-arms battle group and of poor leadership and command in the conduct of the battle, the effect of both being to condemn armour and infantry to fight and be defeated separately without their being able to provide mutual support. The fact that the Alamein position could not be outflanked and was covered by extensive minefields had the effect of forcing the 8th Army to fight a deliberate, setpiece battle, using infantry and artillery to clear the way for and to defend the armour. With a new commander, Lieutenant-General Montgomery, who was determined to exercise the closest possible control of his formations, the tactical plan for the Alamein attack was tailor-made to British numerical superiority and limited tactical capabilities. In singling out Axis infantry for destruction as the means of destroying the cohesion of *Panzerarmee Afrika* as a whole, Montgomery unconsciously adopted the same answer as the Soviet army to the problem posed by superior German technique in mobile operations as it, too, prepared to counter-attack a dead *Schwerpunkt*, stranded at the high-water mark of Axis conquest.

199

These two offensives – the British attack at Alamein in October and the Soviet counter-stroke outside Stalingrad in November – were the second and fourth of four Allied efforts in the space of two months that together marked the ebbing of the Axis tide in the Second World War. The third of these efforts was the Anglo-American landings in French North Africa in November, the first a two-part affair in the south-west Pacific. In the Pacific theatre the period between mid-September and mid-November 1942 witnessed Allied forces move against Japanese beachheads on the Solomon Sea and American forces break a Japanese effort in the Solomons in the course of a campaign that was, with the exception of the struggle for Okinawa in 1945, the most bitterly contested naval campaign of the Pacific war.

The fact that two separate campaigns were fought in the south-west Pacific after 22 July 1942 was the result of diametrically opposing strategic priorities pursued in this theatre by the Americans and Japanese in the immediate aftermath of the battles of the Coral Sea and Midway. After Midway the American High Command, and in particular the navy's chief of operations, Admiral King, sought to develop an offensive in the south-west Pacific in order to deny the Japanese a chance to recover from their defeat and to force the Imperial Navy on to the defensive. King's initial objectives were the Santa Cruz Islands and Tulagi, his long-term aim being to move against Rabaul. In the initial directive of 2 July no mention was made of Guadalcanal. Japanese actions, however, brought this island to American attention because after Midway, as the Japanese planned to develop an offensive against Port Moresby along what their intelligence fondly imagined was a motor road over the Owen Stanleys, they settled upon the establishment of an airfield amid the coconut groves of Lunga Point, on Guadalcanal, as the basis of their defence of the central and southern Solomons. At this time the Japanese staffs calculated that no American offensive in this theatre could be undertaken before the second quarter of 1943, a conclusion shared by American planning staffs, but King's insistence upon an immediate offensive to take the airfield on Guadalcanal as it neared completion, despite the manifest lack of preparation for such an attack, was decisive in ensuring that the Americans secured an initial advantage of timing and position by their occupation of Lunga Point and Tulagi on 7/8 August that ultimately decided the outcome of the campaign for Guadalcanal. This advantage proved decisive in the campaign in eastern New Guinea because, as the Japanese in September slowly awoke to the extent and seriousness of the problems and threats posed by the American occupation of Guadalcanal's airfield, so they abandoned their attempt to secure Port Moresby in order to concentrate their efforts in the Solomons. Thus the Japanese, having advanced to within 30 miles of Port Moresby by 17 September, found themselves unable to continue their offensive because of the demands of the Guadalcanal campaign and thereafter were condemned to certain defeat as the Allies brought overwhelming numbers against the Japanese beachhead around Gona in the second half of November – by which time the outcome of the struggle for Guadalcanal had been decided. Neither in eastern New Guinea nor on Guadalcanal was Japanese resistance brought to an end until early 1943, but with the Japanese forced to move against Wau from their Salamaua beachhead in response to Allied operations even before the Gona position was finally lost, their effort in the south-west Pacific between July 1942 and February 1943 reflected the entire Japanese war effort; an attempt to do too much with too little across too great an area of operations.

The Japanese effort in eastern New Guinea was made in three stages: the landing by a reinforced infantry battalion at Gona on 21 July followed by an immediate advance inland that secured Kokoda on 27/28 July; the reinforcement of this, the main effort, by the arrival at Gona on 21 August of the bulk of Japanese forces committed in this theatre; and the attempt to secure the airfield being constructed at Gili Gili, Milne Bay, by converging amphibious attacks directed at Toupota and Milne Bay itself at the end of August. On the main axis of advance, along the Kokoda Trail, the Japanese were initially opposed by militia which, despite having been on New Guinea since January, was at best semi-trained, poorly disciplined and totally outclassed. It was not until the end of August that the Japanese encountered experienced Australian units, withdrawn from the Middle East in early 1942, and thereafter Japanese plans miscarried both on the Trail and Milne Bay. The Toupota landings never materialised because Allied aircraft destroyed the barges bound for Toupota off Goodenough Island, while at Milne Bay the Japanese were forced to evacuate some 1,300 troops on 6 September after an extra-ordinary episode in which, at the cost of 600 casualties and their assault shipping, the Japanese established themselves in a swamp on a narrow coastal ledge and then proceeded to reduce a defending garrison of 8,800 Allied troops to a state of chaos in the course of night attacks on 26/27 and 27/28 August. Unable to secure their initial objectives, however, the Japanese abandoned the Milne Bay offensive – the first defeat incurred by the Imperial Army in the Pacific war.

The second followed immediately on the Kokoda Trail where the local Australian command sought to fight a series of defensive actions in the

The Southwest Pacific Campaign, August 1942

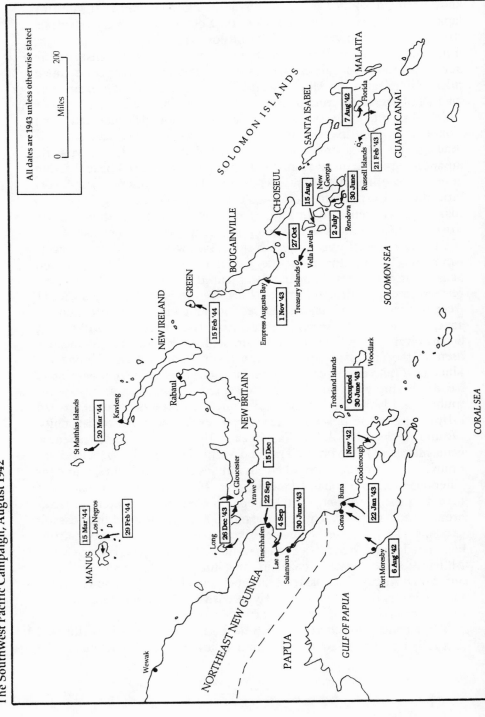

All dates are 1943 unless otherwise stated

0   Miles   200

knowledge that even if its formations were destroyed in the process the Japanese would be reduced to the point where they would lack the strength to take Port Moresby. By this time the Japanese had some 8,500 front-line and 3,000 construction troops on the Trail, the Australians just one infantry regiment deployed between Port Moresby and the Isuraua ridge. While the Australian calculation was realistic, the Japanese inability to maintain such numbers and the collapse of the offensive of 12/14 September to retake Guadalcanal's airfield led the Japanese High Command to order the withdrawal of its forces to the Gona–Buna beachhead despite having come within sight of the sea and Ioribaiwa on the seventeenth. The main Australian position astride the Imita ridge was never assaulted as the Japanese, reduced by starvation to the literal expedient of butchering their prisoners, were forced to retreat to the coast in the face of an Australian advance, with two regiments, along the Kokoda Trail, an American advance along the Jaure Trail, and an airlift of eight Allied battalions to the Pongani area between 5 October and 15 November. By 22 November the Japanese beachheads around Gona, Sanananda and Buna had been reduced to depths of 400 yards, but despite a lack of resupply and reinforcement and the loss of Gona on 9 December and Buna on 1 January, Japanese resistance at Sanananda did not end until 22 January. By this time Allied battalions had been reduced to companies by disease and battle casualties, and front-line troops had been reduced to fighting waist-deep in a swamp during the rainy season. Allied casualties in the course of this campaign totalled some 27,000 of the 33,000 involved in these battles; these returns might well have doubled but for the Australian refusal to evacuate malarial cases.

By the time that fighting in eastern New Guinea ended, the Japanese *2nd* and *38th Infantry Divisions* on Guadalcanal had been reduced to the same physical state as the 7th Australian and 32nd US Infantry Divisions around the Gona–Buna beachhead, but with the rider that unlike the Allied formations at Sanananda the Japanese formations on Guadalcanal were outnumbered and outgunned and had been defeated in their attempts to resecure the island's airfield. In large measure this state of affairs on Guadalcanal was a result of the fact that from the time that the 1st Marine Division secured Lunga Point and Tulagi on 7/8 August both the Japanese army and navy persistently underestimated their separate and common problems in retaking Guadalcanal. The effect of their miscalculations was that while the Japanese commitment at Guadalcanal grew remorselessly between August and November 1942 successive failures left victory that much further beyond Japanese reach. In these circumstances, as the campaign for Guadalcanal lengthened into what was the first test of the Japanese strategy to defend their conquests behind a series of bases supported by the fleet, the Japanese found themselves in the terribly ironical situation of seeing their policy vindicated but at *their* expense by the Americans. By securing Lunga Point and its airfield and then using land- and carrier-based air power to neutralise the enemy's superior sea power, the Americans were able to fight a tactically defensive battle for Guadalcanal and inflict such losses on the Japanese army, navy and merchant marine that the Japanese High Command was forced to abandon the struggle for the island.

Japanese problems in the fight for Guadalcanal were fearfully complicated although they can be stated simply. In what was to be a struggle to dominate the approaches to the island, American possession of an operational air base, Henderson Field, after 20 August denied the Japanese air superiority over the southern Solomons. With no airstrip in the northern and central Solomons south of Buka before November, Japanese air formations based on Rabaul lacked the numbers and technical means to win a battle for air supremacy at the very limit of their aircrafts' range, yet unless either Henderson Field was taken or American air power on Guadalcanal was eliminated the Japanese fleet could not risk closing the island. If it did so it faced the same problems presented by the need to neutralise divergent targets – an air base and any American carrier formations in the combat zone – that had led it to defeat at Midway, but without the commitment of the fleet and the suppression of American shore-based air power any attempt to effect a concentration of the army on Guadalcanal sufficient to drive the Americans into the sea ran obvious and growing risks. For the Japanese army on Guadalcanal, however, an initial underestimation of American numbers and quality on the island was compounded by a failure to appreciate the difficulties of moving and fighting around the Lunga Point perimeter. American possession of the only real estate on Guadalcanal worth holding forced Japanese units to land well away from Lunga Point and to make long, debilitating approach marches to their start lines and to mount attacks on very uncertain lines of supply. In the event these attacks were poorly coordinated and conducted, and executed on too small a scale to succeed. It was not until mid-November that the *17th Army* secured a bare superiority of numbers over the defenders on Guadalcanal, and by that time the Japanese navy had lost the struggle to control the seas around the island because of the neutralisation of its carrier air power and the erosion of Japanese superiority in night fighting over the Americans in the restricted waters of Ironbottom Sound.

For a campaign that ended so disastrously for the Japanese and which was characterised throughout by a sluggish, piecemeal and inadequate Japanese response to the situation that presented itself in the southern Solomons, the struggle for Guadalcanal opened with one of the worst Allied naval defeats of the entire Pacific war. In response to the American landings, the *8th Fleet*, with its headquarters at Rabaul, immediately despatched a cruiser squadron against the beachheads. The resulting clash with Allied forces off Savo Island on the night of 8/9 August ended with four Allied cruisers sunk and a damaged destroyer put down next morning by Japanese aircraft. The Japanese formation failed, however, to attack the transports concentrated off the beachheads and thereafter the opportunity to inflict telling losses on American assault shipping never again presented itself as Japanese difficulties increased with the growing effectiveness of American air power on Guadalcanal.

The commitment of the *Combined Fleet* to the campaign was recognition of the fact that local resources were inadequate for the task in hand, but the first of the three carrier operations staged by the Japanese in the three months after the American landings was a desultory affair. The battle of the Eastern Solomons (24/25 August) witnessed heavy Japanese air losses and one light carrier sunk with no corresponding loss inflicted upon American carrier forces. Accounts were squared by the sinking of an American carrier by submarine attack on 15 September, but the second action induced by Japanese carrier operations, off Santa Cruz, on 24/26 October, again proved indecisive. Damage to two carriers and heavy air losses prevented the *Combined Fleet* from following up its success in leaving the Americans temporarily without an operational carrier in the Pacific, having sunk one and damaged a second carrier in this action.

The naval effort that culminated in the battle off Santa Cruz was but one part of a three-fold Japanese enterprise. The fleet's operations were synchronised with an intensive attempt by Rabaul-based air units to win air superiority over Guadalcanal and with a major effort by the *2nd Infantry Division* to secure Henderson Field. The overall Japanese aim was to secure the airfield and fly aircraft from the carriers to the island, thereby turning the tables on the Americans throughout the southern Solomons. Like the naval effort, both these complementing offensives failed. The air attacks on Henderson Field reached their peak on 25 September without achieving the neutralisation of American air power on Guadalcanal, Rabaul thereafter being left unable to mount offensive operations of any kind for five days. The army's offensive was the third such effort made by Japanese forces to Guadalcanal, the first, by a single unsupported battalion across the Tenaru river on the night of 19/20

August, having been made on the casual assumption that the Americans had some 2,000 poor-quality troops in the beachhead rather than the 10,000 marines put ashore between the seventh and ninth.

The second effort, made by a brigade group of 6,000 men, was more imaginatively conceived than its predecessor in that it involved attacks against each of the three sides of the American beachhead, but as was the case in August American forewarning of attack and overwhelming superiority of numbers, firepower and position resulted in a crushing Japanese defeat despite some soldiers penetrating to the marines' divisional headquarters before being killed. By mid-October, however, the Americans and Japanese each had some 22,000 troops on Guadalcanal and the battle that was fought between 22 and 26 October was correspondingly more closely balanced that the two previous actions, the Japanese offensive penetrating to the last defensive position in front of Henderson Field before being stopped. Poor coordination between the various Japanese attacks, a problem that beset the September offensive and was perhaps unavoidable in the thick jungle beyond the American perimeter, was as important as American advantages of firepower and position in ensuring this third Japanese failure to eliminate the beachhead.

This triple failure in the fourth week of October 1942 led the Japanese High Command to two decisions in an attempt to overcome American resistance in the southern Solomons: to send capital ships against the beachhead and to commit the *38th Infantry Division* to Guadalcanal in readiness for a renewed offensive in November. The growing effectiveness of American air power over the southern Solomons meant that both efforts would involve a large measure of risk, but to date the Japanese had been singularly successful in fighting reinforcement and supply convoys to Guadalcanal with relatively few losses despite American air superiority and had worsted American surface units in a series of minor clashes after the Savo Island action. But the battle off Cape Esperance (11/12 October), when an American cruiser force sank or damaged three Japanese warships in the course of a drawn action, served notice that the clear superiority that the Japanese had enjoyed over the Americans in night fighting was under threat. Just as the effectiveness of American air power grew with the lengthening of the campaign and the acquisition of battle experience, so American light forces absorbed the lessons and techniques of night fighting as a result of the series of defeats they incurred between August and October. By November, and the Japanese decision to send heavy ships into the waters off Lunga Point, there existed a rough equality between Japanese advantages of technique and

206

torpedoes and superior American radar and – in the critical battle of 14/15 November – individual ship quality.

The result of these various decisions and considerations was a series of actions fought off Guadalcanal between 12 and 15 November. On the night of 12/13 November the Japanese intention to use battleships to neutralise Henderson Field was frustrated by American cruisers and destroyers in the course of a furious action, fought at ranges of which torpedoes could not arm and Japanese battleship guns could not depress sufficiently to engage American warships, that ended in the destruction of one Japanese battleship and two destroyers and two American cruisers and four destroyers. Undeterred by their losses, the Japanese conducted an unopposed bombardment of Henderson Field on the following night, but on the following morning the cruiser formation thus committed was badly mauled by American aircraft from Guadalcanal and from a carrier held well to the south of Guadalcanal. Aircraft from the same two sources on this same day (14 November) sank six and damaged one of the 11 transports bringing the *38th Infantry Division* south from Shortland, but that night the American decision to commit two battleships to the defence of the beachhead in anticipation of a further Japanese attempt to bombard the airfield resulted in one of the very few actions in the Second World War between capital ships. As a result of this encounter the Japanese lost one battleship and two destroyers, the Americans three destroyers. Japanese misfortune was completed with daylight when American action accounted for the four transports that reached Guadalcanal and which were beached in the vain hope that their troops and cargoes could be put ashore before the ships themselves were destroyed. Just 2,000 of the 10,000 troops and virtually none of the ammunition and stores that had come south from Shortland reached Guadalcanal, thus ending any Japanese hopes of taking Henderson Field in November.

The battles of 12/15 November decided the outcome of the struggle for Guadalcanal, though the campaign was to continue for another two and a half months in the course of which, off Tassafaronga (30 November/1 December) Japanese light forces inflicted upon the Americans a defeat that would have been every bit as bad as the one sustained off Savo Island but for the wilful refusal of three badly crippled American heavy cruisers to sink. On this occasion the Japanese were able to land troops and supplies on Guadalcanal, but in the final analysis the losses of 12/15 November, and in particular the loss of some 75,000 tons of merchant shipping in a day, could not be sustained. After the mid-November defeats the Imperial Navy came to realise that it could not afford such losses as a matter of course, and with no realistic prospect of securing Henderson Field the navy had to cut its losses at Guadalcanal in order to prepare for subsequent operations in the Solomons. On 12 December the navy formally recommended to Imperial General Head-quarters, the services' high command, that Guadalcanal be abandoned, and despite the opposition of the *17th Army* which wanted to reinforce its depleted divisions on Guadalcanal in February this recommendation was endorsed on 31 December. In reality the *17th Army*'s chance had passed, partly as a result of its own failures and partly because the arrival of two relief divisions in early December brought American strength on Guadalcanal to the 40,000 mark.

The Japanese evacuation of Guadalcanal, however, proved an out-standing success. Beginning on 14 January and ending on 8 February, *Operation KE* resulted in the evacuation of 10,652 troops from Guadalca-nal for the loss of just one destroyer, the Americans not realising that no live Japanese remained on the island until the afternoon of the ninth. In light of their clear superiority at sea and over Guadalcanal the success of *Operation KE* represented a disappointing end to the campaign for the Americans, but there was no altering the fact that overall the struggle for the southern Solomons had resulted in a conclusive American victory. Triumph on Guadalcanal claimed 1,600 American lives while the Allied navies lost 24 fleet units sunk. Some 21,700 Japanese soldiers died on Guadalcanal in addition to an unknown number lost at sea, but while the Imperial Navy lost fewer warships (18) than the Allies, the crippling Japanese losses were those sustained in the air. At a time when the naval air arm numbered no more than 4,000 aviators, the Japanese lost 893 shore-based and ship-borne aircraft and seaplanes and 2,362 aviators in the struggle for Guadalcanal, but even more importantly in the course of this campaign the Imperial Navy lost its moral ascendancy over the US Navy. The battles of 12/15 November completed the rehabilitation of American self-confidence, a process that had begun in the Coral Sea. Tassafaronga notwithstanding, after 15 November the US Navy, and particularly its carrier aviation, knew that the Imperial Navy was theirs for the taking. Another nine months were to elapse before both were able to prove this, and by that time American carrier forces had been trans-formed from those that had helped win a narrow but decisive victory in the southern Solomons. At Guadalcanal the US Navy not only won a campaign but established a supremacy that ensured future success in battle and overall victory throughout the Pacific.

American victories over the Japanese in 1942 were critical in settling the outcome of the Pacific war, but by the Americans' own terms of reference such victories, in the lesser of the conflicts that made up the Second World War, would have lost much of their relevance had Germany in this year won the victory that Hitler knew she had to win if she was to avoid being dragged down to defeat by the combined strength of the enemies that she had arrayed against herself. Germany in 1942, if she was to avoid a war of attrition that she was certain to lose, had either to destroy the Soviet Union outright or to inflict such military defeats and territorial and manpower losses upon the Soviet regime that what remained of Soviet capability was no more than a peripheral irrelevance. The outcome of the entire war, not just the European conflict, thus hinged upon events on the Eastern Front in 1942 where, despite the year opening with German reverses, the *Wehrmacht* won a series of victories in the spring and summer that brought it first to the brink of potentially decisive success and then to disaster.

The course of events on the Eastern Front in 1942 was to be shaped by two decisions – one German and the other Soviet but both taken in the last two months of 1941 – plus the fact that in the winter of 1941/42 the Soviet army failed to register a strategic victory that ensured its retention of the initiative into the spring and summer. This failure was in large measure, however, the product of the second 1941 decision, made by Stalin in December and rubber-stamped by a formal Stavka session on 5 January 1942, that committed the Soviet army to a general offensive along virtually the entire length of the Eastern Front. At a time when Soviet armies faced mounting difficulties in lifting the siege of Leningrad and driving back German formations in front of Moscow, Stalin issued orders for offensives intended to result in the destruction of all three German army groups on the Eastern Front. The significant defeat of *Army Group Centre* represented the only realistic Soviet aim in December 1941, and by insisting upon a series of divergent offensives with inadequate forces Stalin ensured a dissipation of Soviet efforts that ended with strategic failure across the whole length of the front.

   The Soviet effort was divided into two parts: a series of offensives that had largely exhausted themselves by the end of February 1942, and, in April and May, offensives in the north, against Finnish and German forces, and, disastrously, around Kharkov. Though four months separate their starts, the Soviet offensives at either end of the Eastern Front present themselves for initial consideration because unlike other Soviet offensives in early 1942, neither was mounted in the expectation of success other than in a local context. Both Soviet efforts took place in forbidding conditions – during the Arctic winter in the north and in a

Force 5 gale and temperatures of −20°C during the initial Soviet landings on the Kerch peninsula – and while both achieved limited success at the outset both were quickly contained and subsequently defeated with heavy loss. The two Soviet efforts differed, however, in that whereas failure on the Kerch peninsula led the Soviets to double their efforts and thereby only add to the extent of their final defeat, in the north they made no attempt to press their offensives after the first attacks failed to carry their initial objectives, going over instead to the defensive in positions that were barely different from those from which they had begun their offensives in April.

The Soviet attempt to clear the Crimea and relieve Sevastopol involved landings between 26 and 29 December by some 40,000 troops from the 44th and 51st Armies around Kerch and Feodosiya. The immediate Soviet aim was to seal the entrance to the Crimea by taking Perekop thereby trapping the *11th Army*, but the initial landings failed to complete the encirclement of the *46th, 73rd* and *170th Infantry Divisions* with the result that these formations, plus the *8th Cavalry Brigade*, were able to seal off the neck of the Kerch peninsula by 2 January. The Soviet landings nevertheless forced the *11th Army* to abandon its intention to storm Sevastopol, but in turn its counter-attack on the Soviet beachhead on the fifteenth, though held, forced the Soviet High Command to recast its offensive intentions in order to reinforce the Kerch position. Successive Soviet attempts to break the German grip on the beachhead with attacks that began on 27 February, 26 March and 9 April were frustrated by bad security, appalling weather and poor coordination of attacks that were forced by lack of space to develop along channelled axes against tactically strong positions held in depth. These Soviet efforts weakened with each failure but were nevertheless accompanied by a build-up of Soviet forces until no fewer than 21 divisions from three armies were concentrated within the Kerch peninsula by early May.

By this time, however, the Crimean Front was no longer able to save itself from defeat, still less relieve the Sevastopol garrison. On 8 May the *11th Army*, with 10 divisions committed to the destruction of the Kerch beachhead, secured Feodosiya and on the fifteenth took Kerch itself, resistance on the peninsula ending on 21 May. Thus freed from one obligation, the *11th Army* opened its pre-assault bombardment of Sevastopol on 2 June and its assault on the sixth, but it was not until the thirtieth that its formations fought their way into the city and the Soviets began the evacuation of the base. Both evacuation and resistance ended on 3 July, Sevastopol falling after a siege of 250 days.

In the north, issues were resolved in little more than a month and fighting petered out six weeks before the end of fighting in the Crimea. On 24 April three divisions from the 26th Army attacked *III Finnish Corps* around Kestenga and three days later the 14th Army committed two divisions to an attack across the lower Litsa. While the worst blizzards of the winter halted operations in the latter sector at the end of April, the 26th Army, despite committing two more divisions to attacks that came to within two miles of Kestenga and the encirclement of *III Finnish Corps*, was decisively defeated in early May. Piecemeal commitment of formations amidst the swamps north of Kestenga allowed Axis forces to crush the Soviet offensive by 6 May, and on the fifteenth Finnish and German forces went over to the offensive. It was not until 21 May, however, that German forces broke the 263rd Infantry Division by frontal assault on the main track to Louhki, but Finnish unwillingness to support a German advance ended operations in this area on the twenty-third. On the Litsa voluntary Soviet withdrawals on 14 May before the Germans had time to develop a counter-offensive allowed *Mountain Corps Norway* to recover its former positions without a fight, but thereafter the thaw imposed its own check on offensive operations.

In overall terms the fighting around Kestenga and on the Litsa cost the Soviet armies perhaps 30,000 dead, but while five Soviet divisions remained on the Litsa and another three were kept around Louhki there was real compensation for the Soviet High Command (and the Allies in general) as a result of these northern operations that was notably lacking as a result of events in the Crimea. The Soviets lost 176,000 troops in May alone at Kerch and 110,000 at Sevastopol, their only gain being the inability of the German High Command to deploy the full strength of the *11th Army* outside the Crimea before August. In the north the Finns and Germans lost 5,700 dead during April and May, but their real losses came after these actions as Hitler ordered a reinforcement of northern Norway on a scale wholly at variance with the area's strategic importance. The Soviet offensives and Hitler's belief that the British sought to secure this area resulted in 172,000 German troops being stationed in northern Norway by the end of 1942, in no position to influence events in the decisive theatres of operations.

The general offensive between the Baltic and the Sea of Azov that Stalin ordered for the winter of 1942 involved Soviet armies in three major efforts: to lift the siege of Leningrad and break through German positions on the Volkhov and Lovat in order to complete the encirclement and annihilation of *Army Group North*; to extend and intensify operations begun in December against *Army Group Centre*; and to break open the left flank of *Army Group South* by offensives around Orel, Kursk and

211

Kharkov, the ill-fated Kharkov offensive of May 1942 being made from the salient formed to the south of the city in the course of the original January offensive. These efforts were made over a three-month period and their course and outcome, particularly the battles for Staraya Russa, Demyansk, Kholm, Rzhev and Vyazma, are sufficiently well known to need no elaboration, except to note that the Germans' ability to retain these various towns in the face of the Soviet onslaught and mount counter-attacks in strength as early as the third week in January was evidence that Stalin's basic assumption in ordering these offensives was flawed.

Stalin's plans for the winter offensive of 1942 were devised on the premise that a general offensive would complete the rout of an enemy demoralised by the failure to take Moscow and reeling under the impact of winter and the counter-offensive outside the capital. While at least part of this calculation was well founded, the failure to allow the *Wehrmacht* the same powers of recovery that the Soviet Army had shown at Moscow in December provides the starting point for an examination of events on the Eastern Front in the first quarter of 1942. That being noted, three facts about the Soviet winter offensive of 1942 must be recorded. First, and obvious, while the destruction of the *Wehrmacht* on the Eastern Front proved impossible, *Army Group Centre* was driven back to positions between 50 and 200 miles from Moscow, and never again did German armies attempt a direct assault on the Soviet capital. Second, the December counter-offensive and the 1942 general offensive were conducted by a Soviet army that was outnumbered in men and tanks along the length of the Eastern Front and which had no more than equality in the main sectors of operations: the most crucial battles in Soviet history were fought by a Soviet army without any clear material advantage over its enemy. Third, and perhaps surprisingly, German losses in the winter of 1942 were significantly lower than in the first six months of the campaign. On the German army's own figures, *Operation Barbarossa* cost it 830,403 killed, wounded and missing in 1941 and another 277,427 casualties between 1 January and 20 April 1942. German daily losses thus averaged 4,303 during 1941 and 2,893 in the first 16 weeks of 1942. Allowing for German divisions on the Eastern Front entering 1942 perhaps 40 per cent understrength, relative German losses during the winter campaign were no heavier than those incurred during offensive operations in 1941.

Soviet success before Moscow in December 1941 was due to superb strategic timing in that the counter-attack against *Army Group Centre* was unleashed as the German offensive exhausted itself; to the Soviet soldier's superiority over his German counterpart in temperatures of −30°C; and to the ability of the Soviet High Command to move three complete armies into the line in front of Moscow in readiness for the counter-offensive without their being detected by German intelligence. Strategic surprise was critical to Soviet success in December 1941, but with 1942 surprise was a wasting asset: it was not an effective substitute for adequate manpower, armour and artillery and for the logistics and transport needed to sustain prolonged offensive operations. Even in the initial offensives of January 1942 various fronts began operations with no fuel issue, food enough for only one day, and, in one notable case, no ammunition for the field and anti-tank artillery. Such was the haste with which offensives were staged in January 1942 that many fronts were unable to form second-echelon formations for breakout operations, and even where such formations existed and breaches were made in the German line these lacked the fighting power, mobility and range to effect the deep penetration of enemy rear areas sufficient to ensure the encirclement of major German formations. The basic armoured formation with Soviet armies in January 1942 was the brigade, which consisted of two regiments each of two battalions, the theoretical establishment of a battalion being 20 tanks. Such units and formations represented the maximum that could be handled effectively in the field by Soviet commanders, yet they were too small and there were not enough brigades in early 1942 for Soviet armour to function effectively either in the assault or exploitation role.

Without sufficient armour and transport, Soviet offensives could not achieve either a clean breach across an extended front or depth of penetration, and from this emerged the basic pattern of the winter campaign. German retention of certain key positions, most obviously Rzhev and the Rzhev–Sychevka–Vyazma rail line, resulted in the formation of alternating salients in which both sides sought to avoid and effect encirclement. Thus in February the 29th and 39th Armies found themselves partially encircled as they sought to encircle Rzhev and the *9th Army* from the north and west, and the 33rd Army found itself similarly placed as it tried to fight its way to Vyazma from the east. Around Staraya Russa, Demyansk and Kholm the same pattern repeated itself as both sides sought to keep open their lines of communication in the face of enemy counter-attacks. German success in holding these three positions owed much to the *Luftwaffe*'s ability to maintain these garrisons by air – though the maintenance of the German *II Infantry Corps* at Demyansk cost the Germans six months' production of Ju-52 transport aircraft.

Limited Soviet offensive capability in the winter campaign thus produced an increasingly favourable tactical situation for German armies as the initial Soviet advantage of surprise was dissipated, and both became ever more pronounced with the lengthening of days and the coming of March and April. In the Leningrad sector these months saw the collapse of the 2nd Shock Army around Lyuban after a desperate three-month struggle to maintain itself west of the Volkhov, while April also witnessed the complete failure of the 7th Army's attempt to drive the Finns off the Svir. Around Demyansk *Army Group North* was able to re-form its front, trapping and destroying Soviet formations exhausted by their efforts to reduce the pocket. In front of Moscow the end of winter resulted in both sides consolidating their positions around Vyazma, *Army Group Centre* also being able to eliminate the various liberated areas behind its front that had been established during the winter by partisans, parachute forces and isolated columns. Around Kharkov, however, March saw the Soviet decision to proceed with a spring offensive, an extraordinary decision in light of the fact that at the same time Stalin, in what was at this stage a welcome and unusual example of realism, had concluded the Soviet armies would have to assume the defensive in the spring. These contradictory decisions – to mount a massive offensive against *Army Group South* while standing on the defensive in the expectation that the enemy's main effort would be made by *Army Group Centre* – were not untypical of Stalin's planning and conduct of the winter campaign. At various times the Kalinin and Western Fronts before Moscow were stripped of armies for other theatres but were expected nevertheless to secure objectives that they were unlikely to have taken even with their original establishments, and leaving aside obvious command and tactical failures in the Soviet conduct of operations such changes of dispositions and plans, plus Stalin's insistence on a dispersal of effort and the pursuit of a multiplicity of objectives, robbed the Soviet winter offensive of coherence, continuity and realism thereby contributing significantly to its limited results.

The Kharkov offensive of May 1942, however, was to demonstrate other disastrous features of Stalin's conduct of operations at this time, most notably a persistence with offensives despite overwhelming evidence of failure and, in this case, impending defeat. Though certain of the more obvious failings of previous offensives were avoided in the planning and preparation for the Kharkov effort, these were replaced by others, the most important, perversely, being that in sharp contrast to the winter offensives this attack was concentrated on too narrow a front and was not supported either on the ground or in the air by flanking formations. Soviet objectives in May 1942 were moderate in that five armies, with a total of 640,000 men, 1,200 tanks and 13,000 guns, were tasked to recapture the Soviet Union's fourth city. From its start on 12 May, however, the offensive miscarried, the Soviets' own accounts indicating that two-thirds of their artillery were not in range of the enemy and half of the first-echelon formations were at least 10 miles behind their start lines when the offensive opened.

The task of breaking into the German defences around the Izyum salient proved expensive and slow, and it was not until 17 May that second-echelon forces were committed to the breakout and by then it was too late, not simply for such operations, but for the South-west Front to avoid a rout. On this same date *Army Group Kleist*, with the *1st Panzer* and *17th Armies* under command, struck at the left flank of the Izyum salient from positions around Kramatorsk and Krasnoarmeyskoye while the *6th Army*, covering Kharkov, rolled with the punches delivered in the north by the 28th Army and from the Izyum salient by the 6th Army. It was not until 19 May, after insisting that the offensive was pressed even as the 9th Army collapsed, that Stalin gave permission for Soviet forces to try to escape the trap that was closing around them. On 23 May the Izyum salient was eliminated when Kleist's armour linked up with the *6th Army* around Balekleya, and with most of the west bank of the Oskel south of Belgorod cleared by the twenty-sixth Soviet resistance in the Kharkov sector ended on 29 May. The *Wehrmacht* claimed to have taken 240,000 prisoners and to have destroyed 20 infantry divisions and 14 armoured brigades around Kharkov, the battle providing it with the initiative and a clear superiority of numbers over Soviet forces in the eastern Ukraine.*

Soviet errors of planning and execution account in large part for the defeat before Kharkov, yet perhaps the most important single factor in the Soviet failure in the Ukraine in May 1942 was that the South-west Front had no margin of superiority over an enemy that anticipated the Soviet attack and had time to deploy its forces accordingly. The elimination of the Izyum salient, which overlooked the whole German position on the lower Donets, was an obvious German objective for the spring and alone would have justified a major concentration of German forces around Kharkov, but in reality the gathering of German formations in this area was due not to tactical considerations but to a German decision of November 1941 which, with Stalin's parallel decision of December and the subsequent winter campaign, shaped the course of the 1942 campaign. The decision, taken by Hitler a month before *Operation*

---

*It would appear that at Kerch and Kharkov the Soviets lost some 410,000 prisoners and that on all fronts the Soviet army lost perhaps 600,000 men in May alone – which makes the May defeats as bad as Kiev and Vyazma in 1941.

Teifun was abandoned, was that the German main effort in 1942 was to be made in the south.

Hitler's decision was determined by economic considerations. Even before the start of *Operation Barbarossa* he had laid down, and *OKH* had accepted without demur, the principle that as the war entered its third and fourth years the Ukraine would have to feed and support the *Wehrmacht*, the resulting death by starvation of millions of Soviet citizens being accepted by the German military command as a matter of no importance. In the winter of 1942 Hitler identified the mineral wealth of the Donets and the oil of the Caucasus as his primary objectives in the coming year, his calculations being that Germany could not sustain herself in a lengthening struggle without the resources of the Ukraine and southern Russia. It was this decision, put in hand during the spring of 1942, that was to lead the *Wehrmacht* first to victory around Kharkov in May and then to the Stalingrad–Utta–Mozdok–Alagir–Novorossiysk line and general defeat throughout the south between November 1942 and March 1943.

Accounts of this period and campaign have naturally focused upon the military chronology of the German summer offensive, and have generally interpreted events in terms of the notorious inconsistencies within and between *Directives 41* and *45*, issued by Hitler on 5 April and 23 July respectively. These two directives were the German terms of reference for this campaign, and with their fateful confusion of operational priorities and command arrangements do much to explain the German defeat in the south in 1942. Yet much more important developments were at work in this period in producing this confusion in the German conduct of operations, and these same developments provide not just the context of the German defeat on the Eastern Front in 1942 but the explanation of the shift in the balance of forces that took place at this time and which provide underlying reasons for Germany's defeat in the Second World War. It is precisely these factors that explain why, despite all appearances to the contrary and initial German success between May and August, the *Wehrmacht* in the summer of 1942 was singularly ill-placed to win the victory that Hitler expected, demanded and, above all, had to secure in 1942.

In the context and explanation of German failure after December 1941 there are four matters to consider. Arguably the most important was Hitler's own personality and the changes of command and organisation that followed as a result of his assumption of direct command of the army in this month and of his experience in the winter 1942 campaign. This campaign only deepened Hitler's disdain and contempt for the officer corps and served to exaggerate the structural weaknesses within the military establishment that Hitler had devised in order to neutralise a 'politically reactionary' army and ensure his own power of decision in military matters. After December 1941 Hitler combined the roles of head of state, executive, judiciary, party, armed forces and the army, and without the ability to trust competent subordinates sufficiently to delegate authority and without a cabinet system to plan, implement and supervise policy and to coordinate the various aspects of statecraft, Hitler's direction of the German war effort became increasingly arbitrary and erratic with the passing of time. The most obvious example of the growing administrative chaos within the upper leadership was the divisions and overlapping authorities of *OKW* and *OKH*, though in practice *OKH* after spring 1942 was excluded from the strategic direction of the war and, in the words of one distinguished historian, in effect 'no longer existed'. After spring 1942 *OKH* was no more than an administrative office tasked to effect Hitler's orders for the conduct of the campaign on the Eastern Front, though it was increasingly bypassed by Hitler in his direct dealings with field commanders. The army staff remained responsible for the raising and efficiency of army formations, but in most theatres these came under the command of *OKW* and everywhere the cohesion of military forces was weakened by the deliberate sponsorship of the private armies. By June 1943 the *Luftwaffe* deployed no fewer than 24 divisions, the *Waffen-SS* 17 by the end of that year – this total being one fewer than the number of different *types* of division serving with the *Wehrmacht* in 1944, each with its own scales of establishment and equipment. Air and naval formations were responsible to their own commanders-in-chief even in *OKW* theatres, and liaison between the three services existed only in Hitler's person.

Equally serious, there was no effective long-term planning of investment, procurement, manpower resources and research and development programmes that linked industrial output with military requirements, Göring's stewardship of the economy being disastrously incompetent. Croneyism and the promotion of individuals on the basis of loyalty and fanaticism permeated the German war economy, and indeed it was only through the ruthless plundering of occupied Europe that the *Wehrmacht* made war in these middle years. Plunder had its limits, however, and by 1942 some of these limits were imposing themselves upon the *Wehrmacht* for the first time. Some 40 per cent of the German divisions that invaded the Soviet Union in June 1941 were equipped with captured French equipment, and in 1941 the *Wehrmacht* had the amazing total of 2,000 different types of motor vehicle with the armies on the Eastern Front. Re-equipment and standardisation was essential by 1942, but given the state of the German economy was not possible. The most telling indictment of Hitler's direction – or neglect – of the economy was that until 1943 Britain, with half the population and less than half the industrial capacity of Germany, outproduced the *Reich* in terms of aircraft, tanks, artillery and shipping.

Partly as a result of the poor management of the economy, the air and ground forces on the Eastern Front were to begin the summer offensive of 1942 no stronger than they had been a year earlier. However this, the second of those underlying factors that explain Germany's defeats, was more properly the result of Hitler's strategic miscalculations, the failure to register the anticipated knock-out victory over the Soviet Union in 1941 being responsible for leaving the *Luftwaffe* and ground forces without the means and time to add to their strengths in order to meet their widening responsibilities in this and other theatres. The two services were affected differently, but probably the more significant weakness was that of the *Luftwaffe* because of the critical importance that air power held in German war-making. In the course of 1941 the *Luftwaffe* destroyed perhaps as many as 7,000 Soviet combat aircraft, yet the year ended without it being able to exercise even air superiority over much of the Eastern Front. Indeed, by December 1941 the Soviet Union was outproducing Germany 3:1 in front-line fighters, the obvious corollary being that the *Luftwaffe*, with commitments that extended beyond the Eastern Front, could never hope to win air supremacy against an enemy whose numerical and technical capacity and ability to recover from devastating defeats had been hopelessly underestimated. In fact, spring 1942 found the *Luftwaffe* with 2,872 combat aircraft compared to 3,451 in June 1941 and 3,692 in March 1940, but more seriously the same period found the *Luftwaffe* first with a command that never realised that the struggle for air supremacy involved intensive and protracted operations outside the provision of support for the ground forces, and second, without aircraft coming off the production line fast enough to give it any chance of winning more than local and temporary superiority over individual sectors of the Eastern Front. Put at its simplest, in 1942 the *Luftwaffe* did not have the capacity for sustained operations in so vast a theatre as the east and was in any event not the type of air force Germany needed at this time. The pre-war decision to have an air force wedded to *Blitzkrieg* precluded its reorganisation as a general air force of the kind developed by Britain and the United States, and to a much lesser extent the Soviet Union. In 1942 the *Luftwaffe* still retained certain advantages over its Soviet counterpart, most notably better pilots, control and maintenance, but these advantages were small and declining, while the demands of the north-west Europe and Mediterranean theatres made increasingly serious inroads into its strength.

The German ground forces entered the summer campaign in 1942 with similar problems and for similar reasons. Like the *Luftwaffe* the ground forces found in the spring of 1942 extra responsibilities in France and the Low Countries that for the first time made *Army Group D* in the west a competitor with the eastern armies for manpower, but again like the *Luftwaffe*, the real problems of the ground forces stemmed from decisions made by Hitler in anticipation of a victory that then eluded him. In May 1941 Hitler refused to increase the reserve army's training capacity and replacement holdings beyond the levels that had been authorised before the invasion of Poland, and on 14 July he ordered a cut of production of all military equipment other than tanks. Such decisions could not be undone in time for the summer offensive, and indeed the *OKH* assessment in mid-1942 was that ammunition shortages could well halt offensive operations in the course of the summer.

Non-material deficiencies were even more difficult to cover. The *Wehrmacht* lost half of its 500,000 horses in the course of 1941, and while it entered the 1942 summer campaign with about the same number of divisions (179) as it had when it had begun the invasion of the Soviet Union one year earlier, these divisions were 625,000 men under establishment. Placed behind the other two services and the *Waffen-SS* in its call on manpower, the army had no prospect of covering its shortfall, and with armour taking priority on resources the greater part of the army's manpower deficiency was borne by the infantry, which was significantly weaker in numbers and quality than at the start of *Operation Barbarossa*. Moreover, the ground forces as a whole were more cautious in 1942 than had previously been the case, and their command had been impaired by the changes that Hitler had brought about during the winter. In the three weeks that followed his taking command of the army in December 1941 Hitler dismissed 35 senior generals, none lower than corps commanders. With all three army group commanders on the Eastern Front removed in this purge, no commander in the east after winter 1942 was not conscious of the reach of the *Führer* and the force of his orders. But equally pernicious, the emasculation of *OKH* during 1942 included the transfer of the army's personnel branch to *OKW*. Postings and promotions thus came directly within Hitler's patronage, and he used this power to corrupt some to his will, to favour the ardent and the flatterers, and, in September 1942, to undermine the whole principle of hierarchy within the army by the appointment of a major-general as its chief of staff. In fact Hitler's intention to eliminate irritants within *OKH* by appointing a pliant, dependent creature to this still-prestigious post miscarried: the new chief of staff quickly proved just as obstinate as his predecessor, and like his predecessor was progressively ignored for his pains.

The third and fourth factors that complete the context and explanation of Germany's defeats were really separate manifestations of a single phenomenon, though each was of such individual significance as to merit singular consideration. The first was the simple fact that Germany's associates were not capable, either immediately or in the long term, of providing her with *effective* military support in the prosecution of the war and, indeed, were liabilities that had to be supported even though in 1942 five of the six associated powers with forces on the Eastern Front maintained or increased them in this theatre to an extent that covered the worst of Germany's manpower shortages. The one exception was Finland, which had raised 18 divisions in 1941 only by conscripting one-sixth of the entire population in the expectation that the campaign against the Soviet Union would be short. Having dismissed Soviet peace overtures in August, she had to return manpower to the economy as the expectation of a quick victory disappeared. By June 1942 Finland had cut her army nominally by four divisions, but real reductions probably accounted for another two or three divisions.

Finland's weakening effort produced a very special problem for Germany in that Finnish cooperation was essential for the execution of offensives against Leningrad and the Murmansk railroad that were planned for 1942, but in dealing with Finland Hitler found himself exposed to the perils of waging coalition warfare with few of its advantages. Finland's refusal to ally herself formally with Germany, her retention of an independent national command for her forces in Karelia, her maintenance of German forces on her soil and, crucially, her physical separation from Germany meant that Hitler had little leverage over Finland despite her dependence on German arms and grain shipments. The German plans for offensives in the north foundered upon Finnish reluctance to undertake major operations that would involve heavy losses, and Finnish reticence was not overcome by Hitler until mid-1944 when impending defeat forced Finland into alliance with Germany – though the basic ambiguity in Finnish–German relations was maintained to the end by virtue of the fact that the Finns regarded this alliance as one exacted under duress and chose to leave the war rather than abide by its terms.

The position of Germany relative to her other main associates – Bulgaria, Croatia, Hungary, Italy, Romania and Slovakia – was also ambiguous. Hungary, Italy and Romania each massively increased the size of their forces on the Eastern Front in readiness for the summer offensive, Hungary to 12, Italy to 10 and Romania to 22 divisions: Slovakia and Spain maintained their token commitments of single divisions. Further afield, Bulgarian and Italian forces of occupation in Greece and Yugoslavia limited German responsibilities in the Balkans. But the military value of these various contributions was as questionable as the political basis on which the associated powers made donations to what they increasingly recognised not as an Axis but a German cause. The associated divisions were wretchedly equipped, particularly in terms of armour, anti-tank guns, signals and transport, and had to be stiffened by the German formations they were supposed to support. The Hungarians and Romanians had to be kept as far apart as possible because both would far rather fight one another than an enemy for whom they had a dread based upon centuries of having lived alongside.

In fighting on the Eastern Front none of the satellite troops were sustained by nonsensical illusions of grandeur that endowed them with *Herrenvolk* status, and none were not conscious of the contempt in which they and their countries were held by the German system, notwithstanding often good relations at various levels in the field between themselves and the *Wehrmacht*. By 1942 the associated powers knew that their fates were tied to that of Germany, yet they also knew that they had every reason to fear a German victory as much as a German defeat. Nazism abrogated, as the natural right of the German *Volk*, the resources of Germany's associates, an imposition that was ever more ruthlessly applied as defeat came closer, yet the Germans were never able to comprehend the hatred that their demands generated and they could never understand, except in terms of the innate treachery of inferior races, the ease and willingness with which such countries as Italy and Romania defected to the enemy. Germans could not see, and Nazism could never allow for the fact, that Germany's allies had interests that were not necessarily the same as those of the *Reich* and that their primary loyalty was not to Germany.

If in 1942 the worst aspects of German behaviour in the satellite countries were reserved for the future, German cruelty and greed had been given free rein in the Soviet Union from the start of *Operation Barbarossa*. Herein lay the fourth and concluding element in Germany's defeats: an inability in and after 1942 to draw upon the resources of the occupied territories, specifically within the Soviet Union, on a scale that could have made good her various manpower and economic deficiencies. In this fact was Hitler's lasting achievement, perhaps his only lasting achievement, and without doubt this represented the supreme irony of the Second World War. It has already been noted that what made the *Wehrmacht* so formidable in the early years of the war, a racism that provided it with a moral ascendancy over its various enemies, prevented the consolidation of victories by denying the Germans the means to offer the subjected peoples of Europe anything other than slavery and death. In 1941 many sections of Soviet society welcomed the Germans as liberators from Stalinist tyranny, but the barbarism of the *Wehrmacht* in its treatment of prisoners and civilians quickly convinced the various peoples of the Soviet Union not just that they could not look to the outside world for support in overthrowing Stalin and his commissars but that the invader would take away what little they had, particularly their hopes. Herein was the irony of the situation, albeit one that exacted an unimaginable toll of human suffering: by presenting the Soviet peoples with a fight to the death, Hitler legitimised Stalin's rule in a way that Stalin himself failed to do and ultimately ensured the survival of communist rule in the Soviet Union.

The nature and extent of German atrocities in the Soviet Union form no direct part of an account and chronology of the 1942 campaign on the Eastern Front other than to note the political and military consequences of actions that are explicable only in terms of their authors believing that they would never be held to account for their crimes. Apologias that have attempted to justify or mitigate German behaviour by reference to Stalin's own crimes, Soviet treatment of captured German personnel or the very nature of warfare on the Eastern Front can be dismissed with little consideration: the Germans invaded the Soviet Union with the intention of exterminating certain specific social groups and whole populations as a deliberate act of policy. It could be noted, however, that by the terms of reference that the Germans set themselves, the extermination of 30,000,000 people in order to allow German colonisation and control of European Russia, German (mis)rule was both inefficient and a failure. But during and since the Second World War attention has focused upon the more obvious German failure to tap anti-Russian and anti-communist sentiment within the Soviet Union and to turn it against Stalin, it generally being considered that this squandering of a fund of goodwill for the invader was disastrous for the German cause in the east.

There can be little doubt that this was indeed the case, if only in the negative sense. German excesses, and it must be noted that initial pogroms against Jews and communist officials received widespread support and acclaim in Belorussia and the Ukraine, ultimately ensured that the *Wehrmacht* could not win the campaign in the east after 1942. But it cannot be asserted definitively, however, that had the Germans, if only for short-term tactical reasons, adopted a conciliatory policy towards the peoples of the Soviet Union, the *Wehrmacht* would have prevailed on the Eastern Front. A securely held rear area would have been of inestimable value to the *Wehrmacht* after 1942, but partisan activity in 1941 was of small account and scarcely more developed in the next year. Given German equipment problems and transport shortages, the acquisition of manpower in itself was of little advantage to the Germans in 1941 and 1942, and these were the only years in which the *Wehrmacht* had any realistic chance of defeating the Soviet Union. Given these imponderables, perhaps the only safe conclusions to be drawn from the German situation on the Eastern Front on 28 June 1942, the date of the start of the German summer offensive, remain the obvious military ones: that after Kerch and Kharkov the *Wehrmacht* possessed certain clear advantages over the Soviet army in the south; that the *Wehrmacht* was beset by various long-term structural problems that made victory in 1942 essential if final defeat was to be avoided; and that the *Wehrmacht* began its 1942 summer offensive with a confused, incoherent plan of campaign that repeated many of the errors that had characterised the planning of *Operation Barbarossa*.

Perhaps the least obvious weakness of *Operation Blau*, his plan of campaign, lay in the fact that by aiming at economic objectives in 1942 Hitler paradoxically denied himself the chance of recording the very military and political victory that Germany had to win this summer. A more obvious weakness, though one that was not fully appreciated by the German High Command in spring 1942, was that in seeking to secure economic objectives that would both cripple the Soviet Union and provide Germany with long-term insurance against defeat, nothing less than the occupation of Baku, the Donets and the Donbass, plus Voronezh, Saratov, Stalingrad and Astrakhan was essential – and wholly beyond German resources. The obvious weakness of Hitler's *Directive No 41*, however, was that in seeking to wage economic warfare in southern Russia in 1942 Hitler was not consistent because in addition to the offensive in the south the *Wehrmacht* was to mount a simultaneous effort in the north to secure Leningrad and link up with the Finns on the

Karelian Isthmus and on the Svir. Though this effort was clearly secondary to that made in the south, an offensive against Leningrad – to be undertaken on the dubious political grounds of the moral effect of securing the birthplace of the modern Russian state and of communism – represented a major undertaking, the *Wehrmacht* being thus committed to two offensives at either end of an extended front.

This fundamental error was compounded by four further decisions. In order to mount the southern offensive *Army Groups North* and *Centre* in spring 1942 were stripped of armour and denied infantry reinforcements, with obvious strategic implications for both commands, yet in order to proceed with the reduction of Leningrad – *Operation Nordlicht* – the greater part of the *11th Army* was to be moved north, thereby removing from the south the only formation capable of acting as the strategic reserve for *Operation Blau*. Moreover, *Operation Blau* itself involved no fewer than four suspect associated armies two of which, the *2nd Hungarian* and *8th Italian Armies*, were newly raised, while any attempt to develop an offensive into the Caucasus obviously needed the specialist mountain divisions that had been concentrated in the Arctic for *Operation Lachsfang*, the advance on Kandalaksha. With the bulk of Soviet ground and air forces held around Moscow after May 1942, and one-third of the entire Soviet air force held in reserve at this time, the German plan of campaign for the summer of 1942 did not hang together. With the delays imposed upon the *Wehrmacht* by operations in the Crimea and around Kharkov constituting a further, hidden weakness, the German summer offensive was not to begin until after the sun had begun its annual journey to the south.

The plan with which *Army Group South* began its summer offensive envisaged a double offensive to clear Soviet forces from within the bends of the Don and Donets, to secure flanking positions at and between Voronezh and Stalingrad, and to occupy the oilfields of the northern Caucasus, specifically at Maikop. The initial attack, made by the *2nd, 4th Panzer* and *2nd Hungarian Armies* from the Kursk area, brushed aside the 40th Army and reached the Don either side of Voronezh, on the east bank, on 5 July, but in trying to secure the city *Army Group South* encountered serious, sustained opposition for the first time. Possession of Voronezh would provide the *Wehrmacht* with the option of developing an offensive against Yelets and Tula, and at this stage of proceedings the Stavka, despite intelligence to the contrary, suspected that Moscow was the objective of the German offensive. The Soviet High Command thus moved two armies from the Bryansk Front and an army from Tambov to support the 60th and 40th Armies at Voronezh, the result being that the *2nd* and *2nd Hungarian Armies* encountered what German radio admitted was 'ferocious Soviet resistance' before the city was secured on 23 July. By that date, however, the situation in the south had been transformed by two simultaneous developments, one the result of changes of command and plan by Hitler and the other of the unfolding of the battle as the full weight of the German offensive was unleashed and the consequences of Soviet disadvantages of time and position in the south became apparent.

The most important change instigated by Hitler was his decision to split *Army Group South* into two independent commands, *Army Groups B* and *A*, effective from 9 July. It was not until 23 July, and the issuing of *Directive No 45*, that the purpose of this division of forces became clear, it being Hitler's intention to use *Army Group B* to secure the Don and Stalingrad while *Army Group A* crossed the lower Don and secured the northern Caucasus oilfields. On the thirteenth, however, Hitler decided upon the dismissal of *Army Group B*'s commander who, as commander *Army Group South*, was blamed by Hitler for having allowed his forces to become involved in a costly, time-consuming and unnecessary battle for Voronezh and who had had the temerity to dispute his orders. But if the cause of simplicity and continuity were not helped by these decisions, worse was to follow on the sixteenth with one of Hitler's most crucial decisions, as a direct result of the battle within the bend of the Don developing along lines that were overwhelmingly to the *Wehrmacht*'s advantage.

Whatever the merits of the Voronezh argument, the battle for the city did not prevent the *4th Panzer Army* from developing its offensive along the Don as intended, the *6th Army* following behind the armour as it moved southwards. The *4th Panzer Army* as it came south encountered virtually no resistance as it swept through Rossosh and the Kantemirovka–Boguchar gap. The latter had ostensibly been covered by the 28th and 57th Armies, both of which had been shattered at Kharkov and were incapable of offering serious resistance. To their left were the 9th and 38th Armies, similarly depleted as a result of that same battle and then being driven back by an offensive along the Kupyansk–Debaltsevo sector by *Army Group A* after 6 July. This particular offensive had opened with the *1st Panzer Army* shattering the 37th Army in front of Lisichansk before developing a wide sweep on the east bank of the Donets in the general direction of Kamensk-Shakhtinskiy. In the context of this favourable development of the campaign, Hitler on the sixteenth ordered the *4th Panzer Army* southwards, to join with the *1st Panzer Army* in securing and forcing the lower Don.

The German Summer Offensive, 27 June - 6 July 1942

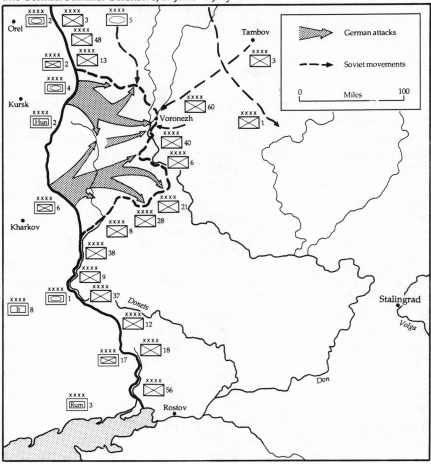

Military commentators and historians have generally identified this decision as the one that cost Hitler victory in the summer campaign, and, if at least one observer is to be believed, victory in the entire war. Neither this campaign nor the entire war was decided as a result of a single operational decision, however important, yet there is no escaping the conclusion that this particular decision was crucial in the unfolding of events because its effect was to throw away a very real chance that the Germans had in mid-July of seizing Stalingrad by a *coup de main* before

The German Summer Offensive, 6 - 24 July 1942

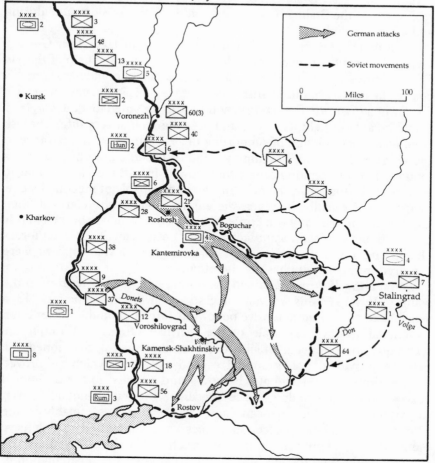

the Soviets had time to prepare the city for an assault and to move formations from the reserve into the region. The fact that on 30 July Hitler ordered the *4th Panzer Army*, then on the lower Don between Razdorskaya and Romanovskaya, to resume its advance on Stalingrad was a tacit acknowledgement that the 16 July decision was wrong, but in reality an attempt to rush Stalingrad with armour in July had no guarantee of success. In the event the *6th Army* was able to estabish itself on the Volga after beating the 4th Tank, 62nd and 64th Armies that had been deployed within the bend of the Volga to stop it. The 16 July decision

227

certainly cost *Army Group B* a very important advantage of tempo, but the real errors of the Stalingrad campaign on the German side came during and after September.

Nevertheless, Hitler's decision of 16 July was a mistake. *Army Group A* was quite capable of securing the lower Don without the help of the *4th Panzer Army*, and the latter's diversion to the south only added to German confusion as two armoured armies converged on a single, narrow sector. The switch of the *4th Panzer Army* southwards assumed that the *6th Army* would be able to fight its way to and over the Don, a very different task from its present mission of supporting the *4th Panzer Army*'s advance to the Volga and thereafter holding ground. With little armour and only a tenuous line of communication that slowed its advance as it came to Rossosh and Boguchar, the *6th Army* was not capable of meeting its new obligations. Crucially, however, the euphoria within the German High Command and the southern armies as the Soviet front was broken in July obscured one very significant fact: a major encirclement of Soviet forces eluded the German armies and relatively few Soviet soldiers were captured in this initial phase of the offensive.

Though the *Wehrmacht* gained the impression of a Soviet rout in the south in July 1942 this was not the case as, for the first time in 1942, a sensible and coherent defensive policy was forced upon the Soviet High Command by the very scale of the German offensive. Without the technique to conduct a mobile defence, the Soviets abandoned the practice of trying to hold ground irrespective of cost – which had proved so disastrous in 1941 and at Kharkov – and reverted to the traditional Russian policy of trading space for time. Inevitably, not all Soviet formations were able to escape and in certain places, notably in the Donets industrial region, certain forces were committed to defensive battles that could only end in their destruction, but the policy of general retreat bought time for the Soviet army to attempt the rehabilitation of formations that were able to escape encirclement and the move of forces from the reserve to the Stalingrad Front.

The course of the summer campaign was to be decided in that, by very slender margins, the Soviet retreat served its various purposes. The greater part of the eight armies west of the Don and Donets in June were able to escape encirclement, though they needed a crash indoctrination programme to steady morale, and in the last 10 days of July two Soviet armies moved into the bend on the Don at the very time when the *6th Army* attempted to rush Stalingrad. A divided command structure, poor coordination between these armies and a supporting tank army, and German domination of the skies over the battlefield resulted in the *6th*

Army defeating the Soviets in the first three weeks of August, but German success was only partial and was costly to *Army Group B* in terms of time and balance. With the *4th Panzer Army* stranded for want of fuel some 40 miles south-west of Stalingrad throughout these battles, it was not until 20 July that the *6th Army* was able to force the Don with *XIV Panzer Corps*, which established itself on the banks of the Volga, just to the north of Stalingrad, on the twenty-third. By 31 July, infantry had been pushed through to the Volga, but with three Soviet armies gathering on the left flank of this corridor and the *6th Army* badly extended along the line of march, *Army Group B* was unable either to close the trap around the 62nd and 64th Armies or to move immediately against Stalingrad itself. Yet as the campaign in the south entered what the German High Command realised would be a crucial phase, the basic weaknesses of the German plan of campaign began to assert themselves with disastrous results for the *Wehrmacht*.

The first of these weaknesses began to appear in early August as the *6th Army* did battle with the 62nd and 64th Armies on the Kletskaya–Surovikino line, the implications of having the *3rd Romanian* and *8th Italian Armies* as flank protection for the *6th Army* causing *OKH* serious concern for the first time. Hitler was persuaded to move a single armoured division into position behind the Italians in order to provide some small insurance against Soviet counter-attack, but this was wholly inadequate given that virtually the whole length of the Don below Voronezh was held by three associated armies which, like the Germans, made no attempt to prepare defences in depth behind the river. Given that at this stage the accent of Axis operations was upon the offensive, the provision of proper defences along the Don called for some strategic prescience, yet failure to show such foresight was to have obvious consequences by the autumn when mobility and the initiative had been lost and *Army Group B* was on the defensive awaiting counter-attack. It was not the case, however, that in the summer the Axis was not given fair warning of the danger inherent in its position. As the *6th Army* advanced on Stalingrad it was obliged to leave various small Soviet bridgeheads on the west bank unreduced, and between 20 and 28 August the 1st Guards Army secured a major foothold over the Don around Ust-Khopershiy, there being no Axis attempt to eliminate this obvious threat to the *6th Army*'s left flank and rear. In the heady atmosphere prevailing at Hitler's headquarters at this time, this development was brushed aside on the assumption that such bridgeheads could be eliminated once Stalingrad had been secured.

The second weakness was one that Hitler could not dismiss so lightly.

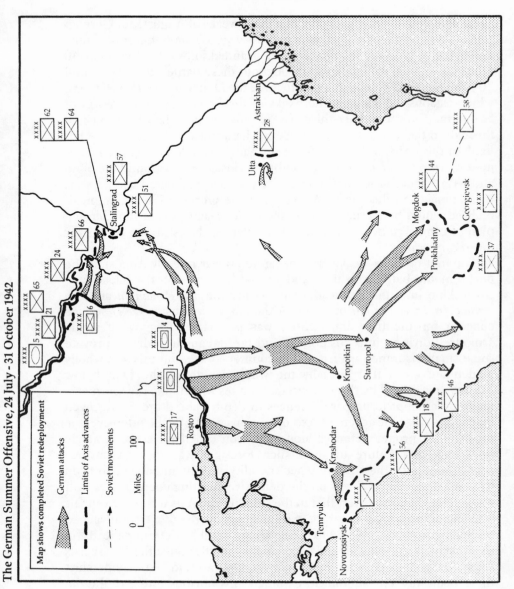

The German Summer Offensive, 24 July - 31 October 1942

Map shows completed Soviet redeployment

German attacks

Limits of Axis advances

Soviet movements

Miles

0   100

As early as the first two weeks in July, at the very time when the 5th Tank Army battered itself to destruction around Voronezh, Soviet forces in front of Moscow had conducted a series of attacks, most notably against *2nd Panzer Army*. From this time dates the Soviet practice of blooding new formations in the quiet sectors of the front, but the July attacks were launched with a somewhat different aim: to pin German armour and prevent its movement to the south and in this the Soviets were successful. In fact the movement was the other way. In July, at a time when it was involved in major anti-partisan operations, *Army Group Centre* received two armoured divisions from – of all sources – *Army Group B*, which also lost two more formations to France at this time, but after August *Army Group Centre* could not release forces to the south as a crisis developed on its other flank with the start of a major Soviet attempt to raise the siege of Leningrad on 27 August. This offensive involved Soviet attacks on both sides of the narrow corridor that *Army Group North* had pushed through to Lake Ladoga, but in the course of one month's fighting some 60,000 Soviet troops were killed around Mga and initial Soviet gains were eliminated. Though the Soviet offensive failed in its objective it nevertheless had one significant result. In order to retain Mga the Germans were forced to commit the forces being assembled for *Operation Nordlicht* in September, and with their commitment ended all German hopes of staging that particular offensive.

The final weakness that manifested itself at this time was the crisis within the German High Command that erupted in early September directly as a result of the various changes of plan that caused the armies in the south to pursue divergent objectives without the means to achieve any single one. Initially German plans had envisaged closing the Volga to Soviet commercial traffic and the occupation of the northern Caucasus, but Hitler's prediction in *Directive No 45* that 'the enemy will probably defend (Stalingrad) tenaciously' seems to have been self-fulfilling as Hitler was increasingly attracted by the prospect of seeking a decision at Stalingrad simply because of the city's name. But while events on the Volga have attracted the lion's share of attention for obvious reasons, it was, in fact, *Army Group A*'s problems that provoked the September crisis.

Directive No 45 widened its objectives to include the occupation of the entire eastern coast of the Black Sea plus the Baku area, but in crossing the Don *Army Group A* abandoned the abysmal road system of European Russia for the non-existent road system of Asiatic Russia. As a result it found itself increasingly dependent upon the *Luftwaffe* for fuel supplies for its armour, and inevitably it encountered mounting difficulties by the end of August as it tried to sustain its advance at distances 300 miles beyond the Don. It had been able to secure Stavropol on 5 August, Maikop and Krasnodar on the ninth, and Piatigorsk on the tenth, but around Maikop and Piatigorsk *Army Group A* was drawn into battles that lasted into the third week of August. It was nevertheless able to fight its way into the Mozdok area by 31 August, but Mozdok represented the practical limits of capacity of a command that had begun its drive from the Don with just 435 tanks and which, by the end of August, faced 20 Soviet divisions in the southern mountains. Given the state of his forces, the commander-in-chief *Army Group A*, Field Marshal von List, disputed Hitler's order that he transfer formations to support the offensive developed in early September by the *11th Army* from Kerch against Novorossiysk. In this protest List was supported by *OKW* which, despite its subservience to Hitler, recognised that this order was impractical. The result was that List was dismissed without replacement on 9 September and the two chief staff officers at *OKW* were deemed to be disgraced by Hitler, who refused any contact with them other than at formal briefing conferences where they were not allowed to speak other than during their reports. On 24 September the simmering disputes between Hitler and *OKH* finally ended with Hitler's dismissal of the army's chief of staff, Hitler's last word in the exchanges being that at this time the army needed Nazi commitment and not professional competence. It was, with Hitler's assumption of direct command of *Army Group A* from his headquarters at Vinnitsa, an incredible way of conducting a campaign, still less a war – and at the very time when the battle for and inside Stalingrad began to go seriously wrong for *Army Group B*.

Other than the struggle for Leningrad, the battle of Stalingrad proved the longest single land battle of the European war and, with the exception of the battle for Warsaw in 1944, was the most ferociously murderous battle of the Second World War. It very quickly degenerated into a series of fragmented actions fought for control of streets, individual buildings and even single rooms, though from its start it exhibited an almost mathematical quality. As the *6th Army* broke into the suburbs, most of which had been gutted by a *Luftwaffe* attack on 23/24 August, retention of the east bank of the Volga and the river ferries enabled the Soviets to feed reinforcements into the city at the minimum necessary to commit the *6th Army* to a battle of attrition inside Stalingrad. By avoiding the temptation to commit the maximum possible numbers to the battle, the trap into which the *6th Army* fell in its increasingly desperate attempt to secure the city before the onset of winter, the Soviets were able to wrest the initiative from *Army Group B* by late October while concentrating reserves on the flanks of a *6th Army* stalled on the banks of the Volga some 35 miles from its only natural line of defence. Leaving aside the obvious German failings in being drawn into a battle in which the *Wehrmacht*'s advantages in mobile operations counted for nothing and the poor conduct of the battle inside Stalingrad itself, the struggle for the city between 23 August and 18 November represented the first occasion in the Nazi–Soviet conflict when the Soviet army outfought and, crucially, out-thought the *Wehrmacht*, and it did so with no margin of superiority over its enemy.

The extent of the difference between German and Soviet conduct of operations in and around Stalingrad in autumn 1942 can be gauged by the fact that as early as the beginning of September, at the very time when German forces broke into Stalingrad and its defenders had no guarantee that they could hold at least part of the city, the Soviet High Command began preparations for a counter-offensive in the winter against *Army Group B*. With nearly half of *Army Group B*'s total of 85 divisions east of the Don, the long and weakly held left flank along the length of the river presented itself as the obvious sector for a counter-stroke, but in planning *Operation Uranus* the Stavka combined elements of deception and surprise with a revised operational doctrine that added a new dimension to Soviet offensive undertakings. The obvious target for a counter-offensive was the sector held by the *8th Italian Army* because any breach made on the middle Don would provide Soviet armies with the opportunity to drive for the Sea of Azov in the expectation of the encirclement of *Army Group A* and most of *Army Group B*. The Stavka plans, however, were tailored to modest Soviet capabilities and phased objectives, *Uranus* aiming at nothing more than the double encirclement of German forces around Stalingrad by converging attacks neither of which had to advance more than 90 miles.

In setting its armies this task, the Stavka sought to mislead the German High Command regarding its intentions by a series of elaborate deception measures that pass under the collective name of *maskirovka* in Soviet military vocabulary. This effort involved very tight signals security, the movement of forces by night into prepared positions and the extensive use of camouflage in those sectors where attacks were to be made, and various ruses, most notably dummy movements and concentrations in other areas, designed to lead German intelligence away from the conclusion that a Soviet counter-offensive would be directed against the *3rd* and *4th Romanian Armies*. The open steppe, the first snows and German superiority in the air made any concentration of Soviet formations along the Don difficult to conceal, but in its attempt to disguise the location, scale and timing of its counter-offensive the Stavka was aided by a chronic division of opinion within the German High Command on the question of Soviet intentions. As winter approached *Army Group B* became convinced that the sector held by the *8th Italian Army* would be where the Soviet counter-blow would fall. The *6th Army* showed ever more concern for its immediate flanks, on the open steppe between the Volga and Don, and *OKH* hardened in the view that the main Soviet effort would be made in front of Moscow. But this uncertainty was compounded by a more fundamental error in the assessment of Soviet capabilities. As the battle inside Stalingrad made increasing demands on German manpower, Hitler convinced himself that Soviet resources were being depleted at a rate that precluded the enemy making any serious offensive effort in the coming winter.

More realistically, *OKH* and *Army Group B* separately recognised that the winter would see a major Soviet offensive operation, but without strong armoured reserves both were reduced to the hope that the Soviets would not be able to tear too many holes in the front.* In effect, both placed their trust in German formations being able to repeat their previous winter's demonstration of tactical superiority over the Soviet army and thereby hold the front together despite local Soviet successes. But in this hope these two commands, like Hitler, failed to realise both the extent to which Soviet operational technique had developed in the course of 1942 and the manner in which the Stavka intended to fight the winter battle.

The Soviet army, which had begun 1942 with the brigade as its standard armoured formation, by the autumn had organised its armour into corps, sometimes with two but usually with three brigades, thereby adding substantially to its offensive power. As important as this organisational change was the evolution of an offensive doctrine that set out to nullify German superiority at the tactical level. The Stavka sought success at the operational level – between army and army group levels of command – in order to compensate for its formations being outfought tactically, the Soviet calculation being that intense pressure across an extended front would bring a potentially decisive success at some point that would offset any number of tactical defeats. In devising this operational concept for *Operation Uranus* the Stavka provided an element of subtlety by selecting the sectors held by the *3rd* and *4th Romanian Armies* as those parts of the front where the main Soviet offensive efforts would be made. In adding this particular ingredient to the *maskirovka*

*See Appendix B

234

concept, the Stavka provided what remained the principal source of German confusion after the winter battles had been decided.

In considering the lessons of defeat the *Wehrmacht* attributed its defeat at Stalingrad and throughout the south during the winter of 1942–43 to 'exceptional circumstances', namely the mistake in having the flanks of the *6th Army* held by weak Romanian armies. Those 'exceptional circumstances' were precisely the reason for the Soviet decision, hence German confusion. It formed no part of Soviet offensive doctrine in 1942 to seek out German armour. Through *maskirovka* the Soviets sought to ensure that strategically the bulk of German armour could be side-stepped whilst offensives were developed along the lines of least resistance, the Soviet intention being to encircle and annihilate enemy infantry – thereby lowering the effectiveness of enemy armour – before German mobile formations could move to support the infantry. In November 1942 the infantry selected by the Stavka was Romanian, in subsequent offensives German, but in noting that the formations singled out for destruction were Romanian rather than German infantry the *Wehrmacht* misled itself about the nature of Soviet offensive doctrine.

These various developments of organisation and doctrine within the Soviet military establishment during 1942 meant that when *Operation Uranus* opened on 19 November *Army Group B* faced an enemy and a threat formidably different from those that had been defeated with such contemptuous ease at Kharkov six months earlier, but by the time that the Soviet counter-offensive opened the German High Command was two weeks into an equally dangerous crisis that demanded its attention and resources – the crumbling of the Axis position throughout the Mediterranean theatre as a result of the collapse of *Panzerarmee Afrika* on the Alamein position and the Allied landings in French North Africa.

In immediate military terms neither the Axis defeat in Egypt nor the Allied landings in Morocco and Algeria were particularly significant. At Alamein a dozen Axis divisions were destroyed or sought safety in flight, their defeat having been ensured by the Allied landings in the eastern Mediterranean where no Axis formations were deployed. The importance of Alamein and the *Torch* landings was nevertheless very considerable. *Torch* marked the first commitment of American combat troops if not to Europe then to the European war, while Alamein was the victory essential to Britain after an otherwise disastrous year and before she was reduced, within the anti-German alliance, to a position of *minor inter pares* by her material weaknesses *vis-à-vis* the Soviet Union and United States. In the longer term, however, the military implications of Alamein and *Torch* were substantial, if somewhat double-edged. Success at either end of the Mediterranean and an increasingly authoritative British naval primacy in the theatre ensured an Allied victory along the entire length of the North African coast despite the arrival of German forces in Tunis on 9 November, one day after the *Torch* landings. With this victory would come a crucial positional change in the conduct of the war to Germany's disadvantage. Control of North Africa and the sea exposed the whole of southern Europe to a threat of invasion that was as potent, indeed more potent, than invasion itself, and it placed a weakened, war-weary Italy in the front line with obvious implications for German commitments. In effect, after November 1942 Germany was fighting a two-front war for the first time, and to this must be added another, no less significant, development. On 27 October, some three months before the first American air raids on the *Reich*, a 1943 production objective of 107,000 aircraft was given priority by the Roosevelt administration.

The battle of Alamein, the British swansong of the Second World War, was fought between 23 October and 5 November. With the initiative and a superiority of 2:1 in manpower, 5:2 in armour and 4:1 in the air, the British were able to fight and win a battle of attrition against an enemy that at the start of this action lacked sufficient fuel for its armour to allow for more than a single tactical redeployment. The slowness with which a decision was reached on the ground despite these overwhelming British advantages was the result of the British desire to win an economical victory, the difficulties in clearing minefields laid to depths of five miles, and the 8th Army's inability until the final stages of the battle to secure the 5:1 infantry superiority on axes of advance that were needed to overcome Axis defences. But for all the time it took to force a favourable outcome, and despite the much-criticised slowness of the pursuit after *Panzerarmee Afrika* abandoned its positions on 4 November, the British victory at Alamein was so comprehensive that not only was Egypt secured but the enemy was rendered incapable of defending Cyrenaica.

Alamein cost the British some 4,500 dead and 150 tanks destroyed, but in return *Panzerarmee Afrika* lost half its personnel killed or captured and was reduced to some 20,000 effectives and 21 tanks at the end of the battle. If the British missed the chance to complete the annihilation of Axis forces in Egypt between 3 and 6 November the 8th Army nevertheless advanced the 700 miles to Benghazi in 15 days. Perhaps a more valid criticism of the conduct of the pursuit lies in Montgomery's refusal to sanction an attack off the line of march against the El Agheila position, reached by *Panzerarmee Afrika* on the twenty-fourth, Montgomery preferring to repeat the Alamein formula with a setpiece assault scheduled for 16 December. This intention was frustrated, however, by Rommel's refusal to be drawn into such a battle, in part because El Agheila's retention was important only for offensive operations which would no longer be undertaken, in part because Axis attention at this stage was concentrated upon Tunisia and western Tripolitania.

By mid-December what remained of *Panzerarmee Afrika* had withdrawn to Buerat, midway between El Agheila and Tripoli, but despite a month on this position Axis forces made no attempt to hold Buerat when the 8th Army assaulted the town on 15 January 1943. Tripoli itself was taken on 23 January. In exactly three months, therefore, the 8th Army fought and won one battle and advanced about 2,000 miles, destroying one Axis army, securing Egypt and conquering Italy's last colony in the process. For all the 8th Army's superiority of strength over *Panzerarmee Afrika* at all stages of this campaign, the sum of its efforts represented no mean achievement and the victory that Britain needed at this time.

The extent of the Alamein defeat was only one factor in the urgency of the Axis withdrawal from Egypt and Cyrenaica: equally important were the Allied landings in Morocco and around Oran and Algiers on 8 November that threatened to roll up the Axis position in Libya from the west even as the 8th Army advanced from the east. In the event, however, this threat was forestalled. The Allied decision to land no further east than Algiers left British forces 400 miles from Tunis and the French forces in Tunisia without immediate physical and moral support in what was a very confused situation. Following Hitler's decision of 11 November to hold Tunisia as a base for future operations in Africa, the Axis powers were able to move five divisions into Tunisia in November and thereby denied the British formations that entered northern Tunisia at the same time the chance to eliminate resistance before it had time to harden. These British formations were able to reach within 10 miles of Tunis at the end of November, but were then thrown back and the *5th Panzer Army* was able to stabilise the situation.

Impressive though these achievements were, they nevertheless had certain implications. The Italian navy's success in moving these divisions by sea to Tunisia without loss was achieved at the expense of any real attempt to support Rommel's forces in Cyrenaica. Axis success in seizing and then holding Tunis owed much to local German air supremacy, but that supremacy existed by default and in the long term the Axis air forces could not match the numbers that the Allies were certain to concentrate over Tunisia. Moreover, whilst the initial movement of forces to Tunis was by air – and German transports were diverted from the Eastern

Front for this task – Axis armies in Tunisia could only be sustained by sea, and by November 1942 the Italian merchant marine in the Mediterranean totalled less than 1.08 million tons. Given ships not in commission, coastal trade requirements and Italian obligations in the Balkans and Aegean, this total represented no more than 350,000 tons of shipping with which to support the armies in Africa – and in effect the end of Italy's capacity to sustain this commitment.

Thus from the start the long-term prospects of the Axis holding Tunisia were somewhat bleak, not unlike the prospects of Germany and Italy themselves, but when the campaign was lost Hitler justified the effort made in Tunisia in terms of its having bought six months in which to prepare for the defence of southern Italy. The effort against time calculation is one that cannot be quantified, but there can be little doubt that if in military terms Hitler would have done better to have followed Rommel's advice to cede North Africa after Alamein, the speed of his reactions to events in the Maghreb and obvious determination to master the situation that had arisen served to hold his various allies in line. November 1942 provided two tests of Hitler's leadership – and twin condemnation of his lack of foresight – and even if Hitler could not prevent Germany's allies realising the implications of events his reaction to them stifled, for the moment at least, the first tentative suggestions in various capitals, notably Bucharest and Rome, that the war was lost.

After the Axis won the race to secure Tunis, the campaign divided into two parts: a period before mid-March 1943 when the Axis armies held the initiative and conducted a series of local but indecisive offensives, and the subsequent phase when the variously assorted British 1st and 8th Armies, constituted as the 18th Army Group, completed the clearing of Tunisia, forcing the last remaining formations of the *1st Italian Army* to surrender at Cap Bon on 13 May. This campaign is best remembered for the battle of the Kasserine Pass, fought between 14 and 22 February, and for the fact that the American 1st Armored Division was cut to pieces in the opening exchanges and II US Corps was badly mauled, yet in reality the Germans were obliged to abandon this offensive on 22 February after being outfought by fresh Allied forces moved into defensive positions behind Kasserine. For all its initial success, the Kasserine offensive left *Army Group Africa* relatively weaker than it had been before the battle, though this was of less significance than the more serious long-term weakening of the Axis armies in Tunisia as more Allied formations were moved into the combat zone after February and Allied naval and air power exacted a prohibitive toll on Axis shipping in the Mediterranean. January 1943 witnessed the destruction of 100,131 tons of Italian shipping, February a further 83,335 tons. In April and May only 58.6 per cent of the cargoes that sailed for Tunis reached their destination, and this constituted only one quarter of *Army Group Africa*'s needs. Between November 1942 and May 1943, as the Allied grip around Tunis tightened, the Italian merchant marine lost 584,081 tons of shipping or 54 per cent of the total available to it when the Tunisian commitment began. To these losses must be added a further 155,497 tons of German shipping destroyed in the Mediterranean in this same period, and this points to arguably the most significant result of the *Torch* venture. The Germans were able to acquire such shipping in the Mediterranean at this stage of the war primarily because on 11 November Hitler ordered the occupation of Vichy France. While this led to the capture of French shipping with which to supplement dwindling Italian resources, this action resolved the conflict of loyalties suffered by the French military as a result of the Allied invasion of North Africa.

It has been argued, and not altogether frivolously, that the crucial German mistake of the Second World War was to have behaved atrociously towards Poland and correctly to France when the reverse would have served German interests to better effect. Be that as it may, while Poland alone in occupied Europe had no quisling regime, only France had a legitimate, legally constituted government that collaborated with Germany to the point of enacting and enforcing violently anti-Semitic legislation. The existence of this government, and the widespread support commanded by Pétain throughout French society and, crucially, the armed forces, was instrumental in preventing the Free French movement, raised by de Gaulle in London in summer 1940, from attracting much support. The New Hebrides and Chad rallied to the Free French in August 1940, but they were virtually alone, and a series of British actions against French forces and colonies thereafter did little to advance de Gaulle's cause with his fellow countrymen.

But the invasions of North Africa by the Allies and of unoccupied France by the Germans in November 1942 presented the military forces that France had been allowed to retain in North Africa with a fresh choice. To date, anti-British sentiment, fear of communism, concepts of duty and obedience, and respect for the state, Pétain and German power had combined to ensure that most of the French military distanced itself from the Free French, and French forces in North Africa fought the invading Americans and British in November 1942, however reluctantly. The German occupation of Vichy France made the Pétain regime a prisoner and effectively broke the ties of loyalty that bound the French military in North Africa to Vichy, but not quickly enough to bring French forces to the Allied side with any positive short-term military results. In the very confused political situation that developed in November, French forces in Tunisia made no attempt to prevent Axis forces landing around Tunis. The fleet at Toulon made no attempt to escape to North Africa and scuttled itself on 27 November when the Germans attempted to seize it. But French forces in Tunisia that avoided being disarmed and interned withdrew into eastern Algeria and linked up with advancing British forces, and the return of the French army to the Allied side dates from December 1942, though perhaps predictably during the final phase of operations that ended with the capture of Tunis and Bizerte on 7 May two rival French forces, one Free French and the other violently anti-Gaullist, were in the Allied line. Politically the last two months of 1942 were very confused as various factions and individuals within the French community sought the mantle of legitimacy and respectability for their own exclusive use, but from this period, and after a six-month gestation, there was to emerge on 3 June 1943 the Committee of National Liberation, a *de facto* provisional government that under de Gaulle represented the reassertion of French rights, dignity and greatness – and endless trouble for Churchill and Roosevelt.

The collapse of Axis resistance in North Africa in May 1943 resulted in the surrender of some 93,000 German and 182,000 Italian troops, a total that was roughly the same as the number of Axis troops killed or captured at Stalingrad during the Soviet winter offensive of 1942–43. Inevitably, accounts of this campaign have been both dominated by the battle for Stalingrad and shaped by German sources. As a consequence, Anglo-American histories of the winter campaign have explained its unfolding in terms of the encirclement of Stalingrad; the actions involving *XXXXVIII Panzer Corps* on the Chir; *Operation Winterstorm* – to relieve the *6th Army*; and Field Marshal von Manstein's counter-offensive at Kharkov in March 1943 that stabilised the front. At best, any account that uses German sources and these events as its framework is inadequate and misleading. The much-vaunted German success on the Chir, for example, has often been presented as an example of German tactical resilience that stabilised a very dangerous situation: what is seldom if ever acknowledged in published Western accounts is the fact that while *XLVIII Panzer Corps* outfought the 5th Tank Army between 2 and 22 December, the Soviet formation, equipped with British tanks and assigned a flank protection role, neutralised the most potent threat to the Soviet offensive that was about to open on the middle Don and which resulted in the destruction of *Army Group B*'s front over a distance of 200 miles. Overall, the winter campaign of 1942–43 saw the German front in the south destroyed throughout its length between Voronezh and Rostov and six Axis armies destroyed in whole or in part. To this must be added the partial relief of Leningrad in January 1943 plus the German withdrawal to the Rzhev salient. Any attempt to explain the events of the winter campaign of 1942–43 in terms of Stalingrad and subsequent German tactical successes – the extrication of *Army Group A* from the Caucasus, the lower Chir operations and the Kharkov counter-offensive – fails to identify the real significance of events, the reality of overwhelming Soviet success at the operational level that more than outweighed various tactical defeats and the reverse at Kharkov in March 1943.

In the course of 1942 the Stavka raised no fewer than 10 reserve armies, each with about 110,000 men; more importantly it refused to commit the majority of these armies to the battles of the summer and autumn. By November most of these fresh armies had been concentrated with the Stalingrad, Don and South-west Fronts, which straddled Stalingrad and reached up the Don as far as Rossosh. It was these fronts and armies, under the command of General Vasilevsky, that were committed to *Operation Uranus*, three tank corps with the 5th Tank and 21st Armies of the South-west Front and one tank and one mechanised corps with the 57th and 51st Armies of the Stalingrad Front being the armoured pincers tasked to close around Stalingrad.

Operation Uranus opened on 19 November with attacks by the five armies of the South-west and Don Fronts though the 66th Army, between the Don and Volga, was committed to holding attacks while the breakthroughs were sought to the west by the 5th Tank, 21st and 65th Armies. Attacks by these formations on the *3rd Romanian Army*, and the various German formations in its company, were fiercely resisted, the 65th Army being singularly unfortunate in encountering the *14th Panzer Division* with the result that its offensive stalled. Such was Axis resistance on this first day of the offensive that the South-west Front was obliged to commit armour detailed for the exploitation phase to the main assault operations, but by the end of the first day's fighting the Soviets had mastered the Axis defences and on the twentieth broke the *3rd Romanian Army* along its entire front.

On the same day, the second part of *Operation Uranus* began with the Stalingrad Front's attack on the *4th Romanian Army*, and in this sector the same pattern of events repeated itself on roughly the same time scale. By 21 November Soviet armour was through the Axis positions and heading for a juncture with the forces pouring from the Don bridgeheads. On the

241

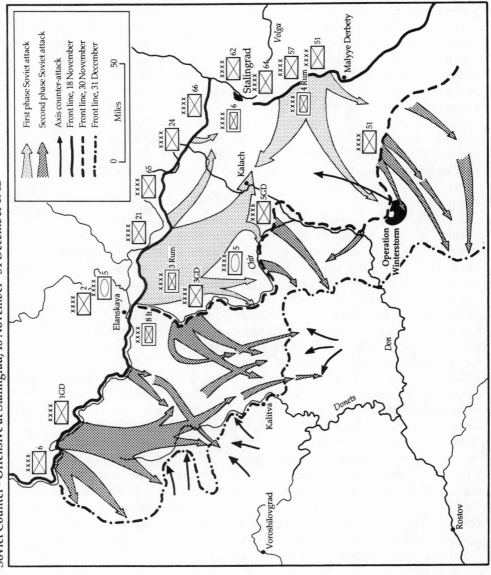

Soviet Counter - Offensive at Stalingrad, 18 November - 31 December 1942

twenty-second, after an advance of 61 miles in three days, units from the 26th Tank Corps, using captured German tanks and attacking from the west, secured the vital bridge over the Don at Kalach. On the following day units from the 4th Tank and 4th Mechanised Corps met around Sovetsky, thus completing the encirclement of Stalingrad, the *6th Army* and parts of the *3rd Romanian, 4th Romanian* and *4th Panzer Armies*. In the course of five days, therefore, the Soviet army had achieved what had eluded it over the previous winter, namely a clean break through the enemy front and a major encirclement – and it had achieved this without any overall numerical superiority over its enemies. Both *Army Group B* and Vasilevsky's forces numbered about 1,100,000 men and roughly the same number of tanks and aircraft, but Soviet success was the result of Soviet advantages of surprise, initiative and concentration, plus a rigid adherence to a simple, realistic aim.

Soviet success in encircling Stalingrad within five days of the start of *Operation Uranus* presented both sides with obvious problems, and predictably the Germans were the first to respond to events even though 19 November found Hitler at Berchtesgaden, *OKW* at Salzburg and *OKH* at Rastenburg in East Prussia. It was not until 22 November that Hitler returned to *OKH*, though by the time he did so he had settled the German course of action. Just as in December 1941 Hitler's response to a Soviet offensive had been one of no withdrawal, so in November 1942 he would not sanction any retreat from the Volga. At the same time, however, he set about the reorganisation of the armies in the south. *Army Group A* received its first commander for three months, and *Army Group B* was stripped of all but the *2nd, 2nd Hungarian* and *8th Italian Armies*. *Army Group B*'s other four armies were placed under the command of *Army Group Don*, and were tasked with restoring the situation within the bend of the Don and around Stalingrad, yet from the start *Army Group Don*'s activities were plagued by ambiguity. With two armoured forces – *XLVIII Panzer Corps* at Termosin and *LVII Panzer Corps* at Kotelnikovo – within striking distance of Stalingrad, *Army Group Don* was expected to effect the relief of the *6th Army*, but with the German position inside the Don crumbling and the *6th Army* under strict orders not to abandon its positions, there could be no question of extricating the garrison and any relief could only be very temporary. Moreover, any relief attempt involved very obvious risks for the formations thus committed. Even if Hitler took the decision to stand at Stalingrad for dubious political and personal reasons, the decision was correct on military grounds if the *6th Army* was left to pin down Soviet formations and thereby buy time for the rest of *Army Group Don* to restore the front. By committing *Army Group*

Don to a relief attempt, and in effect to the restoration of the original front, Hitler both underestimated the strength of the Soviets and threatened to squander the only benefit the *Wehrmacht* could draw from *6th Army*'s encirclement.

That particular benefit was far more substantial than the German High Command appreciated at the time. *Operation Uranus* had been prepared by a Soviet High Command very conscious of the fact that success at Stalingrad could open the way for a general offensive in the south. When Vasilevsky was ordered on 23 November to submit proposals for next-phase operations he recommended *Operation Saturn*, an offensive against the *8th Italian Army* on the middle Don that would be directed against Rostov. Conceived with the aim of encircling both *Army Group Don* and *Army Group A*, the *Saturn* proposal was to involve three Guards formations, the 1st and 3rd Guards Armies in the first echelon and the 2nd in the second, while flank protection would be provided by the 6th Army around Rossosh and the 5th Tank Army on the Chir. Before the end of November, however, Vasilevsky was obliged to scale down his *Saturn* proposals, precisely because of the situation at Stalingrad. Before the start of *Operation Uranus* the Stavka had accepted that any second-stage offensive was dependent upon the success of the effort at Stalingrad, and in recommending *Operation Saturn* Vasilevsky redefined Stalingrad as the Soviet priority in the south. But at Stalingrad in November Soviet armies surrounded 22 Axis divisions and perhaps as many as 290,000 troops, roughly three times what Stavka planning had envisaged. As this fact became apparent so the *Saturn* project died. Though Stalin wanted *Saturn* from the outset and tried to insist upon its implementation, in the first week of December Vasilevsky scaled down his proposals from the strategic to the operational level in order to release the 2nd Guards Army for service at Stalingrad. It was this formation that was to block the German attempt to relieve the *6th Army* in mid-December.

In place of *Saturn* Vasilevsky proposed, and the Stavka sanctioned, *Little Saturn*, an offensive aimed at the destruction of the *8th Italian Army* and the cutting of the railroad through Rossosh that was the main line of supply for Axis forces to the east. The commitment around Stalingrad, where no fewer than seven Soviet armies were tied down by the *6th Army* throughout December 1942, thus prevented the Soviets from making a strategic effort throughout the south in that month. It was, however, this operational effort, which began on 16 December, that provoked the actions on the Chir between *XLVIII Panzer Corps* and the 5th Tank Army as it set about the twin tasks of providing depth to the Stalingrad position

ABOVE: Hitler tapped a romantic strand of German values that repudiated liberal democracy and stressed race and society at the expense of the individual.

LEFT: Benito Mussolini, 'Il Duce'.

ABOVE: Emperor Hirohito of Japan reviewing his troops prior to the outbreak of war with China, 1937.

BELOW: The Anschluss, 13 March 1938: German troops enter Salzburg.

OPPOSITE

ABOVE: The Junkers JU87B – the Stuka – which played a crucial role in German *Blitzkrieg* tactics in the early part of the war.

BELOW: 'Danzig greets its Führer': Hitler's triumphant entry into the Free City, 19 September 1939.

ABOVE LEFT: Josef Stalin.

ABOVE RIGHT: Churchill, in the uniform of Honorary Air Commodore of the Royal Auxiliary Air Force, during the dark days of the Blitz.

Operation Barbarossa, 22 June 1941: with the frontier barriers swept aside, a German troop carrier crosses into Russia.

ABOVE: America enters the war: President Franklin D. Roosevelt.

BELOW: A Japanese pilot's view of the attack on Pearl Harbor,
7 December 1941.

OPPOSITE:

ABOVE: The Battle of the Atlantic. Demonstrating the increasing effect of air power a German U-Boat surrenders to the RAF.

BELOW: The Battle of the Atlantic: Britain's lifeline – t? convoy system.

LEFT: The horror of war on the Eastern Front: the bodies of Russian partisans lie in the snow beneath makeshift gallows.

BELOW: Singapore: a delegatio of British officers on their wa to meet General Yamashita to discuss surrender terms, August 1942.

The approaches to Stalingrad where more than 150,000 German troops were to
lose their lives before surrendering to the Russians on 31 January 1943.

Soviet tanks in action at the Battle of Kursk, July 1943.

The Allied Invasion of Sicily began on 10 July 1943. Six hundred ships and over 2,000 smaller craft were involved in landing troops and arms.

The Battle for Monte Cassino: the devastating destruction incurred as 2,500 tons of bombs rained down on Cassino in March 1944. As the bombardment died down, the fight for the ruins began.

ABOVE: The Teheran Conference, 28 November–1 December 1943. *Front row, left to right:* Stalin, Roosevelt, Churchill; *back row:* Molotov and Eden.

BELOW: On the beaches: the D-Day landings, 6 June 1944.

LEFT: Army Chiefs confer, June 1944: Generals Montgomery, Dempsey and Bradley in conversation.

RIGHT: General Dwight D. Eisenhower, Supreme Commander-in-Chief Allied Expeditionary Force, with James V. Forrestal, US Secretary of the Navy.

BELOW: At Hitler's Field Headquarters, 20 July 1944, within a few hours of the unsuccessful bomb plot. *Left to right*: Mussolini, Martin Borman, Admiral Doenitz, Hitler, Goering, Otto Skorzeny and General Loerzer.

LEFT: The Chindwin Crossing: a loaded pontoon barge makes history, opening the Chindwin way to Tokyo, December 1944.

RIGHT: Planning the final drive to free the Philippines. *Left to right:* MacArthur, Roosevelt, Admiral Chester Nimitz and Admiral William Leahy.

BELOW: Kamikaze attack by Japanese 'Zero' fighter aircraft.

ABOVE: Churchill, Roosevelt and Stalin at Yalta, February 1945.

LEFT: The results of area bombing: Dresden, 1945.

LEFT: Field Marshall Montgomery looks on as General Kinzel puts his signature to the surrender of German land, sea and air forces in Northern Germany, Holland and Denmark.

MIDDLE: The four major Allied military commanders in Berlin. *Left to right*: Montgomery, Eisenhower, Zhukov and the French commander, Lattre de Tassigny.

BELOW: VE Day, 8 May 1945: the gutted remains of the Reichstag in Berlin.

LEFT: A group of Marines raise the Stars and Stripes above the hard-won Mount Suribachi on Iwo Jima island, only 750 miles from Tokyo.

BELOW: Landing craft at the Okinawa beachhead.

LEFT: Smoke billowing more than 20,000 feet in the air from the atomic bomb dropped on Hiroshima, 6 August 1945.

BELOW: Hiroshima: the aftermath.

and protection for the 3rd Guards Army's subsequent operations. Moreover, it was this same effort, *Little Saturn*, that undercut *Operation Winterstorm*. Beginning on 12 December and involving 13 Axis divisions, the Germans attempted to relieve the *6th Army* by fighting their way to positions within 25 miles of the Stalingrad perimeter by 23 December, but in breaking open the Axis front along the middle Don over a distance of 120 miles *Little Saturn* destroyed the basis of an Axis offensive 200 miles further to the east.

If *Operation Uranus* displayed a growing Soviet technique in the art of *maskirovka*, *Operation Little Saturn* revealed an improved Soviet ability in the conduct of offensive operations even though the attack on the *8th Italian Army* was beset by a series of operational and technical errors. Without a second-echelon army, the Soviets stripped much of the front in order to secure massive superiority of force on very narrow attack frontages, the 1st Guards Army concentrating five divisions on an 11-mile sector while its two remaining divisions held 62 miles of front and the 3rd Guards Army four divisions on a nine-mile sector with its remaining divisions each holding 19 miles of front. In fact, the Soviets over-concentrated and created problems for themselves. They also made the error of spreading their artillery across the secondary sectors in order to disguise the attack sectors and pin down enemy forces. More seriously, the Soviets made the mistake of beginning reconnaissance on 11 December, which had the effect of telegraphing Soviet intentions to the Germans while not registering the fact that on the fifteenth various German formations were moved into the line in order to support the Italians. Nevertheless, with nearly 1,200 tanks to the 50 with the *8th Italian Army* and the 70 with the remnants of *3rd Romanian Army* and *XLVIII Panzer Corps* on the Italian right, the Voronezh and South-west Fronts had a material advantage that they used to good effect to crush desperate Axis resistance.

It took the Soviet armies three days to overcome Italian defensive positions that were only three and a half miles deep, lacked a second main line of resistance and were manned by what was in effect light infantry. By 20 December, however, the Soviet armies had split the Axis front along its entire length and were seeking to encircle Axis formations as the two Italian flanks drew apart. In the series of very confused actions that then followed as the Soviets sought to complete the annihilation of various pockets of resistance and newly arrived German formations established themselves at various positions in order to provide the framework for a new defence line, the Soviets destroyed the *8th Italian Army* as an effective fighting force but only at immense cost to themselves. As

The Soviet Offensive, Winter 1942-43

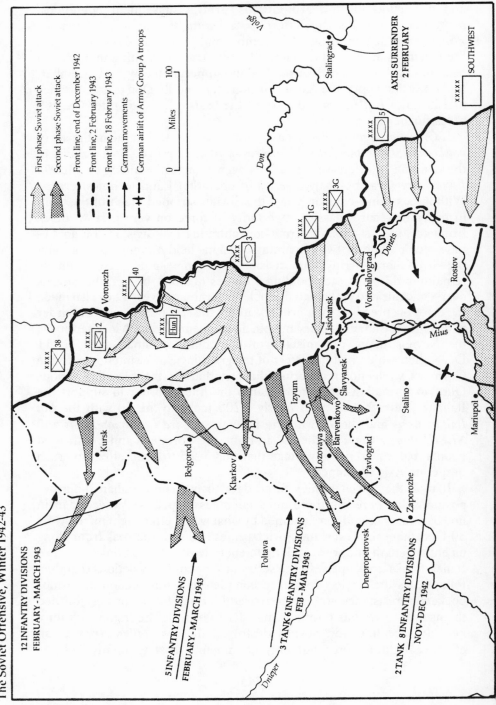

second-phase German resistance hardened and, crucially, the *Luftwaffe* returned to the battlefield with considerable effect, the battle on the middle Don effectively came to an end by 30 December with Soviet armour having lost 90 per cent of its strength.

Costly though the victory on the middle Don was to be, the Stavka decided to develop further its offensive operations in the south once the success of *Operation Little Saturn* was assured. In January 1943, therefore, Soviet armies mounted two more offensives on the Don, first against the *2nd Hungarian Army* and then against the *2nd Army*. But Soviet success in annihilating the *2nd Hungarian Army* between 12 and 27 January and savaging the *2nd Army* between 24 January and 3 February was overshadowed by two developments in the first five weeks of 1943 that determined the course of what remained of the winter campaign. First, as the Stavka developed its plans for these offensives and switched the point of attack in the hope of keeping German forces off-balance, so it came to the idea of widening its effort throughout the south in the search for a strategic victory. Second, at the very time when the Stavka scented the opportunity that it had quite deliberately denied itself in early December, German policy ceased to be simply reactive. The failure of *Operation Winterstorm* meant the effective abandonment both of any future attempt to relieve *6th Army* and of the *6th Army* itself, and with no further commitment at the furthest point of the front *Army Group Don* found itself with a freedom of action previously denied it. Thus the widening of Soviet objectives coincided with a return on the German part to a rational conduct of the battle and to the means of bringing Soviet success to an end.

The Stavka's decision to seek a strategic victory throughout the south was a calculated risk. It realised that any attempt to follow up the success of *Uranus* and *Little Saturn* involved offensive operations with tired and much depleted forces on lines of communication already badly extended as a result of recent advances. More seriously, and in sharp contrast to the situation that had prevailed before the Stalingrad counter-attack, these operations would have to be undertaken by armies and fronts that lacked both second-echelon formations and reserves, while the impact of strategic surprise had been dissipated by January 1943 simply by the passing of time. In the last six weeks of 1942 two armoured and eight infantry divisions were sent to *Army Group Don* by the German High Command, and in the winter of 1942–43 *Army Group D* in France provided the Eastern Front with no fewer than 18 full-strength divisions. By mid-January various German troop movements, either completed or in progress, ensured that the premise on which the Stavka planned for a general offensive – the remorseless and irreversible crumbling of the German front throughout the south – was flawed. But the crucial weakness of the plans developed by the Stavka in January and authorised between the 20 and 23 January was that its two main efforts involved attacks deep into enemy rear areas along divergent axes of advance. While the South-western Front spent January battling its way to the Donets, the Stavka plan of campaign called for this formation and the Southern Front to effect the *Saturn* concept and the Voronezh and Bryansk Fronts to secure Kharkov. The encirclement of Axis forces in the Donbas – *Operation Gallop* – was to be carried out by an advance from the Slavyansk–Voroshilovgrad sector to Mariupol, while the advance on Kharkov – *Operation Star* – was to be followed by exploitation to Poltava and the middle Dnepr. The final stop lines laid down in the Stavka plans tasked Soviet armies with the capture of Kursk, Belgorod, Poltava, Krasnograd, Pavlograd and a bridgehead over the lower Dnepr around Dnepropetrovsk and Zaporozhye.

With *Operation Gallop* scheduled to begin on 29 January and *Star* on 2 February, the Stavka plans allowed little more than three weeks for the securing of these objectives. In setting its armies such tasks the Stavka's planning was a throwback to the events of January 1942 when misplaced confidence led Stalin to order a general offensive in the expectation of a rapid German collapse at the very time when the *Wehrmacht* had weathered the worst that the Soviet army could do. In January 1943 the situation in which the *Wehrmacht* found itself in the south was infinitely more serious than had been its problems in January 1942, but in its desire to beat both the *Wehrmacht* and the March thaw the Stavka made no allowance for the combination of German measures in the first six weeks of 1943 that both prevented the disintegration of the Axis front in the south and enabled Manstein's forces to win a series of tactical successes in the subsequent month.

The first part of this German recovery took place on the furthest part of the front, inside the bend of the Donets, though the process was piecemeal and not completed until 19 February, by which time the focus of attention had switched westwards. Critical to this recovery was Hitler's decision to withdraw *Army Group A* from it positions beyond the Don, a decision that Hitler initially resisted and then took reluctantly because of the long-term implications of the failure to secure the oilfields of southern Russia for the future conduct of the war. But with Soviet forces pressing on the middle Donets and the twin threats to *Army Detachment Hollidt* within the bend of the Donets and to Rostov obvious, Hitler sanctioned the withdrawal of *Army Group A* on 21 January. Partly because of the lateness of this decision and partly because Hitler insisted upon retention of a bridgehead around Taman and Novorossiysk, only one motorised and four armoured divisions of the *1st Panzer Army* were able to withdraw through Rostov before the city fell to Soviet armies for the second and last time on 14 February. Rostov was surrendered by *Army Detachment Hollidt* in the course of a phased withdrawal from the Donets to the Mius between 8 and 18 February that was authorised only as late as the sixth. But thereafter the immediate availability of formations from the *1st Panzer Army* for operations on this part of the front was crucial because in taking command of the *4th Panzer Army*'s formations, the *1st Panzer Army* was able to support the withdrawal to the Mius and to move formations to the Slavyansk–Lisichansk– Voroshilovgrad sector just as the South-western Front sought to develop its drive towards Mariupol through this part of the front.

Voroshilovgrad was not ceded until 15 February, Slavyansk not until the seventeenth, but it was the success of the *3rd* and *7th Panzer Divisions*, moved into the Slavyansk area in the first two days of February, that was critical in shaping the course of subsequent events. These two divisions withstood a series of attacks by the 1st Guards Army between the third and ninth, after which the Soviets abandoned their attempts to secure Slavyansk in favour of bypassing the town to the north. By helping to close the Slavyansk–Voroshilovgrad sector in the first half of February, the *1st Panzer Army* forced the South-western Front off its intended – and for the Germans highly dangerous – axis of advance and pushed it westwards, towards Lozovaya, Pavlograd and the Dnepr bend. By 18 February, when the withdrawal behind the Mius was completed and the *17th Army* began an airlift that was to carry 100,000 of its troops to the northern shore of the Sea of Azov in 17 days, Axis formations on the Mius and Donets had spared themselves the danger of immediate encirclement and had exposed the left flank of the South-western Front to counter-attack.

While the first half of February thus saw an increasingly effective German resistance inside the bend of the Donets, the other half of the Soviet endeavour, *Operation Star*, built upon the success achieved in catching the *2nd Army* in the process of withdrawing from the Voronezh area. Kursk was taken on 8 February and the 3rd Tank and 69th Armies combined to force the upper Donets and to liberate Kharkov on the sixteenth. But the obvious dangers presented by the *2nd Army*'s collapse and the inability of Manstein's command to extend its front beyond Kharkov led to a rationalisation of German command arrangements which slowly brought the situation around Kursk under control. On 13

February *Army Group B* was dissolved and the *2nd Army* was placed under the command of *Army Group Centre*, Manstein's command being redesignated *Army Group South*. By the end of March *Army Group Centre*, having shorted the Rzhev frontage by two-thirds as a result of its withdrawal from the salient, had sent 12 infantry divisions southwards in order to support the *2nd Army*. Along with the *2nd Panzer Army*, the *2nd Army* was then able to retain Orel and to contain the Bryansk and Voronezh Fronts. But by the time that these command changes were effected in mid-February, the breach in the German front along the Donets extended between Belgorod and Izyum. While the existence of this breach enabled the Voronezh Front to retake Kharkov the successful German defence of Zmiyev in the first week of February had the effect of pushing the 6th Army to the south-west, away from the support that should have been provided by the 3rd Tank Army.

Though Zmiyev was subsequently taken, the Stavka failed to plug the gap that opened between the Voronezh and South-western Fronts in the second week of February, and it failed to appreciate the significance of this and other numerous incidents of stiffening German resistance. It continued to believe that German resistance was in its last gasp, and even though it knew that some corps were reduced to just 50 tanks it continued to urge its armies forward in an attempt to clinch a decisive victory before the thaw. On 17 February units of the South-western Front secured Pavlograd and reached the Dnepr opposite Zaporozhye, but by then the main impetus of the Soviet thrusts had been lost and German formations were poised for precisely this eventuality.

By the third week of February the arrival of various formations from the west had allowed the *4th Panzer Army* to be re-formed with corps on either flank of the South-western Front as it pressed towards the Dnepr. With the *1st Panzer Army* withdrawn from the ceded Slavyansk–Lisichansk sector and concentrated against the left flank of the detached Popov Mobile Group as it fought its way southwards towards Krasnoarmeyskoye, the *4th Panzer Army* had *XLVIII Panzer Corps* around Vasilkovka and *SS Panzer Corps* concentrated around Poltava. In making the latter available Hitler specifically ordered that it should be used to retain Kharkov, but Manstein ceded the city in the belief that it could be retaken after the various attacking Soviet armies were destroyed in a battle that would begin once the Soviet offensive momentum was lost.

Having convinced a dubious Hitler of the correctness of his views during their celebrated meeting at Zaporozhye on 17 February, Manstein proceded to vindicate himself. On the eighteenth *XL Panzer Corps* struck at the flank of the Popov Mobile Group and on the twentieth *SS Panzer*

German Counter-Attack at Kharkov, 1943

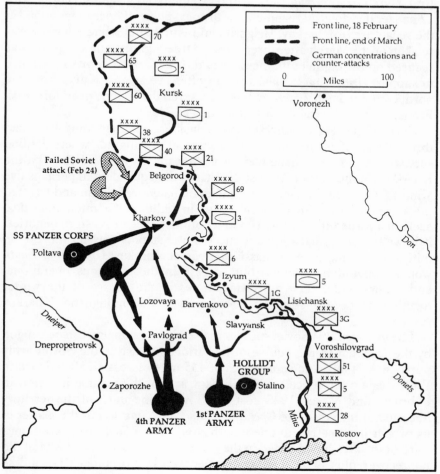

Corps attacked southwards from Poltava, securing Novomoskovsk and ripping a breach of 20 miles across the right flank of the 6th Army. With *XLVIII Panzer Corps* linking up with *SS Panzer Corps* at Pavlograd before moving to secure Lozovaya on 27 February, the *1st Panzer Army*'s success in taking Barvenkovo on the twenty-eighth and reaching the Donets opposite Izyum on that same day completed the destruction of Southwestern Front's three main formations. To compound this defeat, German armour then destroyed the 3rd Tank Army as it came south towards Lozovaya in an attempt to support armies that no longer existed.

251

By 4 March *Army Group South* had regrouped four armoured corps, with 12 panzer divisions, in readiness for the next phase of operations aimed at the recapture of Kharkov, Belgorod and Kursk, but while Kharkov was retaken on 15 March after three days of street fighting and Belgorod was secured on the eighteenth, the thaw and *Army Group Centre*'s reluctance to support *Army Group South* with an offensive against Kursk from the north combined to halt proceedings and saved the Voronezh and Bryansk Fronts from the certainty of further defeat.

German success at Kharkov was considerable. Beginning less than three weeks after the end of resistance at Stalingrad, where 94,000 survivors of the siege made their way into captivity after 2 February, the Kharkov counter-offensive cost the Stavka the equivalent of perhaps five armies,* restored the German front along its entire length, and wrested the initiative from Soviet hands. But in light of the often uncritical acclaim afforded the German conduct of this battle in Western histories, it is well to note that German success at Kharkov was no more than mitigation of an otherwise massive defeat: at Kharkov *Army Group South* won an operational victory, but success in those various operational endeavours undertaken by Soviet armies in the course of the winter together made up strategic success, notwithstanding the Kharkov reverse.

The extent of this Soviet success in the winter campaign can be gauged by the fact that in the course of its various offensives the Soviet army pursued Axis formations distances of 435 miles across a 750-mile front. With specific reference to the Kharkov action, the reverse incurred in February and March 1943 cost the Soviets one-third of the territory liberated in the course of *Operation Gallop* and *Star*: to put the matter in its proper perspective, in one month *Army Group South* recovered one-third of the area it had ceded in the previous three weeks, and what it did not recover, plus all the territory lost between 19 November 1942 and 28 January 1943, was lost permanently. Equally permanent, and perhaps more relevant, the German victory at Kharkov could not undo the Axis military losses of the winter. Whereas the *Wehrmacht*'s material losses between 22 June 1941 and 19 November 1942 has been assessed by a

---

*Soviet losses at Kharkov are not clear, but it is evident that material losses were much heavier than manpower losses, and one of the striking features of the battle was the relative absence of Soviet prisoners. The Popov Group began *Operation Gallop* with 55,000 men and 212 tanks: on the Barvenkovo–Stavyansk–Krasnoarmeyskoye battlefield the Germans counted 3,000 Soviet dead and 251 Soviet tanks but took only 569 prisoners. Other formations, more firmly trapped than this one because of the depth of their advance, lost more heavily, but *Army Group South* took only 9,000 prisoners in the battles around Pavlograd and Kharkov.

German source at 50 divisions, the winter campaign of 1942–43 cost the *Wehrmacht* another 45 divisions and left 300,000 men of the *17th Army hors de combat* beyond the Don: Germany's allies lost about 40 divisions.

Losses of this order could not be absorbed any more than the main instrument of German success at Kharkov, the three *Waffen SS* panzer divisions that fought at Zmiyev and Pavlograd, could cover an entire front held by understrength infantry divisions, inadequate artillery and out-numbered and outclassed armour. The two divisions of *SS Panzer Corps* at Kharkov at the end of January 1943 held half the operational German tank strength on the Eastern Front at that time, and this, plus the fact that this formation had the only Tiger I tanks in service on this front, provide the proper context of the Kharkov battle in terms of the Eastern Front and the European war as a whole: a battle of passing importance won and a campaign of permanent significance lost, plus the concentration of material excellence that was too narrowly based to prevent the overall weakening of the *Wehrmacht* relative to its widening commitments and the growing power of its enemies. The German success at Kharkov may have been an impressive feat of arms, but it was the only type of victory that the *Wehrmacht* could win at this stage of the war and it was no compensation for Germany's failure in 1942 to win the strategic victory that she needed to ensure long-term security. Success at Kharkov partially disguised this fact, but the reality after November 1942 was that Germany was fighting at best a defensive war, at worst a war that was lost: either way, after Kharkov Germany faced the certainty of having to wage a war of attrition, imposed upon her by her enemies, as the result of her failure on the battlefields of 1942 and of Hitler's having broken the eleventh and most important principle of war.

4

1943 AND THE ELEVENTH PRINCIPLE OF WAR

Any year between 1940 and 1945 could be represented as the crucial year of the Second World War. 1943 was a year of special significance in the unfolding of the war, and for one very obvious reason. The flawed strategy with which Britain and France went to war in 1939 and which had laid down that 1943 would be the year when the issue of defeat and victory would be resolved was proved correct: 1943 saw the outcome of the war decided. Paradoxically, however, the battle fronts saw relatively little change in the course of this year, and certainly no changes that compared with those that had occurred in each of the three preceding years and were to be recorded in 1944. In the northern Pacific a couple of islands changed hands; in the south-west Pacific a year that began with battle lines drawn around Sanananda and Henderson Field ended around Finchhafen and the northern Solomons. In Europe Allied successes remained largely peripheral, a fact reflected, not negated, by Italy's invasion, surrender and occupation during the course of the year. Even on the Eastern Front 1943 ended with Soviet armies still far from the borders on which the Nazi–Soviet conflict began 30 months earlier. But if the year ended with Axis leaders and their peoples able to draw comfort and resources from the vast tracts of conquered territory that remained under their control, it also closed with their armed forces having lost a series of battles – on land, in the air and at sea – that left both Germany and Japan without the initiative that was their only compensation for material weakness and without the means to counter the blows that in 1944 were to carry their enemies to their respective borders and coasts.

These defeats, however, were but one of three aspects of the general Axis defeat in 1943: not merely did Axis forces sustain a series of military reverses but the Axis leaderships were out-thought politically and strategically and their countries were outproduced industrially. In 1943, the material weaknesses of the Axis powers, summarised simply in a British cabinet paper that stated that an Allied victory was assured because Germany had factories and no resources and Japan had resources and no factories, were reflected in that the United States, unlike Britain which had global presence but not the power to match, acquired in 1943 the unique capacity to wage global war. In 1943 the United States outproduced the Axis powers, indeed the rest of the world combined, and in this year, in consultation with her three major allies, she settled the main details of the plan by which her power was to be brought to bear against her enemies. Herein was the definition of the relationship between victory and supremacy in the Second World War. In both the European and Pacific wars the Allied victory was the product of supremacy: supremacy was not the product of victory.

The events of 1943 fall under five headings: the five Allied conferences that collectively established the framework for the prosecution of the European war and the war against Japan; the Allied success in mastering the U-boat threat; the gathering pace of the strategic air offensive against Germany; the military operations that re-established the Western allies on the continental mainland and also saw the Soviets clear most of the Ukraine; and the battle of production. Though obviously the Axis conduct of the war and the major part of Soviet deliberations and operations fall outside their terms of reference, the Allied conferences provide the latticework of the year, and, indeed, of the remainder of the war, in no instance more evidently than the decision made at the Casablanca conference (14–24 January) that the United Nations would not accept anything less than the unconditional surrender of the Axis powers.

This decision remains controversial, many post-war commentators condemning it on the grounds that it hardened German resolve and made the task of bringing about Germany's defeat more difficult. This argument is superficially plausible, though there seems no good reason to assume either that had the Allies adopted a less intransigent position German resistance would have been less or that there could have been an end to the German war on other terms. The fact of the matter was that the European war's terms of reference had been provided by the nature of Nazism and by the Anglo-French declaration of war in 1939. Germany showed no restraint either in aim or conduct other than that imposed by the prudence before 1941 in tackling her enemies singly: Britain and

France, rightly calculating that as long as Hitler ruled Germany there could be no peace in Europe, declared total war in 1939, and then failed to wage it. By 1943 theory and practice came together: the declaration merely articulated a fact that all the warring nations recognised. After 40 months of war there could be no changing aims that were stripped of ambiguity and which, when realised, would deny Germans any claim that they had been cheated into surrender. For 20 years the victorious powers of the First World War had been subjected to an orchestrated German campaign of lies and deceit that had denied the reality of defeat in 1918, which asserted that the settlement of 1919 had been imposed by fraud, and which was used by Hitler as cloak for aggression. Just as the Casablanca declaration eased the problems of the Allies by postponing the solution of their various clashes of interest to the post-war period, so this demand for unconditional surrender – issued at the time when the Germans had just set about razing the Warsaw ghetto – made clear to Germany that this time there would be no excuses and no mitigation of defeat. The inter-war experience, the lack of any credible alternative to Hitler within Germany, and the logic of the war itself made the formal Allied demand for their enemies' unconditional surrender inevitable. If there are grounds for criticism of this policy then it lies in it being applied to all of Germany's allies, though given the behaviour of Bulgarian and Italian armies in Yugoslavia it is difficult to see how these two enemies could have been excluded. However, in practice the Americans and British were not consistent. The Italian surrender in September 1943 was not unconditional, and neither the final Allied demands on Japan – the Potsdam Proclamation of 26 July 1945 – nor the final surrender of Japan on 2 September were unconditional.

The Anglo-American conferences of 1943 – Casablanca, Washington (12–25 May), Quebec (14–24 August) and second Cairo (3–6 December) – were primarily concerned with two problems: defining the relationship between and timetable for Anglo-American operations in the Mediterranean and north-west European theatres, and the developing of a coherent strategy in the Pacific – an American monopoly – and relating it to operations in China and south-east Asia. Both problems were fearfully complicated, though their essence can be stated simply.

With regard to the European war, the Americans accepted a Mediterranean commitment grudgingly, convinced that Italy could never be more than a liability to whoever occupied her and that the road up peninsular Italy was one that in military terms led nowhere. When a Mediterranean commitment proved unavoidable, the American High Command tried to limit it in order to ensure that the main Anglo-American effort in north-west Europe proceeded at the earliest possible opportunity. In 1942 the Americans tried to insist upon landings in northern France that year, and when this demand was set aside in favour of *Torch* they tried to insist upon a 1943 invasion. But without command of the sea and air and without the forces and supplies necessary to conduct a subsequent campaign into Germany, there could be no invasion in 1943, though the British were given no credit for their arguments to this effect. But Britain's insistence upon the prosecution of a campaign in Italy to an indeterminate end came to be regarded by the American High Command in 1943, not altogether surprisingly, as reluctance to commit herself to any invasion of northern France, and even after the British did commit themselves to this effort at Quebec in 1943 there remained the questions of whether or not the Italian campaign should remain the main Allied effort in the Mediterranean and how Allied efforts in this and the north-west European theatres should be coordinated. These questions were not resolved until March 1944 and then not satisfactorily: it was not until July 1944 that issues were finally settled, but neither to British liking nor to any useful military purpose.

With regard to the formulation of strategic policy for the war against Japan, Anglo-American difficulties were even more pronounced. Before the outbreak of the Pacific war the American High Command concluded that Japan could only be defeated by coordinated efforts in the Pacific and on the Asian mainland, i.e. in China. But the devising of a strategy for the Pacific proved very difficult for the Americans, in part because Pacific matters had to wait upon the settling of European priorities and timetables and in part because of inter-service rivalries. After April 1942 the Pacific was divided into two American commands, one naval and the other army, and neither would accept subordination to the other. By the end of 1943, however, the weakness inherent in a divided command was partially offset by the American ability to mount coordinated offensives across the central and south-west Pacific, but it was not until September 1944 that immediate American objectives in the western Pacific – in effect, the question of whether the Philippines were to be taken or bypassed – were decided. The arguments on this score, in which the navy lost to the army, obscured the more important question of whether Japan was to be blockaded and bombarded into submission or subjected to invasion and physical conquest. This question was settled in mid-1944, and the decision then set aside by events.

Even without this problem American difficulties in 1943 in trying to formulate inter-dependent strategies for the Pacific and the Asian mainland were severe. At the heart of this problem was how to ensure an effective Chinese contribution to the Allied war effort, but there was no agreement within the American High Command what form this contribution should take. This, however, obscured a more serious matter. In assuming that China would play the role assigned her in an American-devised strategy Washington misunderstood Chungking's intentions and capabilities. Chiang Kai-shek's regime had no intention of accepting any offensive obligation. The outbreak of the Pacific war, which prompted China's formal declaration of war on Japan, vindicated Chiang's policy of waiting until Japan embroiled herself in a general war that she could only lose, and it formed no part of Chiang's policy that his regime should seek to drive out the Japanese occupier when China's victory and liberation would be achieved by nations more powerful than herself *en passant*. American military missions to China in 1942 were scandalised to find what amounted to a '*de facto* truce' in existence between Chungking and Japan. But the Roosevelt administration, having spent years extolling Chiang Kai-shek as the great leader of a mighty struggle against a barbarous invader, could not repudiate Chiang and its previous version of events, and Chungking had its champions in the form of a powerful and vociferous lobby in Washington that, in the final analysis, had the beating of the administration and military.

To compound these problems, this lobby contained within itself an equally strident air lobby. As part of its policy of supporting China in 1941 before Pearl Harbor, the Roosevelt administration had provided credits, aircraft and facilities for pilots to enlist in a surrogate air force in China. This organisation, legitimised once the United States entered the war and headed by Colonel Chennault, embraced extreme air power doctrines, the basis of its 1942 policy being that a strategic bomber force numbering less than 200 aircraft could bomb Japan into submission from bases in China if the entire American effort in China was geared to that end. The patent absurdity of this claim was obscured by the fact that the message itself, with its combination of high technology, low commitment and quick results, was tailored to American public expectation, but it was disputed by orthodox military opinion headed by the highly unconventional Major-General Stilwell, appointed Chiang Kai-shek's chief of staff and made responsible for the entire American effort in China in February 1942. From the start Stilwell recognised that the weakness of the Chennault argument was that before any bombing offensive could become effective the Japanese army in China would move to secure the airfields from which the bombers operated, and his priority was to train, arm and supply a limited number of Chinese divisions for conventional operations against the occupier. As a result, the American military effort in China was divided against itself from the outset, and in this situation Stilwell's arguments were systematically undermined by Chiang. Chiang was not averse to the Americans raising divisions on his behalf, but he was totally opposed to their being used in this war when the more important one, with the communists, would follow in due course.

In China, the American High Command found itself with a political commitment that it could not repudiate; a commitment to supply economic and civil aid that at times seemed limitless; an ally not interested in fighting the Japanese; and no agreed strategic priorities; yet with a persistence that would have been admirable in another context or cause, the American High Command maintained its attempts to devise a coherent, reasoned policy in China even after the Quebec and Tehran conferences that together should have resulted in the Americans cutting their losses. At Quebec the Americans committed themselves to taking the Marianas in summer 1944 and, as the basis of future planning, to seeking the defeat of Japan within one year of the defeat of Germany, which was scheduled for October 1944. Before Quebec the Americans had given no great consideration to the Marianas, and the attraction of the Chennault thesis in part was that no air offensive against Japan could be staged except from China before 1946 under the terms of existing American plans. The inclusion of the Marianas on the list of 1944 objectives thus ended the importance of China as a base for strategic air operations. Similarly, 'the 12-month plan', because it envisaged American forces fighting their way into the Formosa–Philippines–Hong Kong area by early 1945 ended the importance of China as a base for military operations because Stilwell's proposed programme could not be effective by that date. The Soviets' declaration at the Tehran conference (28 November–1 December) that they would enter the war against Japan after the defeat of Germany merely underlined the fact the United States could afford to cut its losses in China, but the ill-defined political commitment to China prevented the United States' leadership, even after the disillusionment of the Cairo meeting between Churchill, Chiang and Roosevelt (22–26 November), from acting upon the logic of events.

China, therefore, presented the American High Command with an 'option of difficulties', but this was not the limit of American problems because the need to support China, irrespective of purpose, involved another set of equally intractable difficulties, this time with the British. The supply of China after March 1942 could only be staged through north-east India, and the Americans insisted that the British should proceed with the reconquest of Burma in order to restore overland communications with China. The Americans also insisted that in the meantime supplies should be airlifted to China from airfields in north-east India. The immediate obstacle to these demands was the fact that north-east India was a backwater, lacking the airfields needed for such an airlift and the communications and military infrastructures needed to support either, still less both, efforts. Moreover, with the British obliged to try to develop these airfields and infrastructures and the Americans unable to decide between the Chennault and Stilwell proposals, American problems were exacerbated by the British unwillingness to undertake a campaign in Burma. The basis of this British reluctance was the calculation that any offensive into Upper Burma from north-east India would involve the movement of formations through the mountains that ring Upper Burma against an intact enemy operating on good lines of communication in the Chindwin, Irrawaddy and Sittang valleys. The British reasoned, correctly, that a victory in Upper and central Burma was at best problematical, and that in any event an advance to Rangoon was out of the question. With these conclusions the American planning staffs reluctantly agreed, particularly after the Guadalcanal campaign revealed the nature of Japanese resistance, but to their subsequent argument that the British should commit themselves to a coordinated offensive with Chinese forces in the Hakawng valley and from Yunnan to clear Upper Burma with a view to building a through road to China the British responded with three unanswerable arguments: that the engineers needed to build a road behind advancing armies were the same engineers needed to sustain the advance in the first place; that such a road could carry no more supplies than those required by the forces needed to guard the road if the Japanese remained intact and undefeated in central Burma; and a road could not be developed before 1946, by which time its usefulness would be negligible given a timetable that scheduled the American arrival in the western Pacific for early 1945. Moreover, an effective Chinese contribution from Yunnan to this effort to secure a road from north-east India was dependent upon the road supplying the wherewithal in the first place.

Burma proved perhaps the most difficult of Anglo-American disputes, worse even than the arguments over Italy, and much of the difficulty stemmed from the manner in which the various problems unfolded. The various problems emerged in turn, and to every successive American attempted solution the British subsequently discovered an insoluble problem. But to this rising American distrust of British sincerity over Burma, 1943 but particularly 1944 added an additional dimension on the question of British naval operations. From July 1942 the British High Command was convinced that the reconquest of Burma could only be effected by an invasion of Lower Burma, the capture of Rangoon and an advance into central Burma. With the surrender of Italy and the freeing of the British fleet for operations in the Far East, British thoughts turned to the possibility of an amphibious assault on Rangoon, only to find that the Americans were adamant that such an operation had to be accompanied by the very effort in Upper Burma that it was intended to avoid.

In fact, at different times the American High Command had its own ideas on the future employment of the British fleet. After Quebec the American planners, caught by their own 12-month schedule and not knowing how their carrier formations would fare as they tackled the Japanese navy's main strength in the next phase of operations, promised to supply and support any British carrier and amphibious formations sent to the Pacific by June 1944. Their intention was to hold British carriers as a reserve for their own carriers, which were expected to sustain heavy losses. The British allowed this offer to pass by default, but as they turned their attention to alternatives to a landing at Rangoon and the Americans to how such alternatives could complement their own operations, so the British slowly came to the realisation that wartime and post-war European demands plus the low birthrates of the 1920s meant that in 1944 Britain would have to choose between naval and amphibious forces in the Far East because she lacked the manpower for both. Moreover, in 1944 Britain also realised that neither Australia nor India had the ability to maintain either a naval or an amphibious force, and that India could not raise the assault divisions needed for any amphibious enterprise. What completed this dismal picture was the fact that what little British assault shipping was in the Indian Ocean in 1943 and 1944 was shore-to-shore, and what was needed for any enterprise was ship-to-shore.

With all these conflicting options, demands, capabilities and limitations and the fact that not all the problems could be seen at a single time, it was small wonder that Anglo-American decision-making with regard to China and south-east Asia was painstakingly slow and characterised by mutual misunderstanding and irritation. In the end, of course, inter-Allied differences were resolved, ironically because the Japanese provided the solution. The Japanese decision to invade north-east India, a course of action that they had considered in 1942 but discounted because of the impossible logistics problems in mounting such an attack, resulted in utter disaster for the *15th Army* around Imphal and Kohima between February and June 1944. It was a defeat that proved the validity of the British arguments against an invasion in the opposite direction: the defeat of the Japanese *before* Burma was invaded destroyed Japanese powers of resistance in Upper and central Burma, and made possible the reconquest of Burma by an overland offensive from north-east India.

The various plans developed at successive Allied conferences in 1943 shared one common characteristic: all were dependent upon the Allies retaining command of the sea, and at the time of the Casablanca conference this remained a seemingly distant objective. By January 1943, however, the Allies had established the basis of overwhelming victory at sea in both the European and Pacific theatres. In the war against Japan 1943 opened with the Americans having secured local naval superiority in the south-west Pacific and beginning to make significant inroads into Japanese mercantile strength. Moreover, with the commissioning of the first of a new generation of fleet carriers on the last day of 1942, the Americans were less than four months away from making good their carrier losses of the year: the Japanese were not to do the same until August 1944, by which time the losses incurred in the battle of the Philippine Sea awaited replacement. In the Mediterranean, superiority of geographical position, numbers, quality and morale, and of intelligence, ensured an Allied victory in the course of 1943, the surrender of the Italian navy in September 1943 and the subsequent incarceration of the battle fleet in the Suez Canal being acknowledgement and consummation of this fact. In the Atlantic and British home waters the threat to Allied shipping from warships and auxiliary raiders had been largely eliminated, and that posed by mines, aircraft and light units reduced to very minor proportions. German surface and air forces stationed in northern Norway remained a substantial menace to Allied Arctic convoys, but the real threat to the Allies were the German submarines still operating in the North Atlantic.

Such was this threat and the success of German submarines in early 1943 that the Admiralty was to record the view that 'the Germans never came so near to disrupting communications between the New World and the Old as in the first twenty days of March 1943'. In these 20 days German action accounted for 107 Allied merchantmen in the North Atlantic, and while the total of 120 merchantmen sunk in this single month was exceeded in eight months in 1942 the significance of the March 1943 losses lay in the fact that 90 ships were lost from convoys, though 13 were stragglers. The U-boat haul of 72 merchantmen from convoys in this single month contrasted with a previous highest monthly toll of 50, and the total of 30 was exceeded only in five months in the whole of the war. What made this month's losses doubly significant was that in March 1943 North Atlantic convoys were afforded protection on an unprecedented scale: on the basis of the Admiralty's quarterly returns of escorts per convoy, 1 April 1943 represented the peak of escort deployment in the North Atlantic in the Second World War.

Such was the extent of German success against convoys in the first three weeks of March 1943 that for the only time in the war the Admiralty questioned the validity of the system itself, and in the absence of any credible alternative to convoy this was tantamount to an admission of defeat as many historians have acknowledged. On 24 May, however, the U-boat command broke off the Battle of the Atlantic and recalled its submarines after unprecedented losses, 32 U-boats having been lost in the first three weeks of May. Perhaps inevitably, the story of this sudden turn-round of fortunes in spring 1943 has been told in most accounts in terms of the convoy battles and related actions of May 1943, but in reality the Battle of the Atlantic was not won and lost in a single month any more than Allied success in May 1943 was sudden and completely divorced from previous events. The events of May 1943 conformed to a pattern of operations that had been established since August 1942, and German success in March 1943 was the solitary exception to what proved an otherwise irreversible process. Moreover, the months of July and August 1943 were perhaps even more significant than May 1943 in settling the outcome of this campaign. German losses in these two months – 37 in July and 25 in August – were fewer than those sustained in May, but they were suffered by a service that had regrouped in an attempt to reverse the verdict of the May fighting, and its failure in these two months was correspondingly greater than its previous defeat.

The Allied losses of March 1943 served to obscure three facts that otherwise indicated that the *Kriegsmarine* was losing the Battle of the Atlantic despite having the numbers after August 1942 that allowed it to form patrol lines for the interception of convoys on a comprehensive basis for the first time. First, and by definition, losses from convoys were sustained only by those convoys that were attacked, and despite the formation of German patrol lines the majority of North Atlantic convoys were not attacked. In April 1943, for example, German submarines attacked 18 convoys totalling 596 ships and sank 25 merchantment, but 19 convoys with 416 ships (and no fewer than 134 convoys with 1,764 ships in American waters and the Caribbean) escaped German attention. Such was the context of the March 1943 losses. Second, in tackling the convoys that they did find, German submarines began to experience significant losses because of the increasing effectiveness of the escorts, and indeed after August 1942 the exchange rate between merchantmen and submarines in the convoy battles was ominously bad for the *Kriegsmarine*. With the exception of March 1943 when the rate reached 12:1, between September 1942 and April 1943 it hovered around the 4:1 level and in September would have been as low as 2:1 but for German success against Arctic convoys. Third, the returns by German submarines in terms of merchantmen sunk per submarine in commission and per submarine per month were in sharp decline. At no stage during 1942 were submarines able to sink one merchantman per month for every one of their number in service, and in the last quarter of 1942 this figure fell below 0.5. By January 1943 the number of operational U-boats exceeded 200 for the first time, and by April 1943 had reached 240: in January 1943 the return per commissioned U-boat per month was just 0.17 merchantmen, in April 0.23.

Thus, even by January 1943 the results obtained by German submarines were wholly inadequate in terms of the *Kriegsmarine*'s own 'tonnage warfare' requirements, but the inadequacy of German performance was worsened by two further matters. Other than in the period between August and November 1941, the majority of German victims were ships sailing independently. In 1942, for example, of the 1,570 ships known to have been sunk by enemy action 962 were merchantmen sailing independently, of which submarines claimed 840. The reduction of the number of independently sailing merchantmen reduced the toll amongst such shipping in 1943 to 215 to all types of enemy action and to 189 to U-boats. Moreover, in the first quarter of 1943 new Allied construction for the first time exceeded losses to U-boats since 1939, and in the third quarter of the year exceeded all losses to all causes since the outbreak of war. What this meant, in effect, was that by March 1943, at which time the *Kriegsmarine* was already six weeks behind its 'tonnage warfare' requirements for the year, German submarines had to quintuple their March sinkings amongst merchantmen in convoy in order to offset the decline in the number of sinkings of independently sailing merchantmen and new Allied construction and still reduce Allied resources by the required 750,000 tons of shipping per month. This was impossible. The Germans simply did not have the numbers to register such results, and even by the end of March 1943 the U-boat command had recognised that its submarines faced unprecedented difficulties in tackling convoys because of the growing effectiveness of Allied escort forces.

These difficulties and the subsequent Allied victory were the result of the balance of technical and tactical advantage in the convoy battles tipping conclusively against the U-boats as a number of Allied counter-measures came together at roughly the same time. It is possible to define these under five separate headings and to note that two, the introduction of continuous air cover for convoys in the North Atlantic and the first appearance (but for a single operation in September 1942) of support groups in the battle, were tied directly to the winding down of the *Torch* commitment, the North African landings having had the effect of delaying both by at least four months. But the Germans' immediate difficulties in late March 1943, and the basis of Allied success in the spring and summer, lay in the continued expansion of escort numbers throughout 1942. By April 1943, when British oceanic strength approached the 600 mark, the British and Canadian navies had 490 escorts in the North Atlantic of which 371 were operational and 347 were assigned. In addition, another 46 were with the Gibraltar and West African commands. With an average of 27 convoys at sea on any day in 1943, the steady increase of escort numbers throughout 1942 allowed the British to raise the average escort per convoy from six to eight in the course of 1943 and to concentrate units in settled formations. Adequate numbers allowed the British to raise and train escort forces as groups and then to commit such groups intact to the battle, and their growing familiarisation with radar and direction-finding equipment, the introduction of the Type 147 contact-holding Asdic in April 1943, and the tactical improvement brought about by changed depth-charge patterns and spacings were the factors that combined to make attacks on convoys so very dangerous for U-boats in spring 1943. Growing escort numbers also allowed the Allies to raise support groups, formations not assigned the protection of specific convoys but tasked to operate in waters used by U-boats and to go to the aid of threatened convoys. Between March and May 1943 one American and five British groups, three with escort carriers, joined the Battle of the Atlantic, but with their accounting for only three of the 41 German submarines sunk in May 1943 their main contribution to victory was in helping to ensure that there was no revival of the U-boat menace after summer 1943: the crucial battles of the spring were won by the ordinary escorts and shore-based aircraft.

The significance of air power in the Battle of the Atlantic in spring 1943 can be gauged from the fact that whereas Allied aircraft accounted in whole or in part for 52 U-boats between 3 September 1939 and 31 December 1942, in May 1943 Allied aircraft sank 20 German submarines and shared in the destruction of another five. The extent of the success of Allied air power in May 1943 in large measure explains the dramatic quality of events in this month, but in reality German losses to Allied aircraft had begun to assume significant proportions even before

May 1943 – 29 were sunk in the first four months of 1943 – and the extent of the German defeat in May was exaggerated by a German operational failure that was continued through the summer. But the significance of air power in May 1943 was that in spring of that year the British were able, for the first time, to tie air power directly to convoy defence in two forms: continuous air cover for convoys in the North Atlantic became possible with the appearance of escort carriers in significant numbers, and Very Long Range (VLR) Liberators similarly became available for the Battle of the Atlantic in telling numbers at exactly the same time.

The first of the new generation of escort carriers entered service in the Atlantic in March 1943, and their impact was immediate if largely negative. Aircraft from escort carriers sank 41 U-boats in the course of the war and shared another 17 with surface escorts and shore-based aircraft, but their main achievement was in providing reconnaissance and contacts for escorts, and also in denying German submarines the ability to track and gather around a convoy without risk of attack. As more escort carriers became available German submarines lost the twin abilities to wait until a convoy drew beyond the range of shore-based aircraft before mounting attacks and to run on the surface in mid-ocean with impunity. Similarly, the intervention of VLR Liberators eroded these abilities which, by spring 1943, were two of the last tactical advantages remaining to German submarines.

In February 1943 the Allies had 312 long, 316 medium and 474 short-range aircraft detailed to maritime duties on both sides of the North Atlantic, but at this crucial stage of the war just 18 VLR Liberators – capable of sustained operations at ranges beyond 650 miles from land – were available for the Battle of the Atlantic. Of this number none were west of Iceland and nine were committed to patrol operations rather than convoy protection. This paucity of VLR numbers was the result of an American reluctance to commit such aircraft to maritime duties in the Atlantic (but not the Pacific) and a resistance on the part of RAF Bomber Command to any diversion of resources from its attempt to bomb Germany into submission. The priority afforded the winning of the Battle of the Atlantic at the Casablanca conference served notice that such intransigence would not be tolerated indefinitely, but it was the losses of March 1943 that finally forced the commitment of VLR squadrons to convoy defence in sufficient numbers that proved so important in May 1943. In the event the number of such aircraft thus committed remained incredibly small, but the total of 49 with RAF Coastal Command allowed between 12 and 15 Liberators to spend an average of three hours with convoys beyond 650 miles from land on every day of May 1943, and their destruction of 10 U-boats either around or *en route* to and from convoys was the final material ingredient in the Allied victory in the convoy battles of the same month. Equally important, but outside the convoy battles, patrol aircraft also accounted for nine U-boats in May. Such patrols were generally unrewarding during the war, though they did account for 12 U-boats in the first four months of 1943, but at the end of April a series of night attacks on German submarines crossing the Bay of Biscay convinced the U-boat command that Allied aircraft were able to locate surfaced submarines from transmissions from their Naxos search receivers. These, fitted throughout the U-boat fleet, since the previous September, were able to detect airborne radar transmissions on the standard 1½m frequencies in use in British patrol aircraft since 1941. By February 1943 the British had developed a 10cm radar that could defeat the Naxos receiver, and on the tenth of that month the centimetric radar provided an American Liberator with a kill in the Bay of Biscay.

The attacks of April 1943 plus the German refusal to believe that the Allies had been able to develop airborne centimetric radar led the U-boat command into a series of operational mistakes over the spring months. Initially, night crossings of the Bay of Biscay were abandoned and submarines were ordered to run on the surface in daylight in order to recharge batteries, but when this only resulted in increased contacts with, and losses to, Allied aircraft the German response was to order U-boats first to stay on the surface and fight their attackers and then to sail in company for mutual protection. With the summer came increased anti-aircraft armament for submarines and, ironically, a system of convoying U-boats across the Bay of Biscay by surface and air escorts, but centimetric radar, shallow-set depth charges and later rocket projectiles for use against surfaced U-boats provided Allied aircraft with a decisive superiority over German submarines throughout the summer of 1943. Indeed, in mid-year, as sinkings by escorts declined with the German withdrawal from the main shipping lanes, Allied aircraft for the only time in the war became the main agent of submarine losses. Between June and August 1943 the U-boats lost 74 of their number in sinking 58 merchantmen, this figure being the same as the number of German submarines sunk by ship-borne and shore-based aircraft. In 1943, as a whole, Allied aircraft registered 140 single kills to the 59 by surface forces.

Thus the combination of increasing escort numbers and effectiveness, the provision of support groups and the timely development of a small but adequate number of VLR aircraft to convoy defence provided the Allies with the material means whereby the U-boat threat was mastered in mid-1943. But this Allied victory was not complete and final in itself. The nature of naval warfare precluded a single, decisive victory, and just as at no time in British naval history had any victory in battle lessened the need for convoy and blockade so the victory of mid-1943 had to be repeated throughout the remainder of the war. Indeed, the effort involved in the struggle to retain command of the sea after mid-1943 was to increase until the peak of British escort strength in the North Atlantic was to be reached, predictably, in July 1944 when no fewer than 619 escorts were operational in the North Atlantic and British home waters: Western Approaches Command did not attain its maximum strength of 296 escorts until April 1945. Even with this considerable growth of numbers after May 1943, the Allies were unable to do more than contain the U-boat threat as German construction kept pace with sinkings. In 1943 the loss of 237 U-boats was countered by 272 entering service: in 1944 losses and commissionings both totalled 242 boats. Like Western Approaches, the U-boat service reached its peak strength – 444 boats – in April 1945, but the outcome of the submarine campaign against shipping was decided not just by numbers but by effectiveness: in 1944 German submarines sank 132 merchantmen of 773,327 tons – fewer ships but a greater tonnage than lost to all causes in June 1942 alone. In the spring and summer of 1943 Allied naval and air escorts secured a stranglehold on the submarines which the submarines never broke, and thereafter the main effectiveness of the U-boat service was in continuing to tie down Allied naval resources rather than in the destruction of commerce.

The fifth and final element that provided the Allies with victory in mid-1943 was the superiority of operational command established by the Allies over the *Kriegsmarine*, and particularly by the Admiralty over the U-boat service, at this stage of the war. This superiority both stemmed from and resulted in decisions that provide the hidden framework of the war at sea, the clear advantage that the Allies secured in research and development being perhaps the most obvious example of German inferiority in the wider aspects of operational detail. In the conduct of the Battle of the Atlantic this Allied advantage extended to operational research, Admiralty studies in autumn 1942 revealing, somewhat surprisingly, that convoy losses were not related to convoy size and that an increase in the average size of convoys from the current 32 merchantment to 54 should reduce losses by 56 per cent. The resultant reduction of the number of convoys as a consequence of the increased size of individual convoys also allowed the number of escorts detailed for convoy duties to decrease even as the scale of protection afforded convoys increased.* As a direct result of such findings, convoy size rose steadily from 32 in January 1943 to an average of 62 in mid-1944: the largest single convoy of the war, HXS300 in July 1944, numbered 164 merchantmen, and such was the measure of escort superiority at that time that its seven oceanic escorts conveyed a million tons of commerce and war material to Britain without loss.

No less significant than development programmes and operational research in the conduct of operations was the fact that in the course of 1943 the British established a decisive intelligence advantage over the *Kriegsmarine*, and by this stage of the war the Admiralty had acquired the combat experience and strength that enabled it to use this advantage to full effect. In part this intelligence advantage derived from the network of agents developed throughout occupied Europe – the first warning of the *Bismarck*'s sortie in 1941 was provided by a French naval source that reported that the Brest dockyard had been ordered to prepare for her arrival – but the most important British source, and the basis of the Admiralty's advantage, was signals intelligence. The British penetration of German naval ciphers began in 1940 but it was not until May 1941, when codes and an Enigma cipher machine were recovered from a U-boat, that the British were able to read signals in the *Kriegsmarine*'s general-purpose cipher on a regular and timely basis. Thereafter, and with only brief exceptions, the British read German naval traffic covering the Baltic and Mediterranean, and signals for coastal and mine warfare units in France and Norway. Until February 1942 the British were also able to read U-boat operational signals, but in that month the U-boats were switched to a separate Triton cipher and it was not until December that this system was broken. For most of 1942, therefore, the British fought the Battle of the Atlantic without access to German operational signals, but after December 1942 – and with a three-week gap in the crucial month of March 1943 when another German procedural change blinded the British – this ability to read U-boat signals, the workings of the Operational Intelligence Centre, and the analyses of the Submarine Tracking Room enabled the British to move to a position in 1944 whereby the Admiralty, on its own claim, knew more about U-boat positions than did the U-boat command. Arguably the most important naval intelligence coups were those that resulted in the destruction of the

*The size of convoys depended upon area, escort numbers upon perimeter. On the basis of average numbers, a mid-1944 convoy of 62 merchantmen was 10.8 per cent better protected by nine escorts than a January 1943 convoy of 32 ships had been protected by six escorts, and the saving of escort numbers was about 22.6 per cent.

battleship *Scharnhorst* off North Cape on 26 December 1943 and the damage inflicted in a carrier raid on the battleship *Tirpitz* on 3 April 1944 at Kaafjord after, and not before, she had completed repairs to damage sustained the previous September, but the most important Allied intelligence successes were those obtained after December 1942 almost on a routine, daily basis at the expense of the U-boats. Thus the German attempt after the defeat of May 1943 to concentrate against American convoys bound for the Mediterranean was countered by the deployment of three American support groups to the Azores where they sank seven U-boats between 13 and 30 July, and the parallel German plan to sail U-tankers in order to develop operations in distant waters was largely frustrated by the hunting down of five of the seven boats in a single three-week period in summer 1943.

The German navy was not without its intelligence successes, though ironically neither of its two most significant coups – the *Automedon* and *Nanking* captures – brought it any direct benefit. Its main successes, however, were concentrated in the first half of the war, and in the critical phase of the Battle of the Atlantic, the first half of 1943, both the British and Germans were reading each other's operational signals. In January 1943 the British realised that their ciphers were compromised though it was not until June that they could be changed. Thereafter German naval intelligence lost its ability to read British naval signals, and though it continued to read British merchant shipping signals until December 1943 the *Kriegsmarine* was to fight the last two years of the war without reliable intelligence and with its own communications compromised. No less seriously, it was to fight these last two years without effective air support and, except in the Baltic, without an effective surface force. After an abysmal failure to attack an Arctic convoy in the Barents Sea in December 1942 Hitler ordered the surface fleet to be decommissioned, but while this instruction was later countermanded, the previous failure to build up the fleet and its current lack of fuel, enforced inactivity and transfers to the U-boat service left the dwindling surface force unable to do more than effect a 'fleet-in-being' strategy that ended, as it had to end, in piecemeal destruction and total defeat.

The U-boat service, on the other hand, survived its defeat of May 1943 because of its numbers, but it could not respond quickly and effectively to the various technological changes that rendered its standard Type VIIC and Type IX boats obsolete. Indeed, by 1943 the submarine, as it had evolved since 1897, had reached the limits of its development, and what Germany needed was a proper submarine of good underwater performance, not a submersible. In 1943, however, the planned Walter boats were some three years from completion, and approval for the construction of two interim classes, the Types XXI and XXIII, was not given until 8 August. By the time that the lead boats were accepted into service in June 1944 Germany's defeat at sea could not be reversed, and somewhat appropriately the first operational mission of an oceanic Type XXI boat began on the day of Hitler's suicide.

In order to continue the war at sea after mid-1943 the U-boat command adopted three measures: the commitment of U-boats to distant waters, specifically off southern Africa and in the Indian Ocean; the introduction of schnorkel breathing apparatus that enabled a submarine to recharge its batteries while submerged; and the introduction of a number of new weapons, most notably the T4 and T5 acoustic torpedoes. None of these proved more than palliatives. No amount of success in distant waters could compensate for defeat in the North Atlantic, and German success in the Indian Ocean lasted no longer than it took to organise a comprehensive convoy system in that strategic backwater: sinkings per month never reached double figures after July 1943. The schnorkel made detection by airborne radar very difficult but only at the expense of greatly degraded performance, while acoustic torpedoes not only had a low rate of success – somewhere between 7 and 11 per cent – but had the singularly unfortunate effect of forcing escorts to use a hitherto little used but one of their most effective weapons properly. In 1941 the British had developed a forward-firing mortar, known as the Hedgehog, in order to allow escorts to engage a submerged boat while still retaining asdic contact. The Hedgehog was first used in December 1941 and made its first kill in February 1942, but its initial training programmes were hurried and inadequate. Moreover, the weapon itself proved unpopular at sea because it could only be used at low speed, and escorts had developed a marked preference for high-speed depth-charge attacks. As a result, the Hedgehog was largely neglected until the use of acoustic torpedoes. The most effective counter to such torpedoes was low speed, and thereafter the Hedgehog and its various successors came into their own and exacted an increasing toll on U-boats after January 1944.

The fact that the *Kriegsmarine* developed various types of homing torpedo in an attempt to provide U-boats with the means of eliminating the escorts preparatory to attacks on merchantmen with conventional torpedoes obliquely raises the question of whether or not the Germans should have sought battle with the escorts from the very start of the campaign at sea. This issue, of course, invites a much wider question of the efficacy of German conduct of both the war at sea as a whole and the campaign against merchant shipping in particular. The verdict of history on both of these highly complicated matters has been generally favourable, allowing for the *Kriegsmarine*'s unpreparedness for war in 1939, its junior status and lack of friends at court, and Hitler's general lack of understanding of and interest in naval matters. Such matters were important, yet any critical assessment of the German navy in the Second World War must note certain facts. The German navy's failure in this war was not its first but its second; it was its second within 30 years and in many ways this second defeat was comprehensive and unmitigated whereas the first most definitely was not. In addition, the conspiracy that seeks to blame Hitler for every German failure is not sufficient to explain this second defeat. Hitler did fail the German navy in many ways, most obviously in terms of the confusion of construction priorities that beset the whole of the German industrial performance in the Second World War, but the German navy was largely free of Hitler's supervision of its attempt to wage 'tonnage warfare'. Even in the one area of naval operations where Hitler was prone to interfere, the activities of major surface units, his often crippling restrictions upon operations were scarcely less stifling than those imposed by the naval staff and were in any event in accordance with the navy's own doctrine that warship raiders should decline action with escorts whenever possible. Moreover, despite the generally uncritical assessment of the U-boat command's conduct of the Battle of the Atlantic, it is at least arguable that throughout the first four years of the European war the German naval command consistently failed to maintain its own selected aim. Allowing for a certain diversion of force as inevitable because Norway had to be defended and Italy supported, the U-boat command's constant switch of the point of attack, the probing for weak spots, was not unlike the surgical knife that cuts away the secondary cancers while leaving the primary growth untouched. Had the U-boat command accepted the losses inherent in attacks on even poorly defended convoys before mid-1942 when screens seldom consisted of more than four slow escorts, it is at least possible that the convoy system could have been overwhelmed before the escorts had time to develop their strength – and perhaps a policy of sea denial might have been made to work.

With all the problems that are presented by the advantage of hindsight in terms of seeing a defeat as inevitable, the jumble of half-digested concepts that the *Kriegsmarine* termed a strategy left the German navy vulnerable to defeat on two counts. It committed the *Kriegsmarine* to a stern chase with an almost non-existent force operating from a position of geographical disadvantage against an enemy of greater resources and with time to counter German moves and make good its losses, if only in part. The handicap of geographical disadvantage was to be eliminated between June 1940 and June 1944, yet even this did not allow the German navy to prevail against an Anglo-American enemy that built 42,485,000 tons of merchant shipping between September 1939 and April 1945. In addition, the idea of sea denial by time or area or both was not an effective substitute for possession of command of the sea, and the concentration of attention upon German failure in the Battle of the Atlantic has served to obscure the full nature of the German defeat at sea during the Second World War.

This defeat encompassed more than failure in the campaign against Allied merchant shipping. It embraced the failure to defend if not Germany then her conquests. The Allied invasions of Italy and of both north-west and southern France encountered negligible and wholly ineffective German naval resistance. Moreover, the *Kriegsmarine* failed in its defence of German seaborne trade, particularly after 1941. Throughout British naval history command of the sea had enabled Britain to use the sea for commercial and military purposes while denying the same facilities to her enemies, and the last two years of the European war saw those three aspects traditionally associated with the use of victorious sea power – the destruction of enemy shipping, the strangulation of enemy seaborne trade, and the razing of enemy ports and coastal towns – put into devastating effect by the Allies even though the main instrument whereby war was carried to German coasts was no longer sea power itself. In the European theatre geography and technology imposed severe restrictions upon the offensive use of sea power, and shore-based aircraft were the primary means whereby the Allied powers completed their naval victory, though it must be noted that the destruction of German ports, as distinct from their immediate hinterland, eluded the victors. Allied air power accounted for eight of the nine major German warship losses of the last year of the European war by direct attack, but such success was belated and had no practical effect upon the outcome of the war.

More importantly, but for the occasional blockade-runner after 1940, Allied sea power drove German commerce from the oceans and deprived Germany of most of her seaborne trade from the very start of the war, but this achievement, in common with the traditional British policy of fighting protracted wars of attrition, only took effect in the last year of the European war when the loss of her earlier conquests finally forced Germany to wage war on the basis of her own resources. The extent of these conquests had largely freed Germany from dependence upon seaborne trade, and allowing for the 89 per cent decline of fishing returns between 1938 and 1942 and the fact that in 1942 Swedish ships carried 53 per cent of Germany's iron ore imports, until 1944 Germany controlled more than enough shipping to meet her trade requirements. In 1944, however, German shipping resources were not sufficient to maintain the level of Swedish ore imports after Swedish shipping was withdrawn from this trade, and by May 1945 a German merchant marine that had begun the war with 4,492,708 tons of shipping had been reduced by 67.23 per cent to just 1,583,151 tons. The greater part of German losses, amounting to 1,052,095 tons of shipping or 42.3 per cent of the German merchant navy on 1 January 1944, was incurred in the last 16 months of the war, but it was not until 1945 that the German minesweeping fleet was finally overwhelmed and German coastal trade collapsed. Apart from the Baltic, where German surface forces continued to operate until the very end of the war and which, for the most part, was beyond the range of aircraft based in Britain, the German defeat at sea in terms of the defence of trade in the Second World War was total. Perhaps one of the most remarkable features of this defeat was the fact that Allied action would seem to have accounted for more merchant ships than did the Axis powers. On the basis of incomplete Admiralty returns with respect to the minor European Axis powers, 5,150 Allied and neutral merchantmen of 21,570,720 tons were captured or lost to all causes, including Japanese action, in the course of the Second World War, but in very quiet contrast to the much-vaunted German submarine performance Allied operations and natural causes accounted for 5,137 merchantmen of 7,823,178 tons in the same six-year period. It was the German navy's failure in defence of trade, coming on top of its inability to resist Allied invasions and to win the Battle of the Atlantic, that points to the conclusion that, for all its acknowledged tactical and technical proficiency, the *Kriegsmarine* understood fighting at sea, not naval warfare.

Examination of Germany's economic collapse as a result of naval defeat and Allied air operations against her seaborne trade leads naturally to consideration of what was – until death and infirmity removed the chief protagonists from the stage – perhaps the most controversial aspect of the Second World War: the Anglo-American strategic air offensive against Germany. To summarise arguments that were fiercely contested well into the third decade after the end of the European war, there was a body of opinion that held that this offensive had little or no effect upon the outcome of the war while a contrary view asserted, with equal certainty, that victory over Germany could not have been won without this campaign. Between these extremes emerged the view that the air offensive made a significant contribution to victory, but in the articulation of this undoubtedly correct assessment obvious problems of fact and interpretation of what was achieved and how the campaign could have been better prosecuted arose to complicate proceedings. Amidst these conflicting claims, however, it is possible to note certain matters which, if not beyond dispute, at least provide the terms of reference for a dispassionate examination of this campaign.

First, and most obviously, the Anglo-American strategic bombing offensive manifestly failed to achieve the independent victory that advocates of air power in the inter-war period and a number of wartime Allied commanders believed was possible, if not certain. Second, the offensive nevertheless resulted in Germany's economic and industrial collapse before her final military defeat was accomplished. The Ruhr was physically isolated from the rest of Germany as a result of the destruction of its canal, rail and road networks, and its factories had been brought to a standstill before it was surrounded by American forces. The difference in time between the two, however, was minimal. Third, the issue of defeat and victory in Europe was decided some time in the second half of 1943: thereafter the German defeat was assured and the only questions that remained to be answered were when, how and at what cost this defeat would be achieved. But the issue itself was resolved before the strategic bombing offensive had registered any significant results whatsoever, and the line of argument used to justify this offensive in terms of 'the decisive destruction of Germany's capacity to continue the war . . . opened her to naval and military defeat' is thoroughly mendacious. Indeed, it is quite possible to argue that the Allied strategic air offensive did not properly begin for a full year after Germany's defeat was guaranteed – not until the autumn of 1944 – and that while it did pave the way for the final advances into the German heartland, whatever success the strategic air offensive achieved was dependent at least in part upon the favourable conditions created for this offensive by the successful advance of Allied armies in north-west Europe during the previous summer. Despite an obvious interdependence of efforts and air power's contribution to its own success in terms of the Americans' winning command of the air, Germany's naval and military defeat opened her to defeat in the strategic bombing offensive, not the other way around.

This third and last observation needs qualification in certain respects. The Allied air offensive predated autumn 1944, and even in the course of 1943 acquired a significance and weight that had important repercussions on the German war economy. In 1943 the Allies attempted to mount a sustained bombing campaign under highly unfavourable conditions and were defeated in their efforts, but the offensive nevertheless forced a diversion of German resources into air defence that had important if unquantifiable consequences on the conduct of the war. By the end of 1943 German air defence numbered 1,000,000 flak troops, and 1,500,000 men were held as labour detailed to the repair of damage caused by bombing raids. German output was increasingly geared to fighters and flak defences at the expense of offensive weapons. In addition, by this time some 70 per cent of the *Luftwaffe*'s fighter strength was committed to the defence of German cities, and German formations on the Eastern Front and in Italy had been stripped of their air cover: in the last two years of the war Allied field armies fought with the advantage of overwhelming air superiority, which was the by-product of the strategic air offensive against Germany. Moreover, between 1940 and 1943 first Britain and then the United States could not take the war to Germany except by bombing, and authorisation of the combined bombing offensive at Casablanca was on the basis that bombing alone promised to provide the Soviet Union with some form of assistance at a time when the Western allies could not undertake the invasion of northwest Europe. The bombing campaign before autumn 1944 thus possessed a political significance infinitely more important than the results obtained in the course of operations, not least because raids, particularly in 1940 and 1941, showed that Hitler had yet to win the war even in this period of German ascendancy. If nothing else, this was a source of hope to those who lived under the tyranny of Nazi occupation and arguably the Allied air offensive justified itself for this reason alone.

The fact that between 1940 and 1943 bombing was the only offensive option available to the British and Americans was important in that it provides the corrective to one of the most important arguments about this campaign which may be discussed at this point in order to dismiss it from further consideration. Both during and after the war the question of the value of the strategic air offensive was inextricably linked with moral issues, and it cannot be denied that Allied claims of moral superiority over Nazism sit uneasily alongside such episodes as the razing of Dresden in 1945. The strategic bombing campaign, with first its acceptance of civilian casualties as the inevitable, if unfortunate, by-product of operations and then the concentration against civilian targets as an act of policy, is not easy to reconcile with the Christian doctrine of the Just War, first defined by Aquinas in the thirteenth century, with its moral imperatives the avoidance of the unnecessary taking of life and the sparing of non-combatants. But in respect to the strategic bombing campaign as a whole, morality existed only in choice, and German civilian casualties could have been avoided only if the Allies had chosen deliberately to deny themselves a means of attack that Germany had employed from the start of hostilities. Moral justification can always be rationalised, not that the Allies considered it necessary at the time to justify the strategic bombing offensive in moral terms, but there existed in the war's middle years neither political nor military reasons, and no good moral consideration, that would have justified the Allies denying themselves their only means of forcing Germany to respond to their initiative by a dissipation of battlefront strength and industrial effort. To have accepted such self-imposed limitation would have constituted a betrayal of the Allied cause itself, of the Allied armies in the field, and – perhaps most important of all – of the peoples of occupied Europe, to whom Britain and the United States owed infinitely more than they did to the German civilian population. Bombing may have embraced a dubious morality, and arguably bombing embraced an increasingly dubious morality as Germany's defeat became reality and other means of taking the war to Germany came to hand, but without recourse to the argument that a just cause permitted the deliberate waging of war against a civilian population as the means of achieving victory the absence of choice in Allied policy after 1940 and the limitations of the air weapon itself at this time precludes morality as a serious factor in any consideration of this campaign. The Allies could not bomb without causing civilian casualties, and they could not afford to deny themselves an offensive that imposed a second front upon the *Wehrmacht* a full year before the invasion of north-west Europe.

Before examining the Anglo-American strategic bombing offensive against Germany it should be noted that the first Allied air raid of the war was on 1 September 1939 when Polish aircraft attacked Berlin, and that the Soviet Union, the first nation to possess four-engine heavy bombers in the 1930s, retained a strategic bombing capability throughout the war and attacked cities in eastern Germany at various stages of the Nazi–Soviet conflict. The Soviet achievement was nevertheless very modest, as indeed was that of RAF Bomber Command before February 1942. Though the British effort before this month divided into several distinct phases the operational pattern established in the first 30 months of the European war revealed that the RAF, which owed its survival in the inter-war period to its presentation of strategic bombing as its *raison d'être*, could not carry out precision attacks on German industrial and military targets as it continued to claim. In part, the reason for this failure was navigational problems, the full extent of which had not been appreciated before 1939, but the fundamental problem that confounded RAF Bomber Command's attempt to develop a strategic offensive was the simple fact that the balance of advantage had shifted in favour of the defensive fighter since the time, in 1932, when the sometime British prime minister, Stanley Baldwin, had made his famous – if heavily qualified – prediction that 'the bomber will always get through'.

For most of the inter-war period this was indisputable: the performance of bombers and fighters in terms of speed and ceiling were roughly equal and indeed the first monoplane bombers of the mid-1930s were considerably superior to fighters, particularly in speed. At a distance of 50 years it is very easy to forget that the reversal of advantages came both late and suddenly, around 1937, with the introduction of high-performance monoplane fighters into service with various air forces. This development, along with radar, airborne radar and combat control centres, provided the defence with the means to detect and concentrate against incoming bomber formations, and the vulnerability of bombers in daylight to fighters designed and tasked to destroy them was confirmed in the Battle of Britain when the *Luftwaffe* was forced to bomb by night in order to avoid prohibitive losses. RAF Bomber Command, however, had suffered the same experience and had come to the same conclusion even before the Battle of Britain.

Despite the fact that inter-war air theory had stressed the deterrence aspect of bomber forces, RAF Bomber Command was singularly ill-equipped to carry out a strategic air offensive in 1939, and at the outbreak of war the British and French governments hesitated to initiate an air campaign partly because of this weakness and German superiority in the air, partly because geography conspired to render British and French cities, particularly London and Paris, more vulnerable to air attack than those of Germany. The lateness of British rearmament meant that the RAF could not come into possession of a sizeable heavy bomber force until 1942, and Bomber Command began the war with just 33 squadrons, 17 of which were equipped with Battle and Blenheim light bombers which were incapable of making an effective contribution to a strategic air offensive. The balance of its squadrons were equipped with Hampden and Wellington light and Whitley heavy bombers which lacked the range–payload combination essential to mounting potentially destructive raids and the self-sealing tanks, armour and defensive firepower necessary for survival over Germany. This fact of life was forcibly impressed upon RAF Bomber Command during December 1939 when two daylight operations each resulted in the loss of more than half of the attacking force. On 18 December, in a raid that involved no real penetration of German air space, radar-directed fighters accounted for 12 of the 22 Wellingtons sent against warships in the Jade Roads and at Wilhelmshaven. Daylight operations between September and December 1939 cost RAF Bomber Command 31 of the 163 aircraft thus despatched.

Before the war Bomber Command had calculated that 5 per cent losses represented the maximum that could be sustained without a decline of operational effectiveness. After the 18 December raid its daylight operations were curtailed drastically and emphasis placed upon night operations. In the winter of 1939–1940 these consisted of dropping propaganda leaflets rather than high explosive on German cities, but in that losses during such missions to enemy action were very few and overall losses totalled only 2.8 per cent lay an obvious conclusion that RAF Bomber Command could not and did not ignore. When the German attack in the west began so, too, did Bomber Command's night offensive against German cities. The first British raid in a campaign that was to last almost five years was mounted on the night of 14/15 May 1940 against communications and military targets in the Ruhr.

Involvement in the fighting in the Low Countries and northern France in May and June 1940 prevented Bomber Command from developing strategic operations in these months, and in the summer weeks that followed its main efforts were directed against aircraft and aluminium factories in western Germany and shipping concentrated in German and Channel ports for the proposed invasion of southern England. These targets, set down in directives issued on 20 June and 4 July respectively, were determined by obvious and immediate needs – to reduce the scale of future attacks on Britain by striking against German air strength at source, and to disrupt German preparations for *Operation Seelöwe* – but they cut across the terms of the directive issued to Bomber Command on 4 June that identified oil as the critical weakness of the German industrial and military effort. This directive ordered Bomber Command to concentrate its efforts against German refineries, storage depots and synthetic production plants as its first priority. A further directive of 13 July restored Germany's aircraft industry as Bomber Command's priority target, but this was changed by yet another directive of the twenty-fourth that presented Bomber Command with a mix of targets. This constant switch of operational priorities throughout the summer of 1940 partially explains the ineffectiveness of Bomber Command's operations – except in its attacks on invasion shipping – in these months, but it was a process that was continued into the autumn. Indeed, this constant change of

279

priority was compounded by Bomber Command's being ordered to attack communications centres and to mine, and also to carry out retaliatory raids on German cities after the raid on London of 24 August. On the night of 25/26 August 81 bombers attacked Berlin, and after the deliberate terror-raid on London on 7 September the RAF was detailed to bombing cities without specific reference to industrial and military targets.

The constant switch of priorities in the second half of 1940 was by no means the major factor in Bomber Command's ineffectiveness at this time, and indeed even if it had been left to concentrate against a single priority target it could not have achieved any significant result for four reasons. At no stage could Bomber Command muster more than 300 operational aircraft, and once maintenance and reserve needs lowered this total to about 150 more than 20 to 30 bombers were seldom available to any single night's operations. Further, the April decision that formally committed Bomber Command to night bombing and the subsequent directives that set out priorities were based upon Bomber Command's carrying out precision attacks at night, and this limited such operations to periods of full moon. Initially, Bomber Command was specifically instructed to avoid indiscriminate attacks on cities, but while the loosening of this restriction and the need to mine and attack communications provided it with alternative targets for the remaining three-quarters of a lunar month, this could not alter the fact that Bomber Command could not carry out a sustained offensive that could inflict cumulative damage upon the German economy. Moreover, the German economy itself was virtually invulnerable to attack in 1940. The pre-war dispersal of industry, the occupation of first Denmark and Norway, then the Low Countries and northern France and last Romania, and trade with Sweden and the Soviet Union meant that the German war economy could easily absorb any damage inflicted by Bomber Command. Indeed, at the time when Bomber Command concentrated its efforts against the German oil industry German stocks rose as a result of increased production and imports and cuts in consumption.

Thus Bomber Command could attack no more than a limited part of the German economy with an inadequate number of bombers on an intermittent basis, but throughout the autumn it continued to claim considerable success in its operations, particularly against the German oil industry. It based its claims on pilot reports and upon theoretical statistical studies, one of which suggested, in the form of a paper presented to the British war cabinet on 16 December, that the German output of synthetic oil had been reduced by 15 per cent despite only 6 to 7 per cent of Bomber Command's effort being directed against it. In making such claims Bomber Command either deceived itself or was deliberately mendacious. In circumstances that demanded success and when Bomber Command had to justify itself and its priority claims on future production, the RAF provided the illusion of success even though by November 1940 the air staff and Bomber Command had become aware that a significant number of bombers failed to find and attack their designated targets. This was indeed the case, and was the final reason for Bomber Command's failure in its offensive at this time. The realisation that the precision attack concept was flawed began to push the new heads of the air staff and Bomber Command towards the conclusion that if bombing could not achieve its aim then the aim had to be changed to take account of what was tactically and technically possible.

In effect, in the last quarter of 1940 the air staff and Bomber Command tentatively recognised that if bombers could not find anything smaller than cities then cities had to be attacked as a matter of policy because neither of the alternatives – either a return to daylight raids or no bombing at all – represented a practical proposition. But another 15 months were to elapse before the logic of this conclusion was accepted by the RAF and Bomber Command in the form of the area bombing directive of 14 February 1942. Meanwhile, four major developments – signposted by three major directives – both delayed and made inevitable the commitment of Bomber Command to attacks intended to break German morale.

The first development was a result of the first Photo-Reconnaissance Spitfires entering service in November 1940 and conducting a recon-naissance of two synthetic plants at Gelsenkirchen on 24 December. At this time Bomber Command, after a double change of priorities in November, was committed to attacks on the German oil industry as its main task and had sent no fewer than 296 bombers against these two plants. This reconnaissance revealed that plants assumed to have been extensively damaged were in full production and bore no obvious signs of major damage. This was the first incontrovertible evidence that aircrew forced to rely upon astro-navigation, map reading and dead reckoning to find their targets were failing in their attempt to carry out a night-time precision offensive, but rather than strengthening the case for area bombing this conclusion perversely led to the decision to concentrate all Bomber Command's resources against just 17 named oil installations in an attempt to ensure their destruction in the course of a four-month offensive. Bomber Command received its formal directive to this effect on 15 January 1941, but despite having the first of the Stirling, Halifax and Manchester heavy bombers in service Bomber Command spent the next 10 weeks vainly trying to succeed in what proved to be its last chance to make precision bombing at night work.

Bomber Command was spared the possible consequences of failure in its oil offensive by the second development, its commitment to the Battle of the Atlantic and specifically to attacks on Brest where German warships gathered in the spring of 1941 for an assault on Allied shipping in the North Atlantic. Throughout that spring Bomber Command carried out a series of raids with a notable lack of success, though in April the battleship *Gneisenau* was hit in dry dock having been torpedoed by an RAF Coastal Command bomber. By July, however, the immediate crises that had provoked Bomber Command's flirtation with maritime matters had passed: the sinking of the *Bismarck* and her intended supply ships, the damage to the *Gneisenau* and the mining of Brest spelt an end to the threat of a breakout into the Atlantic by German warships, and Bomber Command was freed for a resumption of its strategic operations.

This period of commitment to the Battle of the Atlantic coincided with the third development, the debate within the British High Command about Bomber Command's future objectives and operations. Under Air Chief Marshal Portal, until October 1940 C-in-C Bomber Command, the air staff worked slowly towards two conclusions: that area bombing had to be adopted because Bomber Command could not attempt anything else, and that the breaking of German morale by aerial bombardment was the prerequisite for successful military and naval operations against the *Wehrmacht*. For obvious reasons, however, the air staff hesitated to embrace conclusions that amounted to an admission that Bomber Command had been and was a failure but which nevertheless assigned the other services no role other than to watch it try to prove that it was not. With no guarantee that area bombing could break German morale, and Portal for one was not wholly convinced that German morale could be broken before Germany's military defeat was a fact, the commitment of Bomber Command to an offensive against German cities and morale was a gamble with far-reaching implications for the British war effort. The switch from the scalpel, however blunt, to the bludgeon would necessarily involve a massive expansion of Bomber Command. On the air staff's calculations, Bomber Command would need a front-line strength of 4,000 bombers to have any chance of success, and to raise such a force no fewer than 22,000 bombers would have to be built – 17,000 in Britain – between July 1941 and July 1943. Leaving aside the obvious problem presented by a two-year lead-time, to raise such a force would necessarily involve an emasculation of tactical air power and naval aviation plus the further diversion of resources to Bomber Command at the expense of existing military and naval priorities. In short, in spring 1941 a commitment to area bombing threatened to result in Bomber Command swallowing the rest of the RAF and the army and navy being stunted to the extent that they would not be able to capitalise upon the success that area bombing achieved – in two years' time, if indeed it was successful.

These various issues were considered at different levels within the British High Command during spring 1941 with the predictable result that issues were fudged. The 7 July directive that emerged from these deliberations as the fourth development on the road to area bombing committed Bomber Command to attacks on both cities and key communications bottlenecks, but in so doing it evaded the problems at the heart of a strategic bombing policy. By instructing Bomber Command to concentrate against seven transport choke-points and six cities the air staff calculated that bombers that missed their targets would nevertheless inflict worthwhile collateral damage, but the policy of continuing precision bombing by making targets less precise counted for nothing if Bomber Command remained without the navigational aids needed to guide bombers to those targets, and if the aim of operations was to strangle the German transport system then collateral German civilian casualties did not represent a satisfactory *quid pro quo*. Moreover, Bomber Command remained without the numbers needed to raze German cities, and in any event the basis of the directive – that German communications could be paralysed by the destruction of seven key complexes and that German morale could be broken by the flattening of six cities – was somewhat tenuous, by any standard.

The July directive was unsound in its reasoning and unrealistic in the tasks it set Bomber Command, but while Bomber Command was to spend the summer months trying to achieve results well beyond its slender means and capabilities failure on two other fronts combined to force the RAF into unreserved support for an area bombing offensive. First, in June 1941 the RAF began a series of daylight raids over the Pas de Calais designed to force the *Luftwaffe* into a defensive battle that it would lose. In reality, the *Luftwaffe* had the option not to be thus drawn because none of the RAF targets warranted its commitment, and on those occasions when it did fight the superiority of the defence was reaffirmed. Moreover, the RAF found to its surprise that the Spitfire Mark V was outclassed by the new Messerschmitt Bf 109F. By September 1941 escort raids over northern France had obviously failed to make any impression upon the *Luftwaffe* while unescorted raids on

French Atlantic ports had become prohibitively expensive with 10 per cent losses being sustained. By September 1941, with the nights beginning to draw in, daylight operations clearly presented the RAF with no credible alternative to its strategic offensive.

Second, in August 1941 the first scientific analysis of bombing operations became available as a result of bomb-bay cameras fitted to a number of operational bombers. In a report submitted to the war cabinet it was estimated that 65 per cent of all bombers failed to come within five miles of their targets and those that did bombed anywhere within this 75 square miles of the objective. The Butt Report was bitterly denounced by sections of the RAF but it had obvious implications for Bomber Command, and in the immediate aftermath of its submission the policy of attacking communications targets was dropped: Portal, on 25 September, formally requested authorisation of a 4,000-strong bomber force which would end the war in six months by the methodical destruction of 43 major German cities. Churchill dismissed this claim with the observation that there was no good reason to assume that German morale would prove more vulnerable to bombing than that of the British, and he also noted that German defences were certain to improve and that Bomber Command's prime requirement was greater accuracy, not greater numbers. Churchill also suspected, rightly, that there was no sure and single way to victory over an industrialised enemy, but he had little alternative but to admit that bombing remained 'the most potent method of impairing the enemy at the present time'. On 6 October, five days after raids on Karlsruhe and Stuttgart resulted in Bomber Command inadvertently bombing no fewer than 29 German cities, Churchill endorsed the RAF argument in favour of area bombing, the final stage in this journey to an all-out offensive against German morale being reached as a result of the disastrously expensive raid on Berlin of 7/8 November. With 9 per cent losses on this single raid, the air staff took the opportunity on the thirteenth to issue a new directive to Bomber Command restricting its operations in order to conserve its strength throughout the winter in readiness for a full-scale resumption of operations in the spring. The directive authorising this renewal of the campaign, directed against German cities and morale, was issued on 14 February 1942, by which time RAF Bomber Command knew that it would not be alone in carrying the air war to Germany.

The Axis declaration of war upon the United States in December 1941 placed the US Army Air Force in the same position relative to Germany and the prosecution of the European war as RAF Bomber Command since June 1940: without the means to undertake military operations in Europe, the USAAF was the only means by which the Americans could take the war in which they found themselves to Germany. Not until January 1943, however, did American heavy bombers raid Germany, and thereafter a full year was to elapse before American strategic air operations assumed real significance. It was to take the AAF two full years from the time that the United States entered the war to accumulate the strength necessary to undertake sustained offensive operations against Germany, in large measure because after October 1942 the build-up of the 8th Air Force in Britain was checked by the ever-widening commitment in the Mediterranean theatre where the 9th and 15th Air Forces were used primarily in a tactical role. Indeed, such was the drain of the Mediterranean theatre upon American resources earmarked for the European war that throughout the first quarter of 1943 the 8th Air Force averaged no more than a front-line strength of 74 heavy bombers, a number wholly inadequate for the conduct of a strategic offensive.

1942 thus proved to be a year in which the AAF set about the task of creating in Britain the infrastructure for its future operations against Germany, and RAF Bomber Command was not dissimilarly placed. After 22 different directives in the previous 29 months, the 14 February 1942 area bombing directive committed RAF Bomber Command to a task that necessitated major changes of equipment, training and organisation in the course of the year. Thus at a time when the first American heavy bomber formations arrived in Britain (1 July) and began operations against targets in France and the Low Countries on 17 August, RAF Bomber Command was in the process of re-equipping with Halifax and Lancaster heavy bombers, after August raising pathfinder forces in order to mark targets, and devising bomber stream tactics in order to swamp German fighter defences and to ensure saturation attacks. Until the spring of 1942 RAF Bomber Command's attacks had been conducted on an individual basis with aircraft having to find their own ways to their targets, hence the poor returns in terms of navigation and accuracy registered by a force that suffered from inevitable problems of rapid expansion and dilution. The development of pathfinder formations and bomber stream tactics began the process whereby RAF Bomber Command raised overall standards of accuracy by having specialist units lead less well trained and inexperienced units to their targets. This process took time, however, and it was not until 1943 that RAF Bomber Command began to reap the benefits of these changes of tactics and organisation, yet in 1942 it was nevertheless able to record the achievements that established its reputation and ensured that it would be allowed to persist in its attempt to break German morale by area bombing – though 1942 also revealed fundamental differences between American and British bombing philosophies and between Allied air and military commanders.

RAF Bomber Command secured its own future after some 30 months of confusion and failure as a result of raids on Lübeck (28/29 March), Rostock (23/24 April), Cologne (30/31 May), Essen (1/2 June) and Bremen (25/26 June). Lübeck and Rostock were attacked simply because they were medieval Hanse cities that would burn, while the Cologne raid was staged simply as the first 1,000-bomber raid in history. In each of these three operations, plus those against Essen and Bremen which were mounted by more than 900 bombers, RAF Bomber Command sought to burn out city centres in order to demonstrate present capabilities and future intentions, and to provide the Allies with a series of propaganda victories at a time when their fortunes were at a particularly low ebb. Its success in achieving these aims rendered the concept of strategic bombing non-negotiable and also brought RAF Bomber Command a measure of operational freedom relative to the air staff and indeed the British High Command unmatched by any other branch or service. Yet in registering such success RAF Bomber Command found its area bombing policy opposed by an American air command wedded to the belief that daylight precision bombing was the only means whereby a strategic air offensive could be prosecuted to a successful conclusion. With the B-17 Flying Fortress and B-24 Liberator the AAF had equipped itself with two heavy bombers that were supposedly capable of fighting their way to a target in the face of fighter opposition, the American belief being that the formidable defensive armament of concentrated bomber formations would provide the means whereby control of the skies over German targets could be secured. Events proved this concept flawed, and American bomber formations were subjected to prohibitive losses until such time, in the winter of 1944, that American fighter aircraft won control of German airspace in the hours of daylight.

In the differences between RAF and USAAF bombing philosophies lay a possible basis for cooperation, and indeed the different timings of British and American operations gave rise to the 'bombing round the clock' idea. This, however, remained little more than an impressive phrase because the two forces and philosophies were in fact rivals and not complementary. In 1942 and 1943 the American air command clung to its ideas of daylight precision bombing partly in order to prevent being reduced to an adjunct of RAF Bomber Command and partly to ensure distinctive American contribution to the European war: by 1944 and 1945 the situation had reversed itself in that RAF Bomber Command was one of the very last areas of the British war effort not wholly dependent upon US support. Throughout the war the American air commanders were acutely aware that a successful offensive would make the case for an independent air force within the US military establishment irresistible, and on the part of both RAF Bomber Command and the AAF there was a natural desire to secure a victory that did not have to be shared with the other. Given these differences there was relatively little basis for a coordination of the American and British efforts, and the extent of the divergence between the two allies and the fact that 'for most of 1943 there was no combined offensive but . . . a bombing competition' was reflected in the failure to devise a combined bombing directive until 10 June 1943, six months after the combined offensive had been sanctioned at the Casablanca conference. Even after the Pointblank directive was issued, however, both RAF Bomber Command and American air commanders regarded it as the basis for procrastination in their dealings with superiors rather than for mutually supporting operations, and between January 1943 and March 1944 the American and British bomber forces conducted their separate wars even as common problems emerged to frustrate their different efforts.

The first of these problems arose because German cities and industry proved to have unexpected powers of resistance and recuperation. Modern cities, with wide roads and open spaces, were subjected to enormous local damage but could seldom be devastated over an extended area. The 1,000-bomber raid on Cologne, for example, resulted in only 469 German deaths and the destruction of one square mile of the city centre, and even where devastation was more substantial losses of production were usually measured in days and weeks rather than months. Some 8.7 square miles of Hamburg were destroyed in the firestorm raids of 24 July/3 August, but the city's port and shipyards were hardly affected despite the massive disruption of civil life and numbers killed. Manufacturing industry, with its dispersed and diversified centres of production, feeder and specialist industries and complex transportation system, was too extensive to be paralysed or destroyed except as a result of intensive sustained attack that inflicted progressive and irreversible damage. Very few industries, and the synthetic oil industry was one exception, were so concentrated as to be vulnerable to air bombardment, and the fact that throughout 1943 German industry operated well below capacity provided a slack that could be taken up in order to absorb the production losses that were sustained.

Compounding this problem for the Americans and British was the reality that neither had the strength to mount sustained operations that could inflict telling cumulative damage, while bad weather, over Britain or Germany, imposed its own restrictions upon the conduct of operations. Moreover, both the Americans and British were prevented from mounting successive follow-up attacks because of the need to switch targets in order to preserve tactical surprise. This became increasingly important with respect to deep-penetration operations as the scale and effectiveness of German defences grew during the course of 1943. By September 1943 a front-line strength of some 500 day and 350 night fighters (plus over 33,400 flak guns) had been concentrated by the *Luftwaffe* in defence of German airspace, and it was around this time that the German daylight effort peaked with a series of battles that ended with the 8th Air Force temporarily admitting defeat.

The two most important single battles were fought on 17 August and 14 October, the first resulting in the 8th Air Force losing 64 heavy bombers and having another 168 damaged from the total of 376 sent against the ball-bearing factories at Schweinfurt and the aircraft plants at Regensburg while another 67 were lost and 138 were damaged in the October raid on Emden and Schweinfurt by 320 aircraft. Although such losses were exceptional, routine operations in the first 10 days of October 1943 cost the 8th Air Force 139 heavy bombers at a time when its average front-line strength was little more than 400 Fortresses and Liberators, and it was the combination of such losses that finally convinced American air commanders that air supremacy had to be secured as the prerequisite for a successful daylight bombing campaign. At the same time RAF Bomber Command, which had reached this conclusion in 1940 but which had switched to night operations in order to avoid the insoluble problems thus presented, found that the German combination of Freya early warning, Würzburg tracking and Lichtenstein A-1 airborne radars had reversed the previous balance of advantage in night operations and had rendered the bomber stream highly vulnerable to Bf 110 and Ju 88 night-fighters.

In the course of operations that extended across the whole of Germany between 18 November 1943 and 31 March 1944 but which became known as the Battle of Berlin because the German capital was raided on 18 occasions in this period, RAF Bomber Command lost more aircraft – 1,047 with a further 1,682 damaged – than it possessed at any single time during the campaign, and in the last disastrous operation of this particular offensive, against Nuremberg on 30–31 March it lost 108 of the 1,009 aircraft sent against this and other related targets. By the end of March 1944, at a time when RAF Bomber Command had a daily average strength of 974 heavy bombers, the British had exhausted the various counter-measures – fighter–bomber attacks on German airfields, active and passive jamming of German radars, and voice disruption of German communications – that had been developed in order to limit losses. Indeed, by this time RAF Bomber Command had been brought to the edge of defeat and had manifestly failed to bring about the collapse of Germany that its commander, Air Marshal Harris, had claimed on 7 December 1943 it could achieve by 1 April 1944.

This April deadline was critical in the conduct of the Allied strategic bombing campaign because in the winter of 1944 the question of air power's role in the defeat of Germany emerged as the most important single issue confronting the American and British High Commands in the conduct of the European war. The idea of the combined bombing offensive, as settled at Casablanca and in the Pointblank directive, had been a charter, devised by the bomber lobby, for the defeat of Germany by bombing alone, yet as Anglo-American strategic policy evolved in the course of 1943 with the result that the invasion of north-west Europe – *Operation Overlord* – emerged as central to that policy with a timetable settled for summer 1944, so the issues of bomber operations preparatory to invasion and command of the strategic forces during the spring and summer of 1944 presented themselves for solution. At its simplest, *Operation Overlord* had assumed such a priority in the Anglo-American prosecution of the war that it could not be made dependent upon the successful outcome of the strategic air offensive, but while the *Overlord* command sought control of the bomber forces in order to attack German defences and lines of communication in the pre-invasion phase and to support the ground forces once ashore, the bomber commanders, whether American or British, sought to preserve their own freedom of action and insisted that their forces' most significant contribution to an invasion of north-west Europe – privately derided as unnecessary and irrelevant – remained the destruction of German industry and morale.

In the winter of 1944 the bomber lobby lost this argument, in part because the *Overlord* commander, General Eisenhower, made the issue one of personal confidence that could not be resolved except in his favour and in part because by March 1944 the bomber commanders could not hold out any prospect of their forces' achieving decisive results until autumn 1944. In these circumstances, the subordination of the strategic bombing offensive to the requirements of *Operation Overlord* was inevitable, despite the air lobby's insistence that any diversion of effort would grant Germany a reprieve at the very time when the failures and losses of the previous four years were about to be vindicated by decisive success. In the event, during the period between 14 April and 14 September when the strategic bomber forces operated under Eisenhower's direction, the bombing of Germany continued on a very substantial scale, and this period saw the first significant faltering of German industry as a result of the concentration of the American strategic bombing effort against the synthetic oil industry on and after 12 May.

The bomber commanders' March 1944 assertion was overstated, but the fact that on 27 August RAF Bomber Command resumed daylight bombing operations over Germany for the first time in four years was evidence of the Americans having won a victory in the air during the first half of 1944 that was in no way diminished by its not being the victory that they had originally sought. The victory that the Americans won after December 1943 primarily stemmed from the fortunate coincidence of their realising that air superiority had to be won before bombing could be effective and their coming into possession of the means whereby that superiority could be won. Until April 1943 the 8th Air Force had to rely upon short-range P-38 Lightnings and RAF Spitfires to provide its bombers with cover as far as the German border: thereafter the P-47B Thunderbolt was added to the supporting cast and escorted American bombers over western Germany. After July 1943, with the appearance of the P-47C and drop tanks for both Lightnings and Thunderbolts, American fighters operated ever deeper into Germany in defence of the heavy bombers, and the German switch from forward to in-depth defence was partially a response to this development. But while the later Thunderbolts were able to escort the strategic bombers as far as Berlin their overall performance was inferior to that of the Fw 190/Ta 152, the mainstay of the German daylight defensive effort. On 1 December, however, the first P-51B Mustangs arrived in Britain for service with the 8th Air Force, and after flying operationally in Europe for the first time on the thirteenth this aircraft proved that it could do battle with an Fw 190 over Berlin on better than equal terms. Moreover, at this same time, with the 8th Air Force in Britain and the 15th Air Force in Italy brought under a single command in order to subject Germany to coordinated American attacks, the Americans were able to commit their growing numbers of fighters not simply to the defence of the heavy bombers but to seeking out German fighters across the whole of Germany. Such was the success of both fighter efforts that by the spring of 1944 German fighter losses were averaging 500 per week and both the number and quality of the *Luftwaffe*'s daylight effort were in irreversible decline.

American success in writing down the *Luftwaffe*'s day-fighter arm in the first half of 1944 had a beneficial knock-on effect for RAF Bomber Command because as German losses mounted so night-fighter crews were committed against heavily protected American bomber formations with the result that losses amongst the élite of the *Luftwaffe* rose sharply. The German night-fighter service nevertheless retained an effectiveness lost to the day-fighter arm until March 1945, but by the end of 1944 it was not able to man its full operational strength, partly because by that time the cumulative effect of decisions taken in 1941 and 1942 had worked their way through the *Luftwaffe*'s infrastructure with increasingly baleful results. In 1941 the *Luftwaffe* had stripped virtually all its training establishments in order to execute *Operation Barbarossa* in the expectation that the defeat of the Soviet Union would enable it to resume quickly its training schedules and to redeploy formations to western and southern Europe with no serious ill-effects. Failure to defeat the Soviet Union in 1941 along with the disruption of training programmes had serious long-term implications for the *Luftwaffe* that were compounded in 1942 by a refusal to credit declared American intentions with respect to future aircraft construction. By the time that the German High Command realised the depth of American material resources and the constancy of American purpose, it was too late for the *Luftwaffe* to respond effectively to the escalation of the air war explicit in the American commitment to the strategic bombing campaign against Germany.

The result was that while German aircraft production rose dramatically after 1942, from 11,776 in 1941 to 39,807 in 1944, the patterns of both production and deployment became distorted while German operational strength remained more or less constant throughout 1943 and 1944. In 1939 and 1940 fighters formed 32.95 per cent and combat aircraft 61.9 per cent of total German aircraft production. By 1944 these figures had risen to 77.6 per cent and 88.9 per cent respectively, but while the *Luftwaffe*'s offensive capacity slumped in 1943 and 1944 its operational strength of 1,006 single-engine fighters in March 1943 rose to only 1,188 in March 1944 despite the fact that in the first quarter of 1944 German monthly production of single-engine fighters reached four figures for the first time. The massive increase of production in the course of 1944, from monthly runs of 1,236 single-engine fighters in the winter to 2,776 in the summer, came too late for a German air force facing an American air force that had increased its combat strength in Britain from 1,260 aircraft in May 1943 to 4,242 in December 1943 and to 8,351 in May 1944. Despite transferring 15 groups and more than 1,000 heavy bombers to the 15th Air Force after October 1943, the 8th Air Force reached an operational strength of 2,000 heavy bombers on – of all days – 6 June 1944. In the battle of attrition that the AAF imposed upon the *Luftwaffe* after January 1943 but which entered its decisive phase after December 1943, such numbers assured the Americans of a victory over an enemy that by mid-1943 was overcommitted on three fronts, increasingly short of manpower and fuel and beset by long-term structural weaknesses.

Examination of the war at sea and the Anglo-American strategic bombing offensive in terms of their impact upon Germany's capacity to make war leads naturally to consideration of the relative performance of the economies of the great powers in the course of the Second World War. This complicated and highly specialised subject presents problems of presentation and integration within a general history of the war, though the relative performance of the major powers can be summarised simply: the Axis preoccupation with the acquisition of resources contrasted with the Allied practice of expanded capacity and output, and in a protracted war of attrition this conferred on the Allied powers an overwhelming material advantage that was applied on the battlefield to ever-increasing effect during and after 1942. This basic simplicity of definition incorporates, however, a host of matters, peculiar to each of the powers, that defies simple and comprehensive examination. For the purpose of setting out the industrial context of the war, therefore, the economic performance of the great powers in the course of the Second World War will be summarised under two counts: a general statement about selected aspects of individual national performances and a consideration of the common problems that beset the efforts of the Axis powers.

In very different ways the individual performance of each of the five major powers – Britain, Germany, Japan, the Soviet Union and the United States – was impressive, if not in whole then in part. Between 1939 and 1943 Britain outproduced Germany despite Germany's much superior industrial capacity, and even in 1944, when Germany outproduced Britain 3:2 in aircraft numbers, Britain nevertheless continued to outbuild Germany in terms of aircraft weight, which in many ways was the more accurate yardstick of aircraft production than mere numbers. Moreover, despite massive naval construction programmes and increasingly onerous refitting and maintenance commitments, Britain and her dominions built 8,217,000 tons of shipping between September 1939 and April 1945, and with the various contributions provided by the lesser

European Allied powers, such as the Netherlands and Norway, were able to cover the total of Allied and neutral losses to submarines in the course of the Second World War. For her part, Germany in the course of hostilities produced what were arguably the best quality tanks to enter service and pioneered the development of guided missiles, jet aircraft, strategic rockets and high-speed submarines. Japan, despite the smallness of her industrial base, completed 12 fleet and light fleet carriers after December 1941 and built 28,180 aircraft in 1944, figures that compare very favourably to the British wartime completion of 16 fleet and light fleet carriers and construction of 26,461 aircraft in 1944. The Soviet Union's industrial achievement after June 1941, when she outproduced Germany in guns, tanks and aircraft, was remarkable in terms of her lack of a developed automobile industry to serve as the base for the diversification and expansion of production and the loss of her most heavily industrialised regions in the first disastrous months of war.

The United States, of course, was in a class of her own. A nation that between 1922 and 1937 completed just two dry-cargo merchantmen completed in March 1943 alone 140 Liberty ships, the record construction time for one of these pre-fabricated 7,517-ton vessels being $80\frac{1}{2}$ hours. The peak of American aircraft production, a total of 9,113 aircraft in March 1944, was all but equal to the combined production of the other four major powers, and in the course of the war the United States, which raised about 100 divisions in the course of hostilities, supplied her allies with military, industrial and civil aid the cash value of which was equivalent to the sum needed for her to raise either 2,000 infantry or 555 armoured divisions.

In addition, the often forgotten contributions of the lesser powers were no less impressive in light of available resources and were not limited to industrial matters. Australia, perhaps the only country ever to have built a combat aircraft before an automobile, enlisted one in two of her men between the ages of 18 and 45 by voluntary means, and at the peak of her war effort had 89.4 per cent of her male population over 14 years of age either in the armed services or in direct war work. Canada, after many trials and tribulations, raised a navy that after April 1943 provided 49 per cent of the escorts for oceanic convoys in the North Atlantic, a contribution that was only just less than that of Britain in this theatre. India, despite famine, the virtual collapse of much of her coastal trade after 1942 and a rail system that was smaller in terms of locomotives than the largest of the British regional companies, provided the bedrock of the Allied war efforts in the Middle East and south-east Asia and served as the base for support for China. In addition, she maintained some 20 divisions on her own soil and in what before December 1941 had been the military and economic backwaters of the subcontinent. Black African troops of the British and French colonial empires fought in Africa itself, in Europe and in the Far East, and in the victories they helped to secure they sowed the seeds of post-war revolt and independence.

In short, the Second World War witnessed an unprecedented global mobilisation of human and economic resources that was most marked in but not confined to the great powers, and in the process vast political, economic and social changes were effected: the war in effect spelt the end of the European colonial empires; it transformed the United States from a country that covered a continent into a continental power; it altered trade patterns and industrial practices throughout the world, and it contributed, in the same way as the First World War, to concepts of the managed economy and interventionist state; it also contributed to the process of female advancement and saw the principle of racial equality conceded. Moreover, the war years saw various humanitarian developments – such as the synthesis of quinine, penicillin and DDT, the first blue baby operation and the completion of the first cyclotron. Yet these various achievements were significant in terms of the unfolding of the Second World War in one respect: that all were prerogatives of the Allied powers pointed to the fact that the Allies alone had the industrial, financial, intellectual and moral resources to engage in major research and development outside the immediate demands of the war. For all the very considerable German success in weapons development, the Axis powers registered no non-military achievement that compared to those of their enemies.

Common to the three major Axis powers were aspects of political, industrial and administrative organisation that prevented their full and effective mobilisation of resources, the extent of the restrictions upon theoretical potential being demonstrated by the fact that whereas in 1942 the productive capacity available to the European powers was superior to that of the United States the latter outproduced Germany four-fold. The most obvious and persistent factor in Axis difficulties, however, stemmed from the fact that Axis rearmament dated from the mid-Thirties and each of the three major Axis powers embarked upon war between 1939 and 1941 when already at the peak of the production possible within existing political, industrial and financial restraints that effectively precluded simultaneous expansion of industrial capacity. Once the war that they had initiated did not provide the Axis powers with the rapid victories that had been anticipated, the lack of long-term planning for the expansion of industrial output – and it took even the United States an

294

average of 31 months from building site to airframe production – left the Axis powers without the time and means to meet the demands of the wars in which they found themselves engaged. The disparity between the Axis and Allied camps became more pronounced with the lengthening of the war into its fourth and fifth years despite a massive expansion of production on the part of Germany and Japan after 1943.

At the heart of Axis problems in meeting the demands of total war were fundamental difficulties of organisation, most obviously in terms of the political and administrative direction of national war efforts. The German, Italian and Japanese states were modern creations, and all shared a decentralised yet bureaucratic tradition that militated against the highly centralised yet flexible organisation needed to direct a war economy. The position of head of government in all three states was largely constitutional and titular rather than executive, and in Japan the prime minister was obliged to have a law passed that compelled ministers to abide by his instructions. In both Germany and Italy the concept of leadership precluded the development of a cabinet system, and its crucially important sub-committee organisation, that was responsible for the formulation, implementation and supervision of policy and for the effective coordination of ministries and of government with industry and the military. Even when the need for reform was recognised in mid-war, the various institutionalised constraints of the administrative systems in Germany and Italy were too often so entrenched as to prevent major change. In both Germany and Japan highly structured administrative systems, complete with clearly defined and jealously guarded lines of demarcation and established hierarchies, did not lend themselves to close cooperation, not least in Germany because of the rivalries between various different agencies – the party, the SS, Göring's economic ministry and various service interests – that were in large measure deliberately encouraged by Hitler's 'divide and rule' style of leadership. Moreover, there was no tradition in Germany and Japan of the close but often informal cooperation between government and industry as existed in less tightly administered societies such as Britain and the United States, and industry in both Germany and Japan reproduced its organisational and associated problems that further militated against efficiency.

German and Japanese industry were reluctant to accept mobilisation for war, even after the start of hostilities, when in the case of Germany consumer production and in Japan trade continued to offer higher returns on investment, and in both countries industry was not suitably structured to permit a rapid and economic expansion of production.

German industry was concentrated towards capital goods production and Japanese industry to cheap, mass-consumer items: unlike American and British industry, neither was geared to end-manufacture that could be adapted fairly easily to war production and which primarily required the expansion of supply in order to achieve increased output. In the task of conversion to war production, therefore, both German and Japanese industry laboured under difficulties not encountered by Anglo-American industry and neither initially received major state support. In the United States 89 per cent of the aircraft industry's expansion was financed by federal authorities, and this was achieved with the full support of industry itself because the federal authorities were not regarded as inimical to the free-enterprise principle. In Germany and Japan state direction and ownership were regarded with suspicion by industry only too aware of latent hostility on the part of government and the military.

In these countries, moreover, the position and attitudes of the military also served to create other problems of organisation. In Japan the rivalry between the two armed services manifested itself in a struggle for resources that was carried to absurd lengths: both ignored the agencies established in 1943 to plan resources; the army built its own ships; the two services developed their aircraft and radars separately; and Japan was the only major combatant not to have an atomic bomb project for the very simple reason that she had two, one for each service. In both Germany and Japan the armed services consistently sought to control the procurement process and to define the terms of reference, either in the initial specification or subsequent modification, of required weaponry. Without the scientific and technical capability or the necessary cooperation with industry, the Axis powers tied output to changing and often ill-defined requirements at the expense of production, and in both Germany and Japan this problem was exaggerated by the primacy of designers, not production managers, in industry. For example, Japan in the course of the Pacific war produced no fewer than 90 different aircraft compared with the 18 of the United States, and with Japanese production between 1942 and 1945 totalling 64,800 aircraft 104,446 aero-engines and 126,339 tons of airframe to American construction aggregates of 279,813 aircraft, 728,467 engines and 1,029,911 tons of airframe the American advantages in terms of settled production runs, economy of scale and concentrated research and development are obvious. With a highly diluted labour force and a largely imitative as opposed to innovative tradition, Japanese industry faced problems that were more severe than those of Germany, which nevertheless faced the same basic problems as Japan relative to her enemies.

With no supervisory agencies that could assess realistic research and development times against military requirements and machine tool programmes for industry, German research was too widely spread and industry too prone to disruption because of changing requirements to compete with enemies that combined quantity production, economy of scale and concentrated development. Only on the Eastern Front did German weapons retain any qualitative superiority over their opposite numbers throughout the period of hostilities but not by a margin that compensated for numerical inferiority, and with regard to the Western powers German achievements in terms of jet aircraft and rockets were at best double-edged. The Me262 presented fuel, maintenance and operational problems of nightmarish proportions, and the V-weapons programme, specifically the V-2 effort, involved scientific and resource commitments that Germany could not afford and for purposes that were at best strategically dubious. The bombardment of London after June 1944 by V-weapons was irrelevant to Germany's requirements and the outcome of the war, and impressive though certain German development projects undoubtedly were German research achievements were for the most part reactive, never produced antidotes to Allied material superiority, and were strategically defensive in application and of limited value.

In contrast to the position and practices of the Axis powers, the three major Allied powers both collectively and individually enjoyed certain intrinsic advantages and made a number of key decisions that provided them with a decisive material advantage in wars that were fought to Allied strengths after 1941. Most obviously the United States, and to a lesser extent the Soviet Union after spring 1942, had access to domestic resources of continental proportions and enjoyed a geographical isolation and invulnerability against attack on industry denied other countries. No less important, throughout the war the Allied powers enjoyed command of the sea and with it the ability to tap resources globally: in terms of inter-Allied movement of material this same ability to use the sea allowed the United States to supply the Soviet Union with 17,499,861 tons of material, of which 23.77 per cent was moved through the Gulf and Iran and 47.11 per cent across the north Pacific in Soviet ships compared to the 22.65 per cent shipped through White Sea ports. The Soviet Union, with its experience of five-year plans, freedom from normal commercial constraints, docile labour force and minimal consumer demand, was able to concentrate production upon material requirements, and by a ruthless selection of relatively simple but very reliable weapons systems she accepted what was no more than marginal qualitative inferiority for numerical superiority. Whereas the Germans presented problems for themselves in producing tanks and guns *de novo*, the Soviets concentrated tank and self-propelled gun development on existing chassis, and thereby ensured a continuity of production that duplicated that of Britain and the United States in other fields, most obviously in the output of aircraft.

These two powers, Britain in the three years before the outbreak of war in Europe and the United States in 1940 and 1941, separately made the common decision to mobilise for protracted wars of attrition and to concentrate research and development on projects already in hand which could be completed within the expected duration of hostilities. The American decision had one notable disadvantage in that it forestalled tank development by limiting armour to the dimension of projected landing ships, but in other fields these decisions were vindicated impressively. With the exception of the F6F Hellcat, not one of the major American fighters of the Second World War – the P-38 Lightning, P-39 Cobra family, P-40 Hawks, P-47 Thunderbolt and P-51 Mustang and the F4F Wildcat and F4U Corsair – were of post-1940 vintage: perhaps the most famous American bomber of the war, the B-17 Flying Fortress, dated from a 1934 specification, and the other three mainline bombers – the B-24 Liberator, B-25 Mitchell and B-26 Marauder – dated from 1939 programmes and designs: even the B-29 Superfortress predates the war in that she derived from a March 1938 study and 1940 funding. Two of the most successful British aircraft of the war, the Lancaster heavy bomber and Typhoon fighter-bomber, evolved respectively from 1936 and 1937 specifications for other aircraft types and the Americans developed the DC-3 from a 1935 civilian airliner design. The concentration of research and development upon aspects of component performance rather than aircraft type enabled the Americans, and the British to a lesser extent, to engage upon mass production with the minimum of disruption and investment: thus the setting-up of assembly lines for the first Spitfires involved 800,000 man-hours whereas the subsequent 15 combat marks together required a further 69,000 man-hours. Both the United States and Britain possessed major automobile industries that provided about half of the wartime expansion of their respective aircraft industries, and in the United States there were licensing arrangements and pooled production techniques between commercial rivals that were unthinkable in Germany and Japan. Both Britain and the United States possessed labour unions that accepted dilution, and neither country was trapped by self-deluding nonsense about quality production and the exclusion of women from industry that so beset the German war effort.

The Allied powers were not without their failings, most notably the Americans with respect to tanks, the British in terms of carrier aviation and the Soviets with respect to radar development and communications equipment, but in overall terms the three Allied powers utilised certain basic advantages to full effect and fought accordingly. The Americans had a highly skilled manager class, an experience of production-line techniques that was applied to ships and aircraft, and the imagination to work on scales that were beyond the comprehension of those with the limited horizons of central Europe and Tokyo. The Soviet Union, by virtue of scale, and Britain, on account of a system of state control probably without equal amongst the warring nations, supplemented the American effort to the full extent of their resources, and in so doing the Allied powers achieved both a massive increase of production and a balance of production that eluded their enemies. Both Germany and Japan reached the peak of their aircraft production in 1944 at the very time when they had effectively exhausted their fuel supplies and training programmes: the Allied powers were able to raise the manpower to fill the fighting ranks and to provide the necessary support facilities.

The industrial performance of the Allied powers is often slightingly considered as if the fighting and winning of wars of attrition on the basis of superior strength represents no real achievement, but wars between great industrial powers necessarily involve attrition, and in terms of the direction and management of their war economies the Allied powers displayed a more profound understanding of the business of war than enemies that were poorly organised and stressed the political and psychological aspects of conflict at the expense of material.

The outcome of the Second World War was decided, once the Axis powers had failed to clinch victory in the conflicts that they initiated, on the basis of relative resources. The Axis inability to limit and win their separate wars in that period when they held the initiative condemned them to protracted struggles in which their defeat was assured because of their demographic, geographical, industrial and military inferiority to the enemies that surrounded them. In 1943 the Axis lost the industrial and economic struggle, though their armed forces remained to be beaten on the battlefield. In this year, however, the European Axis powers sustained a series of defeats that were significant not simply in terms of the course of the war but in their nature. Western histories conventionally relate the events of 1943 in terms of the defeat of the U-boats, the combined bombing offensive, the clearing of North Africa, the invasions of Sicily and peninsular Italy and, lastly, the battle of Kursk. This battle has been acknowledged as the greatest single engagement of the war, but in accounts that stress its size through repetition of statistics neither the context of Kursk nor the subsequent Soviet offensives that resulted in the *Wehrmacht* being cleared from Kiev and the east bank of the Dnepr by the end of the year have been afforded the consideration they deserve. The outcome of Kursk merits detailed examination of the battle, yet the battle's significance lies in aspects of the conduct of operations on the Eastern Front after March 1943: why it was that the *Wehrmacht*, for all its celebrated technique, was unable to achieve victory on a battlefield 100 miles square despite opening its offensive with a superiority of 7:1 on its selected axes of advance; why it was in the August follow-up actions that the Soviet army was able to break through defences in front of Belgorod and Kharkov that the Germans had had five months to prepare; why it was, if the Manstein counter-offensive at Kharkov in February 1943 was so successful, that *Army Group South* was unable to repeat its feat between August 1943 and March 1944 when it was called upon to fight the same type of battle – and for part of the time over the very same terrain – as it had fought in the immediate aftermath of the Stalingrad defeat.

With respect to this last matter, four possible answers suggest themselves: that by the second half of 1943 the Soviet army was too strong, too well organised and too effective to be caught a second time; that after July 1943 the Soviet army fought in such a way as to prevent an effective German response; that Manstein's success at Kharkov in February 1943 was not all that it was and is claimed to be. The fourth answer combines the previous three and, by removing the element of personality from proceedings, fixes the proper basis of assessment and analysis, namely that in a conflict between systems, 1943 witnessed not simply a massive quantitative growth of the Soviet army but an improvement in terms of command and organisation at the strategic and operational level that condemned the *Wehrmacht* to defeat at Kursk and to a series of local and limited reverses throughout the Ukraine in the following eight months. This qualitative improvement of the Soviet army in 1943 was not completed – by its own terms of reference – until 1944, in which year the benefits of these changes and enhanced mobility brought about a succession of battles of encirclement and annihilation of German formations that had proved beyond the Soviet army in the second half of 1943. In thus explaining the campaign on the Eastern Front in 1943 the underlying factors in the crucial change that takes place during this year – the Germans' loss of the strategic initiative – become self-evident, as does the relative balance of importance between theatres in the sense that an analysis of events on the Eastern Front places the Mediterranean theatre in its proper and lesser, almost minor, context.

Soviet histories divide 'The Great Patriotic War' into three phases, the periods between June 1941 and November 1942 and between January 1944 and May 1945 being respectively those of German and Soviet initiative separated by a period of balance. As a simple guide to events such a division has a certain validity, though the fact that 1944 opened with the initiative firmly in Soviet possession would seem to suggest that this second phase belies its name in that it was a period of growing imbalance as the Soviet army imposed its timetable and will upon an enemy forced to face the reality that it was fighting a defensive war. Such a division of the war into three phases is convenient in that it incorporates the facts that the summer 1943 campaign witnessed a German offensive that compared not unfavourably in size to those of 1941 and 1942 and that thereafter, as many Western historians have noted correctly, the Soviet army was able to mount offensive operations irrespective of season. But this division between the second and third phases is questionable because in the spring of 1943 the Soviet High Command, after considerable argument, abandoned the mainstay of its military philosophy and doctrine and chose to stand on the defensive and await attack rather than undertake offensive operations in the summer. This decision was reached in the aftermath of the Kharkov reverse, which in the spring of 1943 the Stavka acknowledged as stemming from its misreading of the battle. In the course of operations west of the Donets the Stavka had 'situated the appreciation' and had tried to persist in a faltering offensive in the belief that *Army Group South* was seeking to withdraw behind the Dnepr and was unable to assemble armour for anything more than a covering role. But after the reverse at Kharkov the Soviet High Command, far from fearing a German summer offensive as has been suggested in certain Western histories, accepted a defensive battle at Kursk as the means of breaking German offensive power rather than seeking out German armour through offensive action.

This Soviet decision was made on the basis of certain knowledge of German intentions, the current (1988) conventional wisdom being that the source of German intelligence was not the Red Trio network as was widely assumed two decades ago but an ability to read German army signals following the capture of Enigma cipher machines in the course of the winter's fighting. Be that as it may, and it is known that the British passed relevant Ultra information to the Soviets in spring 1943 without disclosing its source, as the spring advanced and the extent of German preparations became clear despite the hesitations and doubts of Hitler and his senior commanders, so Soviet counter-measures in and behind the Kursk salient assumed an extent and nature that finally laid to rest the ghosts of November 1941 when the entire strategic reserve available to

301

the Soviet army numbered just fourteen tanks and of October 1942 when the 4th Tank Army was raised with its numerical designator indicating the number of tanks it had under command. By spring 1943 the Soviet army had acquired the size, organisation and, crucially, the time that enabled it to begin to put into effect the doctrine with which it had gone to war in June 1941. In sharp contrast to pre-war British and American doctrines, that of the Soviet army needed no major revision in the course of the war, but after nearly two years of disastrous defeats and limited successes the Soviet army had acquired the means and combat experience that provided it with a balance, an effectiveness and an element of choice that made it at least the equal of a *Wehrmacht* that, for all its losses in the previous winter, in 1943 was not appreciably weaker in firepower and numbers than it had been in 1942.

By mid-1943 the Soviet army had settled the main aspects of command and organisation with which it was to continue the war for its remaining two years. Nominally, the rifle division had been standardised at 11,700 strength with strong organic artillery and anti-tank groups, and most rifle armies had three, as opposed to two, rifle corps. Armour had become standardised around the corps, which had one motorised rifle and three tank regiments plus a formidable SP artillery and anti-tank support, and by June 1943 the Soviet army had no fewer than five tank armies, each with one mechanised and two tanks corps plus an impressive array of supporting units. At army level the Soviet army had mechanised or armoured corps as mobile groups and had solved questions of fire density and artillery concentrations in the assault to its own satisfaction. It had also accepted the principle of a ruthless concentration of resources and operational talent with mobile forces in order to make maximum use of its limited means with the result that its infantry, despite having organic tank and anti-tank elements at all levels, remained under-invested in terms of training, quality and equipment. The most obvious weaknesses of the Soviet army were its lack of mechanisation for the infantry; the lack of standardisation of armies; an incomplete programme of raising tank and mechanised armies as mobile groups for fronts; its inexperience in deep-penetration operations; and its lack of a tactical air force with a quick-response capability. But by spring 1943 the Soviet air force, which has been generally neglected in Western accounts of the 1943 campaign, had some 5,500 combat aircraft under command and had acquired a size and effectiveness that made it a match for a *Luftwaffe* able to muster only some 2,260 combat aircraft over the Eastern Front at this time.

By mid-1943 the Soviet air force had raised one air army for each of the army's 13 fronts plus a further 19 air corps, with a total of 2,600 combat aircraft, that could be used to reinforce air armies for the duration of specific operations. The result was that whereas throughout 1942 Soviet air armies seldom mustered more than 350 aircraft, by mid-1943 main sector air armies had as many as 1,000 aircraft under command. At the outset of the battle of Kursk, for example, the two air armies with the Central and Voronezh Fronts possessed 1,915 combat aircraft, and were supported by two more air armies, of roughly similar size, in the reserve role. Despite such numbers, however, the Soviet air force was unable to achieve air superiority over Kursk and both sides were able to mount punishing attacks on enemy armour in the course of the battle. While Western attention had fixed on the disastrous Soviet attempt to mount a pre-emptive attack on German airfields on the morning of 5 July the fact remains that the air battles over Kursk in July came as the climax to four months' sustained operations over the Kuban, eastern Ukraine and Kursk that in scale and intensity eclipsed anything that took place during the Battle of Britain. July–September 1943 was one of the very few quarters during the Second World War when the *Luftwaffe*'s overall and operational strengths declined, and by more than 1,000 aircraft. To this decline, at a crucial stage of the air war with the American bombing effort about to increase significantly in scale and tempo, Soviet tactical air power made its full contribution, though not to the extent of the 1,500 air victories claimed in Soviet accounts of Kursk. The Soviet claim that Anglo-American forces 'landed in France in 1944 without much opposition from the *Luftwaffe* chiefly because the bulk of its forces had been smashed on the Soviet–German front the year before' is overstated. Given the fact that the Anglo-American combined bombing offensive is rightly seen as crucial in the process whereby the Allies secured tactical air superiority over all fronts, events on the Eastern Front in that year provide an important corrective in noting the importance of tactical air power – and not just on the Eastern Front – in the progressive weakening of the *Luftwaffe* during 1943. Most certainly the operations over Orel in July and August 1943 were the last occasion when the *Luftwaffe* was able to mount an effort with major repercussions on the course of operations on the ground: thereafter its dissipation and declining quality condemned it to an increasingly ineffective tactical response to a lost strategic situation.

Leaving aside aviation matters, Kursk's significance was profound, most obviously in terms of the erosion of German armoured strength to the point that the *Wehrmacht* was unable to respond effectively to any of the threats that emerged after August 1943. But no less important was that in preparing to fight this battle the German High Command had for the first time faced the problems of conducting a two-front war and had decided upon an offensive conceived, planned and conducted by the army high command with little direction and interference on the part of Hitler, but which ended with a defeat that indicated the bankruptcy of German tactical doctrine. The decision to seek a battle around Kursk was taken despite a body of opinion that insisted that German resources be husbanded and a defensive stance be adopted on the Eastern Front in 1943 in order to concentrate forces in western and southern Europe to meet an anticipated Anglo-American landing on the continental mainland. In setting aside this argument the German High Command sought a battle of annihilation with the main strength of its most formidable foe in order then to free itself to deal with other threats, but implicit in the decision to tackle Soviet armour at Kursk was the possibility of a widening offensive commitment once the battle was won. Like its Soviet opposite number, the German High Command in spring 1943 had a choice between defensive and offensive alternatives on the Eastern Front: partly because of the difficulties of conducting a defensive battle without any clear idea of where the Soviet army might make its effort, partly because the economic importance of the eastern Ukraine to German precluded voluntarily ceding ground, and partly because political considerations demanded a German offensive come the summer, the German High Command chose to attack the very strongest part of the Soviet front.

Had it known the extent and scale of Soviet defences around and behind Kursk the German High Command would probably never have committed itself to this offensive. Indeed, long before 1 July, when Hitler finally ordered the attack to proceed, certain of his senior commanders suspected that successive postponements of the offensive had given the Soviet army so much time to prepare to meet the attack that the German effort was doomed to failure. In fact, by the time that the German attack began on the fifth the Soviet army had prepared eight defensive belts covering the southern approaches to Kursk and the entire Soviet defensive network extended over a depth of 120 miles with the positions occupied by the Steppe Front, in reserve behind the salient, fortified though not on the scale of those held by the Central and Voronezh Fronts within the salient itself. With some 28,000 guns and mortars and 5,000 tanks distributed amongst the three Soviet fronts at Kursk, and tank armies held in readiness for counter-offensives once the German offensive exhausted itself, Kursk was one of the very few battles in which a major armoured offensive began with the defence massively superior in manpower, material and position to the attack. But whilst Soviet success at Kursk can be explained in terms of defence in depth and the weight of fire that was directed against German armour as it tried to fight its way through successive defensive positions, the real point to emerge from Kursk was that the scale of conflict had by 1943 reached a level that effectively marked the end of the superiority of the offence over the defence and of the efficacy of *Blitzkrieg* technique as hitherto practised.

German success between 1939 and 1942 owed as much to the German armed forces' better understanding of the balance between offensive and defensive firepower as it then existed as to any material consideration. Opposed by a number of enemies of limited military resources and inferior doctrine, the *Wehrmacht* had been able to defeat opponents lacking adequate anti-tank and anti-aircraft defences and – crucially – the space and time in which to absorb the shock of a *Blitzkrieg* attack. Despite its obvious battlefield manifestations, *Blitzkrieg* was a psychological as opposed to a material phenomenon, yet by 1943 the Soviet army had survived two *Blitzkrieg* attacks and in the process had learnt to counter this form of warfare with the result that the three main summer offensives mounted by the *Wehrmacht* on the Eastern Front declined successively in terms of frontage, depth of penetration and operational results. In spring 1943 the Soviet army had the choice of countering a German offensive through the use of space or by shock action of its own. But in using the latter, through the concentration of field and anti-tank artillery on unprecedented scales, the development of personnel anti-tank weapons and the use of massed armour in an anti-tank role, plus the proliferation of minefields, events served notice of the growth of defensive firepower at the expense of the offensive with obvious implications for the future conduct of the break-in phase of offensive operations. The British had glimpsed this same development at second Alamein, and with their American allies were to experience to the full the practical difficulties of breaking through a position defended in depth and where surprise and manoeuvre were of limited value. But the main manifestations of this development were to be revealed in the very special conditions of the Eastern Front, where, by 1945, the increase of defensive firepower and the increasing vulnerability of armour to anti-tank systems were such that the Soviet army calculated that an 8:1 superiority of armour was needed to overcome a prepared defensive position and in certain offensives in the last months of the European war armoured superiorities of 40:1 on selected axes of advance were registered by Soviet formations in order to ensure the survival of sufficient force for breakout operations.

After 5 July 1943 there was a continuity of operations on the Eastern Front that prevents the ready division of the campaign into distinct phases either by time or by area. By limiting examination of the campaign to events before 3 November 1943 one can define events on the Eastern Front under three headings: the initial phase of the battle of Kursk when the *Wehrmacht* held the initiative; the Soviet counter-offensives both in the Kursk–Orel area and on the Mius that properly form part of this same battle; and the subsequent Soviet offensives that by November 1943 had resulted in the Germans being cleared from half of the territory occupied by *Army Groups Centre, South* and *A* in June 1943. Of this initial phase little need be considered in light of the mass of literature about this subject other than to note that the line of demarcation between this and the subsequent phase is not precise. The German offensive against the northern part of the Kursk salient, conducted by the *9th Army* of *Army Group Centre*, penetrated only some nine miles of Soviet defences before being halted in front of the Olkhovatka ridge on 8 July, and setpiece attacks on the tenth and eleventh failed to clear this position. By 11 July, however, the *4th Panzer Army* had broken through no fewer than five defensive belts and *Army Detachment Kempf* (later redesignated the *8th Army*) had come abreast of the *4th Panzer Army* for the first time since the battle began. It was on this day that formations from the *4th Panzer Army* launched attacks that resulted, on the twelfth, in the most famous single part of the battle of Kursk, the action around Prokhorovka in which approximately 600 German and 900 Soviet tanks did battle over an area measuring some three miles by four. This single day's action cost the Germans about 300 tanks, the Soviets perhaps as many as 500, but while the *4th Panzer Army* remained holding the battlefield and *Army Detachment Kempf*, by nightfall on 13 July, had fought its way forward to trap parts of the 5th Guards Tank and 5th Guards Armies as they withdrew from Prokhorovka, the German losses in this engagement, combined with developments elsewhere, effectively spelt an end to the German offensive though it was not until 19 July that *OKW* tacitly admitted that the attack had failed.

The most obvious of these developments, and the one usually cited in Western histories as critical in Hitler's decision to end the offensive, was the Anglo-American invasion of Sicily on 10 July, but while this development was given by Hitler as reason to abandon the Kursk offensive during his consultations with his senior commanders on the thirteenth, Hitler did not halt the attack on this day and it was not until the seventeenth that he ordered *II SS Panzer Corps* to be withdrawn from the *4th Panzer Army* for service in Italy. Even then, only the *1st SS Panzer*

Division was moved to Italy, and indeed this was the only German division transferred from the Eastern Front in July and August for service elsewhere. What was far more important in Hitler's decision on the thirteenth to limit the Kursk operation but allow *Army Group South* to continue its attempt to seek out and destroy enemy armoured reserves were indications of an impending attack on the Mius by the South-west and South Fronts and, on 12 July, the start of an offensive by the Bryansk and West Fronts against the *2nd Panzer Army* across a 170-mile sector of the Orel re-entrant. This Soviet effort formed part of the intention to counter-attack at Kursk once the German offensive stalled, but in the event *Operation Kutuzov* began perhaps one or two days too late, the *9th Army* being able to break off operations in front of Olkhovatka on the twelfth. Moreover, the Stavka was apparently unable to capitalise upon the very considerable success registered by *Operation Kutuzov* on the twelfth. *Army Group Centre* diverted reinforcements bound for the *9th Army* to the *2nd Panzer Army* with the result that while the Soviet drive broke into the *9th Army*'s rear areas on the fifteenth *Operation Kutuzov* degenerated into a slow rolling battle of attrition rather than developing into a rapid thrust that cleared the Orel re-entrant and trapped the *9th Army*. *Army Group Centre*'s ability to contain the threat presented by *Operation Kutuzov* – the *9th Army* did not begin to withdraw from its positions until the seventeenth – perhaps suggests that the Soviet effort began too early rather than too late, but the fact that it opened on the day of the Prokhorovka action had the effect of cancelling whatever success the *4th Panzer Army* commanded in this engagement. Without *Army Group Centre* at least holding its positions an encirclement battle was beyond German resources, but on the 14th *XXIV Panzer Corps*, in reserve at Belgorod, was moved by Hitler to a position to cover the newly re-created *6th Army* and the *1st Panzer Army* on the Mius in response to preparations for an attack that the Soviets made no attempt to conceal.

Hitler's decision to reinforce the Mius position was dictated by his concern to hold the Donets industrial area, but his decision was an example of a phenomenon that was to be repeated throughout the remaining 21 months of the war – the settling of strategic policy on the basis of economic (or political) considerations without reference to what was tactically possible. Moreover, by shifting the mobile reserve needed either to consolidate the Prokhorovka position or to exploit the success that had been won there over the previous two days to the threatened Mius sector, Hitler unwittingly acknowledged the loss of the strategic initiative and began a process of chronic indecision that was to persist throughout the remainder of 1943 – and into 1944 – as he tried to switch

307

forces within and between army groups in response to crises but with no very clear view of strategic priorities across the front as a whole. The move of *XXIV Panzer Corps* to the Mius helped to stabilise the position along the river after the Soviets opened their offensive – with considerable initial success – on 17 July, but with two divisions of *II SS Panzer Corps* drawn into this battle and *XLVIII Panzer Corps* obliged to end offensive operations around Prokhorovka at this same time, German success on the Mius was achieved only at the expense of the weakening of the *4th Panzer Army* and *Army Detachment Kempf* to the extent that they were unable to consolidate their recent gains.

By 2 August, when Manstein stated that no Soviet offensive in the Kharkov area could be expected for weeks, the *4th Panzer Army* and *Army Detachment Kempf* numbered some 210,000 men and about 200 battle-worthy tanks: unknown to the German High Command, the Soviets had by that same date concentrated 11 armies and some 90 divisions – excluding reserve formations – for an offensive led by the 5th Guards Tank Army, which had lost two-thirds of its strength just three weeks earlier at Prokhorovka, that was to begin the following day.

The unexpected speed of the recovery of the Soviet army after Kursk came as a shock to the German High Command, but no less surprising were the twin features of *Operation Rumiantsev* in that the initial assault – involving four armies and one corps – was primarily directed against two German infantry divisions that were literally hacked to pieces on 3 August. Thereafter the Soviets developed a rippling offensive along the length of the front in order to confuse the German High Command as to the main direction of the Soviet effort and to prevent a timely and effective German redeployment of armour for the counter-attack. In effect, what the Soviet army attempted in its Belgorod–Kharkov offensive of August 1943 was a concentrated form of its winter operations – and a foretaste of what was to be inflicted upon the *Wehrmacht* over 1,000 miles of the Eastern Front from Velikiye Luki to the Black Sea for the remainder of the year.

Crucially, these various efforts were to differ fundamentally in aim and execution from German offensive operations. The essence of *Blitzkrieg* was a single or double envelopment by armour and encirclement and annihilation by infantry: the aim was to destroy enemy field formations and not, as often suggested, the paralysis of an enemy's command and communications systems. Though there were differences within the Soviet High Command in the summer and autumn of 1943 about how offensive operations should be conducted, what emerged was a broad front strategy that declined deep-penetration operations, in part because of a very considerable Soviet respect for German armoured technique and in part because the Soviet army simply lacked the logistical expertise to mount such operations. In general terms the logistical support available to a Soviet front in an offensive in the second half of 1943 was sufficient for an advance of about 70 miles, and without the means to conduct clear-cut battles of encirclement the Stavka sought to wear down German forces by a series of attacks characterised by advances on one or two axes that would force German formations to withdraw over a much wider operational area. The result was to be not a series of surgical victories but an abrasive sequence of battles to successive river lines in which the Soviet army achieved hard-won victories as a result of their ability to concentrate overwhelming superiority of force on selected axes of attack, to select as these axes the lines of natural weakness presented by inter-army and inter-group boundaries, and to wrong-foot German armour before the start of and during offensive operations. Thus, after a series of violent battles that cost the South-west and South Fronts the equivalent of two tank corps, the Stavka halted the Mius offensive on 6 August, two and one days after Belgorod and Kharkov respectively were lost to a German defence stripped of armour in order to buttress the Mius position: thereafter this armour was to be moved westwards in order to contain the extent of Soviet success in *Operation Rumiantsev* and was able to inflict a series of local defeats upon leading Soviet armoured formations as the latter pressed beyond Kharkov but was not able to effect the recapture of the city for the second time in five months. Subsequently, the German concern to contain the Soviet attacks towards the middle Dnepr, which threatened to and occasionally succeeded in splitting *Army Group Centre* from *Army Group South*, forced the German evacuation first of the Mius position by the end of August and then the Kuban bridgehead at the end of September, but German forces could not prevent the 3rd and 4th Ukrainian Fronts clearing the Germans from the east bank of the Dnepr below Zaporozhye in late October and the isolation of the *17th Army* on the Crimea in the first week of November.

Only in the last days of October around Krivoi Rog was German armour able to gather for a counter-attack that inflicted a sharp defeat upon Soviet forces, the 5th Guards Tank Army from the 2nd Ukrainian Front losing the equivalent of a tank corps in this action. By the time this success came the way of *Army Group South* its intention to develop the Dnepr as its main line of resistance had been compromised throughout the length of the river below its junction with the Pripyat, the Soviets having crossed the Dnepr around Chernobyl on 19 September, on either side of Kiev on the twenty-second and around Pereyaslav, Kremenchug and Dnepropetrovsk on the twenty-sixth. If, as an eminent historian of the Nazi–Soviet conflict has observed of one aspect of Soviet operations in the five months after Prokhorovka, 'the distinguishing aspect' of the Belorussian Front's autumn operations 'was drab pointlessness' because the Stavka could not exploit and had no interest in the operational and strategic possibilities that arose in the course of this formation's offensive, this was not the case with respect to the overall campaign that unfolded after Kursk. While success eluded the Soviet army in *Army Group North*'s area of responsibility, other than around Nevel in early October, south of the Dvina the Soviet army recovered an area between 150 and 200 miles in depth over a frontage of 650 miles by the end of September 1943. In so doing it not only reoccupied the richest areas of the Soviet Union held by the *Wehrmacht* but eroded German strength to the extent that German capacity to form mobile reserves and to man the front properly was hopelessly compromised.

The crisis that developed for the *Wehrmacht* after its defeat in front of Kursk and the loss of Kharkov was the product of three immediate factors: a failure to have prepared defensive positions in the rear areas to which front-line formations could withdraw; Hitler's pathological aversion to withdrawals that were in any event inevitable resulted not in a series of timely withdrawals but a sequence of forced retreats accompanied by ruinously expensive rearguard actions; and the inability of *OKH* to concentrate armoured reserves with both *Army Group Centre* and *Army Group South* in order to counter the several threats presented by successive Soviet offensives against both commands. Of these, which together constituted a long-term failure in the formation of strategic policy on the part of the German High Command, arguably the most important was the last because the absence of armoured reserves reduced the German conduct of operations to mere improvisation with attempts to plug gaps as they appeared and to shift forces between army groups. With the Stavka able to develop offensives against all three German army groups south of the Dvina, if not simultaneously then with sufficient rapidity to deny the German defence the time it needed to regain its balance, this lack of a reserve exaggerated the positional weakness that had hampered all German operations since June 1941. The Eastern Front itself was unbalanced in that it presented the Germans with a mobile commitment in the most distant sector of the theatre, but after July 1943 the *Wehrmacht* lacked the strategic and tactical initiative that had served as the corrective to its positional weakness of the previous two years. In these circumstances the extent of German losses at Kursk assumed its full significance. By 23 August the corps strengths of the *1st*

Panzer Army had been reduced to 5,800 men as a result of the Mius battle while by 7 September, at a time when the effective strength of infantry divisions seeking to gain the protection of the Dnepr was down to 1,000 rifles, *Army Group South* had been reduced to 257 tanks and 220 assault guns, less than one-third of the establishment with which it began its drive on Kursk just two months before.

In trying to piece together an effective defence of the Ukraine in the second half of 1943 the *Wehrmacht* was thus beset by long-term structural and leadership problems that reflected the accumulating difficulties of Germany as a whole as the tide of war turned against the Axis powers, but the *Wehrmacht* nevertheless was to benefit from two developments. The teething and maintenance problems that had attended the introduction of a new generation of tanks and assault guns into widespread service in the first half of the year eased with the passing of time, and the German ability in the autumn of 1943 to master the situation in Italy – at least in defensive terms – meant that after September the Italian theatre did not siphon off German strength on the Eastern Front. In fact, before the end of 1943 as a result of the Anglo-American armies in southern Italy being halted south of Rome the German High Command was able to transfer forces *from* Italy to the Eastern Front. But these benefits were cancelled in that the implications of the German defeat at Kursk were not lost upon Hitler's allies. For the Hungarians, Italians and Romanians the destruction of their armies in the winter campaign was infinitely more traumatic than any defeat sustained by the *Wehrmacht*. In this sense the wavering of Germany's allies in 1943 had origins that predated Kursk and were in any event the product of a combination of defeats on a number of fronts, though the failure of the *Wehrmacht* in the eastern and central Ukraine remained of singular significance. Having been subjected to German contempt because of their inability to resist Soviet arms, Germany's allies could take some wry satisfaction from the defeat of 41 German divisions in front of Kursk, but this was tempered by the realisation that if German power was broken then their own defeat was assured.

The first indication of unsteadiness in the ranks of Germany's allies was provided on 25 July when Mussolini, having been defeated in the fascist grand council, was dismissed by the King of Italy and a new administration headed by Marshal Pietro Badoglio was installed in office: thereafter the German High Command recognised the inevitability of the Italian defection from the Axis camp. Soviet overtures to Finland in the summer of 1943, and the Finns' serious consideration of the possibility of a separate peace, provided confirmation of uncertainty within the Axis camp, and Sweden's withdrawal of transit concessions for German forces in northern Norway and Finland served clear notice of the neutrals' assessment of which powers would win the European war. By September the German plans for the occupation of Hungary and Romania were completed as a precaution against their defection and as their lack of enthusiasm for war – except with one another – became obvious: at the same time Slovakia's contribution to the Axis cause ceased to merit even token status. Only Bulgaria showed any sign of reliability in the aftermath of Kursk, and she had taken the precaution of never having declared war on the Soviet Union. After July 1943, therefore, the German leadership was aware of a weakening of the ties that bound the Axis powers together, and at the very time when the importance of her allies involved widening commitments to ensure their security without any corresponding increase of their contributions to the common cause.

Italy was vital to Germany because of the depth she provided to the defence of the southern *Reich*, and with Hungary and Bulgaria she was crucial to the security of the Balkans: Finland and Romania were no less important to Germany on account of their nickel and oil. But the weakening of all these associated powers after mid-1943 meant that whereas previously all had provided military forces that were useful adjuncts to German power, after this time German attention and resources had to be diverted to ensure their continuing loyalty as German failure at sea, in the air and in two major land theatres became apparent. The need to ensure that Finland remained in the field, for example, prevented the withdrawal of *Army Group North* from the positions it held in front of Leningrad to a shorter and more defensible line that would release formations into the reserve; in the event Finland's economic dependence upon Germany and fear of the Soviet Union were not enough to prevent her in 1944 seeking to ensure her continued existence at the expense of her alliance with Germany. For all the junior Axis powers the dilemma that Finland faced was one that they shared after mid-1943. These powers had good reason to fear a German victory that would reduce them to a status little different from that of more obviously conquered and occupied states, but after summer 1943 these powers, particularly those that lived alongside the Soviet Union, realised that they stood in danger of being dragged down to defeat along with a Germany that would ensure their ruination in an attempt to save herself. What held the European Axis alliance together until 1943 was German power and the prospect of a German victory, and German defeats after mid-year ushered in a period when Germany's allies sought to extricate themselves from alliances that threatened them with disaster while avoiding the German retaliation that was visited upon Italy after September. As Hitler sought to adjust to the reality that Germany would have to wage a defensive war, defeat in the Atlantic and Mediterranean and in Sicily and the Ukraine served to weaken fatally the cohesion and unity of the Axis alliance.

5

TIME, SPACE AND DOCTRINE

By the first week of November 1943 the European war had assumed a balance that prompted Hitler to issue, on 3 November, *Directive No 51*, which set down the principle that henceforth Germany's military priority had to be the strengthening of her forces and defences in the west. Despite Soviet success in previous months and the certainty that further Soviet offensives would be mounted in the winter, Hitler recognised that an Anglo-American landing in north-west Europe would present a direct and immediate threat to Germany's ability to make war and that German resources and attention had to be directed to the defeat of such an invasion. Explicit in this decision was the calculation that on the Eastern Front it remained possible for Germany to cede ground without any danger of being dealt a fatal blow, and in framing this directive Hitler's thinking closely resembled that of a Japanese High Command that had just settled a policy defining 'an absolute national defence sphere' within a perimeter that included the Kuriles, Bonins, the Marianas and Carolines and western New Guinea, east of which was an area in which 'strong defensive actions' were to be fought while defensive positions on the Saipan–Truk–Timor line were strengthened. In fact, by this first week in November the situations in which Germany and Japan found themselves in their separate wars and their responses were curiously similar, as was to be the speed and finality with which their enemies confounded Axis intentions. As early as 5 November one American carrier task group, by striking heavily against air and naval targets at Rabaul, provided evidence that the strategic policy with which the Japanese High Command had equipped itself was flawed: without sufficient air power to cover Rabaul, the Japanese lacked the means to overcome the dilemma presented by the unfolding of a two-front offensive in the Pacific in the second half of the month. This was, *mutatis mutandis*, the same dilemma that confronted Germany at this time, and her efforts to resolve this conundrum were to be no more successful than those of her Japanese associate.

By the end of October 1943 the bulk of their earlier conquests remained to Germany and Japan, and in the still substantial extent of these conquests the Axis powers ostensibly possessed the resources essential to their prosecution of the war and the space that was the prerequisite for the successful conduct of a defensive war. In reality, however, both Germany and Japan, despite having made initial conquests as a result of their ability in mobile operations, were saddled by autumn 1943 with static strategies that involved linear defence upon prepared positions, and neither had high commands with the flexibility that would enable their forces to use to full effect the space that was supposedly the basis of their policies. But no less significantly, neither Germany nor Japan had the means – material and political – that enabled them to exploit the factor of space and the resources of conquered territories to maximum advantage. Neither of the Axis powers had the transport infrastructure, the long-term investment plans and financial reserves, the management techniques and skilled labour necessary to turn economic potential into war material on the scale necessary to meet their widening military commitments, and, crucially, neither had the political will and moral authority to enable them to supplement their own war efforts by enlisting the support of peoples under their jurisdiction.

Throughout the areas that they conquered both Germany and Japan installed puppet administrations, yet in their determination to reserve for themselves the power of decision neither would sponsor client regimes that could mobilise support for the Axis cause even where that potential support existed. German and Japanese attitudes were determined in part by the fact that neither Axis power was prepared to rely upon anyone other than their own nationals for the order and effective exploitation of conquered territories. In essence this failure to tap the potential goodwill of various conquered peoples was the product of philosophies that offered subjected peoples nothing other than slavery and death. As noted elsewhere, herein lay what was perhaps the supreme irony of the war: what made the German and Japanese forces so formidable in the assault – a moral advantage based upon concepts of racial supremacy – ultimately prevented them from consolidating their initial success. Many factors contributed to the final defeat of the Axis powers, but this inability to build upon their initial successes was arguably the most important single ingredient in the defeat of Germany and Japan.

The significance of the German failure is more obvious than that of Japan: relative to their enemies Germany was the stronger of the two Axis powers and commanded in her conquests greater industrial resources, and perhaps even a greater fund of goodwill amongst certain conquered peoples, than did Japan. The Pacific war presents a very different problem of interpretation from the European war in that while it is possible to argue that Germany had the physical but not political means to shape events to her advantage, pervading any examination of the Pacific war is the notion that Japan's defeat was assured from the time that her carriers struck Pearl Harbor. The disparity of resources between Japan and the United States was such that short of the latter sinking into the sea – under the weight of aircraft, ships and tanks built on her soil – there would seem to have been no way in which Japan could have avoided defeat in the war that she initiated in December 1941.

In historical terms it is not without interest to note that for the United States the war against Japan was the second such war she had fought. Between 1941 and 1945 Japan was to the United States what the Confederacy had been 80 years before, and the parallels between these two wars are very considerable. Both wars, each about four years in duration, saw the United States opposed by enemies that relied upon allegedly superior martial qualities to overcome demographic, industrial and positional inferiority, but in both wars the United States' industrial superiority and ability to mount debilitating blockades proved decisive to the outcome. In both wars the United States was able to use the advantages of a secure base and exterior lines of communication to bring overwhelming strength against enemies committed to defensive strategies and which were plagued by divided counsels, while in the military aspects of both wars there were close similarities, though these may not be drawn too exactly. The Union drive down the Mississippi that resulted in the capture of Vicksburg in July 1863 and the separation of the Confederate heartland from Texas has its parallel in the drive across the south-west Pacific to the Philippines which separated Japan from its southern resources area. The battles in the two-way states that culminated in the march through Georgia were not dissimilar from the central Pacific offensive that took American forces to Iwo Jima, Okinawa and the shores of the Japanese home islands; the battles in the south-west Pacific in 1942 and 1943 can be said to have their counterparts in the American Civil War in the campaigns in Maryland and Virginia in 1862 in that both ensured that the enemies of the United States could not win the wars that they had provoked. In the American Civil War the Confederacy looked to support from Europe for success: in the Second World War the Japanese, in an attempt to destroy the Western position in the Far East and to end their dependence upon European events, in effect tied their fate to a Germany victory in Europe, and by autumn 1943 the prospects of a German victory in Europe were as realistic as the Japanese chances of successfully fighting the United States to a standstill in the Pacific.

The battle fronts in the Pacific saw relatively little change between February and October 1943. In the north Pacific theatre American and Canadian forces were involved in a campaign that resulted in the occupation of Adak and Amchitka in January 1943, the reconquest of Attu between 11 and 29 May, and the unopposed reoccupation of Kiska in August. (These two islands had been taken by the Japanese in a postscript to the Midway venture.) Thereafter the Aleutians were a backwater, notably only for Dutch Harbor, which served as a base for submarine operations, and the fitful raids on the Kuriles by the 11th Air Force that represented the first bombing of the Japanese home islands by shore-based aircraft. But despite these efforts, the north Pacific could not be developed as a major theatre of operations because of its forbidding climate and geography, a fact acknowledged in the Japanese decision to abandon Kiska after the loss of Attu in order to concentrate upon the defence of the central and south-west Pacific.

In the south-west Pacific Allied progress during 1943 was slow despite the Americans having speedily followed up the Japanese evacuation of Guadalcanal with the occupation of the Russells by elements of the 43rd Infantry Division on 21 February, and despite the annihilation of the convoy carrying the *51st Infantry Division* from Rabaul to Lae in the Bismarck Sea between 2 and 4 March, after which the Japanese made no major attempt to reinforce their garrisons in eastern New Guinea. The obvious American intention to develop an offensive into the central Solomons provoked the *17th Army* into attempts to strengthen its positions and garrisons in the New Georgia group and there was also a series of major battles for command of the air over these islands between March and June, the Japanese supplementing their shore-based units at Rabaul with carrier groups sent from Truk in April. It was not until 30 June that American forces moved forward to occupy Rendova, units from the 37th and 43rd US Infantry Divisions landing in northern New Georgia between 2 and 5 July. The Japanese airfield at Munda defied capture until 5 August, however, but 10 days later American forces landed on Vella Lavella. With units from the 3rd New Zealand Infantry Division clearing the island after mid-September, the securing of Vella Lavella was significant in that by sidestepping the main Japanese

317

concentrations on New Georgia and Kolombangara the Americans employed for the first time in the south-west Pacific the island-hopping strategy that was to leave Japanese garrisons 'to wither on the vine' and which the Japanese themselves considered to have been one of the most important factors in their defeat.*

Japanese difficulties in meeting the American offensive in the central Solomons were compounded by the fact that the Rendova operation was complemented by Allied landings on Woodlark, in the Trobriands, and in Nassau Bay on 30 June. This last was a feint accompanied by an intensification of operations by the 3rd Australian Infantry Division around Wau that together were intended to distract Japanese attention from operations elsewhere. This Allied ability to stage simultaneous landings across the width of the Solomon Sea served to deny the Japanese the opportunity to counter any of the emerging threats to Rabaul. American progress through the central Solomons was nevertheless punctuated by a series of hard-fought naval actions as the Japanese sought to maintain and strengthen their garrisons, the most notable actions being fought in Kula Gulf (6 July), off Kolombangara (13 July) and in Vella Gulf (6–7 August), but none of these battles witnessed the commitment of heavy forces by either side. Thereafter the net began to close around Rabaul with a series of Allied landings: in Huon Gulf on 4 September and by airborne forces at Nadzab on the sixth that resulted in the Allied captures of Salamaua on the twelfth and Lae on the sixteenth; around Cape Cretin on 22 September which led to the occupation of Finchhafen on 2 October; in the Treasury Islands on 27 October and at Empress Augusta Bay by the 3rd Marine Division on 1 November. The latter operations in the northern Solomons brought the Americans within range of fighter aircraft from Rabaul and prompted the *Combined Fleet* to commit heavy cruiser forces and air groups from its three first-line carriers to the defence of Rabaul, the base being considered a main point of resistance despite the area east of the Saipan–Truk–Timor line having been deemed expendable under the terms of the new operational policy inaugurated in September.

The relative Japanese passivity in the face of the threats that developed before October 1943 against Rabaul, and indeed the whole of the new policy initiated in September, was the product of the realisation that 1943 had to be a year of consolidation and self-strengthening on the part of the *Imperial Navy* in order that the *Combined Fleet* might give battle with its

*The first island-hopping operation in the Pacific was the reconquest of Attu, Kiska having been isolated in the process, but in the case of Vella Lavella the Japanese were able to evacuate their garrisons on the island and on Kolombangara.

full power in the critical engagements that would be fought at some future time on the Saipan–Truk–Timor line. This realisation, however, was belated. The extent of its carrier aviation problems was not appreciated by the *Imperial Navy* until its failures in the battles of the eastern Solomons in August and off Santa Cruz in October 1942, after which time the Japanese cause – not helped by the carrier group deployments to Rabaul in April and October 1943 – was really beyond recall. By 1943 it was too late for the Japanese to restructure their construction programmes and to expand their shipbuilding and aircrew training facilities on the scale needed to conduct an air war in the Pacific that, on the US Navy's calculation, involved monthly air losses of 20 per cent of unit establishment. In fact, 1943 saw not a strengthening of the *Combined Fleet* but its relative decline even without a major battle because in a year that saw it lose one escort carrier, one battleship, three cruisers and 32 destroyers, its commissioning programme of one escort carrier, three light cruisers, 20 destroyers and 37 submarines was dwarfed by the six fleet, nine light and 19 escort carriers, two battleships, four heavy and seven light cruisers, 126 destroyers, 221 destroyer escorts and 56 submarines that entered service with the US Navy in the course of 1943. In fact, in this single year the Americans commissioned in tonnage terms almost the equivalent of the *Imperial Navy* at its wartime peak.

In the war as a whole the *Imperial Navy* commissioned seven fleet, four light and three escort carriers, two battleships, seven light cruisers, 32 destroyers, 31 destroyer escorts and 116 submarines, a not inconsiderable achievement on the part of a nation with such limited construction facilities. But the Japanese achievement in bringing 14 carriers into service after December 1941 was degraded by realities that illustrated not the extent of the achievement but its inadequacy. Only three fleet carriers of the *Unryu* class were laid down, completed and commissioned in the course of the war, and the various conversions on which the *Imperial Navy* had to depend for its maintenance of numbers were of very poor quality and limited performance but were nevertheless put into service at the expense of the escorts needed for the protection of the fleet and trade. The fact was that Japan lacked the resources to maintain a balanced fleet and her merchant marine, and as the balance of Japanese construction was lost so the Japanese found themselves outpaced technically in terms of aircraft and radar development, VT shells, control systems and TBS radios, all of which ensured a massive qualitative improvement of the US Pacific Fleet during and after 1943. The battles that were fought in the Pacific in 1942 were between evenly matched, pre-war navies but in the course of 1943 the US Navy grew into a strength and effectiveness that assured it of victory through its twin abilities to outfight the Japanese on a one-to-one basis and to bring overwhelming numbers to bear against an enemy effectively confined to pre-1942 technology.

The wartime development of American naval power is well known. With yards such as Kaiser launching its fiftieth escort carrier one year and one day after launching its first, a navy that entered 1941 as the equal of the British navy ended the Pacific war with 1,246 fleet units and some 5,250 major combat units, and the staggering total of 67,952 units of all and every size and description with its fleets, amphibious forces, logistics organisation and shore establishments. In 1943, however, when the process of expansion was only beginning to assume significant proportions, the most obvious manifestation of the growth of American naval power was the development of the fast carrier force. The raids on Manus (31 August), the Gilberts (28 September) and Wake (5–6 October) were merely the trial runs of a concept of war that was to be put into effect in November 1943 for the first time when a carrier force with six fleet and five light carriers supported the first amphibious assault on Japan's outer defensive perimeter in the central Pacific.

This operation, which resulted in the American occupation of six atolls in the Gilberts between 20 and 29 November, acquired a notoriety in the United States because of the alleged heaviness of the losses sustained on Tarawa. In reality, American casualties, which totalled 3,301 on this one atoll, were light in relation to the landing force and the overall numbers employed by the Americans in this single operation. The public outcry that followed Tarawa was a reflection of the fact that thus far in the war American casualties had been unconscionably light. Moreover, the losses sustained in taking Tarawa were most certainly not excessive in terms of the strategic results that flowed from the occupation of the Gilberts, namely the securing of a forward base for operations to ensure the isolation of Rabaul, into the Marshalls and into the Carolines. The American gain in securing the Gilberts was very substantial, but this reality was accompanied by two others, one that illustrated Japanese problems in dealing with the offensives that the Americans developed after November 1943 and the other the problems that still confronted the Americans in their conduct of operations. On the first score, American success at Tarawa in November 1943 owed much to the fact that without the air groups and cruisers that had been sent to Rabaul the *Combined Fleet* could not contest the American landings in the Gilberts, but it was these same air groups and cruisers that were mauled in the American carrier raids on Rabaul on 5 and 11 November. Without the ability to determine the place and timing of operations, the *Combined Fleet* could not respond effectively to either of the threats that emerged in the course of November 1943, and in the wider context the Japanese reluctance to cede any single part of their perimeter defence resulted in a dissipation of force that ended in the collapse of another sector for want of effective support on the part of the carrier fleet.

On the second matter, the American assault on the Gilberts illustrated doctrinal problems that were to increase in intensity as the US Navy carried the war into the western Pacific. In the case of all American amphibious operations between August 1942 and October 1944 the critical problem confronting the US Pacific Fleet was that its fast carrier force was tasked with divergent objectives – the covering and support of assault forces plus the destruction of the Japanese fleet in battle should it attempt to intervene. The two objectives were not necessarily one and the same and there was never any guarantee that events might unfold in such a way as to enable the carrier force to do both, as the battles in the Philippine Sea in June 1944 and off Leyte in the following October proved. The key to success in a fleet action was in large measure dependent upon the concentration of a force not tied to a beachhead, but the successful support of an assault landing necessarily involved the commitment of carriers to the beachhead at the same time tackling Japanese air power over an extended area because, as the Americans realised, the outcome of the assault was dependent upon the isolation of the target from effective support. Herein lay a number of related problems. Before the war the US Marine Corps had worked out a comprehensive doctrine of amphibious operations that included close air support, but fleet carriers were too valuable to be risked in protracted operations in the close support role and their air groups were neither trained nor equipped for this specialist task. Moreover, as the American fast carrier force fought its way into the western Pacific and brought the war to Japan's shores, so this enhanced offensive power at the strategic level was countered by a massive decrease in the tactically offensive power of individual carriers.

At the start of the Pacific war the complement of the standard *Yorktown* fleet carrier was 72 aircraft, 18 of which were fighters: by mid-1945 the standard *Essex* carrier had just 18 bombers in a 102-strong air group. This change in the balance of American air groups in the course of hostilities was determined by the need to fight for air supremacy both before and during landing operations and by the scale of attack, particularly by suicide aircraft, to which the American carrier formations were subjected as they fought their way across the Pacific. It was a change

The Pacific Campaign: The Advances Across The Pacific, November 1943 - May 1944

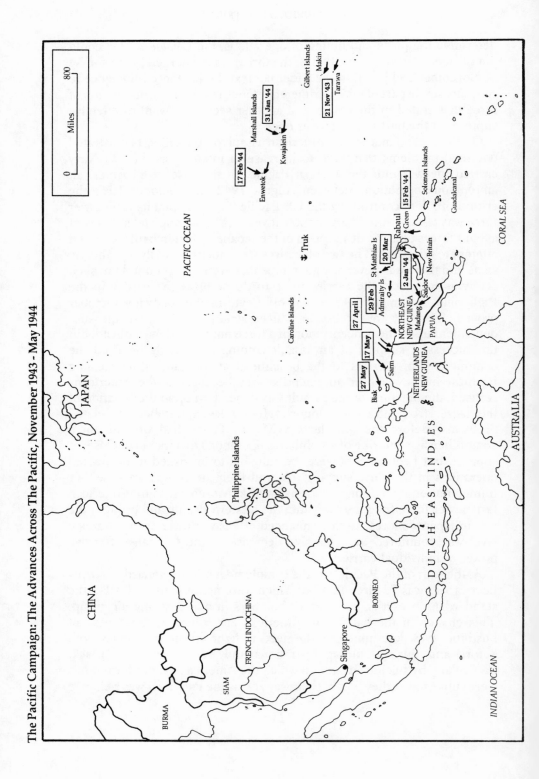

partially offset, however, by the ability of the F4U Corsair to double as a strike aircraft and by the growing number of fleet carriers available to the US Pacific Fleet in the course of the war. In addition, as the Americans advanced into the western Pacific so many of the problems of supporting amphibious operations were resolved by the employment of growing numbers of escort carriers in the close support role. Such was the scale of air and naval operations in the western Pacific in 1945 that in the four months of the Okinawan campaign no fewer than 60 Allied carriers, 26 of them fleet and light fleet units, saw service off the Ryukyus: in the process no fewer than nine fleet carriers were forced to withdraw from the combat zone with battle damage. In the plans that were prepared in 1943 for the possible invasion of the Japanese home islands upwards of 100 carriers were deemed necessary for success, and by 2 September 1944 the US Navy had 99 in commission. Such was the scale of the development of American carrier aviation in the course of the Pacific war and the numbers needed to carry the war to Japan's shores, and it was power on this scale that was beginning to become available to the Americans in the south-west Pacific and the Gilberts in November 1943.

If November 1943 was significant in that it marked the start of the central Pacific offensive and with it the opening of the dual American thrust into the western Pacific, it was also significant in that the two thrusts, though intended as complementary and mutually supporting, were in reality rivals in the allocation of priorities and resources, and in that November 1943 in effect marked the point when the Pacific war properly became an American preserve. These two matters had a common base in MacArthur's south-west Pacific theatre, which in the first two years of the war functioned on the shipping of the twice-exiled Dutch, Australian infantry and MacArthur's egomania: thereafter the latter alone provided an element of constancy and continuity in this theatre.

By the end of 1943 Australia, having shouldered the burden of the fighting in New Guinea, was approaching the end of her resources and could not avoid having to reduce her front-line military strength by a third in order to return manpower to industry and food production. For a nation with only six expeditionary divisions, which found it necessary to hold two divisions as fillers for every division committed to the jungles of New Guinea, this development was disastrous in terms of national prestige and standing with more powerful allies. Even at the peak of her wartime commitment, however, Australia was lightly regarded by the American High Command in general and MacArthur in particular other than by virtue of the fact that as 'white man's country' she had to be denied to the Japanese. By November 1943, South-West Pacific Command possessed sufficient American forces to display an increasingly obvious dismissive attitude towards the Australians whose forces were thereafter assigned rear area duties or secondary operations while American forces assumed responsibility for carrying the war to the Japanese home islands.

This increasingly American aspect of the war in the Pacific, and the clash within the American hierarchy between an army command in the south-west Pacific and a naval command in the central Pacific for primacy in the Pacific theatre as a whole, has received an attention that has obscured the simple fact that the war against Japan was in reality two separate wars – one in the Pacific and the other on the Asian mainland. The latter, by November 1943, was the lesser in importance, but had reached a critical stage in its two main theatres, Burma and China. In Burma, 1943 proved almost as disastrous for the British as 1942 with the collapse of an offensive in the Arakan that was nothing short of shameful with 17 British battalions outfought and harried to defeat by the equivalent of two Japanese infantry regiments (November 1942–May 1943). The only other British undertaking in the dry season, however, proved a more contentious affair: some 3,000 men were formed into raiding columns and spent about three weeks behind Japanese lines in the general area of the Myitkyina-Mandalay railroad before being withdrawn to India. In military terms the first Chindit operations involved 30 per cent losses for minimal return, but in circumstances that demanded a victory this raid was presented by the British as an outstanding and far-reaching triumph, the American response at the Quadrant conference being that if the British could achieve so much with so little there seemed no limit to what they could achieve in Upper Burma if they really tried. At this conference the American High Command offered, as part of a general offensive in Upper Burma for which the British had no enthusiasm, to provide transport and support for a second Chindit operation in the coming dry season.

The British accepted this offer without fully appreciating the significance of a decision that provided the Americans with control of the British operational timetable despite the British wish to develop an amphibious strategy in the Bay of Bengal as an alternative to a Burma commitment. The amphibious alternative, however, proved beyond the British on three counts, excluding American opposition. While the Italian surrender in September 1943 freed fleet units of the Royal Navy from the Mediterranean, the need to refit carriers and capital ships in readiness for service in the Indian Ocean and the cut-off date of May 1944 for operations in the Bay of Bengal left the British without the time to provide fleet support for an amphibious operation before the onset of the monsoon. Further, India by the second half of 1943 was in a state that bordered upon collapse and Bengal was in the grip of a famine that claimed an estimated two million lives. India's greatly overworked railroad system simply could not cope with the civil and military demands placed upon it, and her food and industrial stockpiles by the last quarter of 1943 were measured in days rather than weeks. Militarily, she lacked the infrastructure to increase an Indian army that had already expanded ten-fold since 1939, and the British capacity to develop airfields in south-east India and Ceylon was very limited. Critically, India, with a shipyard capacity less than that of either Southampton or Rosyth, could not service and maintain both a fleet and an amphibious force. Even with South African facilities the British could not escape having to decide between the two. Finally, the amphibious lift in the Bay of Bengal in the second half of 1943 (slightly more than one division) was not the type required by the British as they sought their allies' approval for an assault on the Andamans. In the impasse created by the British desire to move against the Andamans in order to avoid a commitment in Upper Burma and the American insistence that the Andamans operation could proceed only if it involved no lessening of an Upper Burma commitment, the lack of ship-to-shore assault shipping in the Indian Ocean in late 1943 in effect spelt an end to British attempts to bypass Burma.

The unfolding of events in the last quarter of 1943 served only to compound Anglo-American mutual exasperation and misunderstand-ings over Burma. As noted elsewhere, as a result of the Quadrant conference the Americans initiated staff studies based on the premise that the defeat of Japan was to be accomplished within a year of the end of the European war, scheduled for October 1944. These studies envisaged American forces reaching the Hong Kong–Philippines–Formosa area in early 1945, and on this basis the British correctly reasoned that China, and hence Burma, ceased to be serious factors in Allied strategy because China could not be readied for a significant contribution to the Allied war effort since a road could not be pushed through Burma to China by that time. Moreover, as the American planners considered how to develop offensives that would end the Pacific war by October 1945 so they became convinced that British naval and amphibious forces were essential to success. At this time, before the extent of Japanese weakness became apparent and before the American staffs had the chance to absorb the lesson of maximum force and minimum losses, the Americans were prepared to maintain all British forces sent to the Pacific by mid-

1944. On both issues, the two nations found the other not forthcoming, though by the Sextant conferences in November 1943 the British chiefs of staff had realised that the only practical option available to Britain was to accept an inescapable commitment in Upper Burma and to send the fleet to the Pacific, the latter being the surest way of helping to bring the war against Japan to the speediest possible end. In the event, however, British problems of resolving strategic priorities in the Far East were settled by decisions taken in Tokyo.

Burma, for the Japanese, proved a microcosm of their entire war effort: an initial victory that led nowhere except to final, total defeat. After their conquest of Burma the Japanese were willing to regard the Chindwin as a line of exhaustion, convenient to themselves and the British alike, and to turn their attention to other, more important theatres. To the Japanese Burma's importance lay in its provision of depth to the defences of south-east Asia and not as a springboard for an offensive into India, and indeed in mid-1942 the Japanese opportunity to mount an attack on India had passed. In April 1942, at a time when two divisions were sent by sea to Rangoon and carrier forces raided Ceylon, a Japanese landing in Bengal could not have been repulsed by British forces in north-east India, and a British defeat around Calcutta, coming on top of those in Malaya and Burma, could well have destroyed the British position throughout the subcontinent. In the third quarter of 1942, however, the Japanese High Command concluded that any attempt to develop an offensive through the mountains and jungles into Assam and Manipur would prove logistically impossible, yet one year later, under the impact of the first Chindit operation and the realisation that the exhaustion of 1942 was neither permanent nor mutual, the Japanese High Command reversed its earlier decision and sanctioned the *Burma Area Army*'s demand for 'The March on Delhi'. It was this effort, which began in March 1944, that in effect resolved British difficulties in deciding policy with respect to Burma because it forced a defensive battle at Imphal and Kohima on the 11th Army Group and in so doing provided the basis of the British reconquest of Burma in 1945. By breaking the main power of the *Burma Area Army* before entering Burma, the 14th Army won a victory that might well have proved beyond it had it been forced to seek battle in the Irrawaddy valley after a difficult approach against an enemy operating on superior lines of communication. The reconquest of Burma has been attributed in large measure to Allied air supply, and there is no disputing that the 14th Army – the largest British army of the Second World War – advanced further in less time than did the 21st Army Group in north-west Europe largely because it was mainly sustained during its advance by air, but even allowing for the battles that were fought around Mandalay and Meiktila air supply probably could not have met the requirements of an army had it been obliged to confront an intact enemy in the Irrawaddy and Sittang valleys.

British dependence upon the United States and the unfolding of events in the Burma theatre ensured that in a clash of Anglo-American interests and priorities the Americans had the power of decision, but in China, where the Americans faced a situation that was if anything even more complicated than in Burma, the United States was to find herself confounded at every turn by an ally that American liaison missions were shocked to find had been observing 'a special undeclared peace'* with the Japanese even before the outbreak of the Pacific war. In very large measure the difficulties in which the Americans found themselves in their dealings with the Chinese authorities in Chungking were of their own making, specifically with respect to a stubborn insistence that an effective Chinese contribution was essential to the defeat of Japan and to the Roosevelt administration's vulnerability to a formidably organised China lobby in Washington. Complicating the American position, however, was the fact that the US leadership had no clear idea of what it required in China, in very sharp contrast to the Chungking authorities that wanted as small a commitment as was compatible with the continuation of American aid. At the heart of the American dilemma was the question of whether an American effort should be directed to the re-organisation of Chinese nationalist armies in order to raise a small number of very good divisions that could engage the Japanese armies in China or to develop China as an air base for operations against the Japanese home islands.

The latter was an attractive option to considerable sections of the American and Chinese High Commands. It was attractive to Chiang Kai-shek because it would involve relatively little Chinese effort, and it was especially seductive for the US Army Air Force before September 1943 for the very simple reason that under then existing plans its bombers would not be able to conduct operations against Japan except from bases in China until 1947. As noted elsewhere, such an option was singularly alluring to the American High Command as a whole because of its beguiling promise of high technology, low investment and major results. The American air commander in China, Chennault, indicated in 1942 that a single formation of heavy bombers would be able to destroy

*See Appendix C

Japan's capacity to wage war. The weakness of this argument – besides the obvious – was not lost upon Chennault's superior in China, Stilwell, who correctly foresaw that if the Americans developed in China the means to bomb Japan without first raising divisions to defend the airfields from which operations would be conducted then the Japanese would overrun the bases. This argument, however, was undermined on two counts. The Chennault lobby associated itself with the China lobby in Washington, and the latter was bitterly opposed to Stilwell on account of his open disdain for Chiang Kai-shek and his desire to raise Chinese formations for major offensive operations. The nationalist leadership in Chungking was not opposed to a major re-organisation of army formations in order to provide a limited number of first-rate divisions, but it was determined, in accordance with traditional Chinese practice, that such divisions would be used to consolidate nationalist power and for use against the communists, not the Japanese. As the arguments unfolded in Washington in front of an American High Command that did not understand the situation inside China, Stilwell found himself outmanoeuvred by an air lobby that confidently claimed that bombers would be able to halt any Japanese attempt to secure air bases in south-west China and abandoned by an administration that inclined towards the Chennault argument not on military grounds but for political reasons associated with China's and Chiang Kai-shek's symbolic significance in the prosecution of the war.

The issues at the heart of American difficulties in framing policy with regard to China were the basis of the débâcle that overwhelmed the Chinese nationalist armies in southern China after May 1944 when the Japanese began what proved to be their last major offensive of the war. Yet this campaign achieved no long-term strategic result for the Japanese because by the time that the Japanese moved against American air bases around Laohokow, Changsha, Hengyang and Kweilin the American dilemma had been resolved, albeit inconsistently. At the Trident conference the air plan had been endorsed, but after Quadrant and the inauguration of the 12-month schedule the US Navy's selection of the Marianas as a target of attack in mid-1944 provided the Army Air Force for the first time with a practical alternative to China as a base for strategic bombing operations against the Japanese home islands. Moreover, given that a bombing effort from China could only be made after a massive supply effort by air from north-east India, the Marianas offered the Army Air Force a short and easy line of communication without any of the problems inherent in dealing with allies.

Thus the American decision to develop China as a base for air operations against Japan rather than strengthening Chinese ground forces for a campaign on the mainland more or less coincided with a decision to abandon the idea of an air offensive from bases in China, yet this change of policy in no way lessened the American determination that the British should be involved in a campaign to clear Upper Burma – though to no very obvious purpose – while it left Washington with no real power in its future dealings with Chungking. The reality of this situation was lost upon the Roosevelt administration, and hence the double irony of the situation that developed between Quadrant and Octagon: as the American victory in the Pacific assumed reality – and arguably Japan was the only Asian country that the United States could defeat – so the American capacity to influence events in China diminished, and as this reached its nadir so the Roosevelt administration tried to impose increasingly stringent demands upon the Chungking administration only to find, in October 1944, that it could do nothing to back its insistence that Stilwell be given full executive powers in China. An inability or unwillingness to seek an alternative to Chiang Kai-shek left the Roosevelt administration with no power to override the Chinese veto on Stilwell's proposed elevation or, indeed, to resist the demand for Stilwell's recall. In the subsequent transfer of Stilwell from China lay the start of the process of removal from positions of authority and influence of those Americans with no illusions about the corruption, incompetence and essential worthlessness of the nationalist regime, with consequences that were to distort American perspectives of, and policy towards, China and eastern Asia for more than a generation.

By the end of October 1943, the Americans were a matter of weeks away from their offensives into the Gilberts and effecting the isolation of Rabaul, the Japanese some months from operations into north-east India and south-west China. Between them, however, the Americans and Japanese were midway through what was arguably the most important single campaign of the Pacific war, that waged by the Allies against Japanese merchant shipping. At this time the Japanese marine was little smaller than it had been at the outbreak of war – some 5,400,000 tons compared to the December 1941 aggregate of 6,051,660 tons – but by October 1943 the campaign against her shipping was beyond Japan's control and a pattern had been established in this campaign which, continuing until August 1945, resulted in the annihilation of her marine and the collapse of her seaborne trade by the time of her surrender.

The underlying pattern of this campaign can be summarised with relative ease. Japan began the Pacific war with a merchant fleet that was too small to sustain the commitments involved in fighting a defensive war in the central and south-west Pacific while drawing upon the resources of south-east Asia and maintaining the armies of occupation in Manchoutikuo and China, but not only did Japan prove unable to expand her merchant fleet on the scale needed to meet her commitments, she failed what shipping she possessed on two counts: to use it effectively and to protect it from progressive destruction. By the end of the war Japan probably had no more than 900,000 tons of shipping in service; her ports and industries were at a standstill; her population had been reduced to the edge of starvation. The maritime war in which Japan found herself after December 1941 thus involved a total defeat that combined a number of inter-related dimensions: a failure of output and production; a failure of organisation and doctrine; the increasing effectiveness of the American effort against Japanese shipping. Relating the course of events is complicated by the fact that none of these aspects of Japan's defeat manifested itself in isolation and indeed they tended to feed off one another, most obviously in terms of the decline of imports which meant less steel for warship and merchantmen production; this in turn led to fewer ships, more losses and a further decline of imports. In a sense this vicious circle was joined from the day that Japan went to war – perhaps more accurately from the time of the July 1941 embargo on Japan – but obvious evidence of this fact arguably did not come until November 1943 when, in the month that the *Imperial Navy* belatedly introduced a general convoy system, Japanese merchant losses for the first time exceeded not just 200,000 but 300,000 tons, the latter figure being just one-third the total selected by the *Imperial Navy* before the war, for apparently no very good or obvious reason, as the losses that might be appreciated in any given year of a three-year war.

Between 8 December 1941 and 31 October 1943 the Japanese merchant navy lost 552 ships of 2,416,220 tons to all causes, but in this period new construction and captures served to insulate Japan from the full effect of losses that came on top of the deprivation of some 3,250,000 tons of shipping as a result of her decision to go to war. In 1940 Japan imported 22,039,600 tons of food and raw materials (excluding oil) and needed about 9,300,000 tons of shipping to meet her various commitments.* Of this, some 35 per cent of her shipping requirements were met by nations with which Japan went to war in December 1941 and which, apart from captures, was lost to her on the outbreak of hostilities. In the

---

*The total measurement tonnage of inport, collected and coastal shipping in 1941 was 48,705,000 tons: by 1942 this had shrank to 40,531,000 tons and by 1944 to 17,152,000 tons.

course of the war the Japanese captured or salvaged 822,963 tons of shipping, but by October 1943 such sources had ceased to be major factors in Japanese calculations. By mid-war, therefore, Japan had in effect been reduced to dependence upon new construction alone for the maintenance of a merchant fleet that was by any terms of reference wholly inadequate to meet 'peacetime' requirements, still less those of a nation with commitments that widened enormously after December 1941.

Despite other demands upon her resources, Japanese shipyards produced a respectable 3,293,314 tons of merchant shipping in the course of the war – 54.42 per cent of the total shipping available to Japan in December 1941 and, ironically, about the aggregate 'lost' to Japan on the outbreak of war. The peak of Japanese output was reached in 1944 when 1,699,203 tons of shipping were commissioned into service, yet this total formed just 43.67 per cent of the losses – of 3,891,019 tons – incurred in that same year; likewise, the greatest monthly return of 89 ships of about 250,000 tons in March 1944 was placed in context by the destruction of 30 merchantmen of 191,718 tons by American carrier aircraft over the Carolines on a single day during the previous month. Moreover, the construction levels that were achieved by Japanese shipyards were possible only by the neglect of routine refit and maintenance programmes for merchantmen in service, a state of affairs that compounded the long-term consequences of the decision taken in 1940 to postpone refits in order to build up stockpiles of raw material. Even in December 1941 12.6 per cent of all Japanese shipping was laid up; by March 1944 this proportion had risen to 18.96 per cent and by August 1945 to 43.64 per cent. By October 1943 the consequences of a decision to go to war without due consideration of national capacity to wage war, at least in terms of shipping and construction capacities, were becoming obvious to the Japanese High Command under the impact not simply of the inability of industry to cover losses but weaknesses of organisation, doctrine and practices of the Japanese armed services and the quickening pace of American anti-shipping operations.

In terms of organisation, Japan faced two problems that were, in effect, beyond solution though she made no logical or coherent attempt to ease her difficulties. In 1940 some 72.58 per cent of Japanese shipping resources were committed to trade within the yen bloc*, 15.55 per cent with south-east Asia and 11.87 per cent with the rest of the world. War

*Japan with Formosa and Korea, plus Manchoutikuo and occupied China (and coastal requirements).

resulted in an increased demand upon Japanese shipping resources without lessening commitments within the yen bloc, and much of the shipping involved in this trade was small, specialist and short-haul and thus not readily adapted for oceanic requirements. Further, after April 1942 Japan, despite a triangular commitment between the resources area of south-east Asia, the industry of the home islands and the operational zones in the central and south-west Pacific, persisted with sailings to and from the resources and operational areas via Japan, apart from the shipment of oil direct from the Indies to Truk and Rabaul. Thus instead of spending a maximum of one leg in three in ballast, merchantmen sailed empty or only lightly loaded on one voyage in two, the overall loss involved in such arrangements amounting to 8 per cent of Japanese shipping capacity. Even more damaging to Japan's ability to wage war, however, was the division of her merchant navy into three autonomous fleets with 2,000,000 tons of shipping allocated to the army, 1,500,000 tons to the navy and 2,000,000 tons to the civilian economy. Both the army and navy persistently refused to allow their allocated merchantmen to return to Japan with general cargoes unless, as was increasingly the case, these were specifically for their own use and not subjected to central planning controls. Thus even by 1944, when the Japanese shipping position was desperate, merchantmen from the different fleets might sail in ballast in opposite directions on the same route, even in company, and the obvious wastefulness of such arrangements was compounded by the habit of both services of requisitioning merchantmen from the civilian sector without reference to the other and to central planning authority.

These various planning weaknesses reflected a lack of organisation within the Japanese High Command 'that was surely the worst of any great power in modern times', but the wastefulness and confusion that resulted from the absence of authoritative central planning agencies were compounded by the slowness and inadequacy of the *Imperial Navy*'s response to mounting shipping losses. The latter was the direct consequence of an organisation and doctrine that made the *Imperial Navy* the mirror image, albeit on a smaller scale, of the US Navy, hence the relative ease with which it was defeated. The *Imperial Navy*'s *raison d'être* was to fight and win a defensive war in the western Pacific – ironically to secure by force of arms the very position that Japan had repudiated when enshrined in inter-war limitation treaties – but its tactical stance was in fact offensive and its doctrine held convoy and the protection of shipping in low esteem as inappropriate for a service committed to seeking battle. Just as an obsession with 'the decisive battle' indicated that the *Imperial Navy* never understood the nature of the naval war for which it pressed throughout 1941, so its disdain for trade defence served notice of its lack of understanding of maritime warfare and the peculiarities of Japan's national dependence upon the sea. When convoy was introduced on a limited scale in April 1942 the *Combined Fleet*'s opposition to the measure extended to the refusal to allow fleet destroyers on their way to combat zones to serve as escorts *en route*. Even after the *Grand Escort Command* was established in November 1943 it continued to resist demands for the release of units to serve as escorts. Indeed, when the *Grand Escort Command* was established it had just 27 ocean-going escorts of various descriptions, only 12 of which were destroyers, and at its peak strength as an independent command it had only 59 such units, though another 215 local units were distributed throughout the various commands remaining to the Japanese in August 1944.

With such numbers Japanese convoys, usually of between six and 10 merchantmen, were seldom afforded an escort of more than one or two warships, and this failure on the part of the *Imperial Navy* to provide adequate escort numbers, plus the fact that the Japanese did not adopt the big convoy principle as did the British in 1943 and made no scientific study of convoy tactics, meant that with the introduction of general convoy in November 1943 Japan suffered all the adverse effect of convoy in terms of an initial fall of delivery rates without the long-term compensation of better protected shipping and increased chances of safe arrivals. Without an adequate escort force, the *Imperial Navy* was unable to stem the rise in the rate of merchantmen sinkings throughout 1944, when American submarines sank 519 of the 969 merchantmen of 3,891,019 tons lost compared to the 292 sunk in 1943 from totals of 434 ships of 1,820,919 tons. In an attempt to maintain the flow of imports into Japan the *Imperial Navy* resorted to such measures as diversified routing, the use of Chinese coastal waters, movement by night and independent sailings. The American ability to deploy submarines on the basis of deciphered Japanese shipping signals, plus the capacity of American submarines to continue to find targets by virtue of their search receivers and superb SJ radar, largely frustrated such expedients, while convoy itself faltered in the face of the willingness of American submariners to tackle escorts in order to attack merchantmen.

The rise in the rate of Japanese losses as a result of submarine attack in 1944 was the direct result of the growing operational effectiveness of American submarines as the war approached the start of its third year. Between the outbreak of war and 1 October 1943 American submarines accounted for 339 of the 503 Japanese merchantmen lost to all causes, and only in two months after February 1942 – in November 1942 and in

March 1943 – did American submarines fail to account for at least half of Japanese shipping losses. Such results were obtained by boats that were short of torpedoes which were themselves unreliable in terms of accuracy, depth-keeping qualities and firing mechanisms. It was not until 30 September 1943 that an American submarine proceeded on an operational patrol with reliable torpedoes, and thereafter the rate of sinkings by American submarines all but doubled while the number of operational boats increased by only one-tenth. The growing returns of a submarine force that reached its peak wartime strength of 156 boats in the Pacific at the end of 1944 nevertheless formed only one part of an increasingly effective American campaign against Japanese shipping after February 1944, after which time the fast carrier force fought its way into the western Pacific. Thereafter there was a direct correlation between the scale of Japanese losses and either American carrier operations or American amphibious assaults that forced Japanese merchantmen to negotiate waters controlled by enemy air power. Thus February–March 1944 and September–November 1944 witnessed crippling Japanese losses – 179 ships of 782,502 tons and 347 ships of 1,352,516 tons – as American carrier formations first attacked Truk and the Palaus and then established themselves off the central Philippines. The latter in effect marked the end of the Japanese convoy system, though in reality most oceanic convoy routes, already under threat after the loss of the Marianas, were being abandoned by the Japanese because of the shortage of both escorts and merchantmen.

After December 1944 American submarines accounted for just 172 of the 744 Japanese merchantmen sunk, and in July 1945 when more Japanese ships – 145 – were lost than in any other single month of the war American submarines destroyed only 14 merchantmen. A combination of air power and mines completed the destruction of the Japanese merchant navy in the last nine months of the Pacific war, and while this contribution to the final defeat of Japan was not insubstantial it came at a time when Japan had already been defeated at sea. In 1945 the five main Pacific ports of Japan handled just 12.73 per cent of their 1942 traffic and bulk commodity imports into Japan as a whole ran at only 12.45 per cent of 1940 levels; of the 1,551,203 tons of shipping that remained to Japan at the war's end one-tenth was south of the Philippines and for all practical purposes lost to the Japanese while the remainder was all but evenly divided between ships not in service and those committed to bringing food into a country facing mass starvation. Aircraft and mines respectively accounted for 2,543,261 and 618,201 of the 8,619,009 tons of Japanese shipping sunk in the course of the war, but American submarines, with the sinking of 1,113 merchantmen of 4,779,902 tons and the sharing in the destruction of another six ships of 43,921 tons, were the primary agency of destruction, particularly so because submarine success was mainly achieved in the early and middle years of the war and this had a disastrously cumulative effect on the Japanese economy at the very time when output had to be increased far beyond the levels that were achieved. Moreover, American submarines accounted for 201 Japanese warships, including one battleship and eight aircraft carriers, and in at least one battle made contributions that were crucial to American success even excluding the sinkings that they achieved.

At the battle of the Marianas in June 1944 American submarines compromised Japanese intentions on two counts even before the carrier fleets joined action: by halving Japanese oil imports between January and May 1944 through their success against tankers American submarines forced the *Imperial Navy* to deploy its carriers in the southern Philippines before the battle and hence in a position of disadvantage in the action that followed, and the submarines found and reported Japanese forces as they advanced to contact. Overall, however, the success against Japanese warships was secondary to the results registered against Japanese merchant shipping, and this campaign remains perhaps the only example in modern history of the prosecution of a *guerre de course* to a strategically decisive result. By the time that aircraft and mines emerged as the main means by which the campaign was to be concluded, Allied submarines, which accounted for 4,886,991 tons of Japanese shipping in the course of the war, had been primarily responsible for the reduction of Japanese coal imports by 24.10 per cent from 1940 levels, total iron and steel imports by 39.33 per cent, and base metal imports by 41.35 per cent. In so doing submarines fulfilled one part of a strategy that aimed at nothing less than total command of the sea. In their success, the submarines helped to confirm the historical reality that a strategy of sea control and denial, as attempted by the *Imperial Navy*, was only a halfway house to an admission of strategic futility which became self-evident as the failure to limit the duration of the war it had begun left the *Imperial Navy* with nothing but the illusion of power.

When, in mid-1942, the American High Command took the decision that unwittingly committed Allied forces to a six-month struggle for Guadalcanal, *Operation Watchtower* was seen as the first small step in a campaign that would end with the reoccupation of Rabaul. By November 1943, however, the twin American drives across the western Pacific were to begin with Allied forces committed not to the recapture of Rabaul but its neutralisation and isolation, an aim that was achieved by April 1944 as a result of landings by the US 6th Army on western New Britain (15 and 26 December), at Saidor (2 January) and on Los Negros (29 February) and Manus (15 March) in the Admiralties. These operations were complemented by the clearing of the Green Islands by the 3rd New Zealand Division (15–20 February) and the 4th Marine Regiment's occupation of Emirau, in the St Matthias group, on 20 March. This operation, which completed the isolation of Rabaul, was supported by a bombardment of Kavieng by American battleships, but the powerlessness of both Kavieng and Rabaul in the face of these enveloping attacks and bombardment by the 5th US Air Force had already been demonstrated when both had been bombarded by American destroyers three times between 17 and 29 February. Thereafter Australian troops were left to complete the close investment of Rabaul, but by the time that Rabaul's isolation was complete the principle of bypassing rather than tackling the main point of Japanese resistance had been adopted with respect to Truk, the main Japanese fleet base in the central Pacific.

Truk was to be neutralised in the course of two massive attacks by American carrier forces on 17–18 February and 29–30 April, after which only 14 aircraft remained at a base that was isolated from support for the remainder of the war but for deliveries by seven resupply submarines. The first of these raids, however, was conducted by the Americans as part of a covering operation for the assault on Eniwetok, secured between 17 and 23 February, which was itself the culmination of a reduction of Japanese power throughout the Marshalls that had begun on 31 January. On that date Majuro was secured, the first national territory to be lost by Japan during the war, and V Amphibious Corps landed at Kwajalein, the atoll and its submarine base being secured by 7 February. Thereafter the 7th US Air Force operating from Tarawa contributed to the neutralisation of Ponape before Eniwetok was secured, the Americans completing the clearing of the Marshalls, other than the Japanese garrisons on Wotje, Maloelap, Jaluit and Mili, by 23 April. By that time, however, the Americans had been able to capitalise upon their success in driving the *Combined Fleet* from the Carolines as a result of the Truk raid and the subsequent carrier sortie from Majuro that had resulted in the raids on the Palaus (30–31 March) and Woleai (1 April). By forcing the *Combined Fleet*'s withdrawal to Singapore in early February the Americans had left themselves free to use their carriers to support landings in the Hollandia area and at Aitape on 22 April that were intended to sidestep the still formidable *18th Army* in the Markham valley and the Wewak area. In the event, carrier support for *Operation Reckless* was largely superfluous because the 5th US Air Force, at the cost of six of its aircraft, in six heavy raids between 30 March and 16 April accounted for the 351 aircraft of the *6th Air Division* that the Japanese army had concentrated on airfields around Hollandia by the last week of March. The significance of both the landings in Dutch New Guinea and American carrier operations here and elsewhere in the western Pacific was obvious in terms of the breaching of the Japanese defence zone and the capacity of the Americans to develop further offensives into western New Guinea and into the southern Marianas.

The Japanese High Command, in the person of Admiral Koga, C-in-C *Combined Fleet*, correctly read the meaning of events even before they had run their course, and on 8 March he issued the plan that he intended to put into effect, once his carriers had reconstituted their air groups in mid-year, in order to counter further American moves against the hastily redrawn main line of resistance through Saipan, Truk and western New Guinea. The basis of this plan was the strengthening of Japanese air power throughout the Marianas, Carolines, Palaus and western New Guinea with a view to it and the Japanese carrier force complementing one another, hopefully to the extent that any American assault could be met with rough equality of numbers, Koga's intention being to give battle anywhere along the new defence line. Without the initiative and any control over the timing of operations, *Plan Z* was as good as any that could be devised, but its most obvious weakness, as revealed by the raid on Truk and the follow-up attack on the southern Marianas on 22 February that accounted for 168 Japanese aircraft, was that the American carriers could descend on any single part of the line and overwhelm it before it could be effectively supported. Only if the Americans obligingly attacked the Palaus without first making any attempt to clear their flanks would the Japanese be able to give battle on anything like numerical equality, and this begged obvious questions of American qualitative superiority in terms of aircraft and aircrew.

Events in the first week of May, however, forced the Japanese to abandon part of their plan. The landings around Hollandia had rendered the Japanese base at Sarmi untenable, and on 2 May the decision was taken to make Biak and Manokwari the twin centres of resistance in western New Guinea. The loss at sea on the sixth of the equivalent of one of the two divisions being sent to these places ensured that neither could be held in strength and Sorong and Halmahera were designated the new centres of resistance in the Indies. In one month, therefore, and after 21 months in which the Allies moved the battle front forward from Kakoda to Saidor, the front line in New Guinea advanced over 1,000 miles –

from Madang to a toe-hold on western New Guinea, as a result of a single amphibious operation, albeit one ensured by overwhelming Allied superiority in the air and at sea. The *18th Army* remained in the field, indeed it remained in the field until the surrender of Japan herself, but while it held American attention until November 1944 and thereafter denied the 6th Australian Division ownership of Wewak until 10 May 1945, it was reduced to strategic irrelevance by the American occupation of Hollandia and Aitape: its attempt to concentrate against the Americans in no way deflected the latter from continuing their advance along the northern coast of New Guinea by landings on Wakde and in the Arare–Toem area on 17 May and on Biak on 27 May. The extent of Japanese problems at this stage of proceedings was illustrated by the fact that on 17 May an Anglo-American carrier force, operating from Ceylon, raided Soerabaja; for the first time American bombers raided western New Guinea from Australia and Biak from Nadzab; and American surface forces struck at Japanese garrisons in the Marshalls. With Marcus and Wake also taken under attack by American carrier forces in the following week, the Japanese navy by mid-May 1944 faced a series of threats to which it had to respond if it was to preserve the national defence zone and keep the Allies at arm's length from the southern resources area.

Despite the earlier decision to abandon a defence of western New Guinea based on Biak and Manokwari, the American landings on Biak drew that Japanese response. Biak was not the Palaus and thus could not present the Japanese with the battle they sought, but the carrier groups had completed the training of their air groups on 16 May and the *Combined Fleet*'s main strength was in the southern Philippines and in a position to intervene. The Japanese committed themselves to an attempt to force a battle at Biak and to support their garrison on the island, but while the garrison practised cannibalism and continued to resist until 20 August, the manner in which the *Combined Fleet* committed its forces at Biak was wholly at variance with the need to provoke 'a decisive battle' and indeed was a tacit admission that such an action could not be forced upon the Americans off western New Guinea: destroyers that were recalled when sighted by enemy aircraft and destroyers towing barges towards Biak were not the material of which fleet actions in the Pacific in mid-1944 were made. Not until 10 June did the Japanese commit a battle force to support operations off Biak, and by the time this force reached Batjan on the eleventh the Japanese High Command had been made aware of the irrelevance of its faltering Biak moves and its redeployment of some 170 aircraft to western New Guinea: on 11 June American carrier forces attacked Guam, Tinian and Saipan, thereby serving notice of where the main American effort was to be made and where the Japanese could seek their 'decisive battle' if that was their wish.

The battle that was subsequently fought in the Philippine Sea on 19 and 20 June did indeed prove decisive, if any battle other than the last is ever decisive. In reality it was one of the most comprehensive and complete victories won by a fleet in modern history, rivalling Trafalgar and Tsu-shima in its extent and one-sidedness. In the immediate aftermath of the battle, and indeed for many years afterwards, the American victory in the Philippine Sea was regarded by American naval and public opinion as incomplete became the greater part of the Japanese fleet escaped to fight again, and much criticism was directed against the decision whereby the carrier groups of TF58 were held in positions covering the transports and beachheads established on Saipan on 15 June rather than released to seek out Japanese forces until too late to mount sustained attacks on an enemy in flight. In reality, the only chance of the Americans suffering any measure of defeat lay in the Japanese somehow being able to work their way around American flanks and then getting amongst the transports and off the beachheads, and by preventing that possibility TF58 not only ensured itself against defeat but secured an overwhelming victory through its ability to concentrate its fighter squadrons in a defensive battle. Four massed attacks by Japanese carrier aircraft on 19 June cost the *1st Mobile Fleet* about 350 of the 450 aircraft with which it began operations, and only 35 aircraft were left to its carriers after the American strike on the twentieth that accounted for one carrier along with the two sunk by American submarines on the previous day. Moreover, on 19 June the American carriers had enough in hand to account for perhaps as many as 80 Japanese aircraft from the Marianas, and perhaps as many as 200 of the 500 shore-based aircraft that the Japanese had intended to bring into the battle were destroyed between 11 and 24 June as the Americans sealed off the southern Marianas from outside support with operations that extended as far north as Iwo and Chichi Jima in the Kazan Retto. Such were the losses incurred by Japanese carrier aviation in this battle that never again was the *Imperial Navy* able to re-form its air groups and offer battle with a balanced fleet. It was a measure of the extent of a defeat that brought the Americans to a position from which to menace both Honshu and the Philippines that after this battle the *Imperial Navy* chose to resort to its one remaining superiority over the Allies − a moral ascendancy that accepted death in order to fight − in a desperate attempt to stave off further defeats that could not be prevented by conventional means.

At the battle of the Philippine Sea TF58 deployed 15 carriers with 902 aircraft, seven battleships, 21 cruisers and 97 destroyers: the various groups tasked with putting four divisions ashore on different islands in the southern Marianas included in their number seven battleships, 11 escort carriers, 11 cruisers and 83 destroyers and destroyer escorts, plus minor warships, auxiliaries and assault shipping. Impressive though this concentration of naval power was, it was nevertheless but one part of a double American amphibious effort in June 1944: the other was made in north-west Europe. This second effort, however, in its turn formed only one part of a much greater American effort in both the European and Mediterranean theatres that reflected not simply the extent of American power by mid-1944 but the complexities and inter-dependence of these various commitments, and of American relations with Britain, in the prosecution of the war against Germany.

The clearing of Tunisia in May 1943 brought the Western Allies their first irreversible strategic victory over the European Axis powers, and with it an intensification of policy differences that had beset Anglo-American deliberations for more than a year. The American acceptance, or at least the acceptance by the American military, in mid-1942 of a North African commitment was reluctant because of its implications for the policy, agreed with the British in April 1942, for an invasion of north-west Europe in April 1943. As the British had noted in summer 1942, a North African commitment was incompatible with a cross-Channel assault in 1943, but in circumstances that demanded the use of American ground forces against Germany in 1942 the logic of the Allied situation in mid-1942 was that the American commitment had to be made in the only theatre where British ground forces were in contact with the enemy. By the time of the Casablanca conference this same logic decreed that once victorious in North Africa Allied armies would carry the war to the Axis powers, specifically into Sicily, yet in this decision was an ambiguity of military aim that was to plague Anglo-American deliberations and the conduct of future operations in Italy until July 1944.

At the heart of Anglo-American differences was an unwavering American insistence that the Mediterranean theatre in general and the Italian campaign in particular involved a secondary effort that had to be limited and subordinated to the effort that was to be made in north-west Europe: the renaming of this effort in 1943 as *Operation Overlord* was very deliberate on the Americans' part. To the American High Command, the Mediterranean commitment was acceptable only on the terms on which it had been initially proposed by the British, namely the drawing of the ring around the Axis powers, imposing on the latter a war of attrition, and subjecting Germany to a widening commitment that would weaken the *Wehrmacht* in the main theatres – the Eastern Front and, more crucially, in north-west Europe. Against this constancy of American purpose stood a British opportunism that emerged at several times during the Italian campaign, the British intention being to make the campaign into something that it was not and could not be – a campaign fought in a major theatre of operations. No amount of Allied success on peninsular Italy could raise the campaign from its secondary status, and only at the expense of *Operation Overlord* – and perhaps not even then – could Italy be used as a springboard for offensive operations that were both economical and capable of registering strategically significant results. To the American High Command, the British insistence that potentially decisive results were within Anglo-American grasp in southern Europe was at best an illusion, at worst a means whereby the British sought to avoid the one effort to which American resources – at least in theory – were directed: the defeat of the *Wehrmacht* in battle in north-west Europe.

Certain American suspicions of British motives and sincerity in the various arguments about the Mediterranean strategy were overstated, but in essence the American belief that the British sought a peripheral strategy was correct, hence the inability of the Americans and British to agree. Yet even when their views coincided, the idea that the war could be waged but not won in Italy left the Western allies with the problems of defining the aim to be pursued in the Italian campaign and of measuring success or failure in this theatre after July 1943. The Italian campaign certainly imposed a drain on German resources, most obviously by virtue of the fact that after May 1943 – indeed after November 1942, though to a lesser extent – Germany was obliged to assume three major commitments in the Mediterranean theatre where previously she had shouldered but two, each of minor proportions. Whether this drain on German resources was commensurate with the effort that had to be made in order to turn Italy into Germany's 'running ulcer' remains questionable, not least because of the host of unquantifiable considerations that surround virtually every aspect of the conduct of this campaign.

Between May and August 1943 the Italian campaign provided indirect support for the Soviet Union not by diverting German formations from the Eastern Front but in ensuring that 18 divisions that could otherwise have been sent to the Eastern Front had to be despatched to Italy and the Balkans to fill the gaps created by Italy's weakening: in May 1944, on the eve of *Operation Overlord* and the Soviet offensive in Belorussia against

Army Group Centre, eight German divisions, including three already earmarked for service on the Eastern Front, had to be sent to Italy to help prevent the collapse of *Army Group C*. At its peak in 1943, however, the Italian campaign involved 21 Allied divisions (25 in the following year) and throughout 1943 the Mediterranean campaign served as a brake on the concentration of American air power in Britain for the strategic bombing offensive against Germany.

This very considerable investment in the Italian campaign was nevertheless offset in certain ways: unless employed in Italy the ground forces could not have been committed elsewhere; compensation of a kind was secured by possession of air bases in southern Italy for operations over the Balkans and southern Germany; and in any event numerical weakness was but one and not the major problem facing the American bombing offensive before November 1943. Moreover, the Allied effort in Italy imposed upon Germany defensive commitments that extended beyond Italy itself into neighbouring areas of interest, namely southern France and Yugoslavia, Albania and Greece. By summer 1944 no fewer than 55 German divisions were deployed in Italy and these four theatres, though it should be noted that not all the German military effort in these countries was directed to meeting the threat posed by an Allied invasion, and at least in the case of northern Italy and southern France defensive commitments could have been imposed on the Germans at less cost to the Allies simply by the occupation of Sardinia and Corsica. Even the obvious Allied success of this campaign, the defeat of Italy, was of dubious value: the political and psychological benefits of a victory over a major Axis power were dubious and more than counter-balanced by administrative responsibilities that by 1944 involved more shipping being used to meet Italian civilian needs than was available to South-West Pacific Command for the offensive that took it to the Philippines. At best, it might be concluded that while the carrying of the war first to Sicily and then to the Italian mainland by the Western allies was both inevitable and justified for want of an alternative, the campaign south of the Alps after July 1943 served as a distraction to Germany and the Western allies alike, though this was a distraction that the Allies, because of their superior resources, could tolerate more easily than Germany.

Perhaps the ambiguity that surrounded the Italian campaign is best summarised by the fact that when Allied forces landed on Sicily on 10 July neither the Allies nor Germany had resolved their future course of action. Allied planning provided alternative means of proceeding with the Mediterranean campaign after the conquest of Sicily, either by the occupation of Sardinia and Corsica or by a move against the Italian mainland, and it was not until 26 July that the invasion of peninsular Italy was authorised. For a German High Command that had to consider its strategic options against a background of Italy's weakening and uncertain intentions, Italy possessed no intrinsic value that made her defence mandatory though it was in Germany's obvious interest that Allied armies be kept as far as possible from Germany's southern borders. Because of its mineral resources and access to Turkish chrome, the Balkans possessed a significance to Germany that Italy lacked. Nevertheless Italy was important to Germany in terms of the Balkans because, of her 80 divisions in June 1943, 31 were in Yugoslavia, Albania and Greece and were vital in holding down the only part of occupied Europe – other than behind the Eastern Front – where armed resistance to the Axis was open and significant. As the German High Command viewed the situation in summer 1943 it was aware that an Allied invasion of the Balkans would present a potentially greater danger than a landing in Italy for three reasons: its impact on Germany's Balkan allies; the long-term possibility of a juncture with Soviet forces; and the enforced commitment of the *Wehrmacht* in a theatre poorly served by long and vulnerable lines of communication.

The retention of Italy was thus very important to Germany in summer 1943, by her own choice if possible but as a battleground if necessary. As early as May 1943 plans were drawn up for the forcible occupation of Italy if she showed signs of trying to leave the war, and the presence of German forces in Italy was Hitler's security against Italian behaviour. The German ability to move 14 divisions into Italy despite Italian objections after May 1943 denied the Allies quick and significant returns after September, but it was not until the autumn that Hitler resolved the question of whether the main German effort in Italy was to be made south of Rome. In military terms Germany's interests were best served by abandoning southern and central Italy, thereby minimising the danger of Allied landings and leaving the Allies with the responsibility of feeding millions of Italians who could contribute little to their war effort while Germany retained the industrialised north, which accounted for 13 per cent of all German output in the last 18 months of the war. Moreover, evacuation of the south would lessen the demands upon German logistical and administrative services, but in the event Hitler's aversion to any voluntary ceding of ground decided German policy once his forces unexpectedly demonstrated that southern Italy could be held. Throughout the summer of 1943 Hitler was prepared to wait upon events in Italy that could but unfold slowly and which were in any event small change to Germany. The campaign in Sicily was of little account to Hitler compared with Kursk and to the need, after this invasion and Mussolini's fall on 25 July, to ensure the security of the Balkans and the continuing solidarity, if not of Italy's new rulers, then Germany's other allies. In this context the German ability to conduct a successful rearguard defence of Sicily despite the collapse of Italian resistance, and then the inevitable delays before the Allies could move against the Italian mainland, provided immediate respite at a time when the German cause throughout the Mediterranean theatre was at its most vulnerable. Thereafter, the German ability first to disarm the Italian army and then to hold Allied armies south of Rome provided the rationale for the German defensive policy in Italy, though the very success of the *Wehrmacht* in holding the Allies on the Winter Line between October 1943 and April 1944 ultimately involved manpower and material losses that undermined that rationale and brought the German armies in southern Italy within measurable distance of total defeat in June 1944.

The military chronology of the Italian campaign between July 1943 and June 1944 divides into four natural parts: the campaign on Sicily; the Allied landings in southern Italy in September that ultimately carried the 5th American and 8th British Armies to the stalemate on the Winter Line by the end of November; the landing at Anzio in January 1944; and *Operation Diadem* in May 1944. The thread running through the campaign is provided by the argument between the Americans and British on the question of future operations in the Mediterranean theatre and their relationship to *Operation Overlord.*

The campaign in Sicily was overshadowed by Mussolini's fall, but was militarily notable for the fact that the invasion of 10 July involved a concentrated landing on either side of Cape Passero by no fewer than seven Allied divisions, more than were put ashore in Normandy on the morning of 6 June 1944: thereafter two German divisions, reinforced by three more during the campaign, fought a defensive battle and then withdrew intact across the Straits of Messina despite Allied air superiority. Both the German denial of Sicily to Allied armies that numbered between eight and 12 divisions for 38 days and the Allied conquest of an island well suited to protracted defence in some five weeks were creditable achievements, but by the time that the 7th US Army took Messina Allied plans for a triple invasion of southern Italy were well advanced though bound by the American injunction that these and subsequent operations were not to be supported by formations and resources not already available and that in November seven Allied divisions were to be withdrawn to Britain in readiness for *Operation*

The Campaign in Italy, 1943 - 45

Overlord. As finalised and executed, the invasion of southern Italy involved landings in Calabria by two British divisions on 3 September and on the ninth by one British division at Taranto and by one American and two British divisions at Salerno, just to the south of Naples and at the limit of cover provided by fighters based in Sicily. These various landings were preceded by a sustained interdiction campaign, but the inherently unsound nature of the landing plan on account of its dispersal of force between three widely separated objectives was counter-balanced by the fact that after difficult negotiations Italy surrendered secretly on 3 September and promised to support the Allied landings. In the event this intention partially miscarried. The presence of German forces near Rome caused the Badoglio government to go back on a plan for the

345

American 82nd Airborne Division to land in Rome and, with the support of five Italian divisions around the capital, to secure positions to block further German movement into southern Italy and to cut the lines of communication of the two German armoured corps already south of Rome. Moreover, the arrangement between the Italians and the Allies could not get round the fact that the Gulf of Salerno was one of the very few places south of Naples where a major landing could be attempted, and two divisions from *XIV Panzer Corps* were in positions to contest the 5th US Army's landing as a result of their involvement in the disarming of formations of the Italian *7th Army* during the night of 8–9 September.

The nine-day battle that was fought around Salerno provided the *Wehrmacht* with what proved to be its best opportunity of inflicting a major defeat upon the Western allies in Italy, and one that would have been doubly significant in terms of its being won at the start of the campaign and at the expense of an assault landing force. The crisis of the battle developed on 13 September when the *16th Panzer Division* fought its way to within two miles of the sea along the boundary of X British and VI US Corps, but this was only one of the attacks mounted by the German *10th Army* as it brought six divisions, three of which were armoured, against the Allied beachhead within five days of the landings compared to the four put ashore by the 5th Army. In achieving this concentration around Salerno, however, the *10th Army* partially contributed to its own defeat, or at the very least imposed upon itself an all but impossible timetable for securing victory. Because of the divisions it gathered around the beachhead, the *26th Panzer* and *29th Panzergrenadier Divisions* were withdrawn from Calabria and could not oppose the advance of the British 8th Army from the south. Supported by landings at Pizzo on 8 September, Catanzoro on the tenth, Scalea on the thirteenth and Sibari on the fifteenth, the 8th Army advanced some 300 miles in 17 days to link up with the 5th Army around Vallo on 16 September, but in fact the *10th Army* had accepted defeat in front of Salerno on the previous day as a result of its inability to press its attacks in the face of overwhelming naval and air support given to the Allied divisions in the beachhead. On 14 and 15 September alone some 3,400 sorties were flown by strategic and tactical air forces in support of the beachhead, and on the fifteenth, when two battleships joined the support forces, the *10th Army* assumed the defensive. On the following day it was ordered to begin a phased withdrawal intended to hold the Allies south of the Volturno for another month in order to provide time for the preparation of defences in the Winter Line.

The German decision to accept defeat at Salerno, to cede Naples and to withdraw to the Winter Line served to draw the Western allies into the very situation that the American High Command feared: the prospect presented by the capture of Rome generated a political and theatre demand inversely related to progress on the ground. Thus while the 5th Army reached the Volturno on 5 October and the 8th Army the Sangro three days later, the 15th Army Group's two armies were drawn into a series of inconclusive battles on the Winter Line after 13 October with the result that the question of strategic priorities in the Mediterranean theatre assumed two separate dimensions: whether or not the transfer of shipping from the Mediterranean should be delayed in order to allow for an amphibious assault aimed at breaking the stalemate on the Winter Line, and whether the Italian campaign or *Operation Anvil*, the proposed landing in southern France, represented the effort best suited to support *Operation Overlord* in May 1944. The withdrawal of divisions from Italy in preparation for *Operation Overlord* nevertheless proceeded as planned.

Despite certain American reservations, the first issue was resolved at the Cairo conference in December 1943 because the Allied operational timetable for 1944 allowed the retention of assault shipping in the Mediterranean for a landing at Anzio – *Operation Shingle* – in January 1944, the main political complication arising from this decision being that *Operation Shingle* could only proceed if *Operation Buccaneer*, the assault on the Andaman Islands, was cancelled. The latter, however, had been promised the Chinese by Roosevelt as the *quid pro quo* for their participation in the proposed campaign in Upper Burma, and this operation's cancellation provided the pretext for Chiang Kai-shek to go back on his part of the agreement and to demand greater military and financial aid for his regime. The military complication that arose from this decision stemmed from the fact that *Operation Shingle* miscarried, and in the process both increased the commitment that it was to have reduced and jeopardised *Operation Anvil*: ironically, in the process it also provided 15th Army Group with what was arguably a victory second in significance only to the one that was to be secured in May 1944.

The Allied plan to break the *10th Army* on the shortest defence line available to the *Wehrmacht* in Italy involved a series of frontal attacks by the various Allied corps of the 5th Army that were intended to force *Army Group C* to commit its reserves to the defence of the Winter Line, and with the enemy thus committed an Anglo-American force, constituted as VI US Corps, was to be put ashore at Anzio and thence across German lines of communication south of Rome. The Allied hope was that at the very least *XIV Panzer Corps* might be encircled and destroyed and that the *10th Army* be pushed back to the Pisa–Rimini line. The landing at Anzio on 22 January was timed correctly, but Allied intentions foundered because VI US Corps, with only two infantry divisions in its original landing force, lacked the means to secure its own beachhead and to cut German lines of communications simultaneously. Its commitment to its own defensive requirements led quickly to it being contained by German formations hastily assembled for that purpose, and thereafter there was a reversal of roles between the two sides and their respective efforts. In an attempt to buy time for no fewer than 10 divisions of the *14th Army* to crush the Anzio beachhead and thereby inflict upon the Allies a defeat that Hitler hoped would have profound psychological effects as both sides prepared for the Allied invasion of France, the *10th Army* was committed to holding the Allies on the Winter Line: the Allies were forced to intensify their attacks on the Winter Line in an attempt to breach German defences and relieve the beleaguered VI US Corps. The result was a deadlock on both fronts but one that worked to the long-term advantage of the Allies. At Anzio the offensive power of eight German divisions was broken in the course of the *14th Army*'s offensives of 15–20 February and 28 February–4 March by the concentrated firepower of four and a half Allied divisions and Allied naval and air forces: on the Winter Line the Allied attacks of January and mid-February, followed by the offensive of mid-March, inflicted on German manpower reserves an attrition that the *10th Army* could not afford without reinforcement, which was not available despite six divisions having been sent into northern Italy when the *14th Army* moved south to Anzio. As winter gave way to spring, despite its success in holding 15th Army Group on the Winter Line for some five months *Army Group C* lacked the means to continue to offer resistance to the attack that the Allies were to mount in May 1944 in support of *Operation Overlord*. Moreover, by insisting on a policy of rigid linear defence at the forward point of contact, Hitler, who saw only the success and not the cost of holding the Winter Line, imposed upon *Army Group C* a strategy that denied it any measure of tactical initiative and condemned it to defeat in the summer.

The Allied attack of May 1944 was to represent the peak of the Allied effort and achievement in Italy, but it was one mounted only after confused exchanges within the Allied High Command on the question of the competing claims of *Operation Anvil* and the Italian campaign to be assigned the supporting role for *Operation Overlord*. Such was the nature of Anglo-American exchanges at various conferences in 1943 that in February 1944, when this question presented itself for an answer, the American High Command delegated its authority to General Eisenhower – late supreme Allied commander in the Mediterranean theatre but now commander of *Operation Overlord* – to settle the ordering of strategic priorities in the Mediterranean in negotiations with the British High Command. This extraordinary and unprecedented action resulted in Eisenhower postponing a final decision until 20 March, the last date by which shipping could leave the Mediterranean in time for *Operation Overlord*. Eisenhower proposed that in the meantime the Mediterranean command should prepare plans for operations that could complement *Overlord*, *Operation Anvil* being assigned first priority, and that 15th Army Group should continue operations intended to break German resistance on the Winter Line. At the same time, however, Eisenhower insisted that *Anvil* should not proceed at the expense of *Overlord*, and in noting that the latter was under-invested at this time he recognised that the Italian campaign might emerge as the only possible complement to *Overlord*. In effect, these interim proposals gave 15th Army Group four weeks in which to secure the victory that had eluded it over the previous three months but which was nevertheless essential if *Anvil* was to proceed beyond the planning stage: if, however, 15th Army Group again failed then the balance of probability pointed to the cancellation of *Anvil* and the armies in Italy assuming the supporting role for *Overlord* – which, by 22 February when Eisenhower made his proposals, was exactly the role that 15th Army Group sought.

Under the terms of the planning ordered by Eisenhower, 15th Army Group set down a programme for the reorganisation of its armies and the reinforcement of the 5th Army for an offensive that was to begin three weeks before *Overlord* but after various feints had tied down German forces in southern France and northern Italy. The aim of this offensive was to exert the greatest possible pressure upon *Army Group C* in the days immediately before *Overlord* and to force the German High Command to commit additional divisions to the Italian theatre, the prospect of breaking German resistance on the Winter Line and an advance to the Pisa–Rimini line being a secondary, though not unwelcome, consideration. The twin corollaries of this proposed offensive, *Operation Diadem*, were obvious: the reinforcement of 15th Army Group in readiness for *Operation Diadem* could only be undertaken at the expense of preparations for *Anvil*, and with the six divisions needed for the latter requiring two months between withdrawal from a successful *Diadem* and commitment to *Anvil* the earliest possible date for this – given the May schedule for *Overlord* – was mid-July. On 21 March, with 15th Army Group having predictably failed to breach the Winter Line, Eisenhower accepted the logic of these arguments and proposed the cancellation of *Anvil* and the authorisation of *Diadem*. Three days later the American chiefs of staff rejected this proposal and insisted on the execution of *Anvil*, if need be in July but if the British agreed to adhere to the May schedule then with assault shipping already assigned to the Pacific.

While this repudiation of Eisenhower was as extraordinary as his original terms of reference, scarcely less so was the American High Command's insistence on landings in southern France that were shorn of their original military value if they did not coincide with *Overlord*. Moreover, the revelation that the resources needed to execute the full terms of the Germany-first strategy had been earmarked for the Pacific but could be made available on terms was a case, depending on perspective, either of American determination to spare no effort in effecting a Germany-first strategy or an indication that the American High Command's much proclaimed adherence to this strategy was somewhat less than constant. Certainly until the end of 1943 more American servicemen were committed to the war against Japan than were sent to the European and Mediterranean theatres: the army's balance of 15:13 divisions and 76:43 air groups in favour of the war against Germany was more than counter-balanced by the Pacific's claim on the greater part of the strength of the navy and marine corps. In effect, between July 1942 and November 1943 the United States implemented a Pacific-first strategy that was more important than British objections in ending the prospects of a cross-Channel invasion either of these years, but in fact by November 1943 the greater part of American military strength was indeed earmarked for the European war but could not be committed until battle was joined in north-west Europe. Yet the very fact that in March 1944 the American High Command tried to bargain European strategy against Pacific resources at the very least suggests an opportunism that Washington found so objectionable when presented in cables from London. Given the context of the American decision of 24 March – a series of abrasive Anglo-American exchanges on a list of minor issues – the logic behind the American's tirelessness in their *Anvil* demands would appear to have been political: that it was an operation demanded by the American High Command precisely because it was one to which the British High Command had agreed.

Thus evolved the final form of Anglo-American strategic policy for the European war in 1944: an offensive on the Winter Line and a landing in southern France on either side of *Operation Overlord*. With slippage as the latter was strengthened and 15th Army Group took longer than expected to prepare for its offensive, the Allied operational timetable scheduled *Operation Diadem* for May, *Operation Overlord* for June and *Operation Anvil* for August. The overall result of this programme was to ensure that after June the Italian campaign could not develop beyond its existing secondary status: the stripping of six divisions from 15th Army Group's order of battle for *Anvil* drained the command of the formations needed to carry an offensive beyond the Pisa–Rimini line and spelt an end to British illusions of a landing in Istria and an advance on Vienna. Though rationalised in post-war British accounts of proceedings as an offensive that would have had immense political repercussions for central Europe in the post-war era, the Vienna option was never a practical proposition. On 15th Army Group's own calculations 24 divisions would be needed for such an operation, more than both 15th Army Group's strength in Italy and the British army's entire strength, at least in terms of numbered divisions. What this programme did not ensure, however, was that 15th Army Group was prevented from winning a decisive victory in Italy in mid-year. Contrary to some claims that *Anvil* robbed 15th Army Group of the divisions it needed in June and July to complete the destruction of the *10th* and *14th Armies* after the French Expeditionary Corps breached German defences in the Aurunci Mountains between 17 and 22 May, 15th Army Group failed to annihilate these two German armies primarily because the 5th Army, in its desire to secure Rome with American formations ahead of the British, directed VI US Corps northwards on the direct route to Rome rather than eastwards across the German line of withdrawal from the Winter Line. Moreover, it was not until 7 June, two days after the fall of Rome, that 15th Army Group issued orders for the conduct of operations north of the capital.

Operation Diadem, which opened on 11 May, was successful on three counts: it resulted in the destruction of four German divisions and the mauling of another three; it forced the German High Command to commit the equivalent of 11 divisions to *Army Group C* in order to stabilise the situation in Italy after the Winter Line was lost; and it ultimately brought the Allied armies to the Pisa–Rimini line. But the failure of *Operation Diadem* was the result of errors of command in the exploitation phase rather than in the removal of formations for a very successful offensive in another theatre. The fact of the matter was that against a skilled enemy operating in mountainous terrain where Allied material superiority could not always be used to full effect, 15th Army Group even with its full strength in May and June 1944 could not fight and win a battle of encirclement and annihilation on the one occasion when such an opportunity presented itself. Thereafter its failure to breach the Gothic Line positions in the battles of the autumn left the Germans in control of northern Italy, yet paradoxically in this failure was confirmation of the validity of diametrically opposed American and

British views of the Italian campaign that had made the formation of Allied policy so difficult. Throughout the second half of 1944 the number of German divisions in Italy never fell below 26, and while four divisions were transferred to other fronts between January and April 1945 the latter month saw 23 German divisions in Italy to oppose the 17 of the Allies. But if the policy of drawing German forces into Italy and away from the main theatres of operations was vindicated, the fact remained that Italy remained a secondary theatre and one in which strategically significant results could not be and were not registered.

Various campaigns readily lend themselves to the interpretation that their outcome was determined before their start, and in the latter stages of the Second World War there was indeed an aspect of inevitability that attached itself to the Allied offensives that completed the defeat of the Axis powers. The campaign in north-west Europe after June 1944 does not stand apart from this phenomenom: Allied numerical superiority, the German confusion of command arrangements and doctrine, and an Allied initiative that ensured German dispersal at the time of greatest Allied weakness combine to point to the conclusion that the *Wehrmacht* in north-west Europe in 1944 was not unlike the French army in 1940 in that it was beaten before the first shots were fired. But if indeed the Allies operated with such advantages and the *Wehrmacht* under such handicaps that the outcome of this campaign was determined from the outset simply by military criteria, then the element of inevitability based upon relative orders of battle, deployment and command is tertiary to those other aspects of inevitability that provide the proper context of this campaign. In terms of warfare, the defeat of the *Wehrmacht* in France in summer 1944 was the result of the application of victorious sea power against a military power that had lost the initiative and what should have been its greatest advantage over its enemies, an ability to bring superior force to bear against a beachhead by virtue of lines of communication intrinsically superior to those of the Allies. Even more significantly, in terms of the decline of Europe, the invasion of June 1944 marked the emergence of the United States as the major power in western Europe, and discounting the various landings in Italy after July 1943 the American dimension to the Normandy landing represented the first invasion of Europe from the outside world for 590 years. In so many ways the product of American capacity as a continental power, the invasion of Normandy marked the end of the period of European supremacy in the world that had existed for four centuries and pointed to the reality that rather than being the centre of power Europe henceforth would be the object of the attention of those powers that would determine her fate.

Much has been written about *Operation Overlord*, though the name itself is widely, if wrongly, used with reference to the assault landings on the coast of Normandy on 6 June 1944. The codename *Overlord* was used for the planning of the whole of the campaign in north-west Europe, and the operation ended in May 1945 with the surrender of Germany. The assault landings of 6 June 1944 were part of *Operation Neptune*, which officially ended on 30 June and included the preliminary build-up of Allied forces in the Normandy beachhead as well as the landings of the sixth.

In its basic outline the *Neptune* assault plan was determined by considerations of suitable ports of assembly for warships, assault shipping and merchant convoys, of searoom for the invasion force, and of time of passage that precluded any invasion attempt being mounted in the Pas de Calais, which was never seriously considered as a landing area because of its lack of suitably graded beaches with access into the hinterland and because of the relative ease with which German forces could be moved into this part of France. Normandy, opposite the natural assembly ports of Southampton and Portsmouth and the concentration area south of the Isle of Wight, was thus the only part of the north French coast where an invasion could be attempted, and with the *Neptune* plan calling for the assault to be made one hour after low tide in order to keep assault shipping clear of the obstacles sited just below the high-water mark, the date and timing of the landings were dictated by three requirements: for a full moon to aid navigation in the approach to contact phase, for the first low tide of the day to be in hours of daylight in order to allow warships and aircraft to support the landing, and for a second low tide in hours of daylight on the day of the assault for the movement ashore of second-echelon formations. The plan of attack took the form of an assault across a five-division front with three airborne divisions committed to flank protection, the assault involving 2,470 landing ships and craft covered by 713 warships. The strategic air forces were to commit 2,293 bombers to attacks in the hours immediately before the landing, and the various Allied air forces flew another 10,585 sorties in support of the assault in the 24 hours of 6 June 1944.

Of the various factors that contributed to the success of Allied forces in establishing themselves ashore within a secure beachhead in June 1944 four were of particular importance. The Allied ability to isolate the beachhead was critical to the outcome of the campaign; this was the one

Normandy and the Anglo-American Advance to the Seine, June - August 1944

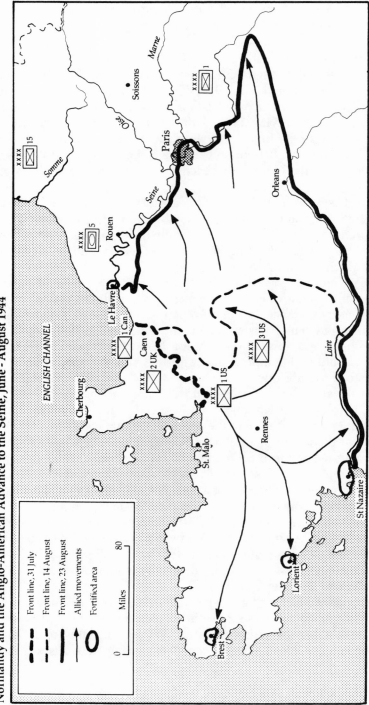

aspect of the conduct of the battle that reversed the natural balance of advantage between maritime and overland lines of communication. In the three months before the invasion Allied air forces set about the systematic destruction of the Belgian and French communications systems with the result that by 5 June 1944 all but two bridges over the Seine below Paris had been destroyed, as had been 27 per cent of locomotive servicing facilities, 13 per cent of the locomotives and 8 per cent of the rolling stock of the Belgian and French railroad systems. By the time of the invasion 75 per cent of the railroad system within 150 miles of the assault beaches had been rendered unserviceable. In the initial phase of the campaign, when the act of landing theoretically allowed the German High Command to strip secondary sectors in order to concentrate against a beachhead restricted in both frontage and depth, this destruction of the German capacity to move forces quickly and intact into Normandy ensured that the *Wehrmacht* did not win the build-up race. The difficulties encountered by *II SS Panzer Corps* in moving into Normandy from Metz in the second half of June is often cited as evidence of the effectiveness of an air offensive that cost the Allies more casualties than were sustained during the landings on 6 June, and most certainly the eight days needed by *Kampfgruppe Heintz* to cover 140 miles to the front was proof of the restriction placed on German movement by Allied bombing and command of the air. The Allied interdiction campaign – which was not directed against the Loire bridges until the invasion itself – could not prevent the movement of 16 German divisions into Normandy and the increase in the number of German divisions in Normandy from 9 to 22 in the course of June, but in that same time 929,000 Allied soldiers – 26 full-strength divisions – were landed in France, and other than the problems created by the great storm of 19–21 June these Allied formations, unlike their German counterparts, operated on an assured line of communication with proper and timely resupply and reinforcement.

The Allied interdiction campaign was only one factor in the German failure to win the race to concentrate forces in Normandy. The Allied supply arrangements ensured the landing in Normandy of 2,052,299 men, 438,471 vehicles and 3,098,259 tons of supplies in the first 87 days after the landing. This logistical achievement was remarkable for the fact that the vast majority of the manpower and material put ashore moved across open beaches or through artificial harbours because no major port was open to the Allies until November, despite the capture of Cherbourg on 29 June and of Le Havre on 12 September. The first resupply convoys alone totalled 15 transports, 74 ocean-going merchantmen and 200 coasters, and *Overlord* planning provided for the supply of fuel by underwater pipelines from Britain. The scale of Allied logistical support was impressive but so, too, were the demands of Allied armies fundamentally different from those that opposed them. Whereas in 1944 about 85 per cent of all German divisions were dependent upon horse-drawn transport, Allied formations in Normandy were wholly motorised, a fact with obvious implications not simply for Allied supply arrangements but for the outcome of a mobile battle. This second consideration raises issues relating to the conduct of the battle in France in 1944 not commented upon by those obsessed with the pernicious myth of German military excellence, of which the defence of Normandy is held to be an example. In Normandy the *Wehrmacht* did indeed display formidable powers of resistance but under a specific set of circumstances – in a static battle on ground of its own choosing in terrain well suited to the defence, against a beachhead with few lines of advance into the interior, and against Allied armies unable to develop their full offensive power until the second half of July. The *Wehrmacht* was no more effective in fighting a mobile battle than had been the French army in 1940, and its relative success in the static conditions of June and early July around the Normandy beachhead owed much to the fact that by this stage of the war the defence had acquired a power and effectiveness denied it at earlier stages of the conflict. Overwhelming material concentration alone provided the means of overcoming a defence prepared in depth and which could not be outflanked, and it was by means of such a concentration that the 1st US Army broke through German defensive positions around St Lô at the end of July. In assessing performance in Normandy the proper context of those claims of German military proficiency is not to be found in selective consideration of one single part of the campaign but by a comparison of the 1940 and 1944 campaigns. In six and a half weeks in 1940 the *Wehrmacht* overran the Low Countries and perhaps three-fifths of France in a campaign that was developed from a secure base across a land frontier some 500 miles in length and over a largely intact communications network. In three months in 1944 Allied armies liberated most of France, Belgium, Luxembourg and the southern Netherlands and entered Germany in the course of a campaign mounted from a base that could not be stocked beforehand and which had a restricted frontage of some 70 miles, the campaign itself being prosecuted across a shattered communications network and costing the *Wehrmacht* about 500,000 casualties. Such was the reality, not the myth, of this campaign.

But while the tactical defence of Normandy by the *Wehrmacht* in June and July proved very effective, the strategic conduct of the battle by Hitler was another matter, and herein lay the third factor of particular significance in the outcome of this campaign: the inability of the *Wehrmacht* to join battle in Normandy with its full strength because of the effectiveness of Allied deception. The remarkable feature of this deception was not the strategic and tactical surprise registered by the Allies on 6 June 1944 but that measures intended to convince the German High Command that the main invasion effort would be made in the Pas de Calais continued to be effective into August. Indeed the war ended with the German High Command convinced that the Allies had intended to attack the Pas de Calais but had switched their point of attack as a result of the unexpected success achieved in Normandy by an attack that had been a feint. For a German High Command that before June 1944 had to consider how France and the Low Countries were to be defended with some 62 divisions against enemies with the choice of where and when to mount their assault, a preoccupation with the Pas de Calais was natural because an Allied landing and advance in this area would immediately expose western Germany, and the critically important Ruhr industries, to direct attack, yet the requirements of the defence and occupation of Brittany, the Cotentin peninsula and Normandy meant that on 6 June 17 German divisions were west of the Seine compared with the 15 in north-east France. This division of German forces reflected an indecision within a German High Command that recognised that north of the Loire only Normandy and the Pas de Calais offered themselves as possible landing areas, but while all three German services at various times came separately to the conclusion that the Allied effort would be made in Normandy for the very reasons that determined the Allied course of action, Allied intelligence trapped the German High Command with a double deception that indicated landings in Norway and the Pas de Calais. When the Norway deception was dropped the German High Command concluded, as Allied intelligence had anticipated, that two simultaneous and contradictory deceptions could not have been perpetrated and that therefore the Pas de Calais effort was genuine and was not the cover for an invasion of Normandy.

On the morning of the Normandy landings, however, the complete order of battle of the invasion force and the warning that the landings were a feint designed to draw the *15th Army* beyond the Seine was fed by Allied intelligence to its opposite number by the latter's most trusted (double) agent in Britain, and this same compromised source continued to send a series of reports that convinced the German High Command not to commit the bulk of the *15th Army* to the fighting in Normandy.

Without these divisions the formations in and sent to Normandy found themselves forced to deploy defensively without being able to keep armour intact and concentrated for the counter-attack, and by the time that defences in north-east France were thinned in order to release formations for Normandy the battle had been lost.

The German intelligence failure to discern Anglo-American intentions – which ran parallel to contemporaneous intelligence failures on the Eastern Front – owed much to institutionalised weaknesses, namely Hitler's practice of 'situating the appreciation' and enforcing his views upon subordinates plus the various inter-service rivalries and divisions that plagued the German military establishment. In terms of the campaign in France in 1944, however, this German intelligence failure was very much part of that institutionalised weakness which affected the strategic direction of both the war and this campaign by the German High Command and which embraced the doctrine, command and organisation of German forces: in their turn these flaws were to be compounded by a succession of all but impossible dilemmas that arose during the Normandy campaign with each German failure – how to contain the Allied beachhead without committing the armour needed for the counter-attack; whether to concentrate against the British or the Americans; whether to cede or try to hold the Cotentin; whether to continue to fight a holding action or to withdraw to a shorter and more easily defended line. German doctrinal problems revolved around the question of whether an invasion should be met on the beaches or inland, it being accepted that the much-vaunted Atlantic Wall could do no more than deny an Allied landing immediate and easy access to certain ports. The orthodox military solution to fight the battle inland – beyond the range of naval gunfire that had been so important at Salerno and Anzio – after Allied intentions had become clear and German concentrations were complete was beset by the problems of divining those intentions and of operating in open country under conditions of Allied air superiority, but to meet an invasion force on the coast involved what was in effect the concentration of the armoured reserve in a tactical role where it could be overwhelmed at the very outset – as happened to German armour opposite the Sandomierz bridgehead at the start of the Vistula–Oder offensive six months later – or bypassed if initial deployment was in error.

The argument over doctrine was never resolved by a German High Command that could provide no answer to the initiative and superior firepower of the Western allies, and this lack of policy led to and was reflected by a hopelessly confused command structure of the *Wehrmacht* in the west. Overall, on 6 June 1944 there were 62 divisions in France and the Low Countries of which nine were armoured, one was mechanised, two were airborne, 13 were infantry, 33 were static and four were provided by the navy. Nominally all were under the command of *Oberbefehlshaber West*, but four divisions in the Netherlands were formed into a command administered directly by *OKW* while the remainder of the military divisions were divided between *Heeresgruppe B*, with the *7th* and *15th Armies* under command, *Armee Gruppe G*, with the *1st* and *19th Armies* under command, and *Panzergruppe West*. *Heeresgruppe B* was commanded by Rommel and was committed to meeting an invasion force on the beaches, but it had only three armoured divisions and of these only one was in Normandy. *Panzergruppe West*, with one mechanised and four armoured divisions scattered between Angers and Brussels, reflected in its deployment and lack of concentration the uncertainty caused by the lack of knowledge of Allied intentions, but these divisions were held for a battle in the interior. In its operational guise as *I SS Panzer Corps*, however, this formation was constituted as *OKW*'s reserve and its divisions could not be moved without direct orders from *OKW*, and while nominally subordinate to *OB West*, *Heeresgruppe B* had direct access to *OKW* and Hitler. To compound arrangements that left *OB West* without direct operational control of the bulk of the forces in its area of responsibility and without a theatre reserve, Rommel's tactical authority extended just six miles inland from the coast, but Rommel himself was tasked by Hitler for an inspector's role over the *1st* and *19th Armies* in the south and to take overall control wherever the Allies landed – which could have been on the Mediterranean coast if the Allied plan of campaign had arranged for *Operation Anvil* to serve as overture to the Normandy landings.

These various arrangements, as *OKW* itself admitted, involved 'some confusion and duplication', commodities that were further aggravated by the confusion and duplication inherent in the *Wehrmacht*'s structure. Even before the Allied invasion, *OB West*'s authority did not extend to the *Kriegsmarine*'s naval and coastal defence forces and to the *Luftwaffe*'s air formations. Of the 62 divisions in the west, 15 were under the administrative control of the *Kriegsmarine*, *Luftwaffe* and *Waffen SS* and all 14 non-army divisions were responsible to their own commands. The final elements of disorganisation in the German order of battle stemmed from the fact that in order to maintain the number of divisions, the German High Command in 1943 raised new divisions at the expense of raising reinforcement formations for existing divisions, but perversely made little attempt to reduce the supporting arms and services of burnt-out divisions even though the new divisions were often under-established as a result. At the same time the *Wehrmacht* opened its ranks to newly recruited prisoners-of-war, to non-German conscripts from annexed territories and to more of the *Volkdeutsch* in an attempt to ease Germany's increasingly acute manpower shortages. These various measures had two obvious effects. They accelerated the proliferation of divisional types within the *Wehrmacht* and with this process the variation of strength and effectiveness between formations. More seriously, they ensured that divisions lacked an effective reinforcement and support system once committed to battle, and in Normandy these weaknesses quickly became apparent: by mid-August the average strength of the 16 German divisions involved in the Falaise battle was about 5,000; between 6 June and 12 July just 6,000 reinforcements arrived at the front to take the place of the 47,000 casualties sustained by 25 June, and by 24 July the reinforcement figure had only reached five figures while battle casualties had risen to 113,000 excluding those lost at Cherbourg.

Such was the doctrinal and organisational state of the *Wehrmacht* in the west before and in the weeks immediately following the Allied invasion of Normandy, and for all the arguments and personality clashes within the Allied High Command that has made the writing of accounts of the Normandy campaign so hazardous there was nevertheless an essential unity of command and purpose that the *Wehrmacht* lacked. Yet at a perspective of nearly 50 years it is pertinent to question whether or not the Anglo-American armies that landed in Normandy possessed a coherent offensive doctrine. What they most certainly did have was a comprehensive plan for an amphibious assault, but the plan for the expansion of the beachhead and the build-up of American armoured forces in its western sector was arguably flawed in several respects, not least because of the correct American insistence before the invasion that British ideas of securing Caen on the day of the assault were unrealistic.

The one episode of the Normandy campaign that raises most questions about Allied offensive doctrine, however, is the Falaise battle. Aspects of command in this battle, on the part of American and British commanders alike, were very obviously suspect, yet what is equally obvious is that on the Allied side there was no doctrinal base for the conduct of a battle of encirclement and annihilation. A comparison with a contemporaneous battle of encirclement and annihilation – of the *German 6th* and *Romanian 3rd Armies* (again) during the Iasi–Kishinev offensive – reveals the extent of a failure that was all the more marked because of the Allied refusal to commit, at the height of the Falaise battle, the airborne forces that could have completed the process of encirclement. The very great strength of the Allied armies in Normandy lay in their ability to win a battle of attrition, but for all the speed of the Allied breakout across France in August the fact that these advances were directed along divergent rather than convergent axes indicate a doctrine geared to a general repulse rather than the encirclement and annihilation of a defeated enemy.

An examination of the Allied conduct of the battle for France in terms of doctrine drains much of the sterile argument about individual commanders from the account of proceedings, but it is an interpretation of events paradoxically strengthened by the two counter-arguments most easily brought against it. An assertion that any allegation of doctrinal weakness fails to account for the fact that some 40 German divisions were destroyed in the course of the battle for France leaves itself exposed to the obvious rebuttal, but the argument that *Operation Market Garden* – the attempt to force the Rhine by XXX British Corps along a line of advance secured for it by airborne forces – represents the attempt to use the dimensions of time and depth to full effect in an offensive operation raises more difficult issues. In the terms of reference generally applied to this September effort, *Operation Market Garden* is set in one of three contexts: the personality setting in that Eisenhower deferred to a self-willed subordinate; the inter-alliance perspective that saw an American supreme commander endorse a British-sponsored plan of campaign at American expense; and, more relevantly, the broad front versus narrow front controversy. This is defined in terms of Eisenhower's preference for an advance to the Rhine across the whole of the front but his support for an operation conceived as the means of encircling the Ruhr and striking into the heart of Germany with a single concentrated thrust, at a time when faltering supplies would otherwise impose a halt upon the Allied campaign. This line of argument is superficially convincing: the Allied armies could not close the Rhine along its length, and if the Rhine was to be crossed and the offensive carried deep into Germany then a concentration of resources on a single sector was unavoidable.

But the real questions to emerge from *Operation Market Garden* are why the Eindhoven–Nijmegen–Arnhem line of advance should have been adopted when this axis leads away from the Ruhr and to nothing more than the Ijsselmeer and why priority should have been given to the 2nd British Army when the 1st US Army was both nearer the Ruhr and faced by a better communications network than its British neighbour. The one very odd fact about the whole *Market Garden* effort is that an offensive aimed at the encirclement of the Ruhr involved logistical demands and distances that were within Allied resources but for this

The German Defeat in the West, August - September 1944

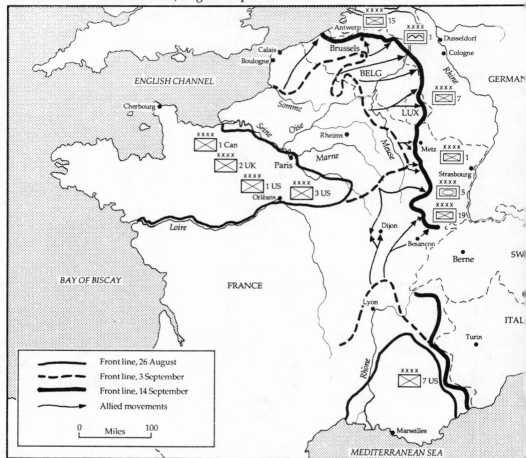

operation. As at least one historian has noted, Düsseldorf was no further from the Normandy beachhead than the distance travelled by the most distant American advance into eastern France by mid-September, and if in logistical terms the Ruhr was within the reach of armies breaking clear of the beachhead then the fact that the Ruhr was not encircled was primarily the result of Allied armies advancing in other directions. Moreover, the real significance of *Operation Market Garden* was that it

362

forestalled any attempt to secure the Ruhr by the one army best placed to take it. Thus by the least exacting standard, the concept of *Operation Market Garden* would seem to support the view that at no stage during the breakout from Normandy did the Allied High Command have a settled doctrine – in terms either of ensuring annihilation in the field or of advancing against geographical objectives of overwhelming strategic importance – to serve as the framework for the conduct of the *Overlord* campaign.

The failure of *Operation Market Garden* in the last week of September in effect spelt an end to strategic operations by Anglo-American armies until March 1945: the autumn and winter were to pass with a series of limited local attacks that ultimately cleared the whole of eastern France and the Rhineland, the German counter-offensive in the Ardennes in December notwithstanding. In strategic terms, therefore, October 1944 – the month when, according to Anglo-American 1943 planning, the European war was to end – marked the start of a lull in north-west Europe, which coincided with a not dissimilar lull on the Eastern Front. Here, however, there was a difference in that after October 1944 the Soviet army undertook a series of offensives in secondary sectors, the efforts on the two main axes of advance – into Poland and into the Balkans – having exhausted themselves by the autumn. These various Soviet offensives in 1944 were of obvious significance for the map of post-war Europe, but no less significant was a military aspect seldom afforded due consideration in Western histories. In 1944 the Soviet army completed 14 major encirclements of Axis forces and – according to Soviet figures – in the process completely destroyed 96 divisions and 34 brigades. In the *Bagration* and Iasi–Kishinev offensives the Soviet army destroyed 28 divisions in 12 days and 22 divisions in 11 days respectively,* and in these and other related facts – advances of 360 miles in the course of the *Bagration* offensive and of 500 miles during the year, plus the Soviet capacity to conduct operations on two major axes of advance – lay evidence of a transformation of the struggle on the Eastern Front of massive proportions and significance in 1944.

Western understanding of the 1944 campaign on the Eastern Front has been fashioned by four phenomena: an ethnocentric consideration of history that naturally focused its attention on the Anglo-American efforts of that year; the political aspects of a campaign that saw Soviet forces carry the war into non-Soviet territories for the first time; the post-war

---

*German accounts generally give losses of 25 and 18 divisions in the campaigns, totals which, with non-German losses, roughly bear out Soviet claims.

confrontation that encouraged the belittling of the achievements of erstwhile allies; and, perhaps most importantly, the passing into Western history, as 'the authorised version', an interpretation of events primarily based upon the highly selective accounts of defeated German generals only too anxious to distance themselves from a discredited regime and from responsibility for German military failure. In essence these accounts portrayed Germany's defeat in terms of Hitler's folly and overwhelming Soviet manpower and material superiority to which there was no effective response, a very convenient interpretation that left intact claims of professional competence at the tactical level and in matters of technique. For its part Soviet history, with its exclusive claims and jarring style, provided no redress to accounts that invariably stressed the German ability to outfight the Soviets at the tactical level, Soviet attacks being portrayed as frontal, unimaginative and hideously expensive. Such was the acceptance of an interpretation of events that was politically and militarily attractive to Western societies that even in the mid-Sixties there appeared what purported to be accounts of the Nazi–Soviet conflict which were in reality little more than uncritical and admiring summaries of what various German generals wrote about themselves. Some two decades later, the memoirs of defeated German generals do not provide answers to the questions that present themselves as crucial to an understanding of events on the Eastern Front.

The claims òf tactical ccmpetence count for little against the fact that German armies were consistently outfought at the strategic and oper-ational levels: an advance of 360 miles by armoured and mechanised forces could not be registered by technically incompetent forces wedded to a doctrine based on brute force and ignorance; an interpretation of defeat based upon overwhelming Soviet numerical advantage sits uneasily alongside the reality that before September 1944 Soviet manpower superiority on the front as a whole was not very marked, perhaps in the region of 1.6:1 over all Axis forces. The apparent contradiction between an interpretation of events based mainly on German accounts and the reality of massive Soviet success in 1944 can be resolved by recognising that the latter was the product of brute force – provided on a massive scale as the Soviets freely admit – allied to very considerable skill, particularly at the strategic and operational levels. It was this that defeated German generals could not understand or would not acknowledge, yet it was most obviously demonstrated in such offensives as *Bagration* in mid-year. The somewhat churlish and patron-ising German assessment of this offensive which stressed that such was the Soviet manpower and material superiority that this attack could have been directed against not simply *Army Group Centre* but also against *Army Group North Ukraine*'s *4th* and *1st Panzer Armies* in the Lublin–Lvov area misses the whole point of Soviet strategic and operational technique as evolved by mid-1944. Leaving aside the failure of German intelligence that discounted the possibility of an attack on *Army Group Centre* and the deployment of German forces that left the mass of the armour in no position to support a command shorn of panzer formations, it formed no part of the Stavka's intention to seek out concentrated German armour when a successful offensive into Belorussia against *Army Group Centre* would jeopardise the position of *Army Group North*, bring about the dispersal of *Army Group North Ukraine*'s two panzer armies with the result that a follow-up offensive could secure Lublin and Lvov regardless, and eliminate the German armoured threat to the planned thrust into the Balkans.

The point that emerges from any detailed examination of the conduct of operations on the Eastern Front in 1944 is that the *Wehrmacht* was outfought at *every* level by an enemy that by this year had acquired the means to fight and win 'the deep battle', a concept of the offensive battle first set down in the Soviet field manual of 1936. In very sharp contrast to the situation in 1943 when the Soviet army failed to effect a single major encirclement, by 1944 it had come into possession of tank and mechanised formations that could provide the speed and depth of penetration needed for the successful conduct of encirclement operations. In so doing, the Soviet army had developed a two-tier structure with the bulk of its combined-arms armies assigned the costly role of mounting massed attacks across an extended front. Because such armies were poorly trained and often inadequately led – it was not unusual for formations to acquire personnel with less than a month's basic training – little was expected of combined-arms armies other than their applying such pressure over the length of a sector of attack that breaches would be made through which the élite armoured and mechanised armies could be committed in the role of operational groups for fronts. The combined armies were generally not capable of flair and initiative, which were not required at the tactical level at which their divisions were fought, but at the operational level, where by 1944 the Soviet army had completed its concentration of human and material resources, Soviet tank and mechanised formations were a match for their German opposite numbers whose quality was in sharp decline by 1944.

Soviet superiority was most marked, however, in matters of doctrine and related aspects of the conduct of operations. Unlike *Blitzkrieg*, which had stressed the rapid encirclement of enemy field armies by armour in order to prevent the reconstitution of a linear defence and then the annihilation of trapped formations by infantry operations, Soviet offensive doctrine aimed at the prosecution of the battle in depth in order to destroy enemy command and control systems and lines of communication – objectives discounted in the German field manual *HDv 300/1*. By 1944 the Soviet army had for the first time the air support and motorised logistical support needed to conduct operations in depth against German command and support systems, and to this were added elements of strategic flexibility and *maskirovka* that had been in evidence at various stages of proceedings. At Stalingrad, during the various offensives on the Don, and in the battles that followed Kursk the Soviet army consistently wrong-footed German armour, and in 1944 the *Bagration* experience was again the rule and not the exception. In the course of 1944 the Soviet army undertook what it termed 'ten linked strategic offensives', each offensive beginning as its predecessor died and each in turn allowed to die as its impetus slackened and the point of attack was switched. It was this ability to alter the point of attack that persistently left German armour wrongly positioned, and it was the parallel ability to deceive that enabled Soviet armies to secure overwhelming numerical superiority at the point of contact. The greatest manpower superiority enjoyed by a Soviet offensive in 1944 was in the region of 2.3:1 at the strategic level, but with the Soviet ability to draw upon the Stavka reserve and to switch formations to support an offensive adding substantially to this superiority, Soviet operational and tactical superiorities were consistently in excess of 4:1 and 10:1 respectively. Moreover, as Soviet overall manpower resources came under strain, Soviet material superiority increased, thereby adding further to the capability of an army that at the end of 1944 mustered 10 fronts, 57 armies and some 560 divisions* and which, in the course of 1944, demonstrated a twin ability to operate offensively through all four seasons of the year and across the greater part of a front line some 2,000 miles in length.

This is not to assert that by 1944 the Soviet army had acquired an immunity to defeat and failure and was invested with some superhuman quality, even though the rhetoric of the Eastern Front did indeed proclaim the Nazi–Soviet conflict in terms of flailing Teutonic and Slavonic supermen. Soviet offensives were often costly affairs, often beset by failure either to secure objectives or to take full advantage of opportunities that arose in the course of operations. The attempted encirclement of the *1st Panzer Army* between the Bug and Dnestr in

---

*These Soviet figures exclude 26 breakthrough artillery divisions and part of the *Stavka* reserve.

March miscarried; the advance into East Prussia in August was repulsed; the crushing of the armoured spearheads around Debrecen and Nyiregy-haza in eastern Hungary in late October represented a bad defeat by any standard. But such was the margin of Soviet superiority over the *Wehrmacht* by the autumn of 1944 that this episode represented no more than a local setback that did nothing to alter the overall imbalance of forces and capabilities on the Eastern Front. It is the failure of Western histories to recognise the dual nature of this imbalance – the acknowledgement of Soviet numerical advantage without the parallel recognition of the military professionalism that underpinned it – that has served to focus Western attention upon the various political aspects of the campaign on the Eastern Front in 1944 while rendering the campaign itself one of the least known episodes of the Second World War.

The narrative of the campaign on the Eastern Front was left with the Soviet offensives that secured the Dnepr and isolated the *17th Army* in the Crimea, the battles around Krivoi Rog and Hitler's decision to switch the focus of German attention from the Eastern Front to the West in order to prepare to meet an Anglo-American invasion of north-west Europe in 1944. These various developments, which bore most heavily upon the German army groups south of the Pripyat Marshes, ran in tandem with other German reverses, most notably the loss of Smolensk on 25 September, but without certain supplementary measures Hitler's re-ordering of Germany's strategic priorities in November 1943 had a three-fold implication for the ensuing conduct of operations on the Eastern Front. Although the preparation of a main line of resistance – known as the Panther Line or Eastern Wall – was ordered in summer 1943 and was well in hand by the autumn, Hitler's refusal to sanction a general withdrawal to prepared positions before Soviet attacks could materialise condemned German forces, and particularly *Army Group North* in January 1944, to fight a series of defensive battles in front of this line that invariably compromised their ability to man the line itself. This same refusal to cede ground voluntarily ensured that there could be no shortening of the front and the timely release of divisions into the reserve, a weakness that exacerbated the absence of a theatre reserve and the inability of *OKH* between November 1943 and March 1944 to draw upon other theatres for more than one armoured division as reinforcement for the Eastern Front. Finally, whereas German doctrine was based on a qualitative superiority of the *Wehrmacht* over its various enemies that was very marked before 1943, the adoption of a defensive strategy on the Eastern Front tacitly ceded the strategic initiative to Germany's most formidable enemy but was not accompanied by any compensatory increase of the mobility of the army as a whole and by a recasting of tactical doctrine. To have accepted a change of doctrine, however, would have amounted to an admission that the war could not be won, but without such a change, without enhanced mobility and without a shortening of the line and the concentration of a reserve, the *Wehrmacht* on the Eastern Front entered 1944 as little more than a disaster waiting to happen, particularly in the south where the ramshackle structure of the army groups was nothing more than an incitement to the Soviet army.

Nevertheless, in the three months after the fall of Smolensk a certain balance was restored to the Eastern Front as a result of Soviet exhaustion, the partial recovery of German forces and the onset of *rasputitsa*, though this did not prevent the Soviet army recovering Kiev on 6 November, beginning in early October an offensive in the Nevel–Vitebsk area against the *3rd Panzer Army* that was to continue until mid-February 1944, and continuing a series of attacks around Kirovgrad that were intended to reverse the verdict of the Krivoi Rog battle and to result in the encirclement of the *8th* and *6th Armies* within the bend of the Dnepr. The continuation of this effort throughout November into December 1943 pinpoints one of the major problems in setting out the military chronology of the 1944 campaign on the Eastern Front: this particular effort, made by two Soviet fronts between the Dnepr and the Bug, in effect merged with the first of the 1944 offensives. This particular offensive began, however, in December 1943 and divided into two quite separate parts, the first being conducted by two fronts into the last days of February 1944 and the second by three fronts, over a frontage of 875 miles, into mid-April. Moreover, the definition of events in 1944 by Soviet criteria as the year of the 'ten linked strategic offensives' is one that has suffered from changing terms of reference, the obvious difficulty of separating the strategic from the operational seemingly being a source of confusion to Soviet history and its Western readers alike.

While 1944 remains in Soviet history the year of the 10 victories – Leningrad, the western Ukraine, Odessa and the Crimea, Vyborg–Petrozavodsk, Belorussia, Lvov–Sandomierz, Iasi–Kishinev, Estonia and Latvia, Hungary and eastern Czechoslovakia, Petsamo and northern Norway – one of the latest authoritative Soviet publications lists 12 strategic offensives for 1944 and does so with lines of demarcation not readily apparent to those unfamiliar with the subtleties of Soviet military dialectics. For example, the Iasi–Kishinev offensive is listed as the seventh of the 1944 offensives, but is dated 20 to 29 August and separated from the tenth and twelfth offensives – Belgrade and Budapest respectively – and from the advances through Romania and Bulgaria to positions from which these latter two offensives could be staged: the chronological definition of this seventh offensive most obviously relates narrowly to the encirclement and annihilation phase of this attack into the Balkans. For the purposes of this narrative, however, the events of 1944 on the Eastern Front are defined under the terms of 10 offensives: first, the western Ukraine offensive between 24 December 1943 and 17 April 1944; second, the Leningrad–Novgorod offensive from 14 January to 1 March; third, the Crimean campaign, 8 April to 12 May; fourth, the Vyborg–Petrozavodsk offensive between 9 June and 9 August; fifth, the Belorussian offensive from 22 June to 29 August; sixth, the Lvov–Sandomierz offensive between 13 July and 29 August; seventh, the offensive through Romania and Bulgaria which began with the Iasi–Kishinev attack and reached into eastern Yugoslavia and the Hungarian plain, the abortive eastern Carpathian offensive being considered part of a general campaign that lasted between 19 August and 14 October; eighth, the Soviet offensive into Estonia and Latvia from 14 September to 20 November; ninth, the Petsamo offensive between 7 and 29 October; and tenth the Budapest campaign, from 20 October to the city's fall on 13 February 1945.

Perversely, however, the most convenient start-line for an examination of the 1944 campaign on the Eastern Front is the second offensive, directed against *Army Group North* which had been weakened over the previous two years by the transfer of its best formations to the south and which, by January 1944, had an order of battle unhealthily dependent upon dubiously rated *Luftwaffe* field divisions and non-German *Waffen SS* formations. This offensive began on 14 January and for the most part had run its course by the end of February, though fierce if inconclusive fighting continued on the Narva–Pskov–Pustoshka line for another month. Its greatest successes were registered in its first two weeks by the Leningrad Front's 2nd Shock Army, operating from the Oranienbaum salient, and the 42nd Army, attacking from positions in front of Leningrad at the expense of the *18th Army*. With the Volkhov Front simultaneously attacking around Novgorod, Soviet forces reached the Luga on 24 January and the Narva by the end of the month, but while this offensive effected the relief of Leningrad on 27 January after a siege of 879 days and at least one million dead and reduced the *18th Army* to just two battleworthy divisions by the end of January, the German ability to retain Narva and Pskov, the enforced shortening of the front and the arrival of reinforcements, particularly from *Army Group Centre*, enabled *Army Group North* slowly to reconstitute its left flank during February

The Soviet Offensives of 1944 - Main Front

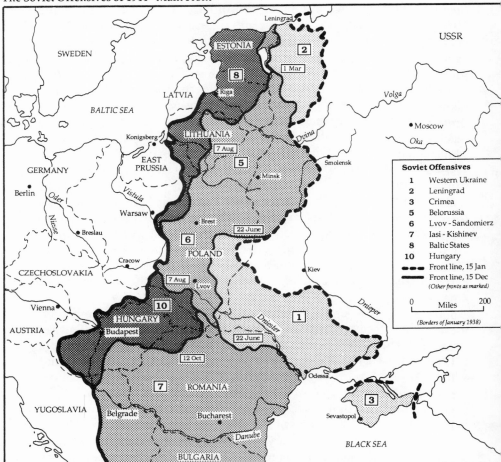

while an early thaw was partially responsible for the thwarting of the 2nd Baltic Front's attempt to break through the centre of the *16th Army*'s front around Pustoshka.

Army Group North thus survived its winter ordeal, but only at the cost of two developments. First, its failure to maintain itself on positions it had held for more than two years had implications that were not lost upon the Finns. Second, whereas in the last week of December Hitler had considered a withdrawal of *Army Group North* to the Narva–Pustoshka

370

line in order to free 12 divisions with which to reinforce an *Army Group South* already in danger of falling apart under the impact of 'the second 1944 offensive', *Army Group North* weathered the Soviet offensive because of its timely reinforcement but ended its retreat in no state to pay back divisions to a reserve needed to counter Soviet advances in the south.

The offensive south of the Pripyat Marshes was opened by the 1st Ukrainian Front on 24 December 1943 against the *4th Panzer Army*'s central sector astride the Kiev–Zhitomir road. With Soviet armour reaching Kazatin on 28 December and succeeding in breaking open the whole of the front between Korosten and Belaya Tserkov by the thirty-first, there was a three-fold development of the offensive. On the right flank, where on 6 January Soviet forces occupied Gorodnitsa on the old Polish–Soviet 1939 border, Soviet formations were directed towards Rovno and Shepetovka, thus threatening both the lateral railroad that supplied the two German army groups in the south and, more distantly, the vital centres of Lvov and Ternopol. The main axes of advance of the 1st Ukrainian Front were directed southwards in an attempt to ensure the destruction of the various corps of the *4th Panzer Army*, and at the same time the 3rd Ukrainian Front entered the battle with a double effort around Kirovgrad on 3 January and in the Krivoi Rog–Nikopol area after the tenth. Like the offensive against *Army Group North*, this overall Soviet effort achieved its greatest success at the outset and thereafter registered only diminishing returns as it reached into February though virtually all of the modest territorial gains recorded at the *6th Army*'s expense came in the latter month. At various stages of the fighting in *Army Group South*'s area of responsibility, Soviet efforts opened a gap of 110 miles between this command and *Army Group Centre* which was never closed entirely and also reduced *Army Group South*'s front to gaps separated by the occasional formation and defended position. But while a major strategic or operational victory was denied the 1st and 2nd Ukrainian Fronts by a combination of skilled defence, the reinforcements made available to *Army Group South* and unusually mild weather, even the limited success enjoyed by Soviet armies in this offensive, have been obscured in Western histories by the no less limited German success in extricating the shattered, demoralised remnants of *XI* and *XXXII Panzer Corps* from the Korsun–Shevchenkovskiy (or Cherkassy) pocket in mid-February.

The fact was that the breakout of some 30,000 troops from this encirclement was no compensation for the loss of some 80,000 troops during this offensive as a whole, particularly in view of the two corps being sent immediately to Poland because their formations were too ravaged to be regrouped. Moreover, the concentration upon one particular episode at the expense of the wider view has served to divert attention from the reality that as a result of this offensive the mines of Krivoi Rog and Nikopol were lost to the German economy and the position of the *6th Army*, and indeed that of the *17th Army* in the Crimea, was compromised not simply by the erosion of *Army Group A*'s strength and holdings within the bend of the Dnepr but by the events on *Army Group South*'s left flank. The loss in February of Rovno, Lutsk, Dubno and Shepetovka, and more seriously the loss on 2 March of Yampol midway between Shepetovka and Ternopol, left 1st Ukrainian Front some 80 miles from the foothills of the Carpathians and the splitting of the entire German front with the *6th Army* still some 300 miles east of the Prut. Moreover, while Hitler and *OKH* believed that the Soviets would not attempt any follow-up offensive because of the imminence of the thaw despite *Army Group South*'s insistence that just such an effort would be made in an attempt to beat the *rasputitsa*, Soviet strength south of the Pripyat Marshes actually increased during this second 1944 offensive. The entire Soviet effort was made without the participation of any of the six élite tank armies, but during February all six were moved into positions opposite *Army Group South* in readiness for the second phase of this offensive.

This phase, like its predecessor, is one dominated in its presentation in English-language histories by the successful breakout of an encircled German formation, in this case the *1st Panzer Army* after it was trapped beyond the Dnestr, at the expense of Soviet gains that were infinitely more substantial than anything recorded in previous Soviet offensives – and not just in 1944. In the course of 42 days the 1st, 2nd and 3rd Ukrainian Fronts advanced between 200 and 300 miles across a 800-mile front, and in so doing effectively split the German front in two, carried the war deep into Poland and beyond the Romanian–Soviet 1939 border and, for the first time since November 1943 and *Directive No 51*, forced the German High Command to reinforce the Eastern Front at the expense of other theatres, including France. Such was the extent of a defeat that is the proper context of the successful extrication of the *1st Panzer Army* from the Dnestr encirclement.

Every one of the 1944 offensives has its own special feature, the first and second, being simultaneous, both displaying the newfound Soviet capacity to mount major strategic operations on two widely separated fronts at one and the same time. The second offensive, perhaps for the first time, revealed the massive improvement of Soviet military capability

– to operate through the thaw, to operate armour *en masse* and in depth, and to conduct offensive operations, particularly encirclement operations, on the basis of a coherent doctrine, though in the event the attempt to trap the *1st Panzer Army* against the Dnestr failed. This was really the first offensive when the various strands of Soviet doctrine and enhanced capability came together in the prosecution of 'the deep battle', though somewhat oddly this was to be an offensive largely ignored in post-war Soviet histories for two reasons: the dead hand of Stalinist orthodoxy after 1947 damned this offensive because of the involvement of certain commanders who by that time had been disgraced, and this offensive was to be eclipsed both in scale and results by the sixth and seventh of the 1944 offensives – Lvov–Sandomierz and Iasi–Kishinev respectively – that came to be regarded, and with good cause, as the high points of the Soviet effort in the south.

The scale of these second-phase operations was nevertheless somewhat impressive. The 1st Ukrainian Front had three tank and five combined-arms armies, the 2nd three and seven, and the 3rd a mere seven combined-arms armies. Despite this order of battle, the weight of the Soviet effort was vested in the 1st Ukrainian Front, which opened the offensive on 4 March with an attack directed at the junction of the *4th* and *1st Panzer Armies*. The 2nd Ukrainian Front joined the attack the following day with an assault aimed at the boundary of the *1st Panzer* and *8th Armies*, and on the sixth the 3rd Ukrainian Front opened proceedings against the *6th Army*. Against an enemy that had had no time to refurbish its panzer formations after the earlier battles, the 1st Ukrainian Front registered a 25-mile advance across a front of 100 miles within two days, and by 10 March the 2nd Ukrainian Front, by taking Uman, effectively destroyed two panzer corps not in battle but by capturing tanks immobilised in the mud or in depots. Between 11 and 13 March, the 2nd Ukrainian Front crossed the Bug, and then forced the Dnestr – one day ahead of the 3rd Ukrainian Front – on 20–21 March: by the twenty-fifth its formations had reached the Prut. By this time, however, two divergent patterns emerged with the 3rd Ukrainian Front ordered to develop its offensive in order to secure Odessa whilst the 1st and 2nd Ukrainian Fronts, after a series of closely coordinated operations to eliminate resistance along their common boundary, were in a position to complete the encirclement of the *1st Panzer Army* around Khotin even as the 1st continued to batter its way against stiffening German resistance towards Ternopol. By 28 March the 1st and 2nd had completed both the internal and external encirclement of the *1st Panzer Army* – the provision against both a breakout and a relief from outside – and were moving to secure positions beyond the Dnestr even though formations on the western sector were thinly spread and low on fuel and ammunition after their advance. Unknown to Soviet intelligence, however, *II SS Panzer Corps* had been transferred from France in order to support *Army Group South*, and at the end of March it was committed to the relief of a *1st Panzer Army* which, with some 200,000 men and 16 divisions, chose to break out to the west rather than attempt the more obvious withdrawal to the south into Romania. As a result, the Khotin encirclement was broken and 1st Ukrainian Front's attempt to harry withdrawing German formations with its 1st and 4th Tank Armies ended inconclusively. At either end of the front, however, results were more clear cut. Ternopol was taken on 16 April in the last gasp of this offensive, Odessa on the tenth, and with Soviet bridgeheads established over the Prut and the 4th Ukrainian Front beginning operations on 8 April against the *17th Army* in the Crimea the Romanians, like the Finns before them, found themselves confronted by a reality that could not be ignored.

The western Ukraine offensive of 1944 cost the *Wehrmacht* 18 divisions wholly destroyed or so mauled that they were disbanded rather than re-formed: another 68 divisions suffered the loss of more than half their strengths. By 12 May these totals had been swelled by the loss of the five German and seven Romanian divisions of the *17th Army* as the result of a disastrous campaign that exacerbated German–Romanian and German inter-service differences: the Romanians had wanted to withdraw the *17th Army* because they saw no point in trying to hold the Crimea as Soviet formations broke into Transdnestr and Romania itself, but Hitler insisted on trying to hold the peninsula because its retention was deemed crucial to ensuring Turkish neutrality; the German army insisted that it was deserted by the *Kriegsmarine* and *Luftwaffe*. The fact remained, as was noted at the time, that whereas Sevastopol had endured an eight-month siege in 1941–42 the *Wehrmacht* in 1944 lost the city and some 70,000 men in 36 days during a Soviet offensive that brought proceedings south of the Pripyat Marshes to a halt for three months.

The first three Soviet offensives of 1944, though divided between two flanks, share certain common characteristics that can be linked to form one of the three categories under which the Soviet offensives of this year can be listed if these offensives are to be presented and considered conceptually rather than chronologically. For the most part they were offensives within the last great *tranche* of occupied Soviet territory as defined by pre-1939 boundaries, though the western Ukraine offensive did involve non-Soviet territory and certain subsequent offensives included the clearing of areas that were indisputably Soviet. The various political aspects of operations that were to arise as Soviet armies entered eastern Europe were largely absent from these three offensives though the implications of the military logic that decreed that the Soviet army would have to move through eastern Europe in order to carry the war into Germany were obvious to all parties. Moreover, though the western Ukraine offensive does not lend itself easily to this definition, until April 1944 the German leadership and those dependent on it could console themselves with the belief that the *Wehrmacht* could handle any crisis that might develop on the Eastern Front. Until April 1944 the hopelessness of Germany's strategic position was concealed by German resilience and tactical expertise, but in the second 1944 offensive this resilience and expertise were not enough even though the *1st Panzer Army* escaped destruction on the Dnestr. This campaign in effect marked the beginning of the end because it was the first Soviet offensive in which German qualitative superiority was clearly at a discount and when the limit of the Soviet advance was defined not by German resistance but by the combination of Soviet choice and local exhaustion.

This definition obviously leaves a number of loose ends with regard to these three offensives and their predecessors that might be considered as being wrongfully treated, but it is perhaps not without interest to note that Soviet histories describe the fifth of the 1944 offensives – in Belorussia against *Army Group Centre* – as 'the first modern offensive of the third phase of the war', a definition that draws a clear distinction between this and the Ukraine offensives but also raises, if only obliquely, a more interesting historical concept that is woven into that theme of German military excellence for which this commentary has shown scant regard. The view of the German military performance in the Second World War that sees the time and effort needed to complete Germany's defeat as evidence of her military proficiency describes a perceived phenomenon rather than explains it, yet if any realistic assessment of this view is to be made then a comparison of like with like is essential. It is at least arguable that the position that Germany enjoyed relative to her enemies between 1939 and 1941 was not equalled by those enemies relative to Germany until mid-1944 – at which time Germany still retained the greater part of the conquests she had made between 1939 and 1942. If, by this reckoning, the period between mid-1942 and mid-1944 was one in which the Allies secured an initiative that Germany had exercised before 1943 mainly because of her psychological preparedness for war and superior military technique, then the obvious question is, what is left of the view of German military proficiency in light of the Allied conquest in one year of both the German homeland itself and the territories that

Germany had conquered before 1943 and which she had held for consolidation purposes for a minimum of two years? This questioning of the conventionally held wisdom of the German performance in the Second World War is mendacious in certain respects: the German defeat involved economic and naval dimensions that took the full length of the war to be realised; German psychological advantage had been eroded by 1943; Germany's military defeat was not achieved in one year even if armies that were spread between Brittany, North Cape, Vitebsk and Rome in May 1944 were reduced to impotent irrelevance in that short time. The reality of the situation, however, was best expressed in the transposition to the European war of a comment made to the Imperial Diet by the Japanese prime minister, Tojo Hideki, on 27 December 1943: 'the real war is starting now.' Both before and during the war the German High Command had shamelessly proclaimed the defensive nature of its aim and actions: in 1944 it found itself committed to a defensive war that was only just beginning.

The seven remaining Soviet offensives of 1944 can be divided between those directed against Finland, against German forces in the Arctic and into Estonia and Latvia (the fourth, tenth and eighth respectively) and those mounted along the main axes of advance across the north European plain and into the Balkans. All of these offensives shared the common theme of operations into territory that lay beyond the Soviet Union's borders of 1938, but in military terms the fifth offensive – against *Army Group Centre* in Belorussia – formed the centrepiece of the entire Soviet effort in 1944. *Operation Bagration* was the greatest single offensive of the year, yet it was planned as but the first of two staggered offensives on the central sector and in the event it was developed, after its main phase ended in mid-July, by secondary attacks that extended into Lithuania and continued into August. It was an offensive that, with these two other efforts, destroyed the German front along its entire length between Ternopol and Lake Preipus and which between June and September inflicted a total of 840,000 dead and missing on the *Wehrmacht*. Twice as destructive in terms of German manpower as the campaign in north-west Europe in these same months, these offensives inflicted upon the *Wehrmacht* losses which could not be covered and which were exaggerated by the simultaneous defection of Romania, Bulgaria and Finland as a result of their defeat at Soviet hands. Moreover, an offensive that demonstrated a massive qualitative improvement in the Soviet conduct of operations over even the western Ukraine offensive, the *Bagration* campaign drawing the comment in the official US Army history that 'in executing the breakthroughs Soviet forces showed elegance in their tactical conceptions, economy of force, and control that did not fall short of the Germans' own performance in the early war years'.

In this fifth offensive the Stavka operations group detailed two senior officers to coordinate the operations of the fronts, and these fronts executed battles of encirclement and annihilation on account of their ability for the first time to complete active rather than passive inner and outer encirclements of enemy formations. By widening attack frontages Soviet fronts were able to achieve 'isolation in depth', while the mechanisation of assault formations and logistics enabled the inner encirclement to begin crumbling operations even before the encirclement was complete while the outer encirclement was directed beyond the trapped centre of resistance in order to prevent the successful sortie to relief. Thus in the *Bagration* offensive alone the Soviet army completed five encirclements of corps-size or greater, and it was this unprecedented Soviet capacity for mass destruction over an extended front and in great depth but little time that rendered *Operation Bagration* so important in the unfolding of the campaign on the Eastern Front in 1944.

Soviet success in their summer offensives had a three-fold basis: a positional advantage that placed their armies around Kovel in May nearer the East Prussian border than the bulk of *Army Group North*; the earlier operations in the southern sector that because of the involvement of 80 per cent of all Soviet armour served to convince the German High Command that the main Soviet effort in the summer would be made in this same area; and an overwhelming superiority of force on attack frontages that manifested itself in densities of between 150 and 204 guns and between 12 and 20 tanks per kilometre in the infantry-support role. In overall terms, the *Bagration* offensive began with the Soviet army commanding a 1,200,000 to 700,000 manpower superiority over an *Army Group Centre* that with 43 front-line and eight security divisions was the largest single German command on the Eastern Front, but through deception tactical superiorities upwards of 10:1 were secured on selected axes of attack and the various reserves available for this offensive allowed the Soviets to double their forces at will.

The Soviet offensives of summer 1944 were so vast, complicated and in the end repetitive that only their main features permit consideration. The *Bagration* offensive, conducted by the 1st Baltic, 3rd, 2nd and 1st Belorussian Fronts with some 4,000 tanks, 24,400 guns and 5,300 aircraft, began on 22 June against an enemy that as late as the fourteenth discounted the possibility of a major attack on *Army Group Centre*: it was a measure of the failure of German intelligence that the presence of the

The Main Soviet Offensives, Summer 1944

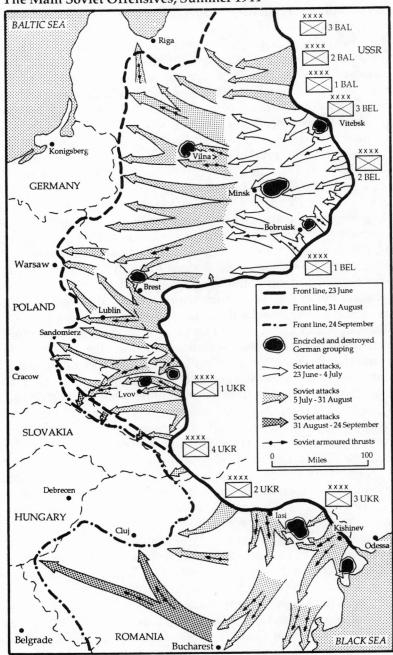

three armies with the 3rd Belorussian Front went undetected before the twenty-second, while on one attack sector where one Soviet division was identified there were 11. By 25 June *Army Group Centre* had been forced to commit its five reserve divisions without any apparent effect upon a Soviet offensive that within the next two days had completed the encirclement and annihilation of four German divisions at Vitebsk, one division at Orsha and two corps at Bobruysk and was in the process of destroying, at appalling cost, two corps around Mogilev. It was only on 28 June, by which time the *9th Army* had collapsed and the *3rd Panzer* and *4th Armies* were reduced to a scarcely better state, that the German High Command began to appreciate the scale of an offensive clearly aimed at the capture of Minsk. Not until the fall of that city on 3 July – and the encirclement of five corps to the east – did *Army Group Centre* realise that its expectation that the Soviet offensive would have to halt for reorganisation and resupply was unfounded: after an advance of 125 miles in 12 days the three Soviet fronts leading the offensive had the capacity to continue their advance and develop it in divergent directions – towards Dvinsk and the rear of *Army Group North*, towards Molodechno and Vilna, and towards Baranovichi and Brest.

The realisation of the extent of the *Bagration* offensive was accompanied by a double command change on Hitler's part: Field Marshal Model took command of *Army Group Centre* in addition to his own *Army Group North Ukraine*, and the commander of *Army Group North* was dismissed, as was his successor within a month, for opposition to orders to move to support *Army Group Centre* while still retaining the command's existing positions. These changes, however, were no substitute for the lack of a theatre reserve and the failure to release divisions from *Army Group North* for the battle in the Polotsk–Dvinsk area, while the expedient of having a single commander of two army groups in order to facilitate the reinforcement of one at the other's expense ran risks all the more obvious for the acknowledged Soviet capacity for an offensive against *Army Group North Ukraine* at this time. Thus despite its success in crushing an armoured lunge by 1st Belorussian Front in the direction of Chelm on 7–8 July, the end of the first week in July found *Army Group Centre* powerless to prevent the disintegration of its front over 200 miles of its length, but even as it sought to re-form itself east of the Dvina–Vilna–Bialystok–Brest line so the Stavka widened the battle. On 13 July, when the *Bagration* offensive completed its last notable encirclement around Vilna, the 1st Ukrainian Front, with 10 armies the largest single front at the Stavka's disposal, began an offensive intended to force the San and the Vistula. With 16,100 guns, 2,050 tanks and 3,250 aircraft, the 1st

Ukrainian Front concentrated its efforts on the Rava Russkaya and Lvov axes with supporting thrusts directed against Zamosc and against Stryi and Stanislav. The main attacks incurred very heavy losses around Brody and on the defensive positions prepared in front of Lvov, but by 15 July the operational technique of massed, sustained attacks across an extended front had yielded results with the exhaustion of German infantry and the erosion of reserves of the *1st Panzer Army*. By the eighteenth the 1st Ukranian Front had partially encircled Lvov and the six divisions of *XIII Infantry Corps*, but while another 10 days were to elapse before the city was cleared and the encirclement battle completed, on the eighteenth the second phase of the *Bagration* offensive began. Having been reinforced by armies transferred from the 3rd Ukrainian Front, the 1st Belorussian Front moved against German forces and positions on the 1st Ukrainian Front's right flank with attacks from the Kovel area towards Chelm and Lublin and towards Brest. To the north the remaining three fronts that had begun the *Bagration* offensive were joined by the 2nd and 3rd Baltic Fronts in second-phase operations that extended across the whole of the front between Bialystok and the Narva.

With only one tank army between these five fronts, this latter effort represented the secondary Soviet undertaking north of the Carpathians in the aftermath of the main *Bagration* offensive. Such status did not prevent, however, the 3rd Belorussian Front from securing Kaunus on 29 July, the 1st Baltic Front from taking Shaulyay and Jelgave in the last week of July, thereby cutting the only railroad supplying *Army Group North*'s formations in Estonia and Latvia; and, perhaps most shocking of all for the Germans, the 3rd Baltic Front from breaking through the Panther Line defences at Pskov and Narva and taking these cities on 23 and 27 July respectively. But by that same last week in July the main Soviet effort had resulted in the splitting of *Army Group North Ukraine*'s front and the securing of the Vistula line by both the 1st Belorussian and 1st Ukrainian Fronts.* Despite the battle around Lvov, the 1st Ukrainian Front reached the San near Yaroslav on 23 July and three days later its forces secured Perermysl: by the thirtieth its armour had crossed the Vistula above Sandomierz. Four days earlier, and in the 1st Belorussian's Front's area of responsibility and following the occupation of Lublin on the twenty-third, the 8th Guards Army reached the Vistula below Deblin: thereafter the 1st Belorussian Front sought to secure a bridgehead over the river and to develop an offensive towards Warsaw as the 48th and

*As its axes of advance diverged 1st Ukrainian Front shed its southern armies to a reactivated 4th Ukrainian Front at the end of July

65th Armies tried to fight their way to the Narew and to positions from which to outflank Warsaw from the north – these efforts being made at a time when Bialystok and Brest remained unreduced in the rear areas and a major German counter-offensive still disputed ownership of Siedlce and control of the main Brest–Warsaw road.

Though Bialystok was cleared on 27 July and Brest the following day, the fact that on these and subsequent days major German counter-offensives were delivered around Siedlce, against the forces advancing on Warsaw from the south and trying to secure a bridgehead below Deblin, and against the bridgehead above Sandomierz was evidence of a German recovery and the faltering of the Soviet offensive after advances upwards of 300 miles across countryside devastated by two years of German anti-partisan operations and recent battles. During August the Soviet advances continued in various sectors: in the south the 1st Ukrainian Front secured Sandomierz on 18 July; in the centre units of the 3rd Belorussian Front reached German soil on 17 July; in the north the 1st Baltic Front fought its way into Tukums and almost to the shores of the Gulf of Riga, while the 3rd Baltic Front punched a massive salient into the *18th Army*'s positions west of Lake Preipus. By the end of July, as the extent of Soviet losses and the drag of logistics took their toll, the main impetus of these various Soviet efforts was spent, and a balance was imposed upon the Eastern Front at the very time when the impasse around the Normandy beachhead was broken. In Western accounts of the 1944 campaign, however, just one aspect of this faltering of the Soviet offensive at the end of July has come to obscure two matters: first, in these various offensives 17 German divisions were destroyed and another 50 halved in strength; second, as the offensives faltered so the Stavka switched the point of attack with the start of its Iasi–Kishinev offensive into the Balkans, an attack that was conducted on a scale only marginally inferior to that of the Lvov–Sandomierz offensive by the 1st Ukrainian Front.

The one aspect of the deadlock on the Vistula Front after July 1944 to obscure these two developments was the Warsaw Uprising. In the rhetoric of the Cold War era, the charge that the Soviet Union had willingly connived or at least acquiesced in the savage German suppression of the Polish resistance in the capital was overlaid by the more general accusation levelled against Western leaders to the effect that in this period, and specifically at the Yalta conference in February 1945, Churchill and Roosevelt abjectly condoned a post-war Soviet hegemony in eastern Europe, a sin of commission and omission that somehow amounted to a supine abandonment and betrayal of countries that had lived in dread of the Soviet Union. The passing of time has served to blunt the more extreme versions of these assertions, and from any reasoned consideration of the realities of the time two points would seem to emerge. First and in military terms, the capture of Warsaw was probably beyond Soviet resources in August and September 1944: the 1st Belorussian Front alone sustained 123,000 battle casualties in July and August. The late summer of 1944 witnessed a number of Soviet reverses and failures that were the direct result of Soviet exhaustion after the *Bagration* and Lvov–Sandomierz offensives. The forces that entered East Prussia were destroyed; the attempt to complete the encirclement of German forces beyond the Dvina was checked and thrown back by the *3rd Panzer Army*; the 38th Army's attempt to force the Dukla Pass and enter Slovakia in order to support and take advantage of the August rising against German rule was narrowly but decisively defeated. Warsaw was not the only objective that proved beyond the reach of Soviet armies in August 1944. Second, eastern Europe was neither Britain's nor America's to abandon and betray: it did not lie within an Anglo-American power of gift. The logic that ensured that the countries of eastern Europe were to suffer the consequences of the Soviet advance through them in order to carry the war into Germany also ensured that Britain and the United States could dispute Soviet mastery of eastern Europe only by force of arms. In mid-1944 Britain and the United States had no obligation to those countries of eastern Europe that had associated themselves with their enemies, and with Germany still formidable even in defeat and a war in the Far East still to be won Britain and the United States had no good reason to risk their present and future relations with the Soviet Union on account of Bulgaria, Hungary and Romania, or even for a Czechoslovakia that had not fought for herself. In the last year of the European war Britain and the United States were powerless to influence events in eastern Europe, and if indeed they did make concessions to the Soviet Union then they did no more than concede what the countries of eastern Europe themselves had already lost.

Poland, however, was somewhat different: her violation in 1939 had been the *casus belli* and, with the exception of Greece and Yugoslavia, she was the only country of eastern and central Europe with fully accredited Allied status. Historically, however, her tragedy had been that she was surrounded by more powerful neighbours that sought not to preserve her against one another but to divide her and assimilate her parts, and in 1944 the latest act in this tragedy was played out against the background of an historical Russo-Polish enmity, the ideological clash between a

Catholic people and an atheistic republic, and the appalling suffering of the Polish people at German hands over the previous five years. At its simplest Poland was, and probably still remains, non-negotiable to the Soviet Union, perhaps the only country of eastern Europe with that unhappy distinction. Astride the historic invasion route into the Russian heartland, Poland's subjugation was a cardinal aim of a Soviet Union presented in 1944 with the opportunity and means to realise this objective. The Warsaw Uprising was the action of those Poles of the Armia Krajowa who recognised this reality, who saw the Soviet version of liberation as barely distinguishable from German occupation. By mid-1944 the issues that had divided the exiled Polish government in London and the Soviet Union – the issue of their common border, the massacre of Polish deportees by NKVD murder squads, the Soviet operations against the Armia Krajowa – came together in the Polish attempt to secure the national capital in the time between the German evacuation and Soviet occupation of Warsaw. In the event the anticipated German evacuation of Warsaw did not materialise and the Polish resistance, having shown its hand on 1 August but having failed to seize the main bridges and installations of the city, was helpless as the Germans put down the rising with a ferocity shocking even by the dubious standards of their normal behaviour in Poland and on the Eastern Front.

The Warsaw Uprising lasted between 1 August and 2 October, and in that time the 1st Belorussian Front made no major, sustained attempt to secure Warsaw and until 10 September the Soviet High Command resisted requests to open its airfields to American aircraft flying supplies to the Armia Krajowa. In these developments lay evidence of a Soviet willingness to allow the Germans the opportunity to destroy an anti-Soviet resistance that the Soviets would otherwise have to destroy themselves, not that the Stalinist state would have flinched from such an eventuality. It was not a case, as was alleged at the time and for many years after the war, that Stalin halted his armies in order to let the Germans deal with the Armia Krajowa, but the deliberate indifference to the fate of the Poles once the battle on the Vistula turned against the 1st Belorussian Front. Herein is the thread of continuity that links these events with the Iasi–Kishinev offensive and with the fourth 1944 offensive against the Finns that preceded *Operation Bagration*.

In the summer of 1944 the Soviet Union stood poised to move against Germany's associates – Bulgaria, Finland, Hungary, Romania and Slovakia – and she regarded each as the legitimate spoils of war, their subjugation the compensation for her losses. There was no pressure from her Western allies to which she was vulnerable, and by the summer of

1944 she was aware that all the minor Axis powers sought their separate exits from the war. Inconclusive negotiations had been conducted with both Finland and Romania; Bulgaria had taken the precaution of never having declared war on the Soviet Union; Hungary, occupied by German forces in March 1944, was gripped by a political crisis that reflected a desire to escape the consequences of her past actions and the realisation that such an escape was not possible. For all these countries Moscow had available docile expatriates ready to be installed in positions of authority but with no real power as and when the Soviet Union chose to impose her will and system upon eastern Europe. In the case of Bulgaria and Romania national capitulations enabled the Soviet Union to work within a framework of legality; in Hungary outright conquest removed obstacles; in Albania and Yugoslavia indigenous communists emerged in the course of the war as the only credible post-war rulers of their countries. In Poland the same pattern of Soviet control and takeover was to be followed but only after the back of the Polish resistance had been broken, and the German willingness to raze Warsaw and with it Polish resistance allowed the NKVD to prosecute an equally ferocious campaign against the Armia Krajowa in those areas already under Soviet military occupation.

Finland, however, proved to be the exception to this general subjugation of eastern Europe to the Soviet Union, which apparently was not prepared to undertake the effort needed to complete the conquest of her neighbour when more important matters were to hand in other areas. As early as July 1943 the Soviet Union made overtures to Finland for the end of their war, but in March and again in April 1944 the Finnish government considered that the terms demanded by the Soviet Union in the February negotiations were too severe for a nation with an undefeated army that stood on Soviet soil. This Finnish position of strength, however, was an illusion. The Finns had been obliged to demobilise part of their army in order to release manpower for the economy, and by spring 1944 Finland's army could muster only 15 divisions, 1,900 guns and mortars, 110 tanks and self-propelled guns, and 248 combat aircraft to withstand an attack by the 41 divisions assembled by the Stavka during the winter and spring for an offensive on either side of both Lake Ladoga and Lake Onega.

The Vyborg–Petrozavodsk offensive began on 9 June with a three-fold aim: to secure the approaches to Leningrad and to clear Karelia; to break if not the Finnish army then the Finnish will to continue the war; and to distract German attention from the imminent offensive in Belorussia. The Soviet intention was to smash the Finnish main strength on the Karelian Isthmus with a setpiece attack by the Leningrad Front's 21st and 23rd Armies and then to clear Karelia with the Karelian Front's 7th and 32nd Armies. With only (*sic*) 450,000 men available for this offensive and confronted by a series of defensive lines that extended over a depth of 110 miles on the Isthmus, the Stavka plan of campaign stressed the need for the 21st Army, with some 80 per cent of the 10,100 guns, 800 tanks and 2,000 combat aircraft assembled for this offensive, to smash *IV Finnish Corps* before it had a chance to withdraw through successive defensive positions. This was to be achieved by a massed artillery attack involving concentrations of 600 to 800 guns per mile on a frontage of eight miles followed by armoured and amphibious assaults. On 10 June the 21st Army broke the first Finnish defence line, but even with the 23rd Army joining the offensive on the following day it was not until the seventeenth that the Leningrad Front's armies mastered the main lines of resistance and forced *IV* and *III Finnish Corps* back to the last line of defences in front of Vyborg, which fell on 21 June.

In Karelia the main Soviet effort was not made until this same day when the 7th Army attacked across the Svir and the 32nd Army secured Povonets, but with a thorough demolition and felling programme impeding the various Soviet advances Petrozavodsk was not cleared until 30 June. These various successes, which involved the clearing of the main Murmansk–Leningrad railroad for the first time since 1941, represented the peak of Soviet achievement. In the last week of June the Leningrad Front, despite being reinforced by a fresh army, registered only minor territorial gains on the Isthmus, while in Karelia Soviet formations struggled through largely featureless country to cross the border on 21 July before fighting died away after two divisions of the 32nd Army were encircled and destroyed around Ilomantsi on 9 August. By the second week of July, however, the Stavka had begun to replace its first-line divisions with garrison formations, an acknowledgement of the approaching end of the Continuation War and the need to move forces to the north for the offensive into the Petsamo area.

In the Vyborg–Petrozavodsk offensive the Soviet army failed in its attempt to destroy the Finnish army but it was successful in realising its other aims, not least in distracting German attention and resources on the eve of the *Bagration* offensive. Indeed, on 21 June, the day before the attack on *Army Group Centre* began and at a time when the *Luftwaffe* had only 40 operational fighters with which to cover the Belorussian sector, the German air force flew 1,000 sorties in support of the Finnish army, at a time when Allied armies in Normandy began the close investment of Cherbourg and were about to begin an attempt to encircle and capture Caen. Moreover, at this same time Hitler despatched ammunition and one division to support Finland which had asked Germany on the nineteenth for direct military assistance in dealing with the Soviet offensive. Hitler's price for assistance was the demand that Finland conclude an alliance that would pledge her not to make a separate peace. The undertaking that no government of President Risto Ryti would conclude such a peace was all that Germany could extract from a Finnish administration that refused to consider itself bound by a promise made under duress, and with the Germans failing to support the Finnish army on the scale that Hitler had promised Ryti's removal from the presidency provided Finland with the technicality whereby she could extricate herself from Germany's clutches. Without the physical means to dominate her as she did her other allies, Germany could not prevent Finland from seeking terms from the Soviet Union at the end of August, an armistice being concluded on 15 September.

The terms under which Finland left the war contained provisions that were the context of the ninth Soviet offensive of 1944: the attack by the 14th Army into northern Norway through the Petsamo area in October. Under the terms of the armistice Finland was to ensure the evacuation of German forces from her soil and to intern those that tried to maintain themselves in Finland after 15 September, if need be with Soviet assistance. The past division of Finnish and German responsibilities north of the Gulf of Finland, plus the sheer impossibility of the *20th Mountain Army*'s voluntary withdrawal from its positions north of Suomassalmi through northern Finland into Norway before this deadline, raised the very real prospect of a major clash between the Finns and Germany, but in the event, with Soviet armies not attempting to cross into northern Finland and despite an ill-judged and unsuccessful German amphibious assault on Suursaari on the fifteenth, the Finns and the *20th Mountain Army* came to an informal arrangement whereby the former did not oppose the German withdrawal from positions around Allakurtti and Kestenga and would follow German formations at a suitably discreet distance through Oulu, Kemi, Rovaniemi, Muonio and Ivalo. At Susasyarvi on 28 September and, more seriously, at Kemi and Tornio between 1 and 8 October this arrangement broke down, and in the battle that developed around the twin ports the *20th Mountain Army* had the worst of the fighting, but the unwillingness of both the Finns and Germans to engage in full-scale hostilities ensured that these incidents were isolated. In part German restraint at this time, which did not extend to the countryside through which German formations passed, was dictated by the fact that by the time the fighting around Kemi came to an end both *XVIII* and *XXXVI Mountain Corps* had withdrawn through

Rovaniemi, and *20th Mountain Army* had a more immediate problem in the form of the offensive of the 14th Army that began on 7 October in front of Petsamo against *XIX Mountain Corps.*

In the course of nearly four weeks the 14th Army was to advance some 120 miles on two diverging axes, securing Petsamo on 15 October, Kirkenes on the twenty-fifth and Neiden on the twenty-seventh, reconnaissance elements pushing forward to reach Tana Fjord by the thirtieth while the 31st Rifle Corps advanced to link up with the Finns at Ivalo on 2 November. Only in the first week of this offensive, however, did the 14th Army achieve any marked success. Originally ordered to clear only the Petsamo area and to defeat, not encircle and destroy, *XIX Mountain Corps*, the 14th Army planned to use two light infantry formations, the 126th and 127th Rifle Corps, in outflanking attacks whilst two corps mounted the main assault against the *2nd Mountain Division* on the Titovka river and a third corps tied down the *6th Mountain Division* on the German left flank. The 14th Army had planned a supporting attack from the Rybatchiy peninsula and amphibious landings to cut German lines of communication behind the *6th Mountain Division*, but a cautious Stavka ordered these efforts to be delayed until the outcome of the main assault was known. As a result, the best opportunity of completing an encirclement of *XIX Mountain Corps* eluded the 14th Army. Its attack on the Titovka broke through German positions within three days, but the 126th Rifle Corps, though it cut the Luostari road on 10–11 October, could not maintain itself on the Tarnet–Petsamo road on the thirteenth. Though Petsamo was captured by converging Soviet formations on the fifteenth, Soviet problems of operating offensively through the tundra and along dirt tracks that restricted attack frontages and lines of communication to one vehicle, plus timely German withdrawals and the commitment of the *163rd Infantry Division* from *XXXVI Mountain Corps* to the battles in front of Salmiyarvo, denied the 14th Army any chance of turning minor tactical successes and territorial gains into operational dividends. By the end of October the main Soviet impetus had exhausted itself, and with the *Army of Norway* committing divisions to Skibotten and Lakselv all three corps of *20th Mountain Army* were able to conduct orderly withdrawals to defensive positions at the head of Lyngen Fjord, *XIX* and *XXXVI Mountain Corps* conducting a thorough scorched-earth policy throughout Finnmark in the process. German detachments remained forward of the Lyngen position at Alta and Hammerfest until the following February and in north-west Finland until April, but after October 1944 – and at a cost of some 9,000 German and 15,000 Soviet dead and wounded – the only Arctic campaign in history was at an end. It reached this end, however, in an irony that Norway shared with the Balkans. What had taken the *Wehrmacht* into Norway and into the Balkans in 1940 was fear of British intentions in these areas, and what shaped much of subsequent German defensive policy in Norway and the Balkans was this same British dimension of the war. Yet the invasion of both was to come not from the sea but by land and at the hands of the Soviet Union, in the case of the Balkans in the form of the Iasi–Kishinev offensive.

This operation was not the largest of the Soviet offensives of 1944 but it was the most complicated. It involved fighting that extended over three months and seven national territories, with effects that extended into Albania and Greece. It involved no fewer than four German army groups and eight Axis armies, most of which were renamed with bewildering frequency, and it involved the fusion of two very different conflicts – the Eastern Front and the series of internecine conflicts that had been spawned across the Balkans after 1941 as traditional national rivalries inside the peninsula, modern social conflicts and the machinations of the great powers came together. It involved, moreover, a sequence of political developments in each of the three Axis countries that were invaded and in the Allied countries that were liberated, these emerging in no set or orderly manner. The Iasi–Kishinev offensive thus does not lend itself easily to narrative and interpretation, especially in light of the fact that the military campaign proved to be merely the prelude to the post-war Sovietisation of all but one of the countries touched by this offensive.

In bare outline the Iasi–Kishinev offensive, conducted by two fronts that between them had some 900,000 men, 1,850 tanks, 16,000 guns and 3,200 aircraft under command, began on 19 August against an *Army Group South Ukraine* that over the previous two months had lost 11 divisions, including three-quarters of its armour, to other commands. In the first five days of this offensive some 250 miles of the Axis front astride the Romanian–Soviet 1939 border were broken, German surprise being compounded by the 3rd Ukrainian Front's main effort being directed south from Tiraspol through some of the most difficult terrain on the entire front. In what was for the *Wehrmacht* a grotesque repeat of what had happened in November 1942 at Stalingrad, the two main Soviet attacks fell upon the *3rd* and *4th Romanian Armies* on either flanks of the *6th Army*, which was split in two and surrounded by 23 August – the day on which the Romanian dictator, Marshal Antonescu, was dismissed by the King and arrested. Romania, which even under Antonescu had sought terms both collectively from the United Nations and bilaterally from the Soviet Union, declared war upon Germany on 25 August after an abortive German attempt to stage a counter-coup and the bombing of Bucharest by the *Luftwaffe* on the previous day.

After 25 August Romanian forces cooperated with Soviet armies as they advanced through Romania on three divergent axes. The 2nd Ukrainian Front, reinforced by armies detached from the 3rd Ukrainian Front, was to advance into Hungary through the passes of two separated sectors, the Carpathian Mountains, and, via Bucharest and Wallachia, the Transylvanian Alps. At the same time the 3rd Ukrainian Front, after arriving on the Danube below Giurgiu on 2 September and following a Soviet declaration of war on Bulgaria on the fifth, crossed the river on the eighth. The Bulgarian response was to declare war on Germany that same day and to install a popular front government in power on 9 September. These two declarations of war coincided with the 2nd Ukrainian Front's capture of Turnu Severin (just south of the Iron Gate) and Sibiu (beyond the Romanian-held Turnu Rosu pass) respectively, but with other formations of this front negotiating the Oituz and Predeal passes at the same time the Horthy government felt obliged to demand that Germany send five panzer divisions to halt these various Soviet advances to the Hungarian plain or allow Hungary to act independently as her situation required. In fact Hitler was prepared to make such an effort in order to ensure that his last genuine ally remained constant to her obligations to Germany. Hitler was also prepared to make a major effort in Hungary in the belief that in so doing he could provoke an Anglo-Soviet clash of interest in the Balkans, but he also took the precaution of ensuring the concentration of German forces near Budapest as an insurance against an Hungarian defection.

The difficulties of moving armour through passes on lengthening lines of communication rather than the strength of Axis resistance served to slow the Soviet advances into Hungary during September. A supporting offensive by the 4th Ukrainian Front after the ninth, directed into northern Hungary via Slovakia, failed to force the Dukla Pass until 6 October. But the military and political developments in Romania and Bulgaria both before the start and as a result of the Soviet offensive had implications for two other German commands: *Army Group F* in Yugoslavia and Albania and *Army Group E* in Greece and the Aegean islands. Both commands were singularly ill-equipped to deal with the threat that developed in the eastern Balkans after 19 August. *Army Group F* had been involved in occupation and anti-partisan operations, and *Army Group E*, while similarly employed, presented an unbalanced order of battle with its better formations committed on the Aegean islands in order to counter any British landings of the kind attempted in the

Dodecanese in October 1943. Though the threat of encirclement by Soviet armies was very real from the time that Romania defected, the local German command in the Balkans delayed for an inordinately long period before ordering the withdrawal of its forces from Greece: not until 2 October, and then only under pressure from *OKH*, was an evacuation ordered, and with Athens abandoned on the thirteenth and Salonika on 31 October, it was not until 1 November that German forces, other than those that remained on certain islands, finally left Greece. By that time the encirclement and annihilation of *Army Group E* should have been assured; the 3rd Ukrainian Front – which secured Varna on 9 September and Sofia on the twenty-third – had crossed the Danube below the Iron Gate on 22 September and had taken Belgrade on 13–14 October and Nis on the fifteenth.

With Belgrade being secured at the same time as the German evacuation of Athens, the 3rd Ukrainian Front seemingly held potentially decisive advantages of time, position and numbers over German forces coming north from Greece, but in the event three matters were to work to German advantage. The Anglo-American offensive against German lines of communication throughout the Balkans that began on 1 September could not be sustained throughout the month and into October at the very time when its efforts could have yielded results. The precautionary occupation of Nis and Skopjle, in Bulgarian-occupied Yugoslavia in late August and the first movement of German forces into Macedonia from Greece in September provided *Army Group E* with sufficient forces to hold the Skopjle–Kraljevo–Visegrad line when Soviet forces attacked into Yugoslavia through the Morava valley in the direction of Belgrade in the first week in October. Finally, and in large measure the key to this second point, both before and after Belgrade fell the main Soviet effort was directed not into eastern and southern Yugoslavia but into the Hungarian plain, and in Yugoslavia itself the Soviet priority was Belgrade and not German lines of communication to the west.

In Hungary, however, Soviet arms had mixed fortunes. Though the 2nd Ukrainian Front secured Arad (in Romania) as early as 20–21 September, the following month saw a series of indecisive battles around Oradea between 26 and 28 September and around Debrecen between 8 and 20 October. In the latter both German and Soviet armour sought the other's encirclement, and, confusingly, at different times both were successful until 14 October when Soviet formations finally freed themselves from the German embrace. Thereafter the 2nd Ukrainian Front at the start of the tenth and last Soviet offensive of 1944 took

Nyiregyhaza on the twentieth, but in trying to develop an offensive towards Budapest three of its corps were trapped around Nyiregyhaza by *Armeegruppe Wohler* between 24 and 29 October in what proved to be one of the last major German tactical successes of the war. As with all such German successes in the last year of the war, however, this victory was swallowed up immediately by operational failure. On 31 October the 2nd Ukrainian Front, attacking along the length of its front between Nyiregyhaza and Arad, secured Kecskemet, and by 5 November the 47th Army had fought its way into the outskirts of Budapest. On the following day, however, a combination of ammunition shortages, exhaustion and perhaps an exaggerated post-Nyiregyhaza caution induced by a modest German counter-attack prompted a voluntary Soviet withdrawal to positions some 10 to 20 miles from the Hungarian capital.

Soviet operations in Hungary did not end with the failure to secure Budapest in the first week of November. As early as 11 November the 2nd Ukrainian Front resumed its offensive in an attempt to outflank Budapest from the north. Thereafter, with the 3rd Ukrainian Front securing Mohacs – the very symbol of Hungarian defeat – on the twenty-sixth, the two Soviet fronts were to complete the encirclement of the capital, appropriately on 26 December, despite desperate resistance. But these and subsequent operations that resulted in the Soviet capture of Budapest, Bratislava and Vienna in 1945 fall well beyond the terms of reference of the Iasi–Kishinev offensive, though the start of the siege of Budapest forms the natural stop line for an examination of the 1944 campaign in Europe, not because of its chronological convenience but in terms of the state of the European war with reference to time, space and doctrine. The most remarkable aspect of the fighting in Hungary between October and December 1944 was not that the *Wehrmacht* was able to re-establish a more or less continuous front in Hungary at the end of October but that there was a campaign, still more a major campaign, in Hungary at all in the autumn.

The end of the war seemed much further away in December 1944 than it had in August. At the height of the summer, as the *Diadem* offensive, the *Neptune* landings, *Operation Bagration*, the Lvov–Sandomierz offensive and the breakout from Normandy followed one another without a break Germany seemed doomed to immediate defeat, and the attempted assassination of Hitler on 20 July was an acknowledgement of that perception. Yet by October Germany had emerged from the crisis and, for the most part, still stood beyond the borders from which Hitler had started the war. But if Germany survived the defeats of the summer she was nevertheless still four months nearer general collapse in December 1944 than she had been in August, not simply because of the passing of time but because by the autumn she had come to the end of her industrial and manpower resources. Without oceanic trade and now deprived of most of her earlier conquests and their resources, Germany's industries in autumn 1944 entered 'end-run production', the stage of manufacture when current output represented the use of the last available materials and stockpiles. The *Wehrmacht* was similarly placed. In the course of 1944 a total of 106 German divisions were destroyed and disbanded, and the *Volksgrenadier* divisions that were raised as the war came to Germany's borders did no more than reflect the hopelessness of her military position. The 66 new or converted divisions raised after August 1944 to replace the 75 line infantry divisions lost in that year stood no detailed comparison with their predecessors, which themselves had been unable to withstand the assaults of their various enemies.

In terms of time, therefore, the *Wehrmacht*'s success in weathering the crisis of summer 1944 availed it nothing because without fresh armies and weaponry that could reverse its battlefield inferiority the *Wehrmacht* could delay but not prevent final defeat. In terms of strategic and operational capacity the Soviet army alone had the measure of the *Wehrmacht*, yet by December 1944, with the last advantages that space had conferred upon her largely lost, Germany nevertheless retained two assets that ensured that her ill-assorted enemies did not allow the interests that divided them to override those that held them together. With the final alignment of the powers complete and only Hungary committed to fight with her to the bitter end, a brittle fanaticism remained to Germany, as did the power of destruction over the various conquered peoples that she still held in thrall. What this power of destruction entailed had become evident in July outside Lublin, at an otherwise obscure little place called Maidanek, and with all too many such places liberated in the weeks and months that followed the revelation of the depths of German depravity and bestiality was enough to ensure that even if allies are not necessarily friends the anti-German alliance would survive to ensure Germany's defeat.

392

6

KĀLO 'SMI

If in the autumn of 1944 a balance reasserted itself upon the main European fronts after the Allied victories and advances of the summer, the Pacific war experienced a quickening of tempo in the aftermath of Allied successes in mid-year in the central and south-west Pacific and in north-east India and Upper Burma. These successes, and specifically that of the Americans in the southern Marianas in June, brought home the reality of national defeat even to the Japanese High Command: the fall of Tojo on 18 July was a tacit recognition that the war would not be won, even that Japan could not respond effectively to a strategic bombing offensive waged from the Marianas and to an American advance westwards that would sever Japanese lines of communication with the southern resources area. Like her German ally, however, Japan in defeat retained a fanaticism and a power of destruction that ensured an Allied advance to the home islands would be a protracted and bitterly contested process.

In addition to the continuing campaign against Japanese shipping, the last year of the Greater East Asia war was to witness five separate campaigns – in Burma, in China, throughout the island groups of the western Pacific, over the Japanese home islands, and in Manchuria – and two battles, one in Tokyo and the other in Washington, on the crucial question, albeit from somewhat different perspectives, of how the war was to be brought to an end. For the United States, and in effect hers was the power of decision in this war other than Japan's right to decide upon surrender, the final year of the Pacific war was to bring victories won on the basis of naval supremacy, yet in this same year the US Navy lost the crucial arguments within the US High Command on virtually every important issue of policy and command appointments. Before the Philippine Sea the US Navy's was the predominant influence in the framing of American strategic policy against Japan, and the navy was unconvinced either of the need to attempt the liberation of the Philippines during the advance to Japan or of the necessity for an invasion of Japan itself. Yet in the aftermath of what was strategically its most complete victory of the war, the US Navy lost the Philippines argument at the very time when Iwo Jima was all but undefended; it was obliged to concede the principle that the invasion of Japan would be needed to complete the defeat of Japan; and it suffered the indignity of having MacArthur earmarked for supreme command in the Pacific. For the US Navy, therefore, there was defeat even in victory, and in this the navy reflected the United States itself: as American power in the western Pacific grew so the American capacity to shape events in eastern and south-east Asia diminished. Throughout Greater East Asia the war had unleashed the forces of nationalism and communism that were to limit the power and influence of the world's greatest state, though 30 years were to pass after the Japanese surrender before the main impetus of change throughout this area was exhausted at the end of a process that generally worked to American disadvantage.

At the time of Tojo's fall Japan found herself defeated decisively both in the Pacific and astride the Indo-Burmese border but in the course of a very successful offensive in central and southern China. This campaign, conducted at a time when the tide of war ran strongly against the Axis powers, was to provide Japan with a victory both double-edged and short-lived, but nevertheless a substantial victory and one with heavy implications for the Chinese domestic scene. The victory was double-edged in that the Japanese effort in central and southern China after April 1944 was possible only by the thinning of forces in northern China and Manchoutikuo, the resultant weakening of Japanese authority in the former and the long-term weakening of the garrison along the Soviet border being unacceptable to the Japanese High Command as 1944 gave way to 1945. It proved crucial in terms of the political situation within China because it produced something more than a defeat for Kuomintang armies that might have been explained away by Chungking with the facility that had been paraded on the occasion of previous defeats. At a time when the Chungking regime had to win victories that would atone for past defeats, the inactivity of recent years and the lack of any clear political programme, the Chungking regime was revealed as not simply corrupt, exploitative and repressive but incompetent and ineffective. Both politically and militarily, therefore, this last major Japanese offensive of the Great East Asia war had the effect of weakening the

Kuomintang relative to the communists at a time when both were looking beyond Japan's defeat to a full-scale resumption of their struggle for power.

The *Ichi-Go* offensive in central and southern China, authorised at the same time as the offensive into north-east India, was planned by the Japanese as two related operations. The first, *Ko-Go*, was to involve converging attacks by the *12th Army* and a detachment from the *China Expeditionary Army* along the 200 miles of the Peking–Hankow railroad in Honan province that remained in Chinese hands: at the same time the *1st* and *12th Armies* were to secure Loyang. The second and main operation, *To-Go*, was scheduled to unfold in three parts: *To-Go I* was to see an offensive by the *11th Army* from the Wuhan salient southwards to Hengyang via Changsha; *To-Go II* encompassed an advance from Hengyang through Ling-ling to Kweilung while the Canton-centred *23rd Army* secured Liuchow; *To-Go III* envisaged converging advances to secure the Canton–Hengyang railroad. After the defeat in the Philippine Sea, however, the scope of operations was extended despite the transfer of two divisions to Okinawa and the Philippines. In order to forestall a possible American landing in China, Foochow, the last major port between Shanghai and Canton still in Chinese hands, was added to the Japanese list of targets, and planning for 1945 set down the development of the Liuchow offensive into an attack on Nanning. Forces in French Indo-China were to support this offensive in order to link and consolidate the various Japanese holdings in China and south-east Asia, but with the Hanoi–Nanning railroad incomplete the Japanese High Command recognised that such a junction of forces could be for liaison purposes only, not for the development of an overland line of communication to serve as a replacement for the maritime links between Japan and the southern resources area.

The *Ko-Go* offensive began on 17 April, and at a cost of 2,150 dead and wounded the Japanese cleared the Peking–Hankow railroad in some three weeks. When Loyang fell on 26 May the Japanese were free to proceed with *To-Go I*, five of the *11th Army*'s eight divisions crossing the middle Yangtse between Ichang and the Wuhan cities on the twenty-seventh. With the main weight of this attack towards Changsha delivered east of the Siang, Liuyang fell on 14 June, Changsha on the sixteenth and Hengyang airfield on the twenty-sixth. Hengyang itself survived an assault on 28 June and then a one-month siege before falling on 8 August. Thereafter the *11th Army* had to pause in order to bring up supplies, but by 1 October it had reached within 40 miles of Kweilung. With Foochow falling to a combined overland and amphibious attack on

8 October, both parts of *To-Go II* struggled very slowly through October to their separate objectives, both Kweilung and Liuchow falling on 11 November. Thereafter, however, the pace of the Japanese advances quickened: the Nanning enterprise was accelerated with the result that Tokyo was able to announce the establishment of 'uninterrupted land communications between Manchoutikuo and Singapore' on 28 November, while simultaneously two divisions from the *11th Army* attacked towards Kweiyang and secured Tushan and Tuyan in the first week of December. Within another week, however, Tuyan had been ceded as the Japanese began to thin out their forces on the Kweiyang road in recognition of their over-extension on this extra front.

The Kuomintang authorities tried to explain away the defeats incurred during the *Ichi-Go* offensive with two contradictory arguments: that the defeats had been sustained by provincial as opposed to government troops, and that the best government troops were committed to battles in Yunnan and Upper Burma. Be that as it may, and both claims were correct, the distinction between provincial and government troops was largely lost upon a peasantry that for years had been ruthlessly exploited and abused by troops indelibly associated with the Chungking regime but who sought safety in flight at the first sign of battle. In Honan an enraged peasantry, abandoned to the Japanese, massacred fleeing Chinese troops, and if at Hengyang the Chinese cause was better served this reflected no credit on Chungking. In the maze of personal and regional in-fighting that characterised the politics of Chiang Kai-shek's court, the commander of the 10th Army that held Hengyang was not a member of Chiang's clique and being unreliable his army was abandoned by Chungking. Chiang's inactivity provoked open talk in Kwangsi of secession which was only checked by the realisation that the United States would not support such a move. Indeed it was in the crisis that the *Ichi-Go* offensive provoked that the United States chose to bind itself hand and foot to Chiang Kai-shek and his regime. Washington's failure to press its demands that Stilwell be given overall command of Chinese forces left the American High Command with no alternative but to recall Stilwell when this was demanded by Chiang, but if the United States lost the greater part of its freedom of action relative to Chungking as a result of this matter then the recall of one American general who was anathema to Chiang was no compensation for defeats that revealed a dangerous anti-Kuomintang undercurrent within Chinese society.

Moreover, the second of Chungking's claims that were paraded as mitigation of defeat really amounted to a massive if unconscious indictment of the Kuomintang regime: the Chinese troops in Upper

Burma were the pick of the nationalist armies in very large measure because they were not subjected to the vagaries of Chungking's mismanagement and corruption. In Burma the five Chinese divisions of the New 1st and 6th Armies of the Northern Combat Area Command, though of somewhat uneven quality, were in the forefront of the Allied effort that in the November 1943–May 1944 dry season wrested the initiative from the Japanese. Between the 1943 and 1944 monsoons the *Burma Area Army* had launched a pre-emptive attack (*Operation U-Go*) against the main bases in north-east India from which a major Allied offensive into Burma would have to be staged, this effort by three divisions of the *15th Army* being preceded by a divisionary attack (*Operation Ha-Go*) against XV Corps in the Arakan by the *55th Infantry Division* of the *28th Army*. This diversionary effort, begun on 4 February, provided the British with their first clear-cut victory over the Japanese: the veteran *55th Infantry Division* lost half its strength after it had encircled the 5th and 7th Indian Divisions at Maungdaw and Buthidaung as a result of these formations holding their positions and being supplied by air while no fewer than four divisions were committed to their relief. Despite its mauling, however, the *55th Infantry Division* succeeded in diverting British attention and resources – and in bringing to a halt a ponderous British advance in the Arakan that had begun in December – at the very time when the Japanese made their main effort across the Chindwin.

The *15th Army* achieved surprise because of the speed and scale of its advance through the rugged terrain between the river and the border, but IV Corps was nevertheless able to withdraw its three divisions into defensive positions around Imphal one day before the Japanese began the siege of the town on 5 April. On the previous day the 31st Infantry Division had reached behind the British garrison at Kohima but here, as at Imphal, once the *15th Army* failed to defeat British formations piecemeal during its initial advance it found that it had no counter to British superiority of firepower and numbers and of strategic mobility that allowed the British to draw upon transport aircraft from as far afield as the Mediterranean theatre to move the 5th Indian Division and other formations to blocking positions behind Kohima. Without the means to sustain a protracted battle and the lateral roads that would allow it to achieve an overwhelming concentration of force on any given sector around Imphal, the *15th Army* found that a stalled offensive constituted a siege of its formations even as it sought to overcome British defences: the refusal of the *15th Army* to admit this reality condemned its divisions to slow, lingering defeat. The siege of Kohima lasted until 20 April though

The Clearing of Burma, 1943 - 45

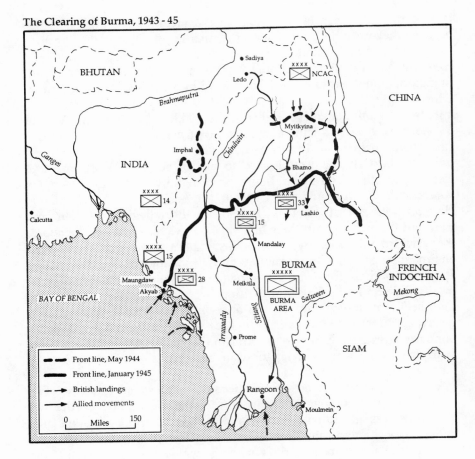

another seven weeks were needed for XXXIII Corps to eliminate Japanese resistance around Kohima: the siege of Imphal was not raised until 22 June.

The defeats in the Arakan and before Kohima and Imphal cost the *Burma Area Army* some 58,000 of the 97,000 men with which it had begun offensive operations: the crippling of four divisions broke Japanese power in Burma. Fought on a scale that eclipsed any land fighting in the Pacific to date, these battles on the borders of north-east India decided the outcome of the Burma campaign because their result was to leave the *Burma Area Army* without the power to resist the British advance from north-east India that was to begin in November 1944. The British victories of February–June 1944, however, were not unaccompanied:

398

two partial victories, and one failure, were secured at this same time by Allied forces on other sectors of the front. In the Hukawng valley the NCAC had begun an offensive in October 1943 that resulted in a series of local defeats for the *18th Infantry Division* and the clearing of the Maingkwan–Walawbaum area by the Chinese 22nd and 38th Infantry Divisions on 7 March, the date when the *15th Army* had begun its *U-Go* offensive. With one American regiment in the line and this effort lavishly supported by transport aircraft, the Sino-American force secured Nhpum Ga in early April, Myitkyina airfield on 17 May and Kamaing on 16 June. In Yunnan, however, the twelve divisions of two Chinese army groups with a total strength of about 72,000 men were outfought by an understrength *56th Infantry Division* in a series of battles along the Salween between April and June. Launched only upon American insistence that the Chungking regime justified the aid it had received, this offensive resulted in the capture of Kufeng and Chiangchu on 19 and 20 June respectively, but at the same time Chinese forces lost the gains that they had made in the Mangshih–Lameng area in the first weeks of their attack. On both this and the Myitkyina front, Chinese forces found themselves by June 1944 committed to protracted sieges, but while the *Burma Area Army* was forced to move the *2nd Infantry Division* from the Arakan to support the *56th Infantry Division* on the Salween the positional advantage gained by the Allies by the development of the Hukawng and Yunnan offensives could not be translated into tangible results until the capture of Tengchung in September and of Myitkyina.

At Myitkyina the Allied occupation of the airfield in May had provided the NCAC with the means whereby fresh British forces could have been moved from north-east India to ensure the rapid capture of the town, but though such forces were requested none were available. As a result the siege of Myitkyina was conducted by exhausted and badly depleted Sino-American formations, and by two British regimental equivalents that were in no better condition and were the most battleworthy of the five formations that had entered Burma in March in the course of the second Chindit operation. Like its predecessor, this operation was a much-proclaimed affair but in military terms achieved little of value. Though Japanese historians have credited the second Chindit operation as having tipped the balance against the *15th Army* at Kohima and Imphal through the disruption of its lines of communication and the destruction of 20 transport companies behind the Chindwin, the fact was that an operation that hung by such a slender thread – and which began after the Japanese right flank had started to crumble and when it was known that enemy forces were operating in the rear areas – had little chance of success. The

British idea of the long-range penetration of Japanese rear areas, as tested by the first and second Chindit operations, proved a fallacy in that it displayed the inherent weakness of light infantry – an ability to move not matched by a capacity to engage in sustained operations – and without the means to hold ground for a protracted period any damage inflicted upon Japanese lines of communication could only be marginal. Part of the Chindit force was withdrawn to India in May, but other formations were involved in the capture of Mogaung on 26 June and of Myitkyina on 3 August.

The significance of the offensive that resulted in the capture of Mogaung and Myitkyina was political rather than military, but in fact the political imperative that had prompted the American High Command to sanction this offensive had been overtaken by events by the time that these two towns fell. Originally, the Hukawng offensive had been ordered in order to enable overland communications between Ledo and Kunming to be established and as the means of dragging the British into an Upper Burma commitment they had resisted throughout 1943. By the second half of 1944, however, the British, having won what they recognised to be an overwhelming victory around Imphal, had come to accept both the political and military arguments for such a commitment though they continued to resist two corollaries. First, contrary to what was proclaimed at the time and which was subsequently paraded as fact, the British command resisted the idea of trying to conduct a general offensive through the monsoon; second, it was unconvinced that Burma could be conquered by an overland offensive from north-east India. British forces were to close up to the Chindwin during the monsoon, and Chindit forces with the NCAC operated through the rains, but it was not until 19 November that IV Corps opened the British offensive into Upper Burma when it crossed the Chindwin at Sittaung. By that time, however, the British inability to release assault shipping from the European theatre as a result of the 21st Army Group's double failure to clear the approaches to Antwerp and to secure the Rhine crossing finally brought to an end the somewhat fantastical scheme to advance into central Burma with armour via Rangoon, the capital and main port of Burma being subjected to an amphibious assault on the scale of the Normandy landings. With the collapse of this wonderland proposal in October the 14th Army found itself committed to the effort that the Allied High Command had dismissed as impracticable for the previous 30 months: the reconquest of Burma by an overland offensive from north-east India.

The campaign in Burma after November 1943 was to be prosecuted to a successful conclusion by the Allies largely on account of two factors: the development of air supply freed ground forces from dependence upon overland lines of communication, the lack of which would otherwise have halted proceedings if not in Upper then in central Burma; and the Japanese High Command could not cover the losses sustained by *Burma Area Army* during 1944 because of the higher priority it had to afford the Philippines, Formosa and the Ryukyus as a result of the defeat of the *Imperial Navy* in the Philippine Sea in June. In Burma, therefore, the Japanese were forced to don a defensive strategy that sought to deny the Allies control of Burma for as long as possible, the prevention of a juncture of Chinese forces from the Hukawng and Yunnan fronts being a secondary objective. By the time that this change was implemented, however, six of the *Burma Area Army*'s 10 divisions had been reduced to 20 per cent effective strength and another two divisions, the *2nd* and *53rd Infantry Divisions*, were fully committed defensively around Wanting and the Mogaung–Myitkyina area respectively. But in the western Pacific the loss of naval and air superiority rendered Japanese holdings untenable, a fact acknowledged by the switch of emphasis of Japanese policy after the June defeat. Whereas Japanese policy had originally set down the aim of securing a negotiated peace that would leave the Empire with its gains of recent years, after June 1944 it was directed to securing a negotiated peace that would avoid unconditional surrender. The hope of the Japanese High Command was not that defeat could be avoided but that an invasion of the home islands could be prevented and that peace would leave Japanese domestic institutions (i.e. the imperial principle) intact. To this aim the Japanese intended to wage protracted struggles in the various islands subjected to assault in order to expose American naval and assault shipping to concentrated naval and air attack, the Japanese thinking being that American willingness to proceed with an invasion of the Japanese home islands would be weakened as a result of their losses.

The immediate problem in the implementation of this revised strategic policy was that the Japanese could only respond to events and had no clear idea of how the Americans intended to proceed after Saipan, a problem that the Japanese High Command shared with its American opposite number in summer 1944. Those operations scheduled as the follow-up to Biak and Saipan were to be executed as planned: after Japanese resistance on Saipan ended on 9 July Guam and Tinian were invaded on 21 and 24 July and cleared by 12 and 1 August respectively; Noemfoor and Cape Sansapor were assaulted on 2 and 30 July and were effectively cleared on 31 July and 31 August respectively. But even by mid-August the Americans were still tied to the 12 March 1944 programme and had no clear idea of whether the main effort in the

The Pacific Campaign: The Advances Across The Pacific, June 1944 - July 1945

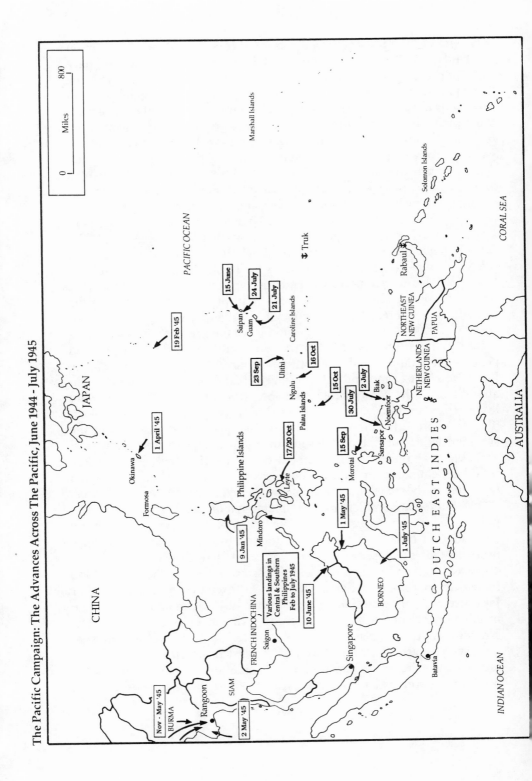

western Pacific was to be directed to Luzon or Formosa: provisional planning set down landings in the Palaus in September, Mindanao in late 1944 and on both Formosa and Luzon in February 1945. As early as 13 June, before the battle of the Philippine Sea was fought, planners in Washington suggested a direct descent on Kyushu after the capture of the Marianas, but this leap of the imagination was too much for Pacific commands who insisted intermediate bases had to be secured in the western Pacific before the Japanese home islands were closed. The Pacific commands agreed in July upon the invasion of Mindanao in November, but with MacArthur insisting that thereafter Leyte and then Luzon be assaulted – in January and April 1945 – and Nimitz proposing to bypass Luzon after the occupation of Leyte in favour of landings on Formosa and around Amoy the most divisive single issue in the settling of American strategy for the war against Japan had to be resolved. At this time three of the four members of the US Joint Chiefs of Staff favoured the navy's plan, but by September the navy's proposals had been weakened by a combination of poor planning for an invasion of Formosa and MacArthur's single-mindedness in championing the liberation of the Philippines *en route* to Japan.

On 8 September, with commitments to land in the Palaus and on islands on the approaches to Mindanao and on Mindanao itself already set down, the JCS sanctioned the invasion of Leyte in December but made no decision on the Formosa–Luzon question. Within five days, however, the issue was in effect settled, to the detriment of the navy's proposals, by the unexpected success of the fast carrier force in action off the Philippines. The basis of American planning had been that ten weeks would be needed before the invasion of Mindanao for the carriers to neutralise Japanese air power in the Philippines, but after preparatory strikes against targets in the Jimas, Wake, Yap, Ulithi, Ngulu and the Palaus, TF38, with 16 carriers under command, raided Mindanao on 10 and 11 September, the Visayans (12–13), and finally Luzon (21–22). In their initial strikes the Americans encountered little opposition and destroyed 58 Japanese aircraft, but in raids over the central Philippines the Americans accounted for 478 Japanese aircraft and a host of minor shipping at the cost of eight aircraft. Even without waiting for the outcome of strikes against Luzon, which resulted in the destruction of an estimated 300 Japanese aircraft, the revelation of Japanese weakness throughout the Philippines invited an acceleration of the American operational timetable. On the recommendation of TF38 command and the endorsement of MacArthur and Nimitz, the JCS cancelled in 90 minutes on 14 September the proposed landings on Yap, in the Talauds and on Mindanao in favour of a landing on Leyte on 20 October.

The change of plan – which came too late to affect the landings on Morotai and in the Palaus which took place within a matter of hours even though their relevance was largely lost with the cancellation of the landings on Mindanao – had one implication: the belief that a Luzon operation would be less demanding on manpower than a Formosa campaign tipped the balance in favour of MacArthur's arguments because a landing on Luzon could be accelerated to meet the new timetable whereas an assault on Formosa could not. Moreover, with the *Ichi-Go* offensive in southern China eliminating the airfields from which any landing around Amoy was to be supported, the naval case for the bypassing of Luzon was lost. Thus was settled the main features of American strategy for the final approach to the Japanese home islands: an advance along the Leyte–Luzon–Okinawa axis and the seizure of Iwo Jima. The question of whether the final reduction of Japan was to be achieved by assault or by blockade and bombardment nevertheless remained to be formally finalised.

Between 14 September and 17–18 October, when the 6th Ranger Battalion landed on three islands in the approaches to Leyte Gulf, US forces conducted four sets of landings in the western Pacific that resulted in the finalisation of Truk's isolation, the capture of airfields from which operations over the Philippines were staged, and the acquisition at Ulithi of a forward base for the carrier force that ended its need to return to Majuro after operations. The landings on Ulithi and Ngulu on 23 September and 16 October were all but unopposed, but Ngulu was abandoned when it was realised that it had no facilities to offer beyond those already available or being developed on Ulithi. On Morotai the American forces that landed on 15 September cleared the island by 4 October, but on Peleliu an operation with two divisions that was confidently expected to last four days continued until 27 November though the island was effectively under American control by the end of September and one of the American divisions was withdrawn during October. Against an enemy that for the first time in the Pacific war conducted a defensive battle in depth rather than try to meet an invasion on the water's edge, the Americans incurred 10,314 battle casualties in the course of an operation that the US Marine Corps assessed to have been as difficult as Tarawa, but which was overshadowed by the unfolding of events in the Philippines.

In its turn, however, the Philippines campaign came to be overshadowed by two of its own aspects. First, in accordance with the mores and history of American society it was portrayed in terms of personality and of MacArthur's triumphant return to Filippino soil, and in the propagation of this heroic image there was no more fervent champion than MacArthur himself. Second, in the recounting of this campaign the naval battles, collectively known as Leyte Gulf, have tended to attract inordinate attention because their conduct on the American side raised issues that continue to be controversial. These aspects of the campaign have obscured a couple of matters which should be self-evident but which are seldom afforded consideration. The Philippines campaign proved to be a protracted, costly affair that was not concluded before the Japanese surrender. Moreover, the battle of Leyte Gulf, which in reality was a series of related actions, was only one of four crushing victories registered by TF38 in the course of this campaign. These matters in their turn raise an obvious issue: if, as was the case, the Philippines campaign was so long and expensive, then the question of whether American interests would have been better served by an invasion of Formosa presents itself.

In the unfolding of the campaign in the western Pacific during the last year of the war it was the naval and air battle, not the course of events on the islands of the Philippines, that held the greater importance, and the operations of TF38 demand initial examination. In effect, the naval–air battle around and over the Philippines was continuous between October 1944 and January 1945, but there were three peaks of American achievement: the raids against Okinawa, Formosa and the Philippines that preceded the landings on Leyte; the battle of Leyte Gulf itself; and the rampage of the carrier force through the South China Sea that represented the postscript to the landings in Lingayen Gulf on 9 January 1945. In addition, there were routine operations and the continuing campaign against Japanese naval shipping by submarines, and what is often forgotten is that whereas between 23 and 27 October in the course of the battle of Leyte Gulf the Japanese navy lost three battleships, four carriers, 10 cruisers and 11 destroyers, American follow-up operations between 5 and 13 November cost the Japanese another two cruisers and eight destroyers while between 5 and 29 November American carrier aircraft and submarines accounted for two carriers, one battleship, four cruisers and 12 destroyers. These latter losses would have been considered grievous in their own right were they not dwarfed by those incurred in one of the greatest battles in naval history. Moreover, these various naval successes were obtained by the Americans in addition to unprecedented losses inflicted upon the Japanese merchant fleet between September and November 1944, most of which were concentrated in and around the Philippines.

The preliminary effort that provided TF38 with its first victory in the Philippine Campaign began on 10 October with the attack on Okinawa; on the eleventh northern Luzon was attacked; and on 12, 13 and 14 October the main American effort was directed against Formosa. On the fourteenth one American carrier group also attacked Luzon, the main American effort in the Philippines being made on and after the eighteenth. With 17 carriers and 1,000 aircraft under command of TF38, the scale of American operations – 1,356 strike sorties on 10 October alone – was unprecedented in naval terms, as indeed was the phenomenon of a naval air offensive against a massed, land-based air force. The latter was crushed in the course of this offensive. Coming on top of the 893 Japanese aircraft destroyed by TF38 during September throughout the western Pacific, American operations accounted for an estimated 600 Japanese aircraft between 10 and 16 October. In the course of the Philippines campaign as a whole the Japanese lost an estimated 3,000 aircraft, but the debilitating losses were those incurred in the preliminary phase because they were sustained by those formations that had to preserve their strength in order to strike at an invasion force if the Japanese were to have any chance of recording even a partial victory in the Philippines. The premature commitment of the *2nd Air* Fleet to the Formosa battle, and its defeat before Leyte was invaded, was crucially important in ensuring that Japanese air power began the Philippines campaign piecemeal and from a position of marked numerical weakness. Moreover, the savaging of the Luzon-based *1st Air Fleet* and *4th Air Army* in addition to the mauling of the *2nd Air Fleet* was accompanied by the destruction of air groups from six carriers that were committed to the Formosa battle despite being made ready for carrier operations in November.

The losses of these groups, which between them numbered 154 aircraft, had two results for the Japanese conduct of the Philippines campaign. In an elaborate attempt to deny the Americans control of the Philippines the Japanese navy had planned to attack an American invasion force first with concentrated land-based air power and then with carrier and surface forces. With only 100 aircraft left to the carrier forces after the Formosan débâcle, the carrier force was given the task of luring American carrier forces away from the Philippines while surface forces fell upon beachheads and assault shipping. Moreover, the destruction of their conventional air power left the Japanese with little real option but to resort to their last moral reserves in an attempt to stave off defeat.

406

Recourse to suicide attacks represented the use of the sole remaining superiority that the Japanese held over their enemies, but if in the event Allied sailors who fought to live proved more than a match for Japanese airmen who died to fight then the long-term implication of the introduction of *kamikaze* attacks in October 1944 was lost on both sides at the time: the inauguration and extensive employment of such attacks over the next eight months pointed to a total collapse of Japanese air power by or in 1946. Without a parallel development of conventional air power the commitment of training schools to this one means of attack foreshadowed a rapid bankruptcy of Japanese aviation. The *kamikaze* option was very literally a one-shot effort that could not be sustained, and in the event it proved singularly ineffective. In the course of 1945 10 American carriers were forced to withdraw from operations with battle damage caused by *kamikaze* attack, but of these only one had not returned to service by September. Such an expedient as suicide attacks was no substitute for adequate, conventional air power and could not defeat enemies that for the invasion of Kyushu planned to have 30 fleet and light fleet carriers with two separate carrier task forces by October 1945.

For this invasion the Americans planned to have 10 carriers with one task force assigned a covering role to ensure the security of beachheads and assault shipping and twenty carriers with a second task force detailed for offensive operations.* It was the absence of such numbers and the ability to discharge two quite separate functions at the one time with a clear definition of responsibilities, that brought the Americans close to a defeat off Samar on 25 October when a Japanese battle force engaged an escort carrier formation at a time when TF38 was not in a position to provide cover. Amongst the various arguments that have continued on the vexed question of individual responsibility for this state of affairs two matters remain beyond dispute. First, off Samar the Japanese could never have registered more than a minor tactical victory that would not have changed the outcome of the campaign in the Philippines, and if the Japanese had broken into Leyte Gulf to attack the transports off the beachhead then their losses would have been even more substantial than was the case, and again, what success they enjoyed would not have altered the outcome of the Philippines campaign. Second, despite the stumble off Samar, American naval forces off the Philippines nevertheless

---

*For the invasion the Americans planned to employ 18 fleet and 8 light fleet carriers divided 7–3, 8–4 and 3–1 between the first, second and reserve forces; the British were to provide 5 fleet and 5 light fleet carriers divided 4–4 and 1–1 between the second and reserve forces.

inflicted crushing defeats on each of the three major Japanese formations committed to battle in October 1944.

The battle of Leyte Gulf was fought over an area and time span without precedence in naval warfare: in terms of numbers and tonnage it was the greatest battle in modern naval history. On the Japanese side it involved four formations: the decoy carrier force operating north-east of Luzon; two battle forces that were to converge on Leyte Gulf after negotiating the San Bernardino and the Surigao Straits; and a cruiser force detailed to enter Leyte Gulf through the southern passage. With the Japanese obliged to divide their fleet because of the oil shortage in the home islands, the carrier and cruiser forces were to sail from Japan, the latter formation via the Formosa Strait while the battle forces gathered off Brunei before going their separate ways. On the American side the landings by two corps of the 6th Army on Leyte on 20 October were supported by TF77 and covered by TF38. TF77, consisting of battle, cruiser and escort carrier groups, came under the 7th Fleet of South-West Pacific Command; the latter, which was assigned the destruction of the enemy fleet as its primary task, was part of Nimitz's command. This lack of an overall commander in a theatre where two separate commands and their forces converged is often regarded as the root cause of American problems during the battle of Leyte Gulf, not that it prevented the savaging of the powerful central force between 22 and 24 October as it approached the San Bernardino Strait and the annihilation of the battle force that tried to negotiate the Surigao Strait on the night of 24–25 October. With the second-echelon cruiser force declining to enter the same strait because of its well-founded suspicion of what awaited it, TF38 sought action with the Japanese carrier force late on the twenty-fourth after both contacting it and noting the withdrawal of the central force in the Sibuyan Sea. This withdrawal, however, was only temporary, and when the central force resumed its advance it found the San Bernardino Strait unguarded, the 7th Fleet having assumed from interceptions of TF38's signals that it had detached forces to close the Straits to a Japanese advance.* The Japanese central force thus encountered an unsupported escort carrier formation when it rounded Samar on the morning of 25 October yet it lost three heavy cruisers in an action that resulted in the destruction of two escort carriers and three other units before it withdrew. The failure to press this action cost the Japanese central force its only possible chance to justify its own losses and the sacrifice of the carrier force, which on the twenty-fifth lost four carriers,

*See Appendix D

one cruiser and two destroyers as a result of carrier aircraft, submarine and surface action.

Arguably, 25 October 1944 constituted the most destructive single day in modern naval history at the end of which, and even without the losses that were to be inflicted on the Japanese navy on the following day, the *Combined Fleet* was an impotent irrelevance, not even deserving the status of a coastal defence force. Other than their losses to the central force off Samar, these successes cost the Americans one light carrier sunk on the twenty-fourth, four Allied cruisers damaged between the twelfth and twenty-fourth, and seven escort carriers sunk or damaged on the twenty-fifth in the first massed *kamikaze* attack. Yet what little success the Japanese achieved was double-edged in that the *Imperial Navy*'s vastly inflated claims of American losses between 10 and 20 October had reinforced the decision of the *Southern Army*, made against the wishes of *XIV Area Army* which was the local command in the Philippines, to meet an American invasion wherever it took place rather than concentrating on the defence of Luzon. As a consequence, the Japanese were to reinforce their single division on Leyte with perhaps 45,000 men drawn from five divisions between 24 October and 12 December, though in the process some 15,000 Japanese soldiers were killed or drowned and virtually all equipment, stores and shipping into Ormoc Bay were lost. A tenacious defence of Leyte forced the Americans to commit a peak combat strength of about 202,000 men on the island at the beginning of December,* but at an obvious cost to the Japanese *35th Army* in the central and southern Philippines. Forces committed to the Leyte campaign represented forces lost even if organised resistance on Leyte did not come to an end until May 1945, but if some 110,000 Japanese troops remained in the central and southern Philippines after the Americans established effective control over the island in late December then the defence of the other islands south of Luzon was nonetheless weakened seriously by the transfer of the *35th Army*'s best formations to Leyte. With the landings of the 77th Infantry Division in Ormoc Bay on 7 December pointing to the rapid collapse of serious Japanese resistance on Leyte, *XIV Area Army* abandoned the struggle for the island on 19 December four days after the 6th Army served notice of its future intentions with landings on Mindoro.

The American move against Mindoro, which was secured against minor opposition by the end of January 1945, was the prelude to the invasion of Luzon and the clearing of the Visayas in order to secure the

---

*American strength on Leyte reached a peak of 257,000 in late January 1945 but this total includes AAF base personnel and troops staged through the island.

sea passage through the islands: it also provoked the last sortie by a Japanese surface force that commanded any measure of success when, on 26–27 December, a cruiser force from Camranh Bay sank a merchantman and patrol boat off Mindoro. The main landings on Luzon, by two corps of the 6th Army in Lingayen Gulf, were followed by secondary landings on 29 January by a corps on the neck of the Bataan peninsula and on 31 January by a formation on the southern approaches to Manila Bay. The Bay, plus the airfields of central Luzon, represented the main American military objectives on the island, but while Clark Field was secured on 31 January and Nichols Field on 12 February, the resistance of Japanese naval troops inside Manila prevented the clearing of the capital until 3 March despite American forces having fought their way into central Manila on 4 February and having completed the encirclement of the city eight days later. With Corregidor secured on 28 February after a 12-day fight, the Americans secured everything of political and military value on Luzon by the first week of March, by which time the 8th Army had begun the process of clearing the Visayas. On 19 February American forces landed on Samar, at Puerto Princesa on Palawan on the twenty-eighth, and in the following seven weeks conducted 38 landings in the central and southern Philippines. For all their numbers the Japanese, scattered across the Visayas and Mindanao, were able to offer prolonged resistance only on Negros and Mindanao itself, and by June, when the 8th Army relieved the 6th Army on Luzon, effective Japanese resistance throughout the Philippines was at an end despite there being some 115,000 Japanese troops still in the field on Luzon alone. By that time the Americans had destroyed or neutralised formations that had numbered between 380,000 and 423,000 men, though this was an achievement that raised issues seldom addressed by histories and accounts of the Philippines campaign other than in terms of the bitter arguments between MacArthur's admirers and detractors.

The natural starting point in setting down the terms of reference for any dispassionate examination of the Philippines campaign is the statement of the obvious: the campaign was fought on MacArthur's insistence. In a situation of uncertainty in Washington, it was MacArthur's single-minded determination that the route to Tokyo lay through the Philippines that ensured that the islands were liberated rather than bypassed. In one sense this was only correct though perhaps not for the right reasons. With the military arguments between the Formosa and Luzon alternatives finely balanced it was proper that political considerations should determine policy, but in the formation of policy the political consideration that should have settled the issue – the need to liberate the

410

Philippines and to atone for the American failure to protect the Commonwealth from invasion and conquest at the start of the war – was subordinate to political expediency on the part of a Washington that, in election year, was not prepared to face the probable consequences of MacArthur being thwarted: it was to need another war and another president, much tougher than Roosevelt, to curb MacArthur's intention to secure for himself the directing of national policy.

In military terms the Philippines campaign did little if anything to clarify the issues that had so beset the formulation of American strategic policy before September 1944. The American effort in the Philippines involved no fewer than 16 US divisions and a sustained commitment over four and a half months followed by a significant residual undertaking over another five and a half: in August 1945 four US divisions remained committed to operations in the Philippines. It is difficult to understand, therefore, how a Formosa campaign could have proved more expensive in manpower and time than the undertaking ultimately made in the Philippines. Moreover, the campaign was expensive in terms of American casualties, and with 52,514 battle and 93,321 non-battle casualties in the course of the fighting ashore the liberation of the Philippines proved considerably more costly than any single undertaking during the central Pacific offensive. This raises two quite separate issues: on the one hand it invites consideration of the relative value of the two American offensives across the Pacific, and on the other hand it prompts examination of the infinitely more difficult question of whether, if not the Philippines, Luzon could have been bypassed.

On the first question MacArthur and his admirers always claimed that MacArthur victories were economical and more cheaply won than those registered in the drive through the island groups of the central Pacific: indeed the 9,694 killed and wounded in the course of operations that took the front line from Aitape to Morotai in five months contrasts sharply with the total of 14,111 Americans killed and wounded on Saipan alone. But the central Pacific offensive was directed against more heavily defended objectives than was the south-west Pacific offensive, and the significance of the former's victories was correspondingly greater than those recorded along the northern coast of New Guinea. The offensive in the south-west Pacific represented no significant threat to major Japanese interests before June 1944 whereas this was most definitely not the case with respect to the central Pacific thrust, and it was most obviously the dependent effort: it could not have been carried into the Philippines without the success provided by the fast carrier force in the central Pacific.

411

The second question presents more awkward problems of interpretation. The fact that Allied arms secured both Luzon and Okinawa lends support implicitly to the view that Formosa could have been secured as the alternative to Luzon, but the existence of a minimum of 145 all-weather and 115 landing strips in the Philippines in August 1944 equally suggests that the extensive harbour and base facilities that were the objectives sought by the Americans from Leyte could not have been secured without the physical occupation of Luzon. Moreover, though both Luzon and Okinawa were secured despite sustained *kamikaze* operations in both campaigns, whether Formosa could have been secured with Luzon unreduced and the Japanese, at least in theory, able to mount concentrated suicide attacks from two directions is clearly problematical. Allied success in meeting the *kikisuis* off Okinawa was partly the result of the Americans having faced and defeated four *kamikaze* offensives before the Okinawa campaign began, an accumulation of battle experience and technique that would not have been available to the Americans if Formosa had been substituted for Luzon. In addition, despite American success over the Philippines in September and October and the fact that some 600 Japanese aircraft were destroyed both in November and in December over the islands, by the end of the year the Japanese still retained about that number of aircraft on the islands. Japanese resistance over the Philippines proved more protracted and effective than had been anticipated. The peak of *kamikaze* achievement was registered on 25 November when four carriers of TF38 were extensively damaged but between 13 December 1944 and 13 January 1945 no fewer than 79 warships, merchantmen and amphibious vessels – including three battleships and five escort carriers – were sunk or seriously damaged by *kamikaze* attack. The scale of these losses suggests that Luzon could not have been bypassed in favour of an assault on Formosa, though perhaps both could have been bypassed by a direct assault on Okinawa that might well have given the Americans an advantage of timing more than offsetting the dangers presented by an intact Japanese fleet and positional and numerical advantages that remained to the Japanese. In any event, such a deep finesse of Japanese possessions in the western Pacific was not attempted, and after Leyte the Americans embarked upon a campaign in the Philippines that would seem to have produced two incontrovertible conclusions. American possession of the Philippines physically separated Japan from her southern resources areas and thus ensured her defeat, though in reality this was already guaranteed as a result of the annihilation of the Japanese merchant fleet: as the official US Army historian of this campaign has noted: 'If no other campaign or operation of war in the Pacific had done so, then Japan's inability to hold the Philippines made her ultimate defeat clear and certain.' It is fairly certain, however, that Japan's defeat was ensured if not before the landings on Leyte then before the landings on Mindoro and Luzon. The latter, however, initiated a campaign that left Manila the most heavily damaged Allied capital in the world after Warsaw. An estimated 100,000 Filippinos were killed in the battle for the city, either caught in the fighting or murdered by the Japanese.

For all the controversy that has surrounded this campaign, the Philippines crusade represented a number of firsts for the United States. It was the first and only occasion during the Pacific war when her forces found themselves committed to a large-scale land campaign, and it was the first campaign in which South-West Pacific Command was committed to operations that involved carrier aviation winning and maintaining air superiority over the battlefield. As such, this campaign was the first in which carrier aviation met and defeated land-based air power as opposed to air power based on scattered island groups, but while this development was peculiar to the Pacific war this aspect of tactical air power was matched by parallel developments of strategic air power in both the European and Pacific theatres.

There are a number of curious similarities between the strategic air offensives against Germany and Japan, most notably in that in real terms both were of extremely short duration. The offensive that began against Germany in September 1944 with the release of strategic bomber forces from *Operation Overlord* and the campaign against the Japanese home islands that began in November 1944 from bases in the Marianas both lasted some eight months. Although the two efforts differed in that the former had been preceded by bombing operations over the previous four years whereas the latter had only the minor introduction provided since June 1944 by XX Bomber Command from bases in China, both offensives succeeded in destroying war economies that were on the point of collapse. Both campaigns built up slowly in their first months before entering their final cataclysmic phase after singularly awesome operations – the only 2,000-bomber raid of the war on 24 December 1944 by the 8th Air Force and the great fire-raid on Tokyo on the night of 9–10 March 1945 that left 124,711 people killed or wounded and 1,008,005 homeless. Both campaigns were brought to successful conclusions in conditions of overwhelming air supremacy, and both bombing efforts were supported by fighters operating from forward bases. (It is an often forgotten aspect of the campaign against Japan that by war's end Iwo Jima, secured as a base for fighters tasked with escorting B-29 Superfortresses to their targets, had been made ready for B-29 combat missions and had an airfield that covered half of the island's eight square miles.) Both offensives, moreover, were conducted on a gargantuan scale. In the Far East, an American effort from the Marianas that was shouldered by just one wing between November 1944 and February 1945 ended on 14 August with the largest single raid of the Pacific war by no fewer than 833 Superfortresses drawn from five wings, and had the war continued and the 8th Air Force been transferred from Europe to Okinawa as planned, Japanese cities would have been subjected to monthly bombardment equivalent to the total November 1944–June 1945 effort.

In the European war in the 115 days between new year and 26 April 1945, the date of the last heavy bomber raids from bases in Britain, RAF Bomber Command, besides mounting the war's largest raid on a single target when 1,108 of its bombers attacked Dortmund on 12 March, carried out operations on 81 days and 100 nights, and on average put 495 heavy bombers into the air in any 24-hour period: in this same phase the 8th Air Force mounted operations on 89 days and 17 nights, carried out no fewer than 55 1,000-bomber raids, and in one two-week period, between 19 February and 4 March, flew nothing but 1,000-bomber raids on each successive day. Even the smaller and unsung 15th Air Force in Italy recorded unprecedented levels of activity in this closing phase of the war. Though it lost 46 days – 24 in January alone – because of bad weather, it bombed Berlin on 24 March while the 8th Air Force flew 1,749 heavy bomber and 1,375 fighter sorties in support of the Rhine crossings, and it recorded its only 1,000-bomber raid on 15 April, though the greater part of this effort was directed against tactical targets. These various strategic efforts in the European theatre were made in addition to those of the tactical air forces, but by April 1945 there was virtually no distinction between strategic and tactical bombing as Allied armies converged in central Germany.

The campaigns against Germany and Japan were also similar in three other respects. First, and at different times, the Allied offensives were conducted by forces in possession of formulae that were proof against failure. In the German context the 25 September 1944 directive presented the Allied air forces with the destruction of the German oil industry as their sole priority: in the case of the Japanese war, victory was to be won after February 1944 by low-level incendiary attacks on urban areas, the form of attack on the civilian population that the American High Command insisted that it declined to use in the European war on

414

moral grounds. Second, and in obvious contradiction to this point of similarity, both campaigns were brought to successful conclusions by area bombardment. Notwithstanding American declarations of principle, in the last months of the European war the American policy of 'blind bombing of communications targets', since it involved an average error of two miles, was in practice indistinguishable from the uncompromising British policy of area bombardment for its own sake; in this last phase of the war American bombers, in the words of one commentator, 'matched the British ruin for ruin'. Certainly any distinction between American and British practices was lost upon the citizens of Dresden, Chemnitz and Berlin after visitations by the 8th Air Force in February 1945. The fact was that while both RAF Bomber Command and the 8th Air Force did attack precision targets in the last four months of the war, such targets became fewer as the progressive German collapse presented the Allied air forces with the choice of bombing area targets or not bombing at all. The latter was an unacceptable alternative both to nations that had lavished so much manpower, money and commitment into the creation of their strategic air forces and to the air forces themselves: these were rivals as well as partners, and neither was prepared to stay its hand as long as the other continued operations.

The remaining point of similarity between the two campaigns was their effectiveness. By the end of 1944 the German war economy had been paralysed and by March 1945 was in ruins: by the end of July 1945 Japan had been reduced to a state of helplessness that even her High Command acknowledged by admitting that if Japan's enemies chose not to invade her but to stand offshore and continue to pound her cities into rubble there was nothing that she could do about a situation that represented 'the most troublesome possible course' that Japan could face. The fear of the Japanese High Command of a collapse of morale, with its obvious overtones of social upheaval and revolution, pointed to strategic air power's success in realising the claim of the pre-war lobby that strategic bombing could destroy an enemy's will to make war: while this never happened in the European war, both the European and Pacific conflicts saw strategic air power achieve its alternative aim of destroying an enemy's ability to wage war. In the case of Germany this achievement was remarkable in light of the size, diversity and dispersal of the German war economy; in the case of Japan the achievement, though scarcely less impressive, was aided by peculiarities of urban and industrial concentration. But neither success was exclusively the property of the strategic air offensives, and whereas the success of the campaign against Japan was very clear-cut and possessed a very obvious finality, the nature, importance and the value of the undoubted Allied victory over Germany in the air are very difficult to assess. Germany's lack of seaborne trade, her loss of foreign resources, and her territorial losses all contributed to her economic defeat, which was assured for the spring of 1945 if only because the October 1944 decision to raise *Volkssturm* formations and to mobilise all manpower even at the expense of industrial production ensured Germany's general industrial collapse in early 1945 even without any bombing in the last six months of the war. The German economic collapse involved a host of related factors, most of which were unquantifiable, but if the exact contribution of the strategic air offensive to Germany's final defeat cannot be stated with any certainty then various aspects of the strategic bombing offensive against Germany can be defined, most obviously the factors that contributed to whatever success the offensive enjoyed and to its most profound failure.

The offensives against both Germany and Japan commanded success because of five factors that were common to both campaigns. First, both bombing efforts benefited as a result of errors of long-term planning and dispersal on the part of Germany and Japan, and both campaigns built on previous achievements, both by sea and in the air. Second, by the time that the strategic bombing campaigns began both Germany and Japan had lost their capacity to absorb damage because the virtual loss of their ability to plunder conquered territory left them with nothing more than their own resources with which to withstand attack: indeed one of the most notable features of both wars was that two nations that for years waged war ruthlessly on foreign soil showed a marked disinclination to sacrifice themselves and their resources when war came to their own soil. Third, the effectiveness of the bombing offensives represented the exercise of a command of the air over enemy cities which was a result of the successful application of fighter power, both defensively in support of bomber formations and offensively in seeking out targets of opportunity. Fourth, the partial elimination of the enemies' air defence systems by the overrunning of forward bases provided the Allied air forces with the means to reach deeply into hostile territory while denying depth and time to the defence: by the end of both wars no single part of either the German or the Japanese home territory was beyond the range of Allied (i.e. non-Soviet) aircraft. Fifth, by the final stages of the wars Allied air forces had for the first time sufficient numbers to mount sustained, large-scale operations and had developed, as a result of years of conflict, navigational and bombardment techniques that ensured an unprecedented accuracy and ferocity of attack.

For all their numbers, however, the Allied strategic air forces in

Europe were too small to prosecute a general offensive to a successful conclusion. The attempt to do so was not achieved by the Allies although in the oil directive of September 1944 they had a plan that might have produced decisive and immediate results had Allied resources been directed to a single task. In sharp contrast to the Japanese war where the plan devised by the Americans was put into effect with the minimum possible diversion of resources, the 25 September 1944 oil directive suffered from two problems of organisation. First, RAF Bomber Command treated the terms of this directive as the basis of discussion and evasion, and its success in so doing was the result of a prestige and status that enabled it to defy superior authority with impunity. The issue on which RAF Bomber Command parted company with its instructions was the same that had been the basis of previous policy disputes, namely whether its efforts were to be directed to the task of breaking enemy morale through the continuation of area bombing or against precision targets, and between October and December 1944 some 53 per cent of its bomb loads were committed to the former task. Even more tellingly, whereas between July and August 1944 when it had operated under Eisenhower's command RAF Bomber Command had committed 11 per cent of its payloads against oil targets, by October 1944 this total had shrunk to just 6 per cent and in the last quarter of the year this particular effort involved no more than 14 per cent of RAF Bomber Command's resources. Second, and a matter of some dispute both at the time and in post-war analyses, any attempt to destroy the German oil industry necessarily involved a concomitant destruction of the German transportation system since success was dependent not simply on the destruction of the means of production and storage but also of distribution. In the case of the Japanese war such problems did not present themselves. Unity of command ensured no dissipation of effort of the kind that characterised the last months of the Allied offensive in Europe, and the attacks on Japanese cities provided collateral damage that ensured the massive disruption of a Japanese railroad system that was not primarily geared to the movement of goods.

By the time that the Americans began their attacks on Japanese oil installations in May 1945 the latter were working at 4 per cent capacity, and American efforts were thus directed against a slack that could never be taken up because of the lack of imports arriving in Japan. But in the case of Germany the identification of the oil industry as the primary target of Allied attention came at the time when German vulnerability to a disruption of her oil supplies, always very marked, was at its greatest on two counts. First, in August 1944 the Soviet occupation of Romania

417

deprived Germany of her only major source of imported natural oil, though in fact Romanian imports had begun to decline as a result of the massive damage inflicted by the 15th Air Force in three raids on Ploesti in April. Second, at the very time when German synthetic production had to make good the loss of Romanian imports the eclipse of the *Luftwaffe* left an oil industry that had concentrated its major plants in the Ruhr without any cover other than that provided by cloud and industrial haze.

Within two months of the 25 September 1944 directive the German output of aviation fuel stood at 25.3 per cent of its May level, and in the course of 1944 German oil stocks fell by two-thirds as reserves were used to cover shortfalls of production. Yet these bare facts conceal what was the very real failure of the Allied strategic bombing offensive against Germany because this November output represented a four-fold increase in production over September's total. The very odd fact was that the September directive that singled out the German oil industry for destruction coincided with its partial recovery from the effects of a highly successful campaign by heavy bomber forces during the time when they were committed to *Operation Overlord*: their release from that commitment and return to their own strategic offensive marked the point of German revival. Unexpectedly rapid German powers of recovery, bad weather, tactical bombing demands, the neutralisation of German V-weapon sites and RAF Bomber Command's wilful refusal to attack 'panacea targets' were amongst the major factors that contributed to an Anglo-American failure that was all the more profound for costing the air forces their last opportunity to achieve a victory that alone would have justified their earlier losses, past efforts and the vast expenditure on their needs. Only briefly, in the course of 1943, had the strategic air forces been afforded the opportunity to wage war independently: both before that time, and in the spring of 1944, the strategic air offensive had been seen by the American and British High Commands as the means of weakening German resistance prior to an invasion of north-west Europe. In the event the strategic air forces had failed this test of their independence, but with the success of *Operation Overlord* they were presented with a second, fleeting opportunity to register decisive success ahead of the advancing armies: in failing this second time the strategic air forces condemned themselves to an increasingly nihilistic campaign after January 1945 against an enemy that was assured of defeat.

Such a state of affairs presented perhaps the greatest single paradox of the war: at a time when the bomber forces failed strategically they were part of an effort that secured the tactical victory that was the essential pre-requisite for the success of *Operation Overlord*; when committed to

Operation Overlord they registered *en passant* a strategic result that came within an ace of decisive success; when released to build upon that achievement they manifestly failed and thus ensured that whatever success they did record was ultimately just one small part of a total Allied victory. To add to this paradox, the strategic air forces confirmed in the process the substance of the RAF claim of September 1941 that Germany could not withstand a sustained, six-month bombardment though it must be noted that operations after September 1944 were not directed solely against those targets that had been the basis of this claim.

Amidst these paradoxes and imponderables, certain aspects of the strategic bombing offensive's achievement cannot be disputed. Its greatest single accomplishment was the means by which the Western allies imposed their will upon Germany and forced her to respond defensively to their initiative. Second, and scarcely less important, the strategic bombing offensive was the most important single factor in the process whereby the Allies secured general air superiority in the course of 1944 and it also ensured tactical air superiority over the various fronts after 1943 as the German armies in the field were stripped of fighter cover because the *Luftwaffe* was forced to give battle in defence of its homeland. By the beginning of 1944 some 70 per cent of the *Luftwaffe*'s front-line fighter strength was committed to home defence: with the *Luftwaffe* suffering in the course of the year a 73 per cent monthly attrition of its fighter strength and the loss of 13,000 aircraft between July and September alone, its defeat in the skies over Germany in 1944 was all but synonymous with the collapse of German air power. By definition, other factors were involved in Germany's defeat. The *Luftwaffe*'s own inability to convert itself from a relatively small, specialised and offensive air force into a large-scale general air force in the middle of a losing campaign in Germany's skies was a major factor in this defeat: the contribution of tactical air power to Germany's defeat was likewise not insubstantial with the Eastern Front alone accounting for 19.2 per cent of all German losses in the first quarter of 1944 as the battle for air superiority over Germany came to its peak. The faltering of the German aviation industry as a result of punishing raids on aircraft factories in August and October 1943 and in February 1944 was also important, but in the final analysis the most important single factor in the defeat of German air power in the Second World War was the Anglo-American strategic bombing campaign and the *Luftwaffe*'s defeat in the battle imposed upon it by the Americans over Germany itself in the course of 1944.

The strategic bombing offensive was also the major material factor in

Germany's industrial defeat and collapse, though the German economy was not reduced to the point where it could no longer support military operations and the requirements of the civilian population until the last two months of the war. The strategic bombing offensive could not prevent German industry achieving unprecedented levels of production in 1944, and German war production reached its peak in the third quarter of 1944 when the index of production stood at 308 relative to a base of 100 in January–February 1942. Nevertheless, a 25 per cent fall in steel output in the course of 1944 had obvious implications and it has been conservatively estimated that even in 1944 German industry worked at some 10 to 12 per cent under capacity because of the Allied bombing campaign. Moreover, this campaign distorted the pattern of German production, most notably in terms of aircraft production. While one-quarter of artillery and ammunition resources, one-third of optical output and half of Germany's electro-technical production was directed to home-based anti-aircraft defence in 1944, German aircraft production rose to 39,807 aircraft in 1944 from totals of 15,556 in 1942 and 25,527 in 1943. In the process, however, German offensive power declined in real terms as the fighter share of output rose from 40.2 per cent in 1942 to 53.7 per cent in 1943 to 77.7 per cent in 1944, yet even this over-concentration of productive effort was insufficient to allow any significant increase in the *Luftwaffe*'s front-line fighter strength during 1944, and most certainly not on the scale needed to allow the *Luftwaffe* to regain air superiority.

The bombing campaign also had the effect of imposing a series of hidden extra costs on German production as a result of enforced dispersal. Delays and loss of production because of this dispersal and subsequent disruption postponed capital programmes as Germany was forced to divert resources to damage repair. The strategic bombing campaign also tied down some 2,000,000 troops and civilians in anti-aircraft defence during 1944, and resulted in 593,000 deaths, 780,000 serious injuries and the destruction of 3,370,000 dwellings. To the lengthening list of German difficulties, therefore, strategic bombing added problems of providing food, shelter, medical care and transportation for hundreds of thousands of people, and in so doing the strategic air offensive provided an element of retributive justice upon a German people only too willing to enjoy the benefits of conquest who had inflicted much greater levels of suffering and misery upon Europe in the confident belief that it would never have to answer for its crimes. In terms of the material balance sheet, however, the strategic bombing offensive ensured Germany's economic ruination through the destruction of her oil industry and transportation system. German oil production, which even in May 1944 was inadequate to meet the requirements of a *Luftwaffe* itself inadequate to meet the demands placed upon it, virtually ceased after January 1945 with two obvious results: German military formations fought their last battles all but immobilised for want of fuel, and the *Luftwaffe* entered 1945 unable to mount large-scale, protracted operations for exactly the same reason. Indeed, the enforced reduction of air training programmes during 1944 carried the same long-term implication for the *Luftwaffe* as the introduction of *kamikaze* tactics had for Japanese air power at this time.

Likewise, the German transportation system virtually ceased to function by March–April 1945 when Allied armies crossed the Rhine and Oder into central Germany. As early as December 1943 the German rail system had begun to come under strain as a result of bombing, specifically with regard to coal deliveries to industry, but in the course of 1944 the dislocation of German rail communications began to assume serious proportions. Throughout this year and into 1945, however, improvisation and movement by night ensured that German military traffic continued to move to and from the fronts but only with increasing delays and at the cost of a damage repair effort that ultimately employed 2,000,000 able-bodied men. In the words of one German economic historian, 'as the year 1944 wore on, German economic terrain came to resemble a transportation wilderness', and one that became ever more desolate with the onset of winter and the flight of refugees from the east ahead of advancing Soviet armies. With the start of the final offensive against rail and canal communications in March 1945 the collapse of the German transportation system was both immediate and total. Though its factories continued to produce arms and ammunition as late as the Rhine crossing, the Ruhr was isolated from the rest of Germany by the destruction of its communications during the last days of March, but this achievement on the part of the strategic bomber forces was superseded by the meeting on 1 April at Lippstadt of the 9th and 1st US Armies to complete the physical encirclement of the Ruhr (and 19 German divisions). In a very real sense what happened to the Ruhr was appropriate comment upon the achievement of the strategic air offensive as a whole, as, indeed, was what had happened to the *Kriegsmarine* under the lash of the strategic bombers' final offensive. By direct and indirect attack, strategic bombing forces accounted for four of the six German battleships sunk during the war, two of the three armoured cruisers, one of three heavy and two of five light cruisers, plus 62 submarines, but of the surface units destroyed by heavy bombers seven were sunk during or after March 1945, some three years after their loss might have had some significance in the war at sea. Technically very impressive, such success, and indeed the whole of the bombing offensive against Germany, was robbed of its value because it came too late to be of real importance.

In the course of the war Anglo-American bomber forces dropped 1,996,036 tons of bombs on targets in Europe, and of this total 1,360,000 tons were dropped on Germany with some 72 per cent of this figure dropped after 1 July 1944. Japan was the unwilling recipient of 160,800 tons of Allied bombs, just 24.5 per cent of the total dropped by Allied aircraft during the war in the Far East and a total modest in comparison with the 133,599 tons dropped by RAF Bomber Command and the 8th Air Force in March 1945 alone. Yet the best available estimates suggest that despite the disparity between the scale of attack to which they were subjected Germany and Japan suffered roughly equal devastation, Japan's susceptibility to damage being much greater than that of Germany because of the greater concentration of her cities with their higher densities of population and household and feeder industries. More obviously, Japan was more vulnerable than Germany to the effects of bombing because she was so unprepared, both psychologically and materially, for such an eventuality. Whereas the German people had four years of small-scale bombing to provide the necessary adjustment to the quickening pace and growing scale of the Allied air offensive, with the defeats of 1942 and 1943 to serve as notice of what was to come, the American strategic air offensive in the Far East was directed against a population misled into believing that victory was assured and which was wholly unaware of the reality and imminence of national defeat. The material damage inflicted upon Japan between March and August 1945 by aerial bombardment was awesome, but arguably the greater damage was to Japanese morale.

For a society that by the beginning of 1945 was rationed at a level only 6 per cent above minimum subsistence levels, that was subjected to various malnutrition-related diseases, and which simply could not obtain consumer durables, the obvious failure of the armed services and the equally obvious failure of government to provide for the homeless and wounded had two immediate repercussions. Under the impact of bombing the discipline of Japanese labour broke. Even in the largely unaffected countryside absenteeism averaged 15 to 20 per cent while in unbombed Kyoto a general 40 per cent rate was noted: in the immediate aftermath of raids munition factories reported absenteeism of 80 per cent of the labour force, thus further depressing an already inadequate level of production. Moreover, defeatism suddenly became widespread through

Japanese society which, according to one noted phrase, 'continued to fight throughout 1945 from habit'. Japanese government surveys at the time suggest that in August 1945, but before the surrender, 68 per cent of the population believed that the war was lost, and if this figure seems rather low in light of the hopelessness of Japan's position at that time it nevertheless contrasts sharply with the 46 per cent of that persuasion in June and the 2 per cent of June 1944. Bombing was by far the most important factor in Japanese demoralisation because it destroyed confidence in the armed forces, not least when the Americans took to the practice of announcing their bombing targets in advance, thereby indicating to the Japanese people that even with this warning their air forces were powerless to prevent the destruction of their cities.

In terms of physical destruction and excluding the nuclear raids of 6 and 9 August, the American strategic bombing offensive devastated 43.46 per cent of 63 major Japanese cities, destroyed about 42 per cent of Japan's total industrial capacity, and killed, wounded and in various ways rendered homeless a total of perhaps 22,000,000 people. This offensive divided into three main phases, and in the eight and a half months between November 1944 and August 1945 it repeated, in concentrated form, the course of the Anglo-American experience of the strategic bombing campaign against Germany. In the initial, three-month phase, XX Bomber Command attempted, as had RAF Bomber Command in the first period of the European war, to carry out daylight precision raids, but without fighter escort and against a defence that peaked in January 1945 when the number of fighter attacks per bomber sortie reached 7.9, the 8th Air Force's experiences of late 1943 were repeated over Japan's cities. Even the formidable Superfortresses incurred a demoralising 5.6 per cent attrition rate, while high-level operations adversely affected payloads, engine life and accuracy of bombing patterns, the latter because of the jet stream over Japan. But even before the first incendiary attack on a Japanese city, by XX Bomber Command on Nagasaki on 10 August 1944, the AAF planning staff in Washington had turned its attention to the possibility of conducting an area-bombing campaign against Japan because of the acknowledged inflammability of her cities, which were mainly of light construction and very heavily congested.* After promising results in two minor fire raids, against Hankow by XX Bomber Command on 18 December and against Tokyo by XXI Bomber

---

*Tokyo had population densities of 135,000 people per square mile in certain areas – the average for Japan's secondary cities was about 49,300 – and of the capital's total surface area 8% consisted of streets compared to London's 26%.

Command on 25 February, the Americans adopted the policy of night area bombing from low altitudes in an attempt to limit their losses and to cause the maximum possible general devastation of Japanese cities.

Thus in March began the second, three-month phase of the campaign, and one in which 105.6 square miles or 41.6 per cent of Japan's six largest industrialised cities were destroyed. This was achieved despite one month in which three-quarters of XXI Bomber Command's efforts were directed against tactical targets in support of operations in Okinawa and a growing commitment to the mining of Japanese waters. In this phase the Americans achieved surprise and overwhelmed air and anti-aircraft defences that were not geared to night operations, though in fact Japanese willingness to give battle in defence of their cities declined after February 1945 as battle was joined first off Iwo Jima and then off Okinawa. After June the Superfortresses were all but unopposed as the Japanese tried to preserve what remained of their conventional air power in readiness for the last battle in defence of the home islands against invasion. It was a measure of Japanese weakness in the air that fighter escort from Iwo Jima, which began on 7 April, was discontinued before the end of the war, and in this final phase, between 17 June and 14 August, 60 Superfortress raids on 57 secondary cities resulted in the destruction of 63.76 square miles of urban areas, 48.13 per cent of the total area of these cities. Of the secondary cities one, Saga in western Kyushu, escaped with negligible damage, eight incurred 75 per cent or more and another 22 between 50 and 75 per cent destruction of their total area. In addition to these operations fighters from Iwo Jima and Okinawa ranged over the Japanese home islands, and in the last seven weeks of the war Allied carrier aircraft and surface units joined the bombardment of Japan, the 20 carriers of TF38 and TF57 bringing some 1,400 aircraft into the battle. In every sense, the scale of attack to which Japan was subjected in the last phase of the war was very literally overwhelming.

What these attacks achieved, however, is difficult to assess for the very obvious reason that because of the decline in imports Japanese industry was in end-run production and much of the American bombing destroyed capacity that was surplus to requirements. In some cases the destruction of capacity and production was related – the Japanese aircraft engine and airframe industries respectively lost 75 per cent and 60 per cent of both capacity and production – but in the case of the oil industry losses of about 84 per cent for both were coincidental. The effect of the naval blockade explains the discrepancy between declines of 75 per cent and 91 per cent in the output of the shipbuilding and aluminium industries during 1945 whereas lost capacity as a result of bombing amounted to 15 per cent and 50 per cent respectively. Conversely, the production of tetraethyl lead increased between March and August 1945 despite reduced capacity, and despite the decline of coal production and the loss of 20 per cent of generating capacity as a result of bombing, the Japanese power industry produced surplus electricity in January 1945 and could have met double actual demand in August, an indication of the extent to which Japanese industry was on short-time working. The bombing and the blockade complemented one another to the extent that Japanese production in July 1945 was probably no more than 35 per cent of its wartime peak, but while the blockade was clearly the more important in terms of the long-term destruction of Japanese industrial power, the strategic bombing offensive played its full part in the destruction of an economy heavily dependent upon small-scale urban suppliers in the electrical component and optics industries that were badly affected by area bombing. But while the various sectors of the Japanese economy suffered different rates of lost production and capacity under the impact of blockade and bombardment, hindsight seems to provide three indisputable conclusions about the situation in which Japan found herself on 26 July 1945 when her enemies, in a declaration that contrary to popular belief did not demand her unconditional surrender, warned of her 'complete and utter destruction' if she tried to continue the war. First, Japan was then but a matter of months, perhaps only weeks, from complete industrial collapse. Second, with a disastrously bad harvest in the offing, she faced the certainty of mass starvation if the war somehow lasted into 1946. Third, Japan had reached the end of her moral and material resources: she had nothing with which to sustain herself as, unknowingly, she faced an American enemy with the means that ensured strategic air power's final victory, that was to dispense with the need for invasion and a campaign of conquest, and that was irresistible as it was all but unimaginable.

In early 1945 there was a very discreet discussion between influential members of the imperial household and certain of the more moderate political leaders of Japan on the most delicate of matters, whether or not the Emperor should abdicate in order to pave the way for an approach to the Allies for an end to a war that was obviously lost. Nothing came of this, nor of the other halting, timorous attempts by members of the ruling hierarchy to act upon the realisation of defeat, and for one obvious reason: those who recognised the inevitability of national defeat were not those with the power of decision within the Japanese High Command.

Within the latter the military held positions of authority and power, and as the war came to the Japanese home islands so the military clung as an act of blind faith to ideas of a final cataclysmic battle that would somehow ensure that the honour and polity of the Empire would be left intact. Amidst the mounting evidence of defeat, perhaps such absurdity was all that was left to the Japanese High Command, but its effect was to ensure that the war was fought long after its outcome could be discerned by all parties to the conflict. Half a world away the same situation – *mutatis mutandis* – prevailed, and for much the same reason and to much the same end. There was no authority in Germany that recognised the reality of national defeat and could attempt to bring the war to an end, and to the very last Germany's leadership clung blindly to illusions of national survival that were no more than failed promissory notes issued by a finance house bankrupted by the Casablanca declaration of 1943. Herein, however, was an obvious point of difference between the end of the war in Europe and the end of the war in the Far East: the contentious 'unconditional surrender' formula was not applied to Japan, and indeed of the three major Axis powers on which this demand was served in 1943 only Germany was allowed no mitigation of the terms of capitulation.

As summer gave way to autumn in 1944 German actions were ever less relevant to the course and outcome of the war. Throughout the second half of 1944 Germany's enemies held the initiative, yet this was an initiative all but unused in the main theatres of operations during the last quarter of the year and indeed by October 1944 the fronts displayed a curiously lop-sided but at the same time balanced picture. In the south, in the only theatre from which Hitler could reasonably draw comfort, the Allied advance from the Winter Line had not resulted in any major German defeat as Anglo-American armies revealed their pre-Clausewitzian characters: by October their lack of infantry and engineers ensured that their attempt to carry the war into the Po valley was to be frustrated on the last line of German defence in northern Italy. In the west, the four-fold Allied failure of the summer – to complete either the close or deep encirclement of German forces in Normandy, to secure Dijon before the bulk of *Armee Gruppe G* completed its withdrawal from southern France, both to complete the annihilation of the trapped *15th Army* and to clear the approaches to Antwerp, and to carry off *Operation Market Garden* – provided a *Wehrmacht* reduced in the west by the end of September 1944 to about 100 tanks and 20 divisions fit for battle with a respite it could not secure for itself by force of arms. Without reserves that were essential to the successful exploitation of the initiative, the three

Allied army groups in north-west Europe could not attempt anything more than limited, local offensives against an enemy that identified retention of the Netherlands as its defensive priority in the west despite the American preponderance amongst the western Allied armies. On the Eastern Front October 1944 witnessed the very odd phenomenon of major German armoured counter-offensives on the extreme flanks, in front of Budapest and around Riga, while the mass of the Soviet armies remained on the defensive along the Vistula.

Various themes have been developed in setting down the course and chronology of the European war, and in this last phase of the war what are arguably the two aspects that provide the basis of understanding why events unfolded as they did are seen to full effect. The lesser of these was the transposition of the German and Soviet armies in the course of the war. The German army of 1944–45, for all its reputation, had the characteristics so meticulously catalogued when displayed by the Soviet army in 1941: erratic and inconsistent direction, a high command packed with place-men and stripped of operational talent, the dead hand of blind obedience imposed by political commissars upon an officer corps despised and distrusted by its political master, failure at every level of command and operations. Conversely, by 1945 the operational and technical quality of the Soviet army was at least the equal of the *Wehrmacht* at its peak, yet historical perversity has produced a casual disregard of the Soviet military achievement in 1945 and presented it as the inevitable product of overwhelming numerical and material superiority. In reality, 1945 witnessed massive Soviet victories in the face of fanatical resistance through the effective application of that superiority, most obviously in the course of the Vistula–Oder offensive of January 1945 that represents perhaps the peak of Soviet military achievement in the course of the European war.

Of greater importance, however, is the theme of Germany's defeat as a result of her inability to understand war. The failure to understand the limits both of military force in the conduct of war and of German national power within the international community characterised Germany's actions in two world wars, almost as if the very success of the one German leader who had understood both – Bismarck – blinded successive generations of Germans to these realities because they saw only his military victories. In two world wars Germany showed an understanding of fighting but not of war itself, and in both conflicts she displayed an ability to conduct campaigns – as long as they were relatively straightforward – but no ability to prosecute war across both space and time. Moreover, and as noted elsewhere at no stage during the Second World

War did the *Führer Prinzip* submit to the structured chain of command emanating from a settled cabinet system that alone allowed the coherent formulation of policy and the integration of political, economic and military efforts and then the supervision of implementation that was essential to German success. While this was of little consequence when Germany was able to dictate the unfolding of the European conflict the later phases of the war demonstrated to the full the consequences of an organisational failure that made Wilhelmine Germany seem a model of efficiency in comparison. Yet this final phase of the war is clearly very different from those that had preceded it in one crucial respect. Flawed though the German system was even at the time of its greatest triumphs, Hitler was if not reasonable then rational: in the final phase of the war he was neither. Much has been written about Hitler's physical and mental state in the last months of his life, not a little of it in the grandest Wagnerian terms that were the dictator's own terms of reference. Suffice to note that in the final months darkness encroached upon and then extinguished an always inadequate light, the penetrating but narrow intellect dimmed and yielded to the same deceptions that had been perpetrated on others, the sense of duty and obligation was inverted. With the certainty of defeat came the escape from reality, yet at the same time Hitler's conduct of the war was very far from being irrational, and his *leitmotif* in the final phase – that Germany had to continue the war until the alliance that opposed her fell apart – was far removed from fantasy. Nevertheless, as his empire crumbled, and his grip on his people tightened as real power slithered from his grasp, so Hitler could not or would not recognise the manner and extent to which the balance of power had changed to Germany's disadvantage in four short years. When at last this reality could not be ignored Hitler made good the promise he had made to the German people on 1 September 1939 that victory would be secured or he would not survive the outcome of the war. Having failed to win a war the terms of which he had provided, Hitler would not accept responsibility for and face the consequences of defeat.

Excluding the Soviet offensive that resulted in the clearing of the Baltic states* and Soviet operations in Hungary, the last seven months of the European war witnessed a series of Allied offensives – and largely irrelevant German counter-offensives – that form a coherent whole because the war had come to assume a singleness as it swept over Germany's borders. There was no synchronisation of Allied efforts on

*This the eighth Soviet offensive of 1944: see pp. 438 *passim*

the various fronts though all tended to be mutually supporting, and each of the three fronts saw the unfolding of events peculiar to itself.

In Italy the 15th Army Group failed in its attempt to break the Gothic Line in a series of attacks between 25 August and 20 October even though its armies were able to overcome the main German defensive positions, but while a British offensive in December secured Ravenna a decisive result in Italy had to await the spring when events on the Winter Line in May 1944 repeated themselves on the approaches to Bologna. The winter erosion of German strength as a result of operations and the transfer of formations to other theatres found *Army Group C*, in April 1945, nominally with 23 German and four Italian divisions with which to oppose the 17 of the Allies, but in real terms *Army Group C* had a total strength of about 600,000 men whereas such numbers were available as the front-line strength of an Allied military establishment in Italy that totalled some 1,500,000 men drawn from 26 different nationalities. Moreover, *Army Group C* was unwilling to commit Italian and other non-German formations to front-line duties and throughout the winter of 1944–45 had to contend with an increasingly effective partisan movement throughout northern Italy. Despite its cosmopolitan character, however, the 15th Army Group split open the *14th Army*'s left flank in front of Bologna between 9 and 21 April after diversionary attacks along both coasts between 2 and 7 April had heralded the start of the final Allied offensive of the Italian campaign, and by the twenty-second the 10th US Mountain Division had reached the Po south of Mantua. As early as 14 April *Army Group C* had recognised the inevitability of defeat south of Bologna but on the seventeenth it was refused permission to withdraw its two armies to positions behind the Po: by the twentieth, when Allied pressure finally forced German formations to begin to abandon their positions in the mountains, it was too late for *Army Group C* to avert a complete collapse of German resistance throughout northern Italy.

Once the battle moved clear of Bologna the conditions of warfare favoured the Allies for the first time in the entire Italian campaign because the developed road system and multitude of bridges beyond the northern Apennines presented the Allies with numerous axes of advance and prevented German formations from conducting a comprehensive scorched-earth programme as they withdrew. Moreover, superior Allied mobility was married to an adequate bridging and logistics support that ensured that the 5th US and 8th British Armies could negotiate river crossings and reach enemy defensive positions ahead of retreating German columns. What little hope *Army Group C* retained of completing a withdrawal of its armies after the twentieth disappeared with the collapse of the *10th Army* around Ferrara on 24 April. Thereafter the campaign in northern Italy was no more than a German rout with Allied forces securing the great historic cities of Piedmont, Lombardy and Venezia, more often than not a day or so after local resistance forces had completed their liberation. Allied forces entered Verona on 25 April, Genoa on the twenty-seventh, Padua and Venice on the twenty-ninth and Turin, Milan and Trieste on 2 May, the first and last of these straddling the assassination of Mussolini by communist partisans on 28 April, the surrender of German forces in Italy on 29 April (effective on 2 May) and the capitulation of the fascist *Ligurian Army* on the thirtieth. In what was among the last acts of the Italian campaign, units of the 5th and 7th US Armies met at Vipiteno, south of the Brenner Pass, on 4 May: at the same time Yugoslavian communist forces sought to occupy Italian territory on the Istrian peninsula that had been the subject of bitter dispute between the two countries in the inter-war period. In May 1945 British forces occupied Trieste in order to separate the two sides and to forestall the possibility of serious disturbances in the city: perhaps surprisingly, 10 years were to elapse before they departed.

The German surrender in Italy was the first in the series of capitulations that brought the European war to an end in mid-spring 1945, but in its last months the Italian campaign, which over its 19 months claimed an estimated 312,000 Allied and 532,000 Geraman casualties excluding those who entered captivity at the end of hostilities, possessed a simplicity denied the two main campaigns that carried the war across the north European plain into the heart of Germany. These two campaigns were very different, not least in scale and intensity: whereas the four main phases of the campaign in the west included only one Allied offensive of major strategic proportions the campaign on the Eastern Front was built around four massive offensives, the first of which in effect embraced related efforts on three separate axes. The two campaigns nevertheless achieved what they set out to – the meeting of Allied armies from the east and the west on the middle Elbe in late April 1945.

In the west the failure of *Operation Market Garden* marked the end of Anglo-American hopes that the war in Europe could be won in 1944. With the failure of the single-thrust strategy and with only 54 divisions available for operations on 1 October, Eisenhower adopted a broad-front strategy aiming to maintain pressure on German armies in the west along the whole of the front, to register a series of territorial gains that together would constitute a significant achievement, and ultimately to close the Rhine along its length in readiness for a general offensive. Between the beginning of October and mid-December, therefore, the three Allied army groups between Switzerland and the English Channel were committed to a series of limited but difficult offensives, the most important of which involved the 21st Army Group clearing the approaches to Antwerp and North Brabant; the 12th Army Group securing Aachen and clearing most of Luxembourg and Lorraine; and the 6th Army Group, which had landed in southern France on 15 August and had advanced up the Rhône valley, securing northern Alsace and the Belfort gap though it was unable to clear the *19th Army* from the Colmar pocket until February 1945. These various offensives registered the territorial gains that Eisenhower sought and also brought important political and military dividends: the American capture of Aachen on 21 October was the first capture by any Allied army of a major German city; the liberation of Belfort and Mulhouse on 21 November and of Strasbourg on the twenty-second was of immense significance for France, particularly because of the prominence of the 1st French Army and the famous 2nd French Armoured Division in these operations in eastern France; the clearing of the banks of the Scheldt between 6 October and 8 November resulted, after the waterway itself was swept, in Antwerp being opened for the resupply of armies hitherto dependent on lines of communication that reached back to Cherbourg and Normandy.

The Allied offensives nevertheless failed in forcing the German armies in the west to conform to the Allies' will. The various offensives were bitterly contested, particularly in the Hurtgen Forest and on the Roer in November and December as the 12th Army Group sought to enlarge its holdings around Aachen, but with the raising of the first of the new *Volksgrenadier* divisions in August 1944, the ruthless combining of units for surplus manpower and extended conscription the German armies in the west were able to cover their summer losses during the autumn, at least on paper. In August and September 1944 no fewer than 44 German divisions were destroyed or disbanded, 20 in the last seven days of August alone, and by September, just before the start of *Operation Market Garden*, the German armies in the west mustered some 63 divisions of which only 13 were battle-worthy. By mid-October, however, the German armies in the Netherlands and Rhineland numbered some 71 divisions of which 33 were fit for battle, and by mid-December the process of rehabilitation was as complete as it could be, allowing for the 107 divisions in the west being some 120,000 men under authorised establishment, which itself had been much reduced in order to provide

431

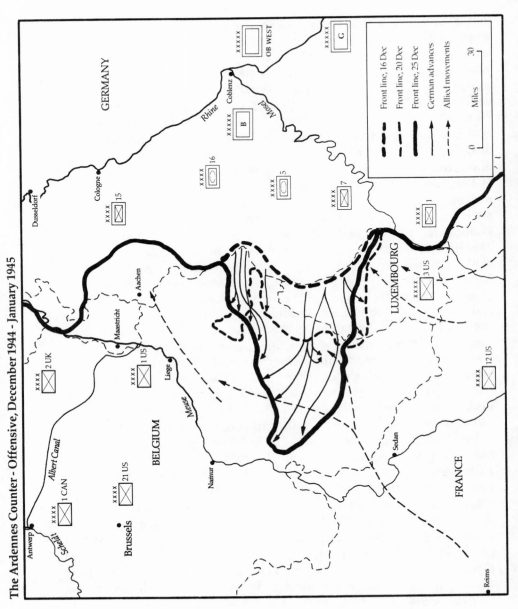

The Ardennes Counter - Offensive, December 1944 - January 1945

numbers rather than quality. In difficult terrain and often appalling weather, however, these formations were able to prevent the Allied armies from registering any major operational success, and they did so while leaving the bulk of the armoured divisions being assembled in the west uncommitted. This fact was crucial to the unfolding of the campaign on the Western Front because Hitler had noted, correctly, that with some 70 divisions available to the three Allied army groups in the west the *Wehrmacht* could still secure a local superiority for an offensive. It was this calculation that provided the terms of reference for the second phase of the campaign in the west – the Ardennes offensive.

This attack is generally regarded as Hitler's last offensive but in fact it was followed by three more before the end of the war. It was, however, the last *major* German offensive of the war, one usually derided as an act of madness, the product of a deranged imagination, that served only to hasten Germany's defeat. The offensive was certainly flawed in every one of its major aspects. Conceptually, the German plan of campaign failed to recognise the vast disparity of force between the two sides, and in terms of space and distance the German armies assembled for this offensive, and the logistical support at their disposal, were at very best marginal to needs. German planning also failed to take account of the closeness of Anglo-American cooperation, and the idea that Germany had to inflict a massive defeat on the Anglo-Saxon powers before the full effects of French mobilisation could be felt was wholly irrelevant: the war was in its last gasp, not about to enter a protracted phase at the end of which French military potential might tip the scales against Germany as had that of the United States in 1918.

Yet the imminence of Germany's defeat was recognised by Hitler; indeed it was the very basis of his decision to undertake an offensive in the west. As early as mid-August, as Allied armies reached across France after weeks of enforced quarantine in Normandy, Hitler had ordered preparations to be put in hand for a major offensive in the west in November, and by autumn, as these preparations began to produce the armoured formations needed for this offensive, Hitler was committed to an attack without which Germany was certain to lose the war. The defensive strategy imposed upon Germany by her enemies could delay but not prevent her final defeat, and, as Hitler correctly appreciated, only an offensive offered Germany any chance of avoiding such an eventuality: equally, Hitler's decision to mount this offensive through the Ardennes against the 12th Army Group was no less correct on political, strategic and technical grounds. The Soviet armies in the east were too strong to be seriously affected by any German offensive mounted at a time when

German resources were divided between two fronts and in any event an accommodation with the Soviet Union was never possible: any attempt to divide Germany's enemies had to be made in the west, and the Americans presented themselves as the natural target of an attack because theirs was the power of decision in the conduct of the campaign in the west and because, in terms of Nazi ideology, they were morally the weakest of Germany's enemies. In seeking a decisive battle north of the Ardennes the German plan of campaign envisaged a strike through this area to Antwerp being complemented by attacks by *Army Group H* that would complete the encirclement and annihilation of 21st Army Group and the 9th US Army. In setting his armies this objective Hitler sought to avoid a commitment to an offensive in which the enemy would have depth in which to manoeuvre and thereby exhaust the attack. This same selection of the theatre of operations also provided German armies with an assembly area largely impenetrable to Allied air reconnaissance. With very strict security enforced before this operation, surprise was recognised by the German High Command to be as important to success as speed of execution: the need to forestall an effective redeployment of Allied forces and to succeed in a period of bad weather that would prevent the intervention of Allied air power in the battle meant that *Army Group B*'s three armies, the *7th* and the *5th* and *6th Panzer Armies*, were allowed only seven days in which to split the Allied front in two.

The German offensive in the Ardennes was the first and only time in the war when unsupported American forces were subjected to major armoured attack, and like so many other armies before it the 1st US Army was broken in the first shock of the assault. In large measure this American failing was the result of an Allied intelligence failure to uncover the presence of the *5th* and *6th Panzer Armies* in the Eifel and to make any allowance for a German offensive, particularly one through the Ardennes, and of an unfortunate Allied deployment that left the Ardennes sector covered by just one armoured and six infantry divisions. With the historic invasion routes running to the north and south, the Americans had used the 85 miles of the Ardennes sector as an area in which to rest formations after action on other parts of the front and to introduce new divisions to combat, but on the morning of 16 December the 1st US Army had just two infantry divisions, one armoured regiment and various minor detachments to cover a 45-mile sector selected as the main axes of attack by no fewer than five armoured and eight *Volksgrenadier* divisions.

This massive disparity of strength at the point of contact accounts for the initial American defeat, but it also accounts in part why this defeat was only partial. Though the *5th Panzer Army* was able to penetrate the American front with relative ease on the first day of the offensive, it was only able to defeat a small part of the forces that the Allies had or could move to the Ardennes, while to the north the *6th Panzer Army* failed to clear the Elsenborn Ridge with the result that its offensive, instead of being developed towards the north-west, made only minor progress towards the west. Moreover, with only minor roads on which to move and hampered by deep snow and the short hours of daylight, the German advance slowed amidst the narrow valleys of the Ardennes as a result of extensive minefields and desperate American resistance, particularly around St Vith and Bastogne, two key communications centres the possession of which was vital to the development of the offensive. By 21 December the *5th Panzer Army* had secured St Vith, was across the Ourthe at Ourtheville, and was advancing on Bastogne having overcome resistance on the part of the 9th and 10th US Armored Divisions. As early as 18 December the *Army Group H* part of the offensive had been cancelled in tacit acknowledgement that the slowness with which the attack had been developed ensured its ultimate failure. By shifting the inter-army boundary southwards to allow the *6th Panzer Army* to move away from the Elsenborn Ridge and through St Vith in order to develop an attack between the Ourthe and the Salm, *Army Group B* hoped to widen the frontage of an offensive that on 23 December reached Celles, some four miles from Dinant and the Meuse.

By the twenty-third, however, and on the day when the weather cleared and Allied air power entered the battle in strength for the first time, the impetus of the German offensive had been exhausted. On the north flank of the German penetration a reorganisation of commands had placed the 9th and 1st US Armies under the orders of 21st Army Group with the result that the two American armies were able to shorten their fronts and British reserves were moved behind the Meuse. With the whole of the American northern front being re-formed as a result, on 25 December the *2nd Panzer Division*, immobilised around Celles for want of fuel, was shattered by attacks by its American opposite number and by Allied fighter-bombers, while the *116th* and the *2nd SS Panzer Divisions*, on either side of the Ourthe, were severely handled by this same combination of ground and air attack. With the northern sector dead-locked, battle was joined around Bastogne, where on 26 December the 4th Armored Division relieved the 101st Airborne Division after a celebrated siege that in reality lasted only two days. With Hitler refusing to abandon the offensive and concentrating forces for the reduction of Bastogne in order to free communications westwards, six American divisions were drawn into a series of battles around the town until 3–4 January when the last German attempt to secure Bastogne was defeated. This German defeat on the southern flank coincided with the start of the 1st US Army's counter-offensive on the northern flank. On 8 January Hitler acknowledged defeat – which he attributed to a failure to follow his orders to the letter – and ordered the withdrawal of his forward formations to the Houffalize area and of the *6th Panzer Army* from the front. By 16 January German formations were back on the start lines from which they had begun their offensive one month earlier, less an estimated 100,000 troops and 800 tanks.

In planning and executing the Ardennes offensive Hitler had calculated that during this operation there would be no Soviet offensive in Poland with which to contend, a conclusion that was correct but hardly for the right reasons: not so badly mauled during their summer offensives that they could not undertake further offensive operations, the Soviet armies in Poland during the autumn were in the process of preparing for offensives on the scale of the previous summer that were to carry the war to the Oder and within 35 miles of Berlin. Moreover, these same offensives were to carry Soviet armies deep into East Prussia, Silesia and the Carpathians, and herein lies the significance of Soviet operations in 1945. Whereas each successive year of the Great Patriotic War had seen a progressive qualitative improvement of the Soviet military art, particularly at the strategic and operational levels, in 1945 the Soviet army for the first time displayed a capacity for conducting simultaneous offensives in depth. There were other aspects of the Soviet conduct of operations in 1945 that showed similar qualitative improvements, most obviously the vast increase in the tempo of Soviet operations as a result of its ability to maintain depth of penetration with a concurrent reduction of time, but it was the increased strategic capacity of the Soviet army that was the most notable feature of operations on the Eastern Front in 1945.

Inevitably, however, a certain controversy has surrounded Soviet operations in the final phase of the European war: the assertions that the Soviet armies need not have stopped on the Oder in February 1945 but could have pressed forward to capture the German capital that month; that in April 1945 the Soviets made a desperate effort to secure Berlin ahead of the Americans, whose 9th Army reached Magdeburg as early as 11 April; and the accusations of Soviet bad faith at the Yalta conference in February 1945. Leaving aside the last two matters until the proper time for their joint consideration, the first point is best examined with reference to the seldom noted fact that four full months elapsed between Soviet armies assuming the defensive on the Vistula at the end of August 1944 and the start of the winter offensive. What would seem an inordinately long delay between operations is explicable on four counts. After advances of some 400 miles through a devastated countryside, the Soviet armies needed time in which to attend to their lines of communication and to move their air bases forward into positions from which to support further operations. The task of reorganising commands after the *Bagration* and Lvov–Sandomierz offensives was enormous, most obviously in terms of time needed to thin out what was the equivalent of four tank armies in the Sandomierz bridgehead in order to achieve the required balance of armour across the front for next-phase operations. Moreover, after October 1944 the Soviet armies were prepared to wait until the winter frosts hardened the ground before attacking. The notorious state of Polish roads in autumn made this a sensible precaution, not that it was an absolute requirement since the Soviet armies themselves had shown an ability to negotiate such conditions in the western Ukraine offensive the previous March. Finally, though the Soviets made no move on the main axis during the autumn they looked to the security of their right flank by clearing the Baltic states between September and November, and then were to make no fewer than six unsuccessful attempts, the last between 17 March and 3 April 1945, to reduce the positions that *Army Group North* retained on the Courland peninsula after its loss of Riga on 15 October. This concern with flank security was a lesson learnt at very considerable cost by the Stavka between 1941 and 1943, and the argument that Soviet armies in February 1945 could have masked the German forces in Pomerania and pressed forward to seize Berlin does not take account of the caution, indeed the professional military prudence, of those responsible for the conduct of Soviet operations in the last months of the war. For the assault on Berlin, and there was never any question in Soviet minds that Berlin would be assaulted and taken by Soviet rather than Allied forces, the Stavka was not prepared to take risks. Though its initial plans for the January 1945 offensive did set down a 45-day timetable that was to result in the capture of Berlin, the Stavka halted its offensive on the Oder in February 1945 because it wanted its flanks secured, its forces balanced across as wide a front as possible, and its air force in position before the start of the offensive that would end the European war.

The Soviet winter campaign consisted of a series of offensives which current Soviet histories number as four, plus the continuing operations in Hungary that culminated with the fall of Budapest in February. Of these

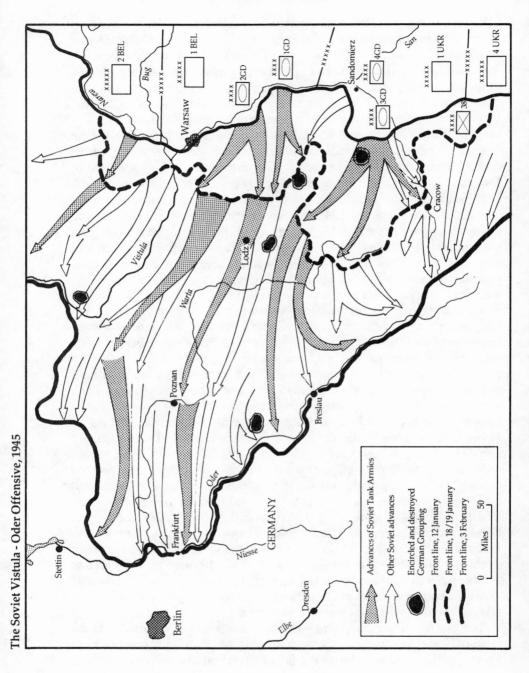

The Soviet Vistula - Oder Offensive, 1945

438

four the last, the East Pomerian offensive, was contemporaneous with the clearing of Silesia to the line of the Neisse, these two operations following from the first and largest of the three Soviet offensives of January 1945 that are normally presented as related. As defined under present Soviet terms of reference, these three offensives, conducted across a total frontage of 930 miles, were the Vistula–Oder, western Carpathian and East Prussian offensives, the first two of which opened on 12 January and the third on the thirteenth. The Vistula–Oder offensive was conducted by the 1st Belorussian and 1st Ukrainian Fronts, and it resulted in the clearing of central and western Poland and the advance of Soviet armies to the middle and upper Oder along its length between Zehden and Casel by 3 February. The western Carpathian offensive was conducted by the 4th and 2nd Ukrainian Fronts and extended across southern Poland, eastern Slovakia and northern Hungary. It was thus linked thematically with the operations against Budapest and with the 3rd Ukrainian Front's success in defeating the various German attempts to raise the siege of the city during January. This offensive is given a closing date of 18 February. The East Prussian offensive, the most protracted and difficult of the three, was conducted by the 1st Baltic and 3rd and 2nd Belorussian Fronts. It resulted in the fall of Memel on 28 January and the clearing of the whole of East Prussia other than the Samland peninsula and certain positions along the Bay of Danzig by 25 April, but the operations of the 2nd Belorussian Front in the old Polish corridor and western East Prussia merged after 10 February with those of the 1st Belorussian Front in eastern Pomerania. The clearing of the northern flank by this drive to the sea was completed in the last week of March and the first week of April, and along with the clearing of lower and middle Silesia by the 1st Ukrainian Front between 8 February and 31 March this provided the required frontage for the final attack on Berlin: in the event this offensive began on 16 April before the Soviet fronts and armies had completed their reorganisation along the middle and lower Oder. The campaign in the east was concluded with operations into Czechoslovakia that resulted in the liberation of Prague. In the south, the collection of capitals made by the Soviet army in the last year of the war included Vienna in April, after the defeat of the last German offensive of the war around Lake Balaton in March, while Yugoslav communist forces reduced Croatia in the last weeks of hostilities.

The Vistula–Oder offensive was the primary Soviet effort of January 1945. Indeed the 4th Ukrainian Front's part in the western Carpathian offensive was in reality a flank support operation for an attack that involved some 2,204,000 men, 6,400 tanks and 46,000 guns, heavy mortars and rocket launchers divided between two fronts each with two tank and eight infantry armies and two cavalry corps, the 1st Ukrainian Front having three tank corps to the 1st Belorussian Front's two. Opposed to this massive concentration of force along a front of 310 miles were three German armies with some 400,000 troops, 1,150 tanks and 4,100 guns, the 1st Belorussian Front being able to match the manpower total and outnumber the artillery and armour by 3:1 and 2:1 respectively in its Magnuszew bridgehead alone. To the north three more German armies faced some 1,670,000 men, 3,300 tanks and 28,000 artillery pieces of the 2nd and 3rd Belorussian Fronts, the 1st Baltic Front's contribution to the East Prussia offensive being limited to a corps against Memel and an army on the Neimen. Though outnumbered 7:2, the forces of *Army Group Centre* in East Prussia nevertheless had the protection offered by an elaborate pre-war defensive system constructed amidst the lakes and forests where the 1st and 2nd Russian Armies had come to grief in the opening weeks of the First World War. The naturally strong defensive positions of East Prussia were in sharp contrast to the positions in which *Army Group A* found itself on the Polish plains. No fewer than seven defensive lines had been sited between the Vistula and the lower Oder and a series of major cities had been designated as fortresses, but the combination of German numerical weakness and concentration in the forward defence zone and the openness of central and western Poland rendered *Army Group A* exposed and vulnerable to attack by an enemy with superior mobility in a way that *Army Group Centre*, operating on internal lines of communication behind permanent fortifications, was not.

Considerations of terrain and communications were to be important in dictating the different speeds at which the Vistula–Oder and East Prussia offensives unfolded, but scarcely less important were factors of German intelligence and deployment plus the manner in which the Stavka planned and conducted operations. By any standard the German deployment north of the Carpathians was questionable on two counts: the concentration of three armies, including the formidable *Panzerkorps Grossdeutschland*, in East Prussia and the dispersal of three armies across the width of the Polish plain, plus the lack of depth of defence on the part of *Army Group A* because of Hitler's insistence that any Soviet attack should be met at the immediate point of contact. On the first matter, the concern with East Prussia was dictated by political considerations: the need to defend German national territory and to deny the Soviet Union control of symbolically important Königsberg ensured that the defence of conquered Polish territory was of secondary importance. This political consideration, however, was compounded by intelligence failure, the much-vaunted *Eastern Intelligence Branch OKH* having predicted that the main Soviet effort would be made in East Prussia and around Budapest and Vienna. In the month before the offensive this estimate changed as German intelligence awakened to the reality that the Soviet army had the capacity to conduct simultaneous offensives north of the Carpathians, and by the time the Soviet offensives opened German intelligence had indeed discerned Soviet intentions. But German intelligence neverthe-less underestimated the Soviet infantry opposite *Army Group A* by 40 per cent and its armour by 60 per cent and had no grasp of the scale of attack to which the *4th Panzer*, *17th* and *9th Armies* were to be subjected. Even the hopelessly understated assessment of Soviet strength, however, was rejected by Hitler. In the weeks before the Soviet offensives began Hitler was obsessed with the Ardennes campaign and with the relief of Budapest, which was marginal to Germany's survival at this stage of proceedings. Moreover, while dismissing intelligence calculations as a successful Soviet deception, Hitler could not appreciate the qualitative change that had taken place on the Eastern Front since 1941.

Both mentally and emotionally Hitler could not progress beyond 1941–42, when the technical superiority of the *Wehrmacht* was at its peak, and this inability to grasp the present superiority of the Soviet army naturally embraced a failure to recognise two aspects of Soviet superiority most marked in the course of the Vistula–Oder offensive. By January 1945 the Soviet air force had developed into a formidable and effective service, capable of saturation tactical raids, deep-penetration operations and provision of on-call support to ground forces. The process of decentralisation of command of the air force in order to provide it with the flexibility for such operations began in late 1943, and the *Bagration* offensive had been the first occasion when the growing effectiveness of the Soviet air force on the battlefield was noted: by January 1945 the Soviet air force had acquired a massive tactical capability, not that this prevented it losing air superiority over the Oder in February. Further, by 1945 the Stavka was sufficiently confident of its armies' strengths and technical proficiency to allow its armour to fight with open flanks and separated from its supporting infantry. This massive disparity between strategic and operational practice was as marked as the physical distances involved in operations during the Vistula–Oder offensive. The maximum advance achieved in a day by any armoured formation – 2nd Guards Tank Army – was 56 miles, the highest average daily advance being 25 miles. But the maximum separation between tank and infantry armies was 62 miles as Soviet commanders, sensing German weakness, drove their armour forward without regard to their flanks and rear in an attempt to get through successive defensive lines ahead of German formations. A practice that would never have been contemplated by the Stavka in 1943 resulted in the realisation of aim: Soviet armour broke through seven defence lines before the latter could be manned in the course of this offensive, and the 5th Shock Army reached an undefended Kienitz on the lower Oder on 31 January. By the least exacting standards, the Soviet conduct of the Vistula–Oder offensive was as impressive as the best (and better known) achievements of American, British and German armour, while in terms of flexibility the turn through 90 degrees of the 3rd Guards Tank Army at Namslau on 20 January in order to clear the left bank of the Oder rather than cross the river was carried out on the march on receipt of a single radio order from front command. Its subsequent advance of 80 miles by the twenty-second places the much more celebrated intervention of the 4th US Armored Division in the Bastogne battle in perspective.

In common with so much of the fighting on the Eastern Front, the scale and speed of events during the Vistula–Oder offensive render any attempt to relate the chronology of proceedings all but meaningless other than as a shopping-list of places, rivers, dates and formations. It suffices to note five aspects of the campaign. First, though the operational practices of the Soviet fronts differed in that the 1st Ukrainian Front committed its armoured formations from the outset whereas the 1st Belorussian Front waited for infantry formations to open the breaches for the armour, the overall result of the initial Soviet blows was much the same: with the 1st Ukrainian Front opening proceedings on 12 January two days ahead of the 1st Belorussian Front, German divisions were, in the words of an eminent American authority, 'literally vaporised'. By the second day of its offensive the 1st Belorussian Front had penetrated German positions to a depth of 25 miles across a front of 40 miles, and by 15 January the German front had collapsed along its length with Soviet armoured formations operating to depths of 60 miles in rear areas. On selected axes of attack, where Soviet artillery concentrations reached 440 guns per mile and 9:1 infantry and 40:1 tank superiorities were registered by Soviet formations, German divisions disappeared without trace, and indeed such was the sheer violence of the preliminary double bombardment mounted by the 1st Ukrainian Front on the twelfth that some German formations broke even before being subjected to assault. By the fifteenth *Army Group A* had ceased to exist other than in name. Second, the Soviets sought to avoid battle in the industrialised areas of Silesia and preferred to manoeuvre German formations from cities rather than subject them to costly infantry assault. With the 4th Ukrainian Front coming into the line in order to reduce upper Silesia, this Soviet aim was largely achieved with the 1st Ukrainian Front reaching the middle and upper Oder as early as 22 January. Such was the finesse of Soviet practice that at Katowice four Soviet armies deliberately left a line of retreat for the garrison, which after evacuating a largely intact city was hammered mercilessly as it withdrew through the forests into the Carpathians.

Third, with the completion of the breakout phase on 17 January – the date of the German evacuation of Warsaw – the Stavka ordered an acceleration of the thrusts to the Oder, and this was achieved on the basis of previous planning. Though there was improvisation in the course of this exploitation phase, the Soviet practice was in sharp contrast to so much of the German conduct of armoured operations which had led to countless problems in 1941 and 1942 because of imprecision in the definition of objectives and routes. The effects of this acceleration were immediately felt on the German side. *Panzerkorps Grossdeutschland*, ordered to move by train to Lodz, arrived piecemeal and was simply bypassed over a front of 100 miles, and by the end of the offensive the *OKH* watch-keepers were reduced to marking situation maps with battalions because larger German formations simply did not remain in the battle zone. Fourth, the later stages of this offensive were conducted in appalling weather conditions. On 27 and 28 January a huge blizzard swept across eastern and central Europe, and on the thirty-first there was a sudden and unexpected thaw. In these conditions the Soviet capacity to sustain the offensive wavered, and the thaw was a major factor in the Soviet loss of air superiority at this time. With the German High Command sending air reinforcements to the east from all fronts, the grass airfields in central and western Poland were no match for the hard strips around Berlin: the combination of mounting supply problems and loss of air superiority over the front, both partly caused by the thaw, appear to have been factors in the Stavka's decision to halt its armies on the Oder.

Finally, the Vistula–Oder offensive was conducted with appalling brutality by the Soviet army once German soil was reached. It has been suggested that the Oder proved the stop-line of the offensive because of the widespread breakdown of discipline within Soviet formations by the time that the river was reached, an obvious historical precedent being the fate of the German offensive of March 1918. Disorder within Soviet formations was rife as the Vistula–Oder offensive brought into Germany a floodtide of murder, rape, arson and pillage, commodities in which the *Wehrmacht* and Nazism had traded for years. The earlier Nazi propaganda theme of the wave of red barbarism descending from the east was justified by events, though perhaps the real basis of post-war German condemnation of Soviet atrocities was their random, indiscriminate nature: the *Wehrmacht* had been infinitely better organised in such matters. Indeed, the evidence of superior German organisational skills in such proceedings had been more than amply demonstrated during the Vistula–Oder offensive following the Soviet liberation of Auschwitz-Birkenau and Chelmno. There they found testimony of a process that was much more than a mere historical footnote to the Second World War. After the losses of the previous months, in December 1944 there remained a network of 13 major and nearly 500 minor camps for the realisation of what was, under the terms of Nazi ideology, the German people's supreme achievement: the purification of the *Volk* and the annihilation of inferior, hostile peoples. How many died in this perverted process is unknown. Recent historical research suggests that perhaps one million of the 1,600,000 people incarcerated in concentration camps between 1933 and 1945 were killed along with perhaps 11 of the 18 millions sent to the extermination camps, but the totals are no more important than the question of which of the peoples selected for the most depraved tortures and appalling deaths – the Jews, the gypsies, the Russians – suffered most in this execrable programme: it was the reality of the process itself, and it being an act of deliberate policy that sprang from the mainstream of Nazi ideology, that was all-important. Nazism, with its concepts of racial annihilation and open-ended commitment to ethnic war, was an absolute with no test of reality other than in places such as Auschwitz, and it had no mitigating features of the kind that had redeemed the only previous upheaval in Europe of similar proportions. In the wake of the French revolutionary and Napoleonic wars there had flowed across Europe ideas of individual liberty, democracy and nationalism that in time had set the peoples of Europe free, E.&.O.E.* Nazism represented no political, social, cultural or intellectual liberating force, quite the reverse: it was a creed devoted to nothing but power and nihilism, and in January 1945 the *Herrenvolk* of eastern Germany, hitherto largely spared the realities of war, was to experience that nihilism as a result of the failing of power. An estimated 2,500,000 civilians died as a result of the Soviet rampage through eastern Germany in 1945 amidst scenes unknown in central Europe since the time of the Thirty Years' War. Soviet terror, though not justified, was at least understandable in light of Germany's behaviour in eastern Europe since 1939.

*Errors and Omissions Excepted

444

The Vistula–Oder campaign came to an end on 3 February with Soviet armies established along the length of the Oder above Kienitz and in certain sectors in bridgeheads over the river: thereafter Soviet attention was directed to the clearing of flanks. In the west a not dissimilar process was in hand with a series of Allied attacks that resulted in the progressive destruction of German forces and the conquest of German territory west of the Rhine. These separate Allied efforts were almost contemporaneous and of similar duration. The Allied effort in the west lasted from 3 January until 21 March, by which time the only German-held territory west of the Rhine was the *1st Army*'s fast-shrinking salient around Landau: the Soviet effort in the east began on 12 January and, except in East Prussia, was concluded between 28 March and 4 April, by which time the only unreduced cities in the rear areas were Breslau and Grudziadz. In their very different ways these two Allied pushes complemented one another and effectively completed Germany's defeat. Some 25 German divisions were committed to the Ardennes offensive and their defeat, in particular the effective destruction of the 10 panzer divisions used in this attack, amounted to the ruination of the last balanced force that Germany could raise. The extent of this defeat, plus the transfer of the *6th Panzer Army* to Hungary, left the estimated 65 infantry and 12 armoured divisions in the west too weak to use to full effect the naturally strong defensive qualities of the Rhineland's difficult terrain. In the east the Soviets claim to have destroyed 35 divisions and to have inflicted between 60 and 70 per cent losses on 25 more divisions during the Vistula–Oder offensive, and to have destroyed another 21 divisions in East Pomerania. With another 37 divisions either having been destroyed or in the process of being written off in East Prussia and another 14 incarcerated in Courland, the movement of 40 German divisions to the Oder from other fronts and from the reserve in January and February 1945 was no more relevant to Germany's needs than the German offensives into Lorraine between 1 and 21 January and on the western approaches to Budapest between 1 and 26 January. Neither offensive provided Germany with any territorial gain or advantage of timing that compensated for losses or in any way altered the strategic situation to her benefit. Having failed in each of the four preceding years to break the strength of the Soviet army, the estimated 103 infantry and 32 panzer and panzer grenadier divisions on the Eastern Front in February 1945 were inferior in numbers, firepower and mobility to the fronts' *reserve* with which the Soviet army opened proceedings in 1945, and the Soviet total excluded front-line strength and the Stavka reserve.

In the west the German salient in the Ardennes was reduced between 3 and 16 January not by converging armoured attacks across or behind its base but by a series of frontal assaults, and in the following seven weeks the three Allied army groups in north-west Europe applied the same formula in a series of local crumbling attacks along the length of the front. Between 15 and 26 January British forces cleared the lower Roer, and thereafter Anglo-Canadian forces combined with the 9th US Army in clearing the west bank of the Rhine below Düsseldorf in readiness for an offensive over the river, it being Eisenhower's intention at this time that the main Anglo-American effort across the Rhine would be made in the Emmerich area in order to develop an offensive across the north German plain. The various clearing operations in the north began between 2 and 8 February, and one month's fighting resulted in the meeting of Allied forces around Geldern on 3 March and the clearing of virtually the whole of the west bank of the Rhine below Düsseldorf by the fifth. At that time, however, the Eisenhower plan of campaign was overtaken by two developments. The first and more immediate arose from the fact that the 1st and 3rd US Armies, assigned flank supporting roles for the offensive over the Rhine by 21st Army Group, developed their own offensives to very great effect. Attacking alongside the 9th Army, the 1st Army had all but cleared the west bank of the Rhine between Cologne and Düsseldorf by 5 March and then, in a sudden breakthrough, advanced to and over the Rhine after the 9th Armored Division captured the Remagen bridge intact. On its right flank, moreover, the 3rd Army, having similarly spent the better part of a month hammering its way through German defensive positions in the western Eifel and around Trier, broke clear of these defences and between 6 and 10 March advanced from the Kyll to the Rhine at Koblenz. Three days later, on the thirteenth, the 3rd Army attacked across the lower Mosel, scattering a weakening defence as it did so. By 21 March the 3rd Army had cleared the whole of the west bank of the Rhine between Koblenz and Mannheim and had captured 120,000 prisoners from *Army Group G* in the process.

With the 1st French Army having squeezed out the Colmar pocket in the four weeks ending in mid-February, the advance of the 3rd US Army to Mannheim brought to an end a phase of operations in which some 20 German divisions were destroyed and virtually the whole of the Rhineland was secured by the Allies at remarkably low cost: whereas the Ardennes campaign cost the Americans 81,000 killed, wounded and missing, the four American armies involved in operations between 8 February and 21 March lost only 6,500 killed. But the purely American aspect of this second phase of operations was concluded with the 3rd US Army, knowing that its action could not be repudiated by an American supreme commander, crossing the Rhine at Oppenheim on 22 March, thereby giving the 12th Army Group two bridgeheads over the river even before the 21st Army Group began its assault. Given the fact that at this time the United States provided 61 of the 89 Allied divisions in north-west Europe, the 12th Army Group's success at Remagen and Oppen-heim made it impossible for Eisenhower to consider anything other than a general offensive across the length of the Rhine as the final Anglo-American contribution to Germany's defeat. US public opinion pre-cluded a deliberate spiking of offensives on the part of the 12th Army Group in favour of an Allied – and British-directed – offensive in the north when American troops were already on the east bank of the Rhine: moreover, by the third week of March sound military reasons underwrote the political factors that dictated a recasting of Allied plans. By the time that the Allied armies reached the Rhine the three German army groups in the west mustered some 60 divisions, but so many were understrength that Allied intelligence assessed their total effectiveness as 26 divisions. With a better than 3:1 superiority in numbers, therefore, there was no good reason for Eisenhower to persist with a single-sector strategy, but even without this military fact of life a recasting of Eisenhower's original intentions was inevitable as a result of the second development – the final wartime definition of Allied plans and intentions at the Yalta conference between 4 and 11 February.

The Yalta accords acquired such disrepute in the Cold War era, and even today continue to be condemned in terms of an alleged Anglo-American betrayal of various eastern European peoples, that it is easy to lose sight of the fact, identified by A. J. P. Taylor more than two decades ago, that the Americans had much the better of the bargains struck at this conference. The United States yielded nothing that the Soviet Union did not already have or could take for herself without seeking American agreement, and in return the Soviet Union undertook to join the United Nations and reaffirmed her promise of October 1944 to enter the war against Japan three months after the end of the European war. Amidst the bitter recriminations that followed the onset of the Cold War, by which time the United Nations had been reduced to a Soviet–American battlefield and the United States was in possession of nuclear weapons that she believed had made Soviet involvement in the Japanese war irrelevant, the reality of the coincidence of American and Soviet interests and the genuine nature of Allied agreement and cooperation at Yalta came to be dismissed – by both sides – as an exercise in mutual and self-deception. In reality, the Americans sought to establish at Yalta the basis of continuing cooperation between the only two powers that could realistically be measured against one another, and this American recognition of the emergence of a bipolar system manifested itself, with respect to the unfolding campaign in north-west Europe, in terms of the confirmation of arrangements that had been prepared on the question of the future of Germany.

As early as July 1944 the three Allied powers had agreed that Germany was to be divided into zones of occupation in order to ensure her de-Nazification and democratisation, plus the destruction of her means to wage war, in preparation for her eventual rehabilitation within the community of nations. The zones of occupation, with Berlin afforded a special reserved status as an Allied city within the Soviet zone, had been settled at this time, and the confirmation of these arrangements at Yalta had one obvious effect: Berlin was removed from the list of Anglo-American priorities. From the time that Berlin's future was decided and the zones of occupation defined, the only justification for an Anglo-American attempt to take Berlin ahead of Soviet forces was either Berlin's possession of such strategic value or symbolic importance – which she did not have – that her capture was mandatory or a Western intention to renege on agreements with the Soviet Union in an attempt to ensure her exclusion from central Germany. The latter was never considered by any responsible Western leader, political or military, at this time. Indeed the whole point of American policy at Yalta was precisely to ensure that the position of the Allied powers was regularised: American policy was geared to the reality that the defeat of Germany could not be achieved without Soviet power being brought into eastern and central Europe and sought to ensure that this did not prevent continuing cooperation between the Allies, not to prevent such an emergence of Soviet power. Moreover, by February 1945 there was evidence that such cooperation was possible. In that strange, almost unreal meeting between Churchill and Stalin in Moscow in October 1944 Churchill had taken the lead in proposing the division of Europe into spheres of influence, and in the winter of 1944–45 the Soviet Union adhered to the eminently practical and sensible terms of agreement decided by the British and Soviet leaders: the British, after landing forces in Greece in August 1944, spent the winter suppressing communist forces in that country with the United States, not the Soviet Union, alone protesting against Britain's action.

The Yalta agreements constituted both a tacit recognition of differences that divided the Allies and a determination not to allow these differences to deflect their attention from the task of completing Germany's defeat: Eisenhower's recasting of plans for the campaign east of the Rhine reflected these political realities and ensured that the final Allied offensives over this river and the Oder complemented rather than rivalled one another. It was on 28 March, however, that Eisenhower issued his revised plan of campaign, and by that date six of the seven front-line Allied armies in north-west Europe were across the Rhine and on this very day effectively ripped open the common boundaries of *Army Groups H* and *B* and of *Army Groups B* and *G*. On 23 and 24 March the 1st Canadian, 2nd British and 9th US Armies of 21st Army Group crossed the Rhine between Emmerich and Duisburg; on the twenty-fifth the 1st US Army began its breakout from the Remagen bridgehead, not to the north as *Army Group B* had anticipated but to the east; between 24 and 27 March the 3rd US Army crossed the Rhine around Boppard and Mainz and broke clear from the Oppenheim bridgehead; on the twenty-sixth the 7th US Army forced the river at Worms. Until the twenty-eighth, by which time only the 1st French Army remained to cross the Rhine, it was the Allied intention for the 9th and 1st US Armies to surround the Ruhr before the 21st Army Group, the strongest of the three commands at Eisenhower's disposal, advanced on Berlin, the general outline of this plan of campaign having been set down in September 1944. On 28 March Eisenhower ordered that the 9th US Army be returned to 12th Army Group and that the latter, with the 1st US Army alone equivalent to both the 21st and 6th Army Groups, should advance on the Erfurt–Leipzig–Dresden and Regensburg–Linz axes with the aim of linking up with the Soviet armies and dividing Germany in two. With the 21st Army Group directed towards Hanover and the north German ports and the 6th Army Group to the industrial cities of southern Germany and to Austria, Eisenhower did not preclude an advance on Berlin but with the concentration of power in the centre the balance of probability was obvious – to the very great irritation of first the British and then the 9th US Army.

The British, with Churchill for the first time beginning a siren song of the perils of a Soviet triumph in central Europe, sought to maintain Berlin as the objective of the Western allies, and their persistence on this matter was not unrelated to the realisation that the change of plan reduced 21st Army Group to a supporting role – as Eisenhower made very clear on 8 April when he rejected that command's request for the equivalent of an army in order to complete the capture of Lübeck and Berlin. The 9th US Army, after it secured Magdeburg and 14 bridge-heads over the Elbe on 11 April, expected orders to continue its advance to Berlin, then some two days to the east at the current rate of advance. It was halted on the Elbe, however, and while there is no substance in the assertion that the consequence of this decision on Eisenhower's part 'constitutes the fundamental theme of world history ever since that day', as has been suggested in a recent account, the rationale for it was contentious. On 28 March Eisenhower's caveat on Berlin was that the city would be taken by the Western allies if its capture could be achieved economically, perhaps a sensible course of action in terms of saving American and British casualties in the conquest of territory from which the Western armies would have to withdraw but one with obvious overtones for the Soviet Union. In the course of consultations with his senior commanders at the time, however, Eisenhower set down the view that taking Berlin could cost the Western allies 100,000 casualties, a figure that seems inordinately high in light of Allied losses thus far in the campaign and mounting evidence of the progressive collapse of German resistance after the Rhine was crossed. In an obvious sense the selection of such a figure almost suggests the search for an estimate that was reason enough not to attempt to take Berlin, and Eisenhower's sudden concern at this time with the possibility of a German withdrawal into southern Germany for a protracted last stand similarly suggests a rationale for a decision taken on other grounds: previous to German radio's announce-ment of the existence of a 'national redoubt' Allied intelligence had no inkling that such a creation existed and indeed German deployment and policy belied its existence other than in Hitler's imagination. Neverthe-less, the Eisenhower figure may not have been too far from the mark, and there is no good reason to suppose that the German armies deployed around Berlin would not have fought in defence of the capital had the final assault come from the west rather than the east: the tacit assumption in the many criticisms of Eisenhower's decision is that the Western allies could have taken Berlin and taken Berlin economically: and while the first is probably correct there is no certainty that the second would have proved the case.

The capture of Berlin, therefore, was to be left to Soviet forces, and on 31 March, when Eisenhower's decision was communicated to Stalin, the Soviet army began its fastest major redeployment of the war. With the Pomeranian and Silesian campaigns effectively over at the end of March, the Stavka began a reorganisation along the Oder that resulted in the concentration of some 2,500,000 men, nearly 45,000 guns and rocket launchers, and 6,250 tanks with the 1st Belorussian and 1st Ukrainian Fronts by 14 April, on which date the former command made an abortive attempt to cross the marshes and secure the Seelow Heights opposite the Küstrin bridgehead. The main Soviet effort was to begin on 16 April with

450

the 2nd Belorussian Front attacking westwards from its bridgehead above Stettin on the twenty-fourth. The primary Soviet objective – contrary to what Stalin told the Western allies on 1 April – was the capture of Berlin by the 1st Belorussian Front while the 1st Ukrainian Front provided flank support, advanced to the Elbe between Dresden and Wittenberg and a meeting with the 1st US Army, and secured a start line for an advance into northern Czechoslovakia. The Stavka plan of campaign fell foul of a combination of the rivalry between Soviet commands that was every bit as intense as more publicised divisions in Anglo-American ranks and the nature and effectiveness of initial German resistance. The 1st Ukrainian Front under Marshal Konev had every intention of involving itself in the taking of Berlin if presented with the opportunity to do so, and by the very nature of things German defences and resistance were at their most formidable on the direct approaches to Berlin that were the axes of advance of the 1st Belorussian Front.

Behind the Oder the Germans had prepared three major defence lines, each with three sets of positions, and with four German armies along the Oder – though both the *3rd* and *4th Panzer Armies* had been deployed to the extreme flanks as a result of Soviet deception measures – the Soviet offensive was opposed by a total of some million men, 10,400 guns and 1,500 tanks in a series of defensive positions which the Germans were able to occupy ahead of the Soviet advances. The 1st Belorussian Front's initial attacks were held in front of and on the heavily fortified crest of the Seelow Heights in the first two days of the offensive, and on 17 April, such was the chaos around the Heights as a result of the 1st Belorussian Front's overconcentration of forces in the Küstrin bridgehead that the two guards tank armies of the 1st Ukrainian Front were ordered to complete the southern envelopment of the German capital while the 2nd Belorussian Front was instructed to prepare to carry out the northern encirclement of Berlin. On the eighteenth, however, the basic logic of the battle on the Seelow Heights began to assert itself: Soviet resources were sufficient to provide insurance against errors and the failures of individual armies and being superior to those of the Germans were certain to prevail in a battle of attrition. By 20 April, Hitler's birthday, the issue on the Seelow Heights, and indeed along the whole of the Soviet front, had been resolved in favour of the attack, and with it the outcome of the battle for Berlin was decided: the German army, having failed with its main strength to hold the Oder, began to fall to pieces as the weight of the Soviet offensive was developed across an 80-mile front. The German defence nevertheless retained sufficient

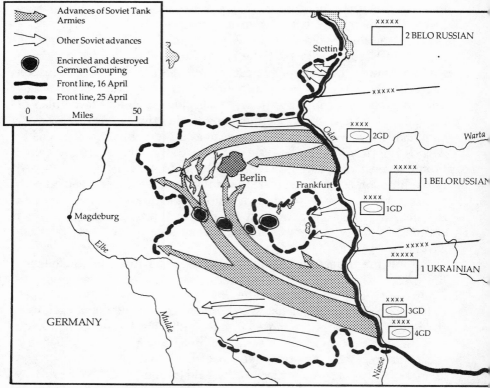

The Final Assault on Berlin, 1945

strength and cohesion to ensure that the Soviet advances were slow and extremely costly.

Whereas the Vistula–Oder offensive had cost the Soviet armies about 15,000 dead and 60,000 wounded as speed and manoeuvre saved casualties, the Berlin offensive (16 April to 8 May) cost the Soviets 102,000 dead and 202,000 wounded primarily as a result of the Soviet inability to manoeuvre clear of a defence sited in depth and the naturally heavy demands of street fighting. Soviet losses in this single offensive exceeded those of the Western allies in the whole of the 1945 fighting and were greater than the total Western killed and missing in the whole *Overlord* campaign in north-west Europe: indeed, Soviet losses in the Berlin offensive were more than the total American dead in the Second World War, and the Soviet High Command most obviously resented having to pay a bill of 10,000 casualties for every mile between the Oder and Berlin that was demanded of its determination to take the German capital ahead of the Western allies. As early as 3 April Stalin complained to his allies that the Germans were ceding vast areas in the west while on the Eastern Front they continued to fight ferociously for obscure, minor positions, not that the Americans and British could be held responsible for the German conduct of operations, but his wholly unwarranted accusation that the Western allies had concluded an agreement with the Germans whereby the Western advance would be unopposed in return for a mitigation of armistice terms served notice on the frailty of the Yalta accords.

The Soviet accusation, while having no substance, nevertheless did accord with what was happening on the ground, and this in turn pointed to a basic ambiguity of German policy in the last weeks of the European war. Hitler and his coterie clung to the belief that the anti-German coalition would collapse, that the Western allies would recognise their folly in bringing the Bolshevik horde off the steppes into central Europe: the death of Roosevelt – 'the greatest war criminal of all time' – on 12 April briefly fuelled this fantasy. It was not until April 1945 that German society realised there were no secret weapons that would redeem Germany's fortunes, that the war was lost, but even in this realisation the German High Command, and not just Hitler, were determined that the war against the Eastern foe had to be continued. While the German military shared Hitler's hope of some form of accommodation with the Western powers that would allow Germany to concentrate her resources on the Eastern Front, as the realisation slowly dawned that there would be no separate peace so the policy of packing the Eastern Front at the expense of defences in the west was tempered by the desire to ensure that the bulk of the *Wehrmacht* was in position to surrender to the Western powers, not to Soviet armies. Right to the very end the German military, which after the First World War had denied its responsibility for, and even the reality of, Germany's defeat and after the Second World War peddled the myth that its defeats were Hitler's doing, tried to have the penny and the bun: it was a measure of the German military's inability to understand the war that it had waged for more than five years that in May 1945 it genuinely did not realise that Britain and the United States would not dance to a German tune.

The reality of Germany's position was that there was no escaping total defeat, though German policy was responsible for the division of the final Allied campaigns into two sharply contrasting parts. In the west, April 1945 was to central Germany what August 1944 had been to France, and indeed the campaign in north-west Europe after June 1944 falls into two very similar phases with a dividing line provided by early December 1944: an Allied advance to contact, deadlock, a self-defeating German counter-offensive and a sweeping Allied advance. Overall, the Allied armies that landed in France between June and August 1944 advanced between 475 and 700 miles during the 11 months of the campaign in north-west Europe. For the most part the Western allies encountered little opposition in the last weeks of the war though German resistance in front of Bremen was protracted and in various places, such as the Harz mountains, was bitter and fanatical. In the north the Canadians cleared the eastern Netherlands while the British advanced to secure Bremen, Hamburg, Lübeck and Wismar by the time that hostilities ended: in the south the 1st French Army, very conscious that national honour was at stake, took Ulm and cleared south-west Germany and the western Tyrol while the 7th Army secured Nuremberg, Regensburg and Linz, Augsburg, Munich and Salzburg, Stuttgart and Innsbrück. Ironically, it was to be a division from VI US Corps of the 7th Army that took the Brenner Pass and linked with the 5th US Army in Italy: VI US Corps had fought at Anzio and the 7th US Army had landed in Sicily. In the centre American forces secured Dessau and Leipzig and cleared Karlsbad, Pilsen and Ceske Budejovice in western Czechoslovakia, but most significant of all was the 1st US Army's meeting with the 5th Guards Army at Torgau on the Elbe on 25 April. By this time both the internal and external encirclements of Berlin had been effected by the 1st Belorussian and 1st Ukrainian Fronts and Soviet armies were ready to complete the reduction of Berlin and the annihilation of *Army Groups Centre* and *Vistula.* On 22 April, the day when Hitler first conceded defeat and made the decision to stay in Berlin to the end, the two main Soviet commands carried out their first major encirclement – of some 180,000 men of the *4th Panzer* and *9th Armies* – in front of Berlin, and on 25 April, the day after Hitler disbanded the *OKH* command structure, Soviet armoured formations reaching around both sides of Berlin met, appropriately, at Potsdam. With the 2nd Belorussian Front having reverted to its original plan of campaign, completing the destruction of the *3rd Panzer Army* around Prenzlau on 25–26 April, the last days of the *Wehrmacht*, which in mid-March numbered nominally some 350 divisions* but which by the

*In the last months of the war the German order of battle became hopelessly confused with the raising of various half-strength formations and the reduction of many existing formations to little more than cadres as a result of losses. Soviet histories, which are normally very reliable in such matters, credit the *Wehrmacht* with 214 infantry, 34 armoured and 15 mechanised divisions on the Eastern Front in March 1945 and with about 60 divisions in the west; along with German garrisons in Italy and Scandinavia the nominal German order of battle would seem to have totalled some 350 end of April represented perhaps no more than a couple of corps under effective command on German territory, were to be spent in the vain defence of 30 square miles of central Berlin and in attempting to mount various counter-attacks in order to relieve the capital. Most of these attacks, however, amounted to very little because the forces that were ordered to carry them out either existed on paper rather than in fact or were so outnumbered and outclassed that they were quickly over-whelmed. In the unreal world of Hitler's last command post below the Chancellory the course and outcome of these offensives were the source of hysterical optimism alternating with hopeless despair until the afternoon of 30 April when, with Soviet troops less than quarter of a mile away, Hitler and his wife of one day committed suicide. Contrary to widespread belief and rejecting a practice with obvious soldierly over-tones, Hitler did not shoot himself but ended his life by poison.

The European war outlasted its author by nine days. The Berlin garrison sought and rejected terms on 1 May only to surrender unconditionally on the second, thus depriving the Soviet High Command of the victory that it wanted to complete on May Day itself. In the next week the government of Hitler's successor, Admiral Karl Dönitz, sought to invest itself with the power and authority of a state that no longer existed and to deal with enemies that would negotiate only in terms of its immediate and unconditional surrender. Just as Hitler had used his senior military officers as pawns, so the Allied powers used the same men in like manner in order to complete Germany's capitulation with the minimum loss of life in the last days of hostilities. When it became clear that the only terms available were those of unconditional surrender, the new German leadership sought to buy time in order to move forces westwards so that these could surrender to the Western powers rather than to the Soviet Union, and Dönitz's government sought to do the same. With virtually the whole of Germany under Allied control* but with German forces still occupying the western Netherlands, Denmark, much of Norway and western and central Czechoslovakia, German plenipotentiaries surrendered unconditionally on all fronts to Eisenhower's representative at Rheims on 7 May. Though represented at this ceremony, the Soviet Union, not to be upstaged and determined that Germany would not avoid a direct surrender to the nation primarily responsible for her military defeat, insisted upon a second surrender in

---

divisions. In the course of the Berlin offensive the Soviets claim to have destroyed 70 infantry and 23 armoured and mechanised divisions, and captured 480,000 prisoners.

*See Appendix E.

Berlin on the eighth. Moreover, the Soviet High Command had a concern beyond mere propriety. In the main theatres the war was over, but by Allied agreement Prague had been assigned to the Soviet zone of operations and on 5 May the Czechs had risen in revolt against their German masters. On that same day the 1st Ukrainian Front began an offensive from the Torgau-Görlitz–Leignitz–Neisse line into western Czechoslovakia: if Prague was only a detail to the Western powers, it was not to a Soviet Union only too aware of the political implications inherent in her liberation of the Czechs. In addition, to the Stavka the war was not ended until the 860,000 men of *Army Group Centre* still in Czechoslovakia were defeated or laid down their arms: a combination of both ensured the liberation of Prague – and the official end of hostilities in Europe – on 9 May, though Soviet mopping-up operations east of Prague continued until the eleventh.* Thereafter the victorious Allied powers were left with the problems of peace – and a final reckoning with Japan.

Other than the continuing campaigns in New Guinea and the Philippines, where Japanese forces remained in the field until the surrender of Japan, the last seven and a half months of the Greater East Asia war witnessed six successful military efforts by the various Allied powers that, together with the naval and air offensives, completed Japan's final and total defeat. In the Pacific the Americans assaulted and took Iwo Jima and Okinawa, and in south-east Asia the Australians, besides securing Wewak in May, occupied Tarakan, Brunei Bay and Balikpapen. In Burma the Allies completed the reconquest of the country – but for Tenasserim and the Shan States – by a combination of an overland advance from Upper Burma and amphibious landings in the Arakan and Lower Burma. In China the greater part of the gains so painstakingly registered by the Japanese during the *Ichi-Go* offensive, which continued into March 1945, were relinquished voluntarily after mid-May as the Japanese High Command began to strip southern China of its forces in order to reassert its control over northern China and to strengthen its garrison in Manchuria, the Japanese correctly interpreting the Soviet Union's notification on 5 April 1945 that the Soviet–Japanese neutrality pact of 1941 would not be renewed in 1946 as a warning that the Soviets would enter the war at the first opportunity. The movement of Chiang Kai-shek's armies into the areas vacated by the Japanese constituted the fifth of the Allied efforts, the last being the Soviet offensive in Manchuria and northern China in August 1945. Together these separate Allied

*See Appendix F.

moves ensured Japan's collapse and defeat despite her armies remaining undefeated and in control of vast areas of northern and central China and south-east Asia at the time of her surrender.

In terms of relative importance in the ending of the war, events in Burma, China and south-east Asia were of secondary consideration: the Japanese decision to surrender in August 1945 was the product of two mainstream developments, namely the nuclear attacks on Hiroshima and Nagasaki on 6 and 9 August respectively – though these were really the culmination of a general and decisive defeat in the Pacific – and the Soviet declaration of war on Japan on 8 August. Indeed, unpalatable though it may be to Americans, a careful consideration of the record of the meetings that led to the Japanese decision to surrender on 14 August reveals that the situation created by the Soviet Union's entry into the war weighed as heavily upon the Japanese High Command as the more obvious American aspects of defeat. In real terms, however, though the shock of the Soviet entry into the war was very considerable and was an important factor in Japan's decision to surrender, the Soviet campaign in Manchuria was largely irrelevant to the outcome of the war: Japan had been defeated, though her leaders refused to acknowledge the fact, before Soviet armies invaded Manchuria, and the fact that the surrender of Japan was signed at a ceremony aboard an American warship was tacit acknowledgement of the primary cause of Japan's defeat.

The most striking feature of the last months of the war in the Far East was not to be found in the course of military events but in the contradiction between public declaration and policy intention on the part of both Japan and the United States, plus the fact that as the war drew to its end both countries shared the common aim of ending it in the shortest possible time and to do so before the Soviet Union entered the conflict. For Japan, the defeat of Germany had obvious implications: within a matter of months the full weight of American, British and Soviet resources would be brought to bear against her, and with the reality of future defeat went the very real fear that military collapse would be followed by a communist revolution. From mid-May dates the start of a futile Japanese attempt first to ensure continuing Soviet neutrality and then Soviet help in ending the war: for her part the Soviet Union, determined to enter the war for reasons of prestige and territorial aggrandisement, rebuffed Japanese overtures in an attempt to ensure that the war did not end before she had a chance to enter it. The United States, which was privy to these Japanese diplomatic efforts because she was able to read signals between Tokyo and the Japanese embassy in Moscow and because she was informed of

Japanese overtures by the Soviet Union in July, displayed an attitude that changed profoundly in the last six months of the Pacific war. Until April 1945 the basis of American policy in the prosecution of the war against Japan was the belief that Japan's defeat had to embrace defeats both on the Asian mainland and in the Pacific, and after the Tehran conference the United States looked to the Soviet Union rather than China to provide Japan's military defeat in Asia. At the same time American planning, as noted earlier, moved to the conclusion that the defeat of Japan could not be accomplished without the invasion and conquest of the Japanese home islands. This conclusion meant in its turn that there could be no invasion of Honshu without a major redeployment of American forces from Europe after the end of the German war because the American military forces already in the Pacific were not sufficient to carry out the various provisions of *Operation Downfall.*

Yet after making various territorial concessions to the Soviet Union at Yalta in order to ensure Soviet participation in the war against Japan, American policy began to change within two months on two separate but related counts. First, in April 1945, even before the defeat of Germany was fact, the distrust of the new Truman administration of Soviet intentions, specifically over Poland, prompted the first American consideration of the undesirability of Soviet involvement in the war against Japan: balance-of-power considerations and the prospects of occupation difficulties if the United States was obliged to share her victory with a lately arrived ally pointed to American interests being best served by Japan's surrender before the Soviet Union could enter the war in the Far East. Second, as spring gave way to summer so the American High Command realised that Soviet intervention, hitherto considered essential to the Allied cause, would be unnecessary, that Japan could be defeated without either a Soviet intervention or an invasion of the home islands. As the American High Command awoke to the reality of Japan's position, her helplessness under the impact of saturation bombardment and naval blockade and her despairing attempts to find a way to end the war, so the very cautious American chiefs of staff hardened in the view the Japan was already defeated and ready to surrender. Moreover, by that same time the American High Command knew that within a matter of weeks the greatest scientific, technical and engineering project in history was likely to place in American hands weapons of unprecedented, awesome power. Less than six years after Einstein had written to Roosevelt warning of the reality of nuclear power and some 30 months after man achieved the first controlled release of nuclear energy by a self-sustaining chain reaction, the Anglo-American Manhattan project had reached the stage of development whereby the construction of three atomic devices – one of uranium and two of plutonium – was nearing completion and scientists were convinced that the dangers of malfunction had been eliminated.

By the summer of 1945, therefore, both the United States and Japan knew that the outcome of the war had been decided, and even before the Allied powers – Britain, China and the United States – demanded on 27 July 'the unconditional surrender of the Japanese armed forces' as the alternative to Japan's 'prompt and utter destruction', the American High Command knew that the only real obstacle in the way of Japanese compliance with Allied demands was the unconditional proviso with respect to the position of the Emperor. It formed no part of American policy to compromise either the person of the Emperor or the imperial principle, yet despite this coincidence of attitudes and interests there proved to be no way in which Japan and the United States could end the war and in which the United States could end it without subjecting Japan to atomic attack and prevent the Soviet Union emerging to administer the *coup de grâce*.

In large measure this inability to do anything but allow things to take their course was the product of the military events of the last months of the war, which obviously did not wait upon these diplomatic and scientific developments. The campaigns primarily responsible for the shaping of attitudes on both sides were those for possession and control of Iwo Jima and Okinawa: though of obvious importance to those involved, the campaigns beyond Japan's inner defence zone had little strategic significance once war came to Japanese home waters. The reconquest of Burma in the 1944–45 dry season did much to restore Britain's tarnished military reputation in south-east Asia, but China's lessening importance to the Allied cause and Britain's recognition that peace would see Indian and Burmese independence meant that the campaign itself had no lasting political or military significance. In China the series of Japanese withdrawals from southern and central China after mid-May were important in terms of the manoeuvring for power as communists and nationalists sought to take advantage of Japanese redeployments but not to involve themselves too closely with Japanese forces: with both Chinese factions observing *de facto* truces with the Japanese events in China had no significance for the outcome of the war. In south-east Asia the Australian operations in Borneo were important in terms of massaging Australian national ego, badly bruised as a result of her being so casually discarded by the Americans as the war receded from her shores, but the Allied inability to rehabilitate the oilfields occupied by the Australians robbed *Operation Oboe* of the logistical returns that alone could have justified this particular military effort.

Iwo Jima and Okinawa, however, were very different. Whereas in Burma and China, and at Brunei Bay and Balikpapen but not at Tarakan, Allied forces were opposed by weakened, weakening or defeated Japanese forces, on the two Pacific islands the Americans found themselves opposed by intact, undefeated formations occupying defences sited in depth and, in the case of Okinawa, backed by powerful artillery. In both island campaigns, moreover, the Americans found themselves subjected to sustained air attack, and on both islands they were involved in costly, protracted campaigns that paradoxically fulfilled and defeated Japanese strategic aims. On both Iwo Jima and Okinawa the Japanese sought to inflict upon the Americans such losses that the Allies would fear to commit themselves to an invasion of the home islands, and while the Allies did indeed heed the lesson of the Japanese defence of these two outposts the nature of their defence only made easier the final American decision to use nuclear weapons against Japan as the means of ensuring her surrender.

Iwo Jima was invaded on 19 February and declared secure on 16 March, but the campaign involved the island's being subjected to the longest pre-invasion bombardment of the war – 72 days – and mopping-up operations continued for two months after the island was declared secure. The whole campaign lasted from 8 December 1944 until the end of May 1945, and with its lengthy preparation phase, the month-long period of intense fighting in which the outcome of the battle was decided, and the subsequent mopping-up phase the campaign on Iwo Jima corresponds so closely chronologically, in terms of duration and even phase timings to the campaign in Burma, that the various differences between the two campaigns are rendered of small account. With Allied forces having secured Myitkyina in the previous August, the main British effort in Upper Burma opened in December 1944 with a three-fold advance from Sittaung and Kalewa, on the Chindwin, that resulted in bridgeheads being thrown across the Irrawaddy at Thabeikkyin and Kyaukmyaung on 11 January, to the west of Ngazun on 13 February and to the east of the town on the twenty-first, and at Nyaungu on 14 February. Leaving aside the second Ngazun bridgehead, the order in which the British campaign unfolded was the key to its success because it was the British intention, presumably based upon an exact knowledge of the Japanese order of battle and intentions, to hold the attention of *Burma Area Army* around Mandalay while striking through Nyaungu at Meiktila, thereby severing Japanese lines of communication and trapping the bulk of the *15th* and *33rd Armies*. There thus developed two separate battles around Mandalay and Meiktila, the one between 20 February and 21 March and the other between 21 February and 28 March that compared to the operational phase on Iwo Jima, which is generally considered to have ended with the last *banzai* charge on the night of 25–26 March.

An immediate point of difference between the two campaigns lies in the fact that whereas on Iwo Jima there was no space in which to manoeuvre strategically and the Japanese garrison had no alternative but to conduct a defensive battle until it was destroyed, on the Irrawaddy the *Burma Area Army* had both space and choice, at least in some measure, and it made the fundamental error of underestimating both the import- ance of Meiktila and the fact that the main British effort was made there rather than at Mandalay. Meiktila was secured by the British on 4 March, by which date V Amphibious Corps on Iwo Jima had secured all three of the island's airfields and had pressed the Japanese survivors back into a narrow belt of defences along the northern coast, and it was not until the middle of the month, with the battle for Mandalay clearly lost and entering its final stage, that the Japanese concentrated against Meiktila. By the time that formations from three Japanese divisions gathered around Meiktila, however, the British possessed a positional, defensive advantage and an aerial resupply capacity that enabled the garrison at Meiktila to survive attack, the cutting of its lines of communication from Nyaungu and even the loss of Meiktila airfield. On 28 March, with Mandalay having been abandoned by the *15th Army* nine days earlier, the *33rd Army* accepted defeat in front of Meiktila and began to withdraw, but by the time that it did so the Japanese defeat throughout Burma was as complete as that on Iwo Jima.

March 1945 saw the final stages of the American conquest of Iwo Jima and of the clearing of north-east Burma, specifically of the old Burma Road, with Allied forces securing Lashio on the seventh, Hsipaw on the twenty-fourth and Kyaukme on the thirty-first. In the Bay of Bengal a series of amphibious landings in the first quarter of 1945 resulted in the British reoccupation of Akyab and Ramree, from which the assault on Rangoon was to be staged and supported, and the clearing of the Arakan as far south as Taungup. Possession of Taungup, and of the An Pass to the north, provided XV Corps with positions from which to develop an offensive through the Arakan Hills into the Irrawaddy valley against a *28th Army* already being dragged eastwards into central Burma as a result of the collapse of Japanese resistance around Mandalay and Meiktila.

By the end of March 1945 Allied advantages of position, numbers and firepower, plus the fact that Japanese forces could be neither reinforced nor provided with effective air support, ensured that the outcome of both campaigns, in Burma and on Iwo Jima, had been decided: by the end of May both campaigns were over, albeit in very different ways. By June all Japanese resistance on Iwo Jima had been eliminated after 2,489 Japanese soldiers had been killed or captured during the two previous months: in Burma the 14th Army's capture of Pegu on 1 May, XV Corps' occupation of Rangoon on the second, and the meeting of the two British formations at Hlegu on the sixth marked the effective end of the campaign, not the end of the campaign itself. The British advances to Hlegu trapped some 30,000 men of the *28th Army* west of the Sittang, and what remained of the *15th* and *33rd Armies* were left to withdraw through the hostile Karen Hills and the east bank of the Sittang respectively. The last weeks of the war witnessed British mopping-up operations and an attempted breakout across the Sittang by the *28th Army* that cost it some 17,000 dead and missing. Though the Japanese lost some 185,000 dead in Burma during the war, the vast majority in the last 18 months of hostilities, in August 1945 no fewer than 118,000 Japanese servicemen remained in Burma, mostly in Tenasserim and east of the Sittang. Japanese military power in Burma, however, had been broken between February and May 1945, between the breakouts across the Irrawaddy and the capture of Rangoon, and in real terms the Allied victory in Burma in these months was as conclusive as that of the Americans on Iwo Jima.

The two obvious points of difference between these two campaigns, those of scale and relative importance, were inversely related. By the time that British forces secured Rangoon and opened communications northwards through the Sittang valley, Burma had ceased to have real significance in Allied strategic deliberations because China had been discounted as a major factor in the prosecution of the war: in sharp contrast, Iwo Jima began to prove its worth to the Allied cause even before the island was overrun by American marines. The American concern in 1945 to complete an overland line of communication to China was the product of an irrelevant, butt-end policy to supply her on a scale – rising from 39,000 tons in March 1945 to a monthly 55,400 tons between May and August – sufficient to raise 34 front-line Chinese divisions, but though the first overland convoys reached Kunming via Tengchung on 20 January and via Bhamo on 4 February the Ledo Road, completed on 20 January at a cost of $148 million, carried only 7.19 per cent of all material supplied to China between February and October 1945. The airlift alone met 113.8 per cent and 99.4 per cent of the respective March and May–August programmes, but to no real effect in terms of the outcome of the war. Conversely, the first of 2,251 B-29 emergency landings on Iwo Jima was on 4 March, at which time roughly a quarter of the island remained under Japanese control, and, as noted elsewhere, fighters from Iwo Jima escorted Superfortresses over Japan for the first time on 7 April. This date was significant, however, not so much for this development but for the shifting of the Pacific spotlight from Iwo Jima: on 7 April the carriers of TF58, having beaten off the first massed *kamikaze* attack of the Okinawan campaign on the previous day, destroyed the last Japanese surface force to put to sea in order to contest Allied control of the Japanese waters.

The campaign for Okinawa proved to be the last of the Pacific war, and in basic outline it conformed to the pattern established by the Americans throughout the Pacific since August 1942: an invasion in overwhelming force accompanied by the isolation of the objective from effective support ensured victory, irrespective of the strength and effectiveness of a garrison that invariably fought itself to total destruction. This campaign nevertheless proved very different from its predecessors. Okinawa was within range of an effective shore-based air force on Kyushu that was both too strong in numbers and too well dispersed to be neutralised by offensive operations, and with the Japanese plan of campaign based upon a protracted defence of southern Okinawa by the *32nd Army* Allied carrier forces were involved in a three-month defence of the beachhead without being able to manoeuvre strategically in order to evade attack. As a consequence Allied losses in this campaign – 22 warships sunk and 259 damaged and 14 landing ships and auxiliaries sunk and another 117 damaged – were the heaviest sustained by the Allies in any campaign of the Pacific war. Further, whereas every previous Allied landing had been directed against objectives beyond immediate local support or distant from Japan itself, Okinawa was only 400 miles from Kyushu, and possession of Okinawa and other nearby islands provided the Allies with overwhelming positional advantages relative to Japan's seaborne lines of communication with the southern resources area, which were severed during this campaign, and relative to Kyushu in that Okinawa yielded a major fleet anchorage and airfields that could be made ready for the final Allied invasion of the home islands. Moreover, the nature of Japan's defeat in the Okinawan campaign was distinctive. It was a total defeat that embraced her air power and her military and naval forces. As a result of the campaign Japan's air forces beyond the inner defence zone were lost to her, and her home-based air power suffered, with the destruction of

463

some 6,900 aircraft during the period, the loss of half its conventional strength and 30 per cent of its *kamikaze* establishment that had been held in readiness for the defence of the home islands. For the *Imperial Navy* the Okinawan campaign marked the end of a long process that had begun with its attempt to free itself from the perceived ignominy of the Washington treaties but which ended with the ignominious reality of American control of Japanese waters and the demise of the *Imperial Navy* itself. For the *Imperial Army*, which provided some 77,000 men of a garrison on Okinawa generally agreed to have numbered perhaps 110,000 men, defeat on the central plains of Burma and Luzon might have been more costly but in both theatres substantial Japanese forces had remained in the field and continued to command the attention of sizeable enemy forces. On Okinawa the Japanese military defeat engulfed the whole garrison but without compensatory return of time, commensurate enemy losses and continued enemy distraction.

The campaign on Okinawa officially lasted between 1 April and 22 June, respectively the dates of the landings and the declaration that *Operation Iceberg* was at an end: in reality the campaign began on 18 March, the date of the first pre-invasion carrier strikes, and closed on 4 August, when final mopping-up operations on Okinawa were completed. The campaign opened with 15 landings on the more important of the Kerama Islands between 26 and 29 March followed by the unopposed American occupation of the Keise Islands on 31 March. Thereafter the campaign on Okinawa divided under four headings: the American advance to the Pacific coast by 4 April; the clearing of the northern part of the island between 5 and 18 April; the occupation of various local islands between 10 April and 26 June; and main-forces operations in southern Okinawa after 6 April.

  With the exception of operations on Ie Shima and a last-ditch stand on the Motobu peninsula, the first three aspects of the campaign presented the Americans with few difficulties: the initial landings on either side of Hagushi were unopposed and in moving through central and northern Okinawa the Americans encountered only scattered, minor resistance. The course of the Okinawan campaign was determined, however, by operations in the south of the island where the *32nd Army* gave battle on a series of defensive lines in front of Shuri that took maximum advantage of the broken, rugged terrain. With the exception of an ill-judged foray on 4–5 May, the *32nd Army* chose to remain on the defensive throughout the campaign in an attempt to prolong the defence of the island and to inflict the heaviest possible losses on the Americans. The inability of the

10th US Army to overcome Japanese resistance quickly as a result of the very deliberate conduct of operations on the part of the *32nd Army* had two very obvious consequences. Until Japanese resistance in southern Okinawa was eliminated the Americans could not ensure the security of airfields on central and southern Okinawa, and in the appalling weather conditions that prevailed for much of this campaign continuing Japanese resistance diverted considerable American engineering resources from airfield construction. Without shore-based air power that could cover the island and beachhead, Allied carrier formations had to remain on station, and their constant exposure to attack, specifically to the eight massed *kamikaze* attacks mounted between 6 April and 30 May, provided a theme to the campaign second only to the battle for southern Okinawa itself.

In addition, American attention came to focus upon the losses and time involved in the clearing of southern Okinawa, both of which were considered excessive though in reality they were not so. The total Allied killed, on land, at sea and in the air, during the Okinawan campaign was 12,605 and Allied battle-casualties numbered 49,319 men. In terms of a three-month campaign against an enemy of 110,000 men on an island of such strategic importance as Okinawa, these losses were not excessive, particularly in light of the fact that at peak strength the Americans had some 249,000 men on Okinawa and overall about 500,000 Allied servicemen saw action during the campaign. The relative lightness of Allied losses was obscured by the inevitable concentration of losses amongst front-line formations, but one significant aspect of Japanese losses was also obscured by this same development. Because of civilian casualties and losses amongst Okinawans conscripted into military formations, Japanese losses are not known with any accuracy, but at the end of the campaign 7,400 Japanese chose to enter captivity rather than die by their own or by an American hand. By Pacific standards this represented a massed surrender, and confirmation of what had happened on Iwo Jima where the Americans took 1,083 prisoners. The latter stages of these two campaigns demonstrated that even Japanese morale could be broken, but not surprisingly Allied attention focused on more obvious facts: that Iwo Jima was secured only after a 36-day campaign and some 22,000 Japanese and 6,821 American deaths, and that on Okinawa the prisoner count came at the end of an 82-day campaign that left some 110,000 Japanese dead. As the Allied High Command considered the obvious question of the casualties and time that would be involved in a campaign in the home islands if Iwo Jima and Okinawa had claimed such tolls, the logic in favour of the use of atomic weapons against Japan in order to ensure her surrender was strengthened – and on 16 July at

Alamogordo in New Mexico an atomic weapon was tested successfully for the first time.

Within the American High Command there was never any doubt that atomic weapons should be used if the alternative was an invasion and conquest of Japan that would involve massive, and politically unacceptable, Allied losses. At this time American planning estimates suggested that a campaign in the home islands could cost the Allies 250,000 casualties: the figure of a million casualties represented the 'worst possible' estimate which, for obvious reasons, came to be used as the rationale for the decision to use nuclear weapons against Hiroshima and Nagasaki in August 1945. In reality, however, the American decision to use nuclear weapons against Japan was the product of three related considerations. First, though the American High Command knew of Japan's attempts to end the war and of the growing importance of the peace faction within Japan, it also knew that the military retained the power of decision within the Japanese ruling hierarchy and that the army remained opposed to any form of surrender. Second, though American possession of atomic weapons was not specified in the Potsdam declaration, the Japanese High Command was given the chance to end the war and its unfortunate manner in its rejection of the Allied ultimatum on 28 July really left the Americans with very little alternative but to use their newly acquired power. Finally, the American High Command, and specifically Truman, was convinced that the use of atomic weapons against Japan would strengthen American diplomacy in dealings with the Soviet Union as Allied differences became increasingly obvious. These considerations, plus the fact that possession generated its own logic in terms of use, settled the American decision to use atomic weapons in an attempt to bring about Japan's surrender.

The atomic raids of 6 and 9 August straddled the Soviet declaration of war on Japan on the eighth, an action subsequently derided by Truman and in various Western accounts of the war as a crude attempt on the part of the Soviet Union to take advantage of the situation created by the American victory in the Pacific and to seize various gains for herself before the war came to an end. Leaving aside the assumption that Japan would have surrendered after the atomic raids and without the Soviet entry into the war, the charge of Soviet opportunism was correct: the whole of Soviet policy towards the Japanese war at and after the Tehran conference was opportunistic, and indeed the whole of the American attempt to ensure Soviet participation in this war encouraged and exploited this fact. Technically, moreover, the charge was also correct in that the Stavka had planned to begin operations against Japan in mid-

August, and it advanced its timetable in order to ensure the start of hostilities before the Japanese had the chance to surrender in the aftermath of the razing of Hiroshima. Ironically, however, the result of this change was to ensure that the Soviet Union began operations against Japan on 9 August, three months to the day after the end of the war in Europe and exactly in accordance with the promises given to that effect by the Soviet Union to the United States at the Moscow and Yalta conferences.

Militarily, the Manchurian campaign was marginal to the outcome of the war: its significance lay in its demonstration of the futility of continued Japanese resistance to Allied demands, its revelation of the emptiness of Japan's political and diplomatic hopes through the destruction of her power in what had been the heartland of her imperialist ambitions for four decades, and its proof of the bankruptcy of Japanese military philosophy. On this point, the Soviet offensive in Manchuria was amongst the most successful undertaken by the Soviet army during the Second World War, but it was an offensive that registered success against an army that had failed to keep abreast of technological change since 1939: as a consequence, the Japanese armies in Manchuria in August 1945 were materially very little different from those that had overrun the province in 1931–32 and northern China in 1937. In terms of armour, mechanisation, firepower and command facilities, the Japanese armies in Manchuria in 1945 were simply not equipped to conduct the mobile defensive battle in the central plains that was the basis of Japanese strategic planning, and in manpower terms the armies in Manchuria were of low calibre as a result of the stripping of the garrison of its better formations in 1944 and 1945 for home defence and service in the western Pacific. Neither in material nor in manpower, therefore, were the six Japanese armies in Manchuria and northern Korea a match for the 11 Soviet armies concentrated for this offensive, most of which consisted of formations moved directly from Europe after the defeat of Germany.

In terms of overall manpower numbers, however, the Japanese armies in Manchuria began the campaign of August 1945 at a marked though hardly decisive disadvantage. They numbered some 1,040,000 men compared with the 1,580,000 troops assembled with the three fronts gathered around Manchuria's borders, but the Soviet margin of manpower superiority was more pronounced than the nominal order of battle would suggest because of the presence of some 160,000 non-Japanese within a military establishment divided between field and garrison formations. Moreover, those same aspects of material advantage and of Soviet practice that had been used to such effect against the *Wehrmacht* in

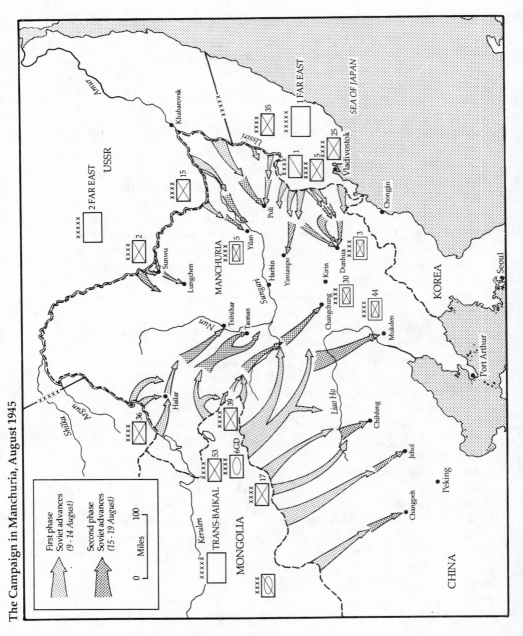

The Campaign in Manchuria, August 1945

the last year of the European war were employed by the Stavka in order to ensure overwhelming superiority of force at the various points of contact. The Soviet armies mustered some 28,000 guns, 5,550 tanks and 4,370 aircraft to oppose the 5,360 guns, 1,115 tanks and 1,800 aircraft of the Japanese, but much greater margins of superiority were sought and achieved by a plan of campaign tailored to ensure strategic surprise. The Stavka anticipated the Japanese calculation that an offensive would not begin until September, after the rainy season, and the Soviet decision to open proceedings in August was made in the expectation of a crucial advantage of timing being secured. More importantly, the central Manchurian plain was covered in the west by the Gobi desert and the Great Hingan Mountains, in the north-east by the swamps around the confluences of the Amur and Sungari and the Amur and Ussuri, and in the east by very difficult, broken and forested terrain. The natural lines of advance into Manchuria followed the railroad through Hailar, Tsitsihar and Harbin and via Heihe, but it was the Soviet intention to make the main effort, with some 40 per cent of total strength and the bulk of the armour, through the mountains and desert to the west. A mixed cavalry-light armoured force was to cross the Gobi desert into the Peking area while three armies were to advance over a mountain range that reached more than 6,000 feet before sweeping into the central plain to secure Changchung and Mukden. On the river lines in the east Soviet commands, lavishly provided with artillery, riverine support and infantry, were to smash through Japanese defences and secure Harbin and Kirin. In order to distract Japanese attention from these main efforts, the Soviet plan of campaign involved two second-grade armies being committed to frontal assaults on Hailar and Sunwu.

Against so refined a plan of campaign, the Japanese armies in Manchuria were effectively defeated before the Soviet offensive began, and indeed the most notable aspects of the campaign related to the extent of Soviet success. In the course of 11 days the lead formations of the Trans-Baikal Front advanced some 560 miles across the Great Hingan Mountains to the outskirts of Mukden (in western European terms the equivalent of an advance from Caen to Milan via Lyon over comparable terrain) from a start line some 300 miles from the nearest railhead. By 19 August, when the *Kwantung Army* formally surrendered to the Far East Command at Khabarovsk, the Trans-Baikal Front's mixed cavalry and armour of the Pliev Group had reached Changpeh and Jehol and its five main armies stood on the Chihfeng–Mukden–Changchung–Taonan–Tsitsihar line. To the east the 2nd Far East Front had secured Lungchen, Yilan and Poli while the 1st Far East Front had taken

Yimianpo and Dunhua and cleared northern Korea as far south as Chongjin. In short, by the time of its capitulation the *Kwantung Army* had been outfought in the east and outmanoeuvred in the west, and its armies could do nothing to prevent their encirclement and annihilation.

The surrender of the *Kwantung Army*, on direct orders from the Emperor on 17 August after it had decided on the sixteenth not to abide by instructions from Tokyo, did not bring an immediate end to the fighting between Japanese and Soviet forces: the collapse of communications and the refusal of some Japanese forces to surrender meant that fighting in Manchuria continued on a declining scale until the end of August. On and after 19 August, however, the Soviet High Command used airborne forces to arrange local surrenders, and to secure towns and airfields, ahead of its advancing columns, and the Soviet occupation of the towns of central Manchuria, of Port Arthur on 22 August, and of Korea north of the 38th parallel was for the most part unopposed, but on Shumshu and in southern Sakhalin the Soviet attempt to reap the rewards of victory was bitterly, if briefly, resisted. On Shumshu, the most northern of the Kurile Islands, Japanese resistance ended on the twenty-third after a six-day battle that provided Soviet forces with an inkling of the island campaign in the Pacific, and fighting on Sakhalin did not end until the twenty-fifth, after which Soviet forces from Otomari moved to occupy Kumashir and Shikotan, the southernmost islands in the Kuriles, on 1 September. With some six other islands in the Kurile chain also occupied by Soviet forces between 25 and 28 August, the various Soviet territorial ambitions at Japan's expense were realised by the end of the war, though at a long-term price that neither Japan nor the Soviet Union could foresee at the time.

The course and detail of the Manchurian campaign were largely unknown to the authorities in Tokyo and were thus isolated from the tortuous process whereby Japan decided, between 9 and 14 August, to surrender to her enemies. What made this process so difficult and protracted was the fact that in these six days the issues confronting the Japanese High Command not only changed and remained ambiguous, but also entered the public domain. At the outset the immediate issue before the supreme war council and the cabinet was the simple question of whether Japan should comply with the terms of the Potsdam declaration or, as the war minister and service chiefs demanded, should seek to negotiate terms – that would disguise the reality of defeat and surrender – as the alternative to continuing the war. The real issue, however, was how best to ensure the preservation of the imperial polity, and though divided on the question of how this was to be achieved the Japanese High Command was united in the view that the war would have to be continued if the Allies refused to guarantee the inviolability of the Emperor and the imperial system. The immediate issue was resolved in the early hours of 10 August when, after council and cabinet meetings on the ninth had failed to settle the matter, the Emperor declared himself in favour of an immediate acceptance of the Potsdam declaration.

By placing the full authority of the throne behind the pro-surrender faction within the government, the Emperor in effect broke the opposition of the military high command, but the subsequent attempt to ensure the position of the Emperor by indicating in notes to the Allied powers that the Japanese government accepted the terms of the Potsdam declaration on the understanding that the Emperor's prerogatives as a sovereign ruler were not compromised only produced a second, more serious crisis for the Japanese government. In its reply of 11 August, the United States indicated that 'the authority of the Emperor and the Japanese government to rule the state shall be subject to the supreme commander of the Allied powers.' This form of words refused Japan a formula whereby she could deny the reality of her defeat, but it was ambiguous in that it presented those who favoured immediate compliance with Allied demands with the oblique, if somewhat unsatisfactory, guarantee that they sought but at the same time provided their opponents within the military establishment with the rationale for a last-ditch defence of the country. The American reply was also unfortunate in that it was broadcast to Japan and was thus made known to an army with a long tradition of removing opponents in government on the pretext of securing the throne against treacherous influences. Coming on top of the publication of the terms of the Soviet declaration of war which revealed for the first time that Japan had sought Soviet help in trying to end the war, the effect of the American reply was to raise the prospect of a military rising before the government could complete the process of surrender.

Between 12 and 14 August, therefore, the issue confronting cabinet and council was whether or not the American note of the eleventh represented a concession sufficient to justify acceptance of Allied terms, and this decision had to be reached against a background knowledge that within the military establishment were factions intent on staging a coup, which sought a final cataclysmic battle that would serve as suitable appeasement of the gods and the dead, and which even produced ideas of raising a 20,000,000-strong *kamikaze* force that was assured of victory. With the prospect of defeat and surrender – and resultant dishonour and

471

dismemberment of the the armed forces – fast assuming real form, what should have been the two compelling arguments in favour of acceptance of Allied terms were lost upon military representatives conscious, first, that they faced a choice between the obligations of duty, obedience and discipline and notions of honour and tradition, and, second, that professions of loyalty on the part of various subordinates were strictly conditional on their taking the 'correct' course of action. On 13 August the pro-surrender faction argued, apparently for the first time, that rejection of Allied terms could only lead to their hardening and that any attempt to fight a final battle of destruction in the home islands could only result in the destruction of the imperial system not in its preservation. Moreover, as the prime minister, Admiral Suzuki Kantaro, told the dissenting war minister, any delay in accepting Allied terms could only end in a greater Soviet involvement in the war and the subsequent peace, and with the start of the Sakhalin campaign on 11 August providing evidence of the danger to the northern islands Suzuki knew that it was essential to comply with Allied demands while the United States remained Japan's chief enemy. Nevertheless, it was to need a second intervention by the Emperor, at the imperial conference on 14 August, to overcome the renewed opposition of the war minister and service chiefs to the acceptance of Allied terms. In the event, this intervention was not sufficient to prevent various attempts by dissident members of the military to stage a coup and kill the traitors surrounding the Throne on the night of 14–15 August. The Voice of the Crane, however, was sufficient to ensure the final unquestioning obedience of senior military commanders during this last crisis, and these efforts to prevent the surrender were quelled and not joined by an army that, for the most part, retained its discipline in the last days of its existence.

There remained, however, the delicate task of how the fact of surrender was to be made public and in a way that would ensure obedience and compliance on the part of a people and army that expected to be told to continue the war. His ministers having failed him in the two greatest crises in Japan's history, the Emperor was prepared to give effect to his decision in two ways: to proceed in person to the war ministry to ensure the army's obedience to his will, and, for the first time, to broadcast to his people. In the event, only the latter proved necessary, yet the broadcast, made at noon on 15 August, in its attempt to avoid reference to defeat and surrender, sought to justify Japan's war of aggression in terms of self-defence and her decision to surrender in terms of saving human civilisation from total extinction in an atomic war. Nevertheless, for all its careful phraseology the imperial rescript left no doubt as to its meaning, and with the appropriate notes sent to the Allied powers war ended on 15 August with Allied carrier aircraft in the air *en route* for Japanese targets. Inevitably, some Japanese chose to die rather than face the reality of defeat and others attempted *kamikaze* operations after the end of hostilities, but by 28 August, when the first American troops landed at Atsugi airfield near Yokosuka, Japanese military discipline was such that there were no incidents. On 29 August American and British warships entered Tokyo Bay, and on 2 September, on the starboard verandah deck of the battleship *Missouri*, representatives of the Japanese government and of *Imperial General Headquarters*, and of the United States, China, Britain, the Soviet Union, Australia, Canada,* France, the Netherlands and New Zealand signed the two formal instruments of surrender against the background provided not just by overwhelming Allied naval power and Japan's devastation but the words of the newly appointed supreme commander:

It is my earnest hope, indeed the hope of all mankind, that from this solemn occasion a better world shall emerge out of the blood and carnage of the past, a world founded upon faith and understanding, a world dedicated to the dignity of man, and the fulfilment of his most cherished wish for freedom, tolerance and justice.

The various peace treaties remained for the future, but the greatest and most destructive war in history was over.

*The surrender ceremony is generally considered to have ended with MacArthur's having declared proceedings to be closed, but the Canadian representative had signed the Japanese surrender document in the French space and the last four Allied signatures were wrongly positioned. This was noted by the Japanese delegation as it prepared to leave the ship, and the document had to be returned for amendment. Only then was peace a reality. On departure the Japanese delegation, which had been received in silence, was afforded naval honours.

7

THE ACCOUNTING

For less than four centuries, in a period that was unique in history, it was easier to sail around than move across the continents. In this fact lay the basis of the transformation of Europe from the least to the greatest of the continents, from the victim of successive invasions from Africa and Asia to a continent that came to extend its power throughout the world. European supremacy did not survive the reversal of the balance of advantage between seaborne and overland lines of communication that came about, very slowly, after the 1840s, and the Second World War completed the process. A war that is generally recognised to have lasted six years and one day saw Europe, which in 1938 had settled its greatest inter-war crisis with reference to outsiders, reduced from the subject to the object of an international struggle for power on the part of extra- and non-European states both infinitely stronger than the greatest of the European nations.

Excluding colonial and imperial territories, 56 nations found themselves at war between 1939 and 1945 but whereas in Europe the comprehensiveness of Axis defeat and the immediate reality of a new balance of power with the end of hostilities precluded further war, in the Far East the end of the Japanese war ushered in a period of upheaval and revolution that was to last some 30 years before the forces of local nationalism and communism and great power interests resolved themselves in such a way as to produce some form of settled, recognised order in the area, though technically it is in this same area that the last unfinished business of the Second World War remains. Nations formally at war with one another remain so until the conclusion of a peace treaty, and in Europe treaties between the Allied powers and the lesser Axis states – Bulgaria, Finland, Hungary, Italy and Romania – were concluded in February 1947. The division of Germany, as her conquerors under the pressure of events created mirror-images of themselves in their zones of occupation, presented problems in the framing of a peace treaty that could not be resolved until the third decade after the end of hostilities, but the Allied powers had earlier solved the problems of normalising the situation in which they found themselves by formal declarations that their state of war with Germany was at an end – Britain on 9 July 1951, France four days later, the United States on 24 October 1951 and the Soviet Union on 25 January 1955. The San Francisco treaty of 8 September 1951 ended the state of war that had existed between Japan and no fewer than 48 of her enemies, but it was not until 28 April 1952 that the treaty came into force and two decades were to pass before Okinawa was returned to Japan by the United States. China, India and the Soviet Union were not parties to this treaty, and it was not until 19 October 1955 that Japan and the Soviet Union, recognising that present circumstances – particularly the USSR's refusal to consider a partial or total return of the Kuriles – did not permit the conclusion of a peace treaty, formally declared that the state of war that had existed between them since August 1945 was at an end.

Though terms of peace eluded the nations for many years, the war nevertheless ended in 1945, and few wars in history provide better confirmation of the observation that

> the final decision of a whole war is not always to be regarded as absolute. The conquered state often sees in it only a passing evil, which may be repaired in after times by means of political combinations.

Indeed, such were these 'political combinations' that within 10 years what had seemed in 1945 to be the most comprehensive and complete aspect of the Allied victory – the military defeat of the Axis powers and the disarmament of Germany and Japan – had been overturned, and such has been the revival of German and Japanese power and influence that many have questioned the worth of the Allied victory in the Second World War. Justification thus exists for the simple statement of the obvious: that the Second World War was not fought about standards of living and levels of individual consumption and comfort but about fundamental values, fought by states that, despite all their imperfections and injustices nevertheless represented concepts of freedom, and opposed the domination of powers that were committed to the realisation of unlimited ambition and to the enslavement and degradation of man. Liberal democracy had little change to show for its efforts in their struggle: in the wake of the defeat of great tyrannies lesser ones emerged in many countries. Yet just as the Democracies evolved into better expressions of their values so even the Stalinist state, no less monstrous and grotesque than the German obscenity that was defeated, survived and slowly allowed those elements of dignity and freedom within communist ideas to emerge.

A German victory in Europe would have changed forever the map of Europe, particularly eastern and south-east Europe. The latter was indeed changed after 1944 by a political, social and economic revolution and a re-orientation of alignment without equal in 500 years, yet a German victory would have resulted in a very different change, one that would have been accompanied by murder on the scale of tens of millions and enslavement of hundreds of millions. In the Far East a Japanese victory – a lesser prospect than a German victory in Europe – would ultimately have seen the wars of national liberation that were to be fought against Western powers after 1945 fought against Japan, and the record of Japan in China after 1937 – and indeed in those areas of subsequent conflict – leads only to the conclusion that these wars would have been infinitely crueller and more bloody than those that were actually fought.

The wars that were fought between 1937 and 1945 saw no power realise the aims with which it entered hostilities. China survived to emerge as a nominal great power: her government did not, though it was not until 1949 that this became fact. Poland lost her national independence. For Britain, the defeat of Germany was only achieved at the cost of national exhaustion and the bringing of a power ultimately greater than Germany into central and eastern Europe. For France, the war brought a defeat redeemed only by powers greater than herself. For the Soviet Union, victory legitimised communism in a way that Stalin's own regime could never have done, but at fearful cost and in a way that was incomplete: the communist regime shared the traditional Russian view of the most powerful European nation's right to decide European matters, as indeed Russia had done with respect to central and eastern Europe between 1815 and 1849, only to find its power and dominance denied. For the United States, the war brought victory but also post-war responsibilities as she was forced to decide between the use to which her power was to be put: to preserve or change the new *status quo*.

For Germany and Japan the attempt to wage wars with unlimited ends but limited means ended in disaster, for Japan predictably but for Germany less so, and of the two Germany's was the greater defeat. The nation that prided itself on military power and prowess lost the war after holding potentially decisive advantages that should have provided her with victory: not merely did she lose the war she ceased to exist thereafter.

The human cost of the war is not known with any accuracy. Germany and Japan lost about 7,400,000 and 2,100,000 dead respectively. The two naval powers were spared the horror of continental warfare and wars of racial annihilation: Britain lost some 430,000 and the United States some 220,000 dead. China lost an estimated 13,500,000 dead and Poland 5,400,000 killed, all but 120,000 after her surrender. The Soviet Union, including the Baltic states, lost perhaps 22,000,000 dead, and recent Soviet statements suggest that this is an understatement. It has been alleged that of all Soviet males born in 1923 only 3 per cent were alive in 1946, and certainly for eastern Europe the war represented a lost generation. Yet compared with the cost that would have been exacted by a German victory in Europe and a Japanese victory in the Far East – the physical, moral and intellectual enslavement of continents – perhaps the human cost involved in the destruction of evil was not great but small, that perhaps 57,000,000 dead was, in the balance of history, a small price to pay for ridding the world of depraved wickedness.

APPENDICES

The Decline in Submarine Effectiveness

The technical limitation of the submarine relative to the escort is best summarised by reference to a comparison of sinkings by German submarines during the First and Second World Wars. In the First World War, German submarines sank 4,837 ships of 11,135,000 tons and in the Second World War 2,771 ships of 14,554,000 tons. Thus, in the First World War German submarines sank on average 95 ships per month compared to 41 per month in the Second World War, and this in spite of the fact that the peak of German strength in 1917–18 was less than average German strength between 1942 and 1945. In addition, of course, German submarines in the First World War did not have access to Atlantic ports and were much inferior in range and capability than their Second World War counterparts.

The decline in submarine effectiveness between the First and Second World Wars was largely the result of two factors: in the First World War convoy was not introduced until 1917 and then only partially whereas it was introduced from the outset of the Second World War and gradually made more extensive; secondly, the escorts secured a technical and tactical mastery of German submarines in the Second World War that was never achieved in the course of the first.

Operation Mars

The *OKH* view, expressed through its Eastern Intelligence Branch's assessments, was not necessarily as wildly inaccurate as it might appear. It is one of the lesser known aspects of the winter campaign of 1942–43 that in November the Soviet army mounted two offensives: *Operation Uranus* around Stalingrad and *Operation Mars* around Rzhev.

The effort around Rzhev began on 25 November, six days after the start of *Operation Uranus*. It involved four armies of the Western and Kalinin Fronts, with a measure of support from four flanking armies, and an attack on Velikiye Luki by the half-strength 3rd Shock Army. The fighting for Velikiye Luki lasted until 15 January 1943 when the town finally fell: the main effort either side of Rzhev also continued into 1943 but was effectively over by mid-December 1942, the Soviets having sustained heavy losses for virtually no return.

Though *Operations Uranus* and *Mars* involved roughly equal Soviet commitments in terms of manpower, the fact that *Uranus* involved about 60 per cent of all Soviet operational armour and one-third of the Stavka's reserve artillery indicates that *Mars* was the secondary, supporting effort. It would appear that *Operation Mars* had two aims: to pin down *Army Group Centre* and prevent its supporting *Army Group B* as the latter's front collapsed, and to make whatever gains it could with the Stavka being prepared to act upon events. The Soviet preparations for this offensive and then its being mounted seem to have been important in the unfolding of the winter campaign in two respects. First, *Operation Mars* most certainly served to confuse German intelligence regarding Soviet intentions and capabilities. For most of the autumn *OKH* held to the view that the Soviet army was capable of only one offensive effort in the coming winter, and reasoning that Rostov and the Baltic were beyond Soviet reach concluded that this effort would be made around Rzhev, where between June and October Soviet armies had launched almost continuous futile attacks. On and after 6 November, by which time the Soviet concentrations in various Don bridgeheads could neither be disguised nor ignored, *OKH* recognised the possibility of a twin Soviet effort but believed that the initial effort would be made around Rzhev. *Army Group Centre* did not believe at this time that it was about to be attacked, and as late as 21 November its *9th Army*, the immediate target of *Operation Mars*, specifically discounted the possibility of a Soviet offensive against itself (i.e. it believed that the Soviets had shown their hand at Stalingrad). Second, while victory eluded the Soviets around Rzhev, *Operation Mars* had the effect of pinning down *Army Group Centre* as the Stalingrad operation unfolded, and indeed it obliged the German High Command to reinforce *Army Group Centre* with three armoured and three infantry divisions before the end of 1942.

Hitler ordered the evacuation of the Rzhev salient on 6 February, and this was carried out between 1 and 23 March. The Demyansk salient was also evacuated at this time, the evacuation being completed on 18 March after Hitler had approved the withdrawal on 31 January.

APPENDIX C
The Japanese in China

The nature and extent of this 'special undeclared peace' has been obscured by the post-war propaganda and disinformation of the various parties involved in these events. Between 1938 and 1944, apart from the Japanese landings in southern China in 1941, there was little in the way of large-scale operations in China, but in these years the Japanese conducted various pacification campaigns in occupied China (usually with great ferocity) and engaged in numerous rice raids at harvest times. From 1942, however, commitments elsewhere began to impose upon China something that approached a *de facto* truce because the Japanese simply lacked the means to conduct large-scale operations against either the communists or the Kuomintang, and both were prepared to accept this situation as they prepared for the eventual resumption of their struggle for power

479

once Japan was defeated. In the case of the Kuomintang the accommodation with Japan extended in time to a flourishing trade across the front lines, and after 1942 the Americans found that they could not purchase Chinese tungsten because they were outbidded by the Japanese. With Japan securing a range of raw materials in return for consumer goods, the balance of this trade worked to her favour, but in 1944 and 1945 the divisions raised, trained and equipped in China by the Americans were mainly fed with food purchased in Japanese-occupied territories.

In the latter the Japanese raised over a million troops in local military and para-military forces, but their aggressive rule, their failure to cede real power to potential collaborators and their ruthless exploitation of exchange rates in order to guarantee access to materials at rock-bottom prices ensured no more than passive compliance with their rule on the part of most Chinese rather than active support. Long before their only major defector from the Kuomintang, Wang Ching-wei, died in 1944, the Japanese political defeat in China was as obvious as their military failure.

APPENDIX D

American Confusion at Leyte Gulf

The argument about responsibility for this state of affairs has been confused by concentration upon the issue of command, which at best was only a minor factor. The crucial matter was role, not command, and TF38 had the task of ensuring the security of TF77 against the very attack that materialised on the twenty-fifth. Its failure to do so was all the more surprising for its commander, in his first major action, had access to all relevant information on Japanese battle procedures, most obviously the invariable use of decoy forces and end runs. At the first opportunity TF38 was taken against a decoy force and not held in a position to cover TF77.

With original strengths given as the second figure, the losses of the various Japanese formations between 23 and 27 October were as follows: Carrier Force – 4/4 carriers, 1/3 light cruisers, 2/8 destroyers and 0/2 battleships; Central Battle Force – 1/5 battleships, 5/10 heavy and 1/2 light cruisers, 3/15 destroyers; Southern Battle Force – 2/2 battleships, 1/1 heavy cruiser, 3/4 destroyers; Cruiser Force – 0/2 heavy and 1/1 light cruisers, 1/4 destroyers. One other destroyer, unattached to these format formations, was sunk on the twenty-fourth off Panay.

APPENDIX E

The Fall of Vienna

Vienna had fallen on 13 April after a Soviet offensive that began after the defeat of the last German offensive of the war. This offensive, around Lake Balaton in defence of the oilfields around Nagkanizsa which did not at this stage produce

480

sufficient oil to meet even local German military needs, was the third German offensive on the southern sector in 1945. The first, a series of attacks, had been made in January in a vain attempt to relieve Budapest: the second, between 17 and 24 February, had eliminated Soviet bridgeheads over the Hron at a time when the bulk of Soviet armour had been withdrawn for refitting. The final offensive began on 5 March against a Soviet defence that had been served one month's notice of German intentions and which had been made ready to fight a riposte battle in the Kursk manner. By the thirteenth the *6th SS Panzer Army*, despite considerable initial success, had all but exhausted itself amidst successive Soviet defensive lines and was subjected to strong, local counter-attacks: the *2nd Panzer Army* barely progressed beyond its start line. As at Kursk, the main Soviet counter took the form of a general offensive against weak sectors. On the sixteenth the full power of the 2nd and 3rd Ukrainian Front was harnessed to an offensive that swept aside the *1st* and *3rd Hungarian* and *13th German Armies*, mauled the *6th SS Panzer* and *6th Armies*, and threatened the *2nd Panzer Army* with encirclement. A general withdrawal by *Army Group South* prevented a complete collapse of the German front, but by the twenty-seventh the Soviet armies had achieved the breakthrough and on the thirtieth crossed the border into Germany: Soviet forces took Vienna on 13 April and the Stavka halted offensive operations two days later.

The Soviets claim to have routed 32 Axis divisions in the course of an offensive noted for widespread 'failures' of German divisions as a 'not-the-last-to-die' attitude began to percolate through *Army Group South*, and Vienna was not defended with anything like the tenacity displayed at Budapest. By the end of the war the only concern of *Army Group South* was to surrender to the 3rd US army, and its withdrawals had allowed Soviet forces to push westwards to the Pisek–Ceske–Budejovice–Linz–Liezen–Judenburg–Voitsberg line.

APPENDIX F
Czechoslovakia and Yugoslavia

As far as the Eastern Front was concerned, Czechoslovakia proved something of a backwater in 1944 and 1945 as the main Soviet offensive efforts were developed north of the Carpathians and through the Balkans, but Soviet forces crossed into pre-1938 Czechoslovakia during the 1944 campaign and by the end of the year had advanced to the Svidnik–Stropkov–Trevisov line. This achievement was registered *en passant*, however, and fell short of Soviet intentions. It had been the Allied aim that as Soviet forces approached Czechoslovakia the London-based government in exile would orchestrate a rising in Slovakia that would facilitate the passage of Soviet armies into the country. This plan miscarried in large measure because the Germans, conscious of her growing importance as the frontline advanced westwards into central Poland, occupied Slovakia on 29 August, and not all Slovak units joined the revolt. With the Soviet 38th Army unable to break through the Dukla Pass in September, the Germans moved some seven divisions into Slovakia and proceeded to crush the Slovak Rising by the end of October. In the course of the west Carpathian offensive in 1945 the 4th and 2nd Ukrainian Fronts, with a Soviet-sponsored Czech corps in the line, pushed the German forces back some 120 miles to the Trstena–Brezno–Levice line, and during the Vienna offensive the 2nd Ukrainian Front liberated Bratislava on 4 April. During April Soviet forces cleared Slovakia, liberating Brno and Ostrava on the twenty-sixth and thirtieth respectively. The final Prague offensive by the 1st Ukrainian Front, in fact, proved a concentric offensive involving the 4th and 2nd Ukrainian Fronts, and ended with the encirclement of German forces between the Jizers and Laba (Elbe) rivers.

Further south, the last German surrenders in northern Yugoslavia did not take place until 15 May, by which date the whole of Yugoslavia was under the effective control of a provisional government that had been formed on 7 March 1945. This government was dominated by the communist resistance, which alone amongst the many factions within Yugoslavia emerged from the civil war and a war of national liberations without any taint of collaboration. In the aftermath of defeat in April 1941 Yugoslavia had been dismembered, and the Axis powers had no difficulty in using the bitter nationalist rivalries with Yugoslavia to sponsor various puppet states. Resistance to Axis occupation came initially from the Cetniks, an organisation that was Serbian nationalist, monarchical and right-wing in character, but given its faith in ultimate Allied victory and its belief that its task was to ensure the return of the monarchy and restoration of Yugoslav and Serbian domination this organisation drifted first into passivity and then into active collaboration with the Axis powers because it saw the communist partisans as the real enemy. The communist resistance proved the only organisation capable of rising above local nationalist rivalries that resulted in a series of civil wars within Yugoslavia after 1941, an estimated 1,500,000 of the 1,800,000 Yugoslavs killed during the Second World War being killed at the hands of other Yugoslavs.

Despite fearful atrocities and a series of offensives aimed at their destruction, the communists survived in the mountains until the decisive moment of the campaign, the surrender and invasion of Italy in September 1943. The Italian surrender in Yugoslavia resulted in the communists' capture of equipment sufficient to arm the equivalent of some nine field divisions, and Allied occupation of southern Italy provided the partisans with a base; Britain, having abandoned the Cetniks, provided the communists with diplomatic, military and logistical support. The Jajce conference of November 1943, at which the communists set down the basis of post-war government in Yugoslavia, was a *de facto* recognition of the communists' supremacy within Yugoslavia, while their allegiance to Moscow and backing from the Western powers provided the basis whereby the Soviets agreed to a limited involvement in the country while the local communists dealt with Yugoslavia's domestic issues. After October 1944 the communists raised four armies and cleared southern Yugoslavia and Dalmatia, but as late as April 1945 *Army Group E* retained Sarajevo and virtually the whole of what is now Croatia, Slovenia having been annexed. In the last weeks of the war communist forces occupied Trieste (1 May) ahead of the British, and Fiume (the third), Zagreb (the eighth) and Ljubljana (the ninth), the process being accompanied by a bloody settling of accounts.

One last aspect of these campaigns in eastern and south-east Europe was the presence of various Czech and Polish formations, and also heavily-indoctrinated Rumanian divisions from their prisoners-of-war. The Polish armies participated in the Vistula–Oder, Berlin and Prague offensives, while four Rumanian armies were involved in the clearing of national territory after Rumania changed sides in August 1944. The 1st and 4th Rumanian Armies took part in operations in Czechoslovakia in 1944 and 1945. The 1st Bulgarian Army was also involved in operations in Yugoslavia, and perhaps surprisingly ended the war in the Wolfsberg area of eastern Austria.

POSTSCRIPT, AND TOWARDS A NEW PERSPECTIVE

This book was initially called *Chaos First: A Re-interpretation of the Second World War, 7 July 1937–19 October 1955*. With this title I intended to set out terms of reference for a fresh examination of the two partially concurrent conflicts that make up the Second World War. On the threshold of the sixth decade since the outbreak of war in Europe, the historian has the duty to provide, and the reader the right to demand, if not new material then fresh evaluation of the available record in accordance with the dictum that 'History is indeed an argument without end'.

The process of re-evaluation and re-interpretation of events is the essence of History: indeed, it is the basis of the truism that anyone who wants to change History should become an historian. But the general and public perception of the Second World War has changed little over the last three or four decades. Many points of detail have not stood the test of time and close scrutiny, and in recent years certain interests that would deny historical reality have made assertions about aspects of this war that are as hideously perverted in terms of integrity as the very events that they would disavow, but for the most part the main themes of historical interpretation of the Second World War remain today much as they were when set down in the first glut of post-war memoirs and the writings of the first generation of historians after 1945. Certainly there has been no major revision of the generally perceived wisdom of the Second World War in the manner, for example, in which Frederick the Great and Napoleon were subjected to critical re-examination of their deeds within twenty years of their deaths.

Why History should have treated the Second World War so differently from its previous material is not clear. Perhaps in the modern world ethnocentric and ideological considerations, either consciously or subconsciously, have affected historiography more than History itself: perhaps the loss of so many potential historians to emergent rival disciplines has stunted the process of historical re-interpretation by the diversion of creative talent that in previous times would have devoted itself to History into other, less rewarding fields. It may be that the power of the spoken word and of image has so impressed itself upon the collective subconscious of successive generations that the written word of the historian no longer commands the power of redress, and it may well be that this is the last book-reading generation. But it is nevertheless legitimate to speculate upon the possible perceptions of future generations and to suggest that with the passing of time the Second World War may well destroy itself as an historical concept. Perhaps in fifty or one hundred years' time the prevailing perspective of the events of 1939–1945 will be that they represent no more than the most intensive part of a series of conflicts, waged between 1931 and 1975, that resulted in the destruction of one world order and the erosion of its replacement to the extent that, for the first time in man's history, no part of the land surface of this planet was not part of indigenous, sovereign territory and the various regional issues brought to the fore between 1931 and 1945 were at last resolved with little reference to the great powers. The diffusion of power and the right of societies to arrange their own affairs with little let or hinderance on the part of the major states arose from the process of which the Second World War – in the sense that the term is generally understood – was the greatest and most important single part, and hopefully this book will be no more than the start-line for the process of re-examination and re-interpretation of these events that must await new generations of historians who alone can move towards a new perspective.

H. P. Willmott
16 January 1989

Recommended Bibliography

In the Preface I noted that over the last two decades there had been a floodtide of publications about the Second World War and that I was aware that any newcomer to the subject is confronted by an intimidating mass of published material, not a little of it of dubious taste and value.

This book represents a distillation of a study of warfare and of the Second World War that has extended over three decades, and any attempt to provide a comprehensive bibliography with respect to sources of fact and interpretation is not practical.

In order to provide both a guide for used sources and, for the student, an introduction to various aspects of the war, this bibliography sets down the most accurate and balanced English-language accounts that are available, biographies, autobiographies and official histories dealing with own national forces being excluded from consideration.

STRATEGY AND POWER
CONWAY, ROBERT H., *The Navy and the Industrial Mobilization in WW2*, Princeton, Princeton University Press, 1951
EARLE, EDWARD MEADE., (ed.) *The Makers of Modern Strategy. Military Thought from Machiavelli to Hitler*, Princeton, Princeton University Press, 1966. Peter Paret (with Gordon A. Craig and Felix Gilbert) (ed.) Revised Edition: *Machiavelli to the Nuclear Age*, 1986
ROSINSKI, HERBERT, *The Development of Naval Thought*, Newport RI, Naval War College, 1977
VAN CREVELD, MARTIN, *Supplying War: Logistics from Wallenstein to Patton*, London, Cambridge University Press, 1977
BIDWELL, SHELFORD and GRAHAM, DOMINICK, *Fire-Power: British Army Weapons and Theories of War, 1904–1945*, London, Allen and Unwin, 1982
BOND, BRIAN, *British Military Policy between the Two World Wars*, Oxford, OUP, 1980
ROSKILL, S. W., *Naval Policy between the Wars*
HOWARD, MICHAEL, *The Continental Commitment: The Dilemma of British Defence Policy in the era of the two World Wars*, London, Temple Smith, 1972
WEIGLEY, RUSSELL, *The American Way of War*, London, Macmillan, 1973

OUTBREAK OF WAR IN THE FAR EAST
BARNHART, MICHAEL, *Japan prepares for total war. The search for Economic Security, 1919–1941*, Ithaca NY, Cornell University Press, 1987
BERGAMINI, DAVID, *Japan's Imperial Conspiracy*, New York, Morrow, 1971
BORG, DOROTHY and SHUMPEI, OKAMOTO (eds). *Pearl Harbor as History: Japanese-American Relations, 1931–1941*, New York, Columbia University Press, 1973
CROWLEY, JAMES B., *Japan's Quest for Autonomy: National Security and Foreign Policy, 1930–1938*, New York, Colombia University Press, 1973
HEINRICH WALDO, *Threshold of War. Franklin D. Roosevelt and American Entry into WW2*, Oxford, OUP, 1988

IENAGA, SABURO, *The Pacific War, 1931–1945: A Critical Perspective of Japan's Role in WW2*, New York Pantheon, 1978

IRIYE, AKIRA, *The Origins of the Second World War in Asia and the Pacific*

JOHNSON, CHAMBERS A., *Peasant Nationalism and Communist Power: The Emergence of Revolutionary China*, Stanford, SUP, 1962

NEWELL, WILLIAM H., *Japan in Asia, 1942–1945*, Singapore, Singapore University Press, 1981

PELZ, STEPHEN E., *Race to Pearl Harbor: The failure of the second London naval conference and the onset of WW2*, Cambridge Mass., Harvard University Press, 1974

TOLAND, JOHN, *The Rising Sun: The Decline and Fall of the Japanese Empire, 1936–1945*, New York, Random House, 1970

OUTBREAK OF WAR IN EUROPE

BELL, P. M. H., *The Origins of the Second World War in Europe*, London, Longman, 1986

DALLEK, ROBERT, *Franklin D. Roosevelt and American foreign policy, 1932–1945*, New York, Oxford University Press, 1981

MACDONALD, C. A., *The United States, Britain and Appeasement, 1936–1939*, London, Macmillan

REYNOLDS, DAVID, *The Creation of the Anglo-American alliance, 1937–1941*

WATT, DONALD, C., *Too serious a business: European armed forces and the approach to the Second World War*, Berkeley, University of California Press, 1975

POLISH CAMPAIGN

BETHELL, NICHOLAS, *The War Hitler Won, September 1939*, London, Allen Lane, 1972

COUTOVIDIS, JOHN, *Poland, 1939–1945*, Leicester, Leicester University Press, 1986

DAVIS, BRIAN L., *German Ground Forces: Poland and France, 1939–40*, London, Almark, 1976

GARLINSKI, JOSEF, *Poland in the Second World War*, London, Macmillan, 1985

ZALOGA, STEVEN and MADEJ, VICTOR, *The Polish Campaign, 1939*, New York, Hippocrene, 1985

BATTLE OF THE ATLANTIC

HEZLETT, ARTHUR, *The Aircraft and Sea Power*, London, Davies, 1970
The Submarine and Sea Power

MACINTYRE, DONALD, *The Battle of the Atlantic*, New York, Macmillan, 1961

MILNER, MARC, *North Atlantic Run: The Royal Canadian Navy and the Battle of the Convoys*, Annapolis, Naval Institute Press, 1985

ROHWER, JÜRGEN, *The Critical Convoy Battles of March 1943. The Battle for HX 229/SC 122*, Annapolis, Naval Institute Press, 1977

ROSKILL, S. W., *The Navy at War, 1939–1945*, London, Collins, 1964

VAN DER VAT, DAN, *The Atlantic Campaign: WW2's Great Struggle at Sea*, London, Hodder and Stoughton, 1988

SCANDINAVIA

ANDENAES, JOHANNES, *Norway and the Second World War*, Oslo, Tanum, 1966

DICKENS, CAPTAIN PETER, *Narvik: Battles in the Fjoirds*, London, Ian Allan Ltd, 1974

LUNDIN, CHARLES L., *Finland in the Second World War*, Bloomington, Indiana University Press, 1957

ZIEMKE, EARLE F., *The German Northern Theater of Operations, 1940–1945*, Washington, Department of the Army, 1959

MOULTON, J. L., *The Norwegian Campaign of 1940*, London, Camelot Press Ltd, 1966

NORTH-WEST EUROPE

ALLEN, PETER, *One More River. The Rhine Crossings of 1945*, London, J. M. Dent & Sons Ltd, 1980

AMBROSE, STEPHEN EDWARD, *Eisenhower and Berlin, 1945: the Decision to halt at the Elbe*, New York, Norton, 1967

BELFIELD, E. M. G. and ESSAME, H., *The Battle for Normandy*, Philadelphia, Dufours, 1965

BENNETT, RALPH, *Ultra in the West. The Normandy Campaign 1944–1945*, New York, Scribner, 1979

BOND, BRIAN, *France and Belgium, 1939–1940*, Newark, University of Delaware Press, 1979

CHAPMAN, GUY, *Why France Fell: the Defeat of the French Army in 1940*, London, Cassell, 1968

D'ESTE, CARLO, *Decision in Normandy: The Unwritten Story of Montgomery and the Allied Campaign*, London, Collins, 1983

ESSAME, HUBERT, *The Battle of Germany*, New York, Scribner, 1969

GLOVER, MICHAEL, *The fight for the Channel ports: Calais to Brest, 1940: A study in confusion*, London, Leo Cooper, 1985

HASTINGS, MAX, *Overlord, D-Day and the Battle for Normandy 1944*, London, Michael Joseph Ltd, 1984

HORNE, ALASTAIR, *To Lose a Battle. France 1940*, London, Macmillan, 1969

JACKSON, W. G. F., *'Overlord'. Normandy 1944*, Newark, University of Delaware Press, 1978

KEEGAN, JOHN, *Six Armies in Normandy. From D-Day to the Liberation of Paris*, London, Jonathan Cape Ltd, 1982

MACDONALD, CHARLES B., *The Battle of the Bulge*, London, Weidenfeld & Nicolson, 1984

ROHMER, RICHARD H., *Patton's Gap: An Account of the Battle of Normandy 1944*, New York, Beaufort, 1981

STOLER, MARK A., *The Politics of the Second Front: American military planning and diplomacy in coalition warfare, 1941–1943*, Westport, Greenwood, 1977

WEIGLEY, RUSSELL, *Eisenhower's Lieutenants: The Campaign of France and Germany, 1944–1945*, Bloomington, Indiana University Press, 1981

THE WAR IN THE AIR

BOWYER, C HAZ, *Air War over Europe 1939–1945*, London, Kimber, 1981

DEIGHTON, LEN, *Fighter. The True Story of the Battle of Britain*, London, Cape, 1977

FRANKLAND, NOBLE, *The Bombing Offensive against Germany: Outlines and Perspectives*, London, Faber and Faber, 1965

HASTINGS, MAX, *Bomber Command*, London, Michael Joseph, 1979

LONGMATE, NORMAN, *The Bombers: The Air Offensive against Germany, 1939–1945*, London, Hutchinson and Co., 1983

MIDDLEBROOK, MARTIN, *The Nuremberg Raid: 30–31 March 1944*, London, Allen, 1980

OVERY, RICHARD J., *The Air War, 1939–1945*, London, Macmillan, 1980

SHERRY, MICHAEL S., *The Rise of American Air Power: The Creation of Armageddon*, New Haven, Yale University Press, 1987

VERRIER, ANTHONY, *The Bomber Offensive*, London, B. T. Batsford Ltd, 1968

BALKANS, ITALY AND AFRICA

BARNETT, CORRELI, *The Desert Generals*, London, George Allen and Unwin Ltd, 2nd edition, 1983

BRADDOCK, DAVID WILSON, *The Campaign in Egypt and Libya, 1940–42*, Aldershot, Gale and Polden, 1964

CARVER, MICHAEL, *Tobruk*, Philadelphia, Dufours, 1964

Dilemmas of the Desert War: a new look at the Libyan campaign, 1940–1942, London, Batsford, 1986

CLARK, ALLAN, *The Fall of Crete*, London, Anthony Bland Ltd, 1962

VAN CREVELD, MARTIN, *Hitler's Strategy, 1940–41: The Balkan Clue*, Cambridge UK, Cambridge University Press, 1973

CRUIKSHANK, CHARLES, *Greece, 1940–1941*, (Newark, University of Delaware Press, 1976

D'ESTE, CARLO, *Bitter Victory. The Battle for Sicily 1943*, London, Collins, 1989

ELLIS, JOHN, *Cassino. The Hollow Victory. The Battle for Rome Jan. to June 1944*, London, André Deutsch, 1984

GRAHAM, DOMINICK and BIDWELL, SHELFORD, *Tug of War. The Battle for Italy*, 1943–1945, London, Hodder and Stoughton, 1986

HIGHAM, ROBIN, *Diary of a Disaster: British aid to Greece, 1940–1941*, Lexington, University of Kentucky Press, 1986

HOWARD, MICHAEL, *The Mediterranean Strategy in the Second World War*, London, Weidenfeld and Nicolson, 1968

JACKSON, W. G. F., *Battle for Italy*, London, Batsford, 1967

MACKESEY, KENNETH, *Crucible of Power. The Fight for Tunisia 1942-43*, London, Hutchinson and Co., 1969

ORGILL, DOUGLAS, *The Gothic Line. The Autumn Campaign in Italy 1944*, London, Heinemann, 1967

PITT, BARRIE, *The Crucible of War – Western Desert 1941*, London, Jonathan Cape, 1980
The Crucible of War – Year of Alamein 1942, London, Jonathan Cape, 1982

SAINSBURY, KEITH, *The North African Landings 1942. A Strategic decision*, London, Davis-Paynter, 1976

SHEEHAN, F., *Anzio. Epic of Bravery*, Norman, University of Oklahoma Press, 1964

SHEPPERD, G. A., *The Italian Campaign, 1943–1945, A Political and Military Re-assessment*, London, Barker, 1968

SIMPSON, TONY, *Operation Mercury: The Battle of Crete*, London, Hodder and Stoughton, 1981

STEWART, I. M. D. G. *The Struggle for Crete*, Oxford, Oxford University Press, 1966

STRAWSON, JOHN, *The Battle for North Africa*, New York, Scribner, 1969
The Italian Campaign, London, Secker and Warberg, 1987

ZAPANTIS, ANDREW L., *Hitler's Balkan Campaign and the Invasion of the USSR*, New York, Columbia University Press, 1987

SOUTH-EAST ASIA

ALLEN, LOUIS, *Singapore, 1941–1942*, Newark, University of Delaware Press, 1979
Burma: The Longest War, 1941–45, London, Dent, 1984

BARKER, A., *The March on Delhi*, London, Faber and Faber, 1963

CALLAHAN, RAYMOND, *Burma 1942–1945*, London, Davies-Poynter, 1974
The Worst Disaster: The Fall of Singapore, Newark, University of Delaware Press, 1977

KIRBY, S. WOODBURN, *Singapore: The Chain of Disaster*, London, Cassell, 1971

LINDSAY, OLIVER, *At the Going Down of the Sun: Hong Kong and South-east Asia, 1941–1945*, London, Hamish Hamilton, 1981

THORNE, BLISS K., *The Hump. The great military airlift of WW2*, Philadelphia, Lippincott, 1965

TSUJI, MASANOBU, *Singapore: The Japanese Version*, (translated by Margaret E. Lake), New York, St Martin's Press, 1961

TUCHMAN, BARBARA W., *Stilwell and the American experience in China, 1911–1945*, London, Macmillan, 1971

THE NAZI-SOVIET CONFLICT

CENTER FOR LAND WARFARE: US Army War College. Proceedings of Art of War

RECOMMENDED BIBLIOGRAPHY

Symposia. *From the Don to the Dnepr: Soviet Offensive Operations – December 1942–August 1943*. (Held in 1984: published in 1985) *From the Vistula to the Oder: Soviet Offensive Operations – October 1944–March 1945*. (Held in 1985: published in 1986.)
ERICKSON, JOHN, *The Road to Stalingrad*
The Road to Berlin. Stalin's war with Germany, London, Weidenfeld and Nicolson, 1983
FUGATE, BRYAN I., *Operation Barbarossa. Strategy and Tactics on the Eastern Front, 1941*, Novato, California, Presidio, 1984
GLANTZ, DAVID M., *The Red Mask: The Nature and Legacy of Soviet Military Deception in the Second World War*
JUKES, GEOFFREY, *Hitler's Stalingrad Decisions*, Berkeley, California, University of California Press, 1985
SEATON, ALBERT, *The Russo-German War, 1941–45*, London, Barker, 1971
SIMPKIN, RICHARD, *Deep Battle. The Brainchild of Marshal Tukhachevskii*, London, Brassey's, 1987
ZIEMKE, EARLE F., *Stalingrad to Berlin: The German Defeat in the East*, Washington DC, Department of the Army, 1971
ZIEMKE, EARLE F. and BAUER, MAGNA, E., *Moscow to Stalingrad: Decision in the East*

WAR IN THE PACIFIC
ALLEN, LOUIS, *Burma. The Longest War, 1941–45*, London, J. M. Dent and Sons Ltd, 1984
Singapore 1941–42, London, Davis and Paynter, 1977
BARKER, A. J., *The March on Delhi*, London, Faber and Faber, 1963
BELOTE, J. H. and BELOTE, W. M., *Titans of the Seas: The Development and Operations of American Carrier Task Forces During World War II*, New York, Harper & Row, 1975
Typhoon of Steel: The Battle for Okinawa, New York, Harper & Row, 1969
BLAIR, CLAY JR., *Silent Victory. The US submarine war against Japan*, Philadelphia, Lippencott, 1975
BRETT-JAMES, ANTHONY and EVANS, LT. GEN. SIR GEOFFREY, *Imphal. A Flower on Lofty Heights*, London, Macmillan and Co., 1964
CALLAHAN, RAYMOND, *Burma 1941–45*, London, Davis-Poynter, 1978
The Worst Disaster. The Fall of Singapore, London, Associated University Press, 1977
FALK, S. L., *Decision at Leyte*, New York, W. W. Norton, 1966
Seventy Days to Singapore. The Malayan campaign 1941–42, London, Robert Hale, 1975
GARFIELD, BRIAN, *The Thousand Mile War*, London, Ballantine, 1975
GOW, IAN, *Okinawa, 1945: Gateway to Japan*, London, Grub Street, 1986
GREGG, CHARLES T., *Tarawa*, Stein and Day, 1983
HOLMES, R. and KEMP, A., *The Bitter End. The Fall of Singapore, 1941–42*, Chichester, Antony Bird Publications, 1982
LINDSAY, OLIVER, *The Lasting Honour. The Fall of Hong Kong 1941*, London, Hamish Hamilton, 1978
LODGE, O. R., *The Recapturee of Guam*, Awans Press
LUNDSTROM, JOHN B., *The First South Pacific Campaign. Pacific Fleet Strategy, December 1941–July 1942*, Annapolis, Naval Institute Press, 1976
MAYI, LIDA, *Bloody Buna*
REYNOLDS, C. G., *The Fast Carriers. The Forging of An Air Navy*, New York, McGraw Hill, 1968
The Fast Carriers. The Forging of An Air Navy, New York, Krieger, 1978
SPECTOR, RONALD H., *Eagle against the Sun. The American war against Japan*, New York, Macmillan, 1985
STEPHAN, JOHN J., *Hawaii under the Rising Sun. Japan's plan for conquest after Pearl Harbor*, Honolulu, University of Hawaii Press, 1984
STEWART, ADRIAN, *Guadalcanal: WW2's fiercest naval campaign*, London, Kimber, 1985

489

SWINSON, ARTHUR, *Kohima*, London, Cassell and Co. Ltd, 1986

WHEELER, RICHARD, *A Special Valor, The US Marines and the Pacific War*, New York, Harper & Row, 1983

WILLMOTT, H. P., *Empires in the Balance. Japanese and Allied Pacific Strategies to April 1942*, Annapolis, Naval Institute Press, 1982

The Barrier and The Javelin, Japanese and Allies Pacific Stragegies: February to June 1942, Annapolis, Naval Institute Press, 1983

Y'BLOOD, W. T., *Red Sun Setting: The Battle of the Philippine Sea*, Annapolis, Naval Institute Press, 1980

Red Sun Setting, Annapolis, Naval Institute Press, 1981

WARTIME DIPLOMACY

ALLEN, LOUIS, *The End of the War in Asia*, New York, Beckman, 1979

FISCHER, LOUIS, *The Road to Yalta. Soviet foreign relations, 1941-1945*, New York, Harper and Row, 1972

HAYES, GRACE PERSON, *The History of the Joint Chiefs of Staff in WW2. The war against Japan*, Annapolis, Naval Institute Press, 1982

PACIFIC WAR RESEARCH SOCIETY / OYA, SOICHI, *Japan's Longest Day*, Toyko, Kodansha International, 1968

READY, J. LEE, *Forgotten Allies: the military contribution of the colonies, exiled governments, and lesser powers to the allied victory in WW2*, Jefferson NC, McFarland, 1985

THORNE, CHRISTOPHER, *Allies of a Kind: The United States, Britain and the war against Japan, 1941–1945*, London, Hamish Hamilton, 1978

The Issue of War: states, societies and the Far Eastern conflict of 1941–1945, London, Hamish Hamilton, 1985

INTELLIGENCE

BEESLEY, PATRICK, *Very Special Intelligence. The story of the Admiralty's Operational Intelligence Centre, 1939–1945*, London, Macmillan, 1977

HOLMES, W. J., *Double-Edged Secrets. US Naval Intelligence Operations in the Pacific during WW2*, Annapolis, Naval Institute Press, 1979

JONES, R. V., *The Wizard War. British scientific intelligence, 1939–1945*

KAHN, DAVID, *The Code Breakers. The Story of Secret Writing*, London, Weidenfeld and Nicolson, 1966

LANGHORNE, RICHARD (ed.), *Diplomacy and Intelligence during the Second World War: Essays in Honour of F. H. Hinsley*, Cambridge, UK, Cambridge University Press, 1985

LEWIN, RONALD, *Ultra Goes to War*, London, Hutchinson, 1978

The American Magic: codes, ciphers and the defeat of Japan, New York, Farrer, 1982

WINTERBOTHAM, F. W., *The Ultra Secret*, New York, Harper, 1975

MISCELLANEOUS

CALVOCORESSI, PETER and WINT, GUY, *Total War: The Story of WW2*, New York, Pantheon, 1972

SEATON, ALBERT, *The German Army, 1933–1945*, London, Weidenfeld and Nicolson, 1982

The Fall of Fortress Europe, 1943–1945, London, Batsford, 1981

STEIN, GEORGE H., *The Waffen SS: Hitler's elite guard at war 1939–1945*, Ithaca, New York, Cornell University Press, 1966

TAYLOR, A. J. P., *Europe, Grandeur and Decline*

The author wishes to acknowledge the help he received in the preparation of the indices from Kevin Boylan, Robert Cameron and Adam Lynde, graduate students with the Department of History at Temple University, Philadelphia. As always in such matters, responsibility for final arrangement and errors of omission and commission lie with the author alone.

There are two indices, the first a campaign index and the other a general index that does not carry any reference cited in the first.

Considerations of space preclude the inclusion in the general index of single page entries; individual aircraft types; formations and units of corps size or smaller; individual ships and items of military equipment. Because of vagaries of rank, title and even name, individuals cited in the text and index are afforded only their surname.

Campaign Index

General Index

491